DOCTOR · WHO

THE WRITER'S TALE

DOCTOR • WHO

THE WRITER'S TALE

The untold story of the BBC series

RUSSELL T DAVIES
and BENJAMIN COOK

BBC
BOOKS

1 3 5 7 9 10 8 6 4 2

Published in 2008 by BBC Books, an imprint of Ebury Publishing. A Random House Group Company.

Doctor Who is a BBC Wales production for BBC One. Executive Producers: Russell T Davies and Julie Gardner. Series Producer: Phil Collinson.

The Random House Group Limited Reg. No. 954009

Addresses for companies within the Random House Group can be found at www.randomhouse.co.uk

A CIP catalogue record for this book is available from the British Library.

ISBN 978-1-846-07571-1

The Random House Group Limited supports The Forest Stewardship Council (FSC), the leading international forest certification organisation. All our titles that are printed on Greenpeace approved FSC certified paper carry the FSC logo. Our paper procurement policy can be found at www.rbooks.co.uk/environment.

Commissioning editor: Albert DePetrillo
Project editor: Steve Tribe
Designer: Clayton Hickman
Cover design: Clayton Hickman
Production controller: Phil Spencer

Printed and bound by Firmengruppe APPL, aprinta druck, Wemding, Germany.

BBC Books would like to thank the following for providing photographs and for permission to reproduce copyright material. While every effort has been made to trace and acknowledge all copyright holders, we would like to apologise should there have been any errors or omissions.
All images © BBC, except:
pages 16, 356 and 502 photography by Dan Goldsmith
pages 29, 37, 61, 75 and 305 © Red Production Company Ltd
page 29 (inset) © Jack Barnes
pages 49, 71, 124, 310, 353, 354 and 404 (top) © Rex Features
pages 51 and 389 © Radio Times
page 58 images © Kudos Film & Television
page 68 courtesy of Rob Francis
page 74 (all) courtesy of Wynnie la Freak
pages 76, 97, 137 (inset), 170 (inset), 181, 214, 222, 258, 267, 297, 302 and 346 courtesy of the *Doctor Who* Art Department
pages 133 and 250 clippings © *The Sun*/NI Syndication
pages 159, 316 and 211 courtesy of William Baker
page 178 © Darenote Ltd. Photographer William Baker
pages 180, 189, 237, 271, 298, 342, 387, 396, 404 (right), 405 (left), 407, 408, 414, 416, 459 (all), 465, 466, 468, 475, 500 and 504 courtesy of Arwel Jones
page 188 courtesy of Steven Moffat
page 212 © Panini Publishing
page 220 © Joss Barratt
pages 248, 268–269 computer-generated imagery courtesy of The Mill
page 278 compilation photos courtesy of Benjamin Cook/Jennie Fava
pages 281 and 474 courtesy of Benjamin Cook
page 282 courtesy Jennie Fava
page 310 © David Fisher/Rex Features
page 313 photograph by Andy Short © *SFX* Magazine 2006
page 353 © Jonathan Hordle/Rex Features
page 354 © Richard Young/Rex Features

CONTENTS

CONTENTS

FOREWORD

PHILIP PULLMAN

I have never met Russell T Davies, but I like him, from the T on outwards. He steals from the best, which proves that he is both discriminating and unscrupulous; he is adventurous and humane, not a common combination; and most of all he's full of a boundless energy, which fizzes out of these pages like champagne. He's a genuine maker. Everybody knows *Doctor Who*, and *Queer as Folk*, and *Torchwood*. They made a difference: they have stamped his authority on the TV screen for a long time to come. My favourite among his stories is *Mine All Mine*, for the simple reason that it was charming, and it confirmed my long-held view that the Welsh are the sexiest people in the world.

But what's this book about? Specifically, it's about the writing – and the re-writing, and the talking about, and the thinking about, and the arguing about the scripts for a series of *Doctor Who*.

However, it's not the theme that's important. What matters are the insights and the vivid and illuminating comments that crop up on the way, as Davies examines the whole business of storytelling. Take the theme itself. Davies says – and he's dead right – 'Maybe that's when bad scripts are written, when you choose the theme first. I consider that I've something to say when I've thought about a person, a moment, a single beat of the heart, that I think is true and interesting, and *therefore* should be seen.'

That's true of novels, stage plays, films, short stories – any narrative that's made up in order to illuminate a theme has a quality of duty rather than joy. It's what Yeats called making the will do the work of the imagination.

He's also right – by which I mean, of course, that his opinion coincides with mine – on the subject of writer's block: 'I don't know why, but I sort of react with revulsion to that phrase. I imagine it to mean sitting there with No Ideas At All. For me, it feels more like the ideas just won't take the right shape or form.'

He's pugnacious, and rightly so, when faced with narrow-minded prejudice: the key is 'not to defend the work, because I think defence always sounds like an apology, but to go on the attack.' But he's also sensitive to the difficulties less experienced writers face when trying to deal, for example, with the relentless and merciless idiocy of internet 'criticism'. His attitude is, again, mine, and therefore resonantly true: 'Creating something is not a democracy. The people have no say. The artist does. It doesn't matter what the people witter on about: they and their response come after. They're not there for the creation.'

In fact, not only is Russell T Davies a great TV writer, a vigorous and creative producer, a wise and perceptive commentator on the profound business of storytelling, and I dare say (I have never met him) a figure of godlike and unearthly personal beauty, he is probably omnicompetent. Reading this excellent book I was more than once put in mind of the old song 'Abdul the Bulbul Amir'. The Bulbul's opponent in that epic conflict was Ivan Skivinsky Skivar, who 'could imitate Irving, play poker or pool, and perform on the Spanish guitar.'

Such a man is Russell T Davies. This book is a treasury of wit, of truthfulness, and of good sound storytelling sense, and well worth stealing from.

PHILIP PULLMAN
May 2008

INTRODUCTION

RUSSELL T DAVIES

I can't drive, so I get a lot of taxis. Which means that five or six times a week I have this conversation:

'So what do you do then?'

'I work on *Doctor Who*.'

'As what? Are you one of the monsters?'

'No, ha ha, that's funny. No, I'm a writer.'

'Oh, right, nice.'

Pause, and then, every time, here it comes…

'So where d'you get your ideas from?'

At that point, I normally say that I buy them from The Ideas Shop in Abergavenny. But in fairness, it's a good question. With no good answer.

Writers never talk about this. You'll see us, in script meetings, talking about plot and character and motivation; you'll see us in the bar, talking about contracts and rivals and fonts; you'll see us in the gutter, complaining about money. (With all of us, all the time, wondering when the good luck will run out.) But the actual writing… oh no, no way, no one talks about that. Like it's sacrosanct. Or just too scary to look at.

But Benjamin Cook wanted to know! And wouldn't give up. So that's what we've tried to pin down here. The ideas. Those mad, stupid, vague, shape-shifting, hot, nagging, drive-you-barmy ideas. And as the idea for this book grew – you'll see it grow, on the page – then it gave me the chance to tackle another thing that was bugging me. Writing is such an industry now. In many ways, that's a good thing, in that it removes all the muse-like mystique and makes it a plain old job, accessible to everyone. But with industry comes jargon. I was aware that jargon was starting to fill those growing shelves of Writer's Self Help books, not to mention the blogosphere. Wherever I looked, the writing of a script was being reduced to A, B, C plots, Text and Subtext, Three Act Structure and blah, blah, blah. And I'd think, that's not what writing is! Writing's inside your head! It's thinking! It's every hour of the day, every day of your life, a constant storm of pictures and voices and sometimes, if you're very, very lucky, insight.

That's what I wanted to capture here, and that's why so much of this book is written at 2am, in the dark hours, when the storm's a-blowing and the rafters creak. It's not writing in theory; it's writing in action, in motion. In anguish! These chapters contain scripts delivered page by-page, night-by-night, to Ben, and Ben alone, ideas written down before anyone else could sit in judgement, or before I could reconsider them in the cold light of day.

I wonder. You might be surprised. It does get a bit wretched and angst-ridden at times. (Steven Moffat, *Doctor Who*'s next showrunner, read the manuscript and said, 'If you still want to be a writer after reading this, then you probably will be.') But for me, that's what writing is, coupled with the enormous joy of actually getting something made. Ben and I tried to capture the process live and unfiltered, in e-mails, and when it came to publishing this, we didn't go back and tidy up. We've tried to leave it as instinctive, impulsive and contradictory as... well, as the inside of your head. Okay, all right, we did go through the finished text to remove the scandal (3,000 words, including My Night With The Slitheen), the lies (2,000 words, including my belief that Arthur Miller nicked my idea for *The Crucible*) and the swearing (28,000 words, including some brand new ones), but, apart from that, we left it intact, to make it as honest as possible. Oh yes, and we removed one or two secrets about the future, because *Doctor Who* is an ongoing show, and hopefully always will be, for ever.

To see writing in motion, means writing as work – a real, proper job, with deadlines and constraints and setbacks, like any other profession. The writer doesn't sit in an ivory tower. Mine's kind of beige, if not nicotine, and the real world is always intruding. No, it doesn't intrude; that real world is part of the writing process too, so a lot of that is laid out for you here, during the most extraordinary year that we've ever had on *Doctor Who*, with the casting of Kylie Minogue and Catherine Tate and Davros and... oh god, I love this job! (Steven, I've changed my mind! Steven? What d'you mean, 'Russell who?')

The only problem with writing on-the-spot e-mails is that I don't stop and pause to give praise where it's due. The personal nature of this book means that I'm not being too objective, or kind. I take a lot of things for granted, so I don't stop to thank David, or Catherine, or the Heads of Department, or Lindsay, as she sews 500 buttons on 75 extras, or Mark the gaffer, as he hauls his lamps around in the rain, or the runners, as they juggle tea and scripts and abuse. They're the people who really get *Doctor Who* made, alongside the brilliant teams at *Doctor Who Confidential* and the Website, and Branding, and... oh, the thanks could fill a whole book. Albeit a rather dry book.

But right here and now, I just want to say thank you to Ebury, for having faith in us, and to Philip Pullman, for his wonderful words, with special thanks to Ben, for the idea, the support, the kindness and the friendship, and to Andrew Smith, the man who's hardly mentioned in here, because he's part of a different world, one which keeps me sane and makes the whole thing possible.

Oh, and then, by the way, the taxi driver always says, 'So do you think up the story and the actors make up the words?' I've gotta learn to drive.

RUSSELL T DAVIES
July 2008

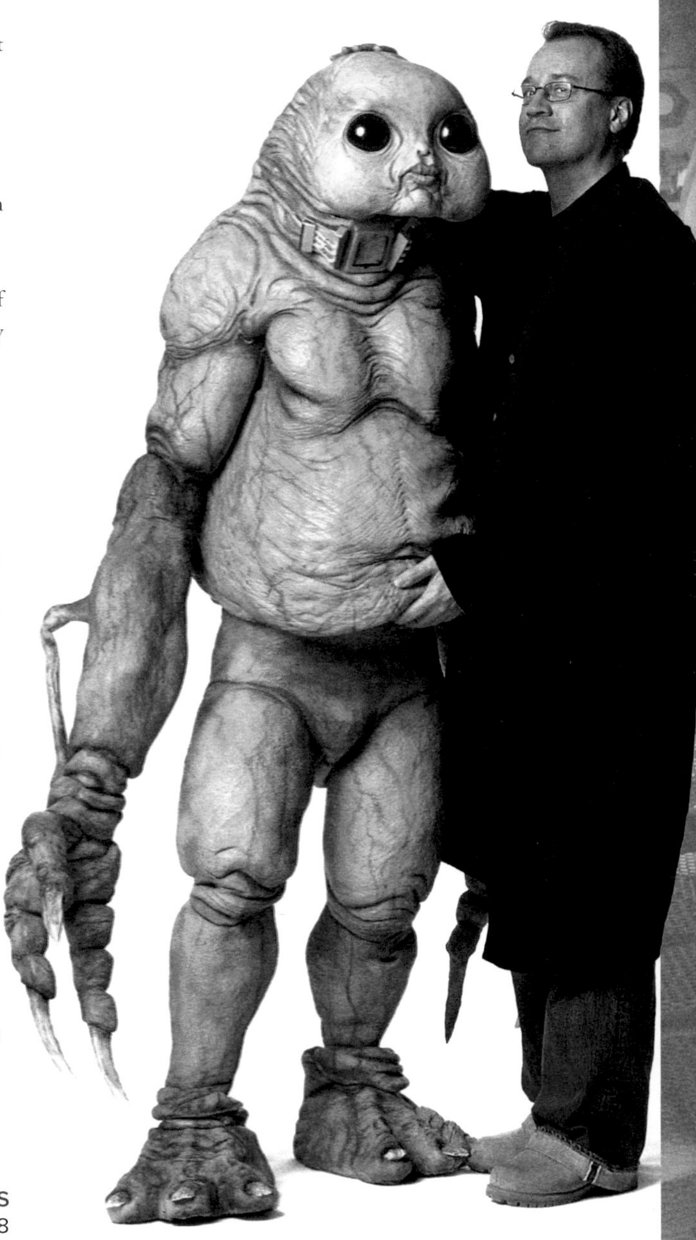

INTRODUCTION

BENJAMIN COOK

As I write this, on a Sunday morning in the first week of July, a nation is reeling from last night's explosive series finale of *Doctor Who*. The Daleks were defeated and the universe saved (well, it was the outcome we'd been rooting for), Rose Tyler got her man (or a facsimile of him – if you missed the episode, we'll explain later), and Donna Noble... oh, poor Donna Noble. We whooped with joy, punched the air in delight, and then broke down in tears. (Much the same reaction, I imagine, as the Controller of BBC One this morning, when she heard the news of the overnight ratings – a staggering 9.4 million people had watched – but then remembered that there will be no new series until 2010!) This was good telly. This was *brilliant* telly. It was also Russell T Davies' last *Doctor Who* series finale as lead writer and executive producer...

I first met Russell in July 2004, outside a department store in Cardiff. I don't live in Cardiff, but I seem to spend half my life there, reporting on the filming of *Doctor Who* (it's made by BBC Wales, you see) for *Radio Times* and *Doctor Who Magazine*. On that evening in 2004, shop-window dummies were coming to life, late-night shoppers were fleeing in terror, and the paparazzi were camped out all night, in the hope of catching a glimpse of Dame Billie Piper. This was her first day on set as Rose Tyler, and the first full day's filming on twenty-first-century *Doctor Who*.

'This is the biggest thing to happen to Wales since... well, I don't know when,' Russell told me that evening, as he was dragged off to chat to local news show *Wales Today*.

'I was very upfront,' he worried, after the interview. 'I was asked why people love *Doctor Who* so much, and how I cope with everyone's expectations. I said, "To be honest, I just ignore them!"'

Four years later, and I now know that this isn't *entirely* true. The weight of expectation seems to be what compels Russell to write. It's what *keeps* him writing. From *Queer as Folk* to *Bob & Rose* to *The Second Coming* to *Doctor Who*, Russell T Davies is driven by expectation – by meeting it, by confounding it, by surpassing it. It's easy to forget, now that his version of *Doctor Who* has proved such a runaway success (9.4 million – Christ!), the pressure that Russell was under, back in 2004, to restore a battered old TV show to its former glory, to make it appeal to a modern audience, without compromising on the original format. It's even easy to forget the expectation that's surrounded Russell ever since – to keep coming up with brave, brilliant, fresh new story ideas, and to never let the standard drop, not even for a moment.

The idea behind this book, then, was to find out exactly what it's like to live, and write, under such a weight of expectation. We wanted to take a progressive look at not just the scriptwriting and storytelling processes, but also Russell's role as showrunner. This is a correspondence, between Russell and myself, spanning a whole year, from February 2007 to March 2008. It's a year-long interview, in effect. Or Russell's personal Series Four production diary… but a diary that answers back! Told through hundreds of e-mails and text messages, this is How It Happened, As It Happened.

Last May, for instance, when Russell was on his way back from Marks & Spencer, in a taxi, and an idea struck him, a sudden flash of inspiration… the first thing he did when he got home (even before unpacking his shopping, I like to imagine) was e-mail me: 'I had a rush of ideas just now,' he enthused, before adding, thrillingly, 'Kylie Minogue should die!' (He can't have meant literally. That would be obscene.) 'I'd never considered that before,' he continued. 'That feels good.' And then, over the weeks and months that followed, we charted the evolution of that initial rush of ideas – many more ideas, too, all bubbling away in Russell's head, simultaneously – into fully fledged characters, and dialogue, and scenes, and a script for a 60-minute *Doctor Who* Special for BBC One on Christmas Day. (That one, by the way, was watched by over 13 million people! Aren't statistics fun?!)

Of course, the nature of *The Writer's Tale* means that the scripts reproduced in this book, for *Voyage of the Damned*, *Partners in Crime*, *The Stolen Earth* and *Journey's End*, are first drafts. In fact, they're pre-first drafts. If you want to read the finished, polished versions, the shooting scripts for all these episodes – along with *Midnight* and *Turn Left*, which we didn't have the space for herein – can be viewed on Random House's website (www.thewriterstale.com), while the episodes themselves are available on DVD from this November. And repeated on BBC Three ad infinitum.

What else? Oh yes, a few thank yous. Firstly, and most especially, to Nick Lane (he knows why), but also to Matthew McCarthy, Neil McRobert, Daniel Holdsworth and Natalie Lambracos. And my mum and dad, or they'll kill me. Further thank yous can be found in the Acknowledgements below, but since no one ever bothers to read them (c'mon, who does?), I'd like to single out Clayton Hickman, for his beautiful designs and continued support, and Julie Gardner, without whom this book might not have seen the light of day in the first place.

But my biggest thank you, of course, goes to Russell himself, for engaging with this project so passionately, so thoughtfully and so honestly, for not telling me to sod off at the start, and for capturing the madness, the fun and the struggle of writing. For telling it How It Is. Even the stuff that contradicts the other stuff. For sharing his thoughts and hopes and fears and worries (if not the cigarettes and coffees and cancelled holidays and late-night walks around Cardiff Bay), and the massive glories of a tiny piece of story clicking together at 4am… which, nine months later, becomes the most watched thing on TV, wowing 9.4 million people. Russell, thank you.

And we're still in touch, Russell and me. We exchange e-mails, now and then. This morning, for instance, when the overnight figures came through, he sent me one that said: '9.4 MILLION!!!!!!!' He really did use that many exclamation marks. 'This writing lark, eh? It's not bad, is it? The most watched programme of the week! Ha ha ha! It's *Doctor Who*'s first time in the Number One position in its whole 45-year history. It's gobsmacking,' he marvelled, and then signed off with this profundity: 'Someone should write a book about how we did it…!'

BENJAMIN COOK
July 2008

ACKNOWLEDGEMENTS

Russell and Benjamin are indebted to a number of very wonderful people. For giving us permission to include them in this book, thanks to Paul Abbott, Pete Bowker, Chris Chibnall, Will Cohen, Phil Collinson, Bryan Elsley, Mark Gatiss, Murray Gold, Steven Moffat, Helen Raynor, Gareth Roberts, Nicola Shindler and David Tennant. Special thanks to James Moran, for giving the authors permission to talk through the rewriting process. For photographic material, design drawings and other illustrations, huge thanks to Ian Bunting, Jennie Fava, Rob Francis, Wynnie la Freak, Dan Goldsmith, Samantha Hall, Arwel Jones, Sandy Knight, Caroline McArthur, Peter McKinstry, James North, Edward Russell, Gill Hudson and Paul Smith at *Radio Times*, Tom Spilsbury at *Doctor Who Magazine*, and Dave Turbitt at BBC Worldwide. Further thanks to Philip Pullman, Catherine Tate, Susie Liggat, Albert DePetrillo at Ebury, Steve Tribe, Bethan Evans at The Agency, the brilliant Clayton Hickman, and the amazing Julie Gardner.

KEY TO REFERENCES

Episodes of *Doctor Who* aren't always given titles until close to transmission, so numerical production codes are used instead. Listed here in order of transmission (with each episode's writer in parentheses), the production codes to date are as follows:

1.1 **Rose** (Russell T Davies)
1.2 **The End of the World** (Russell T Davies)
1.3 **The Unquiet Dead** (Mark Gatiss)
1.4 **Aliens of London** (Russell T Davies)
1.5 **World War Three** (Russell T Davies)
1.6 **Dalek** (Robert Shearman)
1.7 **The Long Game** (Russell T Davies)
1.8 **Father's Day** (Paul Cornell)
1.9 **The Empty Child** (Steven Moffat)
1.10 **The Doctor Dances** (Steven Moffat)
1.11 **Boom Town** (Russell T Davies)
1.12 **Bad Wolf** (Russell T Davies)
1.13 **The Parting of the Ways** (Russell T Davies)
2.X **The Christmas Invasion** (Russell T Davies)
2.1 **New Earth** (Russell T Davies)
2.2 **Tooth and Claw** (Russell T Davies)
2.3 **School Reunion** (Toby Whithouse)
2.4 **The Girl in the Fireplace** (Steven Moffat)
2.5 **Rise of the Cybermen** (Tom MacRae)
2.6 **The Age of Steel** (Tom MacRae)
2.7 **The Idiot's Lantern** (Mark Gatiss)
2.8 **The Impossible Planet** (Matt Jones)
2.9 **The Satan Pit** (Matt Jones)
2.10 **Love & Monsters** (Russell T Davies)
2.11 **Fear Her** (Matthew Graham)
2.12 **Army of Ghosts** (Russell T Davies)
2.13 **Doomsday** (Russell T Davies)
3.X **The Runaway Bride** (Russell T Davies)
3.1 **Smith and Jones** (Russell T Davies)
3.2 **The Shakespeare Code** (Gareth Roberts)
3.3 **Gridlock** (Russell T Davies)
3.4 **Daleks in Manhattan** (Helen Raynor)
3.5 **Evolution of the Daleks** (Helen Raynor)
3.6 **The Lazarus Experiment** (Stephen Greenhorn)
3.7 **42** (Chris Chibnall)
3.8 **Human Nature** (Paul Cornell)
3.9 **The Family of Blood** (Paul Cornell)
3.10 **Blink** (Steven Moffat)
3.11 **Utopia** (Russell T Davies)
3.12 **The Sound of Drums** (Russell T Davies)
3.13 **Last of the Time Lords** (Russell T Davies)
4.X **Voyage of the Damned** (Russell T Davies)
4.1 **Partners in Crime** (Russell T Davies)
4.3 **The Fires of Pompeii** (James Moran)
4.2 **Planet of the Ood** (Keith Temple)
4.4 **The Sontaran Stratagem** (Helen Raynor)
4.5 **The Poison Sky** (Helen Raynor)
4.6 **The Doctor's Daughter** (Stephen Greenhorn)
4.7 **The Unicorn and the Wasp** (Gareth Roberts)
4.9 **Silence in the Library** (Steven Moffat)
4.10 **Forest of the Dead** (Steven Moffat)
4.8 **Midnight** (Russell T Davies)
4.11 **Turn Left** (Russell T Davies)
4.12 **The Stolen Earth** (Russell T Davies)
4.13 **Journey's End** (Russell T Davies)
4.14 **The Next Doctor** (Russell T Davies)

N.B. The transmission order of Series Four was revised after the initial scripting stage, but the production codes remained unchanged to avoid confusion.

On *Torchwood*, the production codes pertaining to specific episodes are as follows:

1.1 **Everything Changes** (Russell T Davies)
1.2 **Day One** (Chris Chibnall)
1.3 **Ghost Machine** (Helen Raynor)
1.4 **Cyberwoman** (Chris Chibnall)
1.5 **Small Worlds** (Peter J Hammond)
1.6 **Countrycide** (Chris Chibnall)
1.7 **Greeks Bearing Gifts** (Toby Whithouse)
1.8 **They Keep Killing Suzie** (Paul Tomalin & Dan McCulloch)
1.9 **Random Shoes** (Jacquetta May)
1.10 **Out of Time** (Catherine Tregenna)
1.11 **Combat** (Noel Clarke)
1.12 **Captain Jack Harkness** (Catherine Tregenna)
1.13 **End of Days** (Chris Chibnall)
2.1 **Kiss Kiss, Bang Bang** (Chris Chibnall)
2.2 **Sleeper** (James Moran)
2.3 **To the Last Man** (Helen Raynor)
2.4 **Meat** (Catherine Tregenna)
2.5 **Adam** (Catherine Tregenna)
2.6 **Reset** (JC Wilsher)
2.7 **Dead Man Walking** (Matt Jones)
2.8 **A Day in the Death** (Joseph Lidster)
2.9 **Something Borrowed** (Phil Ford)
2.10 **From Out of the Rain** (Peter J Hammond)
2.11 **Adrift** (Chris Chibnall)
2.12 **Fragments** (Chris Chibnall)
2.13 **Exit Wounds** (Chris Chibnall)

On *The Sarah Jane Adventures*, the production codes pertaining to specific episodes are as follows:

1.X **Invasion of the Bane** (Russell T Davies & Gareth Roberts)
1.1 **Revenge of the Slitheen Part One** (Gareth Roberts)
1.2 **Revenge of the Slitheen Part Two** (Gareth Roberts)
1.3 **Eye of the Gorgon Part One** (Phil Ford)
1.4 **Eye of the Gorgon Part Two** (Phil Ford)
1.5 **Warriors of Kudlak Part One** (Phil Gladwin)
1.6 **Warriors of Kudlak Part Two** (Phil Gladwin)
1.7 **Whatever Happened to Sarah Jane? Part One** (Gareth Roberts)
1.8 **Whatever Happened to Sarah Jane? Part Two** (Gareth Roberts)
1.9 **The Lost Boy Part One** (Phil Ford)
1.10 **The Lost Boy Part Two** (Phil Ford)

WHO'S WHO

WRITERS

Paul Abbott – credits include *Coronation Street* and *Cracker*, and creator of *Clocking Off*, *Linda Green*, *State of Play*, and *Shameless*

Douglas Adams – 14 episodes of *Doctor Who* between 1978 and 1980, and script-edited the show at the end of the 1970s; best known as the creator of the *Hitchhiker's Guide to the Galaxy* series (initially for radio, later novels and a TV series); also originated the idea for the computer game *Starship Titanic*; died 2001

Lindsey Alford – script editor on *Doctor Who* Series Three and Four, and *The Sarah Jane Adventures*

Peter Bowker – TV credits include *Blackpool*, *The Canterbury Tales*, and *Casualty*

Chris Chibnall – *Doctor Who* 3.7, and head writer on *Torchwood* (1.2, 1.4, 1.6, 1.13, 2.1, 2.11, 2.12, 2.13)

Paul Cornell – *Doctor Who* 1.8 and 3.8/3.9

Richard Dawkins – evolutionary biologist and popular science writer; cameoed as himself in *Doctor Who* 4.12

Brian Elsley – co-creator of and showrunner on *Skins*

Mark Gatiss – *Doctor Who* 1.3 and 2.7; also played Professor Lazarus in *Doctor Who* 3.6

Matthew Graham – *Doctor Who* 2.11, and co-creator of *Life on Mars*

Stephen Greenhorn – *Doctor Who* 3.6 and 4.6

Robert Holmes – 64 episodes of *Doctor Who* between 1968 and 1986, and script-edited the show in the mid 1970s; died 1986

Matt Jones – *Doctor Who* 2.8/2.9 and *Torchwood* 2.7; script editor on *Queer as Folk* and *Queer as Folk 2*

Joe Lidster – *Torchwood* 2.8

Tom MacRae – *Doctor Who* 2.5/2.6

Jimmy McGovern – TV credits include *Cracker*, *The Lakes*, and *The Street*, all of which he created

Robert McKee – screenwriting guru

Brian Minchin – script editor on *Doctor Who* Series Four and *Torchwood*

Steven Moffat – *Doctor Who* 1.9/1.10, 2.4, 3.10 and 4.9/4.10, as well as *Children in Need* mini-episode *Time Crash*, and Russell T Davies' replacement as showrunner from *Doctor Who* Series Five

James Moran – *Doctor Who* 4.3 and *Torchwood* 2.2

Peter Morgan – TV credits include *The Deal* and *Longford*; movie credits include *The Queen*, *The Last King of Scotland*, and the adaptation of his stage play *Frost/Nixon*

Helen Raynor – *Doctor Who* 3.4/3.5 and 4.4/4.5, *Torchwood* 1.3 and 2.3, and has script-edited both shows

Gareth Roberts – *Doctor Who* 3.2 and 4.7, 2005's interactive mini-episode *Attack of the Graske*, and *The Sarah Jane Adventures* 1.X, 1.1/1.2 and 1.7/1.8

Gary Russell – script editor on *Torchwood* and *The Sarah Jane Adventures*; author of behind-the-scenes books on *Doctor Who*

Keith Temple – *Doctor Who* 4.2

ACTORS

Freema Agyeman – Martha Jones in *Doctor Who* Series Three and Four, and *Torchwood* 2.6, 2.7 and 2.8

Howard Attfield – Donna's dad, Geoff, in *Doctor Who* 3.X

Rakie Ayola – the Hostess in *Doctor Who* 4.8

Annette Badland – Blon Fel-Fotch Pasameer-Day Slitheen (alias Margaret Blaine) in *Doctor Who* 1.4/1.5 and 1.11

John Barrowman – Captain Jack Harkness in *Doctor Who* Series One, Three, and Four, and *Torchwood*

Simon Callow – Charles Dickens in *Doctor Who* 1.3

Peter Capaldi – Lobus Caecilius in *Doctor Who* 4.3

Debbie Chazen – Big Claire in *Mine All Mine*, and Foon Van Hoff in *Doctor Who* 4.X

Chipo Chung – Chantho in *Doctor Who* 3.11, and the Fortune Teller in 4.11

Noel Clarke – Rose's boyfriend, Mickey Smith, in *Doctor Who* Series One, Two, and Four; also wrote *Torchwood* 1.11

Camille Coduri – Rose's mum, Jackie Tyler, in *Doctor Who* Series One, Two, and Four

George Costigan – Max Capricorn in 4.X

Lindsey Coulson – Val Cane in *Doctor Who* 4.8

Bernard Cribbins – Donna's grandad, Wilf Mott, in *Doctor Who* 4.X and Series Four

Gareth David-Lloyd – Ianto Jones in *Torchwood* and *Doctor Who* 4.12/4.13

Alan Davies – Bob Gossage in *Bob & Rose*

Peter Davison – the Fifth Doctor in *Doctor Who* from 1981 to 1984, as well as in 2007 mini-episode *Time Crash*

Christopher Eccleston – Steve Baxter in *The Second Coming*, and the Ninth Doctor in *Doctor Who* Series One

WHO'S WHO

Janet Fielding – Tegan Jovanka in *Doctor Who* from 1981 to 1984

Sir Michael Gambon – TV credits include *The Singing Detective*; movie credits include the *Harry Potter* films

Aidan Gillen – Stuart Jones in *Queer as Folk* and *Queer as Folk 2*

Burn Gorman – Owen Harper in *Torchwood* Series One and Two

Mitch Hewer – Maxxie Oliver in *Skins*

Dennis Hopper – American actor and filmmaker; movie credits include *Blue Velvet*, *Speed*, *Apocalypse Now*, and *Easy Rider*

Nicholas Hoult – Tony Stonem in *Skins*

Charlie Hunnam – Nathan Maloney in *Queer as Folk* and *Queer as Folk 2*

Jessica Hynes (née Stevenson) – Holly Vance in *Bob & Rose*, and Joan Redfern in *Doctor Who* 3.8/3.9

David Jason – TV credits include *Open All Hours*, *Only Fools and Horses*, and *A Touch of Frost*

Peter Kay – the Abzorbaloff in *Doctor Who* 2.10

Craig Kelly – Vince Tyler in *Queer as Folk* and *Queer as Folk 2*

Sam Kelly – TV credits include *'Allo 'Allo!* and *Porridge*

Jacqueline King – Donna's mother, Sylvia Noble, in *Doctor Who* 3.X and Series Four

Alex Kingston – River Song in *Doctor Who* 4.9/4.10

Sarah Lancashire – Miss Foster in *Doctor Who* 4.1

James Marsters – Captain John Hart in *Torchwood* 2.1, 2.12 and 2.13

Sir Ian McKellen – movie credits include the *Lord of the Rings* and *X-Men* trilogies

Kylie Minogue – Australian pop star and actress; Astrid Peth in *Doctor Who* 4.X

Georgia Moffett – Jenny in *Doctor Who* 4.6

Colin Morgan – Jethro in *Doctor Who* 4.8

Naoko Mori – Toshiko Sato in *Doctor Who* 1.4 and *Torchwood* Series One and Two

Eve Myles – Gwyneth in *Doctor Who* 1.3, and Gwen Cooper in *Torchwood* and *Doctor Who* 4.12/4.13

Gray O'Brien – Rickston Slade in *Doctor Who* 4.X

Peter O'Toole – Old Casanova in *Casanova*

Geoffrey Palmer – Edward Masters in 1970 *Doctor Who* serial *Doctor Who and the Silurians*, Earth Administrator in 1972 serial *The Mutants*, and Captain Hardaker in *Doctor Who* 4.X

Francois Pandolfo – Quintus Caecilius in *Doctor Who* 4.3

Lynne Perrie – Ivy Tilsley (later Brennan) in *Coronation Street*; died 2006

Billie Piper – Rose Tyler in *Doctor Who* Series One, Two, and Four

Amanda Redman – TV credits include *At Home with the Braithwaites* and *New Tricks*

Clive Rowe – Morvin Van Hoff in *Doctor Who* 4.X

Christopher Ryan – Lord Kiv in 1986 *Doctor Who* serial *The Trial of a Time Lord*, and Sontaran leader General Staal in *Doctor Who* 4.4/4.5

Daniel Ryan – Andy Lewis in *Bob & Rose*, and Biff Cane in *Doctor Who* 4.8

Colin Salmon – Dr Moon in *Doctor Who* 4.9/4.10

John Simm – the Master in *Doctor Who* 3.11 and 3.12/3.13

Lesley Sharp – Rose Cooper in *Bob & Rose*, Judith Roach in *The Second Coming*, and Sky Silvestry in *Doctor Who* 4.8

Elisabeth Sladen – Sarah Jane Smith in *Doctor Who* from 1973 to 1976, reprising the role in 1983 anniversary special *The Five Doctors* and in *Doctor Who* 3.3 and 4.12/4.13, and *The Sarah Jane Adventures*

Brenda Strong – Mary Alice Young in *Desperate Housewives*

Clive Swift – Jobel in 1985 *Doctor Who* serial *Revelation of the Daleks*, and Mr Copper in *Doctor Who* 4.X

Catherine Tate – Donna Noble in *Doctor Who* 3.X and Series Four

David Tennant – Giacomo Casanova in Russell T Davies' *Casanova*, and the Tenth Doctor in *Doctor Who* Series Two, Three, and Four

Russell Tovey – Midshipman Frame in *Doctor Who* 4.X

David Troughton – Private Moor in 1969 *Doctor Who* serial *The War Games*, King Peladon in 1972's *The Curse of Peladon*, and Professor Hobbes in *Doctor Who* 4.8

Indira Varma – Suzie Costello in *Torchwood* 1.1 and 1.8

Jimmy Vee – *Doctor Who* credits include the Moxx of Balhoon (1.2), the Space Pig (1.4), and Bannakaffalatta (4.X); *The Sarah Jane Adventures* credits include Carl Slitheen (1.1/1.2), the Graske (1.7/1.8), and Nathan Slitheen (1.9/1.10)

Lee Williams – TV credits include *Teachers* and *The Forsyte Saga: To Let*

WHO'S WHO

Penelope Wilton – Monica Gossage in *Bob & Rose*, and Harriet Jones in *Doctor Who* 1.4/1.5, 2X and 4.12

Kate Winslet – Reet in *Dark Season*; movie credits include *Titanic*, *Eternal Sunshine of the Spotless Mind*, and *Finding Neverland*

OTHERS

William Baker – Kylie Minogue's creative director

Matthew Bouch – producer of *The Sarah Jane Adventures*

Will Cohen – visual FX producer on *Doctor Who*

Phil Collinson – producer of *Doctor Who* Series One to Four

Robin Davies – driver on *Queer as Folk*, *Queer as Folk 2*, *Bob & Rose*, *The Second Coming*, *Mine All Mine*, and *Doctor Who* Series One; died in 2007

Nick Elliott – Controller of Drama at ITV, from 1995 to 2007

Peter Fincham – Controller of BBC One, from 2005 to 2007

Jane Fletcher – BBC One's Head of Press, from 2005 to 2007

Julie Gardner – BBC Wales' Head of Fiction and Drama, and executive producer of *Doctor Who*, *Torchwood*, and *The Sarah Jane Adventures*

Murray Gold – composer of *Doctor Who*'s musical scores

Neill Gorton – designer of special make-up and prosthetics on *Doctor Who*, *Torchwood*, and *The Sarah Jane Adventures*

Sarah Harding – director of four episodes of *Queer as Folk*

Graeme Harper – director of six *Doctor Who* episodes during the 1980s, as well as *Doctor Who* 2.5/2.6, 2.12/2.13, 3.7, 3.11, 4.2, 4.7, 4.11 and 4.12/4.13, and *Children in Need* mini-episode *Time Crash*

Anna Home – the BBC's Head of Children's Television, from 1986 to 1997

Jay Hunt – Controller of BBC One from 2008

Verity Lambert – *Doctor Who*'s first producer, from 1963 to 1965; other TV producing credits include *Adam Adamant Lives!*, *The Naked Civil Servant*, *Minder*, *Jonathan Creek*, and *Love Soup*

Susie Liggat – producer of *Doctor Who* 3.8/3.9, 4.2, 4.4/4.5, 4.7 and 4.11, and *The Sarah Jane Adventures* 1.X

Freddie Ljungberg – Swedish footballer, and underwear model for Calvin Klein

Euros Lyn – director of *Doctor Who* 1.2, 1.3, 2.2, 2.4, 2.7, 2.11, 3.X, 4.9/4.10 and 2005's *Children in Need* episode

Paul Marquess – TV producing credits include *The Bill* and *Family Affairs*; creator of *Footballers' Wives*

Charles Martin – director of *The Sarah Jane Adventures* 1.5/1.6 and 1.9/1.10, and two episodes of *Skins* Series Two

Charles McDougall – director of the first four episodes of *Queer as Folk*

McFly – pop-rock band, cameoed as themselves in *Doctor Who* 3.12

Peter McKinstry – concept artist on *Doctor Who* since Series Two

Jess Van Niekerk – production co-ordinator on *Doctor Who* Series One to Four

Paul O'Grady – comedian and TV presenter; cameoed as himself in *Doctor Who* 4.12

Louise Page – costume designer on *Doctor Who* since Series Two

Andy Pryor – casting director on *Doctor Who* and *Torchwood*

Tessa Ross – Channel 4's Film and Drama Controller

Nicola Shindler – producer of *Queer as Folk*, *Bob & Rose*, and *The Second Coming*, and founder of independent TV drama production company Red

Tracie Simpson – production manager on *Doctor Who* Series One to Four

Barbara Southcott – make-up designer on *Doctor Who* since Series Three

Richard Stokes – producer of *Torchwood* Series One and Two

James Strong – director of *Doctor Who* 2.8/2.9, 3.4/3.5, 4.X and 4.1

Colin Teague – director of *Doctor Who* 3.12/3.13 and 4.3, *Torchwood* 1.3, 1.7, 2.2 and 2.4, and *The Sarah Jane Adventures* 1.X

Edward Thomas – production designer on new *Doctor Who*, *Torchwood*, and *The Sarah Jane Adventures*

Mark Thompson – the BBC's Director-General

Jane Tranter – the BBC's Controller of Fiction, who – as Head of Drama – oversaw the 2005 resurrection of *Doctor Who*

Piers Wenger – Julie Gardner's replacement as BBC Wales' Head of Drama, and executive producer of *Doctor Who* from Series Five onwards

Wynnie la Freak – Manchester-based drag queen, appeared in *Bob & Rose*

CHAPTER ONE

DEFINITELY MAYBE

In which Mika is inspiring, *Skins* is disappointing, and Russell performs a triple loop on ice

FROM: BENJAMIN COOK TO: RUSSELL T DAVIES
SUNDAY 18 FEBRUARY 2007 07:19:48 GMT

AN IDEA

I've been thinking. I know, I know, but I was feeling dangerous. How about a magazine article on the writing of one or more of your *Doctor Who* scripts? The nuts and bolts of the process, from start to finish. Developing the story, the characters, the dialogue. An exploration of the painstaking creation process. What worked, what didn't, and why. I think it'd be fascinating. Or would it be too intrusive? And is there enough time? I'd want to chat to you about your ideas before you start writing (it could be this year's Christmas Special, or Episode 1 of Series Four, or another episode altogether), and exchange regular e-mails over the weeks and months that you spend scripting, honing, and developing the episode(s). I'd need to read, discuss, and compare various drafts. It'd be a unique and valuable look at the art of the television scriptwriter.

Thoughts?

P.S. Please say yes.

FROM: RUSSELL T DAVIES TO: BENJAMIN COOK
SUNDAY 18 FEBRUARY 2007 12:41:59 GMT

RE: AN IDEA

Well, that's a yes, then. You had me at hello.

Morning, Benjamino! Look at you, typing at first light on a Sunday. You're meant to be waking up hung over in the bed of two strangers called Hans and Milly. London isn't what it's cracked up to be. Anyway, yes to the writing thing. But I'd better warn you – I've never done anything like it before. If it feels too odd, I'd have to stop. My worry is, I never show my stuff to *anyone*. I just lock myself away and work. But the real problem is, I don't do my working out on paper. I don't often do treatments or breakdowns. It all exists in this great big stew in my head, because any story can go in any direction. It's not what you write, it's what you *choose* – and I'm good at choices. Paul Abbott always says that about me, bless him. He says that I make good choices – as opposed to someone who writes a first draft, and *then* focuses on what the story is about, what works and what doesn't. But I doubt that makes me a better writer.

Paul tends to work it out on paper, and he's the Best Writer In The Land.

There's little physical evidence of the script process to show you. No notes. Nothing. I think, and think, and think… and by the time I come to write, a lot has been decided. Also, a lot hasn't been decided, but I trust myself, and scare myself, that it'll happen in the actual writing. It all exists in my head, but in this soup. It's like the ideas are fluctuating in this great big quantum state of Maybe. The choices look easy when recounted later, but that's hindsight. When nothing is real and nothing is fixed, it can go anywhere. The Maybe is a hell of a place to live. As well as being the best place in the world.

I filter through all those thoughts, but that's rarely sitting at my desk, if ever. It's all done walking about, going to town, having tea and watching telly. The rest of your life becomes just the surface, chattering away on top of the Maybe. It never turns off. (And bear in mind, the Maybe isn't just thinking about one episode. Right now, today, I've skipped ahead to Series Four, Episode 12's problem: what do the Lost People of Earth actually *do*? And that'll go on for, oh, the next year or so, until I start writing it in November.) I can't begin to tell you the thousand problems and their possible solutions, bubbling away at the same time. And the *doubts*. That's where this job is knackering and debilitating. Everything – and I mean every story ever written anywhere – is underscored by the constant murmur of: this is rubbish, I am rubbish, and this is due in on Tuesday! The hardest part of writing is the writing.

So, Ben, what I'm saying is: yes, let's do it (judging by how long I've gone on in this e-mail, we might even get a book out of it!), but so much of the process is invisible. When I start typing, those solutions lock in, and create the world of the story very fast – which is terrifying, because you're always waiting for the inevitable day when… they don't! Blimey, that'll happen. One day.

The thing is, you'll have to fight me feeling superstitious about the writing process. My trust in the Maybe feels almost superstitious. (Though I don't actually call it the Maybe; I just made that up now. And I'm not even superstitious. I was born atheist, me.) In considering a script, I might feel that saying those early options out loud to you automatically makes them more fixed, and might unbalance things. It's new territory, and that feels terrifying. Equally, so would the prospect of a night in with Freddie Ljungberg, but I wouldn't say no to that either. (Actually, I don't even fancy him that much, but it's a good name to type, don't you think?)

FROM: BENJAMIN COOK TO: RUSSELL T DAVIES
MONDAY 19 FEBRUARY 2007 00:35:32 GMT

RE: AN IDEA

'There will be no *Doctor Who* this year. Russell was too busy e-mailing Ben.'

I appreciate what you're saying about how you write – more in your head, less on paper – but I reckon it's better like that. It's the bits beyond the documents, beyond what's written down, that interest me the most. Literally, the thought processes. Not just what happened, but what's *happening*. Not just what goes into that great big stew in your head, but also what doesn't. I'm after a more progressive, imaginative, insightful exploration of the scriptwriting and storytelling process. Not much, then!

FROM: RUSSELL T DAVIES TO: BENJAMIN COOK
MONDAY 19 FEBRUARY 2007 01:08:01 GMT

RE: AN IDEA

Right, you're on! I've been thinking about it all day, and it could be really exciting. Also, it's the article on writing that I've always wanted to read. Writers almost never talk about writing. Not ever. Even when I'm sitting there with Paul Abbott, getting drunk at three in the morning (long time since I did that – friendships perish under the *Doctor Who* schedule), we might complain about deadlines and commissioners and directors… but never the actual writing. We guard it. Perhaps it truly is superstition. Like saying Candyman out loud.

Would this year's Christmas Special script work? It's not a typical script: it has to be big and blousy and Christmas Day-y. It's half script, half event. But I'm not sure about the first episode of Series Four either, because that's introducing the Doctor's new companion – I like the name Penny (do you like Penny?) – and I might want to be left alone for that. Plus, you can give away too much information. Maybe discussions about a new companion, if put into print, would become part of fandom's rigid thinking. That actress would, in 20 years'

Continued on page 21

SERIES FOUR BREAKDOWN

This is the Series Four Breakdown, compiled by Russell for the production team early in 2007. 'It's such a scary document, people might resign,' he joked at the time. Episodes 4.X, 4.1, 4.11 and 4.12/4.13 were to be scripted by Russell, 4.2 by Keith Temple, 4.3 by either Mark Gatiss (World War II) or James Moran (Pompeii), 4.4 and 4.5 by Helen Raynor, 4.6 by Stephen Greenhorn, 4.7 by Gareth Roberts, 4.8 by Tom MacRae, and 4.9/4.10 by Steven Moffat...

DOCTOR WHO SERIES FOUR

4.X – STARSHIP TITANIC

The *Titanic* In Space crossed with *The Poseidon Adventure*. The ship is on a Christmas Cruise, gets hit by meteorites, and the Doctor and survivors have to crawl through the wreckage and find out who caused the sabotage, while stopping the ship hitting the Earth below. It's not a proper recreation of the *Titanic*; it's more of a luxury hotel, with Olde Worlde trappings, plus Christmas decorations. The people on board, staff and passengers, aren't human; they're just visiting, like a cruise ship to the Bahamas. I'd like a new, one-off, spiky-faced little alien in black tie to be one of the survivors. Plus, the main monsters are the ship's robot staff – Golden Angels, beautiful, male, blank-faced masks. Also, the Judoon stomp in at the end to arrest the villains.[1] And there'll be a trip down to Earth, to a night-time shopping street with Christmas decorations – but it's deserted! No people. And maybe one scene on moorland at the end. With snow. Gotta have snow.

4.1 – NEW COMPANION

The Doctor meets his new companion, they solve an alien threat, and then sail off together. Modern-day Earth. Possibly a CGI monster.

4.2 – PLANET OF THE OOD[2]

A visit to their home planet, an ice-world, where the poor Ood are being sold into slavery by the human race. CGI-enhanced exteriors – wide-open vistas covered in snow. Factories where Ood are processed. Posh PR-type offices, where the whole enterprise looks legit, but underneath are dark, grimy rooms where the Ood are treated terribly. One huge warehouse space, full of Ood cages. Caves where the giant, pulsating, CGI Ood-brain is fermenting. Plus, a sequence of a man transforming into an Ood.

4.3 – NAZIS

World War II. Monsters on the loose in the Natural History Museum as a Nazi strike-force invades. FIRST DRAFT SCRIPT AVAILABLE, but with changes to come. The museum could be a London shoot for a few days, if we can use the interior of the Natural History Museum, but we'll need Cardiff corridors and rooms as well, if they can match. Plus, an *Indiana Jones*-type chamber hidden beneath, with sliding stone doors and stuff.

OR!!!

I am worried about recreating World War II again so soon.[3] This entire script could be replaced by...

4.3 – POMPEII

God help us! We could build a villa interior, some alien base inside the volcano, and a CGI Vesuvius, smoke and lava and all that, and Fire People might be possible... but the obvious worry is: we can stand in a bit of Welsh countryside and look at a CGI Pompeii from a distance, but I don't know how we can achieve any sort of exterior street/marketplace/whatever. We have to see people running from those ashes! But let's talk about it, because it's possible that we can write a script around our parameters. For once! And 'Pompeii' is such an irresistible headline.

4.4/4.5 – SONTARANS[4]

Martha calls the Doctor back home.[5] A huge British science project to repair the ozone layer is being infiltrated by the Sontarans. Big, sprawling science base. Maybe a military feel. These episodes might

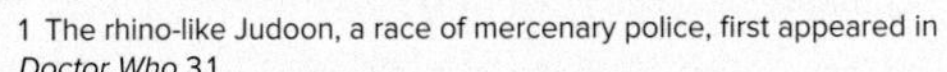

1 The rhino-like Judoon, a race of mercenary police, first appeared in *Doctor Who* 3.1

2 The subservient Ood débuted in *Doctor Who* 2.8.

3 *Doctor Who* 1.9/1.10 were set during the Blitz.

4 A warrior race of dome-headed aliens, the Sontarans featured in four *Doctor Who* serials between 1973 and 1985.

5 Martha Jones (played by Freema Agyeman) was the Doctor's travelling companion throughout Series Three.

SERIES FOUR BREAKDOWN (continued)

have quite a bit of military hardware, open battles between soldiers and Sontarans, guns, trucks, explosions. It's war! Also, secret Sontaran chambers where they're mass-cloning. The science project involves some device being attached to 'Every Home in Britain', like, say, a metal tube running from floor to gutter. Plus, back to suburbia with the companion's family.

4.6 – ALIEN PLANET

The Doctor, Martha, and the new companion. It's not a huge-vistas world; it's more contained. Maybe a broken-down world at war, huddled in bunkers, under fire. I'd love a new race of alien soldiers for this – all identical, like the Ood. Battle-scarred grunts in flight-suit-like costumes. Also, Martha goes back home at the end of this episode, requiring one suburbia-type scene.

4.7 – AGATHA CHRISTIE

The Doctor and Agatha hunt the murderer! Pure Agatha Christie. Country house, drawing rooms, wood-panelled corridors, below-stairs, etc. Nice and smart and gorgeous. It's probably set in 1966, but should feel old-fashioned, like a '20s/'30s thriller. But the gentry don't date much anyway. And a CGI monster on the loose.

4.8 – CENTURY HOUSE

A double-bank episode.[6] All Doctor. Companion-lite (she sits at home and watches the whole thing on TV with her mum; hopefully, one day's filming with her). The Doctor goes live on reality TV show *Most Haunted* to track down the ghost of the Red Widow. A big, old, abandoned, spooky house, like on a cliff top. OB vans and trucks with cables ringed around the house. Certain rooms will flashback to the 1950s or '60s. A big fire sequence towards the end – a couple of rooms burning.

4.9/4.10 – SPACE LIBRARY

An ancient, alien library on another world has been sealed off for centuries, until the Doctor joins an archaeological expedition on a mission to find out why. It's a Steven Moffat script (not available yet), so God help us! He says there are moving shadows (I'm worried that this means actual animation), and he describes the library as dark and dusty, abandoned, creepy, though it's alien and sci-fi at the same time. Events are connected to an ordinary modern-day boy in his bedroom.

4.11 – COMPANION ALONE

Double-bank. Doctor-lite. I'll try to keep this low-cost. Honestly.

4.12/4.13 – THE STOLEN EARTH

The season finale. Earth is transported halfway across the universe as part of a Dalek plot.[7] These episodes feature Martha, Captain Jack, Sarah Jane, Elton, and Rose.[8] Jackie and Mickey?[9] Also, can I have the rest of the Torchwood team, just for a couple of days? Plus, a futuristic space station complex where lots of alien races are gathering for a conference. CGI: Bane, Krillitanes, Gelth, Isolus, everything we've got in the computer.[10] PROSTHETICS: Judoon, Slitheen, the Graske, the Moxx of Balhoon (well, his brother, the Jixx of Balhoon), Sisters of the Wicker Place Mat, plus a new female alien, a wise old counsellor, head of the space conference.[11] And Daleks, en masse. Lots of gunfire and exterminations. And the biggest Dalek spaceship interior ever – more like a Dalek Temple. Christ almighty! The skies over the Earth need to be changed to weird outer space vistas. Also, visible in the sky, a huge Dalek ship exterior. The size of a solar system! This will probably explode. Like they do.

And Davros.[12]

ZAP!

6 Each series contains at least one double-bank episode, featuring nominal appearances from one or more of the regular cast, so that another episode can be shot simultaneously, to save on filming days.

7 The Daleks – with their battle cry of 'Ex-ter-min-ate!' – first appeared in *Doctor Who* in 1963, and have featured in many subsequent episodes, becoming synonymous with the show.

8 Captain Jack Harkness (played by John Barrowman) travelled with the Doctor in Series One and Three, and is the central character in spin-off series *Torchwood*; Sarah Jane Smith (Elisabeth Sladen), companion to the Third and Fourth Doctors in the mid 1970s, returned in *Doctor Who* 2.3, and subsequently the spin-off *The Sarah Jane Adventures*; Elton Pope (Marc Warren) appeared in *Doctor Who* 2.10; Rose Tyler (Billie Piper) was the Doctor's companion throughout Series One and Two.

9 Rose's mother Jackie (played by Camille Coduri) and boyfriend Mickey (Noel Clarke) featured in Series One and Two.

10 The Bane first appeared in *The Sarah Jane Adventures* 1.X; the bat-like Krillitanes in *Doctor Who* 2.3; the Gelth in *Doctor Who* 1.3; the Isolus in *Doctor Who* 2.11.

11 The Slitheen débuted in *Doctor Who* 1.4; the Graske at Christmas 2005, in interactive mini-episode *Attack of the Graske*; the doomed Moxx in *Doctor Who* 1.2, alongside a clan of background aliens nicknamed the Sisters of the Wicker Place Mat.

12 The (fictional) creator of the Daleks, mad-scientist Davros, first appeared in 1975 serial *Genesis of the Daleks*.

time, still be asked in interviews, 'How do you feel about the fact that you were originally conceived to be a blind Sumo lesbian?'

Anyway, off to bed. Not because I'm tired, but because I'm reading a brilliant book, *Prisoner of Trebekistan*. The 'Trebek' is Alex Trebek, who's presented the US quiz show *Jeopardy!* for over 20 years. It's the story of a man who dedicated his life to getting on the show. It's so brilliant, and so funny, and even heartbreaking in small and beautiful ways. A man who's devoted to telly. No wonder I like it.

FROM: BENJAMIN COOK TO: RUSSELL T DAVIES
MONDAY 19 FEBRUARY 2007 02:23:45 GMT

RE: AN IDEA

Yes, I like Penny.

FROM: RUSSELL T DAVIES TO: BENJAMIN COOK
WEDNESDAY 21 FEBRUARY 2007 00:57:02 GMT

RE: AN IDEA

Penny it is! I like that too.

Right. The Great Correspondence. Let's start. I've been sitting here for about two hours thinking, go on, start writing to Ben. With the back of my head going, *EEK!* The scary thing is, it feels so exposed, balanced by the lovely thing that you're one of the few people I'd trust completely to do this with. The only other person I used to show script-in-progress was my Manchester script editor, Paul Abbott's wife, Saskia, because she lives with a writer.[1] She knows how barmy it is.

I'm just going to type and say *everything*. The moment I start censoring, it'll start to become 'written', and I think you need to know everything. I think that's the process you're after. I'm going to type what's in my head, and how it started developing today. No, not developing, but shifting. It's 4.1, the first episode of Series Four, and the creation of Penny. A good, iconic episode, but still a standard 45-minute length –

Of course, this big lump of Maybe coexists with thoughts on my two scripts for *The Sarah Jane Adventures* – which I'm dying to write, but I suspect time is running out. Plus, *Torchwood* Series Two, for which I'm supposed to be writing the Annual Return Of Suzie, coinciding with the 'death' of Ianto, but these plans are being stymied in the preparation stage, because Indira Varma is pregnant and Naoko Mori needs some time off.[2] The schedule is like a spinning wheel of alternative options, intruding into the thinking process. On top of all that there's the *Doctor Who* Christmas Special, the *Titanic* In Space. (*Titanic II* – is that a good title?) For the past few days, I keep focusing on one of the central characters, an old historian-type figure – a nice, funny part, a man who's studied the Earth (these are aliens, sailing above the Earth, on a Christmas Cruise), and he gets all Earth history hopelessly wrong. 'They worship the Great God Santa!' He should wear round pebble glasses. A while back, I read that *Doctor Who* is one of the few programmes that David Jason lets his young daughter watch. Perfect guest star! Yesterday, we asked Andy Pryor, our casting director, to contact David's agent. The agent confirmed that, yes, David's daughter genuinely loves the show, so they'll talk to him, with the caveat that he's very busy, and with our fear that he'd cost a fortune. But that created today's shift onto *Doctor Who* 4.1, because *Sarah Jane* and *Torchwood* problems can park. And David Jason

David Tennant gets himself in the mood for another Christmas Special.

1 Saskia Abbott script-edited both *Bob & Rose* and *Casanova*.

2 Torchwood operatives in Series One and Two include computer specialist Toshiko Sato (Naoko Mori), support man Ianto Jones (Gareth David-Lloyd), and, in 1.1, second-in-command Suzie Costello (Indira Varma).

– well, we'd have to meet him and schmooze him, *if it ever happens*, so I leave that for a minute… and my mind skips onto 4.1, because that's sort of 'clean', untouched, and untroubled –

Well, no, the real truth is, I'm sitting here listening to Mika's album, *Life in Cartoon Motion*. I like Mika. Oh, a lot. Just listen to 'Any Other World', Track 6 of his album. I heard that today for the first time. *Click!* That's what shifted me onto 4.1. A piece of music. '*In any other world / You could tell the difference.*' That's a *Doctor Who* companion song! That's 'I'm going in the TARDIS'! And then those violins start. '*Say goodbye to the world you thought you lived in.*' That's Penny! I'm going to use that track on screen, as she decides to become the companion. The scene is written in my head. I can *see* it – where she is, how she walks, how I write the stage directions, the mood of it, the romance of it, the size of it. I can absolutely see it. Moments of clarity like that, when everything else is in flux, you cling to. You might remind me about that song one day and I'll just be like, 'Oh yeah, forgot.' Or more importantly – 'It didn't work.' But that's today's thought. Never mind schedules, and actors, and bollocks – I've found a companion's soundtrack! And I'm excited about Penny.

Thoughts I've had about Penny, prior to this: a bit older, maybe 30+ (are we losing all the little girls in the audience?), smarter, sassier. All of us loved Catherine Tate and that sort of repartee with the Doctor.[3] At the *Radio Times* Covers Party, Jane Tranter (the BBC's Controller of Fiction) said to me, 'Can't we bring back Donna for a few episodes?' Hmm, no. There are tentative Maybe plans for *everyone* to come back in cameos for 4.12/4.13, including Donna, so let's keep our powder dry for that. But we all liked Donna's equal-status sparkiness, independence, sharpness –

Hang on. Back to Penny. What's her job?! Journalist? It worked for Sarah Jane. In 4.4/4.5, there's going to be an Earth research base that needs investigating. Maybe.

Also, Penny is northern. It's my love of northern, and my ability to write that speech pattern. I actually miss it. But we've told Andy Pryor, 'Don't limit your thinking to northern.' That would be stupid. We've just got to get the best. Andy lives in his great big Casting Maybe all the time. He's already thinking. Sheridan Smith? Someone like a younger Sarah Parish? That ability to

3 Catherine Tate played would-be-companion Donna Noble in 3.X.

Penny meets the Doctor. Illustration by Russell T Davies.

really banter with the Doctor, to match him. And to love him, actually. Under all this is my need to write The Doctor In Love again. I think we've handled it exactly right for Series Three: he'd never fall in love with Martha, because he can't just love the next woman to walk through the door, after Rose. That would cheapen the whole thing. Martha's unrequited love for the Doctor is beautiful. She deserves to grow out of that, so leaves, giving us a nice year-long bridge. Penny is walking into the Doctor's life at just the right time. (It fills me with horror, actor's lives and wages and destinies being decided on my whims, sitting here, looking for the right story. The Maybe isn't just ethereal; it actually employs people. Still, the show is the most important thing.) The first time that the Doctor sees Penny, it should be like – *wham!* Both hearts.

Northern also gives Penny a northern mother. Lovely! Maybe a bit posh. Maybe lottery-winner posh. I miss the funny mum. Little voice in the Maybe, a little doubt whispering away: 'You've *done* funny mum. Lots of funny mums, in fact. Rose's. Even Donna's. What about a funny dad?' But dads aren't funny. Yes, that's not fair, and probably not true. But tough. We're actually close to tackling that question that I always refuse to answer: where do you get your ideas from? *That's* why this correspondence fascinates me. Every writer says that they can't answer that question, but the ideas do come from *somewhere*. That conversation about funny mums happened in the foyer of Claridge's. That's when I thought, let's give Penny a funny mum. ('Where do you get your ideas from?' 'Claridge's!') Or what about a grandfather? Nice old bloke, gentle, sweet, telescope in his shed – he's always been the stargazer. He's the one who waves Penny off, tears in his eyes. It's all unashamed sentiment in the Maybe. I'd planned that grandad for Martha, vaguely, but he never appeared. He lingers on. They do that, the Characters In Search Of An Author.

Other thoughts: the story has to be set on Earth. I've always had this vague image of a housing estate – not a council estate, I mean suburbia – and a great big inverted bowl of a spaceship lands on top of it. Huge ship, covering and sealing off the estate. The space inside becomes night, whilst outside it's day. The ordinary turned into the extraordinary. That's very *Doctor Who*. Turning suburbia into terror. The police and army surround the bowl, but they can't get in, while on the inside – a hunt! An alien hunt. A creature is released – on purpose? Or is it a prison ship? Has the creature run amok and killed the crew, and it's crash-landed here? Nasty alien, vicious, give Penny something to really fight. Fast and deadly. Probably CGI. Make it able to climb on ceilings – that's always scary. Scuttling. Words like scuttling become good and important. I like that.

And in the middle of this estate, there's the Doctor. Taken as read.

That was the thinking… up until today. Thank you, Mika. Today it became: simplify. What if a spaceship crashed, and an alien is on the loose at night? No bowl. A simple, sudden thought of, no, don't contain it; you can make this story wide and free. That made me start to write to you, because the process is starting. The process of going through options. The start of thinking about 4.1. And the stray thought, should Penny start this episode to camera, like a video diary? That's hard to sustain, but it's reaching for a different feel, using the stuff of every other drama. Not being limited to a straightforward telling of a sci-fi or fantasy story. The point is – I don't think that will happen, but I did have an exhilarating moment of thinking it *could* happen. That exhilaration carries over into the rest of the story, and creates these e-mails.

FROM: BENJAMIN COOK TO: RUSSELL T DAVIES
WEDNESDAY 21 FEBRUARY 2007 17:30:09 GMT

RE: AN IDEA

>>*Titanic II* – is that a good title?<<

Do you really want me to answer that, Russell? *Really?!*

I've just downloaded Mika's album. And I Googled him to see what he looks like. I found him in the end, on his official website, sat atop a piano, without shoes. He has oddly shaped toes. The impact of music on your writing, one art form inspiring another (there's a thought – do you see what you do as an art or a craft?), is interesting. Tell me if 'O Mio Babbino Caro' or the Prodigy's 'Smack My Bitch Up' influences today's work.

Also, I'd like to know more about how you name characters. How much importance do you attach to finding the right name? Would Rose have smelt as sweet by any other name? (Do you see what I did there? Eh? *Eh?*) Would we view her differently were she called Natalie? Or Rachael? Or Martha even? Are unusual names better? Can you start writing a character without a name in place?

One other thought, for now. You said, 'Words like scuttling become good and important,' but also you've had 'this vague image of a housing estate… and a great big inverted bowl of a spaceship lands on top of it.' So, do you prefer writing in words or pictures?

FROM: RUSSELL T DAVIES TO: BENJAMIN COOK
WEDNESDAY 21 FEBRUARY 2007 22:17:12 GMT

RE: AN IDEA

I won't be working tonight, because I've had a drink. Never work with drink. (That's me, not a rule. Paul Abbott does the opposite.) I've been for dinner with David and Phil.[4] We had such a good time, with some genuine *Doctor Who* discussion. But that's the first drink

4 David Tennant (the Doctor) and Phil Collinson (producer).

I've had in ages, so cor blimey! I'm not what I was.

Names. As I think of a character, I think of the name. I never spend time debating them, though I can pin all sorts to them in retrospect. Rose Tyler? I'd used Rose in *Bob & Rose*, so that name is like a good luck charm. There's the desire to make the series essentially British, and that's the most British name in the world. I was annoyed with that ridiculous run of female *Doctor Who* companions with boys' or boyish names – Benny, Roz, Charley, even Ace. But that's all hindsight. I just thought, she's called Rose. Instantly, it felt right. On ITV drama *The Grand*, the executive producer made me change the lead woman's name, on a whim, from Judith to Sarah – and that character never felt right from that moment on. I never wrote her well enough. Honestly, I believe that.

Penny's mum is called Moira. There, I just thought of it now! Perfect name.

Look, I'm wary of anyone who's about to start writing ever reading something like this and thinking, that's the way to do it, that's what *I* must do. If you're going to write a script yourself, Ben, please don't think that you have to copy me. I don't think a creative process copies too much anyway. I think it finds its own way. Equally, I know the world is swamped with Robert McKee-type books on structure, and there might be, for all I know, a *How to Choose Your Characters' Names* self-help book. It probably exists. In America. You're just as free to sit down with a *Bumper Book of Baby Names* and choose one with a pin. Whatever works for you.

Now, music is very important to me. I always try to find an album that fits each thing that I write, and then I play it whenever I'm writing, repeating and repeating until I've stopped hearing it, really. It just sinks in, becomes part of the script. There's not always much variance with *Doctor Who*, because most episodes are some sort of action adventure, so often movie scores will do. They equal the size and energy that we try to show on screen. It's much harder with dramas that are more individual pieces of work. (Not that *Doctor Who* isn't personal to me, but there is an essential *Doctor Who*ness that isn't all my own creation.) *Queer as Folk* was Hi-NRG albums, to catch that sheer clubland drive and instil it into the drama. Those characters lived by that beat. *Bob & Rose* was written to *Play*, the classic Moby album. I must have played it tens of thousands of times. That album is urban, sexy, full of lonely hearts at night, just as *Bob & Rose* was full of taxicabs and chance meetings. And *The Second Coming* was Radiohead – experimental, anguish, dark, pain. That was fun!

>>Do you prefer writing in words or pictures?<<

Yes, very pictorial. A visual imagination isn't true of a lot of – very successful – writers, but I can draw, I was drawing before I was writing, so pictures are wired in. It's easy to say that applied to *Doctor Who*, because it's such a visual show, but it's true of everything I've written. *Bob & Rose*, Episode 1, the first ad break, beautifully shot, a crane lifting up as Bob and Rose's respective taxis go their separate ways. That was key. That image was in my head before anything was written. To get pretentious (why am I calling it pretentious, to describe something creative? Shame on me!), that moment sums up the whole show; not the sexuality shtick, but the randomness of it, that two-in-the-morning emptiness, out of which two people make a connection. Of course, sometimes the pictures don't come. It's easy, quoting that scene. There are plenty of ordinary scenes that aren't so memorable. Also, it's not just music + picture + character in separate beats. No, they're all interconnected. The pictures aren't just pictures; they're the tone, the wit, the style, the plot, the people, all in one.

Back to 4.1. As an update, not much has shifted. No real advances. Some days are like that. A lot of days. But I've been playing Mika constantly, always going back to Track 6. If I'm really not going to censor myself, then the sheer fancying of that man, right now, is powerful, ha ha! You see, I just said 'ha ha', because I find it embarrassing to relate. I've got to lose that as I go on, or it'll hold back the honesty. I reckon sex drives a lot of thinking and writing, for everyone. I do think being creative is *immensely* sexual. I think that's true of a lot of writers; they just don't talk about it. It's not just a passive, funny, 'I fancy Mika': it's a very vivid image of him. Oh, in every detail! Just very *real*. (A visual imagination is a great help here.) All those thoughts about sex are really, intrinsically, part of the process – an equal and steady beat underneath Penny's mum, alien hunts, and housing estates. The job is actually sexual. I really believe that.

Perhaps I've made the Maybe sound pure and holy, as though I go into a trance and *think*. People say that to me: Julie is always saying, 'You need thinking time.'[5] But

5 Julie Gardner, executive producer of *Doctor Who*.

Penny must follow in the footsteps of previous companions Rose (Billie Piper), Martha (Freema Agyeman) and Donna (Catherine Tate).

it doesn't exist. The thinking is constant. Never mind Mika with his pants off; this Maybe has a thousand other voices saying, 'Must lose weight. Must stop smoking. Must phone my sisters more often.' Etc. Etc. Etc. Those voices aren't separate from whichever *Doctor Who* plot I'm considering; they're *part* of it. And look – that list is full of doubts. That's the thing about writing. It's all doubt. Doubts about plot, story, character, etc, let in every other doubt, the real doubts, about yourself, your very self.

I'm also sort of… hmm, pausing, wondering how to say this, but I'll say it anyway, it's ground work, and I think you have to know everything to get to the heart of the creative stuff… I'm sort of obsessive. About work, obviously. And smoking. And just look at this e-mail! Proof! A quick chat has turned into an essay. And I get like that about people. I'm not good at handling people. I'm very good at appearing to be Friend To All, but that's easy. But I rarely tell anyone, anywhere, what I'm really thinking, ever. I love my own company. I choose my own company. Because of that obsessive streak. Right now, I think I'm obsessing on these e-mails, and on you. Whether you like it or not. Still, it'll give us material.

Writing isn't just a job that stops at six-thirty. (Well, bad writers can do that.) It's a mad, sexy, sad, scary, obsessive, ruthless, joyful, and utterly, utterly personal thing. There's not the writer and then me; there's just me. All of my life connects to the writing. *All* of it.

That's scared you off, hasn't it? And all we got out of that was bloody Moira! Pages of cheap psychoanalysis, and we end up with a mother's name! That is, equally, why I love this whole bloody thing. Oh, don't think I'm mad and creepy. I'm wondering whether to send, or delete some stuff. Ah, send.

FROM: BENJAMIN COOK TO: RUSSELL T DAVIES
THURSDAY 22 FEBRUARY 2007 05:30:13 GMT

RE: AN IDEA

Dear Mad and Creepy,

Your candidness is definitely A Good Thing. Your frankness is refreshing, and much appreciated. Of course, I would say that. But *really*. It's more than I'd hoped for. Thank you. This is fast becoming the magazine article/book that *I've* always wanted to read.

FROM: RUSSELL T DAVIES TO: BENJAMIN COOK
THURSDAY 22 FEBRUARY 2007 16:46:33 GMT

HERE WE GO THEN…

Good, good, good. I was worried about your reply. Or whether you'd reply or not.

That was a mad e-mail, but also very true. I think I need to do that, to break down the walls a bit, because Glib Funny E-mail Voice is too easy to assume. Well, it's fun. But I need to get beyond that. Even the invention of the Maybe sounds mystical, and possibly glamorous. To make it feel more real, I have to open up that weirdness and compulsion, the darkness of the drive to write, as well as the fun stuff. It *is* painful. And that's good. It's funny, because when I read about other writers' seething fury or alcoholism or whatever, I actually think, blimey, I'm so vanilla. But I'm just barmy in different ways, I suppose.

I had a hell of a time from my mid 20s to mid 30s. Well, everyone does. But I was compulsive and obsessive, and that can get dangerous. I was out every night – really, every night, even Sundays – dancing, drinking, and off my head on God-knows-what. I'd be out till five in the morning, get into work at Granada at nine, throw up in the toilets, then go and be brilliant at my job. What a time! It was madness. (I'll draw a veil over a lot of it or this'll never be printed.) Then I had one calamitous night in 1997, three days after the death of Princess Diana. I actually, really, remember thinking, Jesus, if I die, I won't even make a minor headline, it's all Diana! But that cleaned me up completely. No therapy, no nothing. Just stopped. Well, no, not straight away, it took me three more years, but I got there in the end. I hardly even drink any more. God, I miss it. Really. Compulsive obsessive.

I wrote *Queer as Folk* as a hymn and testament to those days. Not a condemnation of them, but a salute. I'm proud of that. And only I really know that. Well, and you now. But that drive and compulsion, and even the self-destruction, is still there – all poured into the writing now, though still lurking.

Back to the plot! Last night, as I lay in bed, I found myself thinking, Penny should be jilted. In Scene 1. Leaving her raw and open, just ready for a dazzling Time Lord to enter her life. Imagine: a house, full of party guests; Penny is running around saying, 'Ssh, he's coming, hush everyone, lights off!' They all stand in the dark, her boyfriend – Gary, he's called Gary – walks in, lights on, *surprise!* He's standing there, blinking, shocked… as behind him, his *other* girlfriend – Roxanne – walks into the house, which they'd thought would be empty! Nice, cute, needs work.

Practical considerations (because this is where you have to be tough with a scene, and edit it before it's even written): for this scene to work, the lights have to be off, because Gary needs to think that Penny is *away*, assuming that they live together. Problem: you'd have to switch the lights off as he drove into the street, not as he approached the front door, or he'd know. So that means – what? – a minute, two minutes, in darkness, until he actually opens the door. That's a dead two minutes, right at the top of the episode. You can fill that dead time with Penny helping the set-up, whispering to her mate, 'He thinks I'm in Southport for the weekend,' but there's only so much of Penny saying 'Ssh' that you can take. Practical considerations are important when writing for the screen – even simple things, like the time it takes for a person to walk from A to B. Lots of scripts say: 'Gary gets into the car and drives off.' But think about how long that takes. You open the door, get in, adjust the gears and put the key in, do up your seatbelt, ignition, rev up, drive off – that's 30 seconds. The writer intended five seconds maximum, but it can't be done, not without a lot of camera set-ups. You can tighten the length of the process in the Edit by cutting to close-up (CU) keys, CU seatbelt going click, CU exhaust gunning fumes – but that's three extra shots already on what's meant to be a simple, one-line event. A lot of time is wasted on a thousand sets while directors and actors try to fix those sorts of problems.

But the most important worry is this: Penny lives in a house. With a boyfriend. Settled. I don't like that. It feels too old, too remote from those eight-year-old girls watching. Does the scene work in a flat? A flat is more like an eight-year-old's bedroom. Is the scene just too cute? But it's handy for pushing Penny to where I want her to be, emotionally. Alone. Brittle. Sad, but wistful. The result of that scene is a good image: night, city street, lamplight, taxis. Penny is walking along, heartbroken, being funny about it on her mobile to her friend, saying why-oh-why can't she meet the right man… as she walks past a police box.

The Three Who Rule. L–R: Russell T Davies (Head Writer and Executive Producer), Phil Collinson (Producer) and Julie Gardner (Executive Producer).

FROM: RUSSELL T DAVIES TO: BENJAMIN COOK
SATURDAY 24 FEBRUARY 2007 11:47:11 GMT

RE: AN IDEA

I'm home. Manchester. But this is odd: I get welded to a place when I write, because it now feels weird not to be writing to you in my Cardiff flat. Manchester feels wrong, feels like starting from scratch somehow. I try to never carry a script from one city to another, because they feel very specific to either room. (But I left Mika in Cardiff. Damn! I'll have to download that later. I'm making do with Rufus Wainwright.)

I'd better update you on what's in my head. I feel daft calling it the Maybe right now, because it's all pretty empty. The other day, Julie put her foot down, brilliantly, and I am now writing *Torchwood* 2.1! But I've got *no ideas*. No bloody story. And it has to be in by the end of March. It's like looking into your head, into the store of ideas, and there's nothing there. I've a pre-titles sequence – a blowfish driving a sports car – but that's a one-off sequence to reintroduce the show. After the titles… nothing. *Nothing!* And just when I want to be thinking about *Doctor Who* 4.1. It's hard to turn off one story while another is just starting. But it must be done.

There's a funny thing happening, too. This is what's really going on in my head. Yesterday, Julie, Phil and I get into the lift. We all turn to the mirror, fuss with our hair, we all sigh, and then hoot with laughter at ourselves. But then Phil says, 'I've got something terrible to tell you. Have you watched the very first *Doctor Who Confidential* recently? From 2005?' No. Oh God. 'You should see us,' he continues, 'all three of us – we look like *children*.' Ohhhh God! 'We look so young and happy.' And then he looks at me, and says, 'Russell, you're sitting in that old flat, and your hair looks good, and you look beautiful.' Ohhhh. And we're falling apart with laughter, clutching each other in the corridor, but that loud crack you can hear is my vain old heart. I'm telling you this because *that* has been at the front of my head ever since. Right at the front. Blocking anything else. That's what I mean about work and life being indivisible. Never mind 2.1, 4.1, Christmas 2007... my head is full of that first *Confidential* documentary, wondering how knackered I am by all this work, all this sitting. Oh, I could cry. My sister says I lead an incredibly straightforward life. No car to worry about, mortgage paid off, certainly no money worries. But then a simple thing like 'You look beautiful' ruins days of thinking.

That's not entirely true. It works the other way sometimes. When my mum was dying, I was rewriting *The Second Coming*, and work was a good escape. It was nice to retreat into my head.

But I sat in the car back to Manchester yesterday, trying to *make* myself think about *Torchwood* 2.1. Except that doesn't work, it never works, you can't force it. I mustn't buy into that myth of delicate creativity, but that's what's happening. My mind just wriggles off somewhere else. It feels like flinching, to consider *Torchwood*. I *cringe*. And I know already that's a bad start. I'm not sure a truly good piece of writing ever comes from that sort of beginning. Poor *Torchwood*.

FROM: BENJAMIN COOK TO: RUSSELL T DAVIES
SATURDAY 24 FEBRUARY 2007 17:13:09 GMT

RE: AN IDEA

A question (a bit random, but bear with me): have you been watching *Skins*? It's E4's new 'teen drama'. I saw the trailers on TV last month – full of wild, feral, hormonal, house-ravaging revelry – and thought, blimey, this looks incredible! But it's not. Not yet. A few moments of genius aside, *Skins* is a bit of a misfire. It has so much potential, and there are glimpses of genius, but there's a real gulf between the show that everyone involved seems to think that they're making and the show that they're *actually* making. It's fascinating. It deserves to be better. And yet I watch it, week in, week out, hoping that it'll improve. I'm an optimist. Or an idiot.

FROM: RUSSELL T DAVIES TO: BENJAMIN COOK
SATURDAY 24 FEBRUARY 2007 18:08:19 GMT

RE: AN IDEA

I'm watching *Skins*. You do get glimmers of it working. Sid and Cassie are interesting characters (is that her name, the anorexic girl?), and sometimes Nicholas Hoult takes his clothes off, so *come on!* Be fair! What a mouth on that boy. But I do know what you mean.

FROM: BENJAMIN COOK TO: RUSSELL T DAVIES
SATURDAY 24 FEBRUARY 2007 20:54:21 GMT

RE: AN IDEA

Nicholas Hoult the actor is appealing in other stuff, but his *Skins* character, Tony, is so unlikeable. So *improbably* unlikeable. Can that be sustained? Or is Tony heading for redemption? To what extent do lead characters have to be likeable, do you think? Especially in serial drama, where you're asking an audience to stick with them week after week? The Doctor is a likeable character. A modern-day hero. And Rose Tyler – we like her a lot. Mickey and Donna weren't so likeable to begin with, but we warmed to them as they proved their worth. There can't have been many viewers, by the end of *The Runaway Bride*, who weren't rooting for Donna to accept the Doctor's invitation to travel on in the TARDIS. I'm with Jane Tranter on this one. Even the opening of 4.1, still waiting for a ticket out of Maybe, you've planned so that Penny's likeability is, deliberately, right there on screen from the off: she's on the phone to her mate, she's been jilted (we like her *because* she's been jilted – we've all been jilted), and you say she's 'being funny about it'. We like her for being funny about it. How important is it that we like Penny, and Donna, and the Doctor, and how significant is it that I don't like Tony from *Skins*?

FROM: RUSSELL T DAVIES TO: BENJAMIN COOK
SATURDAY 24 FEBRUARY 2007 21:42:09 GMT

RE: AN IDEA

Likeability. I've been thinking about your question during *Dancing on Ice* (did I ever tell you, I was *asked to be on that*? Actually skating! Julie is still laughing, to this day) – and I wonder, should a writer worry about likeability? It tends to be the concern of people outside the script, the producers and commissioners. Years ago, I invented a soap called *Revelations*. At the story conference, one of the commissioners from Carlton said, 'None of these characters seems very likeable,' and Peter Whalley, a wise old soap writer, just sat in the corner of the room, puffed on his pipe, and said, 'Likeability is very low on the list of useable adjectives.' Bless him.

However, *Doctor Who* is designed to incorporate likeable characters, because so much else is going on. You're creating monsters, plots, worlds, environments, so even fairly complicated characters like Rose are sketches, in a sense, to be filled in by good acting. A likeable character is shorthand, to get you into the story, fast. An unlikeable companion, for example, is going to rail against the conventions of the show, so holds you up. Even Donna had to mellow over the course of *The Runaway Bride*. For Penny, being jilted is instantly, automatically likeable, but we're talking about scenes of only a few minutes in duration, because really she's there to be chased by monsters. The jilting is shorthand. If she were awful, if she'd just jilted someone and was laughing about it (well, she's already a bit unbelievable, in this crude example), then she'd be much more complicated, and you'd spend a lot more time trying to get to know her and engage with her, but that isn't actually the point of 4.1. There are stronger voices saying, 'Get on with it! Where are the monsters?'

In other TV dramas… well, first off, most people *are* likeable, or go through the world with some construct of character that they hope is likeable. That's how you get through life. Even if you're an SS guard, you want to get on with other SS guards. The key with characters is to be *honest*. If a character's actions are believable, then that character will work. Notions of like or not-like become irrelevant. One of the finest ever examples of unlikeable characters is the movie *Dangerous Liaisons*. That's the story of two absolute monsters at war – vile, vicious people – and yet you love them, and weep for them both at the end. Brilliant writing. Those characters are so absolutely true to themselves, you end up admiring and understanding monsters.

Stuart Jones in *Queer as Folk* is like that. Without him, that show would have been The Everyday Lives Of Gays, and the whole thing would have died. But Stuart is selfish, cruel, cold, hedonistic… and fantastic! He's the star around which every other character satellites. Stuart is honest and straightforward, and knows himself very well, and knows what he wants. Oh, people *hated* him, vociferously at first, but he's attractive as a character, undeniably, because he's true. How many Stuarts are there on Canal Street? Dozens. *Hundreds!* More importantly, any one of us can, on a certain night of our lives, be like that, exactly like him. There are times when we would all do anything – drop our friends, stampede over people, defy convention – for the sake of getting a man. Or a woman. I don't simply mean that men like Stuart exist; I mean that we can all be like that sometimes. Every one of us. My job as writer is not to worry on behalf of an invisible consensus wondering about sheer bloody boring niceness. Allow the bastards to be lovely, allow the heroes to be weak, and then they'll come alive.

I know that you can't stand Tony from *Skins*, but I can see, or think I can see, what they're trying to do with him. He's got that Stuart Jones certainty, complacency, charm

Above: Stuart (Aidan Gillen), Nathan (Charlie Hunnam) and Vince (Craig Kelly) from *Queer as Folk*. © Red Production Company Ltd Inset: Sid (Mike Bailey), Maxxie (Mitch Hewer) and Tony (Nicholas Hoult) from *Skins*. © Jack Barnes

and good looks, and cuts through everyday events with an absolute ruthlessness – and I think we're meant to admire that, to love the monster. The problem, I think, is that I do not believe a 17-year-old boy like that exists anywhere in the world. *That's* my problem with Tony. I think that's yours, too. He's a collection of ideas, an ideal, a walking wish list, but trapped in the wrong age. If he were 20, 21, then maybe he'd seem more real – but even that's doubtful. In *Queer as Folk*, which was designed to be YOUNG! YOUNG! YOUNG! in its outlook, I had to make both Stuart and Vince 29 to make them believable. Tony doesn't stand a chance. He's simply too young to be that assured.

Maybe I'm wrong. Maybe I'm out of touch. Maybe boys like that do exist. Or maybe boys like that can be invented. It's got to be said, Ben, that *Skins* is popular with Da Kidz. Maybe we're just too old for it. Yes, even you! I just accused you of being old. I'm very happy now. I shall ice-skate away with a triple loop.

FROM: RUSSELL T DAVIES TO: BENJAMIN COOK
MONDAY 26 FEBRUARY 2007 01:51:01 GMT

RE: AN IDEA

I just saw a trailer for next week's *Skins*, in which it seems that Tony is kissing the blonde gay boy, Maxxie. This is good drama, Ben! Stop fighting it! *Skins* wins.

I'm off to Brighton in the morning, Monday to Thursday, selling shows to Johnny Foreigner (it's the BBC Showcase, where Worldwide – the commercial arm of the BBC – flogs all its shows across the world), so that'll be interesting, to have a break, to see what I'm thinking by the time that's done, because my thoughts this weekend have been dominated by *Torchwood* 2.1. It's cancelling out everything else. The sheer white space of it. My mind is blank. It's more like fear and panic. It's so bad that I'm inclined to tell everyone this and pull out of the script. But I won't. I always think like this late at night. In the day, when Julie is looking at me, like I'm the one who can save them, then – I don't know – I'm too polite. That's ridiculous, isn't it? But I'm the man who fixes things. They don't need to hear my problems, just that I can fix theirs. That's more than a production problem. That's me. I don't tell people what I'm really thinking. Maybe things would be better if I did. People would help. But I just don't.

This is a rare problem. It's come along just as we happen to have started this process. It's not typical. But since I've already told you a lot of the things that I don't tell anyone, like the stuff that I got up to years ago (and I've skipped over some of it, and deleted stuff, cos, y'know, dignity and all that), you might as well know this…

In a crisis, another sly snake of a voice starts wheedling away. 'Go out and get off your head, *then* you'll think of a good idea,' it says. I used to do that, go out drinking in a crisis. I used to believe it worked. Actually, I can pinpoint certain evenings when it *did* work. I can point to exactly where I was standing in Manchester's Cruz 101 (downstairs, by the funny little stone well), off my head, when I thought of the frankly brilliant climax to Series One of *The Grand*. The thought was blinding. (It was simply this: both brothers are called Mr Bannerman! They've got the same name! You'd have to see the episode to make sense of that, but it was *so* clever.) It wasn't the alcohol or whatever I was on that night that made me think of that idea – I've created enough stuff since to know that I can do it on my own – but nonetheless the connection is there. Literally, a temptation. 'Just spend one night in Brighton, on your own, out in a club, not talking to anyone, just losing it, and see what you think up.' Bad voice. But it's always there. And I'm not a hundred per cent clean. I don't want to sound like a saint here. Once a year or so, I still go out, on my own, I do get slaughtered, I end up God-knows-where… ha ha, pathetic… but then I can lock it away again.

I thought I'd tell you this because, well, that's the contract, and the things that are past are never really past; they're still going on in my head, all the time. But they're under control now. A lot of nights writing are spent not just thinking of plot, character, pace, etc, but also waiting till 2am or so, just waiting, sitting there with the script open but not actually working on it, finding anything else to do, sending trivial e-mails, eating, watching a bit of telly, whatever, by which time that snaky, tempting voice has given up – and then I can get back to work. It stops by 2am because that's when clubs used to shut, as simple and as literal as that. I know clubs are open all hours now, and I thank God it wasn't like that when I was younger or the pattern would be a thousand times worse.

The Series Two *Torchwood* team. L–R: Toshiko Sato (Naoko Mori), Ianto Jones (Gareth David-Lloyd), Captain Jack Harkness (John Barrowman), Martha Jones (Freema Agyeman), Gwen Cooper (Eve Myles) and Owen Harper (Burn Gorman).

Blimey, this is therapy. And so is writing.

FROM: RUSSELL T DAVIES TO: BENJAMIN COOK
MONDAY 26 FEBRUARY 2007 08:31:34 GMT

RE: AN IDEA

I just read last night's e-mail. How self-pitying! I suppose everyone sounds like that at 2am. I mean, it's all true, but putting that stuff into words sounds sort of fraudulent. Or embarrassing. I suppose I want you to think I'm marvellous, but I sound like an idiot. Hey ho. Still, glad I said it all. Just about.

Anyway, daylight, Brighton, ta-ra!

P.S. This morning, I thought: Penny *Carter*. Sounds nice.

FROM: BENJAMIN COOK TO: RUSSELL T DAVIES
MONDAY 26 FEBRUARY 2007 09:48:16 GMT

BRIGHTON

All writers are self-pitying. Discuss. (No, don't.) Thank you, again, for your openness. If tomorrow morning's headline is 'Family TV Writer Found in Brighton Gutter', I won't half feel guilty. I wonder, though, have you ever pursued 'suffering' in the hope of achieving some sort of, I don't know, creative epiphany? You say that *Queer as Folk* was inspired by your own experiences, but has it ever worked the other way round? Have you ever gone looking for trouble along with inspiration?

FROM: RUSSELL T DAVIES TO: BENJAMIN COOK
WEDNESDAY 28 FEBRUARY 2007 15:32:23 GMT

RE: BRIGHTON

I'm typing from Hull, from a cheap hotel where they've a computer in the bar. It costs a quid for 20 minutes. I was only in Brighton for one night, then my boyfriend's mother died. The poor soul. Oh, it's sad. I've been around to the house and all that, but they're all together now, brothers and sister, so I've retreated. Escaping back into work again.

>>have you ever pursued 'suffering' in the hope of achieving some sort of, I don't know, creative epiphany?<<

No. Honestly, that simple. Never. There's an underlying question of why – why did I end up so drunk and off my face on whatever all those years ago? – but honestly, during those dark times, not one part of my brain was thinking, I'm doing this for research. It's way too scary, too exciting, too mad, too needy for anything that ordered and logical. If only I could use that excuse! Nowadays, it's like I almost entirely disassociate that person from myself. Maybe it's best left sleeping. Just promise me, if it's midnight and I say, 'Sod it, I'm off to buy some Chinese red' or something, you'll say, 'STOP!!!' Mind you, it's been so long, they probably don't call it Chinese red any more. I'd come back with a takeaway sweet-and-sour.

Is that true, though? Did I just lie my way out of that? Okay, so I've never sought out an experience just so that I can use it in a script, but every experience, every single one, I'm thinking, this is interesting. And they do find their way into a script in the end. So which comes first? Blimey, that'll keep me awake.

Meanwhile, I had to take emergency measures. Given the time that I'll have to spend with my boyfriend, I took action on *Torchwood* 2.1 – and stole a plot! Lovely Joe Lidster (nice man, so enthusiastic) is being tried out as a writer on *Torchwood*, so about a month ago I gave him one of my standby plots: Spooky 24-Hour Supermarket. (Have you ever been in one at 3am? Weirdest places in the world – so bright and empty, and staffed by The Damned.) And Joe has been working on this script faithfully, though he has some way to go till it's TV-ready, but then I got on the train to Hull, and thought, clear as daylight – that's *my* plot, I need it, I'm having it. Made the calls. Done. Poor Joe ousted (we'll find him something else), but I've got a story. Smash and grab. Never done that before. Mind you, it's not a brilliant plot – it's more of a standard mid-series plot – and now I have to *make* it brilliant, with precious little time.

Also, on the train down to London on Monday, I was thinking about this year's Doctor-lite double-banker episode. I got an image: Penny and Moira driving into that estate in 4.1… what if, in *Sliding Doors* fashion, they'd turned left that day, but this time we have them turning right? What if she'd never met the Doctor, and 4.11 tells the story of that? Good idea!

There we go. My quid's almost up. Love from Hull.

Left or right? Penny and Moira don't know which way to turn. Illustration by Russell T Davies.

FROM: BENJAMIN COOK TO: RUSSELL T DAVIES
WEDNESDAY 28 FEBRUARY 2007 23:47:13 GMT

RE: BRIGHTON

Greatest sympathies to your fella on the passing of his mum. That's horrible news.

Penny and Moira, *Sliding Doors* style? I think it was Robert Holmes who once said: 'We only ever use original ideas on *Doctor Who*, but not necessarily our own original ideas.' Clever man. With the sheer wealth of sci-fi material coming out of the US over the past 20 years, isn't it near impossible not to touch on story ideas that have been done already? Isn't this equally true for any writer, of any genre, in any medium? How much do you worry about that?

FROM: RUSSELL T DAVIES TO: BENJAMIN COOK
SATURDAY 3 MARCH 2007 16:24:50 GMT

RE: BRIGHTON

Do I worry about finding original ideas? Not at all. Within limits. For a start, there are no new stories, and long-running shows eat up a lot of plots. These plots haven't necessarily been seen on primetime BBC One. Material doesn't have to be new, just good. You might as well ditch all alternative-timeline stories because *A Christmas Carol* did it first. (Just how brilliant was Dickens in coming up with that? It's now replacing the

Nativity as *the* Christmas story. What a man!) I'd feel revolted if the *start* of the process was 'Ooh, I like *Sliding Doors*, so let's do that.' But I went through a genuine sequence of thoughts that led me to a *Sliding Doors*-type of story – the need for a double-banker, Doctor-lite episode, etc – so I feel completely justified. I feel, and the story feels, fundamentally honest. (If I can learn from *Sliding Doors*' precedents, though, all well and good.)

Thursday night, driving back to Hull again, I had a sudden panic about 4.1. I'm thinking it's bollocks. But then last night – a million ideas! I'd been to the funeral, and the result, after a sad, stifling day, was that the Maybe went into overtime. (Later, thinking about that, I fell into that superstition of thinking you have to have a bad day in order to have a good day. Like there's a balance, a pattern, a God, which is bollocks, but you can't help thinking it. All writers are self-pitying, yes. And self-hating.) First off, the *Sliding Doors* episode – it's called *Turn Left* – is *brilliant*. Penny and Moira in that car. Fateful, casual decision: how's it quickest to get to Donna's grandad's? Turn left or turn right? In 4.1, she turns left. In 4.11, she turns right – so Penny never meets the Doctor. And she has a time-psych-thing-creature living on her back, feeding off this alt-life. Ooh, but certain people can see it – old women, psychics, Penny's nervous, quiet friend, glimpsing the beast in mirrors. Is Penny going mad?

Problem: life without the Doctor is dull. Nice idea, the alt-life, but what's *happening*? Apart from simply living that life? And the occasional glimpse-of-monster-in-mirror? Worrying about a monster on your back isn't enough. But what if the Doctor is dead? If Penny didn't meet the Doctor, then the Doctor died. (Which means that I must write a scene in 4.1 where Penny saves the Doctor. But I'd have done that anyway.) Penny in 4.11 becomes a bystander to the events of 4.1, trapped outside the bowl or whatever with the army and police. She sees the Doctor's body being carted away, some soldier saying, 'He gave his life, killing the creature' or something. The story becomes not just What If Penny Never Met The Doctor? but What If The Doctor Were Dead? A world without its protector. While Penny is continuing her 'normal' life, getting paranoid about a glimpsed beast on her back, the weather is getting warmer, strange reports on TV, aliens are moving in; we're getting invaded, and there's no Doctor to save us.

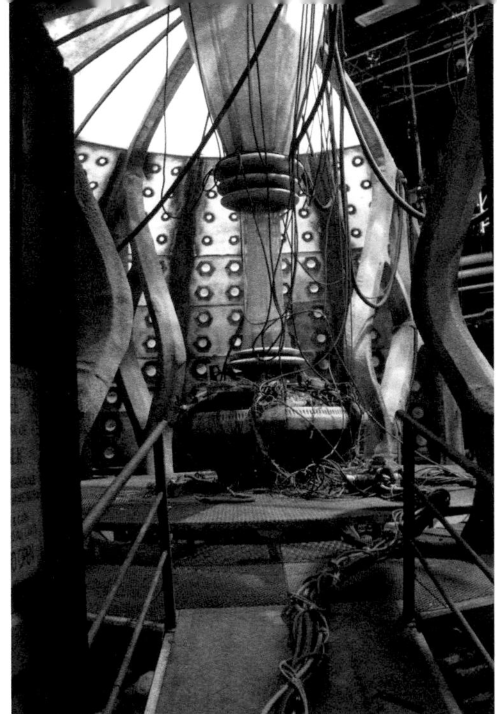

The TARDIS gutted by UNIT, from 4.11 *Turn Left*.

With Earth falling, Penny needs to travel back in time to stop her original self from turning right.

But how does Penny travel in time? The thing on her back? No! The TARDIS! Of course! The Doctor is dead, but he left the TARDIS behind, so UNIT has gutted it.[6] A big empty warehouse, pool of lights at the centre, the police box, innards gutted, scientists all around. They can't really use the TARDIS, because it's beyond them, but they can make one person travel back in time – and they've worked out that Penny is at the heart of the nexus. Penny has to travel back to that road, on that day, to stop herself. But it needs a chase, so Penny is on foot. Running. I love running. Especially if the lead character is running. The cannibalised TARDIS equipment is faulty, she arrives back in time, but half a mile away, it's too late, the car is pulling out, so to stop the original car turning right… she runs in front of the traffic. She kills herself. Alt-Penny has to die. In dying, she fades away, with a blissful smile, because she never existed. The traffic to the right screeches to a halt, original Penny and original Moira can't see what's happened, just some cars tailing back, so they *have* to turn left. And time goes back into its groove. [Major editorial worry – and this is rare, so it has square brackets – the story requires the lead audience-identification character, Penny, to *throw*

6 UNIT (standing for United Nations Intelligence Taskforce – later Unified Intelligence Taskforce) is a fictional military organisation that has featured in *Doctor Who*, on and off, since 1968. Its purpose is to investigate and combat paranormal and extraterrestrial threats to the Earth.

'A big sexy Amazon of a woman' – Russell's original idea for the Doctor's Daughter. Illustration by Russell T Davies.

herself under a car! Don't copy that, kids. Yikes, I can see trouble with that. I'll just have to write it carefully.]

Meanwhile, I was stuck on 4.6, pencilled in for Stephen Greenhorn to write. I really, really like that man. I was due a meeting with him next Friday to talk ideas, but cancelled it yesterday because my head was empty. I'd nothing to talk to him about. Part of me thinks, he's lovely, he loves us, just ask him for his own ideas. But maybe I'm too power-mad for that. Ha! This is interesting, though, because I've just read an interview with him in *Doctor Who Magazine*, which got me thinking.[7] I learnt more about Stephen from that interview than I ever have face-to-face. In *DWM*, Stephen says that it's unusual, writing *Doctor Who*, because the lead character never really changes, like he would in any other drama; he just changes the world around him. Very true. And yet… therefore… wouldn't it be brilliant to ask Stephen to write a story in which,

7 *Doctor Who Magazine* (*DWM*), first published in 1979, is an official, four-weekly periodical about the show.

well, the Doctor really changes? (The text of *DWM* feeds back into the series itself – I *love* this process!) We haven't got a Madame de Pompadour or *Human Nature*-type story in Series Four yet, so let's have something that really stretches David's limitless acting.[8] What can that be? Well, let's really go for broke...

A child. Give the Doctor a child! A daughter. Pre-titles sequence: the Doctor and Penny are trapped underground. Door explodes open. Smoke clears. Great big sexy Amazon of a woman standing there, loaded with guns, and says... 'Hello, dad!'

It's a war-torn world, an Earth colony in mid-invasion, she's leader of the rebels, she and the Doctor have to get to know each other, and lose each other, in the middle of gunfire and barricades and running. But how is she his daughter?! Even I don't want an ex-girlfriend/mother in the background. Ah, but it's sci-fi: she's a genetic scraping extrapolated into a fully grown woman. Somehow. Technically, his daughter. Ooh, technically a Time Lord. (She's got to die at the end, of course.) Or what if some remote probe scans the Doctor and Penny the moment they step out of the TARDIS, and then they meet this fully grown warrior woman who's *their* daughter? From a simple scan, the enemy, the aliens, create fully grown clone soldiers *who are your children*. A form of psychological warfare – you'd find it harder to gun down your own child. Hmm, bit odd. Bit short story. Bit mad. Bit cluttered, if it's Penny's child too. Do you see, in reaching to make something new, you can make it over-complex? At heart, *Doctor Who* is a Saturday night, primetime show. But, but, but... there might be something in there.

Thinking of 4.6 and 4.11 simultaneously made me feel very happy. There's a lot of misery and worry in these e-mails, but last night felt excellent. I went to bed full of adrenalin, letting all these ideas buzz. But then, on the train back to Manchester this morning, I realised: 4.6 *isn't* a blank slate, you dope! It's actually tagged as the Martha Trapped In Space episode. She rejoins the Doctor on Earth in 4.4/4.5, but just as a mate, not as a companion, and then 4.5 ends with the TARDIS spinning off with her on board. The whole of 4.6 is supposed to be 'Take me home!' And I forgot. Damn. How could I forget? I've *promised* that to Freema Agyeman. Ah well. The Doctor's daughter is far, far better.

P.S. You were right, *Skins* is weird. In Thursday's episode, they went to Russia! *Why?!* It's the oddest hybrid of a drama and broad sitcom. Mind you, people say that about my stuff.

FROM: BENJAMIN COOK TO: RUSSELL T DAVIES
SUNDAY 4 MARCH 2007 11:17:56 GMT

'HELLO, DAD!'

The Doctor's Daughter! Well, that'll get some folk hot under the collar. But will they believe it? Go on, Russell, leak *The Doctor's Daughter*, and watch the internet explode! During the 1980s, the *Doctor Who* production team replaced an entry on the office planning board – or so the story goes – with a fake title, *The Doctor's Wife*, in an attempt to identify the culprit leaking information about the series to the press. Sure enough, before long, the redtops were reporting that *The Doctor's Wife* would feature in the next season. (But was the mole caught? That's what I want to know.)

Seriously, though, when conceiving story ideas, are you ever aiming, specifically, to articulate social, political or religious points of view? You've conceived scripts with that in mind before... haven't you? You embarked on *The Second Coming*, for instance, to advocate atheism? And wrote *Queer as Folk* to represent gay men and gay issues on TV? Do you do that on *Doctor Who* ever? Can you? Or is it, above all, about the spectacle, the rush of adventure, the gunfire, the dark tunnels, the tough woman with guns, and all that running?

FROM: RUSSELL T DAVIES TO: BENJAMIN COOK
MONDAY 5 MARCH 2007 01:23:12 GMT

RE: 'HELLO, DAD!'

You do ask tough questions. That's good! It's tricky, that social/political/religious thing, because really that's *life*, that's *people*, that's *what you think about the world*, and that's why you want to write in the first place. It's not like there's a section of my mind that categorises things – like, this scene is about character, the next is all sociology. They're all in there, in one huge continuum.

If you're touching on big issues, you've got to keep turning these things, examining them, looking at the opposite of what you think. For example, as an atheist,

8 In 2.4, the Doctor falls in love with Madame de Pompadour; in 3.8/3.9, the Doctor becomes human.

I set out to include the 'Old Rugged Cross' sequence in *Gridlock* to show how *good* faith can be, regardless of the existence of God – how it can unite and form a community, and essentially offer hope.[9] That was my intention, or my starting point, and yet the real me came bleeding through, because it transpires that hope stifles the travellers. It stops them acting. By uniting, they are passive. The Doctor is the unbeliever. The direct consequence of the travellers in the traffic jam singing that hymn is that the Doctor realises that no one is going to help them. There is no higher authority. That's when he starts to break down the rules of that world by jumping from car to car. You could argue, therefore, that the travellers' faith is misguided.

It's great discussing this with David Tennant, actually. We fell into devil's advocate: he argued for the car-drivers being wrong and passive, and I argued for their goodness. But I think he's right. He got what the script is saying. But I didn't write *Gridlock* thinking, this is my take on religion. My foremost thought, and my principal job, was to write an entertaining drama about cats and humans stuck on a motorway. Everything else just bleeds through. I do have opinions, I do have beliefs, and when I'm writing well – and that hymn sequence is one of my favourites, because the hymn *changes* the course of events – it's synthesised with my worldview. How can it be any other way? Yes, *Queer as Folk* is a massively political drama, and yet barely a political speech is made. Not directly. But every word is loaded. Every scene is about the place of gay men in the world. You could argue that it's entirely political. And it's *my* politics. It's all me, me, me.

Of course, I'm aware of the politics with the cheap, easy lines, like the 'massive weapons of destruction' reference in *World War Three*. But that barely counts: it's quick satire, hardly profound. (Although, it satirises a politician on TV lying to the country about needing a war; men have died for that, are dying now.) More often, I prefer a slyer approach. It boils down to that line in *Tooth and Claw*, my favourite line in the whole series, when Queen Victoria says of the Koh-I-Noor diamond, 'It is said that whoever owns it must surely die,' and the Doctor says, 'Well, that's true of anything, if you wait long enough.' Nice gag, fast, harmless – but actually, under that, it's lethal. That's what I really think about a ton of things: religion, superstition, mysticism, legends, all bollocks. That's a whole belief system, trashed. And I was conscious of that. I wanted to write that line. I was glad that I thought of a way of putting it so precisely, because it wasn't the time for a polemic.

I say the process is inevitable, but also I do think it's your job as a writer to say something about the world. Why else are you writing? I can't think of a script in which I haven't done that. I'm being disingenuous if I imply that it's accidental, because I look for those chances. I create them. Queen Victoria had been expressing her profound interest in the afterlife, ever since the dinner table. That's quite a belief system that the Doctor knocks for six with one fleeting line. The whole thing has a slight awareness of Rational Man versus Head of the Church. Of course, the *real* job of the episode is Man versus Monster (the werewolf, not Queenie), but I can't, I cannot, write just that.

FROM: BENJAMIN COOK TO: RUSSELL T DAVIES
MONDAY 5 MARCH 2007 22:19:55 GMT

RE: 'HELLO, DAD!'

You say that it's a writer's job to say something about the world ('Why else are you writing?'), but do you reckon that's true of all good writers? Or is it perfectly possible to write something brilliant, beautiful or intensely thought-provoking simply out of a desire to tell a ripping yarn, to entertain people? Isn't that why a lot of people start writing? Especially why a lot of people start writing *Doctor Who*? Then again, there are plenty of bad writers out there, so are they the ones that *don't* have something to say? (Even the phrase 'something to say' sounds overtly political.)

FROM: RUSSELL T DAVIES TO: BENJAMIN COOK
TUESDAY 6 MARCH 2007 02:34:07 GMT

RE: 'HELLO, DAD!'

I should start calling this BBQ – Ben's Big Questions. That last one is huge! But BBQs have burgers and sausages and things, so I don't think it fits. Mmm… sausages.

When I say something like 'It's your job as a writer', I'm grandstanding a bit or falling into lecture mode. I

9 *Doctor Who* 3.3 is set on New Earth, a planet in the far future, where the population is stuck in an infinitely huge, near-stationary underworld traffic jam, driving for an eternity in the hope of reaching the real city above.

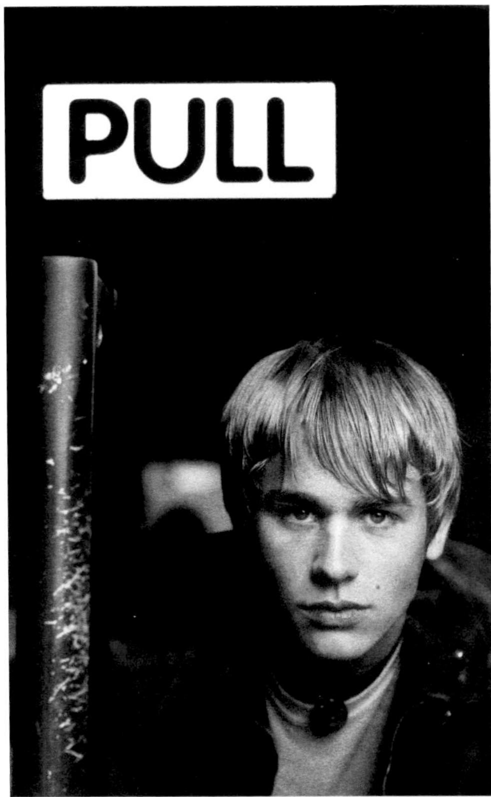

Queer as Folk's Nathan Maloney, 'full of repression and desire, and lust, and martyrdom'. © Red Production Company Ltd

don't think of it as a job. In fact, I've never joined the Writer's Guild, out of some strange belief that this isn't a real job. Partly, I feel a fraud, as everyone does. But also it's because writing, I think, is nothing to do with unions or status or making money; writing is a compulsion. An obsession. You have to be arrogant to be a writer. You have to be able to walk into a commissioner's office and demand six million quid to make something. You have to believe that it's worth that, that it deserves to be made, that it deserves to be seen. I wouldn't be happy just writing this stuff in an exercise book and then leaving it for my own contemplation.

You're right, 'something to say' sounds political, but that doesn't mean I sit here thinking, oh, I must announce my thoughts about gay men, about Christianity, about life. Maybe that's when bad scripts are written, when you choose the theme first. I consider that I've something to say when I've thought of a person, a moment, a single beat of the heart, that I think is true and interesting, and *therefore* should be seen. It's because I can imagine *Queer as Folk*'s Nathan Maloney so full of repression, and desire, and lust, and martyrdom, that I have to write him. It's because I've seen, and sometimes been, Stuart Jones – it's because I understand him and want to convey that life – or because I don't understand him and want to explore him through writing.

Thinking about the show that I'm going to do once *Doctor Who* is over, known only, ridiculously, as *More Gay Men* (I don't even know what it's about, just gay men), I can imagine a man who is so enraged by something tiny – the fact that his boyfriend won't learn to swim – that he goes into a rage so great that, in one night, his entire life falls apart. It's not about the learning to swim at all, of course; it's about the way that your mind can fix on something small and use it as a gateway to a whole world of anger and pain. Huge things in life can extrapolate from small details. That's what I love. That's what I explore. If I write the Learn To Swim scene well – and it could be the spine of the whole drama – then I *will* be saying something about gay men, about couples, about communication, about anger. But that's the result, not the starting point. For me, anyway. You need to be a titanic genius of Jimmy McGovern-level to start with your theme. It might not even be true of him, actually, because look how quickly he boils down the Great Themes to ordinary people making ordinary mistakes in kitchens and pubs.

There's a great big streak of entertainer in me, but the truth is, if you're writing well, if the end result is brilliant or beautiful, then you *are* saying something about the world. You can't not be. *Fawlty Towers*? Comedy genius! But I could write a thousand-page thesis on what it has to say about frustrated middle-aged men, about England, about the 1970s, about dead marriages. It's brilliant because it's honest, and that means that it's resonating. Even something like *Only Fools and Horses*, a much plainer sitcom, is ineffably funny, but it *sings* when Del Boy says, 'This time next year, we'll be millionaires.' That's when people truly take it to their hearts. They recognise it. That's all of us. Even if you're blubbing at the Doctor and Rose on Bad Wolf Bay in *Doomsday*, you're empathising, you're feeling it, and there's an echo of every loss you've ever had in that. If it's successful, it *is* saying something about you, about the world. I'm trying hard to think of something of which that's not true – and can't. Even the bloody *Teletubbies*! That's an extraordinary show, it's true brilliance, because somewhere in there they've captured the sheer strangeness, the joy, the bombardment, of being a toddler in a world of colour and shape and noise.

So why do it? Why write? Well, there's no choice. Thinking of these stories is just the way that my brain is shaped. It's hardwired. If I fell out of favour as a writer, and ended up as a teacher or something, those stories would still be boiling away. I see them everywhere. I think of them all the time. Just today, I met a woman – who shall remain nameless – a nice, smiling, 80-year-old woman, really kind and quiet, and I sat with her waiting for a taxi. But the more we chatted, the more I thought, actually, you're not nice, there's something sour and hard at the heart of you, and you don't let it out; you just sit there smiling. It's not like I solved her conundrum, but she's in my head now, that fixed smile – and I am writing her. She'll pop up one day in something I write. I want to find out why she's like that. I want to push it further, to the day that she cracks. I want to see her let loose with other characters, to see what happens. That's what I do. That's why I do it.

I ended up thinking about 4.1 today. (Hooray! With a boo from the Christmas Special corner.) I thought about Penny's grandad. Way back in the '90s, before reviving *Doctor Who* was real, I had a sort of rough first new episode in my head, should the call ever come. A companion-to-be, all told from her point of view, and she's a young office cleaner, working at night in some sort of smart, high-rise city office, where she can't help noticing… well, maybe they have dinosaurs in the basement! But then I wondered whether dinosaurs are limiting, and I started to think of computer terminals that could move, casings that could ooze and creep after you, even swallow you. This led to thoughts about plastic, and then to Auton twins as the Big Bad Bosses, a man and a woman who would always hold hands, because their hands turned out to be fused.[10] Of course, the would-be-companion meets the Doctor (his first word to her is 'Run!'), and the story had an escape-by-window-cleaner's-cradle sequence – which I ended up using, actually, in *Smith and Jones*, but it was cut well before the final draft. But the point is, the companion had a grandad. He was funny. He played in a skiffle band in the local pub. At one point, the whole

'An echo of every loss you've ever had' – Rose says goodbye to the Doctor on Bad Wolf Bay in 2.13 *Doomsday*.

The Ninth Doctor (Christopher Eccleston) rescues shopgirl Rose Tyler (Billie Piper) from rampaging mannequins in 1.1 *Rose*.

10 The Autons – animated plastic, often in mannequin form – appeared in two *Doctor Who* serials in the early 1970s, and were resurrected by Russell for the first episode of the revived show (1.1).

Penny and her grandad with their 'Alien Watch' gang. Illustration by Russell T Davies.

skiffle band would get involved in… well, I don't know, distracting a guard or something. Funny old codgers. All vague images. Thing is, when they asked me to do *Doctor Who* for real, I junked all that, almost instantly. (Except for the Autons.) That putative companion – she had no name – felt too old, not everywoman enough. But I remembered her grandad today ('Where do your ideas come from?' 'Old ideas!')…

He's now *Penny's* grandad, the stargazer, the man with a telescope in his shed, someone who's been UFO-spotting all his life, now invigorated by this new world in which spaceships fly into Big Ben, Christmas Stars attack, etc. Instead of the skiffle band, maybe there's a gang of old codgers who all meet round his house. Instead of a Neighbourhood Watch, they're an Alien Watch. All a bit hopeless and funny – and then, when faced with real aliens in 4.1, they turn out to be magnificent and brave. Bit schematic. But it could work.

FROM: BENJAMIN COOK TO: RUSSELL T DAVIES
TUESDAY 6 MARCH 2007 02:50:39 GMT

RE: 'HELLO, DAD!'

I'm asking big questions, I know, but they'll get smaller, I promise. (Actually, I don't promise.) I tell you what…

1) What's your favourite colour?
2) If you were a pizza topping, which one would you be?
3) What's it like in space?

Better?

FROM: RUSSELL T DAVIES TO: BENJAMIN COOK
TUESDAY 6 MARCH 2007 02:59:45 GMT

RE: 'HELLO, DAD!'

1) Blue.
2) Pepperoni.
3) Cold.

Much better. Thank you.

CHAPTER TWO

CATHERINE, KYLIE, AND DENNIS

In which Kylie Minogue sings the Muppets, Russell turns down a fifth series of *Doctor Who*, and Charlie Kaufman is told to sod off

FROM: RUSSELL T DAVIES TO: BENJAMIN COOK
TUESDAY 6 MARCH 2007 23:58:01 GMT

RE: 'HELLO, DAD!'

Today was *mental*. I can't even begin to type it all right now. Sorry, Ben. I only got four hours' sleep last night, after watching all of last week's rushes, then getting up at 8am, so I'm exhausted. Mental days like this tend to come to nothing in the end, so we'll look back and think, that was so daft, none of it happened. But it's part of the job, so I'll update you tomorrow. I promise.

FROM: BENJAMIN COOK TO: RUSSELL T DAVIES
WEDNESDAY 7 MARCH 2007 00:11:02 GMT

RE: 'HELLO, DAD!'

Talk about leaving me on a cliffhanger! Never mind e-mailing me, Russell; for Christ's sake, get some sleep, and then you can fill me in on your mental Tuesday.

FROM: RUSSELL T DAVIES TO: BENJAMIN COOK
WEDNESDAY 7 MARCH 2007 12:06:51 GMT

MENTAL TUESDAY

Right. Mental Tuesday. First up, we got interest from Dennis Hopper. Yes, *the* Dennis Hopper. American movie star Dennis Hopper! James Strong met his agent on a plane or something, on his way back from the US, having done ADR with Ryan Carnes for the Dalek episodes.[1] What a showbiz tale! I could fit Dennis Hopper into 4.X, maybe, if I can work out who he can play. A nice little cameo? Or a proper big part, I don't know, like the ship's historian? Mind you, we should be so lucky. I'll believe it when I see it.

Secondly, back in the world of hard facts, Julie said that Billie Piper is up for doing four episodes next

1 US-based actor Carnes, who played Laszlo in *Doctor Who* 3.4/3.5, directed by Strong, was required to record additional dialogue (ADR) after principal photography had wrapped. This is standard practice on TV dramas.

'How Donna-like Penny could be...?' Illustration by Russell T Davies.

year. *Four!* I was hoping for one, two at best. Brilliant. Entirely out of leftfield. What a day! And as if that weren't enough...

As you know, we've been talking to Jane Tranter about how Donna-like Penny could be. Completely by chance, Jane had a meeting with Catherine Tate this week, just one of those general, bigwig, let's-work-together-more sorts of chats. But afterwards Jane phoned up Julie and said, 'All Catherine talked about was what a brilliant time she'd had on last year's *Doctor Who* Christmas Special. She went on and on about it. She could be up for a whole series. I think you're in with a chance.' Bollocks, of course. But it all went a bit mad. This all happened on Tuesday. I bloody love the idea – oh, I love Donna – so we asked Phil, who relished working with her on set, and then we asked David, and he just adores Catherine, and now Julie is booking in a lunch to see her! But it's madness. A woman that busy? With her own TV show? Making movies now? We'll never get Catherine for a whole series. Still, we can but try. At the very least, we might be able to get her back for 4.12/4.13. But this will probably just end up as a wistful paragraph in these e-mails. TV goes crazy sometimes.

P.S. Will you be at tomorrow's Dub of *Doctor Who* 3.4?[2] Murray Gold's Dalek Choir time! Though it might be rather strange to see you, because it feels like you live in my head now. In a good way, I think. See you in Cardiff.

FROM: BENJAMIN COOK TO: RUSSELL T DAVIES
FRIDAY 9 MARCH 2007 09:23:58 GMT

RE: MENTAL TUESDAY

Good to see you at yesterday's Dub, Russell. I love Dubs. How could I not? Watching *Doctor Who* on the big screen, stuffing my face full of BBC croissants, seeing you put your foot down ('You worked on that camera shake for hours, I know. But do you know what? You were wrong!'), and realising that Julie is the biggest *Doctor Who* geek in the room. She'd barely even watched the show three years ago!

Any further news on Catherine?

FROM: RUSSELL T DAVIES TO: BENJAMIN COOK
FRIDAY 9 MARCH 2007 13:49:19 GMT

RE: MENTAL TUESDAY

I'm feeling bleeargghhh. I must have picked up some bug. I've only just got up, after 16 hours' sleep! I feel pale. I want to go back to recording the Maybe, but I'm too busy feeling ill. Again, poor *Torchwood*. This is shameful, but I'm feeling too sick to even worry about it. However, I described the basics of 4.X to David yesterday evening; as I said it out loud, I *really* liked it, what little there is, so that's good. It's David's last day filming Series Three tomorrow. And it's John Barrowman's 40th birthday. I can't believe he's admitting to 40!

One other thing worth noting: in the lift at Broadcasting House yesterday, maybe you heard me turn to Julie and say, 'Wouldn't [name removed – let's call her Miss X] be a brilliant Penny?' She's a marvellous actress, with a rare flair for comedy. So that's snowballed. We've checked with Jane Tranter, and she loves her too. Hmm, we'll see. It might be another of those things that comes to nothing, but thinking about [Miss X] is good, because it sort of merges with Catherine Tate, and makes it clear to me that Penny should be funny. A bit of a klutz would be good. I can see Penny more clearly – not in the magical, pictures-of-the-mind way that radio enthusiasts

2 The Dub is the very first time that the producers view an episode, on a big screen, with finished visuals, sound design, and Murray Gold's score.

bang on about, but a sort of vivid, moving blur. When you think of your friends, you don't *see* them, do you, but you register this strong sort of…? I don't know.

FROM: BENJAMIN COOK TO: RUSSELL T DAVIES
FRIDAY 9 MARCH 2007 15:32:09 GMT

RE: MENTAL TUESDAY

This strong sense of…? What is it that you register at this stage in a character's conception? In what way do you sense Penny? Can you hear her voice in your head already? Her speech patterns? Can you smell her? No, that's silly. (Then again, if I asked you what perfume Penny is wearing, would you know?) Do you know what she'd do in any given situation? And can you really think about her now without the faces of [Miss X] and Catherine Tate flickering away in your mind's eye?

FROM: RUSSELL T DAVIES TO: BENJAMIN COOK
SATURDAY 10 MARCH 2007 21:56:06 GMT

RE: MENTAL TUESDAY

The 'seeing' thing is hard to pin down. Characters really are blurs, but that doesn't mean they're vague; it means they're alive and unpredictable. And I don't carry actors' impressions and characteristics over, thankfully. There's a distinct Donna in my head, separate from Catherine. Even if [Miss X] were to become Penny, Penny has a life of her own. (I get annoyed when other writers say that characters have a life of their own, and now here I am saying it. I suppose what I mean is, Penny has a life beyond the actress that ends up playing her.)

When I wrote *Queer as Folk*, I had strong mental impressions of Stuart, Vince and Nathan, but then when I came to write *Queer as Folk 2*, long after they'd been cast and had acted in eight episodes, I still didn't write Aidan Gillen, Craig Kelly and Charlie Hunnam. The mental versions were far stronger and took over again. I wonder if that's weird. But it *is* like when you picture your friends, isn't it? You imagine their *essence*. I don't imagine their hair colour, or teeth, or clothes, or crow's feet; I sort of imagine their dynamic, the place that they occupy. Penny has that dynamic already. She came born with it. I'm talking, for example, about how to make her funny, but actually that's e-mail rationalisation after the event. Just look at her, from the moment she was conceived: she's jilted, walking past the TARDIS; with her posh mum, going to see her grandad, when she walks into an alien invasion. That's already essentially funny. Even her sadness isn't tragedy; it's light and sweet. She felt like that from the start, from the moment I thought of her.

But there's no smell. You've got me there! And I don't know where she went to school, what she had for breakfast, what knickers she's wearing, unless the scene needs me to know. If I do write Penny having breakfast, I'll write something that will fit her. (It's black coffee. She'd just have black coffee. If it weren't *Doctor Who*, she'd also have a cigarette. Yes, that's very Penny.) Some people draw up huge lists of that background stuff before they start writing. Well, I don't. That doesn't mean you shouldn't. It works for some people.

I suppose I do know already exactly what she'd do in given circumstances… with the proviso that anyone can do anything in any circumstance. You should never mark out a character so formally that their reactions are fully defined, because none of us is like that; we're slightly different every day, with different people, with each different mood. You have to keep turning characters in the light. One of my favourite Doctor moments ever is the opening of *Gridlock*, where he lies about Gallifrey having been destroyed. It's a tiny lie. He omits the fact that his homeworld is gone. But, for the Doctor, that's seismic. I had nothing interesting in that scene until I discovered that. I found a completely new way of understanding the Doctor, a new way of revealing his history, and better still a tiny piece of narrative that sustains the Doctor/Martha relationship throughout that episode. If characters keep turning, moving, thinking, shifting, if they aren't fixed, then they can do anything. Just like real people.

A prerequisite of a good story is that the audience watches the central character – or characters – change, even if the characters themselves aren't aware of that process happening. I'm trying to think of a film or drama in which that doesn't happen. I'm sure they exist, but… do you see? They've been forgotten. Even in something as simple as *High School Musical* – in fact, that's so simple and underwritten, the change is poking out of the carcass so even blind passers-by can give it a good feel. The school jock becomes an arts boy; the geeky girl breaks out of her math class; even the villainous valley girl, in the most appalling and sudden about-turn, becomes nice (that's a failed change, because it comes from nowhere, and demeans her). The template, *Grease*, does it even better, because you really *feel* them change in that. If a story is good, then someone changes. You can apply that principle from *Grease* to *Hamlet* to *Teletubbies*. There is no low-art and high-art divide here. My God, that scene in *Monsters, Inc.* where the monsters realise that their entire world is founded on hurting children – look at that for a change! Two galumphing cartoon characters making a shattering realisation about their world and their role in sustaining it. A truly epic moment. It's stunning.

FROM: BENJAMIN COOK TO: RUSSELL T DAVIES
SATURDAY 10 MARCH 2007 22:41:10 GMT

RE: MENTAL TUESDAY

>>I suppose I do know already exactly what she'd do in given circumstances… with the proviso that anyone can do anything in any circumstance.<<

If a character can do anything, what stops them becoming a sort of Everyman? What makes them distinct?

FROM: RUSSELL T DAVIES TO: BENJAMIN COOK
SATURDAY 10 MARCH 2007 23:15:54 GMT

RE: MENTAL TUESDAY

I suppose what I'm saying is that a character can act in any way *in character*. They can be good, bad, happy, sad, liars, lovers, but in a way that's still unique to themselves. To stretch the metaphor: keep turning them, but not so fast and so often that they become blurred.

FROM: BENJAMIN COOK TO: RUSSELL T DAVIES
SATURDAY 10 MARCH 2007 23:38:19 GMT

RE: MENTAL TUESDAY

Sometimes, surely, the fact that people are incapable of change is enough of a story in itself? Take Madame Ranyevskaya in *The Cherry Orchard*.

FROM: RUSSELL T DAVIES TO: BENJAMIN COOK
SUNDAY 11 MARCH 2007 00:03:44 GMT

RE: MENTAL TUESDAY

Yes, but the realisation of that is a change for the

The Doctor (David Tennant) and Donna (Catherine Tate) in 3.X *The Runaway Bride*.

audience. I don't think Madame Ranyevskaya leaves *The Cherry Orchard* truly aware of herself or really having moved on from Act One, but the world has changed around her and other characters have grown in wisdom, so she acts as a still point – and that's equally powerful.

But I don't know that you can take this principle and apply it to drama too consciously. Can you sit down and say, 'I'm going to write about change! My theme is change'…? Rather, I think it's inherent in a story, any story. That's why they're stories. Things start on Page 1 and are different by the final page, or else why is the tale being told? The Goldilocks who runs away from the three bears is a very different girl from the one who started out into the forest. The change might not last, she might well go back to stealing other people's food and trashing their furniture, but that's why the story ends when it does.

FROM: RUSSELL T DAVIES TO: BENJAMIN COOK
TUESDAY 13 MARCH 2007 22:27:29 GMT

MENTAL TUESDAY II

Let the record state: Julie had lunch with Catherine today, assuming that she'd say she's too busy for a full

series – but she *screamed*, and started planning how to move to Cardiff!!! *WHAT?!* I still don't believe this is going to happen. Surely Catherine's agent is going to rugby-tackle her? Imagine a whole season of Tennant and Tate! It's a casting director's dream. Can't be true. Can't be.

Also, I had to go into Peter Fincham's extremely posh office today, and explain why I will not be doing a Series Five. Ohh, he's not happy. It was very awkward. Mind you, it did strike me that he has no idea how much work *Doctor Who* actually is, how much work I actually do, and absolutely no awareness of the fact that so many of us have had to up sticks and go and live in Cardiff for years on bloody end. Instead, he just supports us with money and publicity and trust and… oh, I shouldn't complain, should I?

Since we started this project, it's been unusually busy and showbizzy on *Doctor Who*. It's normally 'Can we shift that scene to Penarth?' These are weird times. But it does help explain what I'm thinking. Which is not much, because now we're in a Penny/Donna flux. Which woman is it going to be? But the Donna stuff is fun. I imagine that she failed to 'walk in the dust' after *The Runaway Bride*. That's what life is like, isn't it? You meet an amazing man, spend one night with him, think you're going to change your life… then you wake up the next morning and he's gone, there are bills to be paid, your flat needs cleaning, and you never quite get around to it. Poor Donna, she had her chance and blew it. If only she could have a second chance. (I could call 4.1 *Second Chance*!) Mind you, there's no way that Donna could come across the Doctor again by chance; she'd have to be *looking* for him. A very different entry for a companion. I'd have to dump the whole jilted-by-her-boyfriend strand that I'd planned for Penny. But the marvellous thing is, that strand is still true, because we've already done that with Donna in *The Runaway Bride*. Not just jilted, but betrayed by her man.

Anyway. I had a good meeting with Gareth Roberts today, about the Agatha Christie episode. Lovely ideas. But it's going to be tough, that one. I can tell. And a brilliant meeting with Matt Jones about *Torchwood*, leaving me thinking, damn, everyone's episode is better than mine. A rising bile of fear that I'm already *very* behind and will stay like this for months now, maybe for the whole year. I did no proper work at the weekend either. David was the only living soul I saw. But I had some nice thoughts about 4.X – obvious thoughts, but ones that I hadn't crystallised before, namely that a 'disaster movie' needs a supporting cast to climb through the wreckage, some of whom will live, some of whom will die, which means, of course, that some lovely people must die and some bastards will survive. I'm thinking we'll have a sweet, middle-aged or ageing couple – both will die. Heartbreaking. A feisty would-be companion – she'll survive. An arrogant young businessman – he might survive, because you'll want him to die. That sort of thing. Fab.

FROM: BENJAMIN COOK TO: RUSSELL T DAVIES
TUESDAY 13 MARCH 2007 22:54:09 GMT

RE: MENTAL TUESDAY II

Catherine Tate hasn't said no? That is so mad. But oh… Penny! (I almost used a sad smiley there. I feel dirty now.) This will sound pathetic, but I'll miss her. Donna would be AMAZING, and the repartee between Catherine and David to die for, but poor Penny Carter becomes just another Character In Search Of An Author. No second chances for Penny. No *first* chances, even. End of.

FROM: RUSSELL T DAVIES TO: BENJAMIN COOK
TUESDAY 13 MARCH 2007 23:18:44 GMT

RE: MENTAL TUESDAY II

That alone makes this whole e-mail chain worthwhile, because you must be the only other person in the whole world who will miss Penny. No one else had that stuff described to them. Not Phil, not Julie, not anyone. I don't like to flog it, because it sounds daft, but I really do miss her too. That lovely, lonely, wistful scene of her walking past the TARDIS late at night, in a city centre, in the rain – I know I hadn't done much with her, but that moment was crystallised perfectly. In a really strange corner of my mind, I honestly believe that she sort of exists somewhere. It really is that *Six Characters in Search of an Author* stuff. God, when I first saw that play – I'd barely ever written anything at that point – I was stunned by the central conceit, and really took it to heart, and now – and I'm never going to admit this again, and you can't print it anywhere, ever, because I sound like a nonce – I still believe that Penny Carter is walking past that TARDIS, but now she walks on and never meets the Doctor. That feels real.

FROM: BENJAMIN COOK TO: RUSSELL T DAVIES
TUESDAY 13 MARCH 2007 23:31:28 GMT

RE: MENTAL TUESDAY II

Shall we light a candle for Penny?

FROM: RUSSELL T DAVIES TO: BENJAMIN COOK
TUESDAY 13 MARCH 2007 23:37:51 GMT

RE: MENTAL TUESDAY II

You light a candle. I'll light a cigarette.

FROM: RUSSELL T DAVIES TO: BENJAMIN COOK
WEDNESDAY 14 MARCH 2007 22:45:53 GMT

RE: MENTAL TUESDAY II

Catherine's agent phoned today. We expected her to blast us with 'WHAT THE HELL D'YOU THINK YOU'RE DOING?! SOD OFF, CATHERINE IS BUSY!' But no, Catherine is definitely tempted. And then I spent an hour on the phone to Catherine herself. She *so* wants to do it! This is madness.

Penny Carter walks on by. Illustration by Russell T Davies.

FROM: BENJAMIN COOK TO: RUSSELL T DAVIES
MONDAY 19 MARCH 2007 22:52:20 GMT

AN UPDATE

Russell! I'm dropping you a quick line to touch base. I hope all is well. (Has Catherine said yes yet?) I imagine you're extra busy in the run-up to Wednesday's Series Three press launch, and then transmission next week…?

FROM: RUSSELL T DAVIES TO: BENJAMIN COOK
MONDAY 19 MARCH 2007 23:25:25 GMT

RE: AN UPDATE

Mark the date in your diary: today, Catherine Tate

officially said yes! Bloody hell. This is so brilliant. What a cast!

But we've got to get it right. I'm worried about how other writers will handle Donna. Not Steven Moffat, obviously. But it needs a delicate touch not to go too funny or too broad… says the man who, in *The Runaway Bride*, had her swing across the Flood Chamber and smack into the wall! And when do we tell people? Everything leaks. Freema hasn't even débuted as Martha yet. This is going to get very complicated. Announce this too soon and it'll mess up Freema/Martha. We've got to keep that début clean and successful, because Freema is so brilliant. She deserves a big launch. We can't clutter it by announcing the *next* companion. I think Penny will have to live on as a disguise: we'll ask people to write Penny as a placeholder name.

Catherine's casting has, at least, jumpstarted my thinking. I've been worried all weekend, back here in Manchester, because I've done very little thinking. Well, none. I worried that Manchester had become divorced from work, become a place where I switch off. But today I could click back a bit, because the news of Catherine's casting was so exciting. Of course, I also started thinking of problems: Donna would actively have to be looking for the Doctor, so she can't turn right in 4.11, as opposed to left in 4.1, and become The Woman Who Never Met The Doctor. It takes the charm off that 4.11 story slightly now that it's Donna instead of Penny. The magic of it has gone. Oh well. It's a strong story, and strong stories survive changes. (Have I told you that Rose will appear in 4.11, meeting Donna, because the parallel-world walls are breaking down? Bloody glorious.)

Meanwhile, major panic building on *Torchwood*. I'm running out of time. With all the press launch stuff happening this week, I'm just too busy. You wouldn't believe the amount of phone calls and planning that goes into a simple bloody launch. Oh, I don't even want to type about it. It just feels awful.

FROM: BENJAMIN COOK TO: RUSSELL T DAVIES
THURSDAY 22 MARCH 2007 15:13:46 GMT

THE PRESS LAUNCH

Well, last night was fun. I'm still buzzing. It was weird, all those celebs, wasn't it? Looking around and seeing Dawn French and Jonathan Ross and Jo Whiley, like one of those events that you see in the papers, only now it's for *Doctor Who*!

FROM: RUSSELL T DAVIES TO: BENJAMIN COOK
SATURDAY 24 MARCH 2007 16:44:56 GMT

RE: THE PRESS LAUNCH

The press launch was brilliant. Best thing was, I had a good few drinks with you, Phil and Andy, and *didn't* want to carry on and get leathered, which is really good for me. I'm saying this because, when I'm actually writing, I suspect there are going to be a few Dark Night Of The Soul e-mails – oh lordy – so it's good to report the times when I feel happy. And *The Times*' Caitlin Moran was there, too. Did you see her? She said to me, 'You always write about unrequited love.' I've been thinking about that a lot since. Not sure what it says about me. Not sure that it's healthy.

In other news, Kylie Minogue wants to appear in *Doctor Who*.

Yes, Kylie Minogue! Ha ha ha ha.

I wish I could see your face as you read that sentence. Don't worry, it won't happen. Will Baker, Kylie's creative director, was at the press launch and said how marvellous it'd be to get Kylie in *Doctor Who*. He'd had a bit to drink, so I didn't believe it. But then he phoned Julie on Thursday and insisted he'd been serious. (I could waste time fancying Will, but he's way out of my league. He's just nice to look at.) 4.X was always going to have a one-off companion, or maybe a couple of one-off companions, but if it were Kylie… well, no, it won't be. Nothing will happen. But I might have to have lunch with Kylie, and that alone is worth it.

Plus, on Monday, I've got to phone Dennis Hopper, who *is* interested. This is so weird. Kylie Minogue and Dennis Hopper! We really did start this e-mail correspondence at the best time ever. It's never this mad!

FROM: BENJAMIN COOK TO: RUSSELL T DAVIES
SATURDAY 24 MARCH 2007 17:00:10 GMT

RE: THE PRESS LAUNCH

Kylie Minogue? Oh, c'mon! For the next spin-off series, please can I have Kylie and Dennis travelling the universe in a camper van, solving murder mysteries? Thanks.

FROM: RUSSELL T DAVIES TO: BENJAMIN COOK
SATURDAY 24 MARCH 2007 17:32:35 GMT

RE: THE PRESS LAUNCH

I forgot to tell you, I had the strangest clashing of the Maybe/real world the other day, in a way that doesn't happen often. I was walking down Oxford Street, and someone shouted hello, came running up for a kiss and a hug and all that – and it was [Miss X]! In the last days of Penny Carter's short half-life, [Miss X] had advanced *way* up the list of possible Pennys. We'd run [Miss X]'s name past Peter Fincham, and it turns out that he *loves* her, and her dates are free, so for a couple of days, while I never believed that the Catherine Tate thing would happen, the lovely [Miss X] really, really became Penny for me. Meeting her in Oxford Street completely out of the blue… oh, it was bizarre. I'm not kidding, and you're the only person who might properly understand this, I actually found it hard to talk to her. It was like looking at Penny. The fact that Penny would never exist. The fact that [Miss X] would never even *know* this. She was talking about what she was up to, but I was, literally, stumbling and stammering and failing to say all the nice polite things that I should have said. I just mumbled a bit, with this weird collision in my head, and then walked away, thinking how strange it all is…

FROM: RUSSELL T DAVIES TO: BENJAMIN COOK
MONDAY 26 MARCH 2007 23:41:45 GMT

RE: THE PRESS LAUNCH

Crumbs! This has been a mad day. So mad that it's made me say 'crumbs'. All the way to London… TO MEET KYLIE MINOGUE!!! To sell her the next Christmas Special. Then all the way back to Cardiff. This is INSANE!!!

Kylie was lovely. And tiny. I even sang a duet with her. No kidding. We were talking about the Muppets, and she said, 'What's that song that Kermit's nephew used to sing on the stairs?' I sang the first line, she sang the second, and then we both sang the entire verse! Bloody crazy. She liked the sound of Christmas, but visibly baulked at the thought of three/four weeks' filming, so we'll see. Her life seems so barmy and mad that she might forget about it all tomorrow. Although, she's sitting down to watch *The Runaway Bride* tonight. Imagine that! But still, Julie and I were on top form, so I know we couldn't have done more to convince her, and that makes me happy enough. We did good work.

Also, Julie saw Billie yesterday afternoon, and Billie is definitely saying four episodes. Julie ran past her the option of staying on board after 4.13, and then doing the Christmas Special 2008 – filmed as part of our Series Four run, God help us – which would allow her to come back as and when, and film further Specials alongside David. But that's all in a state of flux. If a lot of Series Four is building up to Rose's return, I'm thinking, do we film a scene for 4.1, right at the end, a glimpse of Rose? End of 4.1, story over, danger past, the Doctor standing by the TARDIS, about to give Donna one of those classic 'come aboard' speeches, but Donna interrupts, 'Hang on a minute,' and runs off, leaving the Doctor stranded. That's quite funny. She runs over to the crowd – police, army, ambulances – looking for her mum, just so that she can give her the car keys. In a rush, a panic, Donna shoves the keys at a woman in the crowd – 'Her name's Sylvia Noble. Give her these. It's that red Toyota over there' – and runs off to her new life. Reveal the woman that she gave the keys to: it's Rose! Just standing, watching, waiting. That could be nice. Or too inward-looking? But thrilling! There's an undoubted 'ooooh!' in that moment.

Yes, 4.1 might need tricks like that. I'm worried that the events in the Medusa Cascade in 4.12/4.13 are much harder to foreshadow than 'Vote Saxon' in Series Three.[3] Is Series Four's running thread quite un-runnable? What do you think?

FROM: BENJAMIN COOK TO: RUSSELL T DAVIES
MONDAY 26 MARCH 2007 23:56:02 GMT

RE: THE PRESS LAUNCH

You've met Kylie? (Yeah, well, I met McFly last month, so… er… there! Yeah, Russell – McFly!) Were you able to tell Kylie much about who she'd play?

I've just got back from watching Catherine interview David on stage at the Duchess Theatre, Covent Garden, for Radio 4 show *Chain Reaction*. They were brilliant together. Hilarious. They talked tons about *Doctor Who*, and said nice things about you, which will probably be

3 Mr Saxon is a running reference throughout Series Three, foreshadowing the Master's return at the end of the series in his guise as UK Prime Minister Harold Saxon (played by John Simm).

cut out of the broadcast show, and didn't let slip that they'll be back on our screens, together, for the duration of Series Four. Mad, mad times indeed.

Two things:

1) What is the Medusa Cascade?

2) Rose Tyler at the end of 4.1? Of course I love it! But then, I'm a ming-mong.

FROM: RUSSELL T DAVIES TO: BENJAMIN COOK
TUESDAY 27 MARCH 2007 00:18:33 GMT

RE: THE PRESS LAUNCH

1) The Medusa Cascade is where 4.12/4.13 takes place. It's just an area of space. The Earth is stolen, along with five other planets, and taken to the Medusa Cascade to form a ring that makes up a great big, um, Dalek energy-converter thing to, er, do things. Kill everything, probably. They've always wanted to be the supreme life form, so why not invent a multi-planet-sized energy-converter-bomb thing that sterilises the entire universe, leaving only them alive? Audacious! The Master mentions the Medusa Cascade in 3.13. He says, 'You sealed the rift at the Medusa Cascade,' nicely placing a Big Rift there, because with universe-walls breaking down, and Rose returning, that's going to be needed somehow.

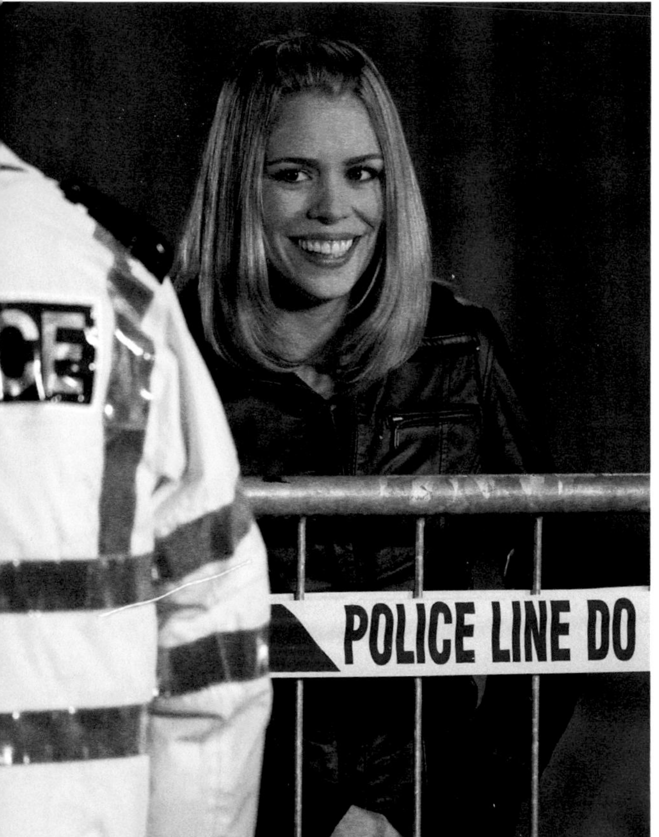

Billie Piper films her cameo as Rose in 4.1 *Partners in Crime*.
Photo © Rex Features

2) Good. Me too.

I just busked with Kylie. I was phoned up at 1am. 'Kylie wants to meet you *today*. She's flying to Stockholm tomorrow.' I got on the train, which turned out to be full of fans on their way to see *Chain Reaction*. (How funny you watched that, knowing what you know.) Then I met the great lady, and I said… well, that they're aboard a spaceship called the *Titanic*, it's hit by meteorites, it destroys Buckingham Palace at the end (she loved that), and her part would be a waitress who joins with the Doctor to escape the wreckage. You think that she's going to be the new companion, but then she does something towards the end, to defend the Doctor, but something rash – she picks up a laser-gun and kills someone – in a situation that the Doctor could have talked his way out of, so effectively she fails Companion Academy. He's disappointed in her. She's left behind at the end, because she's Good But Not Good Enough. For the record, I said, 'I don't know this character's name. Maybe something like Chrissie.' What?! Bollocks to that. *Chrissie?!* What a terrible name. The ship is staffed by aliens – although they'll look exceedingly human – so she should have a nice, simple, sci-fi name.

FROM: RUSSELL T DAVIES TO: BENJAMIN COOK
TUESDAY 27 MARCH 2007 11:19:44 GMT

RE: THE PRESS LAUNCH

I met Kylie! Ha ha ha ha. Fell asleep laughing, woke up laughing. But I'd sooner pull McFly, so you win. Of course, if I met McFly, then I would. This is a fact.

FROM: RUSSELL T DAVIES TO: BENJAMIN COOK
WEDNESDAY 28 MARCH 2007 23:14:25 GMT

RE: THE PRESS LAUNCH

Stray thoughts today. In 4.2 or 4.3, the Doctor should

Dalek Caan, one of the Cult of Skaro, pre-Emergency Temporal Shift, in 3.5 *Evolution of the Daleks*.

be in the TARDIS, talking away quietly, 'I lost my people in the Time War...' He's wandering around the console, all introspective. And then Donna says, 'How d'you spell Dalek?' He looks up – and she's taking notes! Little pad and pencil! He'd hate that. 'You're taking notes?!' 'Well, you talk all the time.' 'I don't have people on board to take notes!' 'Oh, are there rules, then?' 'In this case, yes.' 'Well, I'd better write them down.' These two characters write themselves. But they mustn't bicker for too long. 'I'd better write them down' would be followed by a pause, then a *smile* from the Doctor. He likes her. Without a word, she puts down the notebook and asks him something real. That's how I write – little flashes of dialogue. In fact, 'dialogue' doesn't cover it; that's *them*, that's the dynamic, that's how they are. And then if you use that notebook somewhere vital later in the plot...

Talking of something real, it's about time that someone asked the Doctor, if the Time Lords are dead, why he can't go back in time to find/save them. No one's done that yet. Also, that's a nod to the series finale: Dalek Caan, the last surviving Dalek, will have voyaged into the Time War itself (forbidden! Impossible!) to pull out Davros. It will have sent Caan insane – a weird, broken, strangely holy Dalek, on a plinth, spotlit, revered, talking strangely un-Dalek-ly, more like a mad oracle or prophet. Caan could be a hero in the end. Funny how all these stories flow into each other.

I'm so excited about seeing Donna again, and everything that she can do, the sheer energy she brings to it, so the opening of 4.1 is really taking shape. Oh, the moment that Donna sees the Doctor! The moment that he sees her! (It should absolutely coincide with the appearance of the Big Snarling Beast.) My worry, though, is that 4.1 starts as very Donna-heavy – do we see the Doctor at all, until she does? – which could, given the size of this star casting, make it feel like *The Catherine Tate Show*. I must write up the Doctor more than I usually would when introducing a new companion. Interesting, that sort of worry, because it's

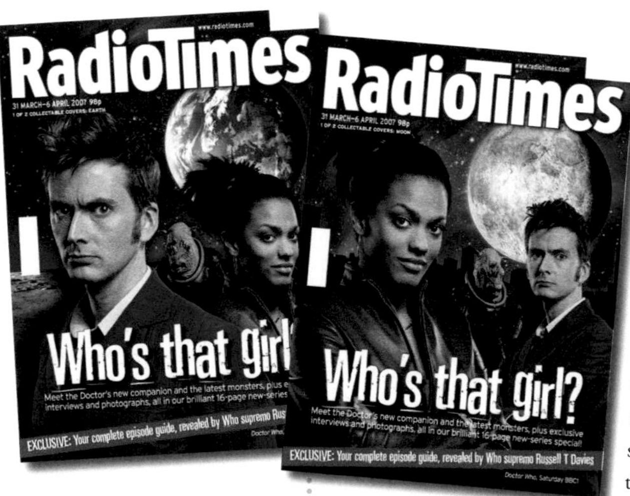

only half a script-worry; the other half is an external, how-this-episode-will-be-perceived worry. That's an equal part of my job, let's not pretend otherwise.

A lot of knives will be out for Donna/Catherine, in that tabloid world. They always are, for successful women. I must, in the script, account for that '*Doctor Who* Becomes Comedy' backlash – give Catherine good, strong, emotional stuff to balance it. This how-the-programme-is-perceived thing is more of a factor on *Doctor Who* than any other show I've ever written. The purist writer in me says that this is wrong, that the story is the thing, that it's not the writer's job to think of external issues – I'm a writer, not a salesman. But also this is the most successful and popular thing that I've ever written, so who says those external worries are bad? Maybe they've *helped*?

Also, since Donna has seen the Empress and the creation of the Earth in *The Runaway Bride*, 4.1 has to be *bigger*.[4] It has to amaze her. I'm wondering about a portal, through which these Big Snarling CGI Beasts come. Yes, they've become plural. I want size. I think seeing 3.1 at last week's press launch, seeing the Judoon stomp across the Moon on the big screen, has put that thought in my head. I want packs of monsters in 4.1.

Big worry about 4.X today: the *Titanic*'s forcefields are deactivated by saboteurs, because someone wants someone dead, so the ship is hit by meteorites; once wrecked, murderous creatures should break out of the hold – but is that the same plan? The same saboteurs? It should be a different plan, surely? Saboteurs upon assassins upon terrorists? Or are the meteorites a coincidence? Maybe the saboteurs should, um, magnetise the hull to attract them? The murderous creatures should be really slim, tight metal. Sexy! Like Kylie's stage-show Cybermen.[5] Or maybe, since this is a Christmas Cruise, the ship could have Robot Angel staff – beautiful golden faces, smiling cherub masks. Polite voices, great for killers. Like butlers. White tunics. Metal wings. Ooh, haloes! Deadly haloes! Maybe they're programmed to go murderous once the ship is hit? Ah, if they're programmed to go mad once the ship is hit, it *is* the same plan. It's part of the sabotage. I'm loving the sound of Robot Angels.

It all feels nice and creative, this. That good mood is persisting. I'm genuinely excited/scared about Saturday's transmission of *Smith and Jones*. That helps. Even seeing the *Radio Times* this week was thrilling. I'm a fanboy at heart.

FROM: BENJAMIN COOK TO: RUSSELL T DAVIES
THURSDAY 29 MARCH 2007 02:41:28 GMT

RE: THE PRESS LAUNCH

I spent three hours this afternoon re-entering numbers into my new mobile phone. My old one was stolen on Saturday. I'm still receiving text messages that were sent to me days ago, but were delayed by the bar on my stolen phone. There's one from you that reads, 'Oh, I hope you've got a new phone to receive texts…' I hadn't. 'I'm on the train to London TO MEET KYLIE!!!'

A question: you know the ending to 4.X already (the *Titanic* destroys Buckingham Palace, Kylie is left behind,

4 The Empress is a half-arachnid, half-human creature – a member of the alien Racnoss.

5 Kylie's 2005 *Showgirl* tour featured dancers in costumes inspired by the design of the Cybermen.

etc), but do you always start writing stories with endings in sight? Isn't a leap into the dark ever more thrilling?

FROM: RUSSELL T DAVIES TO: BENJAMIN COOK
THURSDAY 29 MARCH 2007 23:12:14 GMT

RE: THE PRESS LAUNCH

I always know the ending. Well, usually. Emotionally. I know how it *feels*. I knew, from the first moment, that *The Runaway Bride* would end with the Doctor saying, 'Her name was Rose,' and more particularly that it would end with the Doctor and Donna in an ordinary street, with snow. I knew that *Casanova* would end with Old Casanova dying, and Young Casanova dancing into darkness. Right from the moment that *Queer as Folk* was conceived, I knew that it would end with Stuart and Vince dancing on a podium – and I knew *why*. Everything else – that poor, dumped boyfriend of Vince's, Stuart's loneliness, the circling drug-killer in the club – came later. But the central image – two men, eternally happy in a state of unrequited love – was a given. That was why I was writing the whole drama, right from the start, to reach that moment of happiness. It's as crucial as the first moment of thinking of the story. An ending is what the story *is*. For me, anyway.

I know that 4.1 will end with… well, it's a no-brainer, that one: the Doctor and Donna spinning off into space, in the TARDIS, and happy. And 4.13 will end with the TARDIS circling above the Earth, and the Doctor making an address to the entire planet, welcoming them back home, promising to protect them for ever. Sometimes, I swear, I could write those scenes first. Except I couldn't, because I can never write scenes out of order. I physically cannot do it. Lots of writers do. Paul Abbott does, happily. If he gets stuck on a scene, he skips to a later one. If I get stuck, I sit there, stuck, until it's resolved, because the scenes that come later can't exist if they aren't informed by where they've come from.

I read an interview with Charlie Kaufman, the man who wrote *Being John Malkovich* and *Eternal Sunshine of the Spotless Mind* (both staggeringly brilliant movies), in which he said, *so* forcefully, that any writer who starts a script knowing where it's going to end is morally bankrupt, that they had forfeited their right to stand as a dramatist, because they weren't open to the infinite possibilities of storytelling. I thought, sod off! Firstly, any writer telling another writer how they *must* work can always sod off, no matter how brilliant they are. (That's why I'd never want any of these musings to be taken as a template for How To Write. It happens to be How *I* Write, that's all.) But also I disagree so strongly with Kaufman, I even think he's lying, even lying to himself. If you take away his dictatorial side, it's a fascinating thought; it did make me want to start writing something with no idea of where it's going, just to see what happens. Maybe it would be the best thing I've ever written. But the problem is, I'm not Charlie Kaufman, only he is. Three pages in, I'd have got interested in something, so I'd see the story, my story, the through-line, and immediately that would suggest its ending. I couldn't stop that happening.

It's fascinating how many successful writers start talking like censors – saying, 'You *must* write like this, you must *not* write like that.' The very people that should embrace freedom, and the right to make mistakes, become the people laying down laws. That Bonfire of the Vanities goes on and on. Stoked by writers! Don't they realise that they're becoming dictators?

FROM: RUSSELL T DAVIES TO: BENJAMIN COOK
SATURDAY 31 MARCH 2007 16:26:44 GMT

AND NOW ON BBC ONE…

I've been praying for rain, to increase our *Smith and*

The Judoon rampage across BBC One, in 3.1 *Smith and Jones*.

Jones viewing figures, and I just got back to the flat… and there's a *violent storm* blowing across Cardiff Bay! I am now wondering about the extent of my supernatural powers. I am going to wish for a billion quid and Freddie Ljungberg, and see what happens. Fingers crossed.

FROM: BENJAMIN COOK TO: RUSSELL T DAVIES
SATURDAY 31 MARCH 2007 17:29:54 GMT

RE: AND NOW ON BBC ONE…

It's sunshine here in Chiswick. I might start praying, too. If it gets to 6pm and there's still no sign of rain, I'll offer up my *Mine All Mine* DVD as a sacrifice to Tlaloc. But will he be appeased?

FROM: RUSSELL T DAVIES TO: BENJAMIN COOK
SATURDAY 31 MARCH 2007 18:07:05 GMT

RE: AND NOW ON BBC ONE…

So *you're* the one who bought the *Mine All Mine* DVD? I knew we'd find that mystery shopper in the end. Actually, it's turned sunny again here. My supernatural powers are on the wane. I knew I should have wished for Freddie first.

The Hour Before *Doctor Who*! Exciting!

FROM: BENJAMIN COOK TO: RUSSELL T DAVIES
SATURDAY 31 MARCH 2007 18:16:13 GMT

RE: AND NOW ON BBC ONE…

Don't you ever wish that you *didn't* know what happens next? Isn't this the hour when you wish that you were 'just' a viewer? What are the Judoon? How does a London hospital end up on the Moon? What persuades the Doctor to invite Martha Jones aboard the TARDIS? Right now, aren't you wishing that you didn't know?

FROM: RUSSELL T DAVIES TO: BENJAMIN COOK
SATURDAY 31 MARCH 2007 18:23:47 GMT

RE: AND NOW ON BBC ONE…

Equally, what I don't get is the worry. Will it be crap? Will I be ashamed? Will it let me down? Gareth Roberts called it, marvellously, that sense of 'anticipointment' – all too ready for an episode of *Doctor Who* to be rubbish. That first episode of *Time and the Rani*, that was a deep, dark trough…[6]

Text message from: **Ben**
Sent: 31-Mar-2007 22:02
Full Moon tonight. Dazzlingly bright over Chiswick. How perfect. How many kids must be looking up at the Moon right now, as they draw the curtains before bed, thinking of spaceships and Time Lords and Judoon?

Text message from: **Russell**
Sent: 31-Mar-2007 22:04
That's funny, I just stood on my balcony ten minutes ago and thought the same thing. The Moon is bright and clear over the Bay. It was meant to be.

FROM: RUSSELL T DAVIES TO: BENJAMIN COOK
SUNDAY 1 APRIL 2007 10:30:02 GMT

RE: AND NOW ON BBC ONE…

8.2 million viewers! With a peak of 8.9 million! And a 39.5 per cent audience share! By the time that's consolidated, it'll be higher than last year's series opener. Oh lordy.

FROM: BENJAMIN COOK TO: RUSSELL T DAVIES
SUNDAY 1 APRIL 2007 14:45:20 GMT

RE: AND NOW ON BBC ONE…

Amazing figures! Tlaloc must have appreciated *Mine All Mine*.

FROM: RUSSELL T DAVIES TO: BENJAMIN COOK
SUNDAY 1 APRIL 2007 19:27:08 GMT

RE: AND NOW ON BBC ONE…

I had some 4.1 thoughts last night. It was one of those nights when I thought, right, I'm going to go out and get rat-arsed in some club and end up in a Bute Town gutter. But this town is so bloody small. After an hour in one of the two gay clubs in the whole of Cardiff, I was besieged by *Doctor Who* staff, most of whom I don't even

6 Broadcast in 1987, *Time and the Rani* was Sylvester McCoy's début serial as the Seventh Doctor.

know ('Hello, I'm the man who's building *The Sarah Jane Adventures* website') or, bless 'em, friendly Cardiff gays who'd seen *Smith and Jones* – but *dozens* of them. It was doing my head in, so I left after a few drinks. But Cardiff on a Saturday night is like Beirut, so I had to walk all the way back to the Bay. I wasn't consciously thinking about scripts at all. I was too fed up. But by the time I got to the Bay, lovely and cold and desolate, at about 2.30am, and sat down on the seafront for a cigarette, a few things clicked into place. That often happens. You go for a walk and it's not the walk that clicks things into place, but the *end* of the walk –

I like the idea of the portal – a shimmering circle that you'd step through – to another world. I keep calling the portal the 'Venting'. It's not a good word or particularly appropriate, but that's what my head is saying right now. An alien world beyond the Venting. Nice alien vistas, a bit of a temple, where we discover the last survivors of that world. They've been overrun by these wild dog things. The rest of the population has been eaten. (The wild dogs should be called Vor-something. Vorlax? Vorleen? No, Vorlax is nice.) The survivors have opened the Venting to, literally, vent their world, to give the Vorlax a taste of fresh meat, and so saving their planet. Oh, the Doctor's anger! 'You've got a problem and what do you do? You PASS IT ON!' At the end, he seals the portal, leaving these wise old dying bastards to their fate. That's harsh. But good.

'The wooden boards over the window are straining... moving... buckling...' Illustration by Russell T Davies.

A great image came to me today. In fighting just the one Vorlax, the Doctor is wondering where it came from, and someone points out that the first sightings were in a boarded-up house. The Welsh valleys are full of boarded-up houses. There's something automatically spooky about them. The Doctor and Donna are approaching the house. As they get closer, they realise that the wooden boards over the windows are *straining*... moving... buckling... with a scratching and a scrabbling. In that moment, the boards rip off – and hundreds of Vorlax pour out, chasing and killing! There are people running and screaming. Huge pictures. An ordinary one-monster episode explodes, suddenly, into an epic. On the alien world, an image of an even greater threat to come: wooden gates to the city, behind which there are *millions* of Vorlax, snarling and snapping, threatening to break through any second. Beyond that, huge *plains* of Vorlax. Can we make pictures that big? This is expensive. And how the hell do the Doctor and Donna survive that? Even if the Doctor seals off the alien world, what about the hundreds of Vorlax on the loose on Earth? Does he find a way to kill them? If so, he'd give that solution to the alien world; he wouldn't just seal them off. But I want him to seal them off. I'll think on. Great image, though.

FROM: BENJAMIN COOK TO: RUSSELL T DAVIES
MONDAY 2 APRIL 2007 10:31:53 GMT

RE: AND NOW ON BBC ONE...

How do you know when to start writing? All these images only exist in your head right now, yes? (Pretending for a moment that these e-mails hadn't happened!) At what point do you begin to write the actual script?

FROM: RUSSELL T DAVIES TO: BENJAMIN COOK
TUESDAY 3 APRIL 2007 02:34:17 GMT

RE: AND NOW ON BBC ONE...

How do I know when to start writing? I leave it till the

The Vorlax attack! Illustration by Russell T Davies.

last minute. And then I leave it some more. Eventually, I leave it till I'm desperate. That's really the word, desperate. I always think, I'm not ready to write it, I don't know what I'm doing, it's just a jumble of thoughts in a state of flux, there's no story, I don't know how A connects to B, I don't know anything! I get myself into a genuine state of panic. Except panic sounds exciting. It sounds all running-around and adrenalised. This is more like a black cloud of fear and failure. Normally, I'll leave it till the deadline, and I haven't even started writing. This has become, over the years, a week beyond the deadline, or even more. It can be a week – or weeks – past the delivery date, and *I haven't started writing*. In fact, I don't have delivery dates any more. I go by the start-of-preproduction date. I consider that to be my real deadline. And then I miss that. It's a cycle that I cannot break. I simply can't help it. It makes my life miserable.

My inability to start on time is crippling. Any social event – people's birthdays, drinks with friends, family dos, anything – gets swept aside and cancelled, because there's this voice inside my head screaming, 'I HAVEN'T STARTED WRITING!' I wake up, shower, have a coffee, watch telly, go to town, buy some food, potter about, buy a magazine, come home, e-mail, make phone calls, watch more telly, and it goes on and on and on until I go to bed again, and a whole day has gone. It's just vanished. Every single minute of the day, every single sodding minute, is labelled with this depressing, lifeless, dull thought: I'm not writing. I *make* the time vanish. I don't know why I do this. I even set myself little targets. At 10am, I think, I'll start at noon. At noon, I think, I'll make it 4pm. At 4pm, I think, too late now, I'll wait for tonight and work till late. And then I'll use TV programmes as crutches – ooh, must watch this, must watch that – and then it's 10pm and I think, well, start at midnight, that's a good time. *A good time?!* A nice round number! At midnight, I despair and reckon it's too late, and stay up despairing. I'll stay that way till 2 or 3am, and then go to bed in a tight knot of frustration. The next day, the same thing. Weeks can pass like that. I'm wondering if describing it to you might break the cycle. Probably not.

I've got this *Torchwood* script to write. Although it's a vague mess in my head, I know exactly, very exactly, the first five pages. You'd think, to make my life easier, I'd type out those five pages at least. I could open a file now, right now, and bash them out in about three hours. I'd wake up tomorrow morning so much happier, because a file labelled 'Torchwood 2.1' would exist. But no, I spend all day thinking, start, start, start. But I don't. It's gone 2am now, and I still haven't started. I go to bed in a state of despair, and wake up the same way. Literally, my very first thought when I wake up is a rush of fear and, well, I suppose self-hatred for being so stupid and slow. It's a lousy way to write. Or not write. It wrecks my life. I see my sisters about twice a year, my dad about three times, my best friend Tracy about five times, I might see you socially – what? – twice a year, and it's not like there's a long list of friends who might be taking up other evenings, because this lifestyle has excluded them, slowly, over the years. All the rest of the time, I cancel or simply don't appear. They all think I'm writing. The truth is, I'm more likely to be *not* writing, just sitting on my own, panicking. My boyfriend has the patience of a saint. Or he's a sap to put up with me. No, I'll go for saint.

It's ridiculous, because I can prove, conclusively, that the solutions start to appear every time I *do* start writing. A straightforward example: I spent ages not writing *Doctor Who* 3.11, *Utopia*, just sitting in a black cloud. There was a concrete problem: I had no idea why the TARDIS would end up at the end of the universe. Even though that's where this episode had to be set. Now, with hindsight, it's easy: the Doctor reacts badly to the arrival of Captain Jack, because Jack is an immortal, a fixed point in time, the Doctor can barely look at him, feels it in his guts, *and the TARDIS feels the same*. But imagine that you don't know those words in italics, that they haven't been imagined yet. Without them, the sheer coincidence of a) Jack arrives, and b) at the same time, the TARDIS is thrown to the end of the universe, is an awful, crippling, terrible, un-writable coincidence. The trouble is, because I'm telling you this in hindsight, the solution seems obvious. In fact, the words 'at the same time' spell out the answer. But it wasn't that clear when it was all in a state of flux – where everything is up for grabs and nothing is definite. It wasn't so much a question of how does the TARDIS get to the end of the universe; it was more one of should it? Why? Is that rubbish? Does it need to be connected to Jack? And these doubts were underscored by much bigger ones: is it right to bring back Captain Jack in Series Three? Will he work with David's Doctor? What does Martha do? Have I really got to set this in a lame quarry? How late am I going to be with 3.12/3.13 if *Utopia* is already so late? Does the Master work in this day and age? Can we delay production because I'm so late? Every question was jostling for space.

The TARDIS arrives above the Torchwood hub in 3.11 *Utopia*...

Eventually, the script was so late that I *had* to start work. Two pages in – two bloody pages – it just clicked: Captain Jack arrives, *therefore* the TARDIS goes to the end of the universe. That sounds so simple now, but it was the key to the whole episode. You'd think I'd learn from that example. You'd think that would tell me: start writing and it will begin to make sense. But I never learn. Next script, I'll go through the same process all over again. To make it worse, my career is as successful as it can possibly be, and I'm probably writing scripts to the height of my ability at the moment, so I can only conclude that I've lumbered myself with a painful system *that works*. Is that it? Is it like a superstition that I have to panic in order to write well? It drives me mad.

When I'm out and about and with people, at a production meeting or just bumping into someone and saying hello, I know I'm a funny guy – and I think that's *deliberate*. I am consciously having a laugh, because it's an escape, it's a relief from the cloud bearing down. Truth is, this e-mail isn't scratching the surface. It's worse than I'm describing. I'm not revelling in it; I'm sitting here thinking what a stupid idiot I am, and what a better life I could have, what a good, successful, happy life, and it's all my own fault. What the hell do my family and friends really think of me? I did begin to get slight warning bells at the last *Radio Times* Cover Party, by the

...but Captain Jack is left clinging on for dear life, as the TARDIS flees to the end of the universe.

sheer number of people – about eight separate people, five of whom I hardly knew – who came up to me with an opening gambit of 'Are you all right?' I thought, bloody hell, do I look like a corpse?! But I didn't really, which made me think: how am I spoken of? Like a lunatic?

Well, you did ask.

FROM: BENJAMIN COOK TO: RUSSELL T DAVIES
TUESDAY 3 APRIL 2007 11:42:18 GMT

RE: AND NOW ON BBC ONE...

I recognise – as I think most people would, especially writers – aspects of my own behaviour in what you describe in that e-mail. But would you call it writer's block? It doesn't sound entirely like writer's block, it's more self-imposed than that, and you don't use that term, but I'm interested in how – or whether – you would define writer's block? Some people say that it's a fallacy…

FROM: RUSSELL T DAVIES TO: BENJAMIN COOK
TUESDAY 3 APRIL 2007 22:11:42 GMT

RE: AND NOW ON BBC ONE...

I couldn't help thinking that you might read that e-mail and think, sod off, you self-indulgent tosspot. It's all so me, me, me that I forget, everyone must feel like that. You're right. Well, not everyone. I read an interview with Jeanette Winterson once, in which she spoke about writing with such certainty that she made the process sound so wonderful, clear, pure, confident. It was so beautiful that I cut it out and kept it by my computer. It's now been swept away somewhere. That was stupid. But I remember that she described writing as being like flying. That must be nice. Feels more like falling to me.

I never call it writer's block, though. I don't know why, but I sort of react with revulsion to that phrase. I imagine it to mean sitting there with No Ideas At All. For me, it feels more like the ideas just won't take the right shape or form. Do writers ever run out of ideas? Doesn't the block say that something *else* is wrong? Something bigger? I don't know.

FROM: RUSSELL T DAVIES TO: BENJAMIN COOK
FRIDAY 6 APRIL 2007 10:34:13 GMT

RE: AND NOW ON BBC ONE...

There has been a lot of good, practical work over the past few days – not Maybe thinking, but actual sitting in meetings with writers and sorting out plots. A lot of *Torchwood* and *Sarah Jane*, and a great meeting with Gareth about the Agatha Christie episode. I adore those meetings. I'm in my element.

But in the 4.1 Maybe… I've found that I vividly and profoundly hate the estate, the Vorlax, and the alien planet. I think it's crap. It's very *Primeval*. Too *Primeval*. I like *Primeval*, but I don't want to copy it. Now, lodged in my head, is a simple image of how *funny* it is that Donna is actively looking for the Doctor, that in, say, a new plot there's something going on in an office block (boring setting, but bear with me), something alien, so Donna is investigating, partly in the hope that she'll meet the Doctor, and partly because that's what people who have met the Doctor *do*. They carry on the good work. And the Doctor is investigating too, but separately. This is the crucial image: you play a good 15 minutes at the top of the episode with the Doctor and Donna *not* meeting. She walks out of one door, he walks in another, neither knowing that the other is there. It's got all the fun that the housing estate idea didn't have. And doors! That's why I'm saying an office block – because it needs doors. And lifts. Donna gets in the left-hand lift, doors close, the right-hand lift opens, the Doctor steps out. This story isn't a farce, but it uses the shapes of a farce. That's the starting point, the inspiration, the heart of it. Of course, it leaves me with no story and no enemy, but there we go. Back to square one. Except –

Imagine a moment when the villain is unveiling, unmasking in some swanky office at night, and Donna has been investigating, and so has the Doctor, separately, but with both working out that something crucial is happening in this office. The Doctor has lowered himself down on a window-cleaner's cradle to look into the room (I'm determined to get that cradle back in, the one that was cut from *Smith and Jones*), and Donna is inside the building, outside the office, looking through a glass window. At the moment of the Big Reveal, where the Sinister Boss is revealing himself as a monster, what's *really* happening is: the Doctor and Donna are looking across the room and seeing each other on the other side! Her reaction! His reaction! Upstaging the monster! That makes me laugh, and that's good. It feels more like *Doctor Who* than anything else I've thought up. It's in character for both the Doctor and Donna. The fun of these scenes feels stronger than anything.

FROM: BENJAMIN COOK TO: RUSSELL T DAVIES
TUESDAY 10 APRIL 2007 11:49:51 GMT

EASTER

How was your Easter, Russell? I'm in Nottingham at the moment, heading back to London tomorrow. I was going to go home tonight, but then I realised that I'd miss the last episode of *Life on Mars*, so I'm stopping here to watch it. I bet you've seen it already. I hope it's not disappointing. (Anticipointment?)

Talking of which, how are scripts and that progressing? Dare I ask?

FROM: RUSSELL T DAVIES TO: BENJAMIN COOK
TUESDAY 10 APRIL 2007 23:14:00 GMT

RE: EASTER

I'm just swamped with *Torchwood* and *Sarah Jane* stuff – including Elisabeth Sladen moving into the flat upstairs! Sarah Jane is my neighbour! Oh, but wasn't that *Life on Mars* finale brilliant? Please like it. I hadn't seen it until tonight, and I was amazed. A show that ends with the joyous suicide of a man who'd rather live in his dreams. How often do you get that transmitted on TV? Marvellous!

The suicide of Sam Tyler (John Simm) brings the second series of *Life on Mars* to a close.

FROM: RUSSELL T DAVIES TO: BENJAMIN COOK
WEDNESDAY 11 APRIL 2007 23:48:42 GMT

RE: EASTER

Lordy, what a night! Jane Tranter came to Cardiff this afternoon for a *Sarah Jane* read-through, but then she asked if she could come round my flat tonight, with Julie, for 'a chat', which they did. The chat was to formally convey from the Sixth Floor of the BBC that they want me to stay for a fifth series of *Doctor Who*. The three of us have talked about this before, loads of times, but Jane felt that she'd never really been 'official' about it. I still said no. It's not about the money, and Jane and Julie both know that. They knew my reply even before they'd walked in, and agreed with me, but professionally they had to come and represent the formal BBC point of view.

That's today's news. Hey ho. Turning down a fifth series. The thing is, Ben… a *fifth series!* Did you ever, ever, *ever* think that *Doctor Who* would be this important to the BBC? That's the maddest thing of all, and the best thing of all.

FROM: BENJAMIN COOK TO: RUSSELL T DAVIES
THURSDAY 12 APRIL 2007 02:40:08 GMT

RE: EASTER

Tell 'em that you'll stay on for three million quid and Freddie Ljungberg on a serving dish! Go on, just for a laugh. See what they say. You're probably right to decline, but were you tempted? Just a little bit tempted? A teensy bit tempted? Not because of Freddie on a plate (was that even in the offing? It's late and I'm confused), but just because the BBC really does seem to want you to stay? That must be flattering, at least.

P.S. *Life on Mars* was incredible, wasn't it? But I still can't decide whether the finale should have finished a few minutes earlier, on Sam Tyler's suicide jump, instead of following him, 'alive' and 'well', back into his dream world/the afterlife?

FROM: RUSSELL T DAVIES TO: BENJAMIN COOK
THURSDAY 12 APRIL 2007 03:19:05 GMT

RE: EASTER

Tempted? To do a fifth series? Not for a second. Weird, isn't it? I'm going to go to bed and think that through, and wonder why that is exactly. I'm not sure. I think, really, it's because the option is untenable, because way back, around the time that we filmed *Doomsday*, we promised this course of action to David. And to each other. We decided that we'd have a fourth series (David's third), with a big ending, after which we'd take the show off air, just for a short while, apart from the odd Special, so that we could have a breather, and a new production team could settle in, find its feet, and prepare for Series Five. And there's all sorts of other plans, for the future, but… I'm almost superstitious about putting things into print. Julie, Phil, Jane and I committed to that initial promise, and we're sticking to our word. That promise means that the fifth series option does not exist for me. They *might as well* talk about buying me Freddie Ljungberg. It's flattering and all that, but it ain't gonna happen.

As for *Life on Mars*… well, going out on Sam's suicide would have been such a downer and wasn't the point; he died so that he could live. For ever. In his dreams. The fanboy part of my mind sort of quibbles that the fall would kill him, not put him back in a coma, therefore the fantasy life would stop dead. But that's me being too atheist. That ending is saying that an afterlife can last for ever – or for a split second.

FROM: RUSSELL T DAVIES TO: BENJAMIN COOK
SATURDAY 14 APRIL 2007 16:20:20 GMT

RE: EASTER

The past few days have been so busy. I know that thinking of stories is a constant background beat, but sometimes the sheer volume of work can do a pretty good job at drowning it out. It's like the work *triples* when we're not filming. February and March are sort of my months off from writing, but now it's heading towards Writing Time for the rest of the year. This week, I've been feeling myself sort of withdraw. I'm alone in Cardiff this weekend and next week – very few meetings, just me, locked away. I'm becoming bad at replying to e-mails (I've been telling you less stuff, and I'm making an *effort* to write, though I do still want to), phone calls and messages are going ignored… and I *want* to be like that. I want everyone and everything to sod off.

That Series Five offer didn't help, in a weird way. The next day, I started smoking again (I've been off them for a while), eating really bad food, just sort of guzzling rubbish. I've been browsing Outpost Gallifrey to read how crap I am.[7] I've been watching some of Series Three – not for work, but with a state of mind that says, deliberately, this isn't as good as I thought it was. In fact, it's crap. I've failed. I'm rubbish. I'm lucky. I'm a fraud. I've lost it, and this next script is the script that will expose that. Etc. I am, I realise, making myself miserable. That's the old dark streak of you-don't-deserve-this ticking away, like I punish myself for being successful. Plots and stories in the Maybe are taking a back seat. Instead, I'm focusing on the schedule, because that's already a nightmare. My mind is going 'April, May, June' all the time, because those three months are going to require a script a month, and I *never* manage to complete a script a month. Why-oh-why can't I be happy? Why can't I just love this work? Why can't I feel like Jeanette Winterson in that quote I lost, where writing feels like flying? It's not even falling at the moment; it's sinking. Why do I get like this?

7 Outpost Gallifrey is a fan-run *Doctor Who* website. It spawned The *Doctor Who* Forum, a discussion forum with around 30,000 registered members.

In the real world… yesterday, we said no to Dennis Hopper. He was available for only four days. I was weak and promised to make it work, then came home and realised that I'd lumbered myself with a cameo that doesn't fit 4.X at all. I wouldn't be able to do anything proper with that character because of the limitations. That's where Phil is marvellous. He knows me so well. He phoned on Thursday night, and said, 'Between you and me, I'm worried about the pressure that this is putting you under. Should we withdraw?' He was voicing my every worry. So we nixed that. Good. What does Dennis Hopper mean to an eight-year-old anyway?

It's weird, not knowing if *Gridlock* is on tonight.[8] I'm quite excited.

FROM: BENJAMIN COOK TO: RUSSELL T DAVIES
SATURDAY 14 APRIL 2007 21:51:18 GMT

RE: EASTER

Three cheers for the football not overrunning! It *was* exciting, wasn't it, waiting to see whether *Doctor Who* would be on tonight or not? I wonder what effect the football and 7.40pm start had on the ratings. Well, we'll find out tomorrow.

>>That's the old dark streak of you-don't-deserve-this ticking away, like I punish myself for being successful.<<

You make it sound conscious. Not like, 'Right, I'll piss myself off now,' but like the misery comes first, and then goes in search of stuff that'll encourage it. Is depression too strong a word? Self-induced or otherwise, depression is an affliction with a roll call of writers, poets, musicians and so on. Edgar Allan Poe wondered:

> *whether all that is profound, does not spring from disease of thought, from moods of mind exalted at the expense of the general intellect. They who dream by day are cognizant of many things which escape those who dream only by night.*

I love that. It's from his short story 'Eleonora', which is thought to be semi-autobiographical. Do you reckon this fear that your scripts won't be good enough actually makes them better, ultimately? Does it vanquish complacency? Or would your work be better, do you think, if you didn't harbour such glaring doubts?

8 Had 14 April's FA Cup Semi-Final between Manchester United and Watford gone into extra time, *Gridlock* would have been postponed for a week.

FROM: RUSSELL T DAVIES TO: BENJAMIN COOK
SUNDAY 15 APRIL 2007 14:30:35 GMT

RE: EASTER

That's a great quote. But more important than even Edgar Allan Poe – we got EIGHT MILLION VIEWERS last night! This is a strange and lovely time. That's cheered me up. Talking of which…

The depression thing. I fight shy of the word depression, because real depression is so debilitating and awful that I feel a bit arrogant even to assume that I've touched upon it. Although I go into awful slumps, I do deliver scripts in the end, and I stay on top of work, just about, and I don't think Depression with a capital D has any such luxury. And yet… and yet… I'm well aware of those depression/creativity theories, and certainly I've watched it at work in other writers. Paul Abbott is genuinely bipolar, and that's a frightening and sometimes brilliant thing to behold. I'm nowhere near that. I even envy it, that's the killer. Suffering can seem so admirable and important. There is a widespread theory, propagated by the media and hugely by writers themselves, that writing and suffering are synonymous. With Jimmy McGovern, that seems to be a genuine, heartfelt philosophy – if you haven't suffered, you can't write. But that philosophy actually excludes certain people from the right to write, and that *has* to be wrong. That's a step away from book-burning. You can't have a list of who's entitled to write and who isn't.

When I was starting out, I felt that tyranny. You Must Suffer! It didn't help that one of the first writers I knew well was Paul, because the history of his childhood is so genuinely awful. It looms over his reputation like a monolith, and threatens to become the template for others. In the early 1990s, I used to think I'd never reach his level, because I haven't suffered. That's why *Queer as Folk* was such a breakthrough for me. It took me that long to realise that I had experience of a whole world that no one else was writing. I'm not equating gay with suffering there; I just mean *experience*. Everyone has fallen in love. Everyone has been bullied. Everyone has lost someone, somehow. Everyone has been ecstatic. Everyone has been suicidal, even if only slightly. That 'slightly' is the important thing. You don't need to have had your head shoved in the dirt; you only need to be able to imagine it. 'A moment's imagination is equal to a

Alan Davies (Bob) and Lesley Sharp (Rose) in *Bob & Rose.*

lifetime of experience.' I read that somewhere once, and it's so true. If those sorts of doubts – I'm not important, I haven't suffered, I'm too young/happy/middle-class to be experienced – are ever holding you back from writing, DON'T LISTEN TO THEM! It really is a tyranny, and it's bollocks.

I often get asked to give masterclasses in scriptwriting. I usually turn them down, but once, just once, I gave a great one. If I say so myself! I think I was angry about some recent interview with a 'suffering artist', and it inspired me. It was for the Fast Track people at the Edinburgh TV Festival, the eager ones who *really* want to get into telly, all about 18, 19, 20 years old. I challenged them to admit that they feel, at their age, that they haven't lived, that they don't know enough about the world to write about it. Gradually, reluctantly, lots of nodding heads. And then I played them two clips: one from an episode of *Buffy the Vampire Slayer* (*Out of Mind, Out of Sight*), where a girl has been so ignored that she becomes invisible, and another from *I, Claudius*, where young Claudius is being so ignored that he might as well be invisible. I pointed out that both those scenes are the same thing. One popular culture, one high art, but the same drama. More importantly, who *hasn't* felt like that? Especially at 18, 19, 20, you probably feel more ignored and left out than at any other time in your life. Of *course* you've lived. That's *you!* Which means that you can write *I, Claudius*, and you can write *Buffy the Vampire Slayer*. There's no limit to what you can write. I swear, it was like you could see light bulbs switching on over their heads. I was quite proud of that.

Queer as Folk was ten years of my life put on screen. Just about everything in that happened to me in some shape or form. Except having the baby, and he hardly features! But the best thing I ever did was write *Bob & Rose* next, which had never happened to me, ever, in any way. I've never even slept with a woman. Not once. Well, a bit of rubbing with Beverley Jacobs when I was 15, but that's only because she used to go out with a boy I fancied, and still fancy to this day, so I had my eyes closed, imagining him. Poor Beverley. Of course, in writing *Bob & Rose*, I did go through a long process of imagining the women in my life that I *do* love, the ones that maybe I'd be with if I were straight, and how I'd feel. A lot of that was based on my friend Tracy. When Julie met Tracy a few years ago, she said, 'My God, she's Rose Cooper! She talks like her!' You see, it all comes from somewhere. Every time you think, no, I haven't experienced that emotion, YES, YOU HAVE! In tiny ways. But that's all you need. You imagine and extrapolate from that. Most writers aren't murderers, but an awful lot of them write murders. Who hasn't *wanted* to murder someone? That's what they're tapping into, just that spark. But you certainly don't need to be steeped in blood to write it well.

You asked if the fear makes the scripts better. Well, I have no choice but to think that it helps, or it would be unbearable. To write without that fear is not an option – not yet, not for me – so I have to rationalise it, hope that it helps, or I'd go nuts. I can't imagine writing and thinking, this is easy. I'm marvelling at those words. This. Is. Easy. They're impossible. I might as well say, 'I'm a Martian.'

There I go again, saying that you don't have to suffer, while admitting that the process *is* an act of suffering. Still. No one said that this had to be logical.

Right. I've got to write a synopsis of 4.X for Kylie Minogue's agent. I never write treatments, but I have to this time, because they want to know what they're getting into. Once again, I think the word is 'busk'... ■

CHAPTER THREE

BASTARDS

In which *The People's Quiz* is shunted, the internet is slated, and one beautiful day with Wynnie la Freak makes everything worthwhile

FROM: RUSSELL T DAVIES TO: BENJAMIN COOK
TUESDAY 17 APRIL 2007 01:48:30 GMT

CHRISTMAS IS COMING

Here you go, Keeper of the Matrix. Not a bad read. I hate treatments, but they do make me concentrate. I'm going to bed now, *terrified* about the budget. How the hell are we going to afford this?

DOCTOR WHO CHRISTMAS SPECIAL 2007
STARSHIP TITANIC

The *Starship Titanic* sails above the Earth on its Christmas Cruise. Half original *Titanic*, half floating hotel, it's a luxury spaceship with holidaymakers on board, all decked out for the festive season.

The Doctor comes on board as a curious visitor, and soon makes friends with one of the ship's staff, Peth, a waitress. While everyone wines and dines around her, Peth has to clean up after them. But she's dreaming of a better life. And the Doctor is travelling alone for once – the lonely Time Lord. As he strikes up a friendship with Peth, liking her feistiness, her sense of humour, he wonders... could she join him on his travels in Time and Space, as his new companion...?

Disaster strikes! Meteorites hit the *Titanic* – and it's more like *The Poseidon Adventure* In Space, as the ship is crippled, with oxygen running out. Worse, if the Doctor can't get to the Flight Deck in time, the ship might fall onto the Earth below, with its nuclear engines threatening to explode...

The Doctor joins with Peth to lead a small, brave band of survivors through the wreckage – and in true disaster movie tradition, they're picked off, one by one. But the Doctor soon realises that the meteorites weren't an accident: a saboteur is on board who wants them all dead. But why? What secrets are certain passengers keeping? And the saboteur hasn't finished yet: the ship's robot staff – frightening, blank-faced, golden Christmas Angels – have been reprogrammed to hunt down the living.

It's a race against time, as the Doctor and Peth battle through the ruins of the devastated ship, fighting flying Angels and the ticking clock, to save both the *Titanic* and the planet below. But as the Doctor and Peth are thrown together, can they truly trust each other...?

The *Doctor Who* Christmas Special for BBC One is a fun, scary, full-blooded 60-minute drama, complete with monsters, thrills, chases and terrible deaths, as the Time Lord and his friends battle against the odds to save the day. And they succeed – just in time for Christmas!

FROM: BENJAMIN COOK TO: RUSSELL T DAVIES
TUESDAY 17 APRIL 2007 16:45:14 GMT

RE: CHRISTMAS IS COMING

It's a sci-fi-murder-mystery-Christmas-disaster-movie-epic! With echoes of *The Poseidon Adventure*, *The Robots of Death*, and Kylie's 2001 *On a Night Like This* tour![1] What more could you ask for at Christmas? Good busk. I think it should end on a song, though.

Do you need to appreciate the costs involved in making television drama in order to write it? Or can understanding the expense inhibit invention?

FROM: RUSSELL T DAVIES TO: BENJAMIN COOK
WEDNESDAY 18 APRIL 2007 22:03:50 GMT

RE: CHRISTMAS IS COMING

Did you imagine that there wouldn't be a song? *The Poseidon Adventure* won an Oscar for Best Song for 'The Morning After'. '*There's got to be a morning after / If we can hold on through the night.*' I often sing it at 3am when I'm only on Page 22.

Yes, knowing the cost of television could inhibit invention, but I think writing is a stronger impulse than that; it overrides such plain little worries. Understanding budget isn't strictly necessary for a writer. You're there for the ideas; the production team is there for the making-of. At the same time, the writer-as-producer model is wonderful. The more you do know, the more involved you are, the better the product gets. But getting that production experience in the first place is hard. I was a producer before I was a full-time writer, so I knew all that stuff first. To have a rough understanding of the costs – and, more importantly, the practicalities – has to help.

A lot of budget stuff is common sense. Write an army of 5,000, and it's going to cost. Write a great script set in one kitchen, and producers will love you for ever. *Doctor Who* is expensive to make, but that's because of our ambition. We could have aimed lower. Thankfully, we didn't. But we never relax and throw money around. We're so trusted. I like to think we respect that trust. That's why I went to bed shivering with fear the other night. I was genuinely scared by that 4.X synopsis, and felt a massive responsibility for it. I told Julie, 'I'm deeply worried that my imagination is flying into big-bucks movie territory. If I should pull back, now is the time to say so.' That's a bit disingenuous: I suspected that by offering Julie the chance to cut down, she'd respond by moving Heaven and Earth to get the money that we need so that I wouldn't be compromised. It's all politics. I'm not daft. But neither is she. Julie knows me too well. If she *did* say to pull back, I'd know that she means it, that she'd reached her limits.

Getting out before Series Five is so wise. It'll leave the show at the height of production so that the next, future version *cannot* come back cheaper. Honestly, that's part of the strategy.

FROM: RUSSELL T DAVIES TO: BENJAMIN COOK
SUNDAY 22 APRIL 2007 01:09:17 GMT

RE: CHRISTMAS IS COMING

I keep worrying about 4.1. What the hell is Donna doing? Investigating? What is this high-rise office block? Beauty? Plastic surgery? Cosmetic surgery? The ultimate industrial beauty parlour? Big business, with aliens? In the car on the way up to Manchester (I'm back up north now), I spent a lot of time thinking about Botox. I mean Botox as in an alien spore that bursts out and transforms you. We've never done that creepy green transformation

1 *The Robots of Death* is a *Doctor Who* serial first broadcast in 1977.

'Imagine a scene in a wine bar where they transform, then lurch out into the street...' Illustration by Russell T Davies.

thing – humans turning horribly into aliens. If those humans are 40-something-year-old women who've been Botoxed to the hilt, so much the better. Imagine a scene in a wine bar where they transform, then lurch out into the street. Deadly Ladies Who Lunch! Not camp at all. It's sort of obvious and fun, which is good for a series opener. I'm amazed that we haven't done it before. I think, in my mind, all that 'beauty' stuff had become the sole province of Cassandra, but actually there's so much more that you can do with it.[2]

FROM: BENJAMIN COOK TO: RUSSELL T DAVIES
SUNDAY 22 APRIL 2007 22:08:45 GMT

RE: CHRISTMAS IS COMING

With the investigation of a high-rise city office at night, and the Doctor and companion-to-be criss-crossing but taking time to meet, 4.1 is reverting to the template of that opening episode that you'd planned, all those years ago, were the call ever to come asking you to revive *Doctor Who*. The one with the escape-by-window-cleaner's-cradle sequence, and the grandad who plays in a skiffle band. You've come full circle.

Anyway, I see the *News of the World* is reporting that Kylie has been cast in this year's Christmas Special... as a Cyberwoman! A show spokesman has said: 'Russell is just putting the finishing touches to the episode and it will be TV dynamite.' Well, the spokesman is *half* right.

FROM: RUSSELL T DAVIES TO: BENJAMIN COOK
WEDNESDAY 25 APRIL 2007 22:37:42 GMT

RE: CHRISTMAS IS COMING

I've been silent, I know. I've been glum. Bloody glum. Script glum. It occurred to me – because this was *Torchwood* script glum, not *Doctor Who* glum yet – that it's going to be hard to write to you when I'm glum. I'm not saying that I don't want to; it's just that I'm really going to have to try hard. For one thing, it feels so indulgent. You can't stop that voice in the back of your head saying, 'Miserable? A writer? There are people out there desperately ill, in despair, in genuine, proper, medical Depression – and you dare to be miserable over

2 'Last human' Cassandra, who débuted in *Doctor Who* 1.2, underwent over 700 plastic surgery operations until she was nothing but a piece of skin stretched onto a metal frame, with eyes and a mouth, connected to a brain in a jar.

Torchwood's Gareth David-Lloyd.

a deadline? You actually *want* some of that?' Equally, when I'm in the middle of that worry, I reckon I could wrestle any of those bleeding hearts to the floor and beat them in the unhappiness stakes. Also, there's a fear, a natural fear, of appearing to be an idiot. I don't want to appear to be an idiot to you. And that multiplies because I'm a gay man, and you're handsome and young, so I want to look good anyway. Of course I do. But the fact that this correspondence is scary is a good reason to keep going. Always do what scares you. I'm not flagging this as a call to halt; I'm just trying to explain what I'm thinking.

On Saturday night/Sunday morning, I went to bed at 2am, lay awake, worrying – no, panicking, to be honest – and got up at 3am to work for an hour. And that wasn't typing work. I did anything rather than type. I trawled websites in search of stuff that I could vaguely call research, stared at old scripts, and just sat there doing nothing. Getting up in the middle of the night? I have *never* done that before, which made me realise that this script-panic is something extraordinary. So I took action –

I pulled out of that *Torchwood* script. I'm not doing it.

Poor Julie. She bears the brunt of all this, and protects me from the consequences. It's easy for me in some ways, because with my status as a writer, frankly, I can get away with anything. That's awful, isn't it? No one shouting, no one berating me, no contracts being waved, just everyone running around making that decision easy for me. You could go power mad. Mind you, I'm mild and lovely compared to some of the stuff you hear about other writers. Or maybe this is the start of me getting worse. The truth is, I wasn't not-writing because I couldn't think of anything, but because I'm sick of fixing other people's problems. I sat there at 4am and thought: what am *I* getting out of this? Nothing. Just misery. So sod it, I'm off.

That was severe. First time I've ever done that. As a result, I'm quite cheery again. Nightmare welcome-back-to-Cardiff dinner with the *Torchwood* cast tonight, just when I feel I've abandoned them. (I haven't. I'll try to script-edit more.) Eve Myles got drunk, which was lively. Gareth David-Lloyd is just the sexiest bastard on this Earth. And Johnny Barrowman regaled us with stories of how many Josephs he'd like to sleep with, so it was a bit of a laugh.[3] The panic has abated. Now I'll have to wait for the 4.X panic…

The other thing is, when I do get in that pits-of-darkness mood, it's not quite true that I lock myself away; I can *use* a bad mood. I can use it to say things that I wouldn't otherwise. There's always a game being played, somewhere, somehow, isn't there? So I used that depression to make it very clear that shifting the *Doctor Who* timeslot every week, as has happened this year, is bloody stupid. Squandering, that was the word I used. Good word. So then Julie and Phil told Peter Fincham, using their own glumness too – and it worked! He's shifted *The National Lottery People's Quiz,* and we should go back to 7pm from Episode 6 onwards. The BBC is changing the format of a primetime Saturday-night quiz show just for us. What's more, suddenly, yes, maybe the

3 Barrowman was, at the time, a judge on BBC One's *Any Dream Will Do*, a talent show that searched for a new lead to play Joseph in a West End revival of musical *Joseph and the Amazing Technicolor Dreamcoat*.

Doctor Who budget can allow us to go abroad for the Pompeii episode. (For all of two days, but hey!) And what's this? Extra FX money for 4.12/4.13. The BBC has jumped through hoops to make me happy. That's how it works – and I know it.

FROM: BENJAMIN COOK TO: RUSSELL T DAVIES
THURSDAY 26 APRIL 2007 00:33:23 GMT

RE: CHRISTMAS IS COMING

I'm glad you're okay. You hadn't replied for a few days. I was a bit worried. Not worried about the correspondence (that's like a cockroach: it'd survive nuclear fallout), but worried that you'd thrown yourself into the Bay! I'm glad you haven't. Nonetheless, never feel that you *must* write to me when you're in Script Hell. I'd always prefer that you did, but I wouldn't want these e-mails to make a bad day ten times worse, forcing you to write it all down, to explain yourself.

Having said that (!), can I ask, did you ever feel, even in your darkest moments, that fixing *Torchwood*, that writing a 2.1 that would rejuvenate the concept, was actually beyond you? That you *couldn't* do it? Or was it a dawning realisation that you just didn't want to do it, and that you didn't really have to?

>>Now I'll have to wait for the 4.X panic<<

Of course, you could start writing 4.X now…?

>>They've jumped through hoops to make me happy. That's how it works – and I know it.<<

And that makes you feel… how? Relieved? Disgusted? Humbled?

FROM: RUSSELL T DAVIES TO: BENJAMIN COOK
THURSDAY 26 APRIL 2007 00:57:16 GMT

RE: CHRISTMAS IS COMING

I love that image of this correspondence surviving a nuclear war. The last remnant of civilisation. 'It's… glowing!'

>>did you ever feel, even in your darkest moments, that fixing *Torchwood*, that writing a 2.1 that would rejuvenate the concept, was actually beyond you?<<

Not for a second. Beyond me? Absolutely not. I do feel kind of sad, because I love that cast and I love that show's potential, but really it was eating into *Doctor Who* scripting time. The addition of *The Sarah Jane Adventures* to our schedules has just made me run out of days.

>>Of course, you could start writing 4.X now…?<<

Ha ha ha ha ha ha.

>>And that makes you feel… how? Relieved? Disgusted? Humbled?<<

I don't know. Does that make it more honest or less honest? When did I last do something for one honest, pure reason, instead of calculating how I can *use* it? Then again, *Doctor Who* benefits, so that's worth it.

FROM: BENJAMIN COOK TO: RUSSELL T DAVIES
THURSDAY 26 APRIL 2007 11:57:09 GMT

RE: CHRISTMAS IS COMING

Tell me, then – a serious question – do you have to be a bit of a bastard to succeed in this industry? Some people say that you do. Let's face it, you can afford to be, Russell, because you've achieved a certain status… but have you got where you are today by being nice to the people around you? Similarly, everyone always says how nice Julie is, but… but… I bet she can be a right monster when she needs to be.

FROM: RUSSELL T DAVIES TO: BENJAMIN COOK
FRIDAY 27 APRIL 2007 00:19:27 GMT

RE: CHRISTMAS IS COMING

It's gone midnight! It's my birthday! Do you know, once you're in your forties, you genuinely forget which birthday it is. I used to laugh at old folk and find that impossible. And here I am. Anyway…

Bastards. (Now, that's a chapter title!) No, I don't think you have to be a bastard. Not at all. In fact, people who are bastards – real, genuine, complete bastards – are few and far between, and I've never seen them succeed in TV. They might burn for a year or two, but it doesn't last. Like… hmm… one director, who's long since been reduced to game shows. God, I hated him. And a producer – bloody weird woman – who was put in charge of a very big show, swiftly got sacked, and has never been heard of since. But of course there are thousands of people on a lower level of Bastardom – the pains-in-the-arses, the shouters, the hysterics – and they do all right, because a lot of the industry thinks that's an acceptable way to behave. But why are they bastards? Insecurity, weakness, over-promotion… well, I could just go back and repeat the word 'insecurity' five-dozen times. That's always the problem, isn't it?

If I've learnt one thing, and I keep learning it, it's to be honest. That's seen me through my career. (But not sociopathically honest. There's no point in walking into work and saying, 'Christ, Lynda, you're hideous!') If you don't say what you think, what's the bloody point? Nicola Shindler, who founded Red Production Company, always says that she and I are successful because we know our own opinions, and we say those opinions out loud, immediately.[4] But 99 per cent of TV folk are slow and unsure, or don't speak up, or wait for someone else to speak up first. I remember my first meeting as a storyliner, on a Granada daytime soap called *Families*. I was young then, and terrified of this fabled job that I'd always wanted to do, not having a clue what it actually entailed. I felt out of my depth. I wore a leather biker's jacket, just because I needed armour, I needed to look tough, because I was so scared. The writers were devising the murder of a character, Don McLeod, and they'd cooked up this ridiculous story where – deep breath – the man whose baby had been kidnapped by the pub landlord's wife came into the pub, looking for revenge, and started a fight, and Don joined in, just because he was there, and he got punched and hit his head on the table and died. He was killed by a complete stranger. Despite my fear, I could not stop myself saying, 'No! If Don is going to be killed, it should be by someone who hates him, not some one-episode passer-by.' That sounds like such a small story, but it was huge to me. It was a pivotal moment. I knew that I was in the right job.

Then again, there are plenty of people who think I'm a bastard. Plenty. But I try not to work with them. I hope that's not me surrounding myself with yes-men. I can play the nice guy, and of course I want the world to think I'm nice, but to be honest and tough is going to earn you enemies. Once, I remember, we had to sack a 12-year-old girl from a children's show, because she wasn't good enough. I remember being amazed that people in the office were reeling, horrified, despairing, saying that we couldn't sack a kid… because I absolutely didn't care. It was for the good of the show. I insisted, she went, and the programme got better. I lost no sleep at all over that. Not one second. Seeing people's horror was one of those chilling moments when I thought, everyone else sees this differently – am I a bit odd? But it wasn't chilling enough to stop me.

I'm at the high end of the most expensive area of one of the most insecure, public, high-flown, backstabbing industries in the UK, so I suppose it's kind of disingenuous to say that I'm a nice man. And yet I think I am. (But I can't be.) I think about that a lot, not just prompted by your question. I do wonder. Julie, though… oh, Julie… now that's really, truly, gobsmackingly pure niceness. One in a million.

FROM: BENJAMIN COOK TO: RUSSELL T DAVIES
FRIDAY 27 APRIL 2007 15:34:30 GMT

RE: CHRISTMAS IS COMING

Happy birthday, Russell! You share it with Darcey Bussell, Patrick Stump from Fall Out Boy, and Prince Willem-Alexander of the Netherlands, which means… I don't know what it means. You're by far the tallest?

It's interesting what you say about being surrounded by yes-men. During their interview for *Doctor Who Magazine* the other month, the one where their *Doctor Who* colleagues posed the questions, I asked Julie and

Julie Gardner, Phil Collinson and Russell T Davies record the podcast commentary for 4.X, at BBC Broadcasting House in Cardiff. Photo by Rob Francis

4 Red is a Manchester-based, independent production company, formed in 1998 by Shindler, a successful TV producer. Red's first production was *Queer as Folk*; later dramas include *Bob & Rose*, *The Second Coming*, *Mine All Mine*, and *Casanova*.

Phil *your* killer query: what is it that they like least about your writing? But they wouldn't answer it. Even though they knew how much you wanted them to. That's the drawback, I suppose, of being at the top of your game. Who's going to challenge you? Who can you rely on to be brutally honest with you? Who'll stop you from going too far? Anyone? No one? Doesn't that bug you, Russell? (Look, I've sent you some killer questions of my own, on your birthday. Now who's a bastard?)

FROM: RUSSELL T DAVIES TO: BENJAMIN COOK
SATURDAY 28 APRIL 2007 16:10:47 GMT

RE: CHRISTMAS IS COMING

Julie and Phil do still talk about that question. You're not forgotten, just unanswered, although Phil says, no, he can't think of anything. Julie *gets* the question, she knows what you mean (or what *I* mean – it was my question!), and she's still thinking, I swear to you. Maybe she's worried about saying something that would destabilise me, but I don't think so. She knows me better than that, and she knows it would do me good. It might be a long wait, but I think she'll get there in the end.

I do worry about being surrounded by yes-men. You're right, it happens. But the more able you are to surround yourself with people that you trust, the more likely it is to happen. Not because you want yes-men, but because people that you trust, whose judgement is sound, tend to be people whose judgement is close to your own. That becomes, naturally, a closed circle. I don't think it's happened to me yet. In the end, just as good writers are hard to find, so are good script editors, good producers and good execs. When you find good people like Julie and Phil, their sheer talent cancels out the risk of them yes-ing. I suppose the danger is not 'RTD and the Yes-Men', but a triumvirate of people who are so similar that contrary opinions don't get enough of a look-in. Then again, plenty of shows lack any sort of voice, so maybe our similarities make for a strong show.

But! The fact that Julie and Phil trust me is an equally great pressure. That can be worse than working for someone who thinks you're crap. Julie and Phil give every hour to this show, as do Ed Thomas, Louise Page, Jane Tranter, the gaffers, bloody everyone. That's what's pushing us into Pompeii, the thought of taking the show further, making it better, trying something that's really,

Mark Gatiss, who wrote 1.3 *The Unquiet Dead*, also played Professor Lazarus in 3.6 *The Lazarus Experiment*.

really difficult. I got a great e-mail from Ed the other day, full of the impossibilities and impracticalities of realising Ancient Rome, ending with the words, 'Let's do it!' That brilliant man. He's the best production designer in the business. The thought of them having to work like dogs on a script that isn't quite good enough is awful. That pushes and challenges me. I'm not just being nice; their trust is a great pressure on me, to do well.

But I can't stop wondering – am I a bastard? I haven't been able to shake off that thought. After I activated those couple of anecdotes the other day about sackings and things, it sort of opened a little door onto similar tales, and the list of people I've sacked – well, you don't often get to sack people, but the people I've replaced, or excluded, or had removed, or plainly cut off is, well, it's more than a few. Blimey! Last night, I was on the phone to Julie, and I suggested a new *Torchwood* writer called James Moran to write the Pompeii script, because he's fast and good and new enough to be rewritten by me with no complaints. Julie said, 'Well, give me a few days to sort that out.' I said, 'Why? I could meet him tomorrow.' She said, 'I'll have to talk to Mark Gatiss.' 'Why?' 'Because this script would replace his World War II one,' she said, 'and he's been working on that for over a year.' I went, 'Oh,' and I actually got annoyed with Julie for worrying over something that I thought was trivial. Thing is, I didn't care. And this isn't some stranger; this is Mark! Lovely Mark! Brilliant Mark! A gentleman, and truly a gentle man. He's got one of the wittiest, wildest imaginations in this whole bloody country. I like Mark tremendously, I think he's wonderful, but this is for the good of the show.

I reckon I've got some sort of cut-off point, beyond which I just don't care. In the course of my career, I've faced sacked actors, rewritten writers and banished directors. While I sort of sympathise on a superficial level, it doesn't really touch me. Not at all. God knows what they say about me behind my back! I know of one script editor, who I had booted off a show years ago, who still calls me the Devil incarnate. But he was rubbish. So he was removed. Good. No matter how upset someone is, if it makes the programme better, then tough. That's being a bastard, I suppose. Is the word 'ruthless'? Except 'ruthless' implies a deliberate cutting-off of feelings, doesn't it? I just don't feel them. I do not notice when I've hurt someone. I've spent more time worrying about it in these paragraphs than I do in everyday life.

I've just remembered something. It was 1997, and I copped off with a bloke called Toby. I'll spare you the details. Let's just say it was a great night. But he only had a single bed, because he was a student, and it was a bit uncomfortable, sleeping there, and I'd tons of work to do… so I got up at 5am, got dressed, walked back home. A couple of weeks later, a friend of mine said that this Toby was being all bitchy and calling me stuff. That's a shame, I thought, he seemed really nice. About six years later – it took six years for this little thought to trickle down – I thought, hold on, I got up at 5am after a really great night, got dressed, and just left. Not a word. Not a note. I didn't leave my number. I just went. AND I WONDER WHY HE CALLED ME A BASTARD!!! I didn't think what the whole thing looked like from his perspective, not for one second. I couldn't see what I'd done. Six years it took me to see that. I am blind. I suppose we all do things like that, every day, but it does make me laugh, considering my whole job is based on how people see things.

I just Googled that Toby… and there's nothing. Every name is on Google somewhere. There can't be nothing. Did I make him up? Was I drugged?!

FROM: BENJAMIN COOK TO: RUSSELL T DAVIES
SUNDAY 29 APRIL 2007 12:08:52 GMT

RE: CHRISTMAS IS COMING

>>Is the word 'ruthless'? Except 'ruthless' implies a deliberate cutting-off of feelings, doesn't it? I just don't feel them.<<

You. Would. Make. A. Good. Dalek.

>>I suppose we all do things like that, every day, but it does make me laugh, considering my whole job is based on how people see things.<<

Logically, I suppose, artists should understand us better than anyone – better even than our families, our workmates, our closest friends. Artists are supposed to see us for who we really are. But then art isn't rational, is it? Here is something that Caitlin Moran once wrote in *The Times*. I liked it so much that I cut it out and kept it:

> *By and large, there is a single reason why any artist gains an audience: he talks about us. He explains us to ourselves. While our friends, partners, children, bosses and colleagues will, as a rule of thumb, widely eschew embarking on penetrating analyses of our truest thoughts, or the deepest workings of our hearts, artists wade in there and write whole albums, or fill entire art galleries, or improvise 90 minutes of stand-up comedy about us, and what we're like, and what we think. And this is why we, on many occasions, do things that show we love our artists more than our loved ones. At least they notice us. At least they start conversations.*

I'm not sure that I agree with Caitlin completely, but it does sound like the beginning of a theory that's heading somewhere interesting. What do you reckon, Russell? Do artists understand us better? If that's true, why do they, by and large, make just as almighty a hash of real life as the rest of us?

FROM: RUSSELL T DAVIES TO: BENJAMIN COOK
SUNDAY 29 APRIL 2007 14:49:26 GMT

RE: CHRISTMAS IS COMING

I was at the Welsh BAFTAs last night. *Torchwood* beat *Doctor Who* as Best Drama! And Graeme Harper won Best Director. Oh, it was lovely. He's 60 years old and that's the first thing he's ever won in his whole hard-working life. Just to see him, all smiling and Sontaran-sized under the spotlight, holding a BAFTA mask, it was actually very moving.

Anyway, I love that Caitlin Moran quote. I'm not sure I agree with it either, but I love the way she wades in, never scared of showing her workings in the margin.

God, she's clever. Though maybe she makes the whole process sound more generous and beneficent by saying that an artist 'talks about us'. How kind. But maybe it's 'talks about himself'. He just does it so well that everyone recognises it.

Then again, good writing is basically a good understanding of people. Never mind structure and character and that; just have a good, fundamental understanding of psychology. Not in a psychology-degree sort of way, but in a plain, accurate, human, down-to-earth sort of way. If your friend turns out to be having an affair, there's no point in standing around going, 'No! Never! I don't believe it! That can't be true!' The writer stands there thinking, that's *fascinating!* And even, oh, *of course!* That's not to say that a writer is all-forgiving or non-judgemental, but they're much more interested in *understanding* it, I think. (They? Me? We? Pronoun crisis here! Caitlin's use of the word 'artist' threw me – too scary a word.) The danger is to assume a generosity behind that, like, oh, the writer understands pain, wrongdoing, frailty, the-whole-of-bloody-humanity, therefore the writer must be lovely. In fact, the process is as selfish as… well, as anything else anyone ever does. You might have great insight into your mate's actions, but there's a lot of glee in that understanding, and self-satisfaction, even a feeling of superiority. Actually, are you more interested in your friend in that moment of crisis than on an ordinary day when everything's fine?

The solipsistic, uncaring bastard stands back, studying people and using them. Is that it? Is that what being a writer is?

FROM: RUSSELL T DAVIES TO: BENJAMIN COOK
MONDAY 30 APRIL 2007 15:13:46 GMT

RE: CHRISTMAS IS COMING

I tested the word 'Botox' on Phil earlier. He went, 'Ooh!' – so that's a good sign. I keep thinking of those Ladies Who Lunch, lurching down the High Street, with their Botox lines erupting into green frond-ish stuff. Monsters in fake Chanel suits! And a strong, hard, female villain,

Victory for David Tennant (Best Actor) and *Torchwood*'s Eve Myles (Best Actress) at the Welsh BAFTAs, in April 2007. © Huw John/Rex Features

head of the Beauty Technique, played by someone like Amanda Redman.

I've spent a lot of time thinking about Pompeii, too. The Doctor and Donna arrive… but why do they leave the TARDIS if they know where they are? A quick bit of sightseeing, perhaps, and then they scarper back to the TARDIS – only to see it in the distance, on the back of a horse and cart! It's being taken into Pompeii, so they have to follow. If we can get exterior locations abroad, the Doctor and Donna have to wander through the city in pursuit. The TARDIS will be taken to a villa – our studio-build – and that's where I want a bit of *Asterix*. Roman families on TV are always standing around pontificating, but I want a nice, funny family, like the one in *Asterix and the Laurel Wreath*. A likeable, ineffectual dad, a hapless son, a strong wife, cheeky slaves. Plus, in the villa, to stop the Doctor just hopping into the TARDIS and leaving – Household Gods! I love the idea of Household Gods, like the Romans used to have, God of the Hearth, God of the Atrium… what were they called? Lares? But we can have real 'gods' speaking, issuing forth in flames… which are, of course, the aliens under the volcano. Fire People. (Why are they there?) Somehow, we've got to end up *inside* the volcano, or under it. When it goes off, the Doctor and Donna have to be hiding in a capsule of some sort – maybe a big white ceramic bubble, big enough for two (we might need Sontaran globe-ships later on, so it could double-up) – so they're literally blasted out of the volcano, in the bubble, like a cork from a bottle. That makes me laugh. Christ, the CGI costs…!

Oh, *soothsayer!* I thought of that this morning. You can't go to Roman times without a soothsayer. And what if the soothsayer is right? (And how?) That brings me to the crux of this episode, the interesting new slant: if the Doctor goes to Pompeii and he knows what's going to happen, why doesn't he help? He saves the world, so why not this one? What makes history established? Lord knows, there's never been a good answer to this in the history of the programme, but we could think of some fascinating dialogue – and it's a great attitude for Donna, marks her out as a new companion. None of the others has asked this essential stuff. The sadness of the end, as they have to leave everyone to die! (Everyone? There isn't exactly a list of the dead at Pompeii, so surely the Doctor can nudge someone to safety?)

Mickey Smith (Noel Clarke) – unlucky enough to be killed off?

Also, I keep thinking about 4.12/4.13. That's why, when I get to the end of a series, I can – fingers crossed – write them quickly, because I've had so long to think about them. I wrote 3.13 in four days. *Four days!* Saturday night to Tuesday night. Four days of hell, but all the same…! I'm thinking about Donna, Martha, Rose, Jack, Sarah Jane and Mickey as a team, and the tagline: 'ONE OF THEM WILL DIE!' I'd watch that! Trouble is, I don't want to kill any of them. Rose Tyler was never created to die. None of them was. They were all created to show off *Doctor Who*'s central premise: the world and the universe is wonderful, ordinary people can do great things, and the human race survives. At a cost, yes, but a cost to the *supporting* characters. I mean, really, imagine Martha's death. Or Donna's. Or even Jackie's. It's just wrong. Tonally, wrong.

Maybe Mickey could die? 'Noooo!' said Phil. But Mickey is the only one who seems killable, because he's not quite central, he's unlucky, he's the odd one out. It's inbuilt in Mickey's character. But then I get shivers, because it's always the black guy who cops it. Maybe that's politically correct of me, but political correctness can be political *and* correct. But how do I keep that tagline without delivering? Maybe one of them dies and Martha is on hand with a bit of CPR…? The repercussions of death are so complicated and wonderful to write, but really 4.12/4.13 is about fighting Daleks, not mourning. 4.13 has to have the happiest ending ever. I'm bringing them all back because I want to see six people standing around that six-sided TARDIS console, flying the Earth back home. It's *happy*. You can't mess with that. Then again, I'm perverse and more than capable of ignoring everything I've just said.

I've a great image of Sarah Jane surrounded by Daleks, all shouting 'Exterminate!' That would be thrilling! (Yes, it's fannish, but I reckon I'm allowed to be in my last proper episode.) And then Mickey dimension-jumps in, blasts them with his big gun, and says, 'No one kills a Smith!' Ha ha ha. Also, this thought blazed into my head the other day, as I was walking past Techniquest on the way to Tesco: DAVROS WOULD RECOGNISE SARAH JANE![5] How exciting! And Davros should be the Daleks' slave, because I hate it when he comes in and takes control and reduces the Daleks to soldiers. You could even feel sorry for him.

Have I told you this next bit already? I've put the Doctor's bubbling hand on board the TARDIS so that when David regenerates, one day, he'll grow another self and send it off into the parallel universe, so Rose has a Doctor of her own.[6] Ahh! But then today I thought, why delay? His duplicate will now do this at the end of 4.13, which will be gorgeous, and close off the Rose story for ever. That way, the Specials in 2009 will really be special – no companions, almost no back-references at all. Nice and clean. Never delay gratification if you can have it now. As I said to Freddie Ljungberg last night.

The Doctor's bubbling hand in a jar.

FROM: BENJAMIN COOK TO: RUSSELL T DAVIES
TUESDAY 1 MAY 2007 00:40:40 GMT

RE: CHRISTMAS IS COMING

I saw a book in Waterstones today called *How I Write: The Secret Lives of Authors*. It looked interesting enough, but had hardly any text in it. It wouldn't survive a nuclear war! Is the world ready for *The Secret Life of Russell T Davies*, do you think?

FROM: RUSSELL T DAVIES TO: BENJAMIN COOK
TUESDAY 1 MAY 2007 01:36:14 GMT

RE: CHRISTMAS IS COMING

I've heard about that *Secret Lives* book. It seems a bit intimidating. There was an excerpt in *The Guardian* the other day. Apparently, Alan Hollinghurst has 'a large Piranesi engraving of the ruins of the Baths of Diocletian in Rome' by his desk, while Jay McInerney has 'an Acheulian hand axe, crafted by Homo erectus half a million years ago'. Christ Almighty! I've got a Cassandra action figure on my desk. Still, that's novelists for you.

Did I ever tell you that Zadie Smith once wrote to me to say that *Bob & Rose* is her favourite drama ever, and she watches an episode once a week – and this was years after its transmission – in the hope that she'll create a

5 Davros and Sarah Jane Smith both featured in 1975 *Doctor Who* serial *Genesis of the Daleks*.

6 The Doctor's hand was cut off in 2.X, though he grew another. The original, severed hand, kept in a bubbling jar, appeared in *Torchwood* Series One, the final three episode of *Doctor Who* Series Three, and remains in the TARDIS throughout Series Four.

character as real as Rose one day? *Zadie Smith!!!*

Anyway. I caused havoc on *Torchwood* last night. In 2.6, Ianto is killed, gets revived in 2.7 as the Living Dead – pale, but still sexy – and that strand runs throughout the rest of the series. Last night, I suddenly realised, wrong character. It should be Owen.[7] Seven scripts are now being rewritten, including scenes that are actually being filmed today! Lines handed to the cast on the spot. Someone said, 'We can't do it. It's too late.' I said, 'I'd make you do this at your mother's deathbed on Christmas Day if it makes the show better.' And it does. See, power mad! Still, it meant I had a meeting with Gareth David-Lloyd to explain it all. Christ, he's hot.

I'm talking about sex a lot. That means I'll start writing soon.

FROM: BENJAMIN COOK TO: RUSSELL T DAVIES
WEDNESDAY 2 MAY 2007 10:10:51 GMT

RE: CHRISTMAS IS COMING

I couldn't sleep last night, so I sat in bed and watched *Bob & Rose* on DVD. I've been meaning to for absolutely ages, but never have. That's terrible, isn't it? But I thought I'd find out why Zadie Smith loves it with a passion that borders on insanity. I started watching at 4am, just one episode. Well, I still haven't slept! I ended up watching all six in succession. The whole lot. I cried when Penelope Wilton made that speech at the end of Episode 4 and handcuffed herself to a bus. And then I rewound, re-watched that bit, and cried again.

I'm going to get some sleep now. Slightly embarrassed.

FROM: RUSSELL T DAVIES TO: BENJAMIN COOK
WEDNESDAY 2 MAY 2007 17:01:41 GMT

RE: CHRISTMAS IS COMING

That e-mail means the world to me. Thank you. That scene in Episode 4 is extraordinary, isn't it? I'm going to tell you about that scene. One Sunday, many years ago, I went to a Stonewall Section 28 rally in that same Manchester square. Poor turnout. Bad speeches. But then a glorious drag queen called Wynnie la Freak decided to take action and stood in front of a passing

Wynnie la Freak stops a bus (left) and then recreates the scene for *Bob & Rose* (right), while Russell pops in to watch (centre). © Wynnie la Freak

Stagecoach bus. (Stagecoach's founder had sponsored a lot of anti-gay legislation in Scotland. Marvellously, by accident, it's a Stagecoach bus that Nathan gets on in *Queer as Folk* for his 'I'm doing it!' speech. You can see the Stagecoach logo clearly!) A few camp old things joined Wynnie in the road, everyone danced, the driver shouted, then it cleared and the bus went on. However, during that moment, every political speaker on stage turned their back and pretended it wasn't happening. I just stood there, too, and didn't join in. And then everyone went home – because what do rallies do? Nothing, I suspect. But then, I thought, I can use that...

When we came to film that scene, we ended up in the same square, with a lot of the same people in the crowd – casting went and trawled the Village for the genuine articles – and with Wynnie herself recreating that moment. In full costume. But better! With results! It was a bizarre day. A beautiful day. My favourite day's filming ever. That's not because of the sheer act of recreation, although that was a nice by-product, but because it's Bob and his mum and Holly (oh, poor Holly) who make it work.[8] We went to rehearse that speech, Penelope Wilton on stage, her voice rising... and everyone listened. Even the drag queens were silent. Passers-by were stopping to listen. It was *real*. It was like Monica Gossage's speech was real. And then Jessica Stevenson began to cry. And so did I. Actually, I'm sort of tearful just typing this, no kidding. It was so wonderful. People in the crowd were crying and hugging me, and saying, 'Why can't it really be like this?' Everyone became devoted to that scene and gave everything in every take. Christ, I know I exaggerate, but that's word for word how it happened. Best. Day. Ever.

7 Medical man Owen Harper (played by Burn Gorman) appears throughout *Torchwood* Series One and Two.

8 Bob Gossage (Alan Davies), his mum Monica (Penelope Wilton), and his best friend Holly Vance (Jessica Stevenson), who's madly in love with him.

When it was transmitted six months later, my mum was dying, and that episode was the last thing of mine she ever saw. 'I loved that bit with the mothers,' she said on the phone – and that was the last proper conversation we ever had, because she became insensible after that. The next Monday night, I was pacing up and down in a hospital corridor, just waiting for her to die (the hospital that the Judoon invaded, many years later – how mad is that?), and there in the background was Episode 5 playing out in the patients' lounge, and it just seemed so hugely unimportant. That soured *Bob & Rose* for me for a long time. But do you know what? Not any more.

That was shown at a gay festival thing in LA once, and I held this symposium on scriptwriting afterwards. Some lovely young writer stood up and asked, 'Why did that scene make me cry so much? I described it to my boyfriend afterwards, and I started crying all over again – and I don't know why!' We talked about that for a long time. You could pontificate with 57 theories, but I'm still not sure why. I don't know if I want to know. Other than the simple fact that, in that moment, Monica Gossage is *right*.

Of course, that poor old show died on air. Episode 1 went out on 9 September 2001. Two days later, New York exploded, the world went mad, and so did the TV schedules (the least important thing, I admit), so its timeslot was shifted left, right and centre. The last episode was shown at 11.30pm. But then, a few months later, I won Comedy Writer of the Year at the British Comedy Awards! For *Bob & Rose*! Live on ITV! I thanked my mum, which was nice. Bear in mind, *Bob & Rose* was in competition against the first years of *The Office* and Peter Kay's *Phoenix Nights*. I didn't even think *Bob & Rose* was a comedy, really. For a long time, I thought that award was a sort of 9/11 reaction – the championing of a sweet romance in the middle of what felt like World War III. Or it was a protest vote against bad scheduling. Or it was a gay thing. It's only in the past year or so – you really do spend that long thinking about things that you wrote – that it's begun to occur to me why it won. Maybe it was brilliant. That's why. Yeah.

'You there! Gorgeous creature!' Some things are just perfect, and that's one of them.

Below: Jessica Hynes (née Stevenson) as Holly opposite Alan Davies and Lesley Sharp in *Bob & Rose*. © Red Production Company Ltd
Right: Paul Kasey as the Blowfish in *Torchwood* 2.1.

FROM: BENJAMIN COOK TO: RUSSELL T DAVIES
SUNDAY 6 MAY 2007 05:48:05 GMT

RE: CHRISTMAS IS COMING

Russell! You've topped *The Independent*'s Pink List! You're the UK's Number One Gay! Do you get an actual award? Sir Ian McKellen won it last year. I bet he got an award. Mind you, Peter Mandelson came fifth. *Fifth!* Who'd put Peter Mandelson on a Top 101 list of anything?

FROM: RUSSELL T DAVIES TO: BENJAMIN COOK
SUNDAY 6 MAY 2007 23:37:26 GMT

RE: CHRISTMAS IS COMING

The Number One most… er, most what? I'm not sure. Most influential? Most powerful? Most sexy? Er, no! Still, it's the *most* in the land, and I'm Number One. Ahead of all the other homos in the UK.

On Thursday, I wrote a five-page pre-titles sequence for *Torchwood* 2.1. It's all I can contribute, a five-minute opener. But I love it. That's the blowfish in a sports car. It felt good, and then I felt

DOCTOR WHO IV
DRAWN BY: PETER MCKINSTRY
TITLE STAR CRUISE SHIP
DATE: 08.02.07 EP:
REF PM 01
PRODUCER: DIRECTOR: DOP: PROPS MASTER:
PROD DESIGNER: ASSOC DESIGNER: FABRICATION: CONSTRUCTION:
SUP ART DIR: CHIEF SUP ART DIR: SFX: CGI:
S/B ART DIR: SET DECORATOR: COSTUME: GRAPHICS:
©BBC CYMRU WALES 2006/2007 OTHER:
LOCKED 10/2/07

Peter McKinstry's approved design for the 'Star Cruise Ship' *Titanic* in *Doctor Who* 4.X.

sad that I'm not writing a full *Torchwood* script. Ups and downs. And I spent the weekend rewriting *Sarah Jane* 1.7/1.8, all of which was ignoring the fact that I've about four weeks to deliver 4.X. Except I haven't. At midday yesterday, I realised I'd miscalculated: it turns out that I've three weeks. Bollocks. I read my diary wrong. I'm a bloody idiot. Yesterday just dissolved into panic. I was going to write to you, because I thought it'd be a good thing to describe, but I couldn't even do that. I was just sort of numb.

Sometimes I look at all these scripts piling up, and it defeats me. I love script-editing sessions with writers, but I hate the hours of reading that you have to do beforehand. And I'll tell you what pisses me off most of all: a meeting with a writer has to negotiate a hundred tricky things – the writer's mood, their passion, their style, their ambition, their failures, their idiosyncrasies – but now there's a new element entering the room: writers wondering, 'What will they say about me?' Meaning, online. More and more, with every writer. It's those internet message boards. The forums. They destroy writers. This job is full of doubts already, but now there's a whole new level of fear, shouting at us. It is now a writer's job, like it or not, to put up with it. It's like when Helen Raynor went on Outpost Gallifrey last month and read the reviews of her two Dalek episodes. She said that she was, literally, shaking afterwards. Like she'd been physically assaulted. I'm not exaggerating. She said it was like being in a pub when a fight breaks out next to you. I had to spend two hours on the phone to her, talking her out of it, convincing her that of course she can write, that we do need her and want her. That bastard internet voice gets into writers' heads and destabilises them massively.

The stupidest thing you can say is 'Ignore it', because no one can. Who can resist going in search of their own name on the internet? Coming to terms with it is the key. Helen knows that now. It was the same with Murray Gold during Series One: a massive loss of faith after the first episode leaked onto the internet, because he read the Outpost Gallifrey comments about his music. He was saying, 'I don't know how to do my job any more.' Noel Clarke read the online reviews of his portrayal of Mickey, but at least he got *angry*. Yet none of them has been attacked as viciously as I've been. I always thought I was a big old poof (albeit Number One Poof!), but sometimes I think I must be made of some sort of steel. I read that stuff and it doesn't stop me, not ever. I've got quite high-flown and fancy beliefs about art that maybe put it all into perspective. Principally: it is not a democracy. Creating something is not a democracy. The people have no say. The artist does. It doesn't matter what the people witter on about; they and their response come after. They're not there for the creation.

This is becoming one of the great arguments of the day, for populist writers especially. It taps into the whole debate across journalism about the democratisation of the critic. It was summed up best by Rachel Cooke in *The Observer* recently, where she said that the online voice writes with a deep sense of exclusion. She wrote about that with some anger, but also with a lot of sadness. I don't see the sadness myself. I think it's *right* that they're excluded. Of course, it's always been that way, people have always carped on, but the internet means that we can all read it now. We're taught from childhood that the printed word has authority. If something is typed, it seems official. (History will look back on this as the maddest time – a period of ten years or so in which we all *typed* at each other!) So it can mess up writers when they read that endlessly critical voice. It's completely, *completely* destructive. I cannot see one iota of it that's helpful, except maybe in the toughening up. Helen is in a delicate position in that she's only just started, and she's on the verge of being really very good – and now she finds herself ruined by this wall of hostility. It makes me furious.

FROM: BENJAMIN COOK TO: RUSSELL T DAVIES
MONDAY 7 MAY 2007 04:40:59 GMT

RE: CHRISTMAS IS COMING

Dear Number One,

>>I read that stuff and it doesn't stop me, not ever.<<

But has it ever? Does your resolve not to let the critics affect you come from experience?

FROM: RUSSELL T DAVIES TO: BENJAMIN COOK
MONDAY 7 MAY 2007 10:47:02 GMT

RE: CHRISTMAS IS COMING

It doesn't feel like a conscious resolve; it's just the way I am, I suppose. Only one word makes me furious, and that's 'lazy'. If someone calls me that, I want to rip their head off. Honestly, it's the gap in my armour. It makes me vicious. Writers spend vast amounts of their lives being modest, crippled by doubt, insecure, self-deprecating. Somewhere that has to stop.

It must be experience, though. That experience was *Queer as Folk*. The first three weeks when it was on air, it was like I lived on the radio. I'd sit in my office with calls booked for every half hour, sometimes for the whole day, talking to every Radio Back Yard in the country. I remember not having time to make a coffee. I considered moving a kettle into my office. Some of those were shock-jock radio stations, like the old Talk Radio, where they'd be vile. Much to my surprise, I loved it. I'd weigh in and have a fine old time. I made the *Talk Radio Breakfast* DJs admit to not even having watched *Queer as Folk*. Later on, sitting in the BBC 5 Live studio, facing Nicky Campbell while he complained about the Jill Dando joke in *Queer as Folk 2*, I was defending even that honestly.[9] It toughens you up. There was one caller to that show, a retired teacher from an all-girls school, who said that she'd never taught a lesbian in all her born days. I told her that not only was she a bad teacher, but she'd let down every girl that she'd ever taught – that she wasn't just retired, she was forgotten! The key to get through that whole time was not to defend the work, because I always think defence sounds like an apology, but to go on the attack. It was exciting.

FROM: RUSSELL T DAVIES TO: BENJAMIN COOK
MONDAY 7 MAY 2007 21:31:25 GMT

RE: CHRISTMAS IS COMING

Having wittered on this morning, I've just found an interview with AA Gill in today's *Media Guardian*, and

9 Dialogue in *Queer as Folk 2* mentions a lethal drink named after murdered TV host Jill Dando – 'one shot and it goes straight to your head'.

The budget for 4.X stretches to one spiky alien called Bannakaffalatta. Illustration by Russell T Davies.

he says, of being a critic:

> *Can anyone do it? Is everyone's opinion worth the same? No. My opinion is worth more than other people's. Of course that's a horrendously arrogant thing to say, but that is the nature and basis of criticism. If you are sticking your opinions in front of two million readers every Sunday, then you have to believe that your opinion is worth more.*

So that's a) hooray, and b) oh Christ, I'm turning into bloody AA Gill!

Mind you, later on in the paper, talking about some drama, it says: 'In the most inappropriate piece of casting since Alan Davies was plonked into *Bob & Rose*…' Hmph! You see? You've got to be made of steel or you're flayed alive.

FROM: BENJAMIN COOK TO: RUSSELL T DAVIES
MONDAY 7 MAY 2007 23:07:27 GMT

RE: CHRISTMAS IS COMING

I've found the Independent Television Commission's Programme Complaints and Interventions Report on *Queer as Folk 2*. Apparently, 15 viewers (I know! That many!) complained about your Jill Dando joke:

> *The ITC recognised that some viewers had been very upset by this remark and was sorry for the distress caused. However, given the dramatic context with its serious intent, the ITC concluded that this 'joke' was not in breach of the Programme Code.*

I especially like the bit where they put the word 'joke' in inverted commas.

FROM: RUSSELL T DAVIES TO: BENJAMIN COOK
MONDAY 7 MAY 2007 23:30:18 GMT

RE: CHRISTMAS IS COMING

My favourite complaint was on Channel 4's daily log after Episode 1 of *Queer as Folk* was broadcast: 'My cleaner was so upset, I had to send her home!' Ha ha ha. I swear to God that's true.

FROM: RUSSELL T DAVIES TO: BENJAMIN COOK
TUESDAY 8 MAY 2007 18:11:06 GMT

RE: CHRISTMAS IS COMING

An update: Julie and Phil don't even have to ask how I'm getting on, they know my moods, so they're planning to shift the start of filming back a week. Good. But then they ask me, 'Is that what you want to do?' And I say, 'Don't make it my decision!'

I spent a long time wondering today, as I always do, *why don't I just start?!* I know the 4.X pre-titles: the Doctor pulls the TARDIS off the prow of the *Titanic* (resolving the 3.13 cliffhanger, where the *Titanic* crashes through the walls of the TARDIS control room), the TARDIS materialises in a cupboard on board, he steps out into Reception, wanders through, seeing a lot of our supporting cast, goes out on deck, and the camera pulls out to see the *Titanic* flying above the Earth. Over the ship's Tannoy, we hear: 'Welcome aboard the *Starship Titanic*!' I know that pre-titles. SO WHY DON'T I WRITE IT?

Maybe it's a dreadful decision to cross *Doctor Who* with a disaster movie. A lot of *Doctor Who* is to do with *why* and *who* (why's the *Titanic* been hit? Who turned off the shields?), whereas the narrative of a disaster movie is more about *how* they survive. It's difficult for the Doctor to investigate when he has to follow quite a linear path, simply surviving. It suggests that one of the main characters is involved with the villainy ('Yes, Doctor, it was me! I took down the shields!'), which is a hell of a coincidence, because by definition, to get screen time, that character has to be one of the survivors who happens to be with the Doctor. It doesn't fit. Formats are

The thrilling conclusion to 3.13 *Last of the Time Lords*. With one slight difference. Can you spot it...?

clashing. And why would he (or she?) be on board a ship that he's sabotaged?

But I've decided that 4.X should have an alien called Bannakaffalatta. We've budgeted for one spiky alien – I'd hate everyone on board the *Titanic* to be humanoid – so that's a good name. And I'm hung up on the idea that everyone should be in black tie. Maybe the Doctor, too. And should the Angels use their haloes as weapons? Like killer Frisbees? A nice scene with the Doctor and survivors fighting off flying Frisbees with... well, with anything, with sticks of metal, swinging at them. But how do haloes kill? They can't slice off your head, not at 7pm on Christmas Day! Also, I'm thinking that the Captain is part of the scheme. He's the saboteur – which is revealed early on. He has a young, sexy Midshipman (is that the word, Midshipman?) with him, who discovers the truth and survives. Maybe he's trapped on the damaged Flight Deck trying to control things, while the Doctor is fighting to reach him.

Stray thought: what if the Doctor were *blinded*? That ups the scares, makes him vulnerable. Not permanently, obviously. It'd be brilliant if he were flying the ship at the end, towards Buckingham Palace, and he's blind. Or is that just daft?

Also, I spent ten minutes panicking that the 2008 Christmas Special is a lot closer than I think. Apart from 'Period drama, Cybermen in the snow,' it's blank. Christ!

FROM: BENJAMIN COOK TO: RUSSELL T DAVIES
TUESDAY 8 MAY 2007 21:38:13 GMT

RE: CHRISTMAS IS COMING

Have you heard anything from Kylie yet? It's been a while, but the tabloid rumours persist...

FROM: RUSSELL T DAVIES TO: BENJAMIN COOK
WEDNESDAY 9 MAY 2007 01:41:17 GMT

RE: CHRISTMAS IS COMING

That'll be Will Baker in the papers. Apparently, Kylie *is* still interested, but it's so difficult to get through her layers of agents and managers. It's like that with big stars. Her agent has the synopsis, and then you hear sod all for weeks. But David did go for dinner with her – and to the theatre, to see *The Sound of Music*. How that didn't make the tabloids, I'll never know.

CHAPTER FOUR

INT. SPACESHIP

In which George Lucas is snubbed, Charlie Hunnam's arse is discussed, and a handsome man falls off a balcony

FROM: RUSSELL T DAVIES TO: BENJAMIN COOK
FRIDAY 11 MAY 2007 15:20:45 GMT

RE: CHRISTMAS IS COMING

I thought I should write to you, because I had a rush of ideas just now. I'd gone out to town to buy some food. It's always when I leave this desk, things start clicking. Literally, walking through Marks & Spencer. I know I'm talking to myself. I must look like a nutter. I thought, what if it's an insurance claim? It's the people who own the *Titanic* who have magnetised the hull to attract the meteorites. No, I don't mean insurance – insurance would be insane, since your shares would plummet if your ship crashed. I mean that the Big Boss is on board, he has set it up, he has himself a nice stasis pod, protecting him from harm, so his people can pluck him from the wreckage and he'll be declared dead. Or something. The Angels are pre-programmed to kill the survivors so that no one's left. The ship falling onto the Earth is a by-product, not part of the overall plan. And only the Doctor cares; to everyone else it's just a primitive planet below.

But why not fake a car crash? Why would the Big Boss take everyone with him? In fact, if the ship is going to crash into the Earth, why do the Angels need to kill the survivors at all? They're going to die anyway. But that sort of thing shouldn't stop me. Let it ride. I mustn't bore myself with reasons why not. There are always a million dull reasons why not. Go for the images, the feel of it, the potential, the dynamic. Details come later. I'll think on.

Oh, and Kylie Minogue should die. That struck me like a thunderbolt in the taxi back from town. *Wham!* Disaster movies should always have deaths of people that you don't want to die. She should be the next potential companion, but cops it. I'd never considered that before. That feels good. It's not so much the ideas; it's the fact I'm *having* ideas. That's what feels good.

FROM: BENJAMIN COOK TO: RUSSELL T DAVIES
FRIDAY 11 MAY 2007 17:55:52 GMT

RE: CHRISTMAS IS COMING

So... okay, really, honestly, why don't you start writing now?

FROM: RUSSELL T DAVIES TO: BENJAMIN COOK
FRIDAY 11 MAY 2007 18:30:02 GMT

RE: CHRISTMAS IS COMING

I don't know. Honestly. I'm just sitting here like an idiot. Like a bloody idiot. All day. I'm eating badly, smoking heavily… but that seems to be part of the getting-ready-to-write crap. I worked my way through about 50 cigarettes with the *Sarah Jane* rewrite earlier this week. That's just absurd, even for me. I'm killing myself. I'm looking scruffy, because I'm not bothering to iron shirts. (The Number One Gay!) My VAT needs doing, but I'm ignoring it. I missed my nieces' birthdays last week. I haven't even sent a card. I *still* haven't sent a card. And I'm as horny as hell. Like a stupid teenager. That's more like it, though. That's a better description of what this process actually *feels* like.

FROM: RUSSELL T DAVIES TO: BENJAMIN COOK
TUESDAY 15 MAY 2007 19:01:40 GMT

RE: CHRISTMAS IS COMING

I'm in a stinking mood. Panic, panic, panic. Everyone is giving me a wide berth, because I'm just being vicious to them. They recognise the signs. I suppose I should write it all down properly, but even this correspondence can sod off –

No, it shouldn't. It won't. But that's how it feels. Just bad. I keep telling myself to start work at 9pm, to start typing. That's my latest target.

FROM: RUSSELL T DAVIES TO: BENJAMIN COOK
WEDNESDAY 16 MAY 2007 02:51:27 GMT

RE: CHRISTMAS IS COMING

Hmm, look, I started. Not at 9pm, at midnight. Sheer panic. It'll do me good, waking up tomorrow knowing that a 4.X file exists. That's better than nothing.

```
1. INT. TARDIS - DAY

REPEAT OF 3.13 SC.92. THE TARDIS in
flight. THE DOCTOR walks around the
console. Deep in thought. And then…

EXPLOSION! The Doctor's showered
with debris!

He's on the floor. Coughing. Smoke
in the air. He waves his hand
to clear the air, looking up.
Gobsmacked.

              THE DOCTOR
    What? But… what??

FX: WIDE SHOT, the PROW OF A
SHIP, an old-fashioned liner, now
sticking through the whole of the
right-hand wall of the Tardis,
filling half the space.

The Doctor finds in the debris, a
lifebelt. He flips it over. It says:
TITANIC.

           THE DOCTOR (CONT'D)
    What??!

(End repeat, new material.) He
leaps to his feet, slams away at
the Tardis console.

FX: the prow of the ship withdraws
through the hole.

He slams more switches, the Time
Rotor rising and falling, the sound
of materialisation filling the air…

                              CUT TO:

2. INT. SMALL CUPBOARD - NIGHT

Tiny, dark linen cupboard, just big
enough for…

FX: the TARDIS materialises.

THE DOCTOR steps out, still
brushing himself down. Opens the
cupboard door, steps out -

                              CUT TO:

3. INT. TITANIC RECEPTION -
CONTINUOUS

THE DOCTOR steps out.

Large space, reception desk,
all wood & marble, more TITANIC
signage, STEWARDS passing to and
fro, and GUESTS in their finery,
chatting, laughing. It all looks
very 1912. Almost. And it's decked
out for Christmas, though nothing
gaudy, all very classy. The Doctor
walks through…
```

The TARDIS lands aboard the *Starship Titanic*.

Men in black tie. Ladies in posh dresses. Staff looking immaculate. A WAITRESS in uniform - PETH, young, feisty - walks past the Doctor, carrying a tray. Then he sees -

Two GOLDEN ANGELS, guarding a set of internal doors. THE HEAVENLY HOST. They look like metal statues - tall, with beautiful gold, blank faces, simple tunics, hands locked in a prayer gesture, folded wings, haloes suspended above their metal hair by thin struts. But as the Doctor stares, one of them slowly turns his head. Looks at the Doctor.

Black eyes in a gold face.

The Doctor creeped out, then distracted by seeing -

An alien - BANNAKAFFALATTA - strolling past, in black tie; three foot tall, head like a spiky blue football.

And the Doctor's getting the hang of this now, keeps walking, goes to a metal ship-type door in the wall, marked DECK 15, spins the wheel, opens it -

CUT TO:

4. EXT. DECK 15 - CONTINUOUS

THE DOCTOR steps out. Traditional deck, wooden floor, bronze railing, Titanic lifebelts on display, GUESTS standing with cocktails, enjoying the view. To the left, to the right, all very traditional. But in front…

FX: the Doctor walks to the railing, the night beyond. Revealing that the blackness is not just night, it's SPACE, and below him: THE EARTH.

CU The Doctor - he gets it!

THE DOCTOR
Riiight…

FX: LONG HERO FX SHOT, ZOOM OUT from the Doctor on the deck, pulling back to see the whole ship - A STARSHIP, exactly like the Titanic, but with mighty antigravity engines underneath - keep pulling out wider, to see the vessel sailing majestically above the Earth. Over this:

TANNOY
Starship Titanic is now in orbit above Sol 3, also known as Earth. Population: Human. And in accordance with local customs: Merry Christmas!

CUT TO OPENING TITLES

5. EXT. FX SHOT

NEW ANGLE on THE TITANIC, its sheer beauty.

CUT TO:

6. INT. BRIDGE - NIGHT

Quiet and dark. A long room, rather than deep, the only place with futuristic technology on display, computer banks, etc, though at the centre there's still a big old-fashioned wooden SHIP'S WHEEL. Facing windows, which look out onto BLACKNESS (the view will be GREENSCREEN later).

CREW in smart 1912-ish uniform - NB, everything on board is only an approximation of the period.

CAPTAIN HARDAKER stands centre - 60, wise, calm.

CAPTAIN HARDAKER
Orbit nice and steady. Good work, Mr Cavill. And maintain position.

Crew operate controls, the sound of engines slowing. The Captain relaxes a little:

CAPTAIN HARDAKER (CONT'D)
Now then, gentlemen. According to the traditions of the planet below, Christmas is a time of celebration. I think you might be entitled to a tot of rum. Just the one! Off you go, I'll keep watch.

Smiles, salutes, 'Sir!', and the men head off… Except the youngest, MIDSHIPMAN BLANE, young, nervous.

CAPTAIN HARDAKER
And you, what was it…?

MIDSHIPMAN BLANE
Blane, sir, Midshipman Blane.

CAPTAIN HARDAKER
You're new, I take it?

MIDSHIPMAN BLANE
Only just qualified, sir. First trip out!

CAPTAIN HARDAKER
Then you can stand down, Midshipman. Go and enjoy yourself.

MIDSHIPMAN BLANE
I would, sir, but, um… Regulations say the Bridge has to be staffed by two crewmembers at any one time, sir.

CAPTAIN HARDAKER
Well said. Very good! Just you and me, then. It's only a Level Three planet down below, fairly primitive, they don't even know we're here. Should be a quiet night.

MIDSHIPMAN BLANE
Yes, sir.

CUT TO:

Captain Hardaker (Geoffrey Palmer) at the ship's wheel.

7. INT. BALLROOM - NIGHT

THE DOCTOR, now adjusting his black tie, walks in.

More of a LOUNGE than a ballroom, tables and booths with GUESTS, drinking, milling about; dotted about, more HEAVENLY HOST, standing perfectly still; then a dance floor, and a stage, on which the SINGER & BAND are performing a lounge-music-version of I Wish It Could Be Christmas Every Day.

All normal, until the Doctor looks up…

FX WIDE SHOT: VAST ROOM, levels of seating rising up into a vaulted roof, GUESTS milling about.

The Doctor strolls through, looking around…

His POV: BANNAKAFFALATTA, with some ordinary GUESTS, at a table, all laughing.

His POV: another table, MORVIN (male) & STRUZIE (female), a large pair, tucking into a buffet; they

```
like their food. For some reason,
they're dressed as cowboy &
cowgirl.

The Doctor then distracted by loud
voices -
```

This is weird, showing it to someone at this stage. It feels so odd. But I'd better get used to it. Do you want to read this stuff? I've no idea. So far, I'm thinking… is it a bit dull? The Doctor wandering is deadly dull. The Doctor is best under pressure. But it's hard to generate plot until the meteorites hit. Then again, with all the on-air trailers in December, everyone will know that it's a disaster movie, so there's a pleasure in just meeting the characters. I want to hit the disaster by Page 15 – about 11 minutes in. That feels right.

Other thoughts: Midshipman Blane should be sexy as hell. I don't often think of specific actors, but maybe Russell Tovey. Or posh like Lee Williams. Blane is not a sexy name, though. I'll change it. Struzie should be Debbie Chazen, who played Big Claire in *Mine All Mine*. We offered her a Slitheen in *The Sarah Jane Adventures*, but she begged to be in *Doctor Who* proper. A disaster movie needs a larger woman, and she's a hoot. And Bannakaffalatta? Jimmy Vee. Oh, the thought of little Jimmy and Kylie in a scene together!

FROM: BENJAMIN COOK TO: RUSSELL T DAVIES
WEDNESDAY 16 MAY 2007 03:10:44 GMT

RE: CHRISTMAS IS COMING

How does it feel to have started, Russell? Good, surely? Apart from the strangeness of sending what you've written to me already…

I'm privileged to be the first person to read this. Of course I want to! How could you even ask? But I'll try to resist the temptation to be all subjective and say nice things – or horrible things (you never know) – about what you're sending me. If you decided that something worked because I'd said I think it's great, or that something didn't because I'd questioned it, I'm worried that this project would come crashing down around our ears. At the very least, the world would stop turning. Let's see how long I can remain an impartial observer. Invisible Ben! I will, however, be asking questions. For example –

It's technical, this one, but worth asking, before we go on… you talk about WIDE SHOTS, CUs, FX shots, camera angles and so on, but really who should determine this: the writer or the director? Do you, literally, write each shot into your script? Or do you plan them in your mind's eye but let the director decide?

FROM: RUSSELL T DAVIES TO: BENJAMIN COOK
WEDNESDAY 16 MAY 2007 03:44:51 GMT

RE: CHRISTMAS IS COMING

How do I feel? Scared, because I should have started ages ago. Scared sick. Sick because I gave up smoking again on Saturday, but then I reached Page 2 and went scrabbling through bags and coats, like a teenager at a party, until I found an old pack with four fags left. The script just felt so slow and dead without them. I only stopped writing for tonight because those four have gone. I'm feeling desperate that I'll never write without smoking again. Series One and Two were written without fags, but that feels like five million years ago now.

But I haven't gone to bed yet. I'm too wired by cigarettes and the nicotine patch that I ripped off.

>>you talk about WIDE SHOTS, CUs, FX shots, camera angles and so on, but really who should determine this: the writer or the director?<<

I like to give some camera directions, but not too many, not so many that it reads like a list. When someone is reading a script – principally, the director – they should *feel* it, the pace, the speed, the atmosphere, the mood, the gags, the dread. I'll give camera directions that enhance the mood: WIDE SHOT if something is barren, lost, empty (or huge, busy, epic, if you've the budget), and CU (close-up) when it's focused, intense, when someone's whispering 'I love you'. I never bother with the more ordinary technical shots like MCU (medium close-up) or LONG SHOT (you can see the whole body, but not as wide as a WIDE SHOT), because they don't *feel* like anything, do they? But I'll describe a crane shot, rising up or rising down, if the moment is epic, if you need to feel that huge sweep of events. Also, frankly, then you stand a good chance of the producer setting aside money for a crane, right from the start, for that scene. Cranes are expensive. But it's all emotion, in the end. Scripts can be so dry. *Feel* them. A lot of the time, new writers are told specifically – and strongly – not to write camera angles, because it's the director's choice, but I reckon that's just power games. I've never heard of a director objecting, only power-broking producers and script editors talking on their behalf without consultation.

Stage directions, as opposed to camera directions, are a whole art in themselves. The classic mistake that we get from newer writers, or writers not used to writing action, is something like:

```
The Doctor runs up the stairs,
explosions all around him, and
soldiers appear, but he runs
into a huge white space, with a
glowing blue column rising up into
the sky, and it's crackling like
electricity, and a white halo
surrounds him.
```

Eh? What? *What?!* Calm down. Break it down. Tell me exactly what's happening. I spend huge amounts of time making sure that stage directions match the tone and rhythm of the scene – like in an action scene, where I use dashes instead of full stops to make sure that everything is moving fast:

```
BEN walks into the room, invisibly.
He looks around. Sees the wallet by
the bed.

He walks towards the wallet -

- but it explodes! -

- and he's running, running,
running -
```

Do you see, you *read* it fast? It feels energised. If that gets into the director's head, then you stand a good chance of it working. Funnily enough, a semicolon always looks considered and classy; it slows things down, makes you read more closely:

```
- BEN keeps running -

- and stops. He's in a huge,
beautiful, empty amphitheatre;
classical columns, white marble.
```

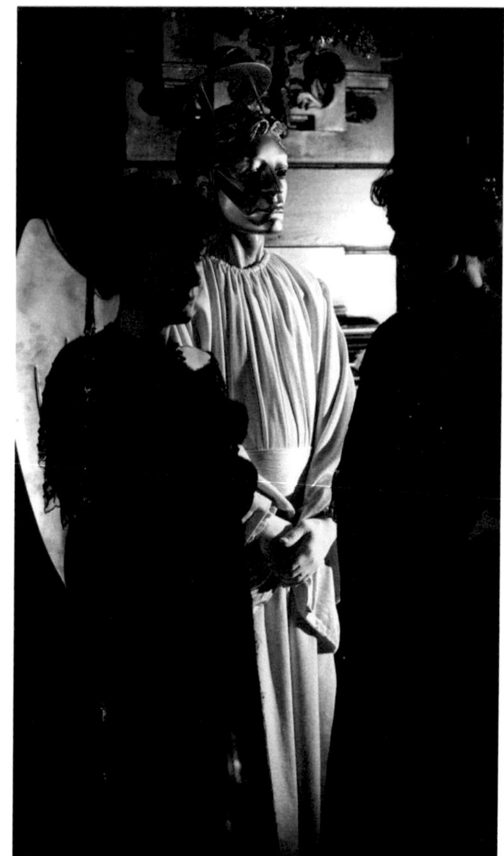

One of the Heavenly Host contrives to look extremely sinister.

Another example: to put 'Pause' on a line of its own makes it *feel* like a pause:

```
BEN looks around. He can hear
singing.

Pause.

Then he moves on...
```

That's much more effective than:

```
BEN looks around. He can hear
singing. Pause. Then he moves on.
```

The first version *feels* the same as what Ben is feeling. I think that's vital. And I strip out adverbs like crazy, because they don't sound dynamic. (This is really personal stuff now. Other writers would be guffawing.) I prefer to write:

```
BEN runs across the amphitheatre,
fast -
```

Instead of:

```
BEN runs across the amphitheatre
quickly.
```

The first one feels faster, whereas the second is too considered. It's not a novel; it's a script and it has to flow. It has to feel like pictures. (I like this new script, by the way. Your wallet exploded and you ran into an amphitheatre. I might add some gladiators in a minute. Be warned!)

I avoid the word 'we', too. It's a real pain to eliminate it – along with 'our' and 'us' – and other writers seem to use it with no ill effects, but it feels wrong to me. 'We see BEN running.' I prefer 'BEN is running', because there is no 'we' inside the script; there's just Ben. Steven Moffat is a good example of the opposite: he's all 'we' and gags in the stage directions, self-referential statements about the actors and stuff. He personally is very present in his stage directions, and it works brilliantly.

Incidentally, we're the only people I've seen who do that FX line break:

```
FX: the prow of the ship withdraws
through the hole.
```

It's a great system, though I'd beware of using it outside of *Doctor Who* circles. People might not get it, because it's unique. I say unique, but I'll probably discover that the whole of Hollywood does it now and always did.

FROM: BENJAMIN COOK TO: RUSSELL T DAVIES
WEDNESDAY 16 MAY 2007 11:02:51 GMT

RE: CHRISTMAS IS COMING

One more anal question (for now): when writing stage and camera directions, which words should you capitalise? Once you've capitalised a word once, should you refrain from doing so for the rest of that scene?

FROM: RUSSELL T DAVIES TO: BENJAMIN COOK
WEDNESDAY 16 MAY 2007 12:29:12 GMT

RE: CHRISTMAS IS COMING

I capitalise every character's name when they first appear, but this is partly a production thing, so that the person drawing up the shooting schedule can spot the name easily in order to break down who's in which scene. That's why, if a character is referred to but they're not in the scene, they're not capitalised:

```
CU THE DOCTOR. He's thinking of
Rose.
```

I used to capitalise names all the way through. A lot of people do. But then I noticed that Paul Abbott changed his system, that he only capitalised them the first time they appear. At about the same time, Nick Elliott (Controller of Drama) at ITV said to me, 'Why do people use all these capitals? Why are they shouting at me?' So I changed, too.

As for other words, it's very indiscriminate, but I tend to do it when it's important:

```
Ben pulls out a LASER GUN.

Then he RUNS!
```

It's kind of telling the director: show this! But a lot of people don't do it at all. If it's worrying you, don't do it. But I do think it gives the script energy, sometimes.

FROM: RUSSELL T DAVIES TO: BENJAMIN COOK
WEDNESDAY 16 MAY 2007 18:48:18 GMT

RE: CHRISTMAS IS COMING

Here's more. I tend to do this, work all day in a panic, then stop at 6pm-ish, catch up with rushes and e-mails, then return to writing at about 9pm or 10pm, depending on what's on telly. But I thought I'd show you this now. I keep changing as I go along, too fast for you to note. For instance, I realised while writing earlier today that I didn't have the Host malfunction at any point – and I was lacking spookiness – so I went back and wrote that into the middle of Scene 7. There's a rewrite that no one ever saw.

7. INT. BALLROOM - NIGHT

THE DOCTOR, now adjusting his black tie, walks in.

More of a LOUNGE than a ballroom, tables and booths with GUESTS, drinking, milling about; dotted about, more HEAVENLY HOST, standing perfectly still; then a dance floor, with COUPLES waltzing, and then a stage, on which the SINGER & BAND are performing a lounge-music-version of Have Yourself A Merry Little Christmas.

FX: CROWD REPLICATION. Then the Doctor looks up…

FX WIDE SHOT: VAST ROOM, levels of seating & balconies rising up into a vaulted roof, GUESTS milling about.

The Doctor strolls through, looking around…

His POV: BANNAKAFFALATTA, with some ordinary GUESTS, at a table, all laughing.

His POV: another table, MORVIN (male) & FOON (female), a large pair, tucking into a buffet; they like their food. For some reason, they're dressed as cowboy & cowgirl.

Passing the Doctor, a BUSINESSMAN - RICKSTON SLADE, late-20s, sharp, ruthless - on his slim, futuristic mobile -

RICKSTON
- it's not a holiday for me, not while I've still got a vone, now just do as I say and sell - !

- as the Doctor heads towards a HEAVENLY HOST, holds up the psychic paper.[1]

THE DOCTOR
Evening, Passenger 57, terrible memory, remind me, you would be…?

Its voice is calm, posh, neutral, movements smooth and controlled, rather than robotic:

HOST
The Heavenly Host, sir. Supplying information and assistance for all passengers.

THE DOCTOR
Robots! Good! So, tell me again, where are we from?

HOST
Starship Titanic is en route from Planet Seth in the Cassavalian Belt. The purpose of the cruise is to experience primitive cultures and celebrate local festivities. This voyage is designated: Christmas.

THE DOCTOR
Titanic, who thought of the name?

HOST
It was selected as the most famous vessel of Planet Earth.

THE DOCTOR
Did they tell you why it was famous?

HOST
I do not have that information.

THE DOCTOR
No, still, lightning, twice, et cetera -

HOST
All designations are approved by Mr Maxitane, President Elect of White Light Cruiseliners.

The Host gestures -

Across the room, in a posh roped-off area, MR MAXITANE, fat mogul with cigar, bodyguards & beautiful ladies.

THE DOCTOR
Oh, you've got the boss on board?

HOST
Mr Maxitane is classified

1 The Doctor's psychic paper, an apparently blank piece of card in a small leather wallet, débuted in 1.2. It allows whoever is holding it to show people whatever they want them to see on the card.

Mr Maxitane, flanked by Heavenly Host, lives it up in his 'posh roped-off area'. Illustration by Russell T Davies.

Guest Number One/One/One/
One/One -

He's broken, Max Headroom, jerks his head with every 'One' -[2]

THE DOCTOR
Oh, hello, bit of a glitch -

He's about to SONIC the Host, but three STEWARDS rush in -[3]

CHIEF STEWARD
Sorry sir, we can handle this -

THE DOCTOR
He just got a bit stuck -

CHIEF STEWARD
Software problem, that's all, leave it with us, sir. Merry Christmas!

He presses a button on the Host's neck -

It instantly snaps rigid, upright, a statue, topples to the side. One Steward catches its torso, the other picks up its legs, and they carry it out, like a dummy. All fast and discreet, no fuss.

As the Chief Steward walks away, he mutters on ear comms, angry (the Doctor still catching this in the b/g) -

CHIEF STEWARD (CONT'D)
Chief Steward to Robotics, we've got another Host down, it's happened *again*. What's going wrong with these things...?

The Doctor turns, distracted by -

RICKSTON SLADE, still on his vone, yelling at the waitress, PETH - she's just dropped a tray of glasses.

RICKSTON
Oh for God's sake, look where you're going! This jacket is a genuine Earth antique!

PETH
I'm sorry, sir -

RICKSTON
Yeah, you'll be sorry when it comes out of your wages, sweetheart -
(walks off, on vone)
Telling you, staffed by idiots! No wonder White Light's going down the drain...

The Doctor scoots over to Peth, gets down on the floor with her, both picking up shards of glass.

THE DOCTOR
There we go, careful...

PETH
Thank you, sir, I can manage.

THE DOCTOR
Never said you couldn't! I'm the Doctor, by the way.

PETH
Peth, sir.

THE DOCTOR
Peth?

2 Max Headroom is an artificial intelligence that originated in 1985 as an announcer for Channel 4's music video programme *The Max Headroom Show*. Max would stutter when the computer program that generated him couldn't render his image fast enough.

3 The sonic screwdriver (sometimes referred to as 'the sonic' or 'the screwdriver') is a tool used by the Doctor since 1968 serial *Fury from the Deep*. Its most common function is to operate virtually any door lock, mechanical or electronic, but it has also been used for everything from repairing equipment to detonating landmines.

PETH
Peth, Peth with a P, Peth Harmone.

THE DOCTOR
Nice to meet you, Peth. Merry Christmas!

PETH
Merry Christmas, sir.

THE DOCTOR
It's not sir, just Doctor. Long way from home then, Planet Seth.

PETH
I dunno, doesn't feel much different. Spent three years working in the spaceport diner. Then I come all this way, and I'm still stuck in the kitchens.

THE DOCTOR
No shore leave?

PETH
We're not allowed. Staff forbidden to leave ship, they can't afford the insurance, or something. It's all cutbacks, these days. I just wanted to try it, just once…

Saying that, standing, both going to the window.

FX (and REPEAT?): EARTH below them. Romantic image, the two framed against the spacescape. Also intercut with:

FX: REVERSE WIDE, from EXTERIOR, the Doctor & Peth framed in the window within the Titanic, the Ballroom behind them.

Both quiet, intimate:

PETH (CONT'D)
Never stood on another world. All those years in the spaceport, watching those ships head off into the stars. Always dreamt of… Ohh, sounds daft.

THE DOCTOR
You dreamt of another sky. A new sun. New air. And life, new life, the whole universe teeming with it, why stand still when there's all that life out there?

PETH
…yeah.

THE DOCTOR
I know.

Smile between them. Hold, then break the moment - almost too intimate! - a bit more professional:

PETH
So! Um. D'you travel a lot, then?

THE DOCTOR
All the time.

PETH
Is that for work, or…?

THE DOCTOR
No, just for fun. My whole life, just for fun. Well, that's the plan. Never quite works.

PETH
You must be stinking rich, though.

THE DOCTOR
Haven't got a penny.
(whispers)
Stowaway.

PETH
Kidding me.

THE DOCTOR
Seriously!

PETH
(laughing)
No!

THE DOCTOR
Oh yes!

PETH
I should report you.

THE DOCTOR
Go on, then.

PETH
I'll get you a drink. On the house.

'Why stand still when there's all that life out there?' 'Peth' (Kylie Minogue) gets a lesson in following your dreams from the Doctor (David Tennant).

And she walks away, smiling.

The Doctor strolls back into the Ballroom, as the SINGER switches to a lively version of I Wish It Could Be Christmas Every Day. The dance floor livens up. The Doctor notices -

A table full of YOUNG GLAMOROUS PEOPLE, all hooting with laughter. They're laughing at -

MORVIN & FOON, cowboy & cowgirl, eating a basket of chicken wings. With dignity. The Doctor slides in to join them.

THE DOCTOR
Something's tickled them.

FOON
They told us it was fancy dress. Very funny, I'm sure.

MORVIN
They're just picking on us cos we didn't pay, we won the tickets in a competition.

FOON
I had to name all five husbands of Joofie Crystalle in By The Light Of The Asteroid. D'you ever watch By The Light Of The Asteroid?

THE DOCTOR
No, not seen it.

FOON
Ooh, it's marvellous!

MORVIN
But according to that lot, we should be in steerage.

THE DOCTOR
Well, we can't have that, can we?

And he gives a discreet whirr of the sonic screwdriver -

PRAC FX: one of the GLAMOROUS MEN

is just pouring champagne, the BOTTLE SHATTERS, all sprayed with drink, WOMEN standing, splattered, dismayed.

Morvin & Foon hooting!

FOON
Was that you?

THE DOCTOR
Maybe.

FOON
Oh we like you!

MORVIN
We do! I'm Morvin Van Hoff, and this is my lady wife, Foon.

THE DOCTOR
Foon! Hello! I'm the Doctor.

FOON
I'll need a doctor, time I'm finished with that buffet. Have a buffalo wing! They must be huge, these buffalo, so many wings!

TANNOY comes over:

TANNOY
Shore Leave tickets Red Six Seven now activated, Red Six Seven…

FOON
Ooh, Red Six Seven, that's us!

MORVIN
Are you Red Six Seven?

THE DOCTOR
(psychic paper)
I think I am, yes.

MORVIN
Come on then! We're going to Earth!

CUT TO:

8. INT. HOST CONTAINMENT CELLS - NIGHT

The damaged, dead HOST from sc.7 is placed upright.

WIDER: the CHIEF STEWARD & STEWARDS with an ENGINEER, in greasy overalls. The Host is being placed in an upright booth with a frosted glass door; lines of booths filling the space. (NB, this is Below Deck, all industrial pipes and steam and oil.)

CHIEF STEWARD
That's five of them now, five of them malfunctioning. One woman, she asked the Host to fix her necklace, it almost broke her neck!

ENGINEER
Can't work it out, I've been over the software, nothing. Like something's got into them, some sort of bug.

CHIEF STEWARD
Well then, fix it!

ENGINEER
I'm trying!

Chief Steward calmer, considers the Host.

Foon (Debbie Chazen) tucks in.

```
              CHIEF STEWARD
    Never liked those things,
    anyway. Doing us out of a
    job.

                 ENGINEER
    Cheap labour. Don't need
    unions, don't need food,
    don't need wages, it's all
    cutbacks.

              CHIEF STEWARD
    Seal it up. And if you can't
    fix it… Throw it overboard.

And they close the frosted door.

As they walk away, closer on the
booth… closer…

And the Host's golden
hand slams against the
glass.
```

My thoughts on it so far: I like the Doctor and Peth; they feel good, nice dialogue. It makes it all feel more real. It's very, *very* strange writing dialogue that might be said by Kylie! Morvin and Foon (I thought Struzie was sayable in too many different ways, so I changed it to Foon) are sweet. Too sweet? These Christmas Specials are so direct, so plain, so on-the-nose. But so they should be. It's Christmas. It's not the time for *The Girl in the Fireplace* or *Human Nature*. But I really should have started weeks ago. Oh Christ! What I'm really thinking is: it's crap, I'm rubbish, this will be a public debacle. Christmas Day, with everyone watching – what a way to fail! That's public execution. But I suppose we can take this insecure crap as read from now on.

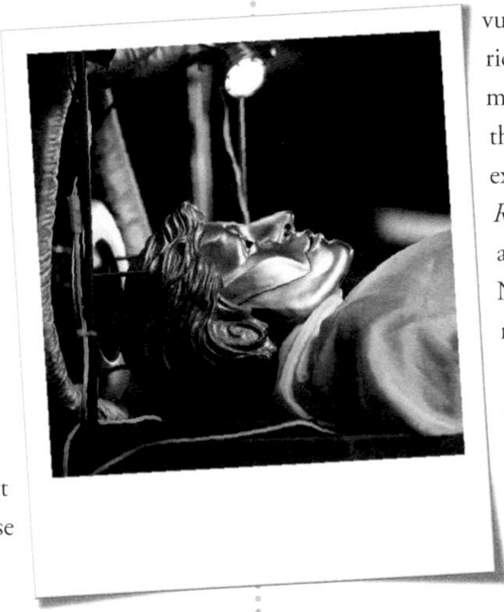

FROM: BENJAMIN COOK TO: RUSSELL T DAVIES
WEDNESDAY 16 MAY 2007 20:37:42 GMT

RE: CHRISTMAS IS COMING

I've just been to Sainsbury's. They're selling *Doctor Who* Petits Filous Frubes. Cyber-Strawberry flavour. Slogan: 'I'm f… f… f… frozen in time!' Is your fridge full of this stuff, Russell?

Thanks for the f… f… f… further instalments of script. A couple of months back, we considered whether lead characters have to be sympathetic, and it's a disaster movie convention that the headlining catastrophe is made more comprehensible by showing it impacting on characters that we care for. But *how* do you make an audience care about your characters? And quickly? Movies in this genre often present 'stock' figures – the star-crossed lovers, the courageous-but-doomed hero – so is that it? Is it identifiability that makes us care? Or universal traits? Must we find aspects of Bannakaffalatta with which we identify? (We're all a bit spiky from time to time!) Or do you focus on your characters' vulnerability? Or furnish them with a rich spectrum of personal details? The more they reveal about themselves, the more we care? To offer another example, at what point in *Bob & Rose* do we start to care about Bob and Rose? And why? We care about Nathan in *Queer as Folk* within two minutes flat – but is that just down to Charlie Hunnam's lost-puppy-dog eyes?

Right. I'd better stop wittering on. My f… f… f… flatmate, Matt, is eating Martha Jones, and I'm enjoying the Moxx of Balhoon. And later I might try a Frube. Boom boom! Mmm… Cyber-Strawberry!

FROM: RUSSELL T DAVIES TO: BENJAMIN COOK
WEDNESDAY 16 MAY 2007 20:52:44 GMT

RE: CHRISTMAS IS COMING

>>We care about Nathan in *Queer as Folk* within two minutes flat – but is that just down to Charlie Hunnam's lost-puppy-dog eyes?<<

Charlie Hunnam's arse, I'd say. Lovely man, Charlie. He's really clever. At his audition, we asked him his favourite actor. He said, 'Christopher Walken,' which is just about the most intelligent reply I've ever heard to that question. Plus, *the arse!*

I am hooting at those Frubes. They're the only licensed product that Julie and I were ever unsure about, but that sort of thing can be worth a fortune for BBC

Worldwide.

The how-to-make-an-audience-care thing is hard. I'll come back to that, I promise.

FROM: BENJAMIN COOK TO: RUSSELL T DAVIES
WEDNESDAY 16 MAY 2007 22:55:06 GMT

CHARLIE HUNNAM'S ARSE

You're mentioned in the new *Radio Times*. TV reviewer Alison Graham says that you and your team 'must be hurt' not to have received BAFTA nominations this year. She has a point. It's an odd list, isn't it? Notable omissions.

FROM: RUSSELL T DAVIES TO: BENJAMIN COOK
WEDNESDAY 16 MAY 2007 23:03:34 GMT

RE: CHARLIE HUNNAM'S ARSE

Let us never change that subject line. Ever. Mmm.

I'm not bothered about the BAFTAs, to be honest. Last year was so extraordinary, it can never be topped.[4] Besides, history decides in the end. Everyone thinks that *Queer as Folk* won a BAFTA, when it wasn't even nominated. Now, *that* was shocking. And the last thing that I need is a night in London. I'm mad and script-obsessed at the moment, therefore a bit destructive. The other day (I didn't tell you this), my agent got a call from George Lucas' people. Apparently, Lucas is in London and he wants to meet me about writing for his new *Star Wars* TV series! But I said no. Well, I can't go to London, I haven't the time, and Lucas didn't exactly beat a path to Cardiff, so he can't be that interested. Mind you, they really want a UK writer, apparently. When I find out who it is, I won't be so snooty, I'll just be jealous.

FROM: RUSSELL T DAVIES TO: BENJAMIN COOK
THURSDAY 17 MAY 2007 02:23:36 GMT

RE: CHARLIE HUNNAM'S ARSE

Phew, 12 pages, almost! That's a good day. It doesn't feel *quite* as terrifying as normal, maybe because a disaster movie has an inbuilt shape: arrive, disaster, climb, safety. That shape helps.

4 At the 2006 British Academy Television Awards, *Doctor Who* won the Best Drama Series category, as well as the Pioneer Audience Award voted for by TV viewers.

```
9. INT. TITANIC RECEPTION - NIGHT

MR COPPER, the SHIP'S HISTORIAN
- 60, shambolic, with Mr Magoo
glasses - holds up a sign, like a
Saga Holidays rep, 6-7 on a red
card. He's already got EIGHT GUESTS
with him.

                    MR COPPER
        Red Six Seven, this way,
        if you could convene, fast
        as you can, Red Six Seven
        departing shortly…

MORVIN & FOON hurrying towards him,
THE DOCTOR following - PETH just
passing by -

                    PETH
        I got you that drink -

                    THE DOCTOR
        And I got you a treat! C'mon -

Said, taking the drink, slamming it
down, grabbing her hand, pulls her
with him, fast -

- to join Mr Copper, the Doctor
shows his psychic paper -

                    THE DOCTOR (CONT'D)
        Red Six Seven, plus one, as
        agreed by the Captain.

                    MR COPPER
        Hurry up then, if you could
        take a teleport bracelet,
        both of you, this will also
        provide translation -

Morvin & Foon are already taking
metal sci-fi BRACELETS off a
STEWARD, the Doctor & Peth do
likewise, muttering -

                    PETH
        I'll get the sack.

                    THE DOCTOR
        Trust me.

                    PETH
        But I can't, I need the
        money.

                    THE DOCTOR
        Brand new sky!

                    MR COPPER
                    (in b/g)
```

Remember the rules, stay within a hundred yards of my good self, do not feed, bully or mate with the locals, thank you, if you could all stand together, thaaat's it…

She thinks: to hell with it!, thrilled, grabs bracelet.

All THE GROUP clusters together, facing Mr Copper.

MR COPPER (CONT'D)
To repeat, I am Mr Bayldon Copper, ship's historian, and I will be taking you to Old London Town. The basic facts: Human beings worship the great God, Santa. A creature with fearsome claws. And his wife, Mary. Every Christmas Eve, the people of Earth go to war, with the country of Turkey. They then eat the people of Turkey, for Christmas dinner. Like savages!

'Do not feed, bully or mate with the locals.' The *Titanic*'s historian, Mr Copper (Clive Swift).

'And me! And me! And me!' Illustration by Russell T Davies.

THE DOCTOR
Excuse me, sorry, but… where did you get this from?

MR COPPER
I have a degree in Earthonomics.

THE DOCTOR
From where?

MR COPPER
Mrs Golightly's Happy Travelling University and Hotel.

THE DOCTOR
Can't argue with that.

BANNAKAFFALATTA
And me! And me! And me!

BANNAKAFFALATTA, running towards them. He barks every word.

MR COPPER
Red Six Seven?

BANNAKAFFALATTA
(shows ticket)
Very good!

MR COPPER
If you could take a bracelet…

THE DOCTOR
Hold on, um, what's your name?

BANNAKAFFALATTA
Bannakaffalatta!

THE DOCTOR
Right, can I call you Banna?

BANNAKAFFALATTA
No! Bannakaffalatta!

THE DOCTOR
Okay, Bannakaffalatta, but -
(to Mr Copper)
Isn't he going to stick out a bit?

MR COPPER
They have a saying on Earth. Spiky blue face is a spiky good face.

THE DOCTOR
No, but really, it's Christmas Eve down there, late-night shopping, there'll be crowds of people, tons of them, he'll cause a riot, the streets are gonna be packed -

But Mr Copper is pressing the switch on his bracelet -

FX: THE GROUP disappears, teleport glow.

CUT TO:

10. EXT. CITY STREET - NIGHT

FX: teleport glow, THE GROUP appears.

WIDE SHOT: absolute emptiness. No people. A low wind; newspaper blowing across, Christmas decorations swaying.

THE DOCTOR
- with shoppers and people and parties and… Oh.

MR COPPER
Spread out! But don't stray too far, it could be dangerous! Any day now, they start boxing.

FOON
I can smell frying!

'Something must be wrong…' The Doctor and company are transported to a deserted London on Christmas Eve.

BANNAKAFFALATTA
Very good! Very good!

As the GUESTS start to spread out:

THE DOCTOR
…but, it should be full, it should be busy, where's everyone gone…?

He sees a WOMAN in a shop window putting up a SALE sign.

THE DOCTOR (CONT'D)
Something must be wrong…

He sees, a distance away, a WOMAN, 50, scuttling past.

THE DOCTOR (CONT'D)
'Scuse me, could you tell me - ?

But the WOMAN hurries away, as though scared.

THE DOCTOR (CONT'D)
What is it, 2007, 2008? No invasions planned, that's weird…

But during all this, PETH looking around, eyes wide.

PETH
…but it's *beautiful*.

THE DOCTOR
Really? D'you think? It's just a street, I mean, the Pyramids are beautiful, and New Zealand, and -

PETH
It's a different planet! I'm standing on a different planet! There's like… concrete! And shops! Alien shops! Real, alien shops! Look, you can't see the stars! And it smells, it stinks, this is amazing! Thank you!

And she gives him a great big hug.

THE DOCTOR
Least I could do.

PETH
Oh, I could get used to this! And all that glittery stuff, that's Christmas, yeah?

THE DOCTOR
Christmas decorations.

PETH
What is Christmas, exactly?

THE DOCTOR
Long story. I should know, I was there - 'scuse me a minute -

A good distance away, he sees one of those freestanding NEWS-SELLER'S BOOTHS. Runs over to it.

On duty, a 50 y/o bloke, STAN, Londoner. Comfy in his booth, with a thermos and a portable TV on a shelf. All the newspaper headlines say: *LONDON DESERTED*, etc.

THE DOCTOR (CONT'D)
Hi there, sorry, obvious question, um, where's everyone gone?

STAN
Scared.

THE DOCTOR
Scared of what?

STAN
Where've you been living? London! At Christmas! Not safe, is it?

THE DOCTOR
But why?

STAN
Why d'you think? It's them! Up above.

And he gestures to the portable, the TV showing NEWS 24, clips of the 2.X SYCORAX SPACESHIP, straplines: *LONDONERS IN FESTIVE FEAR*, etc.

STAN (CONT'D)
Christmas before last, we had that big bloody spaceship. Everyone standing on the roof!

TV: 3.X RACNOSS WEBSTAR, etc; *THIRD TIME UNLUCKY?*

STAN (CONT'D)
Then last year, that Christmas Star, electrocuting all over the place, zapping about. This year, God knows what. Everyone's scarpered. 'Cept me, and her Majesty.

On TV -

CUT TO:

11. INT. ROYAL BACKGROUND - DAY

PRINCE CHARLES being interviewed.

'There is nothing to fear.' HRH The Prince of Wales addresses the nation. Illustration by Russell T Davies.

News strapline: *ROYAL FAMILY WILL NOT BE MOVED.*

PRINCE CHARLES
My mother will be staying in Buckingham Palace throughout the festive season, to show the people of London, and the world, that there is nothing to fear.

CUT TO:

12. EXT. CITY STREET - NIGHT

THE DOCTOR with STAN, CONTINUED.

STAN
God bless her. We stand vigil.

THE DOCTOR
Well, between you and me, I think her Majesty's got it right. As far as I know, this year, there's nothing to worry abou-

FX: teleport glow, the Doctor disappears.

On Stan.

STAN
…then again.

CUT TO:

13. INT. TITANIC RECEPTION - NIGHT

FX: teleport glow, THE GROUP reappears, in original positions.

THE DOCTOR
I was in mid-sentence!

MR COPPER
Sorry about that, um, we seem to have a bit of a problem - if I could have your bracelets, thank you -

The CHIEF STEWARD strides over -

CHIEF STEWARD
Apologies, ladies and gentlemen and Bannakaffalatta, we seem to have suffered a power fluctuation. If you'd like to

```
    return to the festivities,
    normal service will be
    resumed as soon as possible -

PETH - avoiding the Chief Steward
- whispers to THE DOCTOR:

                PETH
    That was the best. The best.

And she runs away, back to work,
the group dispersing:

          BANNAKAFFALATTA
    Very bad! Very bad!

Leaving the Doctor where he is.
Eyes lighting up; he loves a
problem. To the Chief Steward:

             THE DOCTOR
    What sort of power
    fluctuation...?
```

I'm on Page 16, and we're close to the disaster. I keep page-counting. It's a constant tick. I can't help it. The script was 17-and-a-half pages, but I edited it down by cutting lines and shifting stage directions. For instance, I've removed what was basically padding from the dialogue between the Chief Steward and the Engineer in Scene 8. It now reads:

```
           CHIEF STEWARD
    That's five of them now, five
    of them malfunctioning. One
    woman, she asked the Host to
    fix her necklace, it almost
    broke her neck!

              ENGINEER
    I've been over the software,
    nothing. Like something's got
    into them, some sort of bug.

           CHIEF STEWARD
    Well then, fix it!

              ENGINEER
    I'm trying!

           CHIEF STEWARD
    Seal it up. And if it
    can't be mended... Throw it
    overboard.
```

Much better! Can the trip to Earth be cut, too? Is it a diversion? It's only there for the Buckingham Palace gag at the end. Then again, that gag is brilliant. It keeps making me laugh, even now. I love a gag. Oh, and I went back and changed Midshipman Blane to Midshipman *Frame*. Much sexier! Of course, they'll all start dying soon. I'm worried that the dying, though necessary, might be too horrible. Also, I'm thinking it's kind of obvious that Mr Maxitane is behind the whole thing. Good thought tonight, though: the Host are programmed to kill surviving passengers... *but the Doctor is not a passenger!* I like that. Nice.

FROM: BENJAMIN COOK TO: RUSSELL T DAVIES
THURSDAY 17 MAY 2007 08:34:20 GMT

RE: CHARLIE HUNNAM'S ARSE

Hang on... *Prince Charles?!* Kylie Minogue I can believe, but the Prince of Wales? He'll *never* do it.

FROM: RUSSELL T DAVIES TO: BENJAMIN COOK
THURSDAY 17 MAY 2007 23:55:43 GMT

RE: CHARLIE HUNNAM'S ARSE

Hmph, no writing tonight. I came home, had to read seven scripts, watch a *Confidential*, and listen to a podcast. That's enough work for any man. Ridiculous, though, when I'm this behind schedule. I should abandon all that extra stuff. But the moment you do, something goes wrong.

FROM: RUSSELL T DAVIES TO: BENJAMIN COOK
FRIDAY 18 MAY 2007 19:07:02 GMT

RE: CHARLIE HUNNAM'S ARSE

The meteorite has hit! Also, there are some changes to the scene order earlier on, and I've tweaked a few lines. I got that Tannoy speech in Scene 4 right:

```
              TANNOY
    Starship Titanic is now
    in orbit above Sol 3,
    also known as Earth.
    Population: Human. Ladies
    and gentlemen, welcome to
    Christmas!
```

That's better, isn't it? And I've made Bannakaffalatta red, not blue, because he was too Moxx-like.

15. INT. BRIDGE - NIGHT[5]

CAPTAIN HARDAKER at a computer panel, MIDSHIPMAN FRAME at a second one. All calm and normal.

MIDSHIPMAN FRAME
Seems to be power diverted to Host Containment, sir. Flared up, then it stopped.

CAPTAIN HARDAKER
Nothing to worry about, she's an old ship. Full of aches and pains.

A beep from a different panel, Frame goes over -

MIDSHIPMAN FRAME
Picking up a meteorite shower, sir, bearing west 56 north 2.

CAPTAIN HARDAKER
Fairly standard for this part of space. Miles away.

MIDSHIPMAN FRAME
We can probably see it, sir.

Hoists up old-fashioned BINOCULARS.

FX: BINOCULAR POV, through the front windows; the METEORITES just little glimmers of light in space, heading left to right, not towards the ship.

CUT TO:

16. INT. BALLROOM - NIGHT

FX: CROWD DUPLICATION WIDE SHOT. SINGER now starting MURRAY'S CHRISTMAS SONG - so jolly, it's sinister. All fun, lively, the whole party rising in temperature.

CUT TO CU SINGER, the dark Christmassy lyrics…

CUT TO MORVIN & FOON, dancing away.

CUT TO RICKSTON SLADE, chatting up a BEAUTIFUL LADY.

CUT TO BANNAKAFFALATTA, walking along with buffet.

CUT TO PETH, carrying her tray, a smile across the room -

- for THE DOCTOR, who half-smiles back, though he's looking furtive, glances round -

THE CHIEF STEWARD & STEWARDS, the HEAVENLY HOST, dotted about the room, no one looking at him -

- and the Doctor scuttles over to a wall, finds a COMMS BOARD, computer screen & keyboard. Taps in.

THE DOCTOR
Report, recent power fluctuation on Deck 15, define, nature of.

COMPUTER VOICE
You do not have access.

THE DOCTOR
D'you wanna bet?

And he sonics the panel…

CUT TO:

17. INT. BRIDGE - NIGHT

A more insistent beep from the computer panel. MIDSHIPMAN FRAME inspects the radar-type scanner, seeing:

MIDSHIPMAN FRAME
That's a bit odd, sir. The meteorite shower is changing course.

Lifts his binoculars.

FX: BINOCULAR POV, the tiny lights of the far-off burning METEORITES curving round. Towards the ship.

MIDSHIPMAN FRAME (CONT'D)
Strange. Still. We can put shields up to maximum, sir.

CAPTAIN HARDAKER
As you were, Midshipman.

Frame only now turning round to look - CAPTAIN HARDAKER operating computer controls, fixed, grim, quiet.

5 The original Scene 9 has now been split in two: the first part (Scene 9) takes place in the Ballroom, and the second part (the new Scene 10) in Reception. As a knock-on effect, what was Scene 13 – the shore leave group reappearing in Reception – is now Scene 14, followed by this, Scene 15, on the Bridge.

Russell Tovey as Midshipman Frame.

MIDSHIPMAN FRAME
I know we're safe, but all the same…

CAPTAIN HARDAKER
I said, as you were.

MIDSHIPMAN FRAME
Sir? You're magnetising the hull. Is it part of the festivities, sir? Bit of a light-show for the guests…?

CAPTAIN HARDAKER
Something like that.

CUT TO:

18. INT. BALLROOM - NIGHT

THE DOCTOR has now got the control-panel gutted, wires hanging out, though the screen is still working. It shows the same readout as Midshipman Frame's radar-type scanner. Little blips of meteorites, heading in.

The Doctor grim, now. That old feeling. Slides over to a nearby window.

FX: HIS POV, the METEORITES now visible with the naked eye, still just glimmers of light in the distance, but…

CUT TO:

19. INT. BRIDGE - NIGHT

CAPTAIN HARDAKER still working the controls, something strange in his manner. MIDSHIPMAN FRAME worried, now.

MIDSHIPMAN FRAME
I'm only quoting regulations, sir. We should put shields to maximum, just as a precaution.

CAPTAIN HARDAKER
They promised me old men.

MIDSHIPMAN FRAME
I'm sorry, sir?

CAPTAIN HARDAKER
On the crew. Sea dogs. Men who'd had their time. Not boys.

MIDSHIPMAN FRAME
I don't understand, sir.

SCENE CONTINUES, INTERCUT WITH:

20. INT. BALLROOM - NIGHT

THE PARTY livening up now in b/g, lots of dancing and life and colour behind THE DOCTOR, as he sonics, fast, pulls a hand-held microphone out of the wall - it makes the *weeeee-ooo* piping sound of internal ship's communications -

THE DOCTOR
This is Deck 15, to the Bridge, I need to talk to the Captain.

INTERCUT WITH THE BRIDGE, THE DOCTOR'S voice in the air.

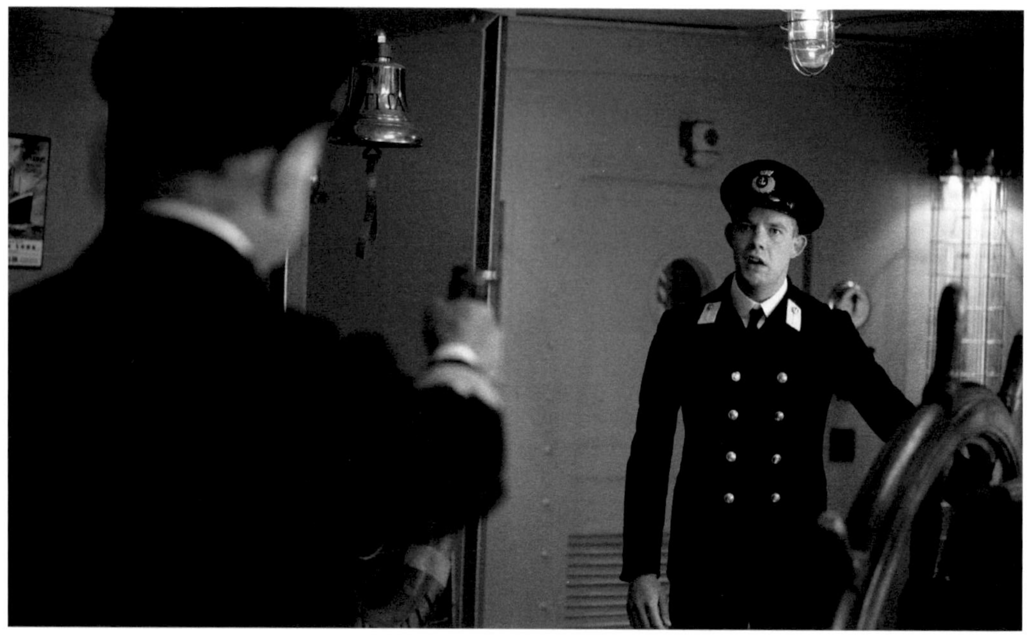

'I said step away, Midshipman.' Captain Hardaker holds Midshipman Frame at gunpoint.

CAPTAIN HARDAKER
Who is this?

THE DOCTOR
You've got a meteorite storm heading in, south zero by north 2.

CAPTAIN HARDAKER
Comms are for crewmembers only.

THE DOCTOR
Yes, but your shields are down, check your scanners - Captain, you've got meteorites coming in and no shielding!

CAPTAIN HARDAKER
You have no authorisation, you will clear the comms at once.

THE DOCTOR
Yeah, did you miss the word meteorites?!

- and the Doctor's grabbed by TWO STEWARDS, the CHIEF STEWARD facing him -

CHIEF STEWARD
If you could come with me, sir -

CUT TO:

21. INT. BRIDGE - NIGHT

MIDSHIPMAN FRAME running to a panel, panicky -

MIDSHIPMAN FRAME
- but he's right sir, the shields have been taken offline - we need to re-energise -

CAPTAIN HARDAKER
Step away from there.

MIDSHIPMAN FRAME
But we haven't got time, sir -

CAPTAIN HARDAKER
I said step away, Midshipman.

Frame only now looking around -

To see CAPTAIN HARDAKER holding a GUN at him.

CUT TO:

22. INT. BALLROOM - NIGHT

STEWARDS discreetly frogmarching THE DOCTOR across the room, towards the doors, THE CHIEF STEWARD muttering:

CHIEF STEWARD
Let's keep this nice and quiet, shall we sir?

THE DOCTOR
- listen to me, you've got meteorites heading towards this ship, and the shields are down -

CUT TO, in amongst all the dancing and fun, MORVIN & FOON, noticing what's happening to the Doctor.

CUT TO PETH, seeing the Doctor being led away...

CUT TO:

23. INT. BRIDGE - NIGHT

CAPTAIN HARDAKER holding his gun at MIDSHIPMAN FRAME.

MIDSHIPMAN FRAME
I'm sorry, sir, but I need to activate the shields.

CAPTAIN HARDAKER
I'm afraid that's not possible.

MIDSHIPMAN FRAME
But they're heading right for the ship, sir, they're gonna hit!

CUT TO:

24. EXT. FX SHOT - NIGHT

FX: *ROAAAAR!!* as five METEORITES - burning balls of fire, trailing thick smoke - race through foreground, heading for, in the distance, the TITANIC, above the EARTH.

CUT TO:

25. EXT. DECK 15 - NIGHT

POSH MAN & FRIENDS still on deck with champagne.

POSH MAN
Oh, that's rather marvellous, look!

FX: HIS POV, the METEORITES, now small balls of flame.

The GUESTS coo and clap!

CUT TO:

26. INT. BALLROOM - NIGHT

THE DOCTOR breaks free - !

- runs back into room -

- STEWARDS run in pursuit -

CUT TO PETH, watching, puzzled -

CUT TO MORVIN & FOON, watching, puzzled -

CUT TO BANNAKAFFALATTA, now noticing -

- the Doctor jumps up onto the stage -

- pushes the SINGER to one side (BAND keep playing) - the Doctor grabs the mic, goes front of stage -

The Doctor invades the stage.

THE DOCTOR
Everyone! Listen to me! This is an emergency! Get to the lifeb-

Whap! A GOLD HAND over his mouth.

A HEAVENLY HOST behind him, super strong - STEWARDS pile in, grab the Doctor, haul him off, Host staying put -

The SINGER grabs the mic, cheesy smile -

SINGER
Sorry 'bout that, folks!

And he goes back to the song -

GUESTS clap, laugh, like it's part of the entertainment -

CUT TO:

27. INT. BRIDGE - NIGHT

MIDSHIPMAN FRAME trapped, frantic.

MIDSHIPMAN FRAME
I'm sorry, sir, it's my duty -

Captain Hardaker fires!

And he runs for the computer panel -

BANG! PRAC FX, CAPTAIN HARDAKER fires -

CUT TO:

28. INT. BALLROOM - NIGHT

THE DOCTOR just being hauled out of the door by TWO STEWARDS & CHIEF STEWARD - one steward's got his hand over the Doctor's mouth, to shut him up, the Doctor pulls free for a second to yell at the nearest man -

THE DOCTOR
- look out the windows - !

- and the Doctor's gone -

The nearest man is RICKSTON SLADE. Hangs up his vone. Curious, starts to walk across to the windows...

PETH running out of the door -

MORVIN & FOON following, concerned for the Doctor -

Rickston reaches the windows. Stares out...

FX: HIS POV, THE METEORITES, closer, closer...

CUT TO:

29. INT. TITANIC RECEPTION - NIGHT

THE DOCTOR being hauled across Reception by TWO STEWARDS - CHIEF STEWARD following -

PETH runs out of the Ballroom -

PETH
Excuse me, sir, I can vouch for him -

CHIEF STEWARD
Get back to work!

MORVIN, FOON & BANNAKAFFALATTA hurry out of the Ballroom -

FOON
- no, Steward, he's with us, he's just had a bit too much to drink -

The Doctor (David Tennant) is restrained by the Steward (Claudio Laurini) and the Chief Steward (Andrew Havill).

BANNAKAFFALATTA
Trouble! Love trouble!

From another direction, MR COPPER to the CHIEF STEWARD -

MR COPPER
Something's gone wrong, sir, all the teleports have gone down -

CHIEF STEWARD
Not now!

IE, THE DOCTOR, STEWARDS, CHIEF STEWARD all being followed across Reception by PETH, MORVIN, FOON, BANNAKAFFALATTA & MR COPPER, towards a door at the far end -

CUT TO:

30. EXT. DECK 15 - NIGHT

POSH MAN & FRIENDS looking out, into space, delighted.

POSH MAN
It's simply beautiful...

FX: a BURNING STONE, in advance of the meteorite shower, zips past them, *whooosh* -

PRAC FX: *WHAP!* punches a small hole in the metal wall.

POSH MAN (CONT'D)
But... what about the shields?

CUT TO:

31. INT. BALLROOM - NIGHT

PRAC FX: small, low pane of glass in the window shatters.

RICKSTON stares down (no one else noticing, the PARTY in full swing in b/g).

On the carpet, a TINY SMOKING STONE.

Rickston worried now, goes to a HEAVENLY HOST.

RICKSTON
You, there. Doesn't this thing have external shielding?

The HOST turns to him, impassive.

The passengers on the *Titanic* are blissfully unaware of the danger they're in...

HOST
You are all going to die, sir.

CUT TO:

32. EXT. FX SHOT - NIGHT

FX: METEORITES *whooooshing* past foreground, THE TITANIC closer, closer, closer...

CUT TO:

33. EXT. DECK 15 - NIGHT

GUESTS now trying to open the closed deck door, but still being stiff-upper-lipped, POSH MAN on a comms:

POSH MAN
Excuse me, there seems to be a little bit of trouble out here, hello? Anyone?

CUT TO:

34. INT. BRIDGE - NIGHT

CAPTAIN HARDAKER operates a final control -

COMPUTER VOICE
External bulkheads closed.

And the Captain is calm, grave, though trembling, as he goes to the wheel, stands there. Captain of his ship.

FX: HIS POV, METEORITES closer, closer...

MIDSHIPMAN FRAME is on the floor. Shot in the side. But alive! Gasping, props himself up on one arm...

CUT TO:

35. INT. TITANIC RECEPTION - NIGHT

RICKSTON SLADE belts out of the Ballroom, yells -

RICKSTON
- where's the Chief Steward?!

RECEPTIONIST
He went that way, sir -

- and Rickston belts towards the far door -

CUT TO:

36. INT. SHIP CORRIDOR #1 - NIGHT

A narrow, metal, behind-the-scenes corridor, now a box of noise, as THE DOCTOR's hauled along by STEWARDS, CHIEF STEWARD following, then PETH, MORVIN & FOON, MR COPPER, then BANNAKAFFALATTA - all simultaneous, wild -

THE DOCTOR
- the shields are down, we're gonna get hit!!

CHIEF STEWARD
You will cease and desist, sir -

PETH
I can take him back to his cabin, sir -

MORVIN
We'll look after him, give him to us -

MR COPPER
- but nothing seems to be working -

BANNAKAFFALATTA
Big noise! Much shout!

- with RICKSTON SLADE bursting through the far end -

RICKSTON
Steward! Oy! *Steward!!*

CUT TO:

37. INT. BRIDGE - NIGHT

CAPTAIN HARDAKER at the wheel, facing front. Brave, ashamed. MIDSHIPMAN FRAME on the floor, in pain.

MIDSHIPMAN FRAME
…you're gonna kill us, sir…

CHIEF STEWARD
I'm dying already. Six months. And they promised me so much money. For my family.

MIDSHIPMAN FRAME
…but the passengers…

CUT TO:

38. EXT. DECK 15 - NIGHT

POSH MAN & GUESTS now hammering on the doors, hysterical, already lit by a red, fiery glow -

POSH MAN
Let us in!! *Let us in!!!*

CUT TO:

39. INT. SHIP CORRIDOR #1 - NIGHT

All bunched in a tight group now, THE DOCTOR still being held by STEWARDS, PETH, MORVIN, FOON, BANNAKAFFALATTA, MR COPPER watching as RICKSTON yells at the CHIEF STEWARD -

THE DOCTOR
Listen to him!

RICKSTON
The shields are down, I saw it with my own eyes, the *shields are down!!!*

CHIEF STEWARD
I can assure you, sir, it's just a little hysteria, caused by this gentleman here, if you'd like to return to the Ballroom…

CUT TO:

40. INT. BALLROOM - NIGHT

FX: CROWD MULTIPLICATION, the PARTY is swinging!

CUT TO the back of the room. One GLAMOROUS WOMAN calling her GLAMOROUS BOYFRIEND over, to look out of the window…

They look up… Aghast…

CU GLAMOROUS COUPLE, red light playing over them…

CUT TO:

41. INT. BRIDGE - NIGHT

CU CAPTAIN HARDAKER. In firelight. So sad.

```
            CAPTAIN HARDAKER
      Forgive me.

   And he closes his eyes.

                                    CUT TO:

   42. EXT. FX SHOT - NIGHT

   FX: WHAAAAAAM!!! WIDE SHOT TITANIC
   as a MASSIVE BURNING METEORITE
   SLAMS INTO THE SHIP!
```

Well, I've solved the coincidence of the Doctor knowing all the survivors, by making him to blame for all the survivors being together at the time of the accident. It's a lot of effort and page count to get them all together in that corridor, but it'll save time later. On the whole, I think it works by being really obvious. Also, I spent a long time thinking that the meteorites wouldn't be burning. They'd be rocks. They'd only burn on entering the atmosphere. But they *need* to be burning, because it looks better, so I gave Frame and the Captain a bit of dialogue saying they were composed of 'flammable nitrofine rock'... and then cut it, because that's dull and I don't care. They're gonna burn!

WHAAAAAM!!! The *Titanic* is hit!

FROM: RUSSELL T DAVIES TO: BENJAMIN COOK
SATURDAY 19 MAY 2007 00:48:06 GMT

RE: CHARLIE HUNNAM'S ARSE

I'm back in Manchester. I doubt I'll be able to work on the script this weekend, because I have to write up my notes on those seven bloody scripts – which are now nine – and watch an edit of 3.12, and... and... oh it's absurd! At least that'll leave next week free to write all the time.

A few notes about that latest draft: in the rush towards the meteorites, I completely forgot to write any more Mr Maxitane. I remembered him in the car on the way up. Whoops! But I love Midshipman Frame. I can't decide if he should live or die, though he'll certainly survive a lot longer. The Captain, too, is quite good and grave – well, again, he's far from subtle, but this isn't about character portraits; it's all about one Big Bloody Smash. It's strong, bold and punchy on Christmas Day. Very blockbuster. Also, in the car, I wondered if the Host should start each speech with 'Information'...? 'Information: you are on board the *Titanic*.' 'Information: you are all going to die.' Nice verbal tic. It makes them 'imitatable'. Kids in the playground and all that. And it helps to keep explaining what they are – information points – because their function isn't really clear. I might try it.

FROM: RUSSELL T DAVIES TO: BENJAMIN COOK
MONDAY 21 MAY 2007 23:40:21 GMT

RE: CHARLIE HUNNAM'S ARSE

Some nights, I'm just wasting my time. I've spent hours sitting here (I'm back in Cardiff now), making poxy little changes to 4.X, but not getting anything more written. For instance, I took out the Doctor showing his psychic paper to the Host, because I'm not sure that psychic paper works on robots. I didn't have a day to lose, but I've lost it. Bollocks. I don't have the energy to write the rest of the meteorites-hitting stuff. I'm scared by the gaping holes, the blank paper, to come.

FROM: RUSSELL T DAVIES TO: BENJAMIN COOK
TUESDAY 22 MAY 2007 19:16:24 GMT

RE: CHARLIE HUNNAM'S ARSE

Kylie Minogue just phoned me!!!

FROM: BENJAMIN COOK TO: RUSSELL T DAVIES
TUESDAY 22 MAY 2007 19:20:40 GMT

RE: CHARLIE HUNNAM'S ARSE

I hope you told her you were busy.

She should go through your agent like everyone else.

FROM: RUSSELL T DAVIES TO: BENJAMIN COOK
TUESDAY 22 MAY 2007 19:25:00 GMT

RE: CHARLIE HUNNAM'S ARSE

I told her we were going for Dannii.[6]

No, I didn't recognise the number, so I didn't answer. *D'oh!* But that means she's on my answerphone, which is better. And now I'm on hers. She wants to chat about Peth – actor-y stuff, I think. She's talking about getting a drama coach. My God, this is really, *really* real! (I still won't believe it until she's in Upper Boat.)[7]

FROM: RUSSELL T DAVIES TO: BENJAMIN COOK
WEDNESDAY 23 MAY 2007 23:47:18 GMT

RE: CHARLIE HUNNAM'S ARSE

Lordy God. No script, again. I spent all day sorting out other people's scripts. I woke up, saw the sunshine, and refused to go into the BBC, so I set up shop outside the Starbucks in Cardiff Bay – and all the Series Four writers came to me, one by one. Me, Julie and Phil, sitting outside, like Starbucks shareholders. It was brilliant. But I spent a total of *nine hours* talking. Talking, talking, talking. Nine bloody hours. It's broken the back of a lot of stories, so it'll pay off. Now, finally, I can get back to work. I haven't written anything new since Friday. Julie said, 'You keep forgetting, it's like this every year.'

Yes, I forget.

6 Dannii Minogue, Kylie's sister.

7 Upper Boat is the Cardiff-based studio complex where *Doctor Who*, *Torchwood*, and *The Sarah Jane Adventures* are filmed. Standing sets such as the TARDIS control room, the Torchwood Hub, and Sarah Jane's attic are stored here.

FROM: RUSSELL T DAVIES TO: BENJAMIN COOK
FRIDAY 25 MAY 2007 02:22:21 GMT

RE: CHARLIE HUNNAM'S ARSE

More script. Nice stuff. I think. It's hard to negotiate eight people in one scene. I can't wait to start killing off the bastards. (I wonder, who do you think is going to die?)

```
43. INT. BALLROOM - NIGHT

FX: WIDE SHOT BALLROOM as a BURNING
METEORITE the size of a house
slams through the entire wall, and
through the room, ploughing through
and obliterating the stage - PEOPLE
and fragments of WALL and GLASS
flying through the air -

FX: WIDE SHOT OF PEOPLE to one
side, not actually hit, but
screaming as a WALL OF FIRE rushes
over them -

                            CUT TO:

44. EXT. FX SHOT

FX: THE METEORITE smashing through
the far side of the TITANIC,
leaving a complete hole through the
centre -

                            CUT TO:
```

Mayhem below deck as the 'meteorites' smash through the ship.

45. INT. SHIP CORRIDOR #1 - NIGHT

THE DOCTOR, CHIEF STEWARD, STEWARDS, PETH, MORVIN & FOON, MR COPPER, RICKSTON SLADE, BANNAKAFFALATTA thrown around as the corridor slams about, lights flicker on and off -

PRAC EXPLOSIONS, WALL PANELS bursting open - SPARKS showering down from the light-fittings -

STEAM jetting out of broken pipes -

- the Doctor grabbing Peth, to shield her -

Madness, chaos, CAMERA SHAKE -

CUT TO:

46. INT. BALLROOM - NIGHT

FX: THE UPPER BALCONIES, tilting, CAMERA SHAKE - STUNT as a HANDSOME MAN falls off the balcony, plunges down -

FX: the GLAMOROUS MAN & WOMAN - to the side of where the meteorite entered - running away, but the GLASS WINDOW behind them SHATTERS, PRAC WIND blasting through, and they fly out backwards, screaming, into the blackness of SPACE -

CUT TO CU GUESTS, holding onto tables, walls, anything, as PRAC WIND blasts through - a MAN, screaming, lets go -

FX: THE MAN tumbles through the SHATTERED WINDOW into SPACE -

CUT TO:

47. INT. HOST CONTAINMENT CELLS - NIGHT

Whole room shaking, the ENGINEER thrown to the floor -

PRAC FX: FIRE and STEAM belching out -

PRAC FX: METAL PIPES falling down from the roof -

- but *sch-chunk!* - the doors on a row of Host Containment Cells open, all at once, like clockwork, THE HEAVENLY HOST standing inside.

CU HOST as it jerks awake!

CUT TO:

48. EXT. FX SHOT - NIGHT

FX: two SMALLER METEORITES punch all the way though, *one!* then quickly, *two!* - the mighty ship rocking -

CUT TO:

49. INT. TITANIC RECEPTION - NIGHT

LIGHTS flickering on and off, chaos, GUESTS & STAFF thrown everywhere as the whole room pitches about -

HIGH SHOT of RECEPTIONIST looking up, screaming -

PRAC FX: *WHAM!* - a huge GIRDER slams down on top of her -

CUT TO:

50. INT. SHIP CORRIDOR #1 - NIGHT

ALL cowering, being thrown about, as -

PRAC FX: RUBBLE hails down on them -

PRAC FX: FIRE ruptures out of the broken walls -

CUT TO:

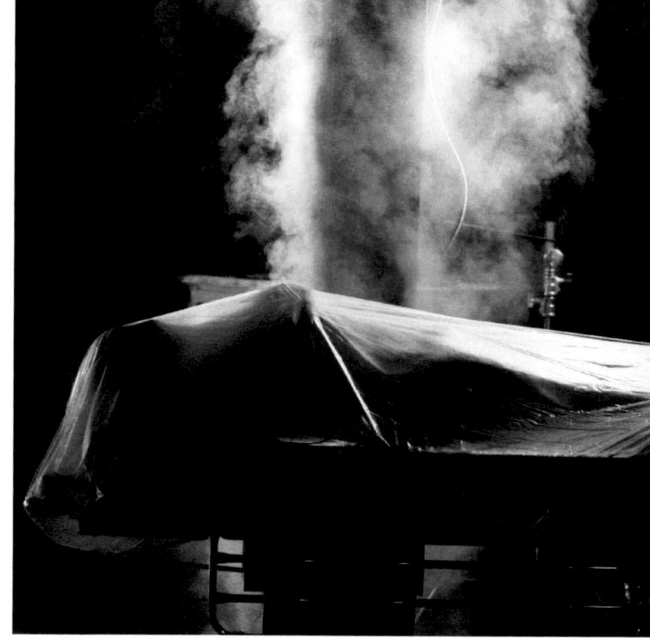

The sleeping Host begin to wake...

51. INT. HOST CONTAINMENT CELLS - NIGHT

PRAC FIRE & STEAM continuing, but -

TEN HEAVENLY HOST step out of their cells, calm, impassive, regimented, unaffected by the chaos -

CUT TO:

52. INT. SHIP CORRIDOR #1 - NIGHT

PRAC FX: STEAM, belches of FIRE, but…

The shaking subsides, slowly.

THE DOCTOR, holding PETH, lifts his head. CHIEF STEWARD, STEWARD, MR COPPER, RICKSTON SLADE, MORVIN & FOON, BANNAKAFFALATTA, all on the floor, covered in dust and grease and bits of rubble… but alive. Foon is screaming.

THE DOCTOR
Hush, hush, hush, shut up! Sorry! But just - just shhhh….

Silence. Pause. All looking round. Then:

THE DOCTOR (CONT'D)
It's stopping…

CUT TO:

53. EXT. FX SHOT - NIGHT

FX: LONG HERO FX SHOT, the TITANIC now with three holes along its length, the space all around the ship glittering with debris. It maintains its position, stays upright, groaning, like an injured beast.

But then all the lights flicker and go off, one by one, like the ship is dying.

CUT TO:

54. INT. SHIP CORRIDOR #1 - NIGHT

(NB, lights off throughout the ship now, but NOT total darkness, just nicely dark!) THE DOCTOR brushing himself down, standing, others moaning, clearing debris.

THE DOCTOR
You all right?

PETH
…yeah. Think so, yeah.

THE DOCTOR
Bad name for a ship. Either that, or it's this suit.

And the Doctor goes to the STEWARD, who's lying flat out, a low babble, recovery, all coming round; PETH going to MR COPPER, clearing rubble off him, he's saying 'Oh dear, bit unfortunate…', MORVIN going to FOON, 'Are you all right, sweetheart?' and she's crying, hugs him, RICKSTON dazed, 'My vone, where's my vone?', BANNAKAFFALATTA grunting 'Not good, not good', with the CHIEF STEWARD standing, dazed.

The Doctor clears metal pipes off the Steward, checks his pulse. Looks across at the Chief Steward. No, he's dead.

Which triggers the Chief Steward into action. (And during this, the Doctor hops over rubble, going from passenger to passenger, checking them out, 'You all right?')

CHIEF STEWARD
Ladies and gentleman, and Bannakaffalatta… I must apologise. On behalf of White Light. Um. We seem to have had a small collision -

Which provokes a sudden hysteria - all improvising round:

MORVIN
What d'you mean small?

BANNAKAFFALATTA
Very bad! Very bad! Bannakaffalatta cross!

FOON
We could've been killed!

RICKSTON
(standing)
D'you know how much I paid for this?!

Over this:

CHIEF STEWARD
If I could have silence.
Ladies, gentlemen, if I could have silence…
(then bellows:)
Qui-et!!!

Which works, they shut up.

In b/g, during the Chief Steward's speech below, the Doctor nips over to Peth & Mr Copper, crouches beside them –

CHIEF STEWARD (CONT'D)
Thank you. I'm sure the White Light Company will be able to reimburse you for any inconvenience. But first, I would point out that we're very much alive, though I would suggest that each and every one of you is given the once-over by the ship's medic. Free of charge. If you could all stay here, while I ascertain the exact nature of the situation –

PETH
It's his arm…

MR COPPER
Nothing to worry about, just a scratch…

THE DOCTOR
Let me see…

And the Chief Steward turns to the door – *shunks!* the handle, releasing the seal –

The Doctor tending to Mr Copper, only just seeing this, yells –

THE DOCTOR (CONT'D)
Don't open it – !!!

FX: THE DOOR – pushed away from the Chief Steward – is ripped off its hinges, door & Chief Steward are *schwupped!* through the air, through a ragged, metal hole beyond, where more corridor should have been, now leading into OPEN SPACE –

PRAC WIND blasts through the corridor – ferocious! –

COMMS PANEL flashing: *VACUUM BREACH.*

PETH, MR COPPER, MORVIN & FOON, BANNAKAFFALATTA holding on for dear life, clinging to anything –

The Doctor, blasted by wind, flings himself against a COMMS PANEL, sonics like mad –

FX: Rickston, as the only one standing, is holding onto a metal pipe and is PULLED HORIZONTAL – yelling – !

The Doctor sonics, frantic – COMMS PANEL blips, reads *OXYGEN FIELD RESTORED.*

FX: *bwip!* over the ragged hole, the ripple of a FORCEFIELD.

The wind stops. Rickston thumps to the floor.

THE DOCTOR (CONT'D)
Everyone all right? Peth? Morvin? Foon? Mr Copper? Bannakaffalatta?

One by one, a grudging 'Yes' from all.

THE DOCTOR (CONT'D)
You, what's your name?

RICKSTON
Rickston Slade.

THE DOCTOR
You all right?

RICKSTON
No thanks to that idiot.

PETH
The steward just died!

RICKSTON
Then he's a dead idiot!

THE DOCTOR
All right, calm down, Rickston, button it – just stay still, all of you, hold on…

Whirrs the panel, a GRAPHIC of the TITANIC comes up, covered with red hazard signs, everywhere.

THE DOCTOR (CONT'D)
Um. Little bit of damage. Just a bit. Oh, blimey.

The Doctor and 'Peth' are thrown together as disaster strikes the *Titanic*.

Minimal oxygen… Just, don't move…

He makes his way down the corridor, towards the hole. Peth follows him (others recovering in b/g).

They squat together at the ragged-metal edge.

FX: REVERSE, SPACE BEYOND full of tumbling fragments of metal and little floating BODIES.

Hushed:

PETH
…what happened…? How come the shields were down?

THE DOCTOR
I don't think it was an accident.

PETH
(upset)
But… how many dead?

THE DOCTOR
We're alive. Just focus on that. Peth, look at me. We're alive. And I will get you out of here. I promise. Look at me. I promise.

And she gives a small smile.

THE DOCTOR (CONT'D)
Yeah?

PETH
Yeah.

THE DOCTOR
Good. Now then. If we can get to that reception area, I've got a spaceship, tucked away, we can all get on board and… Oh.

FX: HIS POV, far-off, the TARDIS in space, gently tumbling.

PETH
What is it, what's wrong?

THE DOCTOR
That's my ship, over there.

PETH
Where?

THE DOCTOR
There, that box, that little blue box.

PETH
That's a spaceship?

THE DOCTOR
Oy, don't knock it.

PETH
Bit small.

THE DOCTOR
Bit distant.

PETH
Haven't you got a remote control?

THE DOCTOR
That would be a really good idea. One of these days.

PETH
But if you can manipulate the oxygen field, can't you just loop it out? Sort of, lasso the box back in?

THE DOCTOR
That's brilliant. Oh, that's brilliant! You're good, you are!

PETH
Try my best!

THE DOCTOR
Trouble is, when it's set adrift, it's programmed to lock onto the nearest centre of gravity. And that would be… the Earth.

FX: THEIR POV, the TARDIS begins to gently fall…

CUT TO:

55. EXT. FX SHOT - NIGHT

FX: the TARDIS, with the WRECKED TITANIC in b/g, tumbles through frame, then falls fast, accelerating, towards the EARTH, becomes a glowing red dot as it disappears below.

CUT TO:

56. INT. SHIP CORRIDOR #1 - NIGHT

THE DOCTOR & PETH in the ragged end-of-corridor hole.

PETH
Maybe not then.

THE DOCTOR
Maybe not.

CUT TO:

57. INT. HOST CONTAINMENT CELLS - NIGHT

FX PRAC FLAMES still burning, SMOKE & STEAM, but calmer.

The grimy ENGINEER shoves rubble off his chest, sits up. But he's trapped under a GIRDER. Heaves. Can't move.

ENGINEER
Don't just stand there, help me!

THE TEN HEAVENLY HOST - untouched by dirt - are simply standing, unmoving, a distance away. Observing him.

ENGINEER (CONT'D)
I said, help me, come on! Host! That is an order! I can't move, for Vot's sake, just lift this thing off me.

HOST
Information: we will help you.

ENGINEER
Well then, hurry up!

HOST
Information: we will help you die.

ENGINEER
(scared)
…what's that supposed to mean?

Midshipman Frame. In his pants. As imagined by Russell T Davies.

```
                    HOST
    Information: all passengers
    must be terminated.

It reaches up, unclips its HALO;
it simply lifts free of the thin
struts supporting it, PRAC LIGHT
halo still glowing

                  ENGINEER
                 (panicking)
    What are you doing? I'm
    ordering you, stop it! Stop
    it, right now!

The Host aims the Halo like a
frisbee - throws -

FX?: HALO whizzes towards CAMERA -

CUT TO REVERSE, FAST ZOOM IN to the
Engineer's face, like a HALO POV,
as he screams his last -
```

FROM: BENJAMIN COOK TO: RUSSELL T DAVIES
FRIDAY 25 MAY 2007 15:26:57 GMT

RE: CHARLIE HUNNAM'S ARSE

You ask who I think is going to die. You've said that Kylie should, but I'm not convinced you'll go through with it. I reckon Rickston will die, because he's young and ruthless. But then maybe that's what you want us to think. Mr Copper is too sweet to snuff it. But the same could be said of Bannakaffalatta, and I'm sure you'll relish giving the conker a *horrible* death. And Morvin and Foon are fat, so they've no chance. Midshipman Frame might die, too. Probably from hypothermia after he accidentally loses all his clothes.

My favourite stage direction so far is: 'STUNT as a HANDSOME MAN falls off the balcony, plunges down.' You introduce and kill off a man in the very same line, but make him handsome – what, to rub it in? Poor Handsome.

FROM: RUSSELL T DAVIES TO: BENJAMIN COOK
FRIDAY 25 MAY 2007 17:18:24 GMT

RE: CHARLIE HUNNAM'S ARSE

Yes, I'll try to take off the Midshipman's clothes. Well, maybe his jacket. Oh God, I think I fancy Midshipman Frame! That's weird, isn't it? It's like fancying a cartoon character – which is entirely possible. Oh, it's all sex. I can never say that enough. Do I only write in handsome men because I think, I honestly think, that we'll cast someone gorgeous, he'll fancy me like mad, and maybe even fall madly in love with me? This has never happened. I'm still thinking of Russell Tovey for Frame, because a) he's brilliant (one of the best young actors in the country), b) he's strangely sexy, and c) he's gay, and therefore d) the above plan will finally happen.

In other news, Dennis Hopper *still* wants to be in it. He's offered to clear three weeks for us. But the only character he could play is Mr Copper, which is hardly a big enough part for him. Oh! Unless he could do a cameo as the Captain? Madness. And Kylie is now leaving me texts: 'Sorry I haven't phoned back. I'm in Cannes and it's crazy.' This is surreal.

And I am thinking about your how-to-make-an-audience-care question…

FROM: RUSSELL T DAVIES TO: BENJAMIN COOK
SATURDAY 26 MAY 2007 03:12:39 GMT

RE: CHARLIE HUNNAM'S ARSE

Just under four pages today. That's poor. It really is a

Captain Hardaker lies dead in the wreckage on the Bridge.

challenge to marshal this many characters in a group, within scenes…

57. INT. SHIP CORRIDOR #1 - NIGHT[8]

THE DOCTOR on the COMMS (in b/g, still recovering, PETH and BANAKAFFALATTA helping MR COPPER, MORVIN & FOON, RICKSTON searching for his vone).

THE DOCTOR
Deck 22 to the Bridge, repeat, Deck 22 to the Bridge, is there anyone there?

SCENE CONTINUES, INTERCUT WITH SC.58 & 60:

8 The original Scene 44 – an FX shot of a 'meteorite' smashing into the *Titanic* – has been cut, to save on expense, shifting all subsequent scene numbers, so the Host killing the Engineer is now Scene 56, followed by this, Scene 57, in Ship Corridor #1.

58. INT. BRIDGE - NIGHT

Shattered. Girders, rubble, computer panels smashed. PRAC FLAMES here and there. THE DOCTOR OOV on COMMS, as…

MIDSHIPMAN FRAME, in great pain, clears debris off himself, hauls himself over to the COMMS.

MIDSHIPMAN FRAME
…this is the Bridge.

THE DOCTOR
Hello sailor! What's the situation up there?

MIDSHIPMAN FRAME
…we've got oxygen…

FX: FRAME'S POV of the FRONT WINDOWS, now shattered, broken glass, but with a *bwip!* ripple of FORCEFIELD outside.

MIDSHIPMAN FRAME (CONT'D)
...but the Captain... he's dead.

Looking across: CAPTAIN HARDAKER buried by rubble. Panicky:

MIDSHIPMAN FRAME (CONT'D)
He did it, oh my Vot, he did it, he took off the shields, there was nothing I could do, I tried, I did try -

THE DOCTOR
All right, just keep calm, what's your name?

MIDSHIPMAN FRAME
- he knew, he magnetised the hull, and I tried to stop him -

THE DOCTOR
- listen to my voice, listen to me - Officer! Tell me your name!

MIDSHIPMAN FRAME
(recovering)
Midshipman Frame.

THE DOCTOR
First name?

MIDSHIPMAN FRAME
Bosworth.

THE DOCTOR
Nice to meet you, Bosworth -

Rickston interrupting, having found -

RICKSTON
My vone's not working!

THE DOCTOR
Yeah, maybe later -

RICKSTON
But I paid a fortune for this thing, and it's not working!

THE DOCTOR
Not exactly top of the list!
(back on comms)
Bosworth, tell me, what's the state of the engines?

MIDSHIPMAN FRAME
They're um... Hold on...

He has to pull himself to another panel, groans with pain -

THE DOCTOR
Are you injured?

MIDSHIPMAN FRAME
I'm all right. They're...
(consults readout)
Ohh, Vot. They're cycling down. Power's gone.

THE DOCTOR
And those are Firesprite Engines, yes? Antimatter core?

MIDSHIPMAN FRAME
Yeah.

THE DOCTOR
And the moment they're gone, we lose orbit?

MIDSHIPMAN FRAME
(realises)
The planet...

THE DOCTOR
Oh yes. If we hit the planet, the antimatter core explodes. And wipes out life on Earth.

CUT TO:

An injured Frame surveys the damage.

59. EXT. FX SHOT - NIGHT

FX: the stricken TITANIC groaning, with THE EARTH below.

CUT TO:

60. INT. BRIDGE - NIGHT

INTERCUT WITH SC.57, SHIP CORRIDOR #1.

MIDSHIPMAN FRAME scrabbling with controls.

MIDSHIPMAN FRAME
But… we've got an automatic SOS, they'll be sending rescue ships, they can stabilise the Titanic, we'll be fine.

THE DOCTOR
Wait a minute… Rickston, did you say your vone's not working?

RICKSTON
Oh, now you're interested!

THE DOCTOR
Give it to me. Give it!
(inspects it)
But this is a Solar Plus Vone. It should work anywhere.

RICKSTON
That's what I was saying!

THE DOCTOR
Bosworth. There's no signal. Someone's transmitting a blanketing field, nothing's getting out, not even the SOS. No one's coming, no rescue ships. We're on our own.

Everyone's listening to this; FOON starts to cry.

FOON
We're going to die.

MR COPPER
Are you saying someone's done this on purpose?

BANNAKAFFALATTA
Bad people! Bad!

PETH
But why? We're just a cruise ship!

THE DOCTOR
Okay, okay, just hush! First thing's first. One, we're gonna climb through this ship. Two, we're gonna reach the Bridge. Three, we're gonna save the Titanic. And coming in at a very low four, why? Right then! Follow me -

He starts heading off, back the way they first came -

RICKSTON
Hold on, who put you in charge? Who the hell are you, anyway?

THE DOCTOR
I'm the Doctor. I'm a Time Lord. I'm from the planet Gallifrey in the constellation of Kasterborous, I'm nine hundred-and-three years old, and I'm the man who's going to save your lives and the lives of all six billion people on the planet below. Got a problem with that?

RICKSTON
…no.

THE DOCTOR
In that case… Allons-y!

I know in rough blocks what comes next: the Shattered Room, where people can pause and have a chat (and make this episode affordable); then the Canyon, where there are Terrible Deaths and a Host Attack; then up to the Bridge, while the Doctor goes to Host Containment; then the plummet down towards Earth, and the ending.

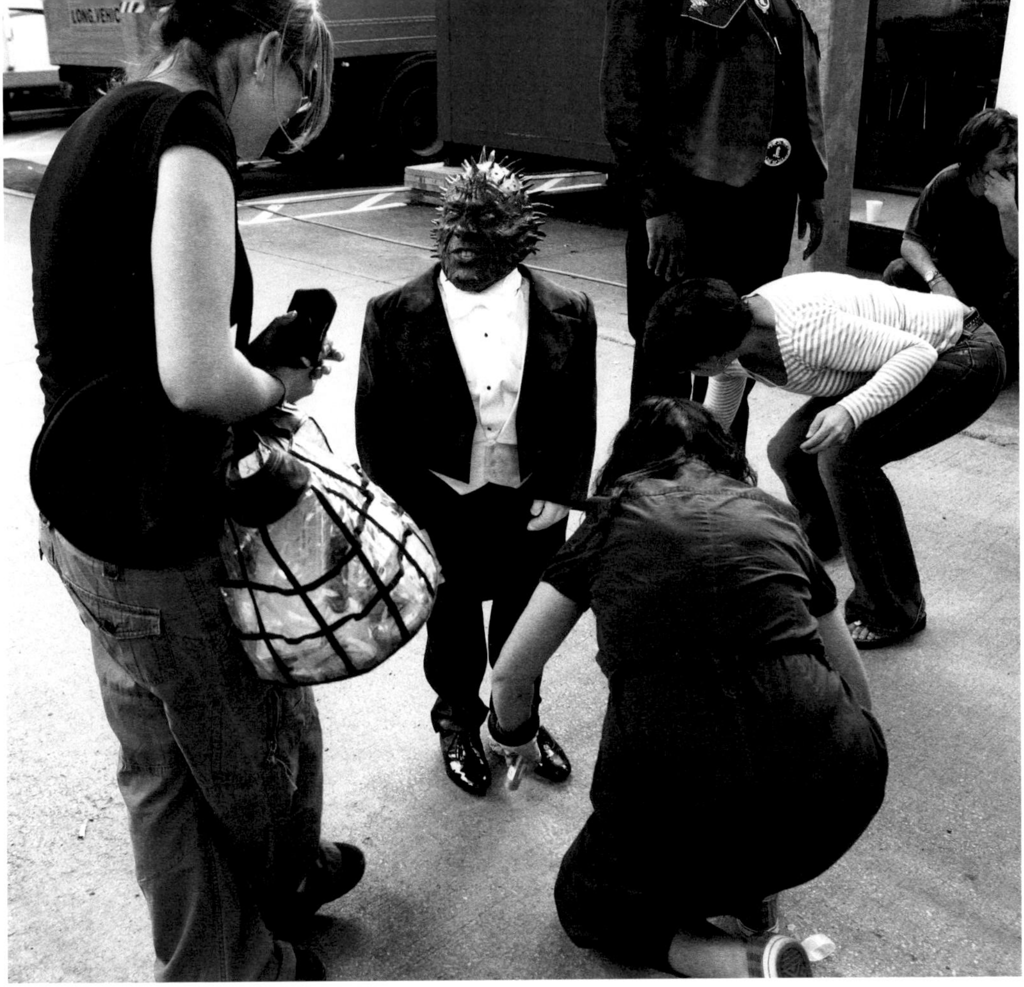

Jimmy Vee as Bannakaffalatta gets the onceover from the Make-Up and Costume Departments before heading on set.

Now, though, I start to worry that it's too long, that it'll end up at a hundred pages. It should be 80 pages for 60 minutes. And the expense is beginning to freak me out. Maybe I could make it cheaper by having Midshipman Frame tie a rope out of all his clothes, and haul up the survivors. Yes, that'll do.

It *feels* all right, though. Worry, fear, deadline, late, budget, all of that, but I've felt much worse at this midway stage. I might keep moaning about the disaster movie format, but I can use it to pull myself along. I think, in the end, it helps. It's a funny old format. It doesn't exactly make room for subtext, which is fine, it's Christmas Day entertainment –

But then, the other night, I saw a repeat of that *Longford*, that Channel 4 drama about the Moors Murders, and it did me no good at all. I sunk into a proper old gloom. I didn't even tell you about it, because it was foul. Peter Morgan is such a fine writer, damn him. All writers hate other writers. It *is* a competition. His *Longford* script was so fine and subtle, so deceptively simple, heartbreaking and true, and I was so powerfully jealous. I thought, I'm sitting here typing 'INT. SPACESHIP'! What am I doing with my career?! The answer is, having a wonderful time, with absolute freedom, I know, I know. All the same, looking at *Longford*, the real tick and beat and pulse that goes on between people, the sheer epic quality of ordinary life, even the lives of Lords and murderers, made me ache.

I'm not knocking *Doctor Who* here, or my love of it. This show *should* be different. But I do wonder – to be sort of snotty about it, I suppose – whether I'm coarsening myself; when I go back to regular drama, it'll be like starting again from scratch. That's why I turned down the opportunity to meet George Lucas the other day. The thought of more years typing 'INT. SPACESHIP' and playing with other people's toys… I mean, no matter how much I love *Doctor Who*, it's not *mine*. I didn't create this show.

Ah well. Lucas might not have liked me anyway. And I can always tell people that I turned him down.

POLICE PUBLIC CALL BOX
POLICE PUBLIC CALL BOX

CHAPTER FIVE

LIVE AND LET DIE

In which Buckingham Palace is destroyed, the Controller of BBC One puts his foot in it, and *Doctor Who*'s long-term future is assured

FROM: BENJAMIN COOK TO: RUSSELL T DAVIES
SATURDAY 26 MAY 2007 21:11:52 GMT

RE: CHARLIE HUNNAM'S ARSE

So. You know in rough blocks what comes next. But do you often change your mind as you write? About big things? Literally, midway through a script? Like whether or not to kill off a character? Originally, in *New Earth*, the Face of Boe bit the dust, but got a reprieve in later drafts.[1] Even JK Rowling, who's had the final *Harry Potter* book (I can't wait!) planned for years now, has said that she's decided to save one key character from certain death, but kill off two others that she'd planned to keep alive…[2]

1 The Face of Boe, a gigantic face in a case, débuted in *Doctor Who* 1.2. Russell intended the Face to die in 2.1, in a hospital on New Earth, after revealing his greatest secret – 'You are not alone' – to the Doctor, but this was removed from later drafts. Instead, the Face died – and imparted his words of wisdom – in 3.3.

2 *Harry Potter and the Deathly Hallows*, released on 21 July 2007, is the final book in Rowling's heptalogy of *Harry Potter* novels.

FROM: RUSSELL T DAVIES TO: BENJAMIN COOK
SATURDAY 26 MAY 2007 22:42:12 GMT

RE: CHARLIE HUNNAM'S ARSE

Old Boe's demise shifted from *New Earth* because that was in the draft in which *everyone* dies, even the patients, and it was miserable as hell for an Episode 1. At the same time, we'd just been commissioned for Series Three, and I realised how huge that 'You are not alone' could be if held back till *Gridlock*. But I don't often change really big things like that as I write. I'd say things *develop*, rather than change…

Holly in *Bob & Rose* was written, in her first scenes, as just The Gay Man's Best Friend. She was the comedy support, nothing more. During Episode 1, Holly went on that date with Bob and the schoolteacher, as best friend and fag hag, and all the way through, literally as I was typing, I was thinking, this character's dull – and how do I make this story last six episodes? And then…

Geoffrey Palmer as Hardaker, with director James Strong on set.

you know how annoyed I get when writers bang on about characters having lives of their own? Well, this is the closest I can ever remember to feeling like that, because Bob, Holly and the teacher were out on that date, and Holly found herself alone with the teacher, and then all of a sudden… she was lying. She was saying things that would split up Bob and the teacher. I can remember that like an explosion in my head – it was as though she started lying in front of me. (I love writing liars. Everyone lies.) Suddenly, on the spot, the show had three lead characters – and, more importantly, I'd enough story for six episodes.

I know exactly who lives and who dies in 4.X, except for Midshipman Frame, although I keep playing with it in my head – because that's the same game that the audience will be playing. (Your list of survivors was interesting, because I've fooled you a *little* bit, which is good for this format.) Actually, Frame is the most interesting one. I love him for not telling the Doctor that he's injured (see, lying again), because that's so selfless and professional – so I swing wildly between thinking, he's so good, he should survive, he's so good, he should die. Poor soul. In fact, I think the character that I've most enjoyed writing in 4.X is the Captain – again, because he's lying. That gives him weight. When he describes the *Titanic* as 'an old ship, full of aches and pains', he's talking about himself, really.

FROM: BENJAMIN COOK TO: RUSSELL T DAVIES
SUNDAY 27 MAY 2007 01:09:47 GMT

RE: CHARLIE HUNNAM'S ARSE

>>I swing wildly between thinking, he's so good, he should survive, he's so good, he should die.<<

And what decides? Well, you do. Obviously. But what's stopping you deciding right now? Or will it come down to how you're feeling on the day? The mood that you're in when you sit down to write his final scene? Or whether there's room in the story for another death? Or are you putting off making a decision because you've become attached? Do you – whisper the word – *care* about La Frame?

FROM: RUSSELL T DAVIES TO: BENJAMIN COOK
SUNDAY 27 MAY 2007 11:25:49 GMT

RE: CHARLIE HUNNAM'S ARSE

Oh, I'm loving La Frame, but the script will decide – the tone of it, the feel of it, the shape of it. Actually, to be blunt, I think Christmas Day will be the eventual decider. Frame's death would be towards the end of the Special, and that would be such a downer. Then again, I *love* writing a good death.

>>Do you – whisper the word – *care* about La Frame?<<

How do you make an audience care about your characters? I've been struggling with that question. 4.X is full of what Hollywood calls 'pat the dog scenes' (an old phrase meaning that if a character pats a dog, that character must be good), and that's because of the disaster movie set-up – or maybe the speed with which you have to introduce any supporting character in *Doctor Who*, given that they're components of a much bigger, much odder format. Frame is young and dutiful, so we like him; Morvin and Foon have won their tickets because they like TV, so we like them; Peth is shining with sheer 'I love the Doctor', so we like her. We like waitresses anyway, because we empathise towards the working classes. That's a whole discussion in itself. In the end, though, I think what you're talking about is *story*, not character. You care about a character *because they're in the story*. You've chosen this story, you've switched on this programme, you've picked up this book, you've paid to see this film, and that's where the caring comes from. Your choice. Your investment. From thereon in, it's up to the story. (That's where it can go wrong: if the story doesn't work, the characters aren't served.) It goes way beyond pat-the-dog moments; it's the space that characters occupy in the story, the role that they fulfil, the *reason* that they're on screen that attracts you...

How can I explain this better? It's pictorial. This is a visual medium, but visuals don't have to mean landscapes, long lenses, stunts, hundreds of extras; it's the ordinary pictures, the sheer existence of people on screen, the fact that I've chosen to put them there and that you've chosen to watch. I realised this on *The Second Coming*, when we spent a million drafts on Steve and Judith's backstory – the fact that they'd always known each other, always sort of fancied each other, she'd got married and divorced, and these two inarticulate idiots were still dancing around each other.[3] An awful lot of thought and script meetings went into that, all of it compressed into their conversation out on the pavement at the beginning, before their first kiss and Steve's awakening as the Son of God. All of that work was to establish, simply and fundamentally, an attraction between them. When I watched it back – well, after I'd watched it many times – I realised the most crucial thing: none of that was necessary. The fact that Lesley Sharp and Christopher Eccleston were on screen, at the same time, together – especially late at night, outside a city-centre club – did all the work. You could lose the sound and still realise what was happening between those two. Put a man and a woman of roughly the same age on screen and you're telling a story. That's a love story. (Storytelling is very heterosexual in that sense. But that's why gay storytelling is exciting, because the images are still new.) The *choice* to put those two characters together on screen, in a story, is the crucial thing. Everything else is just detail. And luck. That's what makes you care. The archetypes. They run deep.

Back to basics: the most important thing is honesty. That's where Tony from *Skins* – your favourite – is interesting, because he's undoubtedly meant to be a Stuart-from-*Queer-as-Folk*, but he doesn't connect with us so easily, because there's barely any recognition. Tony isn't believable. (Perhaps the kids *do* like Tony, but maybe that's wish-fulfilment; they want to be like him, therefore they admire him. But you have to be younger, I think, for that to work. Plus, he did look good in his pants – and there we're back to pictures again!) You can see what they were trying to do on *Skins*, because the plan for Series One, as we now know, was to bring down Tony, to make him suffer, make him realise that he's wrong, and therefore ascend to sympathy. They almost got there by the end, but only by having Tony pat a dog – more specifically, hit a bus! (They had to mow him down in the finale in order to make us care!) I love the fact that everyone expected Stuart to follow that path. So many people wanted him to be brought down. Or run over. Except I never did that. He survived anything thrown at him.

I've gone from dogs, to waitresses, to pavements, to Tony in his pants, all to answer your caring question, when, if I were giving advice to you about your very first script, I'd just say: don't think about it. Ever. Don't sit there thinking, will anyone care about my characters? Put your energy into making the characters real, and honest, and true, and interesting, and three-dimensional – and the caring should follow. Like a dog.

3 Video-shop worker Steve Baxter (played by Christopher Eccleston) and schoolteacher Judith Roach (Lesley Sharp).

FROM: BENJAMIN COOK TO: RUSSELL T DAVIES
SUNDAY 27 MAY 2007 18:23:35 GMT

RE: CHARLIE HUNNAM'S ARSE

>>Put a man and a woman of roughly the same age on screen and you're telling a story. That's a love story.<<

This, I suppose, is why we warm to the idea of the Doctor and Rose in love. But that's pictorial, really. That's all about images. It's because they look right together. If we thought about it reasonably, we'd realise that he's nine hundred-odd years old and she's barely out of her teens, and then it's just *wrong!*

FROM: RUSSELL T DAVIES TO: BENJAMIN COOK
SUNDAY 27 MAY 2007 19:01:58 GMT

RE: CHARLIE HUNNAM'S ARSE

That's so true. How many 'love' lines are there between the Doctor and Rose? About six! And yet it's talked about as the central spine of the series. Well, that's a bit disingenuous, because that's what I wanted, but we didn't really have to try. Man, woman, on screen = love story. Very little work necessary.

I hooked onto that visual thing with the transmission of *The Second Coming*, because ITV was braced for an absolute storm of protest… which never really came. Lots of mad phone calls, a couple of death threats, but all very normal. Quite apart from the theory that maybe it was crap and no one was bothered (that doesn't usually stop the religious hardcore), I think the key was that it didn't disrupt or criticise – or even *use* – the classic religious iconography. No classic pictures. No crucifixes. No angels. That's what people get upset about, when the pictures are played with, especially when the pictures have been there since childhood. If they're that deeply embedded, then they're sacrosanct.

That simple image thing is right at the root of homophobia, too. The fundamental image of life, of family, of childhood, of survival, is man and woman. Every story, every myth, every image reinforces that. Even the images of the real world reinforce that, because statistically heterosexuality is the norm. It's the default. It's the icon. Man/man or woman/woman disrupts a fundamental childhood image. Homophobia does seem to come from some gut instinct that's beyond the religious or the physical act or whatever. It's primal, and I think that's from the pictures. It's from what we see and what we're shown. That's why, in this gay lark, I stress visibility. Change the law, have education classes, do whatever you want, just be *seen*. I don't just mean on Pride Marches, because they're shoved away in an alcove, but I mean everywhere, all the time. I barely ever do an interview without mentioning being gay, and that's deliberate. We have to become visible, especially to the young, as part of the norm, then the picture starts to develop and widen.

FROM: RUSSELL T DAVIES TO: BENJAMIN COOK
SUNDAY 27 MAY 2007 23:37:06 GMT

RE: CHARLIE HUNNAM'S ARSE

I've done little work today. The only things I've changed are… I've renamed the Ballroom the 'Entertainment Lounge', which is more accurate; it's more of a hotel/bar. If I say Ballroom, the Locations Department will look for ballrooms to film in, no matter what the stage directions say. What's more, and rather annoyingly, I've looked it up and strictly those are *meteoroids*, not meteorites. Meteoroids only become meteors when they

Steve (Christopher Eccleston) and Judith (Lesley Sharp) in Russell's ITV drama *The Second Coming*. © ITV/Rex Features

hit the atmosphere, and meteorites are the rocks left behind. Damn it, 'meteorites' sounds so much better! I wrestled with that for a while. I don't normally get so hung up on scientific detail – but I tend to think, if something is bugging my non-scientific mind, then it's indeed a buggable offence and should be corrected.

But I'm still ignoring the fact that the meteoroids wouldn't be burning since they're not in an atmosphere. Burning looks brilliant.

FROM: RUSSELL T DAVIES TO: BENJAMIN COOK
MONDAY 28 MAY 2007 23:49:21 GMT

RE: CHARLIE HUNNAM'S ARSE

I've written nothing today. I know exactly what the next scene is. I'm just feeling sour. Hey ho.

FROM: BENJAMIN COOK TO: RUSSELL T DAVIES
MONDAY 28 MAY 2007 23:52:27 GMT

RE: CHARLIE HUNNAM'S ARSE

But which came first: the feeling sour, or the not writing?

FROM: RUSSELL T DAVIES TO: BENJAMIN COOK
TUESDAY 29 MAY 2007 00:12:24 GMT

RE: CHARLIE HUNNAM'S ARSE

One feeds into the other. It drives me mental. I *think* the feeling sour comes first, though equally it comes from the script, all those voices at the back of my head saying, 'Is this a waste of BBC money?' And then an external trigger allows them dominance. That *Longford* last week really didn't help. Neither did the broadcast of *Human Nature* on Saturday, to be honest – in a really, really selfish way. I had a whole Sunday of people saying, 'That was brilliant,' and specifically, 'What a brilliant script. Paul Cornell is a genius.' Which he is. But I'm thinking, if only you knew how much of that I wrote! But I stifle myself, so it all goes inwards. It festers. People know that I polish stuff, but they think that polishing means adding a gag or an epigram, not writing half the script. I know it shouldn't, but it drives me mad. How selfish. But tiny things like that gang up on me.

FROM: RUSSELL T DAVIES TO: BENJAMIN COOK
WEDNESDAY 30 MAY 2007 03:45:29 GMT

RE: CHARLIE HUNNAM'S ARSE

Back in action! Well, eight pages. They're eminently cuttable – it's the backstory stuff – but that's the way to afford this, lots of chat. If the page count is too long, then these pages will be cut, but it's good to write *anything* to get me over that hump.

62. INT. STAIRWELL - NIGHT[4]

An ordinary lower-decks stairwell, though wrecked, broken pipes & girders & rubble everywhere; the door's pushed open, debris falling away, and THE DOCTOR leads PETH, RICKSTON, MR COPPER, MORVIN, FOON & BANNAKAFFALATTA through.

THE DOCTOR
Careful as you go, now.
Follow me.

He starts going up, carefully stepping over debris, Peth at his side, others slowly following. As they ascend:

MR COPPER
It's rather ironic, but this is very much in the Christmas Spirit, in keeping with the planet below. It's a festival of violence! Humans, they say, only survive the season, depending on whether they've been good or bad. It's barbaric!

THE DOCTOR
Yeah, well it's not quite like that. Christmas is actually a time of peace and thanksgiving and... oh, what am I on about? My Christmases are always like this!

Towards the top of the first staircase, he's found a deactivated, broken HOST, sprouting wires and cables.

THE DOCTOR (CONT'D)
We've got a Host!
(to the Host)
Hello? Information? Anything?

PETH
They've got the strength of ten men. If we can get it activated, we can use it to shift the rubble.

MORVIN
We can do robotics! Both of us!

FOON
We work in the Milk Market, back on Sto, it's all robot staff.

THE DOCTOR
See if you can get it working.
(moves on)
Now, let's have a look...

He and Peth carry on up, reach the landing, look up: the next staircase is relatively clear of debris, but at the top, just before the next landing, it's blocked by a tangle of girders; the tangle is deep, but with a small-ish gap, more of a small tunnel, at the centre.

4 A new Scene 49 – set in the Entertainment Lounge, with a man tumbling through a shattered window into space – has been added, so the Doctor's big speech to Rickston ('I'm the Doctor. I'm a Time Lord. I'm from the planet of Gallifrey in the constellation of Kasterborous...') is now in Scene 61, followed by this, Scene 62, on the Stairwell.

PETH
It's blocked.

THE DOCTOR
So what do we do?

PETH
We shift it.

THE DOCTOR
That's the attitude! Rickston! Come on! And you, Mr Copper - Bannakaffalatta, come here - look, can I call you Banna? It's gonna save a lot of time.

BANNAKAFFALATTA
No! Bannakaffalatta!

THE DOCTOR
All right then, Bannakaffalatta, look, there's a gap - see if you can get through -

They all head up, Morvin & Foon stay with the Host:

FOON
We haven't got a toolkit or anything.

MORVIN
Ohh, we'll do it by hand, just like the old days. Remember those old Zed-grade robots, you'd just clip the brainstem together. These things might be posh, but they're all the same underneath.

FOON
(smiling)
You never give up, do you?

MORVIN
Comes from years of being nagged.

CUT TO Bannakaffalatta - he's climbed through the gap/small tunnel in the tangle of metal, reaching -

The next landing & BIG METAL DOOR.

The Doctor, Peth, Mr Copper & Rickston still on the Staircase 2, INTERCUT both sides:

BANNAKAFFALATTA
Bannakaffalatta through!

PETH
What's it like?

BANNAKAFFALATTA
Good! Big door!

THE DOCTOR
Can we open the door?

BANNAKAFFALATTA
No! Need help!

THE DOCTOR
Don't worry, I'm good with doors.

PETH
I'm small enough, I can get through…

And she heads through the gap, it creaks:

THE DOCTOR
Careful.

PETH
No, I'm fine…

RICKSTON
Yeah, but how are we gonna get the fatsos through that gap?

THE DOCTOR
We make the gap bigger. So start!

As they get to work on the Staircase 2, clearing metal, CUT BACK TO Morvin & Foon on staircase 1, clipping the Host's wires together. But Foon heard Rickston:

FOON
We're holding them up.

MORVIN
I don't care. Soon as we're off this ship, we're going back home, and we'll be happy with what we've got. If this is the high life, you can stuff it!

He's all smiles, to cheer her up. But she starts to cry.

MORVIN (CONT'D)
Heyyy, come on, sweetheart.

Foon (Debbie Chazen) and Morvin Van Hoff (Clive Rowe).

FOON
It's my fault, though. The tickets.

MORVIN
We won them, fair and square.

FOON
I know. But I never told you… I dialled the competition line five thousand times. That's five thousand credits, it's a credit-a-call, we might as well have paid for the tickets. I've been hiding the vone bill for months now.

MORVIN
Five thousand credits…?

FOON
Don't hate me.

MORVIN
You spent five thousand credits?

FOON
I'm sorry.

And Morvin starts to laugh. Really laugh.

FOON (CONT'D)
What's so funny?

MORVIN
Five thousand!

FOON
But we'll never pay that off.

MORVIN
I know! We'll have to work for 20 years! You mad bloody woman! How much??

FOON
(starting to smile)
Five thousand.

MORVIN
Oh my Vot!

FOON
You're not cross…?

MORVIN
Does it matter? Look at us! Who cares about money?! Oh, you drive me barmy - I don't half love you, Mrs Van Hoff! C'mere -

And he gives her a big hug, both laughing.

CUT TO Staircase 2, Morvin & Foon's laughter echoing up, the Doctor, Rickston & Mr Copper clearing the gap:

RICKSTON
What happened, did they find a doughnut?

CUT TO the landing on the far side of the tangle, Peth hauling out a plank of metal, calling through:

PETH
I can clear it from this side, mind it doesn't move…

Putting down the plank, she sees Bannakaffalatta, behind her, sitting on the floor, heaving for breath. Goes to him -

PETH (CONT'D)
Are you all right?

BANNAKAFFALATTA
Good.

PETH
No, you're not, what's wrong, what is it?

THE DOCTOR (OOV)
Everything all right through there?

But Bannakaffalatta puts a finger to his lips; *sssh*.

PETH
(calls back)
...yeah, fine, we're just... Give's a minute.
(hushed)
What is it?

BANNAKAFFALATTA
Can't say.

PETH
Are you hurt?

BANNAKAFFALATTA
Ashamed.

PETH
Of what...?

BANNAKAFFALATTA
Can't say.

PETH
If you tell me, I can help.

BANNAKAFFALATTA
Poor Bannakaffalatta.

And he undoes his shirt.

Underneath, his torso is METAL, with blinking lights.

PETH
...you're a cyborg!

BANNAKAFFALATTA
Had accident. Long ago. Secret.

PETH
No, but everything's changed, now! Cyborgs have got equal rights. They passed a law, back on Sto, you're equal citizens, you can even get married.

BANNAKAFFALATTA
(cheeky)
Marry you!

PETH
Well, maybe you could start with buying me a drink first. But it's different now, you don't have to hide any more.

BANNAKAFFALATTA
Old fashioned.

PETH
Well, I think it looks... nice.

BANNAKAFFALATTA
Must recharge.

He presses a button, his lights blink, he breathes deep.

PETH
There you go. You just sit there for a bit.

BANNAKAFFALATTA
Tell no one.

PETH
I promise.

She gets back to work, grabs another sheet of metal.

THE DOCTOR (OOV)
What's going on up there?

PETH
Oh, I think me and Bannakaffalatta just got engaged.

BANNAKAFFALATTA
Yes yes yes!

'Marry you!' Bannakaffalatta makes a play for 'Peth'.

And he's chuckling away!

CUT TO:

63. INT. BRIDGE - NIGHT

MIDSHIPMAN FRAME has now stripped off his jacket, opened his shirt, has just patched up his bullet wound, using a first-aid kit. In great pain. Then, the *weee-oo* of comms -

He scrambles to the COMMS PANEL, wincing.

MIDSHIPMAN FRAME
This is the Bridge.

SCENE CONTINUES, INTERCUT WITH:

64. INT. KITCHEN CORRIDOR - NIGHT

Same as the Ship's Corridor, only with pots and pans in the debris, the place dotted with PRAC FLAMES. A KITCHENHAND - young lad, only 18 - is on COMMS. Five other KITCHEN STAFF in b/g, injured, dazed, but surviving.

KITCHENHAND
...it's Kitchen Number Five here. What the hell happened?

MIDSHIPMAN FRAME
Meteoroid collision. How many of you are there?

KITCHENHAND
Six of us. Just about. Are we the only ones left alive, sir?

MIDSHIPMAN FRAME
No, there's more on Deck 22, we've got... Wait a minute. If I can cycle the scanner inwards...

He presses buttons. On screen, GRAPHICS: a grid-layout of the Titanic, with tiny blips dotted about.

MIDSHIPMAN FRAME (CONT'D)
Life signs! I can see you, Kitchen Five, six of you! There's about... 50 people, spread throughout the ship. 50 survivors! Listen, everyone's gonna head for the Bridge, can you get out?

KITCHENHAND
No, we're stuck, the doors have sealed.

MIDSHIPMAN FRAME
Can you force them open?

KITCHENHAND
We've tried, they must be jammed or something, we can't get out - no, wait a minute -

Clank! The Kitchenhand and the five survivors turn, look -

The handle on the door is turning, the seal hissing open.

KITCHENHAND (CONT'D)
It's opening, there's someone on the other side!

Door swings open -

FIVE HEAVENLY HOST standing there, impassive.

Kitchenhand - big smile!

KITCHENHAND (CONT'D)
Ohh thank Vot for that, we've got Host! The Host are still working!

Now stay on the Bridge, Kitchen corridor remains OOV:

MIDSHIPMAN FRAME
That's brilliant, tell them to clear a path to the Bridge.
(silence)
Yeah? Did you get that? Kitchen Five, report. Hello, Kitchen Five?

And then, suddenly, OOV: screaming! Blood-curdling.

MIDSHIPMAN FRAME (CONT'D)
Kitchen Five, what's happening? Kitchen Five?! Report!

KITCHENHAND
(screams)
It's the Host! It's the Ho-

And then he screams too -

Comms are abruptly cut off. Silence.

Midshipman Frame looks back at the scanner.

GRAPHICS: Only four blips of light remaining in Kitchen Five. Which then go out, one by one.

Midshipman Frame scared, now, looking as -

GRAPHICS: blips of light going out all over the ship.

FROM: RUSSELL T DAVIES TO: BENJAMIN COOK
WEDNESDAY 30 MAY 2007 23:45:39 GMT

RE: CHARLIE HUNNAM'S ARSE

Bit more. Poxy, really. I thought the Stairwell was going to be a short sequence, but it turned out to be long and bothersome, so I'm up to Page 47 already. A lot of it might have to be cut.

65. INT. STAIRWELL - NIGHT

THE DOCTOR & RICKSTON on the Staircase 2 side of the tangle as MR COPPER heads through the widened gap, but the COMMS gives a *weee-ooo*. The COMMS PANEL is back down on the first landing, the Doctor goes down; MORVIN, FOON & the deactivated HOST on Staircase 1 below.

MORVIN
Almost done!

THE DOCTOR
Keep going.
(on comms)
Mr Frame, how's things?

SCENE CONTINUES, INTERCUT WITH:

66. EXT. BRIDGE - NIGHT

MIDSHIPMAN FRAME on COMMS, urgent.

MIDSHIPMAN FRAME
Doctor, I've got about 50 life signs over the ship, or I did have, they're all going out, one by one -

THE DOCTOR
What is it, vacuum breach?

MIDSHIPMAN FRAME
No, the oxygen's holding - but one of them said it was the Host, it's something to do with the Host -

CUT TO:

67. INT. STAIRWELL - NIGHT

THE DOCTOR turns round in horror as -

MORVIN
It's working!

And the HOST jerks awake!

And grabs Morvin by the neck, throttling him!

FOON screaming, hitting the Host, as the Doctor runs down -

THE DOCTOR
Turn it off, turn it off!

FOON
Let him go, let him go!

Morvin choking, the Doctor sonicking the Host's hand, but -

THE DOCTOR
Won't work - maximum deadlock -

And with a *gaaaah!*, he prises the Host's hand off - Morvin falls back -

FX (PRAC?) SPARKS on the Host's body - still broken, trailing wires - juddering and jerking, it tries to stand -

HOST
Information: kill - information: kill - information: kill -

THE DOCTOR
Go, quickly, get upstairs -

- said, shoving Morvin & Foon up the stairs -

- top of Staircase 2, RICKSTON looking down -

RICKSTON
What the hell's going on?

THE DOCTOR
Get them through!

RICKSTON
No chance!

- and he dives through the gap -

The Doctor backing up Staircase 1 as the Host reaches up, pulls off its Halo - throws it -

FX: the Doctor ducks as the Halo misses, ricochets off the walls, SPARKS flying - though it then spins off and away -

THE DOCTOR
Ohh, out of weapons, now?

The Host lashes out with its metal hand, karate-style -

PRAC FX: banister splinters into pieces -

The Doctor belts up to the first landing, onto COMMS -

THE DOCTOR (CONT'D)
Midshipman, it's the Host, they've gone berserk, are you safe up there?

CUT TO:

68. INT. BRIDGE - NIGHT

MIDSHIPMAN FRAME leaves the comms, goes to the door - but *ahhhh!*, he's racked with pain, sinks to his knees -

From the floor, he looks round -

There's a plain, narrow metal corridor leading to the Bridge - and THREE HOST are walking calmly towards him -

CUT TO:

69. INT. STAIRWELL - NIGHT

On the second landing, PETH and MR COPPER are pulling FOON, squealing, through the gap - BANNAKAFFALATTA still helpless, RICKSTON just standing back - all fast, panicky -

PETH
Come on! You can do it - !

MR COPPER
It's gonna collapse -

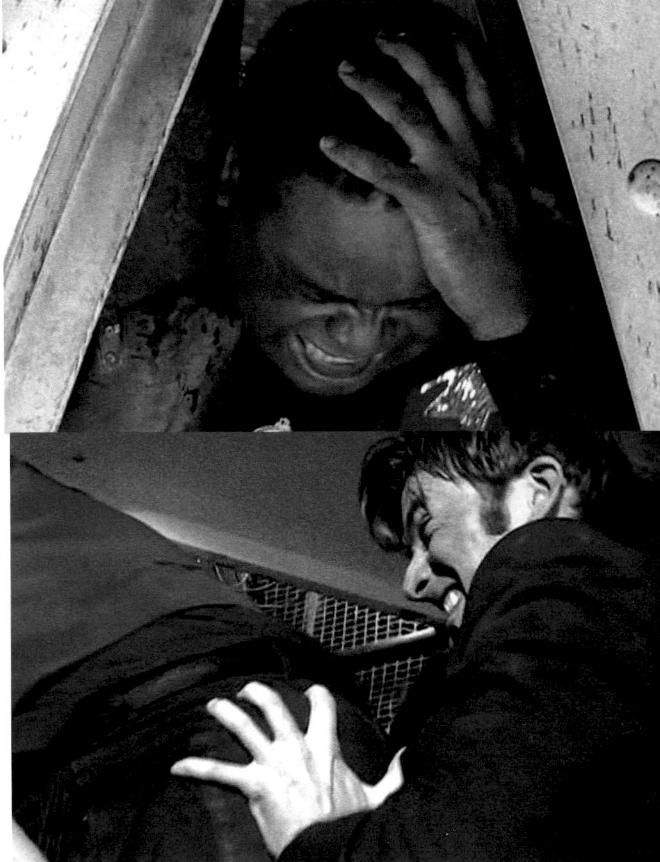

The Doctor attempts to dislodge Morvin Van Hoff.

Mr Copper holds up the tangle, which is creaking ominously, PRAC FX DUST & RUBBLE trickling down from the roof -

CUT TO THE DOCTOR, now backing up Staircase 2, MORVIN behind him at the tangle, the HOST spasming and advancing -

THE DOCTOR
Morvin! Get through!

CUT TO:

70. INT. BRIDGE - NIGHT

MIDSHIPMAN FRAME, in agony, throws himself at a lever in the wall, pulls it -

The metal door *schwups!* across,

cutting off THE THREE HOST -

But *clang!* - a GOLDEN HAND stops the door from closing -

CUT TO:

71. INT. STAIRWELL - NIGHT

THE DOCTOR still backing away -

FX (PRAC) SPARKS from THE HOST, still lurching upwards -

THE DOCTOR
Explain your instructions! I demand information! Tell me why!

HOST
Information: no witnesses.

THE DOCTOR
Says who? Tell me! Who did this to the Titanic?

The Host swipes again, metal pipes go flying -

Morvin's just trying to struggle through the gap - the Doctor backs up to him -

THE DOCTOR (CONT'D)
Mr Van Hoff, we've only just met but you'll have to excuse me -

And he gives Morvin's arse a good shove -

- Morvin is shoved through to the other side -

PETH
Doctor, come on! Get through!

THE DOCTOR
Information override, you will tell me the point of origin of your command structure.

HOST
Information: Level 31.

THE DOCTOR
Thank you!

And he dives through the gap -

Peth & Morvin pulling him through

- Mr Copper holding on -

MR COPPER
- can't hold it - !

THE DOCTOR
Let it go - !

All throw themselves back -

The Host is in the gap/tunnel, its GOLD HAND reaching out -

PRAC FX: huge chunk of GIRDER slams down through the centre of the gap/tunnel - smashing the HOST'S HEAD into pieces!

CUT TO:

72. INT. BRIDGE - NIGHT

MIDSHIPMAN FRAME heaves at the lever, all the way down -

The METAL DOOR closes, cutting off a HOST'S FINGERS -

The fingers clang onto the floor.

Midshipman Frame heaving for breath, recovering. Then he hauls himself round, to look:

The door has a porthole. Now filled with an impassive, unmoving HOST'S FACE. Staring at him.

I spent a lot of time going back through the rest of the script, tidying up nouns and things: sometimes it's called COMMS BOARD, sometimes COMMS PANEL, so I've standardised that. (You'd be amazed how many finished scripts come through – even shooting scripts – that say DINING ROOM, then LIVING ROOM, then LOUNGE, when in fact it's all the same room; the writer has just been careless and given it a different name each time. The Design Department will go out and look for three different rooms!) The collision happens even earlier on Page 24 now. And I went back and put a forklift truck into the Host Containment Cells, because I might need it later. It's introduced in Scene 8:

An ENGINEER is driving up in a small FORKLIFT TRUCK, which has three deactivated HOST stacked up on its scoop, horizontally, like dummies. Engineer brakes, gets out:

ENGINEER
That's four of them now, four of them on the blink.

The forklift's eventual fate is horribly expensive, so that's a worry. It might get cut.

Oh! Forgot to tell you – looking up the real *Titanic* online today, what did I find? A computer game, released in 1998, called – wait for it – *Starship Titanic*! By Douglas Adams! I got straight onto BBC Editorial Policy to see if we're all right copyright-wise. If we're not... oh, damn! I *must* have heard of it, and yet this feels brand new. I got the title *Starship Titanic* off of Peter McKinstry's design sketch for the 4.X vessel. I thought, ooh, nice title. The funny thing is, you can't copyright titles. I could call 4.X *Oklahoma!* if I wanted to, though that would be odd. I've suggested *Voyage of the Damned* instead. Strangely, this does have one benefit: we always end Episode 13 with the graphic 'DOCTOR WHO WILL RETURN AT CHRISTMAS IN...', plus the title, and the word 'Starship' would have given away that it's not the real *Titanic* crashing through the TARDIS at the end of 3.13. The new title might help... if the secret isn't blown by then anyway.

Talking of secrets blown, tomorrow's *Sun* is running our plan to take *Doctor Who* off air after 2008. Bollocks! God knows how they got hold of that. Their contacts are good. With any luck, no one will believe them – or we'll be facing a media storm. It's a nightmare. It's way too soon for this information to be released. Peter Fincham is now talking about overruling Jane Tranter, and doing only one Special for Christmas 2008, then getting a whole new team in place for a full series in 2009, or something. Good luck to 'em. I'll be gone.

All things considered, it's not been a great day.

Time to go . . David

Doctor Who to get axe in 2008

EXCLUSIVE
by GORDON SMART
Deputy Showbiz Editor

HIT show Doctor Who will be EXTERMINATED next year – after the fourth series.

Boss Russell T. Davies has decided to axe the BBC1 sci-fi drama and concentrate on other projects.

He and senior staff have hatched a plot to hand in a group resignation in summer 2008.

A source said: "The heavy workload – nine months of 16-hour days every year – has started to take its toll.

"It was decided the best thing for the show was go out at the top next year."

Davies was behind the relaunch of Doctor Who in 2005 – 16 years after it was originally axed.

The series, starring David Tennant as the Time Lord, is watched by eight million every Saturday.

● **EX Doctor Who star Billie Piper, 24, is due to get her divorce decree nisi from DJ Chris Evans, 41, at the High Court today.**

FROM: BENJAMIN COOK TO: RUSSELL T DAVIES
THURSDAY 31 MAY 2007 12:31:56 GMT

RE: CHARLIE HUNNAM'S ARSE

It's a computer game! Did I know that? I must have heard about Douglas Adams' *Starship Titanic* before now, so why didn't it ring any bells? Couldn't you say that it's a 'homage'? Maybe not. Or give it a subtitle? *Starship Titanic: At World's End...*? Definitely not.

You're right, *The Sun* is reporting that *Doctor Who* is ending after 2008. How that corresponds with the same paper's reports that David is leaving halfway through Series Four, I don't know. What does *The Sun* think will happen for the second half of Series Four? A different guest presenter will play the Doctor each week? (Hey, there's an idea! Copyright Benjamin Cook!) If you know in advance that a story like this is going to appear in the tabloids, isn't there any way that you can spike it? Isn't it in *The Sun*'s interest to keep you guys on side?

As things stand, what *is* the plan for 2009 and beyond? You talk of the BBC taking the show off air for a while, but how long is a while? How long will we be waiting for a Series Five? Couldn't a new production team prep their episodes while you and the current team are still in production? Why can't the show just keep going? Wouldn't that be safer for *Doctor Who*'s long-term future?

FROM: RUSSELL T DAVIES TO: BENJAMIN COOK
THURSDAY 31 MAY 2007 18:42:10 GMT

RE: CHARLIE HUNNAM'S ARSE

The BBC is powerless with the press. No one can control the papers, they'll print what they want, and we need them, so threatening to withhold or punish simply

David Tennant relaxes between takes on set in the *Titanic* Ballroom.

doesn't work. We'll just go crawling back, cap in hand. But the central problem is that the BBC is a public service broadcaster, funded by the public, so we are Not Allowed To Lie – and we end up craven and apologetic. That's why the leak about Christopher Eccleston leaving could not be plugged. Once asked by *The Mirror*, Jane Tranter could not deny it. Even though it ruined the surprise cliffhanger to Series One. How incredible would it have been to keep the Ninth Doctor's regeneration a surprise? But we had to be scrupulously honest. It's all still the consequences of the Hutton Inquiry.[5] But *Doctor Who* is hardly Hutton! This is fiction! I don't give a damn, I'll lie all I like if it safeguards the stories that we're telling. They can't stop me. But there's little point while Peter Fincham has to tell the truth. Madness.

The plan for 2009 and beyond? Well… we'll transmit Series Four next year, then a 2008 Christmas Special, and then two hour-long Specials in 2009, most likely Easter and Christmas Day. Then a third Special in 2010 should segue into a brand new Series Five, with a new production team. We've planned this for ages. I remember discussing it with Julie and David, in Woods Restaurant in Cardiff Bay, a few days before filming began on *The Runaway Bride*. The show, by 2009, will simply need a rest. We need to starve people a bit. We're producing 14 movie-sized episodes a year, which are then repeated ad infinitum, and ratings are bound to decline, even just a little. *Doctor Who* is a phenomenon right now, but nothing stays a phenomenon. Not without careful management. People need to be begging for new *Doctor Who*, instead of just expecting it. That's fine for kids, too. They can wait a few years between *Harry Potter* books and *Star Wars* films. If anything, the wait *increases* the legend.

Meanwhile, a new production team can move in. Hopefully, they can start sniffing around even earlier than 2009, to see us at work on Series Four this year and next, but that's a lot less essential than you'd think. No matter how much we complain that this show is hard to make, it's still a UK drama, with scripts and crews and actors, like any show. The best thing that a new team can do is move in, trample over the way that

5 The Hutton Inquiry was a 2003–2004 judicial inquiry, chaired by Lord Hutton, into the circumstances surrounding the death of Dr David Kelly, an employee of the Ministry of Defence, in July 2003. Kelly had been named as the source of quotes used by BBC journalist Andrew Gilligan, forming the basis of media reports that Tony Blair's Labour government had knowingly 'sexed up' a dossier on Iraq and weapons of mass destruction. The inquiry cleared the government of wrongdoing, but the BBC was strongly criticised, leading to the resignation of both the Chairman and the Director-General of the BBC.

we did things, and find new ways for themselves. While I'm sure that we'll all be around to help and support the newcomers, they'd be better off packing up our stuff and throwing our boxes into the street. New show! New team! New start! The most complicated advice that needs to be passed on is nothing to do with the drama; it's to do with negotiating the BBC. Publicity, funding, merchandising, BBC Wales overheads, all those complicated areas. (Julie's speciality!) You can't really see that in action, but it can be explained over 57 coffees.

But *Doctor Who* can run and run. Definitely. If it's managed this carefully. One day, of course, something will go wrong by accident, and people will look elsewhere, and some mean BBC Controller will take it off air… but only for it to come back blazing a few years later. That, now, is the definition of *Doctor Who*. It's the show that comes back. To the extent that we're building this Glorious Return into the 2010 schedules ourselves. It's not quite like any other show – which has always been *Doctor Who*'s outstanding feature, don't you think?

FROM: RUSSELL T DAVIES TO: BENJAMIN COOK
FRIDAY 1 JUNE 2007 02:40:52 GMT

RE: CHARLIE HUNNAM'S ARSE

Only a few new pages today, mostly chat, but it feels okay. I've sat here for ages, reworking stuff. For instance, I cut Mr Copper's revelation, in his first scene, about the origin of his degree in Earthonomics, and put it in these new pages…

```
73. INT. SHIP CORRIDOR #2 - NIGHT

Corridor as others: wrecked,
rubble, PRAC FLAMES here and
there. RICKSTON, MORVIN & FOON,
BANNAKAFFALATTA (now recovered), MR
COPPER then THE DOCTOR & PETH hurry
through a BIG METAL DOOR, and the
Doctor sonics it shut.

Foon has spotted a shattered metal
hostess-style-trolley -

                FOON
    Morvin, look! Food!

                RICKSTON
    Oh great, someone's happy.

                MORVIN
    Don't have any, then.

But Rickston is starving, joins
them - Peth takes charge -

                PETH
    All right, that's my job,
    share it out, careful with the
    water, we might need that…

All except the Doctor gather round
the trolley, settle, eating, a
moment's rest. The Doctor goes to
the COMMS; a distance away, back by
the door, so this can be sotto:

                THE DOCTOR
    Mr Frame? Still there?

SCENE CONTINUES, INTERCUT WITH:

74. INT. BRIDGE - NIGHT

INTERCUT WITH SHIP'S CORRIDOR #2.

MIDSHIPMAN FRAME back on COMMS.

                MIDSHIPMAN FRAME
    Yes, sir. But I've got Host
    outside, I've sealed the
    door.

                THE DOCTOR
    Someone's reprogrammed them
    to kill the survivors, why
    would anyone do that?

                MIDSHIPMAN FRAME
    That's not the only problem,
    Doctor. I had to use a maximum
    deadlock on the door. Which
    means… No one can get in. I'm
    sealed off. Even if you find a
    way of rebooting the engines,
    you can't get to the Bridge.

                THE DOCTOR
    Okay. Right. Fine! One problem
    at a time. What's on Level 31?

                MIDSHIPMAN FRAME
    Nothing, just storage…

He brings up the TITANIC GRAPHICS
GRID, which also pops up on the
Doctor's comms panel. Both study it.

                MIDSHIPMAN FRAME (CONT'D)
    That's Host Containment,
    that's where we keep the
    robots.
```

THE DOCTOR
But what's that...?

On LEVEL 31 GRAPHIC, a small rectangle of absolute black.

THE DOCTOR (CONT'D)
D'you see? That panel of black, it's registering... nothing. No power, no light, no heat.

MIDSHIPMAN FRAME
Never seen it before.

THE DOCTOR
Completely shielded. What's down there...?

MIDSHIPMAN FRAME
I'll try modulating the scanner.

THE DOCTOR
Good man. Let me know if you find anything.

Hanging up, as Mr Copper brings the Doctor some food.

MR COPPER
Keeps the energy up!

THE DOCTOR
No, I'm fine, you have it.

MR COPPER
You might be a Time King from Gallilee or whatever, but a man needs food in his belly.

Mr Copper tells the truth about his 'qualifications'.

THE DOCTOR
Thank you.

They both hunker down, to eat.

MR COPPER
I was thinking, Doctor... If you could boost the signal on that radio thing, you could send a signal down to the planet below. They could help. Send up a rocket or something.

THE DOCTOR
They haven't got spaceships.

MR COPPER
No, I've read about it, they've got shuffles. Space shuffles.

THE DOCTOR
This degree in Earthonomics, where's it from?

MR COPPER
...honestly?

THE DOCTOR
Go on.

MR COPPER
Mrs Golightly's Happy Travelling University and Hotel.

THE DOCTOR
She sounds marvellous.

MR COPPER
Oh she is! That degree cost me five credits and a night I'll never forget.
(more miserable)
But I lied, Doctor. Pretended I was an expert, forged my way onto the ship. I'd spent my whole life on Sto. Travelling salesman, selling this and that, just junk and tat. I reached retirement with nothing to show for myself. All those years on one planet, and Earth sounded so... exotic.

THE DOCTOR
S'pose it is. In its own little way.

MR COPPER
You seem to know it well.

```
            THE DOCTOR
      Yeah. I was sort of… few
      years ago, I was sort
      of made, well… sort of
      homeless, and… There was the
      Earth.

   Pause.

            MR COPPER
      Thing is. If we survive this -

            THE DOCTOR
      When!

            MR COPPER
      When we survive this! But
      there'll be police, and
      investigations and things…
      I'm not going to come out of
      it very well.

            THE DOCTOR
      Not exactly a master
      criminal.

            MR COPPER
      The minimum penalty for
      spacelane fraud is ten years
      in jail. I'm an old man,
      Doctor. Ten years!

   Whunk! A blow to the metal door,
   from the other side -

   Instant panic!

            THE DOCTOR
      We've got Host! Move!
      Everyone, hup, come on!

   - and they're all up and on their
   feet, moving, hopping and hauling
   themselves over debris -

   PRAC FX: whunk! the metal door
   buckles -
```

FROM: RUSSELL T DAVIES TO: BENJAMIN COOK
SATURDAY 2 JUNE 2007 02:35:42 GMT

RE: CHARLIE HUNNAM'S ARSE

Just rewrites today. A thousand fiddles on a thousand lines. Every day, when I reopen the file, I start right on Page 1 and go through it all again. I never go straight to where I left off last night. I went back to that scene on Earth, in the city street, and gave Mr Copper a credit

A draft design for Mr Copper's credit card.

card. It's handy to place props that you might use later, like the credit card, like the forklift; it's easy to cut them if I don't use them, but their existence sort of seeds them and I start to play with their potential. Also, I added Peth to the chat between the Doctor and Mr Copper in Scene 74, because we're not getting enough Peth and there are rather too many two-handers.

I set myself two new targets today: to get the meteoroids hitting by Page 23 – done! – and to reduce the whole script down from 50 pages. I got to 48. But preproduction starts on Monday. IN TWO DAYS' TIME! The director – it's James Strong – needs to start work. I have to work like hell this weekend.

FROM: RUSSELL T DAVIES TO: BENJAMIN COOK
SUNDAY 3 JUNE 2007 02:24:48 GMT

RE: CHARLIE HUNNAM'S ARSE

More! Lots! About 11 pages! I've been building up to this Canyon sequence for days. Christ, that's tiring. Writing action sequences is exhausting.

```
75. INT. SHIP CORRIDOR #3 - NIGHT

As other corridors, wrecked. The
little gang of THE DOCTOR, PETH, MR
COPPER, RICKSTON, MORVIN, FOON &
BANNAKAFFALATTA hurry over debris -
behind them, the echo of the whunk!

They reach a BIG DOOR & ARCHWAY,
the Doctor sonics the panel, the
door slides back -
```

CUT TO:

76. INT. CANYON - NIGHT

Door slides back, THE DOCTOR stops dead - !

FX: it's a huge Death Star-style CANYON, except the walls aren't smooth, they're all jagged metal, where many floors have fallen through as a result of the collision.

THE DOCTOR, PETH, MR COPPER, RICKSTON, MORVIN, FOON & BANNAKAFFALATTA are safe on a wide, ripped-edge LEDGE, in front of the DOOR ARCHWAY. And in front of that:

FX: THE STRUT. (In fact, a BRIDGE - only called the Strut here to differentiate it from the Ship's Bridge.) Like a huge, long, thick, horizontal piece of metal has fallen, and stuck, lodging across the gap, from their ARCHWAY to an identical ARCHWAY, on the opposite side.

The Strut is jagged & broken, about four feet wide, six feet deep; like a tree across a river. (NB, STRUT is PRAC BUILD in most shots, its surroundings seen in FX shots; for non-FX shots, the Canyon walls around it could be a pitch-black void…?)

RICKSTON
Is that the only way across…?

THE DOCTOR
Yeah, but on the other hand: it is a way across.

PETH
What's that, the engines?

Looking down: FX: at the bottom of the drop, half a mile down: a huge glowing ball, a CORE OF ENERGY, slowly rotating.

THE DOCTOR
Nuclear Storm Drive. It's already slowing down. Soon as it stops, the Titanic falls.

MORVIN
But that thing, it's never gonna take our weight.

'Is that the only way across?'

RICKSTON
You're going last, mate.

THE DOCTOR
It's nitrofine metal. Should be stronger than it looks.

MORVIN
All the same, Rickston's got a point, me and Foon should go la-

- no warning - the floor of the ledge beneath Morvin simply crumbles away under his feet, and he drops like a stone -

FX: MORVIN falls down into the canyon, towards the glowing Core, screaming!

FOON
Morvin! *Morvin!!*

She drops to her knees, screaming over the edge - others shocked, stepping away from the edge - Peth

grabbing Foon, holding her, the Doctor also going to Foon -

RICKSTON
I told you!

MR COPPER
Shut up, just shut up, *shut up!*

FOON
Bring him back! Can't you bring him back? Doctor, bring him back!

THE DOCTOR
I can't, I'm sorry, I can't -

FOON
You promised me!

THE DOCTOR
I know, I'm sorry, I'm sorry…

And he's just hugging her now, as she sobs.

Behind them, from the corridor, louder *whunks!*

BANNAKAFFALATTA
Host coming!

MR COPPER
Doctor, I rather think those things have got our scent.

RICKSTON
Well, I'm not waiting -

And he starts across the Bridge - scrambling -

THE DOCTOR
Be careful - ! Take it slowly!

A few feet across, the Bridge shudders, creaks, Rickston stops, drops to all-fours, terrified -

FX: HIGH SHOT, RICKSTON frozen on the STRUT, the CORE below.

RICKSTON
Oh my Vot, ohh my Vot…

THE DOCTOR
You're okay - Peth -

Meaning, look after Foon, the Doctor standing to call across -

THE DOCTOR (CONT'D)
Step at a time. Come on. You can do it.

Rickston stands. Wobbles. Balances. A step at a time…

In the Archway, louder crashes from the corridor beyond -

MR COPPER
They're getting closer.

THE DOCTOR
I've got to seal us off…

He sonics the door, it slides shut.

MR COPPER
Leaving us trapped, wouldn't you say?

THE DOCTOR
Never say trapped. Just… inconveniently circumstanced.

CUT TO Rickston. Careful steps over the uneven surface…

His foot slips, dislodging METAL SLATES -

FX: WIDE SHOT, Rickston all-fours, SLATES falling down…

RICKSTON
I'm okay, I'm okay…

CUT TO Foon & Peth, on the floor of the Archway.

FOON
He might be all right, maybe there's a gravity shield down there, I don't know, it might have cushioned him, he might be unconscious, or…

PETH
I'm sorry, Foon. Look at me.
(Foon does so)
He's gone.

FOON
What am I gonna do without him?

And she hugs Peth, crying.

CUT TO Rickston - stands, deep breath, and he suddenly runs the last length -

- reaching the OPPOSITE ARCHWAY, hugs the wall. (It has a similar surrounding ledge; its door closed.)

RICKSTON
Yes! Oh yes! Who's good?!

MR COPPER
Luck of the devil.

THE DOCTOR
Bannakaffalatta, you go next.

BANNAKAFFALATTA
Bannakaffalatta small!

And he scampers across the Bridge…

THE DOCTOR
Slowly!

FX: WIDE SHOT, BANNAKAFFALATTA now edging slowly across…

PRAC FX - *whunk!* - the Archway door behind them buckles -

Rickston Slade (Gray O'Brien) makes his way across the Strut.

MR COPPER
They've found us!

THE DOCTOR
Peth, get across, right now -

PETH
What about you?

THE DOCTOR
Just do it, go on!

Peth starts across, one careful step at a time -

The *whunks!* get louder, PRAC BUCKLING of the metal -

THE DOCTOR (CONT'D)
Mr Copper. I don't think we can wait, after you.

MR COPPER
You're more important than me -

THE DOCTOR
Never mind the etiquette, go!

And Mr Copper starts across…

FX: WIDE SHOT, Bannakaffalatta halfway over, Peth following, then Mr Copper, all slow, slipping, stopping, holding on…

The Doctor kneels by Foon, *whunks!* in b/g…

THE DOCTOR (CONT'D)
Foon, you've got to get across.

FOON
What for? What am I going to do without him?

THE DOCTOR
Just think, what would he want? He'd want you safe, wouldn't he?

FOON
He doesn't want anything, he's *dead!*

CUT TO Rickston, in the opposite Archway, yelling across -

RICKSTON
Doctor! I can't open the door! It's locked, we need that… whirring sort of key thing -

THE DOCTOR
I can't leave her!

RICKSTON
You'll get us all killed if we can't get out!

The Doctor trapped - argh! - *whunk!, whunk!, whunk!* -

THE DOCTOR
Mrs Van Hoff. I'm coming back for you. All right?

She doesn't even look at him, just crying.

And he's got no choice, he starts across the Strut…

Bannakaffalatta, just over halfway, calls back:

BANNAKAFFALATTA
Too many people!

THE DOCTOR
Oy. Don't get spiky with me. Just keep going!

FX: WIDE SHOT, Bannakaffalatta, then Peth, then Mr Copper, then the Doctor, all edging across the creaking Strut -

CUT TO Foon, shuffling back into the corner of the Archway, curling into a ball, crying, the *whunks!* above her.

CAMERA SHAKE, the Strut jolts! - they drop to all fours -

PETH
It's gonna fall - !

THE DOCTOR
No, it's just settling. Keep going.

Peth gets to her feet, continues taking careful steps…

CUT TO the Doctor, edging along on all fours, and then…

He stops. Stands. Looking around. Because…

The *whunks* have stopped.

Ominous silence. Hushed:

PETH
…they've stopped.

BANNAKAFFALATTA
Gone away.

THE DOCTOR
But why would they give up…?

RICKSTON
Never mind that, keep going!

THE DOCTOR
But where've they gone?

MR COPPER
Ohh, I'm afraid we've forgotten the traditions of Christmas. That angels have wings.

And he's looking up… The others look up, in dread…

FX: WIDE SHOT, as FOUR FLYING HOST descend upright from above, around the Strut, METAL WINGS UNFURLED, glorious. Arms locked in prayer positions.

FX: CU one HOST descending, serene and deadly.

FX: WIDE SHOT, the FOUR HOST now stopping mid-air, suspended, forming a circle a good few feet above the Strut.

THE DOCTOR
Listen to me. Information override! Examine your primary function, to help, you're supposed to help the passengers, so help us, now.

HOST
Information: kill.

And it reaches up to its Halo…

THE DOCTOR
Arm yourself! All of you!

He rips a stick of metal out of the Strut's loose floor -

Peth does the same - and Mr Copper, and Bannakaffalatta -

CU HOST, it throws its Halo -

FX: WIDE SHOT, all FOUR HOST throw HALOES - the Haloes swoop and glide through the air, deadly frisbees -

FX: (presuming flying Haloes are FX?), the Doctor swings his stick like a bat, SPARKS FLY as he hits a Halo, sends it zinging away -

FX: PETH swings, hits a Halo, spins round to hit a second -

FX: Mr Copper swings, misses, has to fall to the side to avoid the Halo, which whizzes past -

FX: WIDE SHOT, the Haloes not stopping, programmed to keep attacking, swooping up and around the canyon to attack again -

CU Doctor, swinging, hitting -

CU Peth, swinging, hitting -

CUT TO Rickston, cowering back in his Archway -

CUT TO Foon, curled up but watching, crying, in her Archway -

FX: Bannakaffalatta swings, hits a Halo, sends it flying -

FX: the Doctor misses, a Halo slices across his arm - rips the sleeve (PRAC SQUIB?), wounds him - *aaah!* -

FX: Mr Copper on his knees, lashes out - misses, a Halo slices across his shoulder (PRAC SQUIB?) -

INTERCUT all this with CU Host, staring down, impassive -

CU Peth, swinging, but desperate -

PETH
I can't…

But Bannakaffalatta throws down his stick -

BANNAKAFFALATTA
Bannakaffalatta stop!

- rips open his shirt, metal torso -

BANNAKAFFALATTA (CONT'D)
Bannakaffalatta proud!

- he stabs his buttons - his lights flash like crazy -

PETH
(realising)
No, don't - !

BANNAKAFFALATTA
Bannakaffalatta cyborg!

And with a whirr of power - Bannakaffalatta stands proud -

FX: a pulse of energy - a blue circular ripple - blasts out of Bannakaffalatta's body -

FX: WIDE SHOT; the blue circle ripples out from Bannakaffalatta, across the Canyon, over the Host -

CU Host - PRAC SPARKS, it jerks, shudders, malfunctioning -

FX: WIDE SHOT, Host & Haloes deactivated, drop like stones -

'Bannakaffalatta stop! Bannakaffalatta proud! Bannakaffalatta cyborg!' Um... Bannakaffalatta dead.

FX: HIGH SHOT, Host & Haloes tumbling down into the Core.

But back on the Strut, Bannakaffalatta's now lying on the floor. Dying. Peth scrambles over to him, the Doctor also scrambling across, Mr Copper behind them.

THE DOCTOR
Electromagnetic pulse. Knocked out the robotics, Bannakaffalatta, that was brilliant.

PETH
But he used all his power.

BANNAKAFFALATTA
...did good...?

PETH
You saved our lives.

BANNAKAFFALATTA
Bannakaffalatta happy.

PETH
We can recharge you, we can get you to a power point, all we need to do is plug you in.

BANNAKAFFALATTA
Too late.

PETH
No, but you've got to buy me that drink, remember?

BANNAKAFFALATTA
Pretty girl.

He smiles.

Closes his eyes.

And Bannakaffalatta dies.

Silence. All looking down. Peth crying a little, pulls his shirt across the metal, out of respect.

Then Mr Copper steps forward - still stepping carefully on the Strut - gently reaches down to Bannakaffalatta's torso. He starts to unclip a metal baton from the main panel.

MR COPPER
I'm sorry, forgive me, but...

PETH
What are you doing?

R.I.P.

MR COPPER
He'd want us to use it.

PETH
Leave him alone.

MR COPPER
No, but it's the EMP transmitter. I used to sell these things, they'd always give me a bed for the night, in the Cyborg Caravans.

Pulls it free; the baton is a bit like a gun.

MR COPPER (CONT'D)
If we can recharge this, we can use it against the rest of the Host. A weapon! Bannakaffalatta might have saved us all.

RICKSTON
D'you think? Try telling him that.

He's looking up -

FX: ANOTHER HOST is descending.

Mr Copper & Peth frantic, with the baton, clicking buttons -

MR COPPER
There's no power, it's dead -

PETH
It's gotta have emergency!

RICKSTON
Doctor! Give me that key! Throw it! Doctor, throw it to me!

FX: the HOST descends to stand on the Strut, between the Doctor and the original Archway.

The Doctor faces it, Peth & Mr Copper cowering behind him.

THE DOCTOR
No! But! Hold on! Override! Loophole! Security Protocol… ten! Um, 666? Uhh, 21? 45678? I don't know, 42? Oh! One!

The Host, reaching for its Halo, stops, lowers its arm.

HOST
Information: state request.

'Peth' comforts Foon after Morvin falls to his death.

THE DOCTOR
Good! Right. You've been ordered to kill the survivors, yeah?

HOST
Information: correct.

THE DOCTOR
Why?

HOST
Information: no witnesses.

THE DOCTOR
But this ship's gonna fall on the Earth and kill everyone, and the Human Race has got nothing to do with the Titanic, so that contravenes your orders, yeah?

HOST
Information: incorrect.

THE DOCTOR
But… why d'you want to destroy the Earth…?

HOST
Information: it is part of the plan.

THE DOCTOR
What plan?

HOST
Information: you have only four questions under Protocol One, these four questions have been used -

THE DOCTOR
Well you could've warned me!

HOST
Information: now you will die.

And it reaches up…

Peth & Mr Copper scrabble back, the Doctor picks up another stick of metal, readies himself…

The Host unclips its Halo…

Holds it in front, ready to throw…

When a loop of rope goes over its head, around its chest -

Foon, standing behind it - and she's been in her cowgirl costume, all this time - has used the lasso from her belt, the other end wrapped tight around her wrist.

FOON
You're coming with me.

And she jumps -

The Host is *yanked* with her - !

FX: Foon and Host tumble down, down, down, into the Core.

Silence. Peth upset, crying, Mr Copper hugs her. Rickston sinks to the Archway floor, exhausted.

Hold, on the Doctor, looking down. Hold and hold.

Then, grim:

THE DOCTOR
No more.

FROM: RUSSELL T DAVIES TO: BENJAMIN COOK
MONDAY 4 JUNE 2007 02:14:51 GMT

RE: CHARLIE HUNNAM'S ARSE

Here's more. Not as many pages as I'd hoped. But I went back and seeded in Mr Maxitane – now called Max Callisto – throughout. No longer sat in his posh roped-off area in the Entertainment Lounge at the beginning, I've put him instead on the comms panels and wall-screens all over the ship, in a commercial for Max Callisto Cruiseliners, playing on permanent loop. The lead-in to that first scene in the Entertainment Lounge (sans roped-off area this time) now goes:

7. INT. LUXURY OFFICE - DAY

An advert, horizontal lines visible, seen on a TV screen. Smart, posh office, MAX CALLISTO at his desk, to CAMERA - 50, bit of a showman, gold tooth, waxy black moustache.

MAX
Max Callisto Cruiseliners, the fastest, the furthest, the best. And I should know, cos -
(big smile, CU)
My name's Max!

FX: his gold tooth goes *ding!*

Screen blips, footage replays, and PULL OUT TO REVEAL:

CUT TO:

8. INT. CORRIDOR OUTSIDE ENTERTAINMENT LOUNGE - NIGHT

Pulling out, Max Callisto looped on a wall-screen. THE DOCTOR watching as he adjusts his bow-tie; he's back in his dinner suit. He's ready, he walks through -

CUT TO:

9. INT. ENTERTAINMENT LOUNGE - NIGHT

THE DOCTOR walks in.

'And I should know cos – my name's Max!'

And I changed Peth's name to Astrid. Peth is her surname now. I never liked the name Peth, I only came up with it quickly for that treatment, and it's bugged me every day since. 'Astrid' sounds more spacey, more like a futuristic Doctor's companion. Astra was too obvious, I thought.

```
79. INT. SHIP CORRIDOR #4 - NIGHT[6]

An open doorway blocked by a
GIRDER, but with a gaaaah! - THE
DOCTOR pushes it, it topples. The
Doctor leaps into the corridor
- wrecked, as others, some PRAC
FLAMES - ASTRID, MR COPPER &
RICKSTON following. Energy, top
speed:

                THE DOCTOR
    Right! From here, it's up
    three more staircases, get
    yourselves to Reception One,
    the grid says it's still got
    oxygen, once you're there,
    Astrid, you've got staff
    access to the computer, try
    to find a way of transmitting
    an SOS, Mr Copper, give me
    that -
          (takes the baton)
    - once it's charged, it'll
    take out Host within 50
    yards, but then it needs
    60 seconds to recharge, got
    that? Rickston, you take
    this -
             (the sonic)
    - I've pre-set it, just hold
    down that button, it'll open
    the doors, Do Not Lose It,
    got that? Now go and open the
    next door, go on, go!

Rickston runs off.

          THE DOCTOR (CONT'D)
    Mr Copper, you've been
    injured, I need you fighting
    fit -

He grabs the FIRST-AID BOX off the
wall, throws it to Mr Copper -

          THE DOCTOR (CONT'D)
    Astrid, where's the power
    points?

                ASTRID
    Over here -

She runs to a wall, the Doctor
joins her, and as he plugs the
baton into a wall-plug to power
up -

                THE DOCTOR
    D'you see, when it's ready,
    that blue light comes on,
    there.

Both quieter now, more intimate:

                ASTRID
    You're talking like you're
    not coming with us.

                THE DOCTOR
    There's something down on
    Deck 31. I'm gonna find out
    what it is.

                ASTRID
    But what if you meet the
    Host?

                THE DOCTOR
    Oh, I'll just… have some fun!

                ASTRID
                (smiling)
    Sounds like you do this sort
    of thing all the time.

                THE DOCTOR
    Not by choice. All I do is
    travel, that's what I am,
    just a traveller.
```

6 The placing of the Max Callisto Cruiseliners commercial (the new Scene 7) and the Doctor viewing it on a wall-screen (Scene 8) has shifted all subsequent scene numbers, so the Canyon is now Scene 78, followed by this, Scene 79, in Ship Corridor #4.

Astrid (Kylie Minogue) contemplates life in the TARDIS.

ASTRID
Must be nice.

THE DOCTOR
Imagine it. No tax, no mortgage, no boss. Just the open sky.

ASTRID
…I'm sort of… unemployed now. I was thinking, that blue box was kind of small, but… I could squeeze in. Like a stowaway.

THE DOCTOR
…yeah.

Nice smile between them. Then -

CAMERA SHAKE - the corridor lurches, PRAC RUBBLE - and this time, the corridor keeps shuddering, as the Doctor leaps to a COMMS PANEL (screen still playing sc.7):

THE DOCTOR (CONT'D)
Mr Frame, still with us - ?

SCENE CONTINUES, INTERCUT WITH:

80. INT. BRIDGE - NIGHT

BRIDGE SHAKING, MIDSHIPMAN FRAME on COMMS, very ill now:

MIDSHIPMAN FRAME
It's the engines, sir. Final phase! The outer shell's ruptured -

BIGGER CAMERA SHAKE -

CUT TO:

81. EXT. FX SHOT - NIGHT

FX: THE WRECKED TITANIC, creaking, groaning, small GOUTS OF FLAME around the ENGINES, fragments flying out -

CUT TO:

82. INT. SHIP CORRIDOR #4 - NIGHT

CAMERA SHAKE slowly subsiding, THE DOCTOR on COMMS:

THE DOCTOR
How long have we got?

MIDSHIPMAN FRAME
Eight minutes. If that.

THE DOCTOR
Don't worry, I'll get there.

MIDSHIPMAN FRAME
But the Bridge is sealed off!

THE DOCTOR
Yep! Working on it! I'm gonna get there, Mr Frame. Somehow.
(the baton beeps)
All charged up!

He shoves the baton to Astrid, runs back to the first door -

THE DOCTOR (CONT'D)
You lot! Keep going. Mr Copper, look after her. Astrid, look after him. Rickston… look after yourself. And I'll see you again. All of you. That's a promise.

Presses the button, the door slides shut, he's gone.

CUT TO:

83. INT. CANYON - NIGHT

FX: WIDE SHOT, THE DOCTOR runs back across the STRUT.

CUT TO:

84. INT. STAIRWELL #2 - NIGHT

Rubble, etc. ASTRID, MR COPPER & RICKSTON heading up…

CUT TO:

85. INT. STAIRWELL - NIGHT

THE DOCTOR hurrying down…

CUT TO:

86. INT. SHIP CORRIDOR #5 - NIGHT

RICKSTON sonics open the door, it slides back -

THREE HOST standing there!

Rickston runs back -

RICKSTON
Do it - !

```
MR COPPER & ASTRID are further
back, he holds up the baton -

              MR COPPER
    Stand by!

FX: THE BLUE RIPPLE bounces out
from the baton -

SLAM! CU HOST'S HEAD hitting the
floor, deactivated.

Mr Copper, Astrid & Rickston
overjoyed, whooping!

                             CUT TO:

87. INT. KITCHEN CORRIDOR - NIGHT

THE DOCTOR heading along, as fast
as he can - bodies of kitchen staff
in the debris (no faces visible)
- when -

THREE HOST appear at the far end.

The Doctor turns back -

THREE MORE HOST at the opposite
end. They unclip Haloes…

              THE DOCTOR
    Wait wait wait, Security
    Protocol One! D'you hear me?
    One! One!!

They pause.

              THE DOCTOR (CONT'D)
    And that gives me four
    questions, right? So! You
    have orders to kill the
    survivors, yes?

              HOST
    Information: correct.

              THE DOCTOR
    And the survivors must
    therefore be passengers, or
    staff, yes?

              HOST
    Information: correct.

              THE DOCTOR
    Well, not me! I'm not a
    passenger, I'm not staff, go
    on, scan me, you must have
    biorecords, no such person on
    board, am I right?
          (terrible pause)
    Please be right.

              HOST
    Information: correct.

              THE DOCTOR
    Then you can't kill me! Goes
    against your programming!
    Oh, I'm good. In fact,
    I'm a stowaway, and I bet
    your programming says that
    stowaways must be arrested
    and taken to the nearest
    figure of authority, and I
    reckon the nearest figure of
    authority is on Deck 31,
    question number four, am I
    right?

              HOST
    Information: correct.

              THE DOCTOR
    Brilliant! Take me to your
    leader! Always wanted to say
    that.
```

FROM: RUSSELL T DAVIES TO: BENJAMIN COOK
TUESDAY 5 JUNE 2007 02:42:56 GMT

RE: CHARLIE HUNNAM'S ARSE

Almost finished. About 13 pages today. That's good. All those random props are paying off – the forklift truck, the teleport bracelets, the commercial. Max Callisto is now called Max Capricorn – much better! And Midshipman Frame is Alonso, not Bosworth. But this is still so expensive, there might have to be major cuts. Anyway, you're not alone now, because I handed in these first 61 pages to the production team today, to start prep. Lordy God, it's real…

```
87. INT. TITANIC RECEPTION - NIGHT[7]

Door opens, MR COPPER bursts
through with the baton -

FOUR HOST scattered around the
room, all turn -

FX: BLUE RIPPLE bounces out of the
baton -
```

7 A brief scene (numbered 31) of the Posh Man and friends watching the approaching meteoroids ('It's simply beautiful,' says the Posh Man. 'Thank you, Max Callisto!') has been deleted, shifting all subsequent scene numbers, so the Doctor encountering the Host in the Kitchen Corridor is now Scene 86, followed by this, Scene 87, in Reception.

PRAC FX SPARKS on one Host, it judders, drops dead.

WIDE SHOT, all four Host lying dead in the rubble, as ASTRID & RICKSTON follow Mr Copper in. The room's wrecked, but not too bad. (NB, this is a different Reception to sc.3, 12, 16, etc, which was lower down in the ship. But all Receptions look the same!) Mr Copper in charge now, like it's been the making of him.

MR COPPER
Rickston, seal the doors, make this room secure. We have sanctuary! And keep an eye on the Host, first sign of rebooting, I'll blast them, Astrid, try the computer, we need that SOS!

ASTRID
Yes sir!

CUT TO Rickston, who runs to a second door, sonics it.

That done, he stops. Gets his breath. Sinks to the floor. Curls up. Quietly, Rickston starts to cry.

Astrid puts Bannakaffalatta's EMP transmitter to good use.

CUT TO ASTRID, on the far side of the room - Mr Copper in b/g, checking each dead Host. She's going to the COMMS PANEL (still playing sc.7 on a loop)… But it's right next to the RACK OF TELEPORT BRACELETS.

She picks one up. Realises…

Uses the comms.

ASTRID (CONT'D)
Bridge, this is Reception One.

SCENE CONTINUES, INTERCUT WITH:

88. INT. BRIDGE - NIGHT

MIDSHIPMAN FRAME on COMMS - throughout, wrestling with controls, trying to get more power.

MIDSHIPMAN FRAME
Who's that?

ASTRID
Astrid Peth, I was with the Doctor, tell me, can you divert power to the teleport system?

MIDSHIPMAN FRAME
No way. I'm using everything I've got to keep the engines going.

ASTRID
Just one trip, I need to get to Deck 31. The Doctor's gone down there, he's on his own. Mr Frame, he's done everything he can to save us. I can't leave him.

Frame hesitates. Damn it! Then stabs buttons…

CUT TO:

89. INT. TITANIC RECEPTION - NIGHT

MR COPPER ripping wires out of a dead Host, when -

ASTRID
Mr Copper. I'm going to find him.

FX: at the far end, teleport glow, ASTRID disappears.

'I like a funny man. No one's been funny with me for years.' Max Capricorn (George Costigan) reveals himself to the Doctor (David Tennant).

MR COPPER
...good luck.

CUT TO:

90. INT. HOST CONTAINMENT CELLS - NIGHT

TWO HOST lead THE DOCTOR in, as guards. A THIRD HOST already there, standing sentinel. The Doctor looking up...

FX: DMP WIDE SHOT, looking up, a hole ripped through the floors of the Titanic, leading up above, huge height.[8]

THE DOCTOR
Wow. That's what you'd call a fixer-upper. Come on then! Host with the most. This ultimate authority of yours, who is it?

Two Host go to the BOOTHS; two of them are still closed, but now revealed to be a false front - the two booths are actually a DOOR, which the Host now slide back.

PRAC STEAM blasting out, like a seal has been broken. Beyond, black space. But with lights glinting from inside...

THE DOCTOR (CONT'D)
Ohh, clever, that's a Omnistate Impact Chamber. Indestructible! You could survive anything, in there, you could sit through a supernova. Or a shipwreck.

Something glides out, into the light...

Clanking, whirring, lights shining...

It is a METAL BOX, five feet tall, three feet wide, blinking with computer panels, though driven by great big industrial wheels. Laced with tubes; it's a mobile life-support for the SEVERED HEAD on top: pale and ghastly, white cataract eyes, it sticks out of the top of the box, plugged into the tubes, a ventilator hissing away. As it glides out:

8 A digital matte painting (DMP), added during post-production, is used to create virtual sets and backdrops.

THE DOCTOR (CONT'D)
But only one person could have the power and the money to hide themselves on board like this.
(imitates advert)
And I should know, cos…

MAX
My name's Max.

And the HEAD OF MAX CAPRICORN smiles -

FX: his GOLD TOOTH goes *ding!*

THE DOCTOR
Oh, it really does that!

MAX
Who the hell is this?

HOST
Information: stowaway.

MAX
Kill him.

THE DOCTOR
No! But! That's such a waste! I mean, you're giving me so much material here! Like… how to get a head in business. D'you see? Head? Head? No? Head?

MAX
Ohhh, the office joker.

THE MAX-BOX trundles towards the Doctor, wheels clanking, gears grinding, the box hissing STEAM.

MAX (CONT'D)
(smiles)
I like a funny man. No one's been funny with me for years.

THE DOCTOR
Can't think why.

MAX
A hundred-and-seventy-six years of running the company have taken their toll.

THE DOCTOR
Yeah, but… nice wheels.

CUT TO the far end of the room, ASTRID sneaking through a gap in the wall. Crouching down, hidden by debris, watching -

MAX
A life-support system, in a society that despises cyborgs. I've had to run the company by hologram since the late five-thousands.

THE DOCTOR
And it's showing. The company's not doing too well, yeah? Going down the drain, they say, can't even afford staff insurance.

MAX
(ignoring this)
Host! What's the schedule?

HOST
Information: time-cycle nine.

MAX
We should've crashed by now, what's gone wrong?

He turns, whirrs, clanks…

Going to a ledge, with a railing, at the end of the room.

FX: WIDE, LEDGE, THE MAX-BOX perched above canyon walls.

MAX (CONT'D)
The goddamn engines are still running, they should have stopped.

FX: HIS POV, the drop, then the CORE OF ENERGY far below.

THE DOCTOR
You've got a very good man up on the Bridge. Midshipman Frame. Better than you deserve.

MAX
Just a delay, that's all. They're still gonna fail.

THE DOCTOR
And when they do, the Earth gets roasted, I don't understand, what's Earth got to do with it?!

MAX
This interview is terminated -

THE DOCTOR
No, but hold on, wait wait wait! I can work it out, just

watch me, I'm brilliant,
I could've been your
apprentice, I'll prove it -

MAX clanks back towards him, fascinated…

THE DOCTOR (CONT'D)
- so! The business is failing, then you wreck the ship, so that makes things even worse… Oh! Yes! No. Yes! The business isn't failing, it's failed, past tense! You've been bought out! Max Capricorn doesn't even own Max Capricorn any more!

MAX
My own board voted me out. They stabbed me in the back.

THE DOCTOR
If you had a back.

CUT TO Astrid, creeping carefully across the space, just a few feet, keeping low, heading for something…

THE DOCTOR (CONT'D)
So! You wreck the ship - wipe out any survivors, just in case anyone's rumbled you - and the company they just bought halves in value. Ohh, but that's not enough, no! Cos then, a Max Capricorn ship hits the Earth, it destroys an entire planet, outrage and scandal back home, the business is wiped out!

MAX
And the board thrown in jail, for mass murder.

THE DOCTOR
While you sit there safe, inside the Impact Chamber.

MAX
I have men waiting to salvage me from the ruins, and enough offworld accounts to retire to the beaches of Penhaxico Two. Where the ladies are fond of metal, so they say.

The Doctor *furious* now:

THE DOCTOR
So that's the plan. A business plan. A retirement plan!! Two thousand people on this ship, six billion underneath us, all of them slaughtered, and why? Because Max Capricorn's a loser!

MAX
(furious)
I never lose!

THE DOCTOR
Titanic's still afloat, you can't even scupper!

MAX
Just watch me. I can cancel the engines from here -

CU Max's panel, a BIG RED LIGHT flashes, *veep-veep-veep* -

CUT TO:

91. INT. BRIDGE - NIGHT

BIG RED LIGHT flashes, *veep-veep-veep* -

PRAC EXPLOSIONS on the computer banks!

MIDSHIPMAN FRAME
No no no - !

CUT TO:

92. INT. TITANIC RECEPTION - NIGHT

SLIGHT CAMERA SHAKE, the room trembling, just a little. MR COPPER & RICKSTON look up, PRAC FX DUST trickling down…

RICKSTON
What's happening…?

CUT TO:

93. INT. HOST CONTAINMENT CELLS - NIGHT

SLIGHT CAMERA SHAKE, room trembling -

ASTRID hidden, but looking round, making up her mind…

THE DOCTOR furious -

THE DOCTOR
You can't do this - !

'I never lose!'

MAX
Hold him!

The TWO HOST flanking the Doctor grab his arms, iron grip.

THE DOCTOR
Max, you can disappear, that's fine, just take the money and go, I don't care, but leave the Earth alone - !

MAX
I wish we could have worked together, Doctor, you're rather good. All that banter, and yet not a word wasted. But it's time for me to retire. The Titanic is falling; the skies will burn; let the Christmas inferno commence.

He turns away, hissing, clanking.

MAX (CONT'D)
Host. Kill him.

While the two Host hold the Doctor, the THIRD HOST, standing across the room, takes down its Halo.

The Doctor struggling like mad -

The Host takes aim…

When…

ASTRID
Mr Capricorn!

Max turns -

The Doctor turns -

CU ASTRID.

JUMP CUT WIDER, Astrid in a seat.

JUMP CUT WIDER, Astrid in the seat of the FORKLIFT TRUCK!

ASTRID (CONT'D)
I resign.

CU her hand slamming off the handbrake -

CU FORKLIFT TRUCK WHEELS, racing -

The FORKLIFT TRUCK speeds across the room -

CU THE MAX-BOX grinding, Max furious, turning to face it -

CU ASTRID, driving, fierce -

CUT TO THE DOCTOR, trapped -

THE DOCTOR
- Astrid, don't - !

WHAM! CU Astrid thrown forward, jerking back -

WIDER: THE FORKLIFT TRUCK and THE MAX-BOX, slammed up against each other, two machines, both with engines at full throttle, both straining, neither one giving way -

CU MAX-BOX WHEELS, spinning, PRAC FX SMOKE & SPARKS -

CU FORKLIFT TRUCK WHEELS, spinning, PRAC FX SMOKE -

The Host throws its Halo at Astrid -

FX: Astrid flinches, but the Halo hits the cage of the driver's seat, SPARKS, zings away -

CU Astrid, cranking the gears up…

CU MAX, snarling at her…

FX: the *ding!* of his GOLD TOOTH.

THEN SLOW MOTION: ASTRID looks across at the Doctor.

SLOW MOTION: the Doctor, trapped, looking at Astrid. Knowing what she's going to do. He says quietly, no…

Normal speed again - she cranks the gear up to maximum -

CU FORKLIFT WHEELS, PRAC SMOKE, but they suddenly SHOOT FORWARD, fast -

WIDE SHOT, the FORKLIFT TRUCK scooping up the MAX-BOX, and racing forward, fast -

FX: THE WIDE SHOT OF THE LEDGE, MAX-BOX & FORKLIFT TRUCK breaking through the railing and tipping down -

Both HOST suddenly release the Doctor, jerking hands up in a surrender position (ie, control over them broken), leaving him to belt forward -

THE DOCTOR (CONT'D)
Astriiiiid - !

At the edge, his POV -

FX: with the MAX-BOX furthest down, screaming its way down into the depths, the FORKLIFT TRUCK beside it, on ASTRID: she's free of the driver's cage, but is falling, falling, falling, down, down, down, looking up at the Doctor…

On the Doctor. His horror.

FX: THE SHAFT empty now. A last flare of power from the CORE, then it dies, fades to black.

And now HOLD THE CU ON THE DOCTOR. Devastated. Staring down. CAMERA SHAKE increases.

But the noise fades down, to silence.

And the music soars.

On the Doctor.

MIX his CU with images from…

MIX TO:

94. INT. BRIDGE - NIGHT

SLOW MOTION. SOUNDLESS, music only.

PRAC EXPLOSIONS from the computer banks, beautiful in slow-motion, sparks arcing, with MIDSHIPMAN FRAME desperate, trying to use the controls, but having to shield himself.

And though there's no sound, he is yelling 'Doctor! Doctor, help me!' over and over again…

MIX TO:

95. INT. TITANIC RECEPTION - NIGHT

SLOW MOTION. SOUNDLESS, music only.

MR COPPER & RICKSTON cowering against a wall.

PRAC RUBBLE & DUST falling down, as they look up, imploring. Both shout 'Doctor!', again and again. Begging for help.

MIX TO:

INT. HOST CONTAINMENT CELLS - NIGHT

SLOW MOTION, SOUNDLESS. Music only. On THE DOCTOR, as he walks back into the room.

Astrid makes the ultimate sacrifice.

Lost. Alone.

PRAC RUBBLE falling around him, but it's like he doesn't notice, doesn't care.

NORMAL SPEED, though still soundless, music only, as the Doctor stands between the TWO HOST again. They stand erect, locked into the default prayer position, heads bowed.

He stands there. So tired.

Then, eyes dead, he just lifts his hand.

Clicks his fingers.

Both Host slowly raise their heads.

Still grim, the Doctor offers out both his arms, the crook of his elbows. Both Host hook arms round his elbows.

The Doctor looks up, cranes his head right back.

The two Host look up.

FX: WIDE SHOT, the two HOST now with WINGS UNFURLED, and they FLY! Carrying the Doctor with them, three-in-a-row, whooshing up, up, up into the DMP heights -

CUT TO:

97. INT. FX SHAFT - NIGHT

FX: TWO HOST, holding THE DOCTOR between them, all looking up, fly up, up, up, through the gutted ship - the shaft in b/g whizzing past behind them, floor after floor -

FX: TIGHTER THREE-SHOT, B/G WHIZZING PAST, all still looking up as both Host raise their arms, fists clenched in a punch -

FX: CU GOLD FIST, B/G WHIZZING PAST -

CUT TO:

98. INT. BRIDGE - NIGHT

CAMERA SHAKE, PRAC RUBBLE falling, MIDSHIPMAN FRAME cowering on the floor, in pain, but then -

PRAC FX: The two Host with arms aloft PUNCH THROUGH THE FLOOR! Floorboards shattering, flying away -

The top half of their bodies staying in the hole as THE DOCTOR hauls himself up the rest of the way. All smiles!

THE DOCTOR
Midshipman Frame! At last!

MIDSHIPMAN FRAME
But the Host -

THE DOCTOR
Controller dead, emergency protocol, they revert to the next highest authority. And that's me!

CUT TO:

99. EXT. FX SHOT - NIGHT

FX: THE TITANIC groaning, beginning to tilt downwards towards the Earth, more GOUTS OF FLAME from the engines -

CUT TO:

100. INT. BRIDGE - NIGHT

CAMERA SHAKE - ROOM TILTING DOWN - THE DOCTOR grappling with the controls, MIDSHIPMAN FRAME on his feet -

MIDSHIPMAN FRAME
But there's nothing we can do -

THE DOCTOR
What's your first name?

MIDSHIPMAN FRAME
Alonso.

THE DOCTOR
You're kidding me.

MIDSHIPMAN FRAME
Why…?

THE DOCTOR
That's something else I've always wanted to say. Allons-y, Alonso!

And he slams a big lever -

CUT TO:

101. EXT. FX SHOT - NIGHT

FX: THE TITANIC tilted downwards at 45 degrees, suspended for a second - and then it drops! Hurtling towards EARTH!

CUT TO:

102. INT. BRIDGE - NIGHT

THE WHOLE ROOM TILTING DOWN - WIND BLASTING THROUGH - THE DOCTOR leaps to the WHEEL - spinning it!

MIDSHIPMAN FRAME holding onto the computer banks for dear life - yelling all the way - !

A FIERCE RED LIGHT flares up, fills the room -

CUT TO:

103. EXT. FX SHOT - NIGHT

FX: THE TITANIC now plummeting through the upper atmosphere, at 45 degrees, BURNING, HULL GLOWING RED HOT -

FX: TITANIC POV, hurtling down through clouds, Britain appearing down below -

CUT TO:

104. INT. TITANIC RECEPTION - NIGHT

TIGHT ON MR COPPER & RICKSTON pressed against the wall, all now TILTED DOWN at 45 degrees, yelling, helpless, as DEBRIS shifts and tumbles down on top of them -

CUT TO:

105. INT. BRIDGE - DAY

Red light gone, stark daylight now streaming through - THE DOCTOR at the WHEEL, yelling with exertion as he spins it - the TILT of the room lessening a fraction -

CUT TO:

106. EXT. FX SHOT - NIGHT

FX: THE TITANIC no longer glowing - not burnt, it's a tough old ship - now levelling up a few degrees, but still plummeting down, down, down through blue skies -

CUT TO:

107. INT. BRIDGE - DAY

THE DOCTOR at the WHEEL, manic, spinning it, MIDSHIPMAN FRAME holding on, as the Doctor glances down -

ON SCREEN GRAPHIC: a map of LONDON, zooming in to one particular spot, marked with a red *DANGER* sign.

The Doctor holds the Wheel with one hand, gets out Rickston's vone with the other, bleeps it -

THE DOCTOR
Hello, yes, could you get me Buckingham Palace?

CUT TO:

108. INT. NEWS 24 STUDIO - DAY

HORIZONTAL LINES VISIBLE, NEWSREADER to CAMERA:

NEWSREADER
…and as dawn rises over Great Britain, it seems that, this year, the City of London has escaped intact…

CUT TO:

109. EXT. BUCKINGHAM PALACE - DAY

WIDE SHOT, with roads empty. The flag is flying.

NEWSREADER OOV
The Queen has remained in residence, in defiance of extraterrestrial incursion…

Voice fades down, SLOW ZOOM in, sound of a RINGING PHONE.

CUT TO:

110. INT. BRIDGE - DAY

THE DOCTOR on the vone -

THE DOCTOR
- listen to me, Security Code 596, now get out of there!!!

CUT TO:

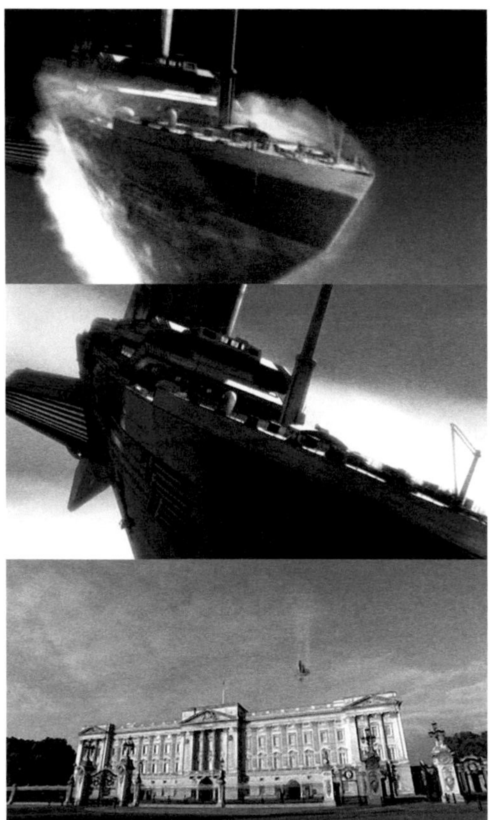
The *Titanic* hurtles through the clouds, plummeting down, down, down towards Buckingham Palace...

111. EXT. FX SHOT - DAY

FX: blue skies, THE TITANIC levelling, levelling, levelling, but still racing downwards -

CUT TO:

112. INT. POSH MARBLE STAIRCASE - DAY

BACK TO CAMERA, an OLD WOMAN in a nightie & curlers running downstairs with TWO LIVERIED COURTIERS & A CORGI -

CUT TO:

113. INT. BRIDGE - NIGHT

CU THE DOCTOR, heaving at the WHEEL, teeth gritted, like he's physically pulling the Titanic up, the room levelling back slowly towards the horizontal...

CUT TO:

114. EXT. BUCKINGHAM PALACE - DAY

The Palace stands proud....

FX: THE TITANIC, reaching the perigee of its downward curve, swoops in from behind the Palace and *SMASHES THROUGH THE ENTIRE BUILDING!!!*

CUT TO:

115. INT. BRIDGE - DAY

Room now tilting slightly upwards, as the FLAGPOLE shoots through like a javelin - *whannng!*, it spears into the back wall, right through the portrait of Max Capricorn, UNION JACK fluttering.

CUT TO:

116. EXT. COURTYARD - DAY

TIGHT HIGH SHOT looking down on the OLD WOMAN in nightie & curlers, on the floor, covered in dust, BRICKS all around her, the TWO COURTIERS just helping her to her feet.

LOW ANGLE, the old woman standing, now framed against the sky. She waves an angry fist in the air.

THE QUEEN
Damn you, aliens! Damn you!

CUT TO:

117. EXT. FX SHOT - NIGHT

FX: THE TITANIC, more graceful now, on an upward incline, heading back to space, though at less steep an angle, sailing through the blue skies of Christmas morning.

CUT TO:

118. INT. TITANIC RECEPTION - DAY

Daylight now streaming in, the room tilting upwards a little, debris falling away from MR COPPER & RICKSTON, still pressed up against the wall.

```
They can't believe it; they made
it. Both start to laugh.

And they hug each other, crying,
overjoyed.

                          CUT TO:

119. INT. BRIDGE - DAY

Room now tilting upwards.
MIDSHIPMAN FRAME slumped against
the back wall, shattered,
recovering. And THE DOCTOR
slides down to sit with him.
Exhausted:

            THE DOCTOR
   Used the heat of re-entry to
   fire up the Secondary Storm
   Drive. Unsinkable. That's me.

         MIDSHIPMAN FRAME
   ...but... we made it.

            THE DOCTOR
   Not all of us.

                          CUT TO:

120. EXT. FX SHOT - NIGHT

FX: THE TITANIC suspended in space,
back in a peaceful orbit above the
Earth. Damaged, but serene.
```

I was going to bring in the Judoon at the end, wasn't I? Not enough time. Also, it'd just feel odd now, like they've walked in from another adventure. Too big. Too comic. The allocated Judoon costumes refurbishment money can go into some prosthetics for Max, I hope. We've allowed for ten Host, too, but I don't think we need more than six. That's good. Tiny savings.

In other news… Peter Fincham walked into a meeting with Catherine Tate today, with loads of executives from Tiger Aspect Productions (a huge London indie) and said, 'So you're going to be the new *Doctor Who* companion?' *Noooo!* Jaws dropped. Secret out, all round London. Christ! The real reason this is bad is that the tabloid reports are going to be 'FREEMA SACKED!' with a vengeance, which isn't true; we've so many plans for her. I can't believe it. After all these months of secrecy. Catherine is gutted. She'd told *no one*. Damn.

FROM: BENJAMIN COOK TO: RUSSELL T DAVIES
TUESDAY 5 JUNE 2007 10:32:10 GMT

RE: CHARLIE HUNNAM'S ARSE

YOU *DO* KILL KYLIE!!! And oh – you saved the Queen. Well, you couldn't kill her on Christmas Day. I'm sure it says so somewhere in the BBC Charter.

Here's a curious thing: Astrid plummets to her death; two pages later, the Doctor is joshing about Midshipman Frame's first name; another two pages, and the Queen is in a nightie and curlers, running downstairs with two courtiers and a corgi! Back in March, you said with regards to E4's *Skins*: 'It's the oddest hybrid of a drama and broad sitcom. Mind you, people say that about my stuff.' Comedy and Drama (or Comedy and Tragedy – the more traditional division) are common bedfellows in a Russell T Davies script, but is it a mistake to think of them as diametric opposites? Does the genre 'comedy-drama' (or 'dramedy', I've heard it called) really exist outside of BBC press releases and whatnot? Are there occasions when you'd consider it unworkable to blur the line between Comedy and Drama in this way? I mean, if you can progress suddenly and speedily from heartbreak as Astrid is killed, to a deliberately daft, tangential cutaway gag… what *won't* you do, Russell?

FROM: RUSSELL T DAVIES TO: BENJAMIN COOK
TUESDAY 5 JUNE 2007 13:09:56 GMT

RE: CHARLIE HUNNAM'S ARSE

Yes, I hate saying Comedy and Drama, because it automatically assumes that Drama = Tragedy. Big, big mistake. Drama encompasses the whole range. But I believe passionately that Comedy and Tragedy exist alongside each other. No way are they diametric opposites; they're right next to each other, and they overlap in a thousand different ways. *Queer as Folk* Episode 3 is like a thesis on that. There's a huge comedy sex scene, which results in a slapstick fall off a window ledge, intercut with the horniest threesome in the world, intercut with a drugs overdose in which a man dies. I chose to intercut Tragedy with Comedy and Sex. The whole world is compressed into that; the coexistence of all those things.

Pause for a weird story. That overdose scene really happened to me, in my kitchen, with a man like that

Kylie Minogue relaxes in her trailer. (How could you kill off this lovely lady, Russell? How *could* you...?)

– and I wrote it into the script. The existence of that scene was one of the great engines of *Queer as Folk*. A week before filming, the location fell through, and the production team said, 'Can we use your house?' Honest to God. So there's a man, acting out what could have happened to me, but dying, in the place where it actually happened. I can't tell you how that makes my head explode. Funny thing is, I believed that coincidence until about a year ago, when I realised that the director, Charles McDougall, who was a truly mad genius, was so intent on accuracy that he must have changed locations on purpose. I bet there was no 'other location'. It took me eight years to realise that. (They painted my house and redecorated, by the way. It's not really that awful hippy colour.)

But I have to write like that. Funny, sad, all at once. That's how life is. You can have a pratfall at a funeral. You can laugh so much that you choke to death. The Master is dark and genuinely, drum-beatingly insane, and therefore can be funny as hell. Jackie Tyler makes us laugh, but I knew that I'd uncover something sad at the heart of her. Her sadness over her absent daughter is there as early as *Aliens of London*, but you don't really get to see it properly until *Love & Monsters*. Idiots will say, 'Ah, that character is developing now' – what, like you were going to play it all in the first 30 seconds?! – but that capacity was always there. It had to be. Even in *Rose*, when Jackie is ostensibly 'funny', telling her daughter to get a job in the butcher's, Jackie is one of the things that's holding Rose back – and that's quite dark, at its heart. 'Funny' is hiding a lot of other stuff.

Many people hate that in my writing. Not just the fans, but also commissioners. Tessa Ross at Channel 4, who axed the greenlit *The Second Coming* before it was picked up by ITV, did so because she thought that my writing is essentially lightweight. Nicola Shindler has warned me about that: she says there are a lot of people who don't take my scripts seriously, because of the level of comedy. But I don't worry about that. It's how I write, it's me, and I'm not changing it. I think having a sense of humour is a powerful and human thing, it's one of our survival mechanisms, and it's never destroyed. Equally, a sense of humour can be cold, almost ruthless, but I've never found a single situation – not my mother's death, not my overdose, not anything – in which something funny hasn't happened. That's why I think it's so, *so* wrong to write with a Comedy or Tragedy label in your head. Life isn't like that. Indeed, I think *Mine All Mine* went wrong because I actually thought, I'll make this funny. Conversely, I took *Bob & Rose* incredibly seriously, and won Comedy Writer of the Year for it!

Anyway, more script. I've finished. It feels okay...

121. INT. TITANIC RECEPTION - DAY

Lighting restored. Still filled with rubble, but with some order restored.

WIDE SHOT, THE DOCTOR, MR COPPER & RICKSTON scattered across the space, just sitting there, stunned, still recovering.

Hold the pause, the silence. Then Mr Copper looks up. Still holding the baton. A weary smile, at the Doctor.

MR COPPER
I was quite a fighter in the end.

The Doctor just nods, flat now, lost in thought.

MIDSHIPMAN FRAME enters - now patched up, proper bandages. During this, on the Doctor, as he wanders over to the row of TELEPORT BRACELETS, picks one up, idly.

MIDSHIPMAN FRAME
Gentlemen. I've sent the SOS. Rescue ships should be here within 20 minutes. And they're digging out the records on Max Capricorn. Should be quite a story.

MR COPPER
But… they'll want to talk to all of us?

MIDSHIPMAN FRAME
Should think so, yeah.
(to the Doctor)
They'll want to know who you are, Doctor. As would we all.
(the Doctor just nods)
Is there any of that water left…?

MR COPPER
Of course…

He hands him a water bottle. Midshipman Frame swigs, wanders to the far end of the room, tired.

Mr Copper goes to the Doctor, sotto:

MR COPPER (CONT'D)
I think one or two inconvenient truths might come to light. Still. My own fault. And ten years in jail is better than dying.

THE DOCTOR
S'pose.

RICKSTON
Doctor…

Rickston's walking towards them, holding out the sonic screwdriver. And he's still tearful, broken, honest.

RICKSTON (CONT'D)
This is yours.

THE DOCTOR
And this is yours.

He hands him the vone, takes the sonic screwdriver.

RICKSTON
I never said… Thank you.

And he suddenly hugs the Doctor, tight.

But then, as he pulls out of the hug, wiping his face, the old Rickston is recovering, that glint in his eye.

RICKSTON (CONT'D)
Funny thing is, I said Max Capricorn was falling apart. Just before the crash, I sold all my shares. Transferred them to his rivals.
(smiles)
It's made me rich. How about that?

Rickston wanders away, more his old self, on his vone:

RICKSTON (CONT'D)
Salvain? Yeah, I know, just listen - check the Stock One Thousand, tell me the price on Majestic Cruises…

The Doctor still staring. Boiling. Mr Copper quiet, wise:

MR COPPER
Of all the people to survive. He's not the one you would have chosen, is he?

(no reply)
But if you could choose, Doctor. If you could decide who lives and who dies. That would make you a monster.

The Doctor looks at him properly. Smiles.

THE DOCTOR
Mr Copper.

Hands him a teleport bracelet.

THE DOCTOR (CONT'D)
I think you deserve this.

Mr Copper realises what he means, puts on the bracelet, as the Doctor gets a second bracelet, puts it on.

Then the Doctor looks across the room. Midshipman Frame far across the space, knows what he's about to do.

And Midshipman Frame stands tall. Salutes the Doctor.

The Doctor salutes him.

And then…

FX: TELEPORT GLOW, the Doctor & Mr Copper disappear.

CUT TO:

'Between you and me, I don't even think this is proper snow…'

122. EXT. HILLSIDE OVERLOOKING CITY - NIGHT

WIDE SHOT. SNOW falling. TWO SMALL FIGURES trudging across the barren, empty hillside, THE DOCTOR & MR COPPER.

MR COPPER
…so, Great Britain is part of Yooropee, and just across the British Channel, you've got Great France and Great Germany…

THE DOCTOR
No, just France and Germany, only Britain is great.

MR COPPER
And they're all at war with the continent of Hamerica?

THE DOCTOR
No, well, not yet, you could argue that one… There she is!

Far off, in the snow: THE TARDIS.

JUMP CUT TO THE DOCTOR & MR COPPER next to the Tardis. The Doctor patting it, wiping snow off. They're on the brow of the hill, the lights of a city glittering far-off.

THE DOCTOR (CONT'D)
Survive anything!

MR COPPER
Between you and me, I don't even think this is proper snow, I suspect it's the ballast from the Titanic's salvage, entering the atmosphere.

THE DOCTOR
Yeah. One of these days, it might snow for real.

Which is just chat, to delay the awkward moment:

MR COPPER
So!

THE DOCTOR
Well then.

MR COPPER
I take it, you'll be going?

THE DOCTOR
The open sky.

MR COPPER
And… what about me?

THE DOCTOR
Sorry. I travel alone. It's best that way.

MR COPPER
Then what am I supposed to do?

THE DOCTOR
Give me that credit card.

Mr Copper hands it over, the Doctor studies it, sonics it.

MR COPPER
It's only petty cash. Spending money. All done by computer, I didn't really know the currency, I thought a million might cover it.

THE DOCTOR
A million pounds?

MR COPPER
Enough for trinkets.

THE DOCTOR
Mr Copper, a million pounds is worth five million credits.

MR COPPER
How much…?!

THE DOCTOR
Five million, and fifty six.

MR COPPER
…I've got money.

THE DOCTOR
Yes, you have!

And Mr Copper takes the card. Incredulous. Then stands back, exultant, laughing to the skies.

MR COPPER
Oh my word. Oh my Vot. Oh my goodness me, *yee hah!*

THE DOCTOR
It's all yours. Planet Earth. Now that's a retirement plan. Just you be careful, though!

MR COPPER
I will, I will, oh I will!

THE DOCTOR
No interfering. I don't want any trouble. Just… have a nice life.

MR COPPER
I can have a house! A proper house! With a garden! And a door! Oh, Doctor! I'll make you proud!

He grabs the Doctor, kisses his cheek -

Then runs off, into the snow, towards the city, yelling:

MR COPPER (CONT'D)
I can have a kitchen! With chairs! And windows! And… plates!

THE DOCTOR
Um… where are you going?

MR COPPER
No idea!

THE DOCTOR
Nor me.

The Doctor turns to the Tardis, gets out the key.

But Mr Copper stops, calls back, a silhouette in the snow.

MR COPPER
Oh, and Doctor!
(pause)
I won't forget her.

The Doctor just nods.

Pause.

MR COPPER (CONT'D)
Merry Christmas!

THE DOCTOR
Merry Christmas, Mr Copper.

And the Doctor goes into the Tardis.

FX: the ancient grind of engines, and the Tardis fades away, obscured by the snow, gone.

END OF EPISODE 4.X

I'm off to London now. It's the *Jekyll* launch. It's Steven Moffat's new drama for the BBC. I can't wait to see it. I had to get up early and work like hell to finish this script, all so I can have a night out. In London Town!

FROM: BENJAMIN COOK TO: RUSSELL T DAVIES
THURSDAY 7 JUNE 2007 22:30:36 GMT

RE: CHARLIE HUNNAM'S ARSE

You've finished! What's been the early feedback? Do you even get feedback? From Julie? From Phil? Do you take notice of it? Are you back in Cardiff now? How was London? How was *Jekyll*? Any good? All these questions!

Astrid handles the forklift.

FROM: RUSSELL T DAVIES TO: BENJAMIN COOK
FRIDAY 8 JUNE 2007 01:26:56 GMT

RE: CHARLIE HUNNAM'S ARSE

I'm back in Cardiff. In fact, I've just got in from the BBC Worldwide Licensees' Dinner, at the St David's Hotel. I can see them all from my window, still dancing. It's a jamboree junket for all the *Doctor Who*, *Torchwood* and *Sarah Jane* merchandise licensees – over 200 of them! I had to talk to the man who makes the Frubes. I wanted to say, 'My friend said his flatmate was eating Martha Jones!' But I didn't. Frubes Man said they're a resounding success. Flying off the shelves, he said. Imagine being Frubes Man! I'm knackered from smiling. Christ, it's exhausting.

Now, *Jekyll* was wonderful. I loved it. It's well worth watching. I fear that the BBC might neglect it a bit, because it's a tricky one to sell, but of course it's *so* clever. Steven is over at the St David's now, pissed. Paul Cornell is there, too, and said that he'd heard from Kate Bush, because she loved his two Series Three episodes so much! *Kate Bush!* How funny.

Anyway, I've no time off, because *Torchwood* is in crisis – one script down, blah, blah, blah. That poor show lives in a state of crisis. But *Voyage of the Damned* has been well received, thank God. Julie loves it. Phil loves it. I think. I'm never sure, because they're just glad to get a working script. Of course I get feedback, I'll have any note going, although there hasn't been time for a proper notes session yet. But *I'm* happy with it. It's a sort of 7/10 script at the moment. It's kind of lame having Max as the villain, I suppose, but it's the only possible solution. It's not credible that one of the survivors could go 'ha ha!' in a sudden reveal, and turn out to be part of the evil plot. That's why I had to turn Max into a cyborg box, because the dramatic reveal of... *a businessman!* was too rubbish for words. Also, I loved the forklift once I'd planted it on, ooh, whichever draft, but to have Astrid use that against a human Max would have been ridiculously violent.

The real editing will come with the expense. It's a nightmare. Ed Thomas has about, I don't know, £20,000 to £30,000 to spend on a Christmas Special. I saw him just now at the licensees' dinner. He said, 'I've costed up to Page 66, and it's already £87,000!' That's just what I didn't want to hear. Oh well, we'll think of something.

CHAPTER SIX

THE REWRITER'S TALE

In which Buckingham Palace is saved, Kylie Minogue plays gooseberry, and Russell makes do with a single porthole

FROM: RUSSELL T DAVIES TO: BENJAMIN COOK
FRIDAY 15 JUNE 2007 17:19:55 GMT

FW: MEETING NOTES

We had a 4.X script meeting today. Here, for the record, are the notes from the script editor, Brian Minchin:

> DOCTOR WHO 4.X DRAFT ONE NOTES
>
> Dear Russell,
>
> Thank you again for such a lovely meeting. There are very few notes on such a wonderful script. I've summarised this morning's discussion below:
>
> BUILDING UP THE ROLE OF ASTRID
>
> Finding more time with Astrid and the Doctor. We should almost believe that she could be the next companion. If possible, more moments when we learn more about Astrid: her history, her family, her perception of the Doctor.
>
> Astrid kissing the Doctor.
>
> We talked about everyone being a bit in love with Astrid, and that it would be great to have a moment between her and Mr Copper.
>
> Making more of the moment when Astrid decides to follow the Doctor to Deck 31.
>
> Spelling out her sacrifice at the end: she's doing something that the Doctor wouldn't do in killing Max. Pushing her heroism: Astrid doesn't want to go over the edge with Max, but she needs to keep her foot on the pedal/hold onto the gear stick. Making this sequence explicit so that we understand why she can't leap off the forklift before it propels her into space.
>
> MAX CAPRICORN
>
> Should the Doctor have a plan in mind when he's confronting Max?
>
> Also, we discussed whether there is a way to build up Max before we see him, but didn't have any useful thoughts.
>
> LOCATION CHANGES
>
> The Titanic Reception is CUT. All action from these scenes will be relocated to the

Entertainment Lounge, corridors, and Deck.
Please note that ALL corridors should be shot in ONE corridor location, but redressed/ with different lighting.

COSTUME AND MAKE-UP

In order to signify that all the guests on board are 'alien', each character has a small bindi on their forehead.
The Stewards will be in naval costumes.

There were some specific scene notes, too. For example, the ledge beneath Morvin should 'snap away', rather than 'crumble'; the Doctor should tell Midshipman Frame what he has to do to stabilise the ship; we talked about clarifying the attempts to send an SOS (if the signal has been blocked, does the Doctor need to tell Astrid to do something cleverer?), and so on.

FROM: BENJAMIN COOK TO: RUSSELL T DAVIES
SATURDAY 16 JUNE 2007 12:50:34 GMT

RE: FW: MEETING NOTES

Are you nodding in agreement at the meeting notes, or shaking your head in disgust? Or did you kick out any note that you didn't agree with during the meeting? (And Brian's opening paragraph – is that how *all* notes from script editors begin? Are they told to do that? Or do some notes to writers start with: 'Thanks for nothing, you talentless bastard. Your script was a terrible piece of rubbish. Here is the first instalment of notes'…?) Also, Ed must have costed the whole script by now, so what's the damage?

FROM: RUSSELL T DAVIES TO: BENJAMIN COOK
MONDAY 18 JUNE 2007 14:21:53 GMT

RE: FW: MEETING NOTES

Script editors are *trained* to write an opening paragraph like that, with compliments, on any set of notes, on any show. It's polite and gets things off to an agreeable start. Of course, if you know that, the compliments are useless. But they're good notes. Though, as you say, I kicked out any that weren't good. I'm trying to think of an example… oh, I remember, a tiny thing: someone suggested that the Doctor and Astrid, in Scene 3, should look at each other as they pass for the first time. *Duh!* Stupid note. The whole joy of that passing is that they don't acknowledge each other; the audience knows more than the characters do.

In a way, with Kylie cast (provisionally), I relaxed slightly with Astrid and didn't work hard enough at her, because I thought that the sheer iconic imagery of her casting was enough. I'm a fool. I can see that now, and I'm happy to bump up her part. Also, if you know how a character is going to end, sometimes that can rob them of energy. I tell off other writers for this, then go and make the same mistake myself. Since I knew from the start that Astrid would die, there's an ever so slight indifference towards her. It feels as though any Astrid Could Be A Companion scene is *false*. I've got to fight that. Making Astrid more of a hero, though? Unfortunately, that's buggered – because now we *are* offering Mr Copper to Dennis Hopper. If Dennis Hopper should, in a mad world, accept the part, we'll have a similar set of notes – doubtless from his agent – asking for Mr Copper to be bumped up further in the heroic stakes. This is one of the problems of casting before writing: it starts to affect the production. In fact, when I explained this to Julie, she said, 'I wish you'd told me, because then we wouldn't have sent the bloody script to Dennis!' Julie wants Astrid absolutely central, quite rightly.

Should the Doctor have a plan in mind when confronting Max? That's a great idea, but I can't imagine what it is. The Doctor is weak in those scenes, I've compensated with verbiage, and I've no idea how to fix it. But I'm confident I'll think of something. And building up Max before we see him? That's tricky. It's a slight disappointment as Max unveils himself, I admitted as much in my e-mails to you, but the Big Reveal *can't* be anyone else in the cast. If that scene were the absolute climax, I'd have to rethink, but we still have the plunging *Titanic* – the proper, adrenalin-filled climax – to come. I think we have to live with it. But I'll keep thinking. Often, with things like that, you realise the solution… in

DESIGN CUTBACKS

This is Russell's reply to Phil Collinson's e-mail about the Design Department's cutbacks. 'I was officially sulking,' recalls Russell, 'because I had to make so many cuts. Every time Julie or Phil phoned me up, I was all monosyllabic and clipped. "Yeah. Fine. Okay. Bye." What a child! But I couldn't help it. And then I e-mailed them, and was all agreeable and full of exclamations! Like! This! That reinforces the sulking, because they know those exclamations ring false. How ridiculous – especially since I know full well that they're out there, banging the phones, scrimping and saving every last penny for me...'

FROM: RUSSELL T DAVIES TO: PHIL COLLINSON
DATE: TUESDAY 19 JUNE 2007 18:08:44 GMT

RE: EP. X

>> Hi Russell,

Sorry to bombard you, but I've just had a budget meeting with Ed. We have our work cut out, and all of these are just suggestions, but I wonder if we could make some cuts and trims, and we discussed the following possibilities: <<

Don't worry, Phil, it must be done.

>> Deck 22 has gone altogether, which is a good saving. We left some money to build windows into the Entertainment Lounge, but how many do you think we need? <<

I could make do with a single porthole.

>> The Bridge. At the moment, this set is budgeted to be built on a rostrum. A good saving could be had if we build the main set on the ground instead, but then build a small section – say, a six-foot-square corner – on a rostrum, and shoot the Host/Doctor breakthrough, in medium close-up, on that. We could cheat a way of getting a shot with Frame and the ship's wheel in the foreground, so that it feels like the same set, and then close-up shots of the Doctor climbing out. We'd build both sets side by side, and match the main set to the breakaway one for all action after the breakthrough. It'll save us a good few grand. <<

Of course that'll work. Simple!

>> Host Containment Cells. That's a big build, to construct individual cells as scripted. Could we rethink this and have a kind of robot deactivation area – an industrial space, a big console, some kind of operating table in the centre, with a robot on, and other robots standing against the wall but 'plumbed in'? This would mean we could find an industrial-type location, and avoid big construction costs. The console – or one of the walls – could part to reveal Max. <<

Lovely!

>> Do we ever go back to the Entertainment Lounge after the meteoroid crash? It'll save us money if we don't have to redress this room. If you cut the big shot as the meteoroid rips through, will you still keep Sc.44/2 (people consumed by flame), Sc.46/1 (stuntman falling over balcony), Sc.46/2 and Sc.46/3 (handsome man and woman's death), and Sc.51/1 (man tumbles through space)?[1] <<

44/2 is gone. 46/1 is gone. 46/2 and 46/3 are gone. In fact, I'd better cut 51/1, too. This does mean I have to keep the Chief Steward's death in full, or the meteoroids hit the *Titanic* and we see no one die. *No one!*

>> Morvin's death is going to be very expensive as written, as we have to construct a mechanism to tip part of the set. Instead, could he lean against the railing, which breaks and causes him to fall? <<

Railing it is!

1 Scene designations are now from The Mill's FX list, so 44/2 means Scene 44, FX Shot 2, and so forth.

12 months' time!

Also, Phil tapped into something that I've worried about from the start: the passengers on the *Titanic* are going to look human, like the *Titanic* has time-travelled from 1912 or something, or like humans from the future have time-travelled back for a laugh. It doesn't matter how many times you say that they're from the planet Sto; it's the *pictures* that matter, and this looks like a bunch of humans partying. I suggested that everyone wears bindis. It's all that I could think of. We can't afford alien prosthetics on every single extra. I'll try to write it into the dialogue somehow. If we'd a huge budget, everyone would have gills.

The script has been costed – and Ed reckons that we're £45,000 over budget! This is terrifying. This is major. Cutting the Reception will only lose us about £10,000, so another £35,000 has to be found. We won't have all the answers for the next draft, so I'll just rewrite as is and we'll come back to it. We've about three weeks to sort it all out, but we've never been faced with such an overspend from the Design Department. This is serious.

FROM: RUSSELL T DAVIES TO: BENJAMIN COOK
MONDAY 18 JUNE 2007 23:42:15 GMT

RE: FW: MEETING NOTES

Tonight, I got told that 4.X has 197 days of CGI FX too many![2] It's only supposed to have about 350 in total – and that's big – so I'm more than 50 per cent over. Problem is, The Mill is so busy, they've taken a *fortnight* to work this out. But I have to move on fast, not wait for number-crunching. I'm frozen with terror at the amount of time I have to write 4.1, and polish Gareth Roberts' Agatha Christie script, Keith Temple's Ood script and James Moran's Pompeii script. It looks like I have about four weeks to do all that!

So. Big cuts to 4.X. Poor old Buckingham Palace has to go. We need to convert the cost of building – and destroying – a scale model into money for The Mill. I might keep the flagpole smashing through the window of the *Titanic*, because that makes me laugh, though Ed's department is £45,000 over, so, um, I might not. Plus, I've just worked out a new end sequence for Astrid – her death isn't very sad at the moment, is it? – which requires even more FX, at least another eight shots or so. When I described the new ending to Julie – it's lovely, sentimental, Christmassy – she said, 'Well, we've got to keep that!' But how are we going to find the money?

FROM: BENJAMIN COOK TO: RUSSELL T DAVIES
WEDNESDAY 20 JUNE 2007 06:38:12 GMT

RE: FW: MEETING NOTES

I'm off to the Glastonbury Festival this afternoon, so I'll be without e-mail access for a few days. (Five nights in a tent – bliss!) Best of luck with the FX cuts and Astrid's new death. Can I ask, before I go, is it preferable for a writer to edit his or her own work, do you think, or for a script editor to do it? A writer knows their script better than anyone, but a script editor provides an alternative eye and a fresh perspective.

P.S. The Saturday after next, they're showing *Last of the Time Lords* on a giant screen in Trafalgar Square! Did you know? Will you be there?

FROM: RUSSELL T DAVIES TO: BENJAMIN COOK
WEDNESDAY 20 JUNE 2007 08:45:14 GMT

RE: FW: MEETING NOTES

That Trafalgar Square thing is barmy, isn't it? I'm half-torn whether to go or not. It's part of Gay Pride – it's so that the gays won't have to miss the series finale – except it's likely that everyone will be drinking and dancing and snogging instead, and *not* watching *Doctor Who*, which would upset me. But Johnny Barrowman and Freema will be there, on stage.

Script editing. An editor is *vital*. Everyone should have one. You can't always edit something yourself; you need that fresh pair of eyes. (Not a friend. Or your mum. That's no good.) The 'second death' that I'm about to write for Astrid seems absolutely intrinsic, and it's weird to think that I didn't put it there in the first place. I felt dissatisfied with the original, but only in a vague, shoulder-shrugging way. I could ignore that nagging voice. All writers do. It took a proper meeting with others to express that dissatisfaction. Even a stray remark can make all the difference: just chatting before the meeting, Brian Minchin said, 'I didn't expect Astrid to die. I thought the teleport bracelet would save her.' I thought, ah ha! I'd forgotten that she was even wearing it. Instantly, I knew what to do. I didn't say anything during the meeting, I just agreed with the general dissatisfaction and promised to fix it, knowing full well what I was going to do…

You're dealing here with a script that works, essentially, but the process of writing isn't an exact science. It's imprecise, moody and instinctive, so you need people to keep you on track and remind you why you're writing in the first place. Of course, finding the right people is key. The industry is full of rubbish script editors. The

2 Post-production company The Mill is responsible for the (computer-generated) visual effects on *Doctor Who*, *Torchwood* and *The Sarah Jane Adventures*. An FX day equals a day's work for one person at The Mill. 'Theoretically, if The Mill had 350 FX days allocated and 350 people working on *Doctor Who*, they could finish an episode in a day,' explains Russell. 'Except it's not quite literal. The Mill's definition of a day must include… well, payment for talent, genius, planning, and all that.'

bad ones are vandals. They don't just destroy scripts; they destroy writers. It takes a lot of work when you're young, or starting out, to survive those people. Well, to even recognise them in the first place. That's hard work.

FROM: RUSSELL T DAVIES TO: BENJAMIN COOK
FRIDAY 22 JUNE 2007 23:48:54 GMT

4.X DRAFT TWO

I've been watching the Glastonbury coverage on BBC Three. Isn't Amy Winehouse stunning? I hope you're having a good time. I eagerly await tales of drugs and sex. In a tent. With Kasabian. I just got a text off John Simm – he's there, too. And so is Freema. Have you met up? The Master could have hunted down Martha Jones at Glastonbury! With you watching!

Here's the revised 4.X for you to read on your return. It's still over-budget. I haven't cut enough FX shots. More changes to come, I suspect. Maybe we'll have to reconsider that whole forklift death, because that's eating into our budget hugely. Still, I'm pleased with the new Buckingham Palace sequence and Astrid's second farewell…

108. EXT. BUCKINGHAM PALACE - DAY[3]

WIDE SHOT, with roads empty. The flag is flying.

NEWSREADER (OOV)
The Queen has remained in residence, in defiance of extraterrestrial attack…

Voice fades down, SLOW ZOOM in, sound of a RINGING PHONE.

CUT TO:

109. INT. BRIDGE - DAY

THE DOCTOR on the vone -

THE DOCTOR
- listen to me, Security Code 771, now *get out of there!!!*

CUT TO:

3 A new scene (numbered 34) of the Posh Man and friends applauding at the approaching meteoroids ('Absolutely wonderful,' says the Posh Man. 'Thank Vot for the shields, eh?') has shifted all subsequent scene numbers, so the Doctor calling Buckingham Palace is now Scene 107, followed by this, Scene 108, with the Newsreader.

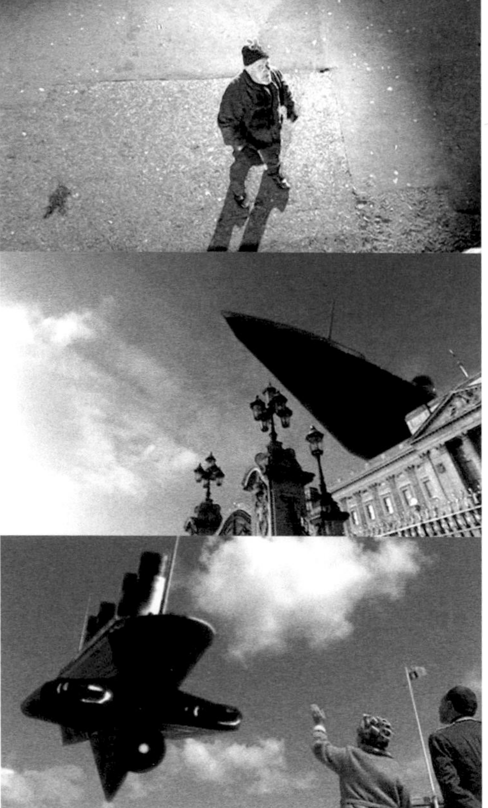

'Thank you, Doctor! Thank you!'

110. EXT. FX SHOT - DAY

FX: blue skies, THE TITANIC levelling, levelling, levelling, but still racing downwards -

CUT TO:

111. INT. POSH MARBLE STAIRCASE - DAY

BACK TO CAMERA, an OLD WOMAN in a nightie & curlers running downstairs with TWO LIVERIED FOOTMEN & A CORGI -

CUT TO:

111A. EXT. CITY STREET - DAY

HIGH ANGLE on STAN, running from his NEWS-SELLER'S BOOTH, waving an angry fist at the sky.

STAN
Don't you dare! Don't you dare!!

CUT TO:

112. INT. BRIDGE - DAY

CU THE DOCTOR, heaving at the

WHEEL, teeth gritted, like he's physically pulling the Titanic up, the room levelling back slowly towards the horizontal…

CUT TO:

113. EXT. BUCKINGHAM PALACE - DAY

The Palace stands proud…

FX: THE TITANIC, reaching the perigee of its downward curve, swoops in from behind the Palace…

And just misses, by an inch! Sails overhead!

CUT TO:

114. INT. BRIDGE - DAY

Room now horizontal, beginning to tilt slightly upwards, THE DOCTOR heaving at the wheel, now grinning -

CUT TO:

115. EXT. AGAINST SKY - DAY

FX: LOW ANGLE, TITANIC heading slowly upwards in b/g; the old woman standing, now framed against the sky, waving.

THE QUEEN
Thank you, Doctor! Thank you!

CUT TO:

116. EXT. FX SHOT - DAY

FX: THE TITANIC, more graceful now, on an upward incline, heading back to space, though at less steep an angle, sailing through the blue skies of Christmas morning.

CUT TO:

117. INT. TITANIC RECEPTION, DECK 1 - DAY

Daylight now streaming in, the room tilting upwards a little, debris falling away from MR COPPER & RICKSTON, still pressed up against the wall. They can't believe it. They made it! Both start to laugh.

And they hug each other, crying,

Even boosting the molecule grid with the restoration matrix can't bring back Astrid for good.

overjoyed.

CUT TO:

118. INT. BRIDGE - DAY

Room now tilting upwards. MIDSHIPMAN FRAME slumped against the back wall, shattered, recovering. And THE DOCTOR slides down to sit with him. Exhausted:

THE DOCTOR
Used the heat of re-entry to fire up the Secondary Storm Drive. Unsinkable. That's me.

MIDSHIPMAN FRAME
…we made it.

THE DOCTOR
Not all of us.

Pause. Then suddenly -

THE DOCTOR (CONT'D)
Teleport! She was wearing a teleport bracelet!!

And he's running - !

CUT TO:

118A. INT. TITANIC RECEPTION, DECK 1 - NIGHT

(The Titanic is back in space now, dark outside; stable, but with lights still off.) MR COPPER & RICKSTON recovering, as THE DOCTOR runs in - going straight to the

TELEPORT PLINTH, starts stabbing controls -

THE DOCTOR
Rickston! Sonic - !!!

Rickston throws the sonic, the Doctor catches it -

THE DOCTOR (CONT'D)
- Mr Copper, the teleports, have they got an emergency setting?

MR COPPER
I don't know, they should have -

THE DOCTOR
She fell, Mr Copper. She fell. What's the emergency code?

MR COPPER
Let me…

And he runs to the plinth, helps the Doctor, both frantic.

MIDSHIPMAN FRAME enters, still in pain.

MIDSHIPMAN FRAME
What the hell are you doing…?

THE DOCTOR
We can bring her back!

MR COPPER
If a passenger has an accident, on shore leave - if they're still wearing their teleport, their molecules are automatically suspended and held in stasis… if we can just trigger the shift…

THE DOCTOR
There!

And they look, in awe:

FX (AND REPEAT): centre of the room, with a beautiful, blue star-like shimmer, ASTRID appears. Transparent; like a ghost. She just stands still, lost, her voice faint.

ASTRID
…I'm falling.

THE DOCTOR
Only halfway there, come on!!

And he's ripping out wires and sonicking like crazy.

FX: Astrid stays transparent.

ASTRID
…I keep falling.

THE DOCTOR
…feedback the molecule grid… Boost it with the restoration matrix, no no no! Need more phase containment…

MR COPPER
(quiet, kind)
Doctor…

THE DOCTOR
No, if I can just link up the surface suspension…

MR COPPER
Doctor, she's gone.

THE DOCTOR
I just need to override the safety, I can do this, I can do it -

MR COPPER
Doctor. Let her go.

THE DOCTOR
I can do *anything!!*

And he kicks the plinth, savage.

And then stops.

Looks across the room.

FX: Astrid, fading a little.

ASTRID
…stop me falling.

MR COPPER
There's not enough left, the system was too damaged. She's just atoms, Doctor. An echo, with the ghost of consciousness. She's stardust.

Mr Copper, Midshipman Frame, Rickston look on in respectful silence. As the Doctor walks forward.

THE DOCTOR
Astrid Peth. Citizen of Sto. Born with a jewel in your forehead, so you might travel among the stars.

He faces her.

FX: Profile to profile, the Doctor and a transparent Astrid; she stares at him, lost, begging for release.

THE DOCTOR (CONT'D)
There's an old tradition.

FX: they kiss.

Then as they separate, the Doctor lifts up the sonic.

THE DOCTOR (CONT'D)
Now you can travel for ever.

He whirrs it.

Across the room, the PORTHOLE opens - black space beyond.

FX: blue ripple of the oxygen field outside.

THE DOCTOR (CONT'D)
You're not falling, Astrid. You're flying.

'There's an old tradition...' The Doctor kisses Astrid goodbye.

FX: Astrid loses corporeal form, becomes a shimmer of blue light, tiny stars, blowing gently across the room, towards the porthole...

CUT TO:

119. EXT. FX SHOT - NIGHT

FX: THE TITANIC suspended in space, back in a peaceful orbit above the Earth, damaged, but still majestic. And the shining STARDUST of Astrid Peth sails away from the ship, swirling past CAMERA for a second...

Then spiralling away into space, dispersing, gone.[4]

FROM: BENJAMIN COOK TO: RUSSELL T DAVIES
TUESDAY 26 JUNE 2007 18:20:55 GMT

RE: 4.X DRAFT TWO

I'm back from Glastonbury. I spent most of it stuck in the mud (I think some folk are still there, stuck fast), but I had the most awesome time. You'll be saddened to hear that I didn't have sex with Kasabian. (Would you, though? *Really?!* It'd be like making out with Topman's entire autumn range. Plus, you'd get stubble rash.)

I returned from The Mudbath to find an invite to the 4.X read-through next Monday, in London. Cheers for that, Russell, since I'm sure you had something to do with it. I've just read the revised 4.X, and I almost prefer the new version of the Buckingham Palace gag, though not quite. But Astrid's second death is stunning. (Invisible Ben isn't supposed to tell you things like that, is he? Oh well!)

Once you'd started, you wrote 4.X at a fair lick, didn't you? Barring the occasional day or so when not much happened, you rattled off the thing pretty damn fast. You started at midnight on 15 May and finished Draft One on 5 June, just three weeks later. That's speedy. Is that a necessity of your workload? Would you have liked longer? If you'd had an extra week, or a month, would you have filled it constructively, do you think? And have you always written that quickly?

Continued on page 175

4 Hereafter the action continues as per Draft One: a scene in Reception with Midshipman Frame explaining that he's sent an SOS, Rickston thanking the Doctor, and Mr Copper and the Doctor teleporting off the *Titanic*.

DRAFT TWO CHANGES

In addition to Buckingham Palace's alternative fate and Astrid's new departure, other changes in Draft Two included an explanation for the bindis, in Scene 9:

THE DOCTOR
I'm the Doctor, by the way.

ASTRID
Astrid, sir, Astrid Peth.

THE DOCTOR
Nice to meet you. Merry Christmas!

ASTRID
Merry Christmas, sir.

THE DOCTOR
Just Doctor, not sir.

ASTRID
Enjoying the cruise?

THE DOCTOR
Yeah, I suppose, I dunno. Doesn't quite work, a cruise, on your own.

ASTRID
You're not with anyone?

THE DOCTOR
No, just me, just… Used to be, but, um… No.

ASTRID
You're not from the homeworld, then?

THE DOCTOR
How d'you know that…? Ah. No…

He indicates his own forehead, looking at her bindi.

ASTRID
The Jewel of Sto. It's embedded in the Sto-kind, when we're children, a tiny piece of the Sapphire Moon. To remind us that we're born to fly.

THE DOCTOR
And here you are. Miles from home.

Also, the Doctor's demonstration of how to power up the EMP transmitter, in Scene 77, was extended to include:

ASTRID
…I'm sort of… unemployed now. I was thinking, that blue box was kind of small, but… I could squeeze in. Like a stowaway.

THE DOCTOR
…I suppose.

ASTRID
Was that a yes or a no?

THE DOCTOR
It's not always safe.

ASTRID
Then you need someone to look after you. And I've got no one back on Sto, no family. Just me. What d'you think? Can I come with you?

THE DOCTOR
Yeah. I'd like that, yeah.

Big smile between them. Then –

In Scene 80, the Doctor hands Astrid the EMP baton and is about to leave when:

ASTRID
Hold on a minute. There's an old tradition on Planet Sto…

DRAFT TWO CHANGES (continued)

She's taking a BOX out of the rubble, carries it to him.

THE DOCTOR
I've really got to go -

ASTRID
Just wait.

She plonks the box in front of him.

Stands on it.

Then grabs his jacket, pulls him in for a good kiss!

Then lets go, both smiling.

THE DOCTOR
That's a very old tradition.

ASTRID
See you later.

THE DOCTOR
Oh yes.

He stands back, still looking at her. Presses the button, the door slides shut, he's gone.

Scene 92, set on Deck 31, was extended to include:

THE DOCTOR furious -

THE DOCTOR
You can't do this - !

MAX
Hold him!

The TWO HOST flanking the Doctor grab his arms, iron grip.

MAX (CONT'D)
Not so clever now, Doctor.

THE DOCTOR
Oh d'you think? Like I said: watch me.
(at the third Host)
You there, Host! Security Protocol One! Three questions! You work for Max Capricorn, yes?

HOST
Information: correct.

THE DOCTOR
Max Capricorn is a cyborg, yes?

HOST
Information: correct.

THE DOCTOR
But according to your society, cyborgs are inferior, so you should accept my commands instead of his, yes? Yes? What d'you say, yes??

HOST
Information: no.

THE DOCTOR
What?! Why's that then?

HOST
Information: your three questions have been used.

MAX
But I can answer that. They're robots, Doctor. To them, cyborgs are practically family.

THE DOCTOR
Information: damn!

MAX
Nice try, though. I wish we could have worked together, you're rather good.

Russell Tovey takes five between takes.

FROM: RUSSELL T DAVIES TO: BENJAMIN COOK
TUESDAY 26 JUNE 2007 23:13:50 GMT

RE: 4.X DRAFT TWO

A read-through with Kylie Minogue! Marvellous, isn't it? She's going to watch *Last of the Time Lords* on Saturday with David. Madder and madder! And we've cast Clive Swift as Mr Copper. That's brilliant! (Dennis Hopper, it turned out, isn't available for *that* many days.) And Geoffrey Palmer is Captain Hardaker, which is glorious. Also, Russell Tovey as Midshipman Frame, which is my favourite casting of the lot, because he's going to be huge, that man. He's amazing. I think I'd make him the Eleventh Doctor.

I love that new Astrid ending. Pure sentiment. Pure Disney. It would be way too sentimental if she weren't dead, but since she still cops it, well, I reckon it's grand. I'm gutted about Buckingham Palace, though. Always will be. It's a big set-up for a gag that never happens. We've almost reached an FX compromise: lost a few more shots, but kept Astrid's death and all the major stuff. I think we've about 40 more FX days to lose, but that's doable. Phil came over tonight, and we found a possible 40 days or so. He'll take that back to The Mill tomorrow and I'll get sent a report tomorrow evening so that I can do the final rewrites overnight.

Would I have liked longer to write 4.X? Well, I've always written fast. The second drama script I ever wrote, *Dark Season* Episode 2, I completed in two days flat – which makes it sound like a piece of piss, but I hope this correspondence is making it clear that it's the thinking beforehand, not the typing, that takes up my time. You're right, though, give me more time and I'd waste it – not consciously, but just because the adrenalin isn't there. In the old days, I had so little faith and so much fear, I used to write out the entire episode in longhand first, on one sheet of A4. Well, it was 'tiny hand', not longhand. I can write very small. Microscopic writing. It's a handy skill. (In wartime.) I loved those pages, but they were a crutch. As the years went by, they became just scribbled headlines, then a few words and maybe a drawing, until slowly, over about ten years, I abandoned the paper and wrote straight onto the screen. I can't remember that transition actually happening – there was no great Paper-Less Ceremony – because it just evolved. But today the notion of writing a line, pausing, taking a walk, in mystic contemplation, feels alien to me. Once I'm into a script, I hurl myself into it and stay there. The quiet days in the middle are more tiredness than anything. The fear of screwing it up wastes time, too.

FROM: RUSSELL T DAVIES TO: BENJAMIN COOK
WEDNESDAY 27 JUNE 2007 22:39:01 GMT

RE: 4.X DRAFT TWO

It's been another bastard of a day. We realised… well, to fill you in, when David finishes Series Four, he's off to the Royal Shakespeare Company to play Hamlet. *Wow!* (Equally, *bah!* I've never been able to sit through *Hamlet*. Have you?) Oh, and that's very, *very* top secret. Don't even let David know that you know. Anyway, we realised today that the RSC needs to announce David's casting in September, which, because of the dates, will immediately make it obvious that there won't be a Series Five with him in 2009. The secret will be out. Heaven knows what we're going to do.

FROM: BENJAMIN COOK TO: RUSSELL T DAVIES
FRIDAY 29 JUNE 2007 22:55:31 GMT

RE: 4.X DRAFT TWO

David's doing *Hamlet*? Wow indeed. No *bah!* from me. He'll be magnificent.

FROM: RUSSELL T DAVIES TO: BENJAMIN COOK
SATURDAY 30 JUNE 2007 00:43:52 GMT

RE: 4.X DRAFT TWO

Sad news: Robin Davies has died. Do you remember Robin, Chris Eccleston's driver on Series One? Lovely, brilliant, laughing Robin. He died of a heart attack just the other day. I suppose he didn't suffer, but it was out of the blue. I loved that man. He became my comrade on *Queer as Folk* – a nightmare shoot with an insane/genius director, endless night shoots, and there was Robin, laughing away, offering me sanctuary in his car at 4am. Then he did *Bob & Rose* and *The Second Coming*. He came to Swansea and got to know my family during *Mine All Mine*. Chris Eccleston adored him, too. When the history of *Doctor Who* is written, no one is going to know how much Robin was a part of that team.

FROM: BENJAMIN COOK TO: RUSSELL T DAVIES
SATURDAY 30 JUNE 2007 00:52:43 GMT

RE: 4.X DRAFT TWO

Of course I remember Robin. He was so kind. He wasn't a bullshitter, and Chris liked that. Such sad news. He can't have been that old either.

Text message from: Ben
Sent: 30-Jun-2007 19:40
I'm in Trafalgar Square for *Last of the Time Lords*... and it's not on! Some brain-dead pop band is playing instead. The crowd grows impatient...

Text message from: Russell
Sent: 30-Jun-2007 19:44
On BBC One, the Doctor just saved the world. You missed it!

Text message from: Ben
Sent: 30-Jun-2007 19:47
Are all Gay Prides this dreadful? I'm not impressed.

Text message from: Russell
Sent: 30-Jun-2007 19:51
Captain Jack just revealed he's the Face of Boe!

Text message from: Ben
Sent: 30-Jun-2007 19:53
Still no *Doctor Who*. :-(We're being showered in sequins.

Text message from: Russell
Sent: 30-Jun-2007 19:54
I hate to tell you this, but sequins suit you.

Text message from: Ben
Sent: 30-Jun-2007 19:57
They've cancelled *Doctor Who*! The crowd is booing! I predict a riot.

Text message from: Russell
Sent: 30-Jun-2007 20:00
You're the reporter on the front line.

Text message from: Ben
Sent: 30-Jun-2007 20:02
I'm covered in sequins. No news agency will take me seriously. I'm going home.

If Captain Jack really is the Face of Boe, then the Doctor (David Tennant) and Novice Hame (Anna Hope) witness his death in 3.3 *Gridlock*.

FROM: BENJAMIN COOK TO: RUSSELL T DAVIES
MONDAY 2 JULY 2007 21:33:01 GMT

THE READ-THROUGH

Wasn't today's read-through AMAZING? Can you believe Kylie, walking around, introducing herself to everyone?

I always thought, in my naivety, that read-throughs were for the actors' and director's benefit, primarily, so that they can get a feel for the script as a whole before shooting it all out of order? But afterwards, once the cast had left, you, Julie, Phil and James got together for script notes. So do you often rewrite the script as a result of the read-through? Heavily, ever? Do you amend scripts based on each actor's performance? Their portrayal? Their delivery? Or is it just for technical stuff, like the timing of an episode? This is a question of the actor's relationship with the script: should the script shift to fit the actor, or is it the actor's job to fit the script?

FROM: RUSSELL T DAVIES TO: BENJAMIN COOK
MONDAY 2 JULY 2007 22:04:28 GMT

RE: THE READ-THROUGH

It was an INCREDIBLE read-through. Best of all, *Kylie can act!* I always knew she could – I was a faithful viewer for all those years of *Neighbours*, and she never delivered a duff performance – but she really nailed Astrid, didn't she?

Tell you what, though, there was an even greater revelation for me: I love that 4.X script. Really, properly love it. I'd been a bit unsure about it till now – I always am, I suppose – but I felt the format clicking into place. That was magical. It's so obviously a disaster movie that I'd got used to the idea, way back, and even got over it. I'd forgotten its impact. The thrill of it was overwhelmed and absorbed into all the problems of writing it. Yesterday, it was like seeing it as new. All that moaning to you about the disaster movie format… and I was forgetting that I love them.

>>do you often rewrite the script as a result of the read-through?<<

That's what they're for – for performance and timing, but also to make the script better. That's why a Pink Draft is issued after a read-through. The pink pages are any pages that have been revised at all. At a *Doctor Who* read-through, we all scribble down notes. Small performance things – tone and pitch, don't shout this, be quiet with that, emphasise that gag – but also proper drama notes. Why is she so cross? Can we explain why he runs? Do we even need that scene? Etc.

>>Heavily, ever?<<

If need be. I sat in the read-through of *The Grand* Series Two, Episode 1, and realised I'd got a major plot

DRAFT THREE

This is Russell's e-mail to the production team, accompanying the final draft of 4.X, amended after the previous day's read-through...

FROM: RUSSELL T DAVIES
TO: JULIE GARDNER; PHIL COLLINSON; BRIAN MINCHIN; EDWARD THOMAS
TUESDAY 3 JULY 2007 15:25:22 GMT

4.X PINKS

Here we go. All done!

I got a bit hung up on Rickston's vone at the end, when the Doctor calls Buckingham Palace, because we've been told clearly that the vone doesn't work. I'd always presumed that when the Doctor takes control of the Bridge, he slams a few controls that stop the blanketing of signals so the vone is reconnected – but there's no room or need for him to say so, so that's not going to work. It's going to look odd. Instead, in this draft, I've got him using the ship's phone. I've described it as a Bakelite receiver, but I'm not sure if that fits the computer-bank designs, so I'll copy this e-mail in to Ed, too. (Hello, Ed!) The Bakelite would need to be near the ship's wheel, since the Doctor is still holding on.

David Tennant and Kylie Minogue pose for pictures after the *Voyage of the Damned* read-through, in the Central Baptist Church on London's Shaftesbury Avenue. Darenote Ltd. © 2007. Photographer: William Baker

wrong. We were axing two main characters, so I wrote them having an affair that would lead to their exit in Episode 4. But I realised, sitting in the read-through, that it was just crap. Wrong actors, wrong characters, wrong story. In the meeting afterwards, I chucked it out – and it was about 50 per cent of the script. Not only that, but the next three scripts, with the characters in mid-affair, were lined up to be shot. They all had to be rewritten. It had to be done, overnight! It doesn't matter how much work it is; there's no point in filming a mistake.

>>should the script shift to fit the actor, or is it the actor's job to fit the script?<<

You cast someone to fit the script; lines and emphasis can change. Unfortunately, a lot of scripts are loose and vague, therefore the actor has too many options, or no options, so the performance swings away from the script, the director swings away from the actors, and… oh, a mess. That's bad TV drama. Actually, that's just ordinary TV drama. The sheer not-quite-ness of it all.

FROM: BENJAMIN COOK TO: RUSSELL T DAVIES
WEDNESDAY 4 JULY 2007 00:21:34 GMT

RE: THE READ-THROUGH

The BBC has just announced Catherine Tate's casting in Series Four, in a press release issued at midnight. Eh?! Why announce it this soon? Mind you, the internet is going into meltdown.

```
PRAC FX: SPARKS & SMOKE from
BEN's computer.
```

FROM: RUSSELL T DAVIES TO: BENJAMIN COOK
WEDNESDAY 4 JULY 2007 01:52:45 GMT

RE: THE READ-THROUGH

The Sun got wind of Catherine Tate, so we've fought back, for once, and spiked their exclusive by releasing Catherine's name to everyone. Hah! But there's worse to come. The *Daily Mail* has got wind of David's booking as Hamlet. We're battening down the hatches. None of us is quite sure what to say. In amongst all this, Julie and I reflected with horror today that we haven't been able to tell the staff what's going to happen after Series Four. People who have moved to Cardiff, with mortgages and everything. It's a bloody hurricane. Of our own making. I can't imagine another show with this trajectory or adrenalin.

Here's a quick update on everything else: in the next 17 days, I have to rewrite Keith's script, plus Gareth's, plus James', which then gives me eight days to write 4.1. This is impossible. It's a bloody mess this year; we are *so* behind. I don't know why that is. Maybe I'm slowing down. Being ground down? I feel sick with worry. When I slow down, the whole engine slows down, the whole *Doctor Who* factory. I know, for example, that I'm not bullying anyone about the other writers' deadlines, when I should be. It's all my fault. Realising that makes me feel *more* sick, which then, I suspect, slows me down further. Vicious circle.

On a more positive note, I had a script meeting with Gareth after the read-through, so he can rewrite as much of his episode as possible while I'm rewriting Keith's – and Gareth was *brilliant*. He learns, and learns, and learns. We went in with the biggest problem: why is Agatha Christie caught up in a murder mystery? Isn't that a bit of a coincidence? Agatha's sheer presence had to become part of the plot. I said, 'We're not leaving this room until we solve this, even if we're here for ever.' We'd cracked it within ten minutes. 'Hang on,' we said, 'if we make one of the characters a Christie fan and they're reading a Christie novel as the alien activates… then the alien mentally inherits the murder mystery as a template and bases its actions on that!' Problem solved.

And then Helen Raynor came in to discuss her two-part Sontaran adventure. I had to give away one of my favourite ideas ever: Evil Cars! With Evil Sat Nav! I've been dying to write that for years. In fact, Evil Sat Nav was in the first draft of *The Runaway Bride*, on board the speeding taxi, with the Empress of Racnoss using it as her eyes and ears on Earth – though I junked that idea before I even delivered the script. Now someone else gets it. Damn.

Also, we cast Max today: George Costigan. It was almost on the cards for Dennis Hopper to be Max, because it's fewer days on set than Mr Copper, but we just ran out of time. He had the script and apparently was willing, he's even in the country now, but we didn't hear back (it's hard to nag American agents), and we needed Max for a prosthetic fitting on Wednesday, so it all fell through. But George Costigan is perfect.

That's about it, update-wise. Oh, except I e-mailed Julie today saying:

> *It almost goes without saying, but… in the climax to Series Four, with Donna, and Martha, and Rose, and Sarah Jane and Captain Jack, all battling away to save the Doctor… I suppose you'd want a mysterious shimmer of blue stardust to make an appearance at some point, wouldn't you?*

She e-mailed back with an 'OH YES!' So that's a laugh.

Captain John (James Marsters) and Captain Jack (John Barrowman) in *Torchwood* 2.1 *Kiss Kiss, Bang Bang*.

FROM: RUSSELL T DAVIES TO: BENJAMIN COOK
SUNDAY 8 JULY 2007 21:30:00 GMT

JAMES MARSTERS' ARSE

It's not often that I'm sat in a Cardiff bar with Spike from *Buffy*, and Kylie Minogue walks in![5] This city is now, officially, insane. And James Marsters is the sexiest bastard alive, much more so than he is on screen. As straight as the day is long, and yet every single conversation came back to sex with him. I wasn't complaining.

For all that, I'm back in the flat now, rewriting *Planet of the Ood*…

FROM: BENJAMIN COOK TO: RUSSELL T DAVIES
SUNDAY 8 JULY 2007 21:59:33 GMT

RE: JAMES MARSTERS' ARSE

Kylie Minogue playing gooseberry. Who'd have thought it?

How are the Ood coming along?

5 American actor James Marsters, best known as Spike in *Buffy the Vampire Slayer* and its spin-off series *Angel*, was in Cardiff to film three episodes of *Torchwood* Series Two, in which he plays Captain John Hart, a rogue Time Agent.

BZZZZ!

FROM: RUSSELL T DAVIES TO: BENJAMIN COOK
SUNDAY 8 JULY 2007 22:34:07 GMT

RE: JAMES MARSTERS' ARSE

The Ood are… late. Bloody Ood. Must keep going, though, because I'm rewriting Agatha next week. She's fighting a giant wasp. We really couldn't think what sort of enemy she should fight. Dickens? Ghosts. Shakespeare? Witches. But Agatha…? Then Gareth came up with a wasp – and I remembered the old paperback cover of *Death in the Clouds*, which has a plane being attacked by a symbolically giant wasp. 'That'll do,' we said. Our most tenuous link yet.

FROM: BENJAMIN COOK TO: RUSSELL T DAVIES
SUNDAY 8 JULY 2007 22:49:04 GMT

RE: JAMES MARSTERS' ARSE

A Giant Wasp? I'll be happy so long as you've a posh butler, a country house, and someone murdered by a poisoned dart. Oh, and Agatha should be played by Madonna.

When you get a moment, can you explain the 'rewriting' process on *Doctor Who*? Do you ever worry about treading on other writers' toes?

FROM: RUSSELL T DAVIES TO: BENJAMIN COOK
SUNDAY 8 JULY 2007 23:05:56 GMT

RE: JAMES MARSTERS' ARSE

No dart, damn it. But a poisoned sting – that's close! And death by lead piping, just because that's so irresistible. (Donna: 'Who uses lead piping?!') How we're going to get a Giant Wasp – a Vespiform, to be precise – to wield a piece of lead piping is going to make for a fun Tone Meeting.[6]

Rewriting? I write the final draft of almost all scripts – except Steven Moffat's, Matthew Graham's, Chris Chibnall's and Stephen Greenhorn's – and that draft becomes the Shooting Script. I might change at least 30 per cent of the material, often 60 per cent, sometimes almost 100 per cent. I go over every line of dialogue, either adding new stuff or refining what's there; sometimes that means enhancing a line that the original writer hasn't realised is good. I'll bring out themes, punch up moments, add signature dialogue, clarify stage directions and make cuts. To every single scene, if need be. Usually, the basic shape remains intact, but sometimes I'll invent brand new characters and subplots… while at the same time remaining faithful to the original writer. I'll even impersonate them.

Sometimes, yes, this does mean treading on other writers' toes. I'm sure some of them think of it as vandalism. Equally, to be fair, others are very grateful. But my job is to get the Best Possible Script on screen, even if that means stampeding over someone. The viewer at home doesn't care who wrote it; they just want it to be good. My job is to make it as good as it can be. Take no prisoners! And it's got to be done fast, so I haven't time to pussyfoot around, transplanting lines of dialogue, delicately. Even interesting stuff has to go sometimes, because I can only find room for myself by shifting back all the furniture, making it my own. This is a multi-million quid show that has to be the absolute best it can be.

Hey, filming on 4.X starts tomorrow. The first of three days on the Strut. That's in at the deep end.

FROM: BENJAMIN COOK TO: RUSSELL T DAVIES
MONDAY 9 JULY 2007 07:49:44 GMT

RE: JAMES MARSTERS' ARSE

Today's *Guardian* says you're the fifteenth most powerful

The construction of the Strut at Upper Boat Studios is overseen by camera operator Julian Barber and director James Strong.

6 Tone Meetings are where the heads of departments, the producers and the director, gather to work out, scene by scene, how the episode can be made.

player in the media industry. (You have to question the choice of the word 'player', don't you?) You're up from Number 28 last year. You're the highest-ranking TV producer on the list. Well done! Again! You're making a habit of these polls, aren't you?

FROM: RUSSELL T DAVIES TO: BENJAMIN COOK
MONDAY 9 JULY 2007 08:30:09 GMT

RE: JAMES MARSTERS' ARSE

That gives me a year to murder 14 people. It can be done.

FROM: BENJAMIN COOK TO: RUSSELL T DAVIES
MONDAY 9 JULY 2007 08:45:55 GMT

RE: JAMES MARSTERS' ARSE

I wondered why you were so hung up on lead piping the other night.

FROM: BENJAMIN COOK TO: RUSSELL T DAVIES
TUESDAY 10 JULY 2007 10:20:48 GMT

RE: JAMES MARSTERS' ARSE

Have you seen yesterday's rushes yet? How's the Strut looking? Can you explain why it's important, as showrunner, that you view each day's rushes?

FROM: RUSSELL T DAVIES TO: BENJAMIN COOK
TUESDAY 10 JULY 2007 11:30:24 GMT

RE: JAMES MARSTERS' ARSE

The rushes are wonderful. The Strut is an amazing set. I watch the rushes to correct things, if they can be corrected in time; sometimes it's too late. For example, Foon has a daft hairstyle – but it's too late to change, because of continuity, so there it is. In extreme circumstances (if she were the lead), I could demand for it to be re-shot, but not in this instance. It can be toned down, though. Babs Southcott can do anything! We can get away with it, because Foon is a big, funny character. She can support big hair. You can even argue, when Morvin dies, the funny hair is marvellously contradictory; she's a tragedy in clown's clothes, which has a nice sort of resonance.

Mainly, I'm looking at the rushes for tone. The pitch of it. The height. The broadness. The speed. The precision. For example, the moment they arrive on the Strut is too hysterical. 'Look! Big drop! Eek! Oh no!' It's all full-pitch. When Morvin falls to his death, the pitch has nowhere to go. They're already squealing, so there's no contrast. That led me to a note that I'd never given James until now, because it hadn't occurred to me: don't make it too hysterical. Disaster movies thrive on that grim tone, that quiet fear, that bravery in the face of death, small people in big events, not screaming and shouting. There are blunter notes, too. Debbie Chazen is wonderful. More of her, please. Favour her. Gray O'Brien (Rickston)'s accent is brilliant. He's Scottish playing posh. Design, Wardrobe and Make-Up have

ood operations

Service with a smile

PLANET OF THE OOD

This is Russell's e-mail to his fellow producers (including Susie Liggat, overseeing five episodes of Series Four, with Phil Collinson becoming exec for those episodes) and script editor Lindsey Alford, accompanying his completed rewrite of *Planet of the Ood*...

FROM: RUSSELL T DAVIES
TO: SUSIE LIGGAT; PHIL COLLINSON; JULIE GARDNER; LINDSEY ALFORD
CC: BENJAMIN COOK
TUESDAY 10 JULY 2007 04:09:40 GMT

EP. 4.2

Here we go. Finished. I haven't had time to check for typos and stuff, but...

Remember I promised you no new locations, Susie? But then Mr Halpen had to go and mention a cinema... so now there's a cinema, and an Ood attack within the cinema.[2] Ideally, it's one of those posh press-launch cinemas, but do they even exist in Cardiff? It could always be a real cinema, one of the smaller ones, but I worry that it's going to look like we filmed in the local Odeon. Not very Forty-Second Century! But it's worth trying. We've the same old sets revolving around this story, so it makes a nice change – and great for kids, to imagine monsters romping through a cinema.

2 Mr Halpen is Chief Executive of the Ood-Sphere, which markets and sells Ood to the galaxy in the Forty-Second Century. The cinema is the setting for a scene where Ood kill a visiting party of sales reps. Although this scene makes the transmitted episode, the location has been altered to a less costly Sales Reception Room.

done a brilliant job… so I pass on the praise. Those teams work so hard and they love to hear that we're happy. Everyone is overworked – and people like Louise Page worry so much, she *needs* that text to say thank you. And me and Julie text all the lead actors – they need it and deserve it. It's a blizzard of texts from midday onwards.

Best of all, watching rushes does *me* good, because when I see them standing there, dirty, grimy, scared, the Time Lord, the pop star, the fat couple, the old man, the businessman, the red conker, all looking down at the terrible drop, with the viewer knowing – oh, just knowing – that some of them will die, it makes me think, really, powerfully: I love this episode. My confidence in this script is growing.

FROM: BENJAMIN COOK TO: RUSSELL T DAVIES
TUESDAY 10 JULY 2007 12:01:07 GMT

RE: JAMES MARSTERS' ARSE

So is it only during filming – and afterwards – that tone can be assessed properly? How far, really, can tone be established at the scripting stage? Or at the Tone Meeting? And how does a TV show, as opposed to any individual episode, find its overarching tone? Its voice? New *Doctor Who* found it within five minutes, whereas *Torchwood*… well, that show may have found its voice, but it's hard to tell, because it keeps losing it. In the opening five minutes of your *Torchwood* episode, the Series One opener, a character uses the f-word – and it really jarred, I thought. It stuck out, sorely. It felt wrong. Like watching K-9 hump a lamppost.[7]

FROM: RUSSELL T DAVIES TO: BENJAMIN COOK
TUESDAY 10 JULY 2007 13:11:24 GMT

RE: JAMES MARSTERS' ARSE

Above all, tone comes from the script. (I would say that!) You get 57 dozen people working on a drama, at key stages, and they all wander off. No, it's not fair to call it wandering, because they're creative people, they're employed to use their imaginations, but everyone creates in a slightly different way, sometimes in a radically different way. The director, the producer, the design teams, etc, should be interpreting the show in the *same* way, so the script should convey the tone in every adjective, in the layout of its pages, in the names of its characters; everything should transmit the tone. I mean, if Rose Tyler had been called 'Ace', what would the design teams have thought? Street-smart, tough, DMs, rough mother, nasty flat, etc. From one word, the tone starts to go wrong. All the smaller stuff – the words, the names, the style – conspire together to make a show that works, or a show that doesn't.

Even then, it's amazing how often the script is forgotten. *The Second Coming* had devil-possessed people and the script said, specifically, that they have 'tiny white glints of light in their eyes'. Then you bring 57 dozen more imaginations on board, and everyone but everyone who read that script – the producer, the exec, the channel, everyone – said to me, 'How are we going to do the red eyes?' Red? *Red?!* I spent months going, '*Red?!*' The script never said red, anywhere, but people thought instinctively that devil = red. A natural assumption, but wrong. Even having hammered home 'white', the FX guys went off and came back with… green cats-eyes! I had to keep saying, 'No, no, no,' until I sat down with a pen and paper and drew exactly what we needed. It worked. It was a fantasy element, and I was the only person on that team who really knew his fantasy, from TV sci-fi to B Movies to the best that cinema has to offer. I know what looks tacky and what looks creepy. All those years of watching sci-fi pay off. And deciding that fine line, deciding why red and green are bad and white is good, that's a judgement call. That's tone.

Of course, that's a tiny example, but that's what we're talking about, a whole string of tiny examples, which gather together to form the whole. If it's not controlled, you end up with a mess. To take *Skins* as another example – they did get the tone right, bang on, spectacularly right… in their trailers. They were fantastic, weren't they? You've said so yourself. It looked like it was going to be the most mind-blowing drama, because of those images – wild, feral, sexy, *new*. If the drama had looked like the trails, it would have been magnificent. A lot of people worked very hard on that series, I'm sure, but I don't think the tone was controlled enough. I'm lucky in that I'm given the authority to control. I'm 6'6", loud, compulsive, pedantic, deliberately gregarious, and I get my point across. I

7 The Doctor's robot dog K-9 débuted in 1977 *Doctor Who* serial *The Invisible Enemy*, remained with the show until 1981, and returned, alongside Sarah Jane Smith, in *Doctor Who* 2.3.

A subservient Ood from 4.2 *Planet of the Ood*.

describe my job as 'transmitting'. You have to transmit all the time what this show is. To do that, you can't talk too much about the vague concept of the show; you have to talk about the cutlery, the sound effects, the colour of that light in the background, and what sort of jeans Martha is wearing.

Then again… my first *Torchwood*? Yes, I agree, I'd take out that f-word now. It was trying to set a tone. It was saying, 'Go away kids' – as if that ever works! Swearing rarely feels natural on TV. There's still so little of it on that the words stand out artificially. When I hear a swear word on telly, I look at my watch. I think, oh, 20-past-nine. It takes me right out of the scene. It needs to be judged carefully. It's hard to imagine *Queer as Folk* without it – it's part of the energy – but I won't do it again on *Torchwood*. I don't think it sits well with sci-fi. (Why didn't I remember that when I was *Torchwood*ing? Trying too hard, I suppose.) Someone used the f-word in the first episode of *Bob & Rose*, and Paul Abbott told me to take it out. He was so right. Such a delicate word, it jarred.

See? You never learn.

FROM: RUSSELL T DAVIES TO: BENJAMIN COOK
TUESDAY 10 JULY 2007 13:43:20 GMT

RE: JAMES MARSTERS' ARSE

I've been thinking. That last e-mail – a lot of it was crap, the tone stuff. It was based on the assumption that the script is good, and then gets ballsed up by various levels of creativity. It was written too much from the writer's point of view. Truth is, tone goes astray not because of interference, but because, simply, most scripts don't work. That doesn't mean it's anyone's fault. Many scripts don't work because… well, because they're scripts. They're not an exact science. Just as most things in life don't work – machines, marriages, friendships, paper planes, everything. It's so easy, with hindsight, to say what went astray, much harder to pinpoint it at the start; otherwise 99 per cent of dramas would be brilliant. In fact, 99 per cent of life would be brilliant! And that's never going to happen. Everyone should have permission to fail and to try again.

If you listen to Bryan Elsley, the co-creator and driving force behind *Skins*, talking about the future of drama and the need for a narrative for a young audience, he is absolutely fascinating – and maybe absolutely right. He did the most brilliant interview about this, maybe two or three years ago, I think for the *Sunday Times*. That interview was so memorable because it *frightened* me. It said that the people running TV now are of the generation that grew up with it – we know it, we know TV, its forms and potential – but for the generation coming up, those brought up not so much on TV but on video gaming and user content, etc, TV is archaic. Soon, Bryan said, we – meaning me and him, and all of us of a certain age – would be as redundant as the generation before us. It was a real call to arms, to say that new forms of storytelling were on their way. Maybe we won't like it, but that change, that shift, will and must happen. (Will it? Aren't certain rules about drama, about storytelling, as old as the hills? Aren't there some truly fundamental needs that will never change?) Looking back, that was the path that led Bryan to *Skins*. He really is amazing, and *Skins*' uncertain tone just means that he's stumbled slightly on the first step. And stumbled bravely. Like you, I am looking forward to Series Two, despite Series One's shortcomings – so *Skins* is far from a failure.

But hey, I loved your *Torchwood* criticism. Invisible Ben does make me laugh: I'm telling you all sorts of things and you might be thinking, *blimey*, or *yeuch*, or *you bastard*, and yet you have to stay invisible. You're like Rose and her dad sneaking into the Cyberfactory in *The Age of Steel*: give yourself away and… well, you'll be taken to the Cybercontroller and given plenty of time to destroy him. Never got that quite right, did we? But when you describe *Torchwood*'s failure of voice – which is my fault, I suppose, though they're all working hard to fix it for Series Two – then I sort of know where we stand, and can go further. ■

CHAPTER SEVEN

FIRE AND BRIMSTONE

In which JK Rowling is offered a part in *Doctor Who*, Russell begins the search for his successor, and Emergency Protocol One is activated

FROM: RUSSELL T DAVIES TO: BENJAMIN COOK
TUESDAY 10 JULY 2007 22:49:33 GMT

SAD NEWS...

I just heard that David's mum is very ill. He's left the set and driven north, heading home to Scotland. Oh, bless the man. Filming in ruins, schedule buggered, and no insurance, because you can't insure against that sort of thing, but never mind that – poor David. Poor mum.

FROM: BENJAMIN COOK TO: RUSSELL T DAVIES
WEDNESDAY 11 JULY 2007 13:34:12 GMT

RE: SAD NEWS...

When you hear the news that David has to dash off, when Phil or whoever breaks it to you, and you realise that the making of one of your scripts is, unavoidably, compromised – what do you do? Do you shrug and move on? Are you too busy worrying about writing to get caught up in such production problems? Is that Phil's job? Or do you have a moment, however brief, of sinking your head into your hands and weeping uncontrollably?!

FROM: RUSSELL T DAVIES TO: BENJAMIN COOK
THURSDAY 12 JULY 2007 21:35:06 GMT

RE: SAD NEWS...

Still no news on David's mum. We've managed to rearrange stuff so far, to fill in with non-Doctor material, but tomorrow we run out! The whole set – Kylie, too – on standby. But imagine David, with his work ethic, *knowing* that. Poor bastard.

Production crises are a world apart from plain old script worries, probably because a production crisis is shared. There's almost no problem that you can't write your way out of. Location falls through? Lose a cast member? Camera fault? They can all be written around. That training comes from working on the soaps, I think. I was on *Coronation Street* when Lynne Perrie (who played Ivy Tilsley) was forever falling sick or off the wagon, and always at least one actor, in an ageing cast, needed a sudden day off. Soaps are great big ruthless machines that simply can't stop, so you have to find a way to cope. The only *Doctor Who* example I can think of is *The Shakespeare Code*, when the Doctor and Lilith were meant to have a sword fight. On the day of filming, the stuntwoman hit the stuntman's eye with her sword – yikes, his eye! – and filming had to stop on the spot. But while the ambulance came in, and he was taken away (and it was horrific – the whole crew was shaken up), Phil phoned me up, explained the situation, and I started typing away with a new version, as transmitted, replacing the sword fight completely; Lilith tries to seduce the Doctor instead. It only took me 20 minutes. A few hours later, we were filming the alternative version. Horrible and awful, but the show must go on.

That can happen, in a small way, all the way through production. Constant rewriting. Normally, it's because a scene has been dropped at the end of a day; they simply ran out of time. If it can't be rescheduled, I'll type away to adjust yet-to-be-filmed scenes, to remove the original scene from existence. But it's never face-in-hands weeping time. Even now, I'm half-thinking of a version of 4.1 that would be *very* Donna-heavy, in order to give David a fortnight off. He's not asking for that, but I think it's our responsibility to at least offer it. He has nine months ahead of him of being the leading man, and he won't get a proper break until Christmas now, so we have to consider practical ways of helping him cope. A Donna-heavy episode would be completely wrong for the show, but we could make it work. To hell with art.

Anyway… I go on a month's holiday next Friday, in Italy, which is obviously buggered because I'll still be rewriting James Moran's Pompeii episode. I've said to my boyfriend, 'I'll have to work a bit on the laptop,' but I haven't admitted that I'll have to work about 12 hours a day, every day, no weekends. That's not going to go down well. Truth be told, if it's a nightmare, I'll just come home. I've worked on holiday before – Episode 5 of *Mine All Mine* was written in France – and it was truly awful. Typing in that heat. Typing while your mates are frolicking in the pool. That episode of *Mine All Mine* is easily the worst, and that fact is haunting me now.

When I get back, I now have a fortnight to write 4.1. I'm looking at it with terror, especially because it should be a fast, dynamic, funny episode, and this bad mood is the worst to be in when writing in that style. I'm not saying you have to *be* happy to *write* happy – I don't think writing is ever happy – but you do need energy. You need to be galvanised. I feel a long way from that. I feel old, and fat, and slow. If I knew what happened in 4.1, that would help. I have some ideas, like the first two scenes:

Sc.1. Donna leaves her house, locks the door.

Sc.2. The Doctor leaves the TARDIS, locks the door.

I know that sounds small, but it took a long time for it to arrive in my head. It sets up the crux of the episode: the symmetry of them both on the same mission, neither knowing that the other is there, and the fact that they're destined to meet. Apart from that, I've a nice image of Donna going to visit someone who's been Botoxed (I still like the Alien Botox idea), having stolen something – say, a vial – from Alien Botox Inc. Donna talking to this other woman and fiddling with the vial, which activates the alien inside the woman! Donna chases the alien into the street, but it's whisked away by an Alien Botox van (alerted by Vial Activation), which races along… past the Doctor, who's also running to the crime scene! High shot: the Doctor and Donna, standing in parallel streets, literally, both giving up and walking away, not realising that the other is there. That's good. It's still not a story, though.

I had another idea this morning. You know how, in 4.13, I'm going to regenerate the Doctor's hand-in-a-jar into a second Doctor, which can then travel off into the parallel universe – in the blue suit! – to live with Rose for ever? This morning, I suddenly thought, well, if you've two Doctors in 4.13, why not use them both? Properly? You've fleets of Daleks, and a red Dalek (I fancy a red Dalek – might look good), and Davros, and the End Of All Life In The Universe… so what can possibly save the day? *Two Doctors!* 'This situation needs two of us.' One in brown, one in blue, sparring off one another. It's so irresistible to end 4.12 with the Doctor, shot by a Dalek bolt, saying, 'I'm regenerating!' All that regenerative energy shoots out, but he channels it into the hand-in-a-jar, so his original self is healed, not changed, and the regeneration power creates a whole new Doctor around the hand. (Hmm, the new Doctor would be naked. I'll have to be clever with that. I'm all in favour of nudity… but not the Doctor!)

Other thoughts… Christmas 2008: Cybermen rising from the grave. We haven't really done rising from the grave before. Not fully. A Victorian funeral, in the snow, all the mourners and headstones, when hands start reaching up from the graves. Cyberhands! The humans are pulled into the earth. End on a silent graveyard, snow falling. That could be the pre-titles sequence.

'All that regenerative energy shoots out...' Illustration by Russell T Davies.

FROM: BENJAMIN COOK TO: RUSSELL T DAVIES
FRIDAY 13 JULY 2007 11:58:01 GMT

RE: SAD NEWS...

So whereabouts in Italy is your 'holiday'? Aren't you just a little bit tempted to say, 'Screw this, I'm not flying back for anyone. Somebody else can sort out this mess'...? Or are you too much of a control-freak?

>>I don't think writing is ever happy<<

Do you really believe that?

FROM: RUSSELL T DAVIES TO: BENJAMIN COOK
FRIDAY 13 JULY 2007 20:12:54 GMT

RE: SAD NEWS...

The holiday villa is in Sorrento. Frankly, it's palatial. But today I made the terrible decision: I booked myself a flight home after just seven days out there. I simply can't stay away. That's not control-freakery; that's genuine panic. The rest of the team is brilliant at sorting out problems, but I'm the only one who can rewrite an entire episode. I need to be here. I can holiday when all this is over.

Do I *really* believe that writing is never happy? (What a day to ask me!) Well, I think that was a grandiose thing for me to say. I must have been in martyr-mode. It can be unhappy, certainly. Writing can be a hell of a load of misery. It's such a hard job. Writers never talk about how hard it is, out of the fear of being pretentious. 'Try being a nurse or a teacher,' people say. No, sod you – try being a writer! Try sitting with every doubt and fear about yourself and everyone, all on your own, with no ending or help or conclusion. I know I'm sort of a happy man and love a laugh, but I think that's because the job is so hard. At the same time, writing can be the most wonderful job in the world. When I'm happy with a script, I'm happier than you can ever imagine. Delirious! I think what I mean is, writing is never *easy*. Yes, that's what I meant. Moffat sent me a great e-mail about this the other day, in which he wrote:

> *John Cleese once said (at the time of* Fawlty Towers, *when he* owned *comedy) that he thought his main advantage as a writer was that he knew how hard it was supposed to be. That's what I mainly think when I read scripts – I think, you have no idea how hard this is.*

'You have no idea how hard this is.' I could have that as a tattoo.

FROM: RUSSELL T DAVIES TO: BENJAMIN COOK
SUNDAY 15 JULY 2007 23:23:52 GMT

RE: SAD NEWS...

David's mum died at noon today. So sad. He's back at work tomorrow – because he wants to be – and will stay until the funeral, which is Saturday. I can see what he means, he'd rather be working, although I worry that – having been through it myself – he doesn't know how huge and never-ending it is, the death of a parent. To be going through that with a bloody great camera shoved in your face...

FROM: BENJAMIN COOK TO: RUSSELL T DAVIES
MONDAY 16 JULY 2007 00:49:27 GMT

RE: SAD NEWS...

I hope David is all right. It's easier to throw yourself into work, I suppose, but all the same a brave decision to continue working.

She must have been so incredibly proud of him.

FROM: RUSSELL T DAVIES TO: BENJAMIN COOK
TUESDAY 17 JULY 2007 12:25:49 GMT

RE: SAD NEWS...

David says the hardest thing is having to learn lines at night. Poor bastard.

I told Julie today that I was cancelling most of my holiday. She just said, 'Well, yes.' Hmph. I was expecting some protestations, even if they were faked, but I think, in her head, she's been assuming for ages that the holiday is cancelled. Still, this does mean I'll be in Cardiff for Russell Tovey's Midshipman Frame scenes. How is a man with sticky-out ears so completely beautiful? And he's gay – I can't bear it! Matt Jones said to me yesterday, 'You're the only exec I've ever met who talks openly about fancying his cast.' I said, 'Yes, but I'm the only one who's not actually shagging them.' I'm all talk.

I could bring back Midshipman Frame in 4.12/4.13, actually. I have been wondering, but the cast list is already so huge that Russell would only have time for six lines. Well, we'll see...

Oh, and for the record, I just e-mailed Moffat and finally spoke about the Elephant in the Room. I asked him: is he interested in the job? I'm fascinated to know what his reply will be. As is the whole *Doctor Who*-loving world.

FROM: BENJAMIN COOK TO: RUSSELL T DAVIES
TUESDAY 17 JULY 2007 12:51:37 GMT

RE: SAD NEWS...

Wow. Okay. Who actually chooses your successor, then? Do you really have a say?

FROM: RUSSELL T DAVIES TO: BENJAMIN COOK
TUESDAY 17 JULY 2007 13:11:02 GMT

RE: SAD NEWS...

It's not like I've got a say; it's just that I'm here, now, in the job, so of course I'm part of it.

Silence from the Moff, though. He usually writes back straight away. It's a cliffhanger!

STEVEN MOFFAT

This is Steven Moffat's reply to Russell's 'Elephant in the Room' e-mail. It would be a couple of months before either Russell or Steven had a chance to follow this up...

FROM: STEVEN MOFFAT TO: RUSSELL T DAVIES
THURSDAY 19 JULY 2007 11:59:42 GMT

RE: HELLO

I hope you don't think I'm being weirdly reticent here. I am, of course, thrilled to my socks. It's not only a dream job; it's *my* specific dream job since I was about seven. But there's so much to process – kids, Hartswood, Cardiff, other projects, that giddy mountain of Things I'm Never Going To Write And I'm 45 Already, and Sue and I haven't worked together since *Coupling* stopped, and we're keen to.[1]

But I love *Doctor Who* to tiny bits, I know I'm good at writing it, and I *so* want it to continue. And if there were a way to make this work, I know it would be – to coin a phrase – the trip of a lifetime. So, total turmoil in my head. Probably something you're not unfamiliar with.

Of *course* I'm going to talk about it, and hear what the offer is (assuming there *is* an offer, which I won't until there is), and add that to the general confusion. If you don't mind, I'd need to talk to you too, so I can hear the Horrid Truth and the Hidden Wonders. And listen – don't get reticent on advice. You get stuck right in.

But never mind that for the moment. Russell, seriously, it's a *huge* honour even to be in the frame as the guy who follows you. Bloody terrifying, but a huge honour. Thing is, you've really got big shoes. It's not a metaphor – you've actually got enormous shoes. They may haunt my dreams.

Reproduced with kind permission

1 Hartswood Films is an independent production company founded by Steven Moffat's mother-in-law. Moffat's wife, Sue Vertue, is a producer and board director at Hartswood. Her producing credits include BBC sitcom *Coupling*, which Moffat created and wrote.

Text message from: Ben
Sent: 18-Jul-2007 16:52
I'm on set with Kylie Minogue! In Cardiff's old Coal Exchange building! Ha ha ha! Mind you, on such a sunny day, trust us to be filming inside.

Text message from: Russell
Sent: 18-Jul-2007 17:56
Kylie just asked me if I wanted dinner in the hotel tonight. I turned her down, because I'm rewriting Agatha bloody Christie. I'm telling you this just so you can make a note of my pain in The Great Correspondence. Oh, my life!

Text message from: Ben
Sent: 18-Jul-2007 20:31
You chose Agatha over Kylie? Are you sure you're gay?

Text message from: Russell
Sent: 18-Jul-2007 20:45
I think choosing Agatha over Kylie is a whole new level of gay. Gay Mark II.

FROM: RUSSELL T DAVIES TO: BENJAMIN COOK
WEDNESDAY 18 JULY 2007 22:07:16 GMT

AGATHA CHRISTIE

I'm now amusing myself by trying to get as many Agatha Christie titles into the dialogue as possible.

FROM: BENJAMIN COOK TO: RUSSELL T DAVIES
WEDNESDAY 18 JULY 2007 22:25:56 GMT

RE: AGATHA CHRISTIE

I'll give you £20 if you can slip in *Ten Little Niggers*.

FROM: RUSSELL T DAVIES TO: BENJAMIN COOK
WEDNESDAY 18 JULY 2007 22:33:43 GMT

RE: AGATHA CHRISTIE

Actually, I did try:

```
DONNA
It's like Ten Little -
```

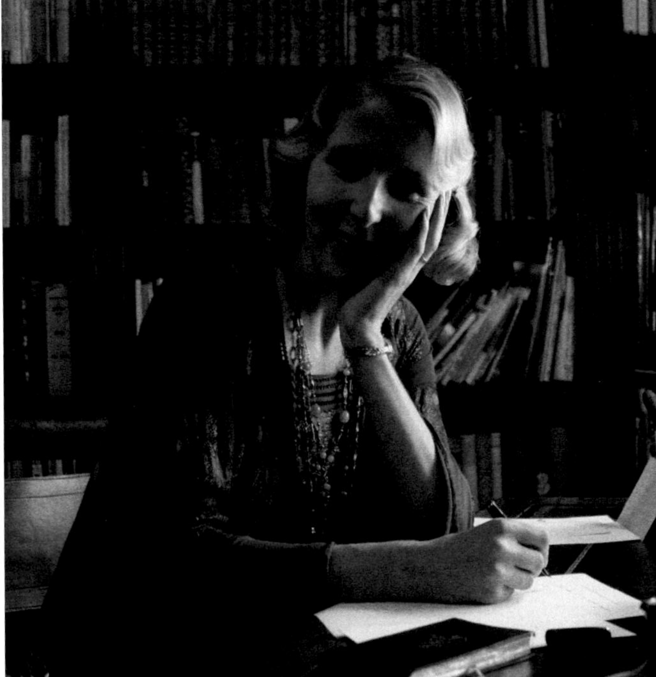

Fenella Woolgar as Agatha Christie in 4.7 *The Unicorn and the Wasp*.

```
THE DOCTOR
Niggles aside, let's look in
the library.
```

But I thought it was too risky, so cut it.

FROM: RUSSELL T DAVIES TO: BENJAMIN COOK
THURSDAY 19 JULY 2007 17:24:18 GMT

RE: AGATHA CHRISTIE

Well, I've finished 4.7. That was hard. Bloody hard. Gareth's version is much more intricate than it would first appear, so I had to be really, really careful, filtering through it. I couldn't just blunder in, adding explosions and monsters. I had to keep the lightness and the cleverness of Gareth's original. That's exhausted me.

I'm off on my holidays in half an hour. I'll have my mobile on me in Italy, but only my BBC e-mail while I'm away. I've never used that account before. You get given it when you join the BBC. A lot of people have presumed that it's working all the time. The IT man opened it up yesterday, for the first time, and there were 24,000 e-mails waiting for me! I told him: 'Delete.'

THE ADIPOSE

This e-mail exchange, on 18 July, between Russell and visual FX producer Will Cohen, from The Mill, regards the monsters in 4.1. 'I blabbed to someone else,' Russell told Benjamin later that day. 'I feel unfaithful. I've been having various thoughts and worries about 4.1 for about three days now, and simply haven't had time to write to you about them all. But then Will came blundering in with a production question, and I sang like a canary...'

FROM: WILL COHEN TO: RUSSELL T DAVIES
WEDNESDAY 18 JULY 2007 11:47:43 GMT

EP. 1 – SERIES FOUR

I know you're insanely busy, but I'm just wondering, for my own advanced scheduling purposes, if you think there may be a CGI creature in Ep 1...?

FROM: RUSSELL T DAVIES TO: WILL COHEN
WEDNESDAY 18 JULY 2007 11:59:21 GMT

RE: EP. 1 – SERIES FOUR

I'm beginning to think there might be. I'd been thinking of a green vegetable/seaweedy monster, creeping over human skin... but that's been done to death, hasn't it? And now I'm quite excited by the idea of a different sort of CGI creature – depending on the cost. Have you seen that car advert with those sinister little puppets/knitted soft toys chasing after a car?[1] They're only a few inches tall. I think they're meant to be funny, but they creep me out. I was thinking along similar lines as that, but spongy creatures – almost cute, rudimentary, blank blobs, maybe eight inches tall, with stumpy arms and legs, and a mewling mouth. No lip-sync; they just mewl. They'd trot along, seemingly cute, like a kid's soft toy – but deadly! And they'd be white – or a sort of marbly white – because they're actually made out of fat. Don't laugh, they are! It's modern-day Earth, a sinister weight-loss plan. 'Your fat just walks away from you.' And it *does*! People take a pill, which turns out to be an egg, then, while you're sleeping, a little creature grows out of your fat, comes alive, separates away from you and walks off. Yikes. Horrible.

Trouble is, for some shots, we'd need hundreds of them. Trotting along the streets. Mewling. Clambering over people. We've never done that hordes-of-little-creatures shtick. I'm quite excited by this idea. I'm worried that we might, in our fourth year, start to repeat ourselves with CGI Big Monsters, whereas little, scuttling, cute-but-horrible white blobs, with stumpy legs and mewling mouths... well, it feels new. But also it feels difficult, problematic, expensive, and a nightmare. I rather like that!

1 The C.M.O.N.S., a band of woven hand puppets, featured in adverts for the 2007 model Vauxhall Corsa.

FROM: WILL COHEN TO: RUSSELL T DAVIES
WEDNESDAY 18 JULY 2007 12:06:01 GMT

RE: EP. 1 – SERIES FOUR

I absolutely love this idea. It's fresh, exciting, scary and fun. We want to blow everyone away with the series opener. Heading outside the comfort zone – exactly where we want to be! If we keep the amount of FX shots to a minimum, we may be able to use this crowd software, Massive. We have an exclusive western-

'Your fat just walks away from you.' The Adipose in 4.1 *Partners in Crime*.

hemisphere license for Massive, which uses AI to tell the models what to do, to step over or move around things in an environment. I'll get to thinking about time, costs, etc, and e-mail you back later.

FROM: WILL COHEN TO: RUSSELL T DAVIES
WEDNESDAY 18 JULY 2007 12:29:33 GMT

RE: EP. 1 – SERIES FOUR

Sorry to bombard you, Russell, but we're having chats. How about if the fat doesn't take any one shape, but can change to a multitude of forms? When the creatures attack people, they can transform into a head, mirror people screaming or laughing, etc? My worry about a white blob is how it would look, a few pixels in size, in a daylight street scene…? Check out on YouTube our Tooheys Extra Dry commercial – I'll send you the link – where someone's tongue leaves their body while they're sleeping and heads off to a party.

FROM: RUSSELL T DAVIES TO: WILL COHEN
WEDNESDAY 18 JULY 2007 12:46:15 GMT

RE: EP. 1 – SERIES FOUR

OH MY GOD, THAT TONGUE! That's brilliant. That's what the Adipose – yes, they're called Adipose (I remember from O Level Biology, 'adipose' is a posh word for fat) – will do. They'll separate off from someone when they're sleeping. They distend out of the stomach, the stomach skin stre-e-e-etching, and then *plop!* – divide off into separate little creatures. I'd like them to be expressive, but I think they might start to lose their identity if they morph into any shape. I think the sheer, weird, freaky *cuteness* of these things is the key.

Back when we very first started, in 2004, I wanted to use the best imagery from current adverts and pop videos. Like Cassandra, inspired by stick-thin celebrities, etc! But ever since her, I think I've become a bit traditional, and it's time to remember core values, to remind myself of why I'm doing this, and to push things further than Yet Another Monster.

Text message from: Russell
Sent: 25-Jul-2007 10:13
Nice and hot here. Very hard to work. I have to lock myself away to write. Bah! But I'm 70 pages into the new Harry Potter book. Blimey, what a return to form. Good old JK! I can't read fast enough.

Text message from: Ben
Sent: 25-Jul-2007 12:33
I finished it in 24 hours. Just wait till you reach Chapter 36!

Text message from: Russell
Sent: 26-Jul-2007 17:37
Dobby just died! I am RIDICULOUSLY sad. It's turning into a bloodbath. But so exciting! I'm abandoning Pompeii. Blame JK.

Text message from: Russell
Sent: 27-Jul-2007 11:53
I finished it last night. What a book! Mrs Weasley fighting Bellatrix! 'NOT MY DAUGHTER, YOU BITCH!' Ha ha ha.

FROM: BENJAMIN COOK TO: RUSSELL T DAVIES
SUNDAY 29 JULY 2007 18:13:16 GMT

HOLIDAY!

Good holiday?

FROM: RUSSELL T DAVIES TO: BENJAMIN COOK
SUNDAY 29 JULY 2007 20:21:48 GMT

RE: HOLIDAY!

Holiday fine, yes. Gone now. Mind you, I was even recognised in a tiny restaurant on a godforsaken cliff top on the Amalfi Coast, by a little girl called Molly. One of these days, I'm going tell 'em to sod off, just to see the look on mum and dad's face!

No, I won't. But I dream of it.

I was back in this flat for five minutes – *five bloody minutes* – before Julie was at the door. Lovely to see her and all that, but *c'mon!* It's like walking into a blizzard. I've a mountain of work. I have to rewrite the end of 4.7, because David thinks – quite fairly – that ramming a car into the Vespiform is the Doctor committing murder.[1] Good point, but… any ideas?

But! I had an idea on holiday. Such a mad idea that I phoned Julie, to start setting it in motion. I was in the shower on Saturday morning (you may avert your eyes), thinking about how much I'd enjoyed that last *Harry Potter* book, how I'd love to write something like that, remembering that, back in 2004, I asked JK Rowling to write an episode of *Doctor Who*, though she politely declined, and reflecting that we can't possibly get someone to star in next year's Christmas Special who's as famous as Kylie… when all those things coalesced. *BAM!* I thought, don't ask JK to write a *Doctor Who*, ask her to *be in* a *Doctor Who*! We've done Dickens, Shakespeare, Agatha Christie… why should kids think that all great authors are dead?

Imagine it. A cold Edinburgh Christmas Eve. JK Rowling walking through the snow, pursued by a journalist. 'What are you going to write after *Harry Potter*? The difficult second album…' Later, JK sits down to write. At the same time, a Space Bug (maybe the same as Donna's time-psych creature in 4.11), probably put there by the Rita Skeeter-type journalist, leaps onto her back.[2] *ZAP!* JK's imagination becomes real! A world of Victorian magic replaces the present-day world. The Doctor arrives and has to battle through a world of witches and wizards, with wands and spells and CGI wonders, to reach JK Rowling at the heart of it all…

That's either brilliant or more like a *Blue Peter* crossover. But worth trying. It's different, certainly. So, Julie is trying to set up a meeting with JK. It's easier getting into Fort Knox at the moment, but that's Julie's skill. (Fort Knox? Is that still true? Or are my allusions getting old?) Imagine those opening titles: 'DAVID TENNANT' flying at you, then 'JK ROWLING'! She's the only name in the whole wide world who's bigger than Kylie right now. Imagine the Doctor in a world of magic made real – that would be glorious. So, there we go. That's under way.

FROM: BENJAMIN COOK TO: RUSSELL T DAVIES
MONDAY 30 JULY 2007 01:38:37 GMT

RE: HOLIDAY!

That would be – Oh God.

Do you really think she'll consider it? Did you see her on *Blue Peter* the other week, a couple of days before *Harry Potter and the Deathly Hallows* was released? She was shown a clip from *The Shakespeare Code* – the bit where the Doctor tells Martha about crying when he read Book Seven. JK seemed tickled.

But can she act?

FROM: RUSSELL T DAVIES TO: BENJAMIN COOK
MONDAY 30 JULY 2007 02:15:24 GMT

RE: HOLIDAY!

That was Julie's first question. After she stopped laughing. I said I'd write around it. Besides, did you see JK being interviewed by Jeremy Paxman on *Newsnight* before the release of Book Five? She's the only person I've ever seen run rings around him. That woman is ineffably cool and self-assured. Anyone who can do that can act. (I just made up that rule, but I'm sticking to it.) Even if

Fantasy publishing? Illustration by Russell T Davies.

1 The script had the Doctor driving an open-top tourer into the Vespiform, which falls into a lake, where it drowns.

2 Rita Skeeter is a reporter of dubious repute in the *Harry Potter* novels.

Another good reason for Russell to visit the *Voyage of the Damned* set on 31 July 2007: a visit from Sixth Doctor actor Colin Baker (centre).

it never happens, it's enough to keep me going through the dark hours. Well, that and Bel Ami porn.

FROM: RUSSELL T DAVIES TO: BENJAMIN COOK
MONDAY 30 JULY 2007 23:51:51 GMT

RE: HOLIDAY!

I've just been for drinks with Kylie and cast and crew. Everyone's ridiculously excited about Bernard Cribbins' day on set tomorrow. It's a pity, really, that Stan the newsvendor is just a cameo. Kylie had never heard of Bernard, until we told her that he was the voice of the Wombles! I'm tempted to come on set with you all tomorrow, except I'm so short of time. Not a word of Pompeii rewritten. I haven't even opened the file. But I'm getting interested in soothsayers, in a sort of Sisterhood of Karn way, or the Seeker in *The Ribos Operation*, or that wonderful Fortune Teller in *Snakedance*.[3] Thank Christ for *Doctor Who*'s rich history! There's a wealth of ideas to draw from in a crisis.

3 The Sisterhood of Karn appeared in 1976 *Doctor Who* serial *The Brain of Morbius*; the Seeker in 1978's *The Ribos Operation*; the Fortune Teller in 1983's *Snakedance*.

FROM: BENJAMIN COOK TO: RUSSELL T DAVIES
TUESDAY 31 JULY 2007 08:45:45 GMT

RE: HOLIDAY!

You really should come on set tonight. You might never again get the chance to see Kylie Minogue on the streets of Cardiff. Unless her career takes a real turn for the worse.

FROM: RUSSELL T DAVIES TO: BENJAMIN COOK
TUESDAY 31 JULY 2007 15:16:25 GMT

RE: HOLIDAY!

Oh, all right, I am coming tonight. I couldn't resist. Pompeii can burn.

FROM: RUSSELL T DAVIES TO: BENJAMIN COOK
FRIDAY 3 AUGUST 2007 12:38:55 GMT

RE: HOLIDAY!

Christ and damn and bollocks. It's August.

This is a new low: I'm resorting to going into a Tone Meeting on Monday – it's for Block Three – with a few paltry pages (I hope) of 4.3, and a three-page synopsis of 4.1.[4] This is bad. It's bordering on an emergency. It feels awful – literally, makes me feel sick. I've just flagged up to Julie that we could abandon Pompeii, and bring in Mark Gatiss' World War II/Natural History Museum script instead.

FROM: RUSSELL T DAVIES TO: BENJAMIN COOK
FRIDAY 3 AUGUST 2007 21:45:41 GMT

RE: HOLIDAY!

Emergency Protocol One has been activated! Block Three has been split in two. Colin Teague will now direct 4.3 on its own (instead of 4.1 and 4.3 together), and James Strong will come back to direct 4.1 in a brand new Block Four. In other words, while Colin is shooting the Pompeii episode, that's the prep time for James on the Adipose one.

This takes the pressure off scripts, because now 4.1 doesn't have to be ready until the beginning of September. This is a huge relief for me, but also chronic; it means paying off Colin and his editor for the work that they'd have done on 4.1, plus finding a new chunk of money to pay James. That's money that won't be seen on screen. Technically, that's terrible. In practice, it's the only way that we're going to get on air. Bloody hell.

FROM: RUSSELL T DAVIES TO: BENJAMIN COOK
SATURDAY 4 AUGUST 2007 14:17:53 GMT

POMPEII

Finally, I've started on Pompeii. Five pages in. That's five pages better than this morning. (I woke up in abject terror.) But what do these bloody soothsayers want? What and why and how? I think by breathing in the gases from the hypocaust, people in Pompeii are turning into stone… because the Stone Aliens (yes, really!) aren't really stone, they're *dust*, and they need to be inhaled to become, gradually, their stone selves. Well, that's my idea for now, but it still doesn't decide what the soothsayers do. I just like soothsayers.

4 Each series is split into filming blocks of one, two, or three episodes, overseen by the same director. Block One of Series Four comprised 4.X only (directed by James Strong), Block Two comprised 4.7 and 4.2 (Graeme Harper), and Block Three comprised – at this stage – 4.3 and 4.1 (Colin Teague).

(RE)WRITING POMPEII

In this extract from James Moran's original script for 4.3, the Doctor and Donna have just arrived in Pompeii (which they've mistaken for Rome) in AD 79, in a bustling Pompeian marketplace…

```
                DONNA
      This is - this is not
      today.

                DOCTOR
      Course it's today. Every
      day is today, as long as
      it's today. Basic time
      theory, that.

He strides off, exploring.
Donna has trouble speaking.

                DONNA
      No, it's not 'today'-
      today. It's before today.
      Not present day. The
      past. We're in… the past.

A market trader holds out a
gourd to Donna.

             MARKET TRADER 1
      Gourd, madam? Very
      reasonable.

                DONNA
      No, thanks, I… I've
      already got one. Doctor!

                              CUT TO:

4. EXT. SIDE STREET OF MARKET

An offshoot of the market,
filled with interesting fruits
and foods. Donna struggles to
keep up with the Doctor.

                DONNA
      We're in the past!

                DOCTOR
      You don't want to see
      the boring old present,
      do you? We want to see
      what it was really like.
      In the past. Soak up all
      that past-y goodness.
      Look at it.

Donna touches a wall, picks up
a vase. Tears in her eyes.
```

DOCTOR (CONT'D)
Ah, good old Rome! The Colosseum! The Pantheon! The Circus Maximus!

He looks around at the surrounding area, standing on a box to get a better view. It's obvious that none of the things he just mentioned are anywhere in sight. He frowns.

DOCTOR (CONT'D)
Well, somewhere around here, I'm sure. Might be a tad off course.

DONNA
And it's safe? You've been here before?

DOCTOR
Once, yes. Didn't go very well, had to leave in a bit of a hurry… And I had NOTHING to do with Rome burning down, before you ask, that was entirely not my fault at all. Mostly.

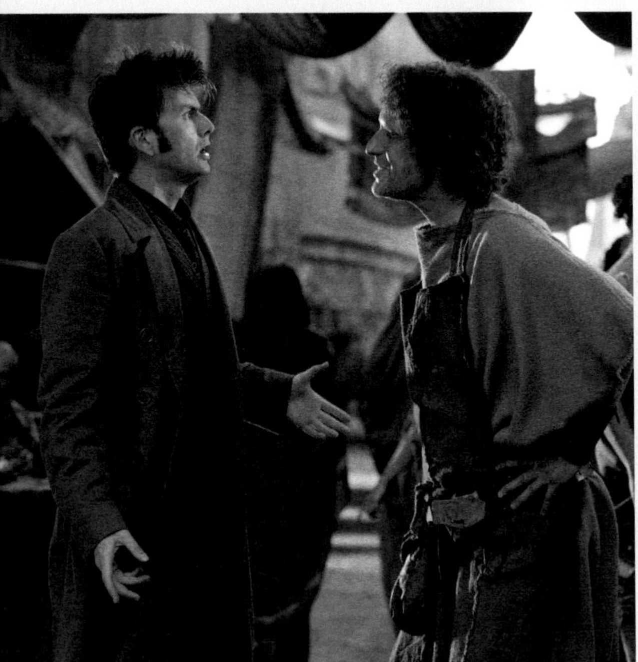

The Doctor (David Tennant) meets a Pompeian trader (Phil Cornwell).

Anyway, it's all been rebuilt now.

DONNA
Simple 'yes' would be fine. Hold on - I spoke to that man. You! Can you understand me?

She addresses another trader.

MARKET TRADER 2
Course I can.

DONNA
Doctor! I'm speaking Latin! I must be one of those language geniuses. You know, like how Einstein was rubbish at school, but then it turned out -

DOCTOR
No, that's the TARDIS. Translation thingy, gets inside your head.

DONNA
Oh. I'm not a genius, then?

DOCTOR
Not as far as I know. Where is everything?

He's still trying to get his bearings, nothing looks familiar. Donna is still staring at everything, taking in the sights, sounds, smells, madness.

DONNA
Okay, so we're in ancient Rome. I can handle this. I can do this.

This is Russell's rewrite (on 4 August) of that section…

DONNA
I'm here, in Rome, Donna Noble, in Rome! Me! This is just weird. I mean, everyone here's dead!

THE DOCTOR
I wouldn't go telling them that.

(RE)WRITING POMPEII (continued)

DONNA
No, but… Hold on a minute, that sign over there's in English. You having me on, are we in Epcot?

Hand-painted stall-sign, *Two amphoras for the price of one.*

THE DOCTOR
No, that's the Tardis translation circuits, just makes it look like English. Speech as well, you're talking Latin, right now.

DONNA
Seriously? I just said 'seriously' in Latin? But… what if I said something in actual Latin? Like, 'veni vidi vici', my Dad says that when he comes back from the football, if I said 'veni vidi vici' to that lot, what would it sound like?

THE DOCTOR
Um… I'm not sure. Have to think of difficult questions, don't you?

DONNA
I'm gonna try it…

Goes up to a STALLHOLDER, a cheery Cockney, selling fruit.

STALLHOLDER
Afternoon sweetheart, what can I get you, my love?

DONNA
Veni vidi vici!

STALLHOLDER
(like she's dumb)
Ah. Sorry. Me no speak Celtic. No can do, missy.

DONNA
Yeah…
(back to the Doctor)
How's he mean, Celtic?

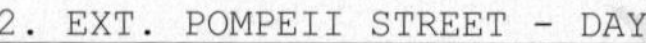

THE DOCTOR
Welsh. You sound Welsh. There we are, I've learnt something.

As they stroll away -

CUT TO A SOOTHSAYER, good distance away. Woman, 20s, in robes, face painted white, with strange patterns. Part-witch, part-priestess. She's hiding in the shadows of a doorway, staring at the new arrivals.

And she keeps to the shadows, as she follows them…

CUT TO:

2. EXT. POMPEII STREET - DAY

THE DOCTOR & DONNA walking along.

Throughout: a good distance away, the SOOTHSAYER follows.

DONNA
Don't our clothes look a bit odd?

THE DOCTOR
Naaah, Ancient Rome, anything goes. It's like Soho, but bigger.

DONNA
Have you been here before, then?

THE DOCTOR
Ages ago. And before you ask, that fire had nothing to do with me, well, not very much, well, a little bit, well… But I never got the chance to look around properly! The Colosseum! The Pantheon! The Circus Maximus! Although… you'd expect them to be looming by now, where is everything? Let's try this way…

FROM: BENJAMIN COOK TO: RUSSELL T DAVIES
SATURDAY 4 AUGUST 2007 15:33:41 GMT

RE: POMPEII

Who has the horrible job of telling the writers that you're taking over their scripts?

FROM: RUSSELL T DAVIES TO: BENJAMIN COOK
SATURDAY 4 AUGUST 2007 15:56:23 GMT

RE: POMPEII

That's always Julie's job. The writers are told in advance that it *might* happen. It's a condition of the contract. They've all got my number and e-mail address, if they want to have a pop at me. Once it's done, I do phone them up to explain how and why and wherefore. Keith Temple was absolutely delightful about my rewrites on his Ood script. Such a nice bloke.

FROM: RUSSELL T DAVIES TO: BENJAMIN COOK
TUESDAY 7 AUGUST 2007 23:31:10 GMT

RE: POMPEII

Donna Noble arrived today! She was glorious. We had the read-through for 4.2 and 4.7, Catherine sat right next to David, and she was dazzling! After all that Penny/Donna development, I just sat there and thought, this is *exactly* what I wanted. All that work, all that thinking, all those e-mails to you, actually had a result. She's an equal to the Doctor, a friend, a mate, a challenge. It struck me – this is how Barbara Wright would be written, if she were a 2007/8 character.[5] That feels good. Catherine takes a funny line, makes it five times funnier, and aims it like a dart – which makes David raise his game. He throws back a javelin! I'm so happy. I realised how scared I'd been all this time, because you never really know if something is going to work.

Catherine Tate as Donna Noble.

Anyway, this has all interrupted the writing of Pompeii. It's annoying, when writing gets interrupted, because you lose the energy, the drive, the flow. It's hard to summon it back. I'll have to smoke-and-coffee myself back into that state tomorrow. I sat here for hours today – all day, really – and managed little more than reducing the length from 33 pages to 32, then I wrote one new page, which is all right-ish, and added a joke for Donna about going to the shops in Pompeii ('T K Maximus')... but I promised to deliver the script tomorrow! Especially with Colin and Phil heading off to Cinecittà Studios on a recce this week.[6] (It looks as though filming in Rome really will happen!) Not the best time for me to slow down. But I'll have to panic tomorrow. Of course, while I pause, the problems and worries are stirring. How come the Stone Aliens' presence in Pompeii is allowing the city's soothsayers to tell the future? In *Doctor Who* terms, there must be a scientific explanation, even if it's not *real* science. Is Pompeii on a Time Rift? Don't laugh, it's a quick solution.

FROM: BENJAMIN COOK TO: RUSSELL T DAVIES
WEDNESDAY 8 AUGUST 2007 00:10:26 GMT

RE: POMPEII

So what does a normal day consist of, to stop you writing? What's a typical day, in your role as showrunner?

5 Barbara Wright (played by Jacqueline Hill) was one of the original *Doctor Who* companions, joining the show at its inception in 1963 and staying until 1965.

6 Rome's legendary Cinecittà Studios is where HBO/BBC series *Rome* was filmed, on five acres of outdoor sets comprising elaborate reconstructions of Ancient Rome.

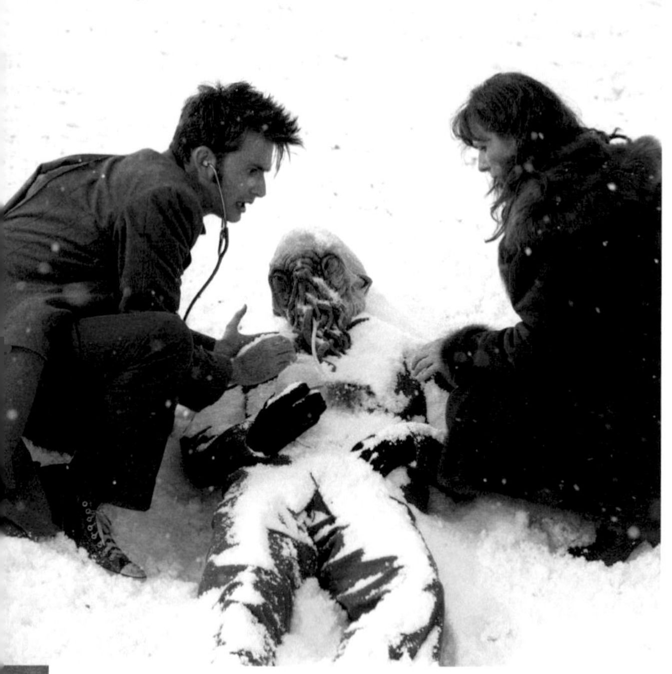

The original Episode 2, *Planet of the Ood* (left), was swapped in the running order of Series Four with Episode 3, *The Fires of Pompeii* (right).

FROM: RUSSELL T DAVIES TO: BENJAMIN COOK
WEDNESDAY 8 AUGUST 2007 00:38:34 GMT

RE: POMPEII

Well, there's no such thing as a typical day. But today? Um… a read-through. Plus, talking Catherine and Phil through what will happen in 4.1 so that everyone knows where Donna is coming from. (I enjoyed describing it – it sounds fun and weird – but I'm acutely aware that it has no ending.) I sorted out *Sarah Jane* Dub dates with Julie. A compulsory set visit, if only to see Russell T. Ovey. (He told me that *Bob & Rose* is one of his favourite shows ever, and actually *quoted lines* from Episode 6. He loves me. It's official.) I had to sort out the end of *Doctor Who* 4.7, because of David's worry about killing the Vespiform. (David T. Ennant: clever, sexy *and* good on scripts. Why don't I hate him?) I had to come home and do that rewrite, as well as some further rewrites on 4.2. I had to clear the press release for Friday – we're releasing a photo of David and Catherine on set for 4.7. This involved 20 e-mails. I noticed that the BBC *Doctor Who* website has a new page of artwork, which we'd promised exclusively to Worldwide for books and magazines, so I alerted Julie – that's a major storm on the way.

What else? I decided to swap 4.2 and 4.3 in the transmission order – Pompeii first, then Ood – so I set that in motion. Since the Ood tale is surprisingly dark, I'd thought that it would undercut people's comedy expectations of Life With Donna, but then, at the read-through, I thought that the Ood episode was dark to the point of grim. It's a very macho, testosterone-fuelled script, and they're never my favourites, so, yes, it's better as the third episode. Also today – I watched rushes, *Doctor Who* and *Torchwood*, all good, no notes, and the online edit (the finished picture with FX added) of *Sarah Jane* 1.3/1.4. I worried about the decision to kill Tosh and Owen at the end of this year's *Torchwood* (I'm happy to kill the characters, not happy to lose the actors – but that show needs a shock), so I sent concerned e-mails to Julie. Also, I'm still debating with Julie whether to leave Mickey Smith in this universe at the end of 4.13, so he can guest in *Torchwood* and *Sarah Jane* as a sort of roving character – and in *Doctor Who*, if the next production team fancy a link with the past. Yes, I think we're going to do it.

Also, and this is top secret (do not tell anyone), Phil has been offered the job as producer of *Coronation Street*! I'm so happy for him. He loves *Coronation Street*. It's possibly the only job in the UK that could replace *Doctor Who* in his heart. He'd be the king of Manchester! And it wouldn't be till the beginning of next year, so he'd only miss the filming of the final two episodes of Series Four. But… but… Jane Tranter wants him to stay at the BBC (of course she does – he's brilliant), so she's throwing a brand new North-West Drama job at him. He'd be based in Manchester, as Head of Drama for the entire region. Well, Phil doesn't know what to do. What a dilemma! Today was talking him through that. Russell T Counsellor.

And then more work – I disagreed with Peter McKinstry's design of Ood Sigma's hip flask. It's too tricky for a blind and gloved actor. Lovely design, though. I ate a lasagne, cold, because I didn't have time to heat it up. That's bad, isn't it? I saw a second hip-flask design, and approved it. I was asked to sign off on the Series Three DVD boxset cover, but didn't, because it's terrible. I texted Russell Tovey, just… because. I read and approved three BBC Novel proposals and one BBC Audiobook proposal. I suggested a commission for Joe Lidster for a *Torchwood* radio play. I e-mailed Ben –

Oh. That's you.

Bloody hell. And this is a normal day. It's barmy. Mind you, every time I say to myself, 'I can't wait for it all to end,' something grabs me. Julie and I spent the car journey to Upper Boat today talking about the New Studio. They're thinking of building it from scratch next to the St David's Hotel. Near my flat! To house *Doctor Who*, *Torchwood*, *Sarah Jane*, and various other BBC shows. That's vast. They're even talking about having Universal Tours-style visits! Just as I contemplate leaving, they go and make the empire bloody tangible, right on my doorstep. Oh, so tempting, to stay and help set that up. That's *thousands* of jobs, literally. It's only a plan at the moment, but a plan that's hastening every day. Ed Thomas is drawing up designs. It would be his masterpiece. And I'll miss it. Well, I'm going to keep this flat on, so I can press my nose up against the windows and cry.

I really can't keep working at this rate. It'll kill me. It has to stop.

FROM: RUSSELL T DAVIES TO: BENJAMIN COOK
FRIDAY 10 AUGUST 2007 02:14:55 GMT

RE: POMPEII

I'm on Page 43 of Pompeii. Not enough. Colin and company are in Rome right now, screaming for pages. Well, tough. It took all day to think of the water pistol. The Doctor uses it to face off the alien-possessed High Priestess, the head of the Sibylline Sisterhood in Pompeii. That's where the time goes. Or rather – I thought of the water pistol at about midday (in the middle of a *Sarah Jane* Edit), and it took the rest of the day to *convince myself* it can work. A lot of doubt. Eventually, I realised it's a great scene; it's very Doctor to face an alien with a water pistol. His character allows you to get away with murder. Sometimes.

FROM: BENJAMIN COOK TO: RUSSELL T DAVIES
FRIDAY 10 AUGUST 2007 22:51:04 GMT

RE: POMPEII

There are reports on the news that a fire last night destroyed part of the Cinecittà Studios in Rome. Isn't that where Colin and Phil and the team are at the moment, on the recce? According to BBC News:

> *Flames leapt 40m (130ft) into the air at one point before the blaze was brought under control. The fire engulfed about 3,000sq m (32,000sq ft), firefighters said. There were no reported deaths or injuries. Firefighters fought the blaze all night and prevented the fire spreading to the densely populated urban area around the film studios. The fire began in a store for film sets, destroying sets used in a television series about ancient Rome, produced by HBO and the BBC.*

Phil didn't nip outside for a smoke, did he, and drop his cigarette? Will *Doctor Who* still be able to film at Cinecittà?

FROM: RUSSELL T DAVIES TO: BENJAMIN COOK
SATURDAY 11 AUGUST 2007 02:50:16 GMT

RE: POMPEII

The fire! Yes, bloody hell. The reports from Rome are that there's still enough of the set left standing for us to film on. Of course, I did ask if they had footage of the burning, because that could look brilliant for us! Phil harrumphed at me. Well, it's an idea. How mad, though. And thank God, otherwise we'd have to go to Malta instead.

In fact, I've just finished the 4.3 script. I'm knackered. I need sleep.

FROM: BENJAMIN COOK TO: RUSSELL T DAVIES
SATURDAY 11 AUGUST 2007 03:58:19 GMT

RE: POMPEII

Why exactly don't you insist on a co-writer's credit for 4.3?

FROM: RUSSELL T DAVIES TO: BENJAMIN COOK
SUNDAY 12 AUGUST 2007 18:33:52 GMT

RE: POMPEII

I know, I know, that credit thing… but it just crept up on us, really, until it became a sort of policy. It was never planned that way. Back in 2004, we'd always talked about my rewriting as a possibility ('polishing' we called it, when we were young and naive, before we actually had scripts in our hands, and I'd never rewritten anyone before, ever), but Andy Pryor kick-started the whole process when we wanted to offer the part of Charles Dickens to Simon Callow. We really *needed* Simon

Simon Callow as Charles Dickens in 1.3 *The Unquiet Dead*.

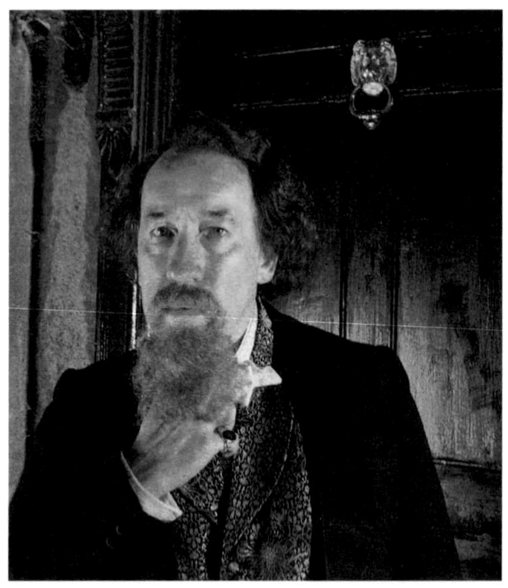

JAMES MORAN

After reading Russell's rewrite of his Pompeii episode, James Moran e-mailed script editor Brian Minchin...

FROM: JAMES MORAN TO: BRIAN MINCHIN
MONDAY 13 AUGUST 2007 11:20:15 GMT

RE: 4.3

Had a quick read, through half-closed fingers – such a strange feeling, I knew it would be different, because it's always weird being rewritten. But it's bloody brilliant! Once I got used to reading it – by Page 20, I was just enjoying the story. It belts along, it's funny, it's clever, some of my jokes are still there, some are Russell's new ones, and I nearly wet myself at the water pistol gag. I wish I'd thought of that.

Normally, being rewritten is a horrible experience, but in this case, while it feels slightly odd (which it *always* will – it can't be helped), every single change is right, right for the story, makes it feel more part of New *Who*, and is done to make for a better episode, instead of competing for lines. (I had a few bad months on a different project, where it felt like the other guy was changing stuff just to try to stamp himself on it, rather than to make it better – and some stuff suffered.) Everything in RTD's rewrite serves the story and builds on the stuff that I set down, instead of throwing it out. I can see *why* everything has been done, rather than 'what the hell are you thinking?!' – which has happened to me on other things.

I've learned a lot from seeing my version magically transformed into a proper *Who* TV episode. It's really bizarre, and quite fantastic, and I don't know how RTD has managed to do a rewrite where I feel enriched, and educated, and happy. Clearly, he has evil mind-melding powers.

Reproduced with kind permission

Callow for that part – but Mark's script for *The Unquiet Dead* wasn't ready.

After that, in some ways, it became a trap. I'd be rewriting an episode and I'd be thinking, well, if I didn't get a credit for the last script that I rewrote, why should I single out this one? And I have to be fair to the original writers: they work so hard and deserve that credit. It's partly arrogance as well, because I don't think my rewrites are as good as my actual scripts. (With the exception of *The Impossible Planet* and *The Satan Pit*. God, I love that story!) For instance, I think the Pompeii episode works now, though it's curious how still it's inherited the linear shape of James' original. I reckon I'd still have written it better had it been mine from the start. Instead of all those months of thinking and consideration, rewriting somebody else's script is more like plate-spinning – keeping lots of things in the air, making them look pretty, hoping that they won't crash. In an emergency, I throw lots of things in there – soothsayers, psychic powers, prophecies, funny squares of marble – and hope that I can make a story out of them as I go along, like an improvisation game. When you've a big, central conceit like a volcano, as long as you make sure everything streamlines into that (it's not plate-spinning; it's a maypole – it's a multi-metaphor!), then it should hang together. The psychic powers are caused by the dust, which is the aliens, and the aliens are thwarted by the volcano erupting, etc, etc, etc. Ram them all into each other. It's not a maypole; it's a car crash! Fun, though.

FROM: RUSSELL T DAVIES TO: BENJAMIN COOK
SATURDAY 18 AUGUST 2007 00:29:47 GMT

RE: POMPEII

I was doing further production rewrites on Pompeii today, and thinking about our e-mails earlier in the year, and what I said about characters, that you should keep turning them, keep seeing them in new lights, so they live a bit more. Now, James didn't have time to get his Pompeii script to that stage of finessing, so he only got the Caecilius family to first base – the father was henpecked, Metella was a nag, Quintus was sullen, Evelina was girlish.[7] Fine, good starting point, and James made them much more distinct than a lot of writers

Quintus (Francois Pandolfo) in 4.3 *The Fires of Pompeii.*

would have done. But then the turning must start. Take Quintus (who only has 25 or so lines, so theoretically a small part, but it's true that no parts are small) – a lot of my rewrite consisted of turning him, like a barbecue, making sure that he's cooked all the way through. Metaphor heaven! In my rewrite, he's sullen and hung over when he first appears, but then he deepens as he defends his sister before his parents ('But she's sick!'), then greedy when the Doctor offers him money to take him to where Lucius lives, then as scared as a little kid when they break into Lucius' quarters ('Don't tell my dad!'), then brave when he throws the burning torch at the soldiers to escape Lucius, then magnificent back at the Caecilius' villa when he kills the Pyrovile with the bucket of water.[8] And then he's transformed at the end: the sullen youth has become a doctor himself, the image of his hero. That's what I mean by turning. No one is fixed. They're all capable of change – not just once in some plot-reveal, but all the time. They become more distinct by allowing them a fuller life. Quintus goes through a lot of stuff, but there's still an essential Quintus-ness to him, which only gets richer as he turns.

In other news… Peter Capaldi agreed to play Caecilius today. Brilliant casting! And with the most handsome Quintus you could imagine: a young actor called Francois Pandolfo. Julie said, 'Does his skin-tone

7 The Roman family in 4.3 consists of a father (Lobus, listed as Caecilius in the script), mother (Metella), son (Quintus) and daughter (Evelina).

8 Lucius Petrus Dextrus is Chief Augur of the City Government; he serves the alien Pyroviles, rock creatures born out of magma. At the end of 4.3, set some time after the eruption of Pompeii, Quintus is training to be a doctor.

A world descending into anarchy – Donna takes a stroll through an alternative Britain in 4.11 *Turn Left*.

match the rest of the family?' Me, Phil and Andy: 'Shut up! Who cares?'

FROM: RUSSELL T DAVIES TO: BENJAMIN COOK
TUESDAY 21 AUGUST 2007 23:04:21 GMT

RE: POMPEII

It's dawning on me that 4.11 and 4.12/4.13, which once felt nice and distant, are approaching at the rate of knots. It all has to be done by Christmas! Judging by my work rate this year, that's impossible. A bed of panic is building up, which is a shame, because the past few days have seen good 4.11 thoughts. For example, just how much should this alt-world of Donna's change? It really should be a World Descending Into Anarchy. I've been thinking that we should bring back Chipo Chung (Chantho in *Utopia*), without her alien prosthetics, as one of Donna's real-world mates. Donna could find her being carted off in a truck, by soldiers, to the internment camps, because she's 'not British'. That sort of world. 'It'll be the redheads next,' says Rose to Donna. Is that going too far? For a world without the Doctor? No.

For 4.13, I keep playing 'Live and Let Die'. That's how exciting the finale should be. Not the lyrical bits; the fast bits where that song is so epic and dynamic. It sort of makes me want to stand up. Sometimes, I do. I'm listening to it right now, on repeat. It's exhausting. Noisy old song. End of 4.13, the whole place exploding, everyone running for the TARDIS – Donna, Martha, Rose, Captain Jack, Sarah Jane, Mickey, Jackie, everyone – and the Doctor shoving them through the TARDIS door. He counted them out; he counts them back in again. He saves *all of them*. Yes, we're back to that 'One of them will die' prophecy, but I'm sorry, Ben, I can't. I just can't. I can't kill any of them. There's no room for anyone to die. That's why it's worth bringing back Midshipman Frame, because he can die, and they'd be sad for, ooh, a minute, but that's all.

And Christmas 2008 is steaming up on the horizon! I should be writing that in January. That's like *tomorrow!* That could be JK Rowling, or Cybermen in Victorian London. David doesn't like the JK idea, he thinks it sounds like a spoof, so we've paused slightly, wondering whether to win him round or just abandon something that he's not going to be happy with. We've got to keep him happy. He keeps *us* happy. (You should see the rushes of him and Catherine chasing Agatha Christie in vintage cars – it's a hoot!) Plus, he might be right. So that idea has parked itself, while Julie tries to find ways to approach JK anyway. And I doubt we'd ever get JK – she doesn't *need* to do it – so Cybermen in the snow are hauling themselves back into my head. Workhouses.

Starving children. At Christmas. The Little Match Girl. That's the companion, the Little Match Girl. Well, maybe a bit older and foxier. The Foxy Match Girl.

But we've production problems already: we worked out – no, Julie worked out – that we've only really time to shoot *two* Specials after Christmas 2008. We wanted three: Christmas 2009, New Year's Day 2010 (instead of Easter 2009, which was the original plan) and Easter 2010, which then would lead directly into Steven's (or whoever's) Brand New Series. Except that doesn't work, does it? The Brand New Series needs a brand new start. Clean sheet. Not following on seven days after us. So what if we only do Christmas 2009 and New Year's Day 2010? But! We're all geared up for three Specials. We don't want to drop one. I did suggest Halloween 2009, which lands on a Saturday, but then I realised that it would transmit in the middle of *The X Factor*, which is way too scary. Even if we reverted to the original plan of an Easter 2009 Special, there's no time to film it, what with David going off to do *Hamlet* next summer. I mean, if we added it onto the end of this Series Four production run, that'd only give David a week off in between *Doctor Who* and *Hamlet*. That's inhuman. After that, he won't be free until January 2009. We wouldn't be able to complete post-production in time for Easter on a Special filmed in January and February 2009.

So now – and this is mad – Julie is suggesting that we film an Easter 2009 Special in two halves: two weeks at the end of this Series Four production run, following straight on from the Christmas Special 2008 (and shooting all the FX stuff first, if we can), then picking up the rest of the story in January 2009. I think that's *insane*, but I love Julie's nerve. Really, though! I mean, cast availability and all that. That's asking for trouble. Let alone David's hair! If he filmed in January 2009, immediately after *Hamlet*, that'd mean his Hamlet would have to have Doctor-length hair, and I bet you a million quid he's going to want to look very different. But Julie keeps saying, 'We'd be ahead! Imagine being ahead! I love being ahead!' And that, Ben, is how she builds empires. It's not just money and schedules; she loves introducing *risk*.

And so it goes, round and round and round... with no idea what these stories actually are, by the way. I'd better start thinking!

Meanwhile, 4.1 is forging its way to the front of my head. But I can't think of an ending. I can think of a *story* ending, that's Donna joining up, but I can't think of a straightforward *plot* ending, the defeat-the-aliens ending. That's normally in place by now. And do I or do I not have Rose appear towards the end of 4.1? Yes, it's irresistible, but I'm worried that Rose might upstage our This Is Catherine Tate publicity. It'd be brilliant, just brilliant, to have two edits: one a false scene, where Donna hands over her car keys to any old woman, and that's the version we issue to the press and show at the launch, so no one, but no one, knows about the real, second version *until it's actually transmitted!* I love that idea.

FROM: BENJAMIN COOK TO: RUSSELL T DAVIES
TUESDAY 21 AUGUST 2007 23:23:17 GMT

RE: POMPEII

A false scene for publicity purposes? Wouldn't The All-New We Never Lie BBC consider that deceitful?

FROM: RUSSELL T DAVIES TO: BENJAMIN COOK
TUESDAY 21 AUGUST 2007 23:48:41 GMT

RE: POMPEII

Well, stories *are* deceitful. That's my answer. Having two versions of a show is expensive and ridiculously paperwork-heavy, but I think we can cope. Very tempting.

CHAPTER EIGHT

STRUCTURE & COSMETICS

In which Billie Piper's honeymoon causes problems, Ken Barlow's death is anticipated, and Russell contemplates a *Doctor Who* movie

FROM: RUSSELL T DAVIES TO: BENJAMIN COOK
WEDNESDAY 22 AUGUST 2007 22:07:19 GMT

TIME-CHECK

I went out for a walk this afternoon. I passed a woman and heard her say to her husband, 'What time-check is it?' He said, 'Half-past-five.' I thought, *time-check?!* That's a word now? Is it hyphenated? Whatever happened to 'What's the time?' But instantly that rattled off into dialogue, in my head, as I was walking along…

```
                MAN 1
    What's the time-check?

                MAN 2
    Um... Half past five.

                MAN 1
    Right. We'd better get going.

Pause.

                MAN 2
    What did you say, time-check?

                MAN 1
    Yeah.

                MAN 2
    Where's that from?

                MAN 1
    Why, what's wrong with it?

                MAN 2
    Everyone else says 'time'.

                MAN 1
    Oh, do they? Well, I
    apologise. Is there a list of
    words I can and can't use?
```

And off they go, straight into an argument! The term 'time-check' is irrelevant, it's just a hinge; it's the relationship that matters. It could be a man and a woman, any combination, but they sound like either a couple who have been going out for a few months, so the initial shine has rubbed off and now they're *really* getting to know each other, or a couple who have been together for far too many years and are now disintegrating. The former, I think. The latter would be more stark. But I like the fact that they're heading out somewhere. It's about 6.30pm, 7pm, they're putting on ties, like they're going somewhere posh. Dialogue, mood, location, all there, all vague, but at the same time precise. I might use that exchange in a script one day. I might not. But I bet I will. The opening family dialogue in *Mine All Mine* ('What colour is linen?') was overheard and stayed in my head for about 15 years before I used it.

Anyway, I thought I'd write and tell you that, because after tens of thousands of words, trying to tell you what writing is like, it struck me: *that's* what it's like. All the time, in my head. Writing!

FROM: BENJAMIN COOK TO: RUSSELL T DAVIES
WEDNESDAY 22 AUGUST 2007 22:16:30 GMT

RE: TIME-CHECK

Maybe the woman was from up north and you misheard her say, 'What's the time, *chuck*?' Ho ho. Interesting that the dialogue in your head changes, immediately, to Man 1 and Man 2, rather than Man and Woman as per the original. You're so gay.

When you're writing dialogue, do you say the lines out loud to yourself? How do you develop an ear for certain speech rhythms, dialogue patterns and accents? Could you hear Kylie's Australian twang when you were writing Astrid's lines?

FROM: RUSSELL T DAVIES TO: BENJAMIN COOK
WEDNESDAY 22 AUGUST 2007 22:32:11 GMT

RE: TIME-CHECK

I couldn't hear Kylie's Australian twang, but I could hear *Astrid* – young, innocent, inquisitive. If I tried to write Australian, I think we'd end up with cod nonsense. I think all my characters speak with the same rhythm, essentially. My rhythm. Sarah Harding, who directed the second half of *Queer as Folk* and who's very knowledgeable about music, used to say that she could sing my scripts. The loon. Some people say it's a Welsh thing. I don't know.

I do say the lines out loud, but I don't *stop* and do it. I don't finish a scene and give it a reading. You'd find me muttering away constantly, sitting here. All night. Always testing for the rhythm, to make it sound right, to find a better way of saying it. It's good to read stuff out loud. You can find all sorts of problems. The tiny details that make dialogue better. My favourite pet hate (can you have a favourite?) is the list of three adjectives: just watch a week's telly and see how often it crops up, dialogue that goes 'I felt hurt, angry, betrayed'. It's just the writer listing, showing off his so-called understanding of motive. It doesn't exist in real life. People don't talk like that. It's much more accurate, more believable, more sayable, if you make the simplest rephrasing: 'I felt angry. God, I was so hurt. You betrayed me!' Much better. Instant polish. Even then, I bet the scene would be more interesting without it. Whatever's going on, you can pretty much assume those emotions.

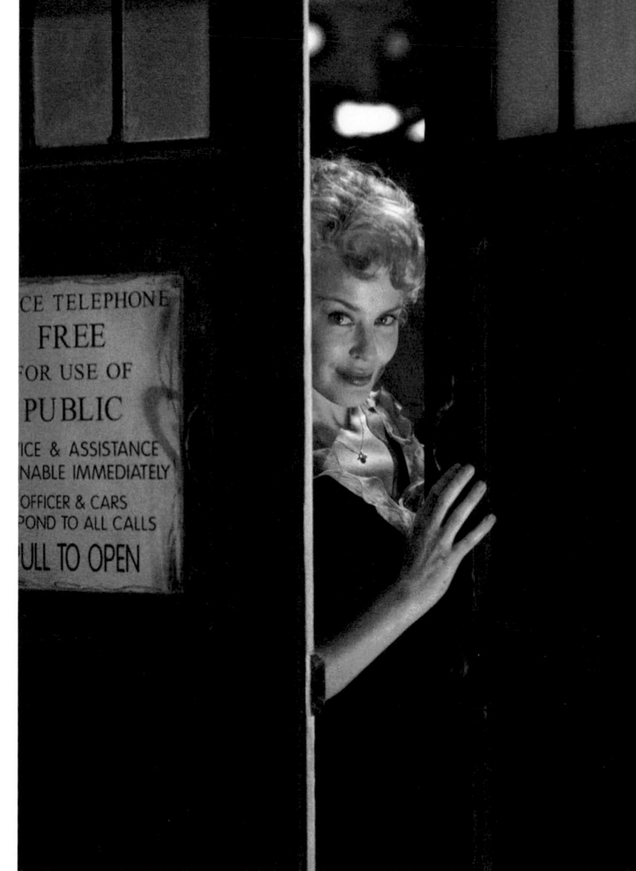

Kylie Minogue as 'young, innocent, inquisitive' Astrid.

FROM: BENJAMIN COOK TO: RUSSELL T DAVIES
WEDNESDAY 22 AUGUST 2007 22:39:45 GMT

RE: TIME-CHECK

Would you agree, though, that every character is always talking about him- or herself? Every character has their own agenda and it's the centre of their world, especially in dialogue with other characters. Is that true?

FROM: RUSSELL T DAVIES TO: BENJAMIN COOK
WEDNESDAY 22 AUGUST 2007 23:14:21 GMT

RE: TIME-CHECK

Yes, absolutely true. Remember what we were saying about Captain Hardaker in *Voyage of the Damned*, 'full of aches and pains'? Thing is, to think about yourself all the time isn't necessarily selfish; the self is all we've got. We might touch on other people, glance off them, and sometimes, maybe once in a while, *maybe*, see deeply into them. But the other 99 per cent of the time? It's just yourself. There's no other option.

Dialogue is just two monologues clashing. That's my Big Theory. It's true in life, never mind drama! Everyone is always, *always* thinking about themselves. It's kind of impossible to do otherwise. I just hate dialogue that goes:

```
                RUSSELL
I went to town.

                BEN
Why?

                RUSSELL
Because I needed to see Stan.

                BEN
And what did he say?

                RUSSELL
He said you knew the truth.

                BEN
Yes, I do.

                RUSSELL
Why didn't you tell me?

                BEN
Because I was scared.
```

Captain Hardaker, 'full of aches and pains'.

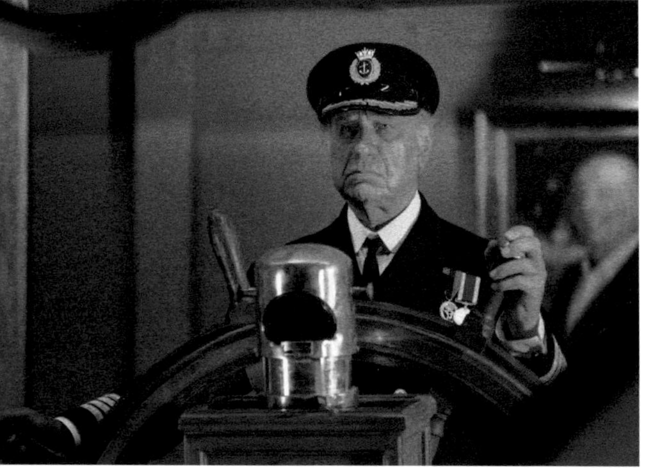

It's like they're both *listening* to each other. Rubbish! Appalling amounts of TV dialogue is like that, especially on the soaps, whereas in reality we're all waiting to say the next thing that we want to say. Truest phrase ever: 'The opposite of talking isn't listening. The opposite of talking is waiting.' Fran Lebowitz said that, and I bloody love it.

FROM: BENJAMIN COOK TO: RUSSELL T DAVIES
WEDNESDAY 22 AUGUST 2007 23:25:49 GMT

RE: TIME-CHECK

We're all talking about ourselves... and yet our instinct is to *guard* our inner selves, sometimes even from those we love. Wouldn't you have thought those two ideas are mutually exclusive?

FROM: RUSSELL T DAVIES TO: BENJAMIN COOK
WEDNESDAY 22 AUGUST 2007 23:47:32 GMT

RE: TIME-CHECK

The opposite of exclusive: they're the same thing, in a way. We think of ourselves, but reveal ourselves through what we say. I think 'reveal' is the crucial word there. We don't actually *say* what we're thinking, not deliberately, not consciously. We're revealing and guarding at the same time. You hear it, every day, in the way people say other people's names. If someone fancies someone, but hasn't said so out loud – and might not even be hugely conscious of it themselves – the way that they say that person's name just gives it away. More importantly, the number of times they say that person's name, every day. Oh, don't you just *love* people, for all their transparency and hopelessness?

That's what dialogue is: it's tapping into those tides and urges, revealing glimpses of it, though never revealing any one final truth, because there isn't any one final truth; we're many things, to many people, and a great unknown to ourselves. I love that bit where you say that we guard ourselves 'sometimes even from those we love'. I think it's *especially* from them. All the time. Or maybe I'm a cynic. But I don't think 'love' is the cure-all, the great honesty; it's the most complicated area of the lot. Hence, thousands of years of love stories. It's the centre of fiction, with no sign of exhaustion.

It really is crass to use Captain Hardaker as an example, because he's hardly the finest fictional creation ever (though I look forward to presenting the annual Hardaker Award), but he *is* doing what we're talking about. 'It's an old ship, full of aches and pains' is talking about himself both physically and – if you want to get wanky – morally. But he's not saying, 'Actually, I'm going to kill myself.' Revealing and guarding at the same time – don't we always? I don't actually imagine that Hardaker is thinking, aha, I'll talk about myself metaphorically. It's more of a mood than that.

FROM: BENJAMIN COOK TO: RUSSELL T DAVIES
THURSDAY 23 AUGUST 2007 00:04:07 GMT

RE: TIME-CHECK

Dialogue should be character-driven, but how naturalistic should it be, do you think? It depends on the show, I suppose, and *Doctor Who*'s dialogue is often heightened, but completely naturalistic dialogue would be so clotted with 'ums' and 'ers' and clichés and 'at the end of the days' and 'oh my Gods' that it'd be unbearable to read or listen to. Should dialogue in TV drama reflect day-to-day speech?

FROM: RUSSELL T DAVIES TO: BENJAMIN COOK
THURSDAY 23 AUGUST 2007 00:41:51 GMT

RE: TIME-CHECK

How you want your dialogue to sound is entirely personal. That's one of the things that defines a writer. I think the strongest writers in the land write dialogue that sounds like themselves. Paul Abbott's characters sound like Paul. Kay Mellor's sound like Kay. Alan Bennett's sound like him. Within that, they might be writing posh lords or checkout girls or mystic swamis or cruel murderers, and each of those characters would be distinct, with their own speech patterns, rhythms, habits… and yet there's a fundamental Abbott/Mellor/Bennett that creeps through.

I'd always aim for naturalism, within reason. I mean, let's not pretend, all the speeches in a script are chosen, honed, shaped, edited, so it's always going to be a faux-realism. (If only your real-life-blather could go through that process. We'd sound wonderful!) It just depends which faux you fancy and how you use it. It depends on the drama. The dialogue in *The Second Coming* was unusually stripped down for me – sparse, blunt, few jokes – because it was a cold world. *Queer as Folk* was foul, savage, funny – very gay! *Doctor Who* has much more bantering, a witty tone, because that fits the Doctor. That's how he survives. And so on. But –

I'm not answering this too well, because I don't think about it much. And yet I sit here all day trying to choose the right words, so I think about it all the time, I suppose. Hmm. I just think that dialogue has to be sayable. It has to sound real, while being highly artificial. Blimey! No one said it was easy.

On a practical level… avoid repeating words. That's the simplest advice, and yet it's what I must spend 50 per cent of my time doing. Like the word 'just'. I can use that word night and day. I just fall into it. 'I just thought I'd pop in and say hello, cos I was just thinking about you, just the other day.' Cut the 'justs'! How many months of my life have I spent cutting 'justs'?! But word repetition – and those clichés that you mentioned – can be dangerous. Make sure that every speech doesn't start with 'Well' or 'So' or 'Right'. 'Well, I think we should go to town.' 'Well, I don't.' 'Well, you would.' Easy trap to fall into. And watch out for the repetition of words across scene divides. It's really easy to end a scene with 'I hope you find him', and then you go and make a cuppa, come back and start the next scene with 'I hope you find the room comfortable'. When that runs as one, you go ouch!

The second thing I do is trim dialogue down into blocks. Discrete sentences. What I mean is, when I started writing – and was a lot more florid – I would have had the Doctor saying, 'I'm gonna go back to the TARDIS, and find the Daleks, and then I'll stop them, and then have a cup of tea.' Nowadays, I'm more likely to write, 'I'm gonna go back to the TARDIS. Find the Daleks. Stop them. And then, tea.' I spend a lot of time trimming down like that. Although, evidently not as much as I'd like to think. I remember Peter Kay phoning me from the set of *Love & Monsters* and saying, 'Did you buy a job lot of commas somewhere? It's all bloody

Peter Kay as Victor Kennedy in 2.10 *Love & Monsters*.

commas! How am I supposed to learn this? Never seen so many bloody commas in my life!' (Mind you, then I read his autobiography and realised that I could have sold him some. Ha ha.) But even the commas are a way of breaking down dialogue into blocks. I wouldn't have a character say, 'I'm going to Deck 31 to find whoever's behind all this.' I'd have them say, 'I'm going to Deck 31, to find whoever's behind all this.' Better or worse? I don't know, but I can't stop myself doing it. Comma mad. But what the commas and full stops are doing is imposing a rhythm, my rhythm, on the words, deciding when they're fast, when they're slow, when they stop. That's not the quest for naturalism; that's the quest for the drama, to decide when it's hard, when it's witty, when it's throwaway, when it's stark, how a scene rises and falls and builds and declines. That's rhythm.

I do put in 'ums' and 'ers', to an extent. An 'um' or an 'er' indicates that the character is hesitant, scared, out of their depth, whatever. But do it constantly and it drives people nuts. Never make a script annoying to read. I gather 'ums' are unpopular and frowned on now, particularly in the US. I think it's seen as a bad habit. I've even seen it argued that you shouldn't start speeches with filler words like 'Right' or 'Well' or 'So', that you should let the actors add that sort of thing, to naturalise it themselves. I find that ridiculous. If no one is regulating it, that's just asking for every speech to start with 'Well'. That's why you can't leave it to the actor. They don't have an overview of the whole script and its rhythms. If an actor adds a 'Well' to the last line of a scene, they won't necessarily have realised that the first line of the next scene starts with a 'Well', particularly if they're not in that scene. Besides, those words are important. In fact, they aren't just filler. 'Right' is decisive. 'Well' is calmer. 'Well!' is flouncy. 'So' is deliberate. Every word says a lot.

I am at that stage of my career when the script editor or producer will phone me up for approval if an actor wants to swap something as tiny as an 'and' for a 'but'. This means that I'm a despot and will soon fall.

FROM: RUSSELL T DAVIES TO: BENJAMIN COOK
THURSDAY 23 AUGUST 2007 21:26:22 GMT

BILLIE

Bad news. Billie's agent phoned yesterday. Now, this is a hugely powerful man, but he called in a genuinely regretful voice. I didn't think he had a genuinely regretful voice. Billie is getting married on New Year's Eve… and wants to go on honeymoon for the whole of January! That's when we film 4.12/4.13! That's when Freema, and John, and Lis Sladen, and Euros Lyn (who's going to direct) have all been booked for. *Nooooo!!!* The whole series finale is lying in disarray. Further updates to follow…

FROM: BENJAMIN COOK TO: RUSSELL T DAVIES
THURSDAY 23 AUGUST 2007 21:39:45 GMT

RE: BILLIE

Oh no! How can you get around that one? Write her out? Change the filming dates? What are your initial thoughts? This time, surely, you're sinking your head into your hands and weeping uncontrollably? No? You *must* be!

FROM: RUSSELL T DAVIES TO: BENJAMIN COOK
THURSDAY 23 AUGUST 2007 22:29:31 GMT

RE: BILLIE

For about ten seconds, I was just sad. Really sad.

Mourning for a lovely story that's gone. It'll never be seen. Not angry, though. That's a waste of time. Leads nowhere. But that deep keening feeling lasts ten seconds, and then I get on with fixing it. Immediately. Within about ten minutes last night, I'd thought, right, move the story where the Doctor's hand-in-a-jar grows another Doctor and he sends it to Rose in the parallel world to David's very last episode. Even if it means only seeing Billie on Bad Wolf Bay, we can always manage *one* day's filming with her. It wraps up a whole era nicely. And less people in 4.12/13 will make life easier for me. It's one hell of a cast list. In a way, it makes Rose-being-lost-for-ever even more poignant, because she can't even be there for the grand reunion.

Julie greeted me today with a sad 'How are you?' She thought I'd be glum, but really I'm not. I'm not just putting on a brave face. In fact, my greatest sadness is for Mickey Smith/Noel Clarke, because now there's no way to bring him back. That's a shame. But it could all change tomorrow. That's the other thing I've learnt. Like with all that Penny/Donna stuff. Keep on your toes. Julie is on red alert. If anyone can solve this, it's her. I think about the only problem we couldn't cope with is if David disappeared off to Guatemala tomorrow. But then we'd have to close down, so it wouldn't even be my problem –

Ahh, bollocks, what am I saying? I'd even find a way around that.

Funny thing is, Julie, Phil and I have all been invited to the wedding. We'd just stand there glowering. Good old Billie, though – I do love her. She's a phenomenon, and this is what dealing with phenomena is like.

FROM: BENJAMIN COOK TO: RUSSELL T DAVIES
THURSDAY 23 AUGUST 2007 22:38:14 GMT

RE: BILLIE

You say that absolutely anything can be written around. If you wanted Mickey to come back, but you can't feature Rose, well, why can't you write around that? What's stopping you?

FROM: RUSSELL T DAVIES TO: BENJAMIN COOK
THURSDAY 23 AUGUST 2007 23:29:47 GMT

RE: BILLIE

Hmm, anything can be written around… with integrity.

Above: Rose Tyler's return to Bad Wolf Bay is looking uncertain. Opposite page: Kylie Minogue and Benjamin Cook (and a Dalek!), at the Worx Studio, in London. Picture by William Baker

You have to be ruthless with the logic of it. If Mickey came back, it would mean that travel between universes is possible – so where the hell is Rose? Why hasn't she come back for the Doctor? You start to think of dialogue like Mickey saying, 'We invented a universe-hopping machine, and I was the first one to try it, but it turns out it could only work once – and here I am!' Do you see, it's just getting silly? That dialogue is lame. Not one word of that is interesting or heartfelt. It's bending the rules too far. And that integrity is what makes the story good.

FROM: RUSSELL T DAVIES TO: BENJAMIN COOK
FRIDAY 24 AUGUST 2007 14:21:39 GMT

RE: BILLIE

First viewing of 4.X today. Interesting. Let's shove in the caveats first: it's an early viewing, there's much more work to be done, it's running at 78 minutes and really should be reduced to 65-ish, and first viewings are often a bit unnerving and off-putting. Every edit after that is dedicated to lifting the programme to what it should be, what it deserves to be, and we always get there. But beyond the cut-this, cut-that, tighten-the-whole-thing-up-and-give-me-more-Frame notes, I'm sitting there, as writer, wondering what the hell I've done and why I did it.

A great sense of dismay at watching the disaster movie format fight the *Doctor Who* format. Yes, the very thing that I worried about as I wrote it. Do you remember, at the end, I was really proud that I'd combined them? The funny thing is – and I learn this lesson every time, yet forget it – if a fault is fundamental, any problem-solving is only papering over the cracks. The cracks always show. Faults persist. They always do. The disaster movie fights the essential nature of the Doctor, because he becomes just Any Old Survivor – a clever one, the leader, yes, but a hapless victim of events. He's *lacking*. Now, when the plot turns and he changes ('No more!' he says), then he's in charge again and good old *Doctor Who* kicks in; next thing you know, he's outwitting Host, battling the Max-Box, saving the ship, and he's the hero. Everything feels right. But that's a good 50 minutes in.

The Edits next week will go back to papering over the cracks. The fight goes on, long after it's been shot. Maybe none of this will be too evident by the time we're finished. (It will, though. I'll see it.) But… what do I think now? If a fault is fundamental, if it's in the *concept*, you can never fix it? Not without a *complete* rewrite, which has the Doctor on board for very different reasons? In the end, I think you're left facing the fact: there's no such thing as a perfect script. But is that just giving up?

I'm skipping all the excellent stuff, too. Kylie driving a forklift truck, fighting the Max-Box, is insanely fantastic. Her death is wonderful (and what a performance – she's amazing). Lots of good laughs with Morvin and Foon. And loads of sequences, like the Strut, that won't truly work until the FX are in place. And pace is the key – at the moment, it's leisurely, so you've time to dwell on the faults. Phil came up with a wonderful phrase: 'Edit it like you're ashamed of it.' We were hooting at that, but he's right. Don't dwell, don't luxuriate, don't show off, don't rely on FX, or Kylie or David. Be blunt, be fast, be ruthless. We had the same problem with *Tooth and Claw*: it ran at 55 minutes, and we made them cut it down, without losing a single line or scene, to 45 minutes, just by taking out every pause, every pan, every relax, until it moved like lightning. And it was magnificent. So we'll get there.

FROM: BENJAMIN COOK TO: RUSSELL T DAVIES
SATURDAY 25 AUGUST 2007 22:49:14 GMT

RE: BILLIE

I interviewed Catherine yesterday, on location for the Ood episode, at Twin Peaks Hangar (honestly, that's what it's called) at RAF St Athan, in the Vale of Glamorgan. There were soldiers with guns on the gate. We weren't allowed to use our mobile phones inside or we'd be shot at. 'I genuinely couldn't believe they'd asked me,' she said about being asked to come back as Donna. 'Even now, I just can't believe it.' Apparently, she didn't have to think twice about signing up for Series Four: 'It was a bit of a no-brainer for me, really.' Bless her.

And then – blimey – I spent this morning in a London photo studio with Kylie Minogue, posing and pouting with a Dalek (her, not me) for her exclusive *DWM* cover shoot. 'I've had to gracefully accept second billing today,' she said of the Dalek, adding: 'Well, at least I'm younger!' She was full of praise for you and Julie, too. Apparently, she fell in love with the two of you after that first meeting in London. It must have been your Muppet duet, Russell. (She said it was your 'humour, talent and passion for the show', but I still reckon it's the duet.) What a couple of days! Oh, and I had my photo taken with Kylie. It was obligatory.

How's your day been? Have you started 4.1 yet? I'm surprised at your latest assessment of *Voyage of the Damned*. 'Any problem-solving is only papering over the cracks.' Well, isn't that true of the storytelling process full stop? If you're inventing something artificial, something false, and yet you're wanting to convince people that's it's real so that they can suspend their disbelief sufficiently, surely you're 'papering over the cracks' from the moment that you start writing?

FROM: RUSSELL T DAVIES TO: BENJAMIN COOK
SATURDAY 25 AUGUST 2007 23:26:25 GMT

RE: BILLIE

I like your version of papering over the cracks. I'm going to cling to that. Maybe the cracks are more evident with 4.X because it's so clearly a hybrid. You're right, most stories require the writer to wallpaper like crazy, especially those stories that demand so many suspensions of disbelief. Often the wallpapering is sleight of hand – like in *Tooth and Claw*, taking the incredible coincidences of Queen Victoria, the Koh-I-Noor, and a werewolf all being in the same place, at the same time, and fighting hard to make that *essential*, rather than just an accident. I am a wallpaperer. Yes, that's what I am.

I'm so glad you interviewed Catherine. That Ood stuff is looking wonderful, isn't it? A quarry in the snow! And I'm loving the thought of Kylie's photo shoot. My God, if that isn't the best-selling *DWM* cover ever, I don't know what is… though I'd buy a few copies more if it were Midshipman Frame posing with a Dalek.

I'm making a promise, here and now, to start 4.1 on Monday night. Hold me to it! Mind you, I went and saw *The Simpsons Movie* this afternoon (not bad, not brilliant), and thank God I dropped that original 4.1 plot, the inverted-bowl-over-the-Estate plot because that's what happens to Springfield!

FROM: BENJAMIN COOK TO: RUSSELL T DAVIES
MONDAY 27 AUGUST 2007 20:31:09 GMT

RE: BILLIE

So. Have you started yet?

FROM: RUSSELL T DAVIES TO: BENJAMIN COOK
WEDNESDAY 29 AUGUST 2007 23:54:48 GMT

RE: BILLIE

No, I haven't started. Problems with *Torchwood* have sort of got in the way. The future of the show's looking a bit scary. Chris Chibnall isn't doing a third series – and I don't blame him, he's brilliant, he should fly free! – but I don't know how we'd make it without him. He's just delivered 2.12. Best. *Torchwood.* Ever. I swear, it's wonderful. And he puts in the hours, which few do. So, Julie has a series with no lead writer. That puts me in a tricky position, because I love Julie, and I did invent the bloody show, so how can I *not* help? This is really beginning to bug me. I lay in bed last night, thinking, I'll never be rid of this bloody place. What do I do? Oh, there are worse problems to have.

Even while I'm scared and terrified, and berating myself for not having started 4.1, my head is filling up with all sorts of 4.1 scenes. Have I told you the bit where the Doctor admits that he wants a travelling companion, but with no strings, no Martha-fancying stuff, and he sighs, 'I just want a mate'…? And Donna says, horrified, 'You want *to mate?*' He says, 'No, I said *a mate!*' Ha ha. Dialogue like that keeps me going. That won't be said until right at the end, but it's something to look forward to.

FROM: RUSSELL T DAVIES TO: BENJAMIN COOK
FRIDAY 31 AUGUST 2007 01:44:09 GMT

4.1

Look! I've started! Weird, actually, because I'd promised myself I'd start at 8pm, and then, at 7.55pm, I was clicking through the channels, desperate to find anything that I could watch so that I could put it off until, oh, 10pm or so… and there on BBC Three was the final scene of *The Runaway Bride*. Donna in the snow. Like a sign! At the end, she turns away, walks back into her house, and I went to the computer and started typing:

1. EXT. FX SHOT - EARTH

As 1.1, the Earth, suspended in space.

ZOOM IN, down through the clouds, down, down, down…

Heading towards Chiswick!

CUT TO:

2. EXT. DONNA'S HOUSE - DAY

DONNA steps out of her front door. Smart, ready for work, but more than that; she's on a mission. Head held high. As Donna heads left to right -

CUT TO:

3. EXT. CITY STREET - DAY

- heading right to left, THE DOCTOR steps out of the TARDIS. Heads off. On a mission.

CUT TO:

4. EXT. CITY STREET 2 - DAY

DONNA walking along, left to right, through COMMUTERS.

CUT TO:

'On a mission' – Donna heads to Adipose Industries.

5. EXT. CITY STREET - DAY

THE DOCTOR walks along, right to left, through COMMUTERS.

CUT TO:

6. EXT. ADIPOSE INDUSTRIES - DAY

DONNA stops in the street, looks up…

A TOWER BLOCK looming above. Cool, sleek, stylish, the London HQ of Adipose Industries.

Deep breath, Donna heads towards it.

CUT TO:

7. EXT. ADIPOSE INDUSTRIES - DAY

THE DOCTOR stops in the street, looks up…

THE TOWER BLOCK looming above, Adipose Industries. But this is the opposite side to Donna's, the back.

Deep breath, the Doctor heads towards it.

CUT TO:

8. EXT. ADIPOSE INDUSTRIES FOYER - DAY

DONNA walks through the revolving doors.

CUT TO:

9. EXT. ADIPOSE INDUSTRIES, BACK YARD - DAY

Concrete, bins, deserted. THE DOCTOR is down a flight of steps, finding basement access. He sonics a door, SMALL PRAC EXPLOSION on the lock, and he slips inside.

CUT TO:

10. INT. ADIPOSE INDUSTRIES FOYER - DAY

Posh foyer. DONNA shows her ID pass to the SECURITY GUARD.

DONNA
Donna Noble, Health and Safety.

And she strides on her way.

CUT TO:

11. INT. ADIPOSE INDUSTRIES, DOWNSTAIRS CORRIDOR - DAY

'Backstage' corridor, all concrete and pipes. THE DOCTOR passes a WHITE-COATED TECHNICIAN, shows the psychic paper.

THE DOCTOR
John Smith. Health and Safety.

And he strides on his way.

CUT TO:

12. INT. ADIPOSE INDUSTRIES FOYER - DAY

Two lift doors, next to each other. DONNA gets into the left-hand lift, heading up. Doors close. As they do…

The doors on the right-hand lift open - it's come up from the basement - and THE DOCTOR steps out. He heads off…

CUT TO:

13. INT. CINEMA

Part of the Tower Block, with Adipose Industries logos on the walls. Slogan: *The Fat Just Walks Away.*

The logo is spinning on screen, and stays there as MISS RATTIGAN steps forward, at the front. She's in her 40s, handsome, strong, very Amanda Redman.

She addresses the audience. It's not full, but a good 40 PEOPLE or so scattered about, taking notes - they're JOURNALISTS; this is a Press Launch.

MISS RATTIGAN
Adipose Industries. The twenty-first-century way to lose weight. No exercise, no diet, no pain. Just lifelong freedom, from fat. The Holy Grail of the modern age. And here it is!

Holds it up, an ordinary white pill.

MISS RATTIGAN (CONT'D)
You just take one pill. One pill, once a day, for three weeks. And the fat, as they say…

ON SCREEN, GRAPHIC (animation?!), the logo now has a mouth, and sings: *The Fat Just Walks Awaaaaay!*

CUT TO DONNA, in amongst the audience, as a WOMAN near to her pipes up - PENNY CARTER, late 20s, sharp.

PENNY
Excuse me. Penny Carter, Science Correspondent for The Observer. But there have been a thousand diet pills on the market, and a thousand frauds. How can we be sure the fat isn't going into your bank account?

MISS RATTIGAN
Of course, if cynicism burnt up calories, we'd all be thin as rakes. But if you want the science, then I can oblige…

She nods up to the PROJECTION BOOTH.

The next reel starts up, GRAPHICS showing a pill, and a layout of the Human body, with arrows going from the pill, to the body, then flowing round the bloodstream.

VOICEOVER
The Adipose Pill is composed of a synthesised mobilising lipase, bound to a large protein molecule. The mobilising lipase breaks up the triglycerides stored in the adipose cells, which then enter the bloodstream… [etc.]

But during this, on Donna, looking ahead, fascinated. And then PAN UP to see behind her, THE DOCTOR, in the PROJECTION BOOTH WINDOW. (Not seeing Donna, just watching the screen.)

CUT TO:

'Of course, if cynicism burnt up calories, we'd all be thin as rakes.' 'Miss Rattigan' (Sarah Lancashire) addresses the press.

14. INT. PROJECTION BOOTH - DAY

THE DOCTOR staring through the window, a big FILM PROJECTOR whirring away, manned by KEITH, 40s, Londoner.

KEITH
You supposed to be in here?

THE DOCTOR
Health and safety. Just checking the projector doesn't get too… hot. Is it hot?

KEITH
Not really.

THE DOCTOR
Good! Not hot! You get a big tick! Funny though, using film. Bit old-fashioned, these days.

KEITH
I know, we've got all the digital equipment, stored in the back. But no, she says, got to be film.

THE DOCTOR
And she would be…?

KEITH
Miss Rattigan. Her down there.

The Doctor looks back through the window, fascinated.

THE DOCTOR
Miss Rattigan…

CUT TO:

15. INT. CINEMA - DAY

Film over, the screen reverting back to the spinning logo, as MISS RATTIGAN steps forward again. CUT BETWEEN THE DOCTOR & DONNA watching, separately.

MISS RATTIGAN
All sanctioned by the World Health Organisation. 100% legal, 100% effective.

PENNY
And how many people have taken the pills?

MISS RATTIGAN
We've already conducted trial runs on 500 people in the Greater London area. Just for marketing purposes.

PENNY
Then if anything does go wrong… For those 500 people, it's already too late.

MISS RATTIGAN
I can promise you, Miss Carter, for those 500 people… Life will never be the same again. And from Monday, we start rolling out, nationwide. The future starts here. And the United Kingdom will be thin!

CUT TO:

Penny Carter (Verona Joseph) asks the difficult questions.

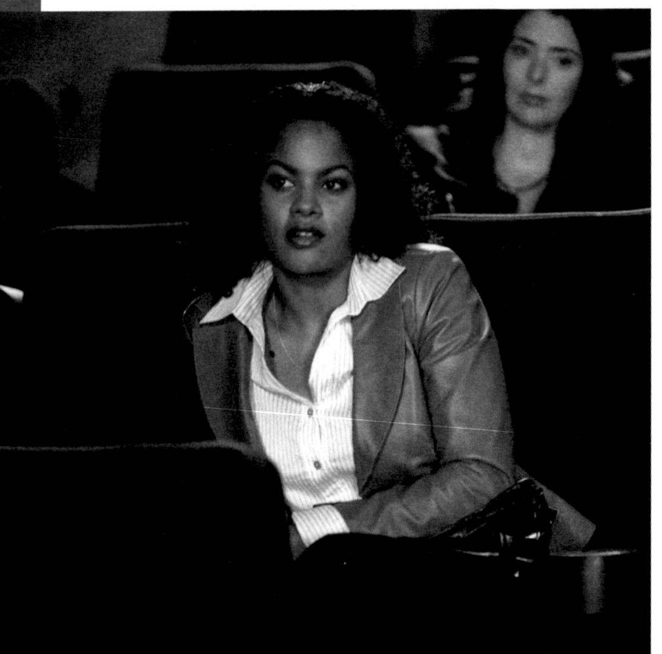

16. INT. SALES CUBICLES - DAY

The sales floor. Divided into those American-style cubicles, as functional as possible, like Keanu Reeves' office in The Matrix. Just a desk, a computer, a phone. TRACKING along, passing one SALESPERSON after another, all on headsets, all delivering the spiel. 'Good morning, I represent Adipose Industries…' 'Good morning, I represent Adipose Industries…' 'Good morning…' etc.

TRACKING TO FIND DONNA, walking in - on edge, cautious, armed with a clipboard - she grabs a spare chair, pulls it over to a CUBICLE, where CRAIG, 20, is at work, on headset.

DONNA
Donna Noble, Health and Safety, don't mind me.

CRAIG
(on headset)
That's a three-week course of pills for the special introductory price of 45 pounds…

Hand over headset mic, he hisses at her -

CRAIG (CONT'D)
What have I done wrong?

DONNA
Nothing. Just observing.

CUT TO the opposite aside of the room, THE DOCTOR entering - cautious, on edge - he grabs a spare chair, slides it across to CLAIRE'S cubicle. She's 20, on headset.

THE DOCTOR
John Smith, Health and Safety, don't mind me.

CLAIRE
…we can deliver within three working days, registered post -

Hand over headset mic, she whispers to him -

CLAIRE (CONT'D)
Health and Safety, what for?

THE DOCTOR
Keyboard injuries. Very nasty. Keep going! I'm here to help.

And he gets out a tape measure, measures from her elbow to the keyboard, pretending it's important.

CUT TO Donna & Craig. He's now taking off his headset, as Donna indicates a sign saying -

DONNA
'No mobiles', why does it say that?

CRAIG
I dunno, microwaves or something, you're Health and Safety, not me!

CUT TO the Doctor & Claire. She's taking off her headset. Her booth, and every booth, has the 'NO MOBILES' sign.

THE DOCTOR
No mobiles, anywhere?

CLAIRE
Not even at lunch, no mobiles allowed in the building, they sack you on the spot.

THE DOCTOR
No digital signals…

CUT TO Donna & Craig.

DONNA
I just need a list of your customers, can you print it off?

CRAIG
S'pose so.

DONNA
Where's the printer…?

CRAIG
Just over there, by the door.

WIDE SHOT, as she pops her head up over the partition. The only face visible among the rows of cubicles.

DONNA
Which door, that door?

The Doctor turns on the charm.

CRAIG OOV
That's the one.

DONNA
Lovely.

She pops back down, gone - and in that second -

- THE DOCTOR pops his head up, far across the room.

THE DOCTOR
And that's the printer, over there?

CLAIRE OOV
By the door, yeah.

THE DOCTOR
Brilliant!

And he pops back down -

- as Donna pops back up, looking towards the printer.

DONNA
Does it need a code? Last place I worked, the printer needed a code.

CRAIG OOV
No, I can do that from here.

DONNA
Off we go then!

And she pops back down -

- as the Doctor pops back up, looking round.

THE DOCTOR
How many people working here?

CLAIRE OOV
I dunno, there's six floors of us, and Executive sales above that, must be loads.

The Doctor gives an 'oops!' and ducks down, seeing -

MISS RATTIGAN striding in. TWO WHITE-COATED TECHNICIANS either side, like guards. She goes to the centre of the floor, claps her hands.

MISS RATTIGAN
Everyone! Excuse me! If I could have your attention!

Heads pop up all around the cubicles, some standing, some just with eyes over the partitions. Donna stands up…

As the Doctor slowly stands up…

Miss Rattigan takes a single step forward, just in time to completely mask the Doctor from Donna's POV, and Donna from the Doctor's POV.

MISS RATTIGAN (CONT'D)
Now, which one of you fine people is Terrance Maloney?

LITTLE GEEKY MAN puts his hand up. All look at him.

MISS RATTIGAN (CONT'D)
I'd like to announce that Mr Terrance Maloney has made one hundred sales in his first day of trading. I think that deserves a round of applause.

All clap, the Doctor & Donna half-hearted. Terrance embarrassed, but sort of loving it too. A modest wave.

MISS RATTIGAN (CONT'D)
And a little extra something in your pay packet, I think. Well done, Terrance! Now, back to work! See if you can beat him!

All heads duck down, Donna sinking back down as -

Miss Rattigan clears Donna's previous POV, revealing the Doctor, who ducks back down into the cubicle. To Claire:

THE DOCTOR
Anyway! If you could just print that off, thanks.

CUT TO Donna & Craig.

DONNA
Print off the list, and I'll get out of your way.

Craig operates his mouse -

CU CURSOR clicking on PRINT.

CUT TO Claire, operating her mouse -

CU CURSOR, clicking on PRINT.

CUT TO PRINTER, churning out PAPERS. Yellow sheets.

DONNA (CONT'D)
Lovely, thanks, see you.

WIDE SHOT, as she stands, hurries over to the printer -

The Doctor pops up for a micro-second, about to go -

THE DOCTOR
Thanks then -

But he's pulled back down again, fast! Claire's grabbed his arm, and is holding out a piece of paper.

THE DOCTOR (CONT'D)
What's that?

CLAIRE
My telephone number.

THE DOCTOR
…what for?

CLAIRE
(foxy)
Health and Safety. You be health. I'll be safety.

'You be health. I'll be safety.' The Doctor (David Tennant) gets more than he bargained for from flirty Claire (Chandra Ruegg).

```
                THE DOCTOR
        ...right.

    CUT TO Donna, at the printer. She
    grabs all the papers, heads for
    the door, and as she swings it
    open, foreground, and disappears
    through - in background, the Doctor
    stands -

             THE DOCTOR (CONT'D)
        ...that contravenes paragraph 5
        subsection C, sorry, thanks,
        bye.

    And he hurries away, going across
    to the printer.

    No papers, nothing. Eh?! He lifts
    the photocopier lid, checks all
    round, no sign of them. Damn.

    CUT TO CLAIRE, as the Doctor
    reappears. Big smile.

             THE DOCTOR (CONT'D)
        Me again!
```

Penny Carter lives! She's in there! And destined to die horribly, I suspect. A bit like she could have been the companion, but gets murdered instead. I like that.

It feels… okay, at the moment. Only okay. This opening sequence is funny, I hope, but it's been in my head for weeks now (the whole shtick of the Doctor and Donna crossing paths, but not meeting), so I just don't find it so funny any more. It stopped amusing me way back. So is it still funny? I just don't know. Also, I'm still a good few pages off seeing a monster. That feels bad. I could have a pre-titles sequence of someone being horribly murdered by an Adipose, but the pre-titles murder is wearing a bit thin now, and I loved the energy of starting Series Three with no pre-titles. Last year's opener went straight from the continuity announcer into the titles into Martha, and that had a real welcome-back energy to it.

Still, thank God I've begun – this script that we've been talking about since February!

FROM: BENJAMIN COOK TO: RUSSELL T DAVIES
FRIDAY 31 AUGUST 2007 13:25:58 GMT

RE: 4.1

YOU'VE STARTED! I want to ask you about beginnings. I'm wondering about when to start a narrative. At what point should the story begin? Is the answer, simply, just as it's about to get interesting? Back-story can be filled in later, right?

FROM: RUSSELL T DAVIES TO: BENJAMIN COOK
FRIDAY 31 AUGUST 2007 21:23:02 GMT

RE: 4.1

The job of a first scene is to make you watch, and to keep you watching. My friend Patrea, a lovely writer, argues the opposite: she says that first scenes are bums-on-seats time, that they should give you time to come in from the kitchen and settle down. Nothing too vital. Mind you, she said that to me 15 years ago. I wonder if she's changed her mind now that TV is faster and louder and there's much more choice.

If the first scene grabs you, it shouldn't do so by lying or creating a false premise. Any old script could start with an explosion, but the explosion has to be integral. The real reason that 4.1 can't open with a murder by an Adipose is that I'm not yet convinced they *do* murder. Well, they will do later on, when they're ordered to, but their first appearance will be more weird and unnerving than murderous. Instead, the opening of 4.1 is setting out the stall for the whole episode: the Doctor and Donna meeting again. That's the story. The aliens are just the plot that gets in the way. The cutting between the Doctor and Donna is played as a sort of cute conceit, but that's dressing up on the surface; underneath that, it's absolutely fundamental.

In *Queer as Folk*, the meeting of key characters marks the start of the story, I suppose – Stuart and Nathan, with the third part of that eternal threesome, Vince, watching them. Of course, if you mean *literal* start, then that's Vince talking direct to camera. Unusual technique. I was experimenting – and I never intended that to go past Episode 1. I did that because... well, I was younger, and that's when you try out the tricks. You learn to lose them, I think, as you go on. You'd think that narrative tricks were the domain of the experienced scriptwriter, but I tend to find that they're used by the newcomer, thrilled with all these brand new toys, mastering them. As you get older, you learn to trust the story a bit more, just tell it. Maybe. But since the drama was throwing you head first into The Gay Scene, I wanted those pieces to camera so that you'd connect with those boys and get the humour of the piece –

Ah, but crucially, although the bits to camera came first, they existed for the ending. It was impossible to get a proper cliffhanger out of Episode 1's story. Stuart and Vince drop Nathan off at school. It's hard to imagine that they'd ever see him again, because he's just a kid. It could have looked like the end of the story, so the pieces to camera bookending the episode allowed me to drop in Nathan, at the end, saying (of Stuart), 'Six months later, he was *begging* me to stay.' And that worked. People were intrigued. In that instance, the ending of Episode 1 decided the start.

In fact, there's a second start to Episode 1: after Vince's piece direct to camera, we cut to Stuart, Vince and Phil hitting the streets, copping off, funny dialogue, something I very much wanted to show.[1] All bloody gay dramas have scenes inside clubs – we had surprisingly few – and so I wanted to show something new, that extraordinary street life when the clubs shut (in the days when clubs did shut), when the streets would come alive with a whole different sort of gay life. I suppose that's an anthropological choice, not a story choice – except the anthropology is laying out the whole style and intent of the show, and it's that Walking The Gay Streets that

So where did the story of *Queer as Folk* actually begin...?
© Joss Barratt

1 Phil Delaney (played by Jason Merrells), friend of Stuart and Vince, in *Queer as Folk*.

leads Stuart to Nathan. Plus, it looks good. Then there's start number three: Nathan on Canal Street, asking Bernie what's the best place to go, and Bernie's foulmouthed reaction.[2] That was absolutely laying out my other agenda: in contrast to Vince's funny piece to camera, you get a virtuoso destruction of the entire gay scene from a bitter old man. Not like me at all, ha ha! Finally, start number four (*four!*): Stuart spotting Nathan, Vince seeing this… and off we go for eight weeks!

It's funny, that list, because it makes you ask – so what *is* the start? Where does the story start? It doesn't have to be the first scene. But should it be? I can imagine a *Queer as Folk* that begins with that fourth start, with Stuart strolling past Nathan, stopping, going back. I could make that work, although I'd worry that I wasn't invested in any of the characters. So, starting where the story starts isn't as obvious as it sounds. A lot of the story revolves around Stuart and Nathan, but also the story of *Queer as Folk* is the story of that whole world, so that's what I laid out first.

Oh! I was just reading back this e-mail, and I'd completely forgotten that there *was* a different start. Long since lost. *Queer as Folk* Episode 1, Draft One, started with Nathan and Donna (I've used the name Donna before – I didn't even realise that until now) in an ordinary teenage party – drink, snogging, vomit, etc – and Nathan watching while everyone around him cops off, but he has to stay quiet and closeted.[3] The turning point comes when he sees someone's 12-year-old brother snogging a girl in the alley outside – like, 12-year-olds are getting some and he isn't! Nathan makes his mind up on the spot, goes to the room where everyone has dumped their coats, ransacks them until he finds £20, and just walks out – abandoning poor Donna – and gets the bus to Canal Street. (My favourite bit in that is the stealing the money. There was always a danger that Nathan would be the sweet, innocent victim of *Queer as Folk*, but actually he was fabulously selfish and ruthless, and the theft set that up, right from the start.) I think, in that version, he'd come out to Donna already, so he got on the bus saying where he was going in a scene that then must have become, in the transmitted version, Episode 2's 'I'm *doing* it! I'm really doing it!' scene. That Draft One opening was a good start. It was great. But Nicola Shindler said, quite rightly, 'Cut it. Get on with it.' All the scene is doing is saying that Nathan is young, closeted, a virgin. But when you see him sitting on his own, on Canal Street, when he approaches Bernie and is spotted by Stuart… well, Nathan looks young, closeted, a virgin, so there's no need for any establishers. You can't say that dropped opening scene was *wrong* exactly, but the main imperative was: get on with the story.

Similarly, *The Second Coming* had to start before Steve's revelation… though we did always wonder, even sitting in the Edit, whether it would have been better to start with a bedraggled man, a stranger, running over the moors, gasping, panting, collapsing in front of a car and proclaiming that he's the Son of God. That was tempting. I think the big-screen version would start there, but again, on TV, I wanted a bit of backstory, a bit of real life, and the kiss from Judith, which is *really* when Steve's life changes. Then again, when *The Second Coming* was adapted for HBO (they commissioned a trial script for a potential series, never made), they had a good 30 minutes of backstory at the top, the revelation came right towards the end of the first episode, and it worked. In fact, I did wonder if it was better. It was a very good adaptation.

And new *Doctor Who*… well, it had to start with Rose Tyler. Except it didn't, actually. It started in outer space, zooming in on her flat. We needed that. It gave her whole world an outer-space context, with the promise of weird things to come. I drilled into the production team that the whole montage of Rose's life had to last only two minutes (we failed with the two minutes, I think, but we came close) before things turned sinister, with shop window dummies coming to life in the basement. That's when the world of *Doctor Who* arrived. That was the real start.

In the end, I think what I'm saying is, start with the story *and its context*. Its surrounding world. But that's just me. Maybe I worry about context too much.

In other news… we spent all day hammering 4.X into place. I like it much more now. We took out all the flab and the pauses, so it's ten minutes shorter now – 71 minutes – and much better. Also, right now, David and Julie are being police-escorted down the motorway to get to the Blackpool Illuminations! David is switching on the lights. The traffic was so bad that they've got

2 Bernard Thomas (played by Andy Devine), a cynical veteran of the gay scene, in *Queer as Folk* and *Queer as Folk 2*.

3 Donna Clarke (played by Carla Henry), Nathan's best friend, in *Queer as Folk*.

outriders clearing the way. I wish I could have been there. Meanwhile, I texted Russell Tovey, to tell him how good 4.X was, and he replied: 'I'm in Ibiza with my boyfriend.' I'm in Cardiff. Life is a bitch.

FROM: RUSSELL T DAVIES TO: BENJAMIN COOK
SATURDAY 1 SEPTEMBER 2007 02:39:37 GMT

RE: 4.1

That's enough work for tonight. I'm too tired. The monster is about to appear, and then the action starts, but that needs a lot of energy to write. Monster on Page 13! That's late. Bollocks. I'll try to trim it down. There's a lot of adult chat so far, which doesn't feel very *Doctor Who*-ey at all. It's more like a detective yarn. Still, that's the story. Follow the story. But I'm worried that it's a bit dull for kids. Mind you, the monster is revolting, so that'll make up for it.

```
17. EXT. STACY'S HOUSE - NIGHT

STACY HARRIS, 20s, bit plump -
harassed, running late - opens her
front door (it's an end-of-terrace
house).

DONNA is standing there, with
clipboard & yellow papers, just
flashes her ID card so it can't be
seen properly.

                DONNA
    Stacy Harris?

                STACY
    Who wants to know?

                DONNA
    My name's Donna, I represent
    Adipose Industries, and
    you're on the list of our
    valued customers - I wonder,
    could I ask you a few
    questions?

                STACY
    Um, well, not now, I'm going
    out, I'm going into town,
    I've booked a taxi, it's on
    its way.

                DONNA
    Tell you what, I'll get in
    the taxi with you, I'll pay
    for it on expenses, how does
    that sound?

                STACY
    Um. Brilliant, yeah. Okay!
    I'm still getting ready, I'm
    in a bit of a rush -

                DONNA
    You just carry on, don't
    mind me!

And Donna heads inside -

                                CUT TO:

18. EXT. ROGER'S HOUSE - NIGHT

ROGER DAVEY, 40, a thin & happy
man, opens his front door (nice
semi, with a small drive).

THE DOCTOR is standing there,
clutching his yellow papers, and he
shows the psychic paper -
```

THE DOCTOR
Mr Roger Davey?

ROGER
That's me!

THE DOCTOR
John Smith, I'm calling on behalf of Adipose Industries, I just need to ask you a few questions -

ROGER
Oh, brilliant, come in, those pills, they've been like magic! If you want me to do adverts, anything, testimonials, I'm your man -

And the Doctor heads inside -

CUT TO:

19. INT. STACY'S LIVING ROOM - NIGHT

Nothing posh, but a nice house. STACY is on her feet, grabbing clothes, money, all that about-to-go-out stuff. DONNA sitting there with clipboard.

STACY
- it's been fantastic, I started the pills on Thursday, five days later, I've lost ten pounds!

DONNA
Two pounds a day, that's amazing. And no side effects or anything?

STACY
No, I feel fantastic, it's a new lease of life - what d'you think about the earrings, do they work?

DONNA
Lovely, yeah. Going on a date?

STACY
I'm doing the opposite, I'm gonna dump him! I can do better than him now, I'm almost slim! Hair up or hair down?

DONNA
It's fine, like it is.

STACY
No, I should wear it down, I want him to see me looking gorgeous -

As she heads out, to go upstairs -

STACY (CONT'D)
- won't be long, if the taxi beeps, give me a shout -

And she's gone. On Donna, wondering what she's doing here.

CUT TO:

20. INT. ROGER'S HOUSE - NIGHT

THE DOCTOR with ROGER.

ROGER
I was one of the first, I've been on the pills for two weeks now, I've lost 14 kilos!

THE DOCTOR
In two weeks? That's a bit drastic, doesn't it worry you?

ROGER
It's government approved.

THE DOCTOR
Suppose, yeah. Although, when it comes to the government, you have just lost a Prime Minister who vanished shortly after assassinating the President of the United States.

ROGER
Yeah, what was all that about?

THE DOCTOR
We may never know. But this weight loss, is it regular, is it the same amount every day?

ROGER
One kilo, exactly. You wake up in the morning, and it's gone. Well, technically speaking, it's gone by ten past one in the morning.

THE DOCTOR
…what makes you say that?

```
                    ROGER
    That's when I get woken up,
    so I weigh myself at the
    same time. But ten past one,
    every night, bang on the dot,
    without fail… the burglar
    alarm goes off.

                                    CUT TO:

21. EXT. ROGER'S HOUSE - NIGHT

THE DOCTOR & ROGER looking up at
Roger's burglar-alarm box, high on
the wall above the door.

                    ROGER
    I've had experts in, I've
    had it replaced, I've tried
    everything, but no! Ten past
    one, off it goes.

                 THE DOCTOR
    But with no burglars?

                    ROGER
    No, first night, I came
    running downstairs. With my
    cricket bat. Nothing! I've
    given up looking now, there's
    no one there.

                 THE DOCTOR
    Tell me, Roger… have you got
    a cat flap?

                                    CUT TO:
```

'I've met cat people. You're nothing like them.' The Doctor (David Tennant) investigates Roger (Martin Ball)'s late-night disturbances.

```
22. INT. ROGER'S KITCHEN - NIGHT

THE DOCTOR on the floor, prodding
the back door's cat flap with the
sonic. The flap swings to and fro,
harmless. ROGER kneeling beside
him, fascinated.

                    ROGER
    It was here when I bought the
    house. Never bothered with
    it, really, I'm not a cat
    person.

                 THE DOCTOR
    No, I've met cat people,
    you're nothing like them.

                    ROGER
    Is that what it is, though?
    Cats, getting inside the
    house?

                 THE DOCTOR
    Well, that's the thing about
    cat flaps. They don't just let
    things in. They let things
    out as well.

                    ROGER
    Like what…?

                 THE DOCTOR
    The fat just walks away.
```

I'm not sure about the Prime Minister reference. Is that going too far? It's a bit of an in-joke. Still, eight million people watched that Series Three finale, so it's not *that* much of an in-joke. It's harmless enough to leave in for the moment.

Also, I'm sending you a scene that I've cut already. (Normally, I'd just delete it, but for you, Benjamino…) I needed a gizmo inside every customer's house, to activate the Adipose. I couldn't think what it could be. That's why I stopped last night, because I was stuck. I spent all day trying to invent something. Sitting in the 4.X Edit, just thinking, what activates the Adipose? What gizmo? Originally, I'd thought of mobile phone signals – something about banning digital signals from Adipose HQ, because they needed one, clear signal to activate all the Adipose at once. But that's rubbish, isn't it? Like other digital signals would interfere! Like a big, modern building with computers and sales floors would be digital-free! But I had no better idea. I delayed writing tonight until 10pm – still no idea, but I sat down to write anyway. The moment I started writing, I just thought, oh, it's a free gift! It's a pendant. You always get free gifts with these mail-order things. Anyway, I had to introduce the free gift, so I wrote this separate scene:

```
INT. SERVING HATCH - DAY

Like a postal depot counter, within
the building - a hatch, behind which
are shelves, piled high with stock.
DONNA with clipboard, talking to the
HATCH GUY, 20s, Welsh.

                 DONNA
     ...so the customer orders
     three weeks' worth of pills,
     you process the forms, and
     you send them out from here,
     registered post.

                 HATCH GUY
     You gonna try them?

                 DONNA
     You saying I need to lose
     weight?

                 HATCH GUY
     The fat just walks away!

                 DONNA
     I'm reporting you. So you send
     out the pills, the info pack,
     the Sign-Up-A-Friend leaflet...

                 HATCH GUY
     And the free gift.

                 DONNA
     What's the free gift?

He holds up a pendant, gold chain
with a gold Adipose pill.

                 HATCH GUY
     Pendant. I said, they'd be
     better off giving away pens.
     Everyone needs pens.

                 DONNA
     I'll take that. Health and
     Safety, thank you.

She walks away, disappears off left.

Hatch Guy tidies things, just for
a second. Then THE DOCTOR appears,
from the right.

                 THE DOCTOR
     John Smith, Health and Safety.

                 HATCH GUY
     You're like Nazis, you lot!
```

Terrible scene. I don't need anyone to tell me that. It's long-winded. The location is sort of unbelievable. Hatch Guy is fake-funny. The scene doesn't have a punchline. Typing a scene that you know is bad is a terrible feeling. I put it after the Sales Cubicles scene – but the Sales Cubicles scene, with its yellow customer lists, cuts so nicely to Stacy's House, because she's a customer, that it was a crime to place it there. It ruined the flow. And so I placed it in between the Cinema and the Sales Cubicles, but it was just holding up the action. When a scene doesn't fit anywhere, you know that you're in trouble. (This is why I can't write scenes out of order. They have to *fit*.) I worried. I got miserable. I carried on writing, introducing Stacy and Roger, loving them, so they cheered me up. But still I sat here for hours, stuck with a scene that I hated. And then I stood up to go to the bathroom – I'm only telling you that because so often it's *when I stand up and walk away* that an idea hits me – and *ding!* Instant thought: I don't need the hatch and the Hatch Guy, I don't need the scene at all, I've got the bloody Sales Cubicles, so introduce the pendant there! Completely obvious, in hindsight. Lost me hours tonight, to realise that. I went back and took out the mobile phone rubbish and Keith's stuff about digital projection equipment, and inserted the following into Scene 16:

```
CUT TO Donna & Craig. He's on his
headset, with the spiel; he's got
a script, and a sample Adipose
Industries box at his side - a
small white cardboard box, full of
21 pills in packets, information
leaflets, etc. Donna observing.

                 CRAIG
     ...the box comes with 21 days'
     worth of pills, a full
     information pack, and our
     special free gift, an Adipose
     Industries pendant...

Donna takes the pendant out of the
box. A simple gold chain, holding a
gold representation of an Adipose
pill.

CUT TO the Doctor & Claire. He's
already taken the pendant out of
the box, holds it up, examines it.
```

CU on the gold Adipose pill. Claire just in b/g:

CLAIRE
…it's made of 18 carat gold, and it's yours for free… No, we don't give away pens. Sorry. No, I can't make a exception, no.

CUT TO Donna & Craig. He's now taking off his headset, to look at her properly, as she puts the pendant in her pocket.

DONNA
I'll just keep this for testing. And I just need a list of your customers, can you print it off?

CRAIG
S'pose so.

Also, I fixed Miss Rattigan's speech to the sales force later in Scene 16, because I felt that it was too like Yvonne Hartman's speech to the Torchwood workforce in *Army of Ghosts*.[4] So I've changed it. She's telling them off now. It makes her slightly more generic-villain, but that's no bad thing when we need a bit more *Doctor Who*-ness:

MISS RATTIGAN
We've collated the initial sales figures - on average, you're each selling forty Adipose packs per day. It's not enough! I want one hundred sales, per person, per day, and if not, you'll be replaced. Cos if anyone's good at trimming the fat, it's me. Now back to it!

Right, to bed! I must write loads tomorrow, but it's Cardiff Mardi Gras. I'm the patron, so I've got to go. Charlotte Church is the other patron, but she's too pregnant.

FROM: RUSSELL T DAVIES TO: BENJAMIN COOK
SATURDAY 1 SEPTEMBER 2007 16:06:48 GMT

RE: 4.1

Here's this afternoon's work. Now I must go and address the gays at Cardiff Mardi Gras. I'll come back and continue tonight. I'm in an unusual position with this script, because preproduction starts on Monday (Christ!), so I'll have to hand in however many pages I've finished by then. You won't be the only one seeing it in its raw state.

23. INT. STACY'S BATHROOM - NIGHT

Nice bathroom, bit cluttered. STACY has her hair down now, is checking herself in the mirror, just putting a different lipstick on. Calls down:

STACY
Won't be long!

INTERCUT BATHROOM & LIVING ROOM -

CUT TO:

24. INT. STACY'S LIVING ROOM - NIGHT

INTERCUT WITH BATHROOM.

DONNA sitting there, calls up:

DONNA
That's all right!

She's fiddling with the Adipose gold pendant. Just out of boredom. She holds it up, in the light. Nothing special.

Then she just holds it normally as she sits there, looking round the room.

CU Donna's hands as, without thinking, she starts to unscrew the two halves of the gold capsule…

CUT TO THE BATHROOM. Stacy gasps. Not pain, but a sudden *feeling* in her stomach. She clutches it.

CUT TO LIVING ROOM, Donna stops fiddling with the capsule.

CUT TO BATHROOM, the sensation's gone, Stacy recovers, holds her stomach. What the hell was that…?

CUT TO LIVING ROOM, Donna starts to fiddle again, unscrewing the capsule…

4 Yvonne Hartman (played by Tracy-Ann Oberman) was the director of Torchwood One, the London branch of the Torchwood Institute, in *Doctor Who* 2.12/2.13.

Donna examines the free Adipose gold pendant. All 18 carats of it.

CUT TO BATHROOM, Stacy feels something again, holds her stomach. What's happening…?

CUT TO LIVING ROOM, Donna still screwing & unscrewing the two halves, without even looking at what she's doing.

CUT TO BATHROOM, Stacy lifts up her top. Smoothes the skin of her stomach.

CUT TO LIVING ROOM, Donna still fiddling…

CUT TO BATHROOM, Stacy horrified, as…

FX: the skin on her stomach moves. Like something is writhing underneath. Pushing the skin out…

She's not in pain, just scared, as she looks in the mirror.

FX: her stomach keeps moving, just one central area, like a little fat mole is buried underneath, trying to get out.

CUT TO Donna, still fiddling, as…

CU, the two halves of the capsule come apart!

CUT TO:

25. INT. MISS RATTIGAN'S OFFICE - NIGHT

Smart, shiny, windows looking out onto the city. But an alarm blares! MISS RATTIGAN spins round in her chair -

On her COMPUTER SCREEN, a map of London, with one red light flashing in synch with the alarm.

Miss Rattigan stabs the intercom -

MISS RATTIGAN
We have an unscheduled activation!

CUT TO:

26. EXT. ROGER'S HOUSE - NIGHT

THE DOCTOR just saying goodbye, ROGER in the doorway.

THE DOCTOR
Thanks for your help, tell you what, maybe you could lay off the pills for a week or so -

Alarm sounds!

The Doctor gets out a little gizmo from his pocket, like a palm-pilot, with a red flashing light.

THE DOCTOR (CONT'D)
Gotta go, sorry!

And he belts off - !

Roger left waving.

ROGER
Always welcome!

CUT TO:

27. INT. STACY'S LIVING ROOM/ STACY'S BATHROOM - NIGHT

DONNA holds up half of the capsule, now noticing…

CU, tiny wires hanging out of it.

CUT TO BATHROOM, STACY breathing hard, in terror, as…

FX: the skin of her stomach is stretching out now, like a big bump is pushing through…

CUT TO:

28. INT. MISS RATTIGAN'S OFFICE - NIGHT

MISS RATTIGAN on intercom, fast -

MISS RATTIGAN
Send out the Collection Squad. Bring them back!

CUT TO:

29. EXT. ADIPOSE INDUSTRIES, CAR PARK - NIGHT

A big, black POLICE PRISON VAN, with barred windows, scorches out of the underground car park -

CUT TO:

30. EXT. ROGER'S ESTATE - NIGHT

THE DOCTOR, running, running, running -

CUT TO:

31. INT. STACY'S LIVING ROOM/ STACY'S BATHROOM - NIGHT

STACY, standing there, horrified, as…

FX: the shape in her stomach is stretching out, slowly…

Stacy lets out a little scream.

CUT TO LIVING ROOM. DONNA looks up.

DONNA
You all right up there…?

CUT TO BATHROOM, as…

FX: STACY'S skin stretches out - and nothing is actually breaking through, no broken skin, no blood - instead, the stretching skin is whitening and dividing off into a separate entity, like an amoeba separating…

FX: and the lump plops free! With Stacy standing by the sink, it just drops down into the bowl, and her stomach just twangs back to normal. And the lump is…

FX: an ADIPOSE, standing in the sink-bowl. About the size of a bag of sugar, and almost the same shape. A white lump of fat, Pillsbury Doughboy in texture, with rudimentary arms and legs, no eyes, a little mewling mouth.[5] It's strangely sort of cute. Like a soft toy. And it seems to be waving, with little stumpy arms, at Stacy.

Stacy is just *boggling.*

LIVING ROOM, Donna's standing, goes to the door, calls up:

DONNA (CONT'D)
You all right up there?

BATHROOM, Stacy stunned. And crucially, too embarrassed to call for help.

STACY
…yeah.

FX: the ADIPOSE is mewling at her, a bit like 'mummy!'

CUT TO:

32. INT. MISS RATTIGAN'S OFFICE - NIGHT

MISS RATTIGAN now with TWO WHITE-COATED TECHNICIANS standing in front of her desk.

MISS RATTIGAN
The Adipose has been witnessed. Activating full transmutation.

And she's holding a GOLD CAPSULE, twists it -

CUT TO:

33. INT. STACY'S LIVING ROOM/ STACY'S BATHROOM - NIGHT

STACY alarmed, feeling something… looks round, and down…

She's in jeans. And one of her buttocks is now starting to move, a shape squirming under the denim…

CUT TO DONNA, by the living room door, calling up.

DONNA
I like what you've done with this hall.

5 The Pillsbury Doughboy is the advertising mascot of the Pillsbury Company, appearing in many of their commercials. He is a small anthropoid character, apparently made out of dough.

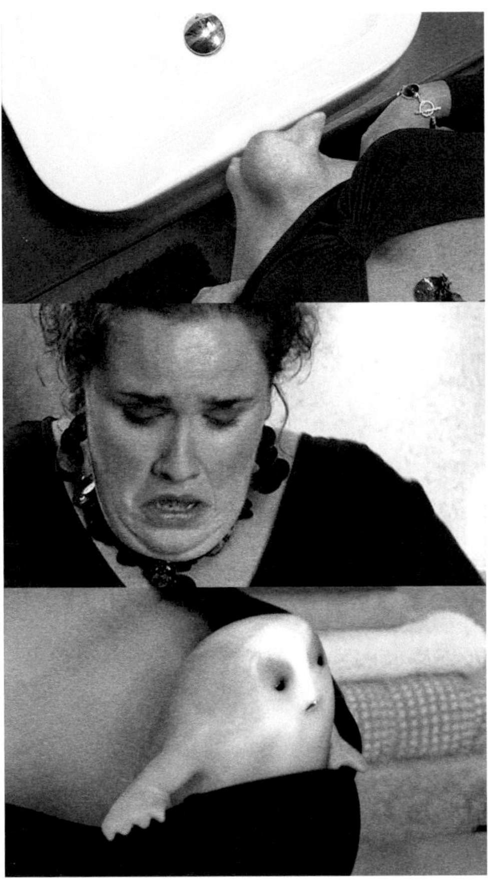

Stacy Harris (Jessica Gunning) feels a little off-colour...

STACY twisting round to see in the mirror, as...

FX: an ADIPOSE struggles up over the waistband of the back of her jeans! Mewling! Free!

CUT TO Donna, getting a bit concerned now -

DONNA (CONT'D)
Have you lived here long? Stacy? You all right?

FX: in the BATHROOM, the TWO ADIPOSE now in the sink, waving.

STACY staring, shaking now, terrified. Whispered:

STACY
What are you? *What are you?*

But then - oh God - more movement - under her T-shirt, more shapes, lots, shifting, her stomach, at her shoulder, on her back, on her thigh, writhing under her clothes.

FX: the two Adipose in the sink, gleeful, waving, excited!

CUT TO STAIRS, DONNA now heading up.

DONNA
Wouldn't mind a little visit myself. Everything okay in there?

CUT TO BATHROOM, Stacy desperate, now trying the press the bumps in her clothing back in to her skin...

Donna now outside the door, little knock.

DONNA (CONT'D)
Only me. D'you mind if I pop to the loo? Stacy?

STACY
(quiet)
...help me.

DONNA
I'm sorry?

STACY
Help me. Oh my God, *help me!*

DONNA
What is it, what's wrong - ?

Donna rattles the door, it's locked -

Inside, Stacy is still struggling with the writhing bumps -

Donna starts to thump the door. Bangs it. Shoves it.

DONNA (CONT'D)
Stacy! *Stacy!!*

Then Stacy shudders, lets go of the bumps, screams -

FX: in a second, her whole body divides into separate pieces - 20 separate ADIPOSE, plop!, falling to the floor, in amongst her falling, empty clothes -

Donna now shoving herself at the door, frantic -

CU on the inside lock, it's only a bolt, beginning to give -

FX: on the FLOOR, in amongst the fallen clothes, THE 20 ADIPOSE now waddling about, heading for the walls...

FX: with their fat little ploppy legs, the Adipose can walk up the wall!

Donna shoves, shoves again, hard -

The bolt breaks, door flies open - !

Donna in the doorway, stares.

Her POV: first of all, Stacy's clothes on the floor. Then she looks up...

FX: the bathroom window is open. And just one ADIPOSE remains, on the windowsill. It gives Donna a little wave, like 'bye bye!', then hops out of the window, gone!

Donna runs to the window -

CUT TO:

<u>34. EXT. STACY'S HOUSE - NIGHT</u>

HIGH ANGLE, DONNA'S POV from the upstairs bathroom window.

FX: down below, 22 tiny little shapes, casting long shadows in the streetlight, scurry along in the dark, like plump little imps, heading for the street -

CUT TO:

<u>35. EXT. NEAR STACY'S STREET - NIGHT</u>

Terraced houses, close to Stacy's house. The BLACK PRISON VAN scorches along -

CUT TO:

<u>36. EXT. NEAR STACY'S STREET - NIGHT</u>

THE DOCTOR runs - stops, checks the signal on his gizmo, *bleep bleep*, changes direction, runs back -

CUT TO:

So near and yet so far... The Doctor and Donna miss each other by yards.

<u>37. EXT. NEAR STACY'S STREET - NIGHT</u>

The PRISON VAN has stopped, SECURITY GUARDS leap out. With BUTTERFLY NETS.

CUT TO:

<u>38. EXT. STACY'S HOUSE - NIGHT</u>

DONNA runs out of the house - panic - no sign of the little shapes, but she runs in the direction they were heading -

CUT TO:

<u>39. EXT. NEAR STACY'S STREET - NIGHT</u>

THE DOCTOR, running, running, running -

CUT TO:

<u>40. EXT. NEAR STACY'S STREET - NIGHT</u>

FX: a STEEL BOX now packed full with little mewling ADIPOSE - *slam!* The lid is shut!

Slam! The Doors on the van shut!
CU wheels, scorching off -

And the van races away -

CUT TO:

41. EXT. STACY'S STREET - NIGHT

DONNA just reaching the end of the street, as the PRISON VAN roars past her. She doesn't pay it much attention, but stops, breathless, looking round. No sign of anything.

CUT TO:

42. EXT. STREET PARALLEL WITH STACY'S - NIGHT

THE DOCTOR runs to a halt, as the PRISON VAN scorches past - he looks at it, suspicious of it - but then he's distracted by his gizmo, the bleeps have stopped. Damn!

CUT TO:

43. EXT. STACY'S STREET - NIGHT

DONNA lost, shaken, wandering back down the middle of the street towards Stacy's house. A BLACK CAB is just pulling up, beeps, then the Driver calls out -

TAXI DRIVER
Stacy Harris?

DONNA
No.
(pause)
She's gone.

TAXI DRIVER
Gone where?

DONNA
She's just… gone.

TAXI DRIVER
Thanks for nothing.

The taxi drives away. As it does so…

HIGH SHOT, from above the houses, revealing the layout: Donna standing in the middle of Stacy's street. And parallel with her, in the next street along, THE DOCTOR standing in the middle of the road.

Both just stand there. Look round. Then give up. Donna walking off one way, the Doctor the other, into the night…

This is revolting! The Adipose are disgusting. For the first time ever on this show, I'm typing something wondering what Editorial Policy will make of it. In fact, I went back through it and took out most of Stacy's pain. Originally, I had her writhing and suffering and stuff, and it was too horrible to watch.

FROM: BENJAMIN COOK TO: RUSSELL T DAVIES
SATURDAY 1 SEPTEMBER 2007 16:32:07 GMT

RE: 4.1

Browsing the BBC Writersroom website the other day, I found some guidelines – on Situation Comedy, but I wonder whether the same rules apply to Drama – that state:

> *It is useful to think of organising a story in three acts. The first act […] sets up the major story of the episode, and introduces the major sub-plot. The final act […] resolves both main plot and sub-plot. The middle act […] develops the narrative but, around halfway through the script, pushes things off into an unexpected direction.*

Do you agree? Is there a formula for determining what happens when? Do all self-contained stories follow a three-act structure? I'm trying to think of exceptions, but it's difficult, because three-act structure is, in effect, Beginning, Middle and End. All stories have that, don't they? (But not necessarily in that order?) I ask because the end of Scene 43 in your latest instalment… well, that's the end of Act One, isn't it? It's an advert break, if the BBC were a commercial station. I'm not saying that you thought, right, this is the end of Act One. But perhaps an experienced scriptwriter organises his story in such a way without even thinking?

FROM: RUSSELL T DAVIES TO: BENJAMIN COOK
SATURDAY 1 SEPTEMBER 2007 22:41:28 GMT

RE: 4.1

That's funny, I just opened the script again for the first time in hours, and that bit you mention – the Doctor and Donna in the street, alone – is on Page 20, exactly a third of the way through a 60-page-ish script! It *is* the end of Act One! I hadn't realised. Oh, that's weird. I wonder if I like knowing that.

The language of scripts has now become so formalised,

Donna (Catherine Tate) and her father Geoff Noble (Howard Attfield) in 3.X *The Runaway Bride*.

it's losing its mystique (and that's good – there shouldn't be mystique), but along with that comes all the deconstruction, and then the textbooks, the experts, the catchphrases. I've never read any of those how-to-write books. They scare me. I was once bought a copy of Robert McKee's stuff. I opened it at a stray paragraph, flinched at what I read, and closed it. I've never opened it again. But not because I disagreed with it. Rather, the paragraph that I read was so accurate that it sort of shocked me. I thought, I don't want to know! I'd rather think about that stuff myself than be taught it. I don't want some tutor's voice intruding into my head when I'm trying to write. I've enough voices already, thank you.

And here I am, talking about how to write. So sue me.

This script language wasn't really around when I was starting out, certainly not in TV, so I'm not versed in it. It's not how I think about scripts. I don't think, Act One, Act Two, Act Three. It's just not wired into my head. (But I'm 44. If I were 18, maybe I'd be rattling off Third-Act-B-Plot-Denouement theories like a good 'un.) I do think about shape and rhythm, though, and the direction and velocity of a script – and, crucially, I do think of Beginning, Middle and End. As you said, that's the same thing as Act One, Act Two, Act Three, but in a different language. Every story ever told has a Beginning, a Middle and an End. It's fundamental. But this is where I'm wary of a formula, because I don't think of the Beginning, *then* the Middle, *then* the End. They're all connected, they're all the same thing, each dictates what the other is. It's back to that big soup of Maybe in my head. Soup is shapeless.

Julie and I argue about this. When she reads 4.1, she'll say what you said: the Doctor and Donna in the street, walking off into the night, in opposite directions, that's the end of Act One. And I suppose you're both right. There's a clear break, we shift location, we shift mood. But *I* never think of it like that. I just know that the story has to pause there. It has to earth itself and get a bit more real and heartfelt. That's when Donna will go and visit her dad on the hillside (we're inviting back Howard Attfield, who played Geoff Noble in *The Runaway Bride* – along with Jacqueline King, who played Donna's mum, Sylvia), where he sits with his telescope. After that, Donna goes back to Adipose Industries. Whatever her dad says on that hillside has consequences, pushes Donna onwards. Every scene should advance the story, even if the advance is tiny. (People often mistake this for 'every scene should *change* the story', so you get labyrinthine scripts full of plot twists and sudden shocks and reveals, which is the path to nonsense.) The scene must change Donna's mind – so she goes to work, meets the Doctor, and then it's a hell-for-leather race to the finishing line. But I don't sit with diagrams or cards or a sheet of A4, working that out. I just feel it.

Maybe it's inbuilt. Maybe I'm more disciplined than I realise. Maybe that's why I run away from a single Robert McKee paragraph, because I like the arrogance of imagining that I've worked it all out for myself... when, in fact, it's commonplace.

I worry a lot about that formal structure language, because it's the one thing that the inexperienced cling to. A learnt language. Like a set of crutches. Meetings throughout the industry now consist of script editors and producers sitting there saying, 'Where's the Second-Act Reversal?' Idiots. Really, they should be saying, 'Who is this man? Why is he scared? Does his wife really love him? Can he really kill her?' They talk about the shape, not the essence, obscuring valid discussion of the actual story – and story is far more important. In fairness, as I've said from the start, it's hard to talk about actual writing – the ideas, the scariness, the exhilaration – so I shouldn't be surprised if the formal language is a substitute, but I really do start to react violently when the substitute begins to take control...

It's easy to mock something that a lot of writers find useful, but those BBC guidelines that you quoted say 'halfway through the script, [the narrative] pushes things off into an unexpected direction.' Really? Must it? Things like that start to become rules, not suggestions. But *Goldilocks and the Three Bears* doesn't do that. (And I'm not using a fairytale lightly; that's a classic story that will outlast us all.) The bit where Goldilocks eats the bears' food and tries out their beds and goes to sleep (the 'middle act') doesn't surprise us; it's clearly setting us up for a 'final act' in which the three bears return home. And we bloody love it, because we just know what's going to happen. Equally, who's to say that you can't spin off in an unexpected direction a few minutes into the 'first act'? That's what great, modern films do, like the Charlie Kaufman stuff, like *Being John Malkovich* or *Eternal Sunshine of the Spotless Mind.* (I'm sure someone could draw up a list showing how those stories do, in fact, conform to absolute rules, but to hell with 'em. I'm not listening.) If you're a writer, don't fret away the hours worrying about this structure stuff. All the joy and fear and fun and despair is in the writing, not in the flowchart.

P.S. Cardiff Mardi Gras was barmy. I ended up on stage with Lisa from *Big Brother 4* and Faye from Steps. Oh, and a Dalek. Then I got mobbed outside the park. One person, then five, then ten, then 20, and they were all drunk, and I was getting pushed onto the road and grabbed by short drunk Welsh men. Ever so slightly scary. Imagine being David Tennant!

FROM: BENJAMIN COOK TO: RUSSELL T DAVIES
SATURDAY 1 SEPTEMBER 2007 23:21:51 GMT

RE: 4.1

You met Lisa from *Big Brother 4*?! OH! MY! GOD! So jealous!

End irony.

A question: how do you think the structure of a story written for TV differs from that of, say, a movie? The shape must vary depending on the length of the story being told, even within TV formats? Is it a 25-minutes-a-day serial drama, a 13-week run of 45-minute episodes, a 60-minute Christmas special, or two 90-minute episodes shown over a bank holiday weekend, probably starring Robson Green as an ordinary man with a mildly interesting job, who's pushed to the limit when his child, wife or girlfriend is murdered, kidnapped or involved in a car crash? But does the narrative structure of television drama, regardless of length, stand distinct from other storytelling mediums? If you're watching a movie, the chances are that you're sat in a cinema or you've purchased a DVD or... well, you're less likely to walk out or turn off. This must make a difference.

Also, what is it that attracts you, Russell, to telling stories on television as opposed to writing a novel or film script or radio play?

FROM: RUSSELL T DAVIES TO: BENJAMIN COOK
SUNDAY 2 SEPTEMBER 2007 03:52:10 GMT

RE: 4.1

Films are a whole different world. I'm often asked to write films, and it scares me a lot, because it's a whole new regime. That's why I *will* write one eventually; scary and new is good. I was thinking today about a *Doctor Who* movie, should it ever happen, because suddenly it occurred to me that something that we take for granted about the Doctor becomes a huge selling point in a movie: the fact that he doesn't use weapons. That's just a given on TV (well, bar the odd moment where he has to blow everyone up!), but in the cinema, a cinema full of action heroes with Uzis and blades and bullwhips, the Doctor becomes a truly extraordinary figure. You'd actually centrepiece that, rather than assume it. There's something of some sort of Film Theory at work in there; that movies have more focus, less sprawl, more of a centre; a simple characteristic can become a movie's entire purpose.

This whole formality about structure in storytelling has really evolved from the movies, and sometimes, I suspect, it just doesn't fit television. Television can ramble and pause and deviate and accelerate. It really is a different art form. With the soap opera, we've a brand new form, which is still evolving. We've had 47 years of Ken Barlow's life.[6] *Forty-seven years!* Like it or not, no fictional character has ever existed in such everyday detail. Not ever. Brand new form of fiction! And utterly shapeless – a couple of dozen different production teams, with different agendas, over all those years, with no overall plan – and yet time is going to impose on Ken Barlow a Beginning, a Middle and an End, as we move from his youth, through his adult life, to his death one day. Fascinating, isn't it? Structure imposes itself, just through the passage of time. There has never been a fictional form like the soap opera before. It's hugely underrated and unconsidered.

As for whether structure differs depending on the length of the story – well, again, every script is different, and every show is different. That's another reason for my distrust of blanket rules. Look at the rambling shape of *The Royle Family* or *Early Doors* – idiosyncratic, shambling, eccentric and genius. I think standard sitcom rules would decree that those shows shouldn't exist. At the opposite end of the scale, there's Steven Moffat's *Coupling*, which is plotted as tight as a drum, with the precision of a Swiss watch. All different. Again, though, they all have some sort of Beginning, Middle and End. Every story does, just in the telling of it.

The worst thing that happens these days is that channels and commissioners think that a shape is flexible. They take a two-hour drama and split it into two one-hours. That's a profoundly different shape. It happened with *Casanova*. That was written as two 90-minute episodes for ITV, but when it shifted to the BBC, who don't really have 90-minute slots, it became three 60-minute episodes. I rewrote it to a certain extent, but there wasn't time to rewrite from scratch, so the 90-minute shape remained inbuilt – and the finished drama staggered a bit as a result. (It's still two 90-minute episodes on the DVD, for boring overseas-licensing reasons, which *almost* restores it.) Very often, shows are written, or at least conceived in detail, or even completely shot, but then a new duration or slot is imposed – and it really can ruin something. That script has been through a writer's head, he's forged his way through his own personal Beginning, Middle and End, and then the whole thing is fractured and pasted back together. Terrible.

>>what is it that attracts you, Russell, to telling stories on television as opposed to writing a novel or film script or radio play?<<

I watch TV. I love TV. If there's a big movie on TV tonight, I'm still much more likely to be hopping my way between *The X Factor*, *Casualty* and *Smallville*. TV is my first choice. Always. Therefore, I *think* TV. When I think of *More Gay Men*, I don't think of a one-off story; I think of a six-part TV series, immediately. That's instinctive. I like looking at new televisual shapes, too. I'd love to write a drama in 52 episodes. Once a week, half an hour, on BBC Three or Four, just the simple story of a man and his life, so you can see how character and story develop over a whole year. That idea sprang out of the conversations we're having here. (No, you can't have ten per cent!) I'd call it *365*. Or maybe *Happy Birthday*, if you started and ended on the man's birthday. I like that, because I think a lot of telly still apes film, and not enough says, look, here's a sprawling, constant, available-to-all art form that doesn't often take advantage of its uniqueness. A story can last a year. Literally. I find that exhilarating – and knackering, because I'd have to write them all, God help me. Imagine having to write a half-hour script every week! I'm interested in what would happen to *me*.

Anyway, here's a bit more of 4.1. Nice last scene. Sentimental. But it's meant to be. It's funny, you defining that street scene as the 'end of Act One', because then I thought of the next scene as the 'start of Act Two' – and wrote it accordingly! This e-mail correspondence is having a direct effect on the actual script. Is that weird? I think it's good. And now it means that posters on Outpost Gallifrey will be allowed to blame *you* for the downfall of Western civilisation, too!

6 Ken Barlow (played by William Roache) is the only surviving character from the first episode of *Coronation Street* in 1960.

44. INT. NOBLES' HOUSE - NIGHT

DONNA comes in, still shaken. A pause. She gathers herself, exhausted, then....

Real life slams back in! Mum, SYLVIA, in the kitchen -

SYLVIA
And what time's this?

DONNA
How old am I?!

SYLVIA
Not old enough to use a phone!

CUT TO:

45. INT. TARDIS - NIGHT

THE DOCTOR hurries in, goes to the console, fast, starts pressing buttons, preparing a scan. Then, carefully, he gets out, dangling on its chain...

The GOLD ADIPOSE CAPSULE.

CUT TO:

46. INT. NOBLES' HOUSE - NIGHT

SLOW TRACK IN ON DONNA, just sitting there, as SYLVIA busies herself all around her, passing to and fro.

'It's no good sitting there dreaming...' Sylvia Noble (Jacqueline King) gives her daughter a piece of her mind.

SYLVIA
...I thought you were only moving back for a couple of weeks, but look at you! You're never gonna find a flat while you're on the dole! I mean, it's not the 1980s, no one's unemployed these days. Except you! How long did that job with Health and Safety last, two days? Then you walk out! 'I have other plans.' Well, I've not seen 'em! And it's no good sitting there dreaming, no one's gonna come along with a magic wand and make your life all better -

DONNA
Where's Dad?

SYLVIA
Where d'you think he is? Up the hill! Where he always is!

CUT TO:

47. EXT. HILLSIDE - NIGHT

DONNA trudging up a lonely hillside.

FX: beyond her, the lights of London, glittering.

But she's not here for the view. There's her dad, GEOFF, sitting on a little camping chair, with a telescope - nothing too expensive, the amateur astronomer. All nice and quiet; she loves her dad.

GEOFF
Aye aye. Here comes trouble.

DONNA
Permission to board ship, sir.

GEOFF
Was she nagging you?

DONNA
Big time. Brought you a thermos. And a Mars Bar. Seen anything?

GEOFF
I've got Venus, with an apparent magnitude of minus 3.5. At least, that's what it says in my book. Come and

see. There you go…

She puts her eye to the telescope.

(FX?) Her POV through TELESCOPE. Venus just a dot.

GEOFF (CONT'D)
The only planet in the solar system named after a woman.

DONNA
Good for her.

Donna leaves the telescope, looks up into the night sky.

DONNA (CONT'D)
Imagine if you could go out there.

GEOFF
We will. One day. Bit late for me, I suppose. But a hundred years' time, there's gonna be people like you and me, striding out amongst the stars.

DONNA
Don't suppose you've seen a little blue box?

GEOFF
Is that slang for something?

And she sits on the grass, next to him.

DONNA
No, I mean it… If you ever see a little blue box, flying up there in the sky… You shout for me, Dad. Oh, you just shout.

GEOFF
(smiles, kind)
I don't understand half the things you say, these days.

DONNA
Nor me.

Pause.

GEOFF
Fair dos. You've had a funny old time of it, lately.

DONNA
You can talk.

GEOFF
Oh, I'm on the mend. But you had poor old Lance, bless him.[7] That mad old Christmas.

DONNA
S'not the half of it. You wouldn't believe the things I've seen.

GEOFF
Then tell me.

DONNA
Just tonight, I was…
(pause)
Doesn't matter. Sometimes I think I'm going mad.

GEOFF
Well, you're not yourself, I'll give you that. I dunno. You just seem to be drifting, sweetheart.

DONNA
I'm not drifting. I'm waiting.

GEOFF
What for?

DONNA
The right man.

GEOFF
Oh, it's always a man.

HIGH SHOT, slowly pulling out, Donna & Dad looking up.

DONNA
No, I don't mean like that. But he's out there somewhere… And I mean for real, he exists, I've met him. And I just let him fly away. But I'm gonna meet him again, Dad. One day. If I have to wait a hundred years. I'll find him.

CUT TO:

48. INT. TARDIS - NIGHT

CU on THE DOCTOR with glasses & attachments like in 3.12, studying the opened CAPSULE, tiny wires trailing out.

7 Donna's fiancé in *Doctor Who* 3.X, Lance Bennett (played by Don Gilet), was revealed to be working for the Empress of the Racnoss, who later murdered him.

Catherine Tate and Howard Attfield film the hillside scene in 4.1.

```
                THE DOCTOR
      Fascinating. Seems to be a
      bio-digital relay specifically
      for…

   Looks up, looks round, aware that
   he's talking to himself.

   WIDEST SHOT POSSIBLE of the Tardis.
   The ancient, slow creak of the
   vast, empty space.

   The Doctor alone.
```

It is an absolute nightmare explaining what Donna has been up to since *The Runaway Bride*. What did she tell everyone happened to Lance? I have a version worked out (London was attacked by the Empress' Webstar, so Donna would have said that he died because of that), but it's a five-page speech – no, worse, it's a fake speech, because she would have had that out with her parents long ago – and I just don't want to stop for that amount of exposition. No wonder the Doctor never went in for that Christmas dinner with her folks!

FROM: RUSSELL T DAVIES TO: BENJAMIN COOK
SUNDAY 2 SEPTEMBER 2007 15:48:45 GMT

RE: 4.1

I've been sitting here for two hours, fiddling over rewrites to Donna and Geoff's chat in Scene 47. I'm sending you the new version. I thought you might like to see what I'm up to…

FROM: BENJAMIN COOK TO: RUSSELL T DAVIES
SUNDAY 2 SEPTEMBER 2007 16:00:03 GMT

RE: 4.1

Cheers for that, Russell. If you've time to answer this, I'm interested in why you've made each of those changes to Scene 47. Despite all the thought processes that I keep asking you about, we haven't answered exactly what it is that you do, 'tweaking' and 'fine-tuning', when sat in front of your computer, with last night's script on the screen…

FROM: RUSSELL T DAVIES TO: BENJAMIN COOK
SUNDAY 2 SEPTEMBER 2007 17:17:12 GMT

RE: 4.1

Well… the opening to Scene 47 remains unchanged, as things stand, right up to Geoff telling Donna that Venus is the only planet in our solar system named after a woman. 'Good for her,' says Donna, and then she adds: 'Imagine if you could go out there.' When I went back to that today, I realised that last line of Donna's was *way* too on-the-nose. This is the new, subtler version:

```
                DONNA
      Good for her.

   Donna leaves the telescope, looks
   up into the night sky.

                DONNA (CONT'D)
      How far away is that…?
```

And then I spent about half an hour on the internet, trying to find the distance from Earth to Venus – in miles, because Geoff wouldn't use kilometres! I discovered that on the transmission date of this episode – say, roughly, early April 2008 – Venus is too far away, behind the Sun, so Geoff wouldn't be able to see it. Damn. So I changed Venus to Mars – and changed Donna's line about a Mars Bar to a Twix, or there's too much Martian talk, but I really hated cutting the 'only planet named after a woman' line. But then I realised that this is actually 2009, in story terms, since *The Runaway Bride* was set at Christmas 2007, and this episode takes place a little over a year later. I entered that April 2009 date – and Venus *is* close! Hoorah! The 'only planet named after a woman' line went back in. If I've got the calculations right…

```
                GEOFF
About 26 million miles. But
we'll get there! One day.
Hundred years' time, we'll
be striding out amongst the
stars. Just you wait.
```

You'll have noticed that I took out Geoff's 'Bit late for me, I suppose' line. That lovely actor, Howard Attfield, has been ill and had chemotherapy. That's why there's that reference later on in the scene to him having been ill ('Oh, I'm on the mend'), though even that makes me shiver, so I might take it out. But 'Bit late for me, I suppose' is equally grim, isn't it? Also, I had Geoff saying 'there's gonna be people like you and me, striding out amongst the stars', but I thought that was, again, a bit unsubtle, since we all know that Donna *will* be flying off into space by the end of this episode.

The scene continues unchanged until:

```
                DONNA
That's not the half of it.
Things I've seen. Even
tonight, I was…
            (pause)
Doesn't matter. Sometimes I
think I'm going mad.
```

I took out a line of Geoff's – 'Then tell me' – interrupting Donna's speech. It was just fluff. No, it wasn't fluff, it was meant to be a little bit insistent, to suggest that there has been a lot that Donna hasn't been telling her dad since Christmas, but only a CSI forensic-style examination would get that amount of meaning from a simple line, so it's gone. And it saves space.

```
                GEOFF
Well, you're not yourself,
I'll give you that. I dunno.
You just seem to be drifting,
sweetheart.

                DONNA
I'm not drifting. I'm
waiting.
```

I keep worrying about that line. Is it too poetic? It's staying for now, but it's on a caution.

```
                GEOFF
What for?

                DONNA
The right man.

                GEOFF
Oh, it's always a man.

                DONNA
No, I don't mean like that.
But he's out there somewhere…
And I mean for real, he
exists, I've met him. And
then… I just let him fly away.

                GEOFF
Well then. Go and find him.
```

Now, that line of Geoff's is the biggest change. I made a mistake, because Donna came to this scene with a very fixed state of mind. She could have delivered her big 'I'll find him' speech from the moment that she arrived. I'd forgotten the point of the scene, which is that contact with her dad *changes* Donna. She's lost, upset over Stacy… so now, I hope, there's a slight sense that she's sort of given up, and then a quiet word from her dad puts her back on track. Funny thing is, I was rereading our e-mails and I saw that yesterday I said to you, 'Whatever her dad says on that hillside has consequences, pushes Donna onwards.' Clear as day. But when I came to write that scene… I forgot! Sometimes, I can get too close to a script and lose sight of why I'm there. I wander away from my original intention. Or maybe I've lived with that intention for so long that I take it for granted and forget to actually say it. That one, I forgot overnight! Thank God for these e-mails.

That's what rewriting is: discovering the point of a scene. If it has no point, cut it. Unless it's got a great gag. Or a naked man. And you'll see that Donna's 'He's out there somewhere' line has been shifted from her earlier speech, because it sounds better here. And Donna's speech here needs to be longer, for the camera move and for the mood. The scene continues:

```
Donna lies back. HIGH SHOT, pulling
out on the two of them, both Donna
and Dad looking up at the night sky.

                DONNA
Yeah. That's what I'm gonna
do. If I have to wait a
hundred years. I'll find him.
```

Donna and Geoff watch the skies. Illustration by Russell T Davies.

```
                    GEOFF
                  (laughing)
          God help him.

                    DONNA
          Oh yes!
```

I'm not sure about the last couple of lines. I thought Donna's big speech was a bit too 'written', so those two little grace-note lines take the edge off it. It's more natural now. Less pretentious. It was too Disney before, and now it's more me. Plus, it's nice to see them laughing. Laughing in the dark. But I still might go back to the original, because Disney is good and I'm worried that the throwaway laughter undercuts the drama of a woman dreaming of the Doctor. I don't know. Also, ticking away in my head: how upset is Donna over Stacy? Did she call the police? Did she leave the front door open?! It's a big problem. There are all sorts of scenes and lines that I could put in, but they don't lead anywhere. Nonetheless, it's bugging me.

FROM: RUSSELL T DAVIES TO: BENJAMIN COOK
MONDAY 3 SEPTEMBER 2007 03:43:03 GMT

RE: 4.1

I've done more. Lots of trims to what I'd already written, though. Keith the projectionist has gone. Poor Keith. He's just a BLOKE now, and he no longer has any lines. Also, I changed Miss Rattigan's name. I used it because Rattigan was the name of the family in *Revelations*, the old soap that I invented at Granada. It's kind of a lucky charm. But it kept making me think of the villain, Professor Ratigan, in Disney's *The Great Mouse Detective*! Plus, I thought of a nice gag for her new name, Miss Foster. Finally, she's getting a bit of life to her. She's a *mother*. That's much less Yvonne Hartman-like. In fact, I've inserted a couple of new scenes in between the 'end of Act One' (the Doctor and Donna in the street) and the scene where a shaken Donna arrives home. These new scenes are now the 'start of Act Two', I suppose (dear God, don't say that those How To Write books are telling the truth!):

```
43. INT. SALES CUBICLES - DAY[8]

B&W HIGH-ANGLE CCTV footage of the
cubicles, fast-forward, PEOPLE
jump-cutting as they go to and fro…
including THE DOCTOR & DONNA, and
also CRAIG, CLAIRE & OTHER WORKERS,
including the events of sc.15.

                              CUT TO:

44. INT. MISS FOSTER'S OFFICE -
NIGHT

REVEAL that sc.43 is playing on a
PLASMA TV in the office. MISS FOSTER
sits at her desk, studying the
screen. TWO SECURITY GUARDS either
side of her.

                MISS FOSTER
      All these Humans look the
      same… But one of them did
      it, that was no accident.
      Each capsule is bio-tuned to
      its owner, someone must have
      introduced a second capsule.
      One of these people is a
      thief…
```

8 A knock-on effect of the cutting of Scene 14 (in the Projection Booth) is that the original Scene 43 – the 'end of Act One' – is now Scene 42, followed by this, the new Scene 43, of CCTV footage of the sales cubicles.

(suddenly)
There!

She presses the remote, to freeze it.

MISS FOSTER (CONT'D)
Oh yes. There she is.
(looks down, babyish)
Shall we get her, baby? Shall we?

FX: an ADIPOSE on the desk waggles with joy, 'wheee!'

MISS FOSTER (CONT'D)
Shall we get the lady? Shall we, liddle moo-moo? Shall we kill her? Yes we will. Oh yes we will!

FX: she leans over, gives the Adipose a kiss. It goes 'aww!'

This is followed by Donna arriving home (now Scene 45), but I've cut the original Scene 45 of the Doctor hurrying into the TARDIS to study the Adipose capsule. It wasn't adding anything. Scene 46 is still of Sylvia having a go at Donna, and I revised – yes, further – the scene of Donna and Geoff on the hillside. After her line 'You can talk', it now goes:

GEOFF
Oh, I'm on the mend. But you had poor old Lance, bless him. That mad old Christmas.
(beat)
I wish you'd tell us what really happened.

Finally! *That's* the missing line. After all that wondering what Donna did or didn't tell her parents after *The Runaway Bride*, I realised this morning, walking to Tesco, that a lot of Donna's unhappiness comes from not being able to tell anyone about the Doctor. Geoff's line – 'I wish you'd tell us what really happened' – encompasses all that, and Donna's next speech flows a little better as a result:

DONNA
I know. It's just… The things I've seen. Sometimes I think I'm going mad. Even tonight, I was…
(pause)
Doesn't matter.

Donna Noble visits her dad on the hillside, in the original version of 4.1 *Partners in Crime*.

GEOFF
Well, you're not yourself, I'll give you that. You just seem to be drifting, sweetheart.

DONNA
I'm not drifting. I'm waiting.

And then the scene continues as before, until Geoff says, 'Well then. Go and find him.' To which Donna replies:

DONNA
Ohh, I've tried. He's… nowhere.

GEOFF
Oy! Since when did you give up? I remember you, six years old, I said, no holiday this year, so you toddled off, all on your own, and got on the bus! To Strathclyde! We had police and everything!
(both laughing)
Where's she gone, then? Eh? Where's that girl?

Donna lies back. HIGH SHOT, pulling out on the two of them; Donna and her Dad, looking up at the night sky.

DONNA
You're right. I'll do it. Just you watch me! He's out there somewhere. And I'll find him, Dad. Even if I have to wait a hundred years… I'll find him.

In working and working through this scene, *that's* what it's all about. Dad changes Donna's mind by inspiring her. (Interestingly, didn't I once say that I didn't write funny dads? Because dads aren't funny? But here he is – Geoff is funny and sweet. This proves that I talk bollocks.) However, I cut the two grace-note lines (Geoff: 'God help him.' Donna: 'Oh yes!'), which hurt, because I loved them, but they distracted from this irresistible on-screen cut from 'I'll find him' straight into Scene 48 of the Doctor in the TARDIS.

Right, here's the new stuff:

49. EXT. NOBLES' HOUSE - DAY

Back to the fast, cheeky music.

DONNA leaves the house, galvanised, determined to succeed today - she's got car keys, heading for the CAR.

SYLVIA is in the doorway, in her nightie.

SYLVIA
It's my turn for having the car! What do you need it for?

DONNA
A quick getaway!

JUMP CUT TO CU CAR KEY, turning in the ignition.

CUT TO:

50. INT. TARDIS - DAY

CU THE DOCTOR turning a key in the TARDIS console.

WIDER, the Time Rotor starts to rise and fall, in flight…

CUT TO:

51. EXT. CITY STREET - DAY

DONNA just slamming the door shut on the parked car, striding away, and as she clears -

FX: PULL FOCUS, and way down the street, the TARDIS appears.

CUT TO:

52. EXT. ADIPOSE INDUSTRIES FOYER - DAY

DONNA walks through the revolving doors -

CUT TO:

53. EXT. ADIPOSE INDUSTRIES, BACK YARD - DAY

THE DOCTOR sonics the lock, PRAC EXPLOSION, in he goes -

CUT TO:

54. INT. SALES CUBICLES - NIGHT

DONNA strides through, not stopping -

CUT TO:

55. INT. ADIPOSE INDUSTRIES, DOWNSTAIRS CORRIDOR - DAY

THE DOCTOR strides along the corridor -

He's heading for a door, opens it. A tiny little storeroom, mops & buckets, etc. No light. He gets inside, his hiding place, and he sonics the lock. A big *clunk!* Locked.

CUT TO:

56. INT. LADIES TOILETS - DAY

Clean, smart, large room. DONNA hurries in. There's at least five cubicles in a row. She goes to the furthest one.

Inside, she locks the door. Then lowers the lid on the toilet, to just use it as a chair. Sits.

Looks at her watch.

CUT TO:

57. INT. SALES CUBICLES - DAY

MISS FOSTER & TWO SECURITY GUARDS striding through. Sotto:

MISS FOSTER
She's in here somewhere...

As they clear, PAN UP to the CLOCK on the wall. 09.30.

MIX TO:

CLOCK reading 18.10.

CUT TO WIDER, STAFF standing, putting on coats, CRAIG heading off, CLAIRE calling to a MATE:

CLAIRE
See you tomorrow!

CUT TO:

58. EXT. ADIPOSE INDUSTRIES FOYER - NIGHT

CLAIRE & WORKERS heading out, into the NIGHT.

PAN UP. (FX?) Lights going out all over the Tower Block.

CUT TO:

59. INT. ADIPOSE INDUSTRIES, DOWNSTAIRS CORRIDOR - NIGHT

INSIDE THE STOREROOM, THE DOCTOR sonics the lock, *clunk.*

He steps out, a bit aching...

The corridor's darker, now. He heads off. Runs!

CUT TO:

60. INT. LADIES TOILETS - NIGHT

DONNA still in the cubicle. She stands, aching, ooh. Then unlocks the bolt, steps out, the toilet empty -

Then her mobile rings! She panics, hisses -

DONNA
Shut up shut up shut up -

- hurries back into the stall, locks the door, getting out her mobile, whispering -

DONNA (CONT'D)
Not now!

CUT TO:

61. INT. NOBLES' HOUSE, LIVING ROOM - NIGHT

SYLVIA on the phone, GEOFF in his coat in b/g, armed with TELESCOPE & THERMOS, about to head off.

SYLVIA
I need the car, where are you?!

SCENE CONTINUES, INTERCUT WITH LADIES TOILETS.

CUT TO:

62. INT. LADIES TOILETS - NIGHT

DONNA sitting on the loo, whispering on her mobile.

DONNA
I can't. I'm busy.

SYLVIA
What are you whispering for?

DONNA
...I'm in church.

SYLVIA
What are you doing in church?

DONNA
Praying.

SYLVIA
Too late for that, madam!

GEOFF
What's she in church for?

SYLVIA
Hush! Go to the hill!
(to Donna)
But I need the car, I'm going out with Suzette, she's invited all the Wednesday Girls, apparently she's been on those Adipose pills, she says she looks marvellous -

But Donna suddenly hangs up - she's heard footsteps -

CUT TO OUTSIDE THE CUBICLES, as the door slams! open -

MISS FOSTER & TWO SECURITY GUARDS stride in, like Stormtroopers, the guards now armed with GUNS. Miss Foster stands centre, utterly

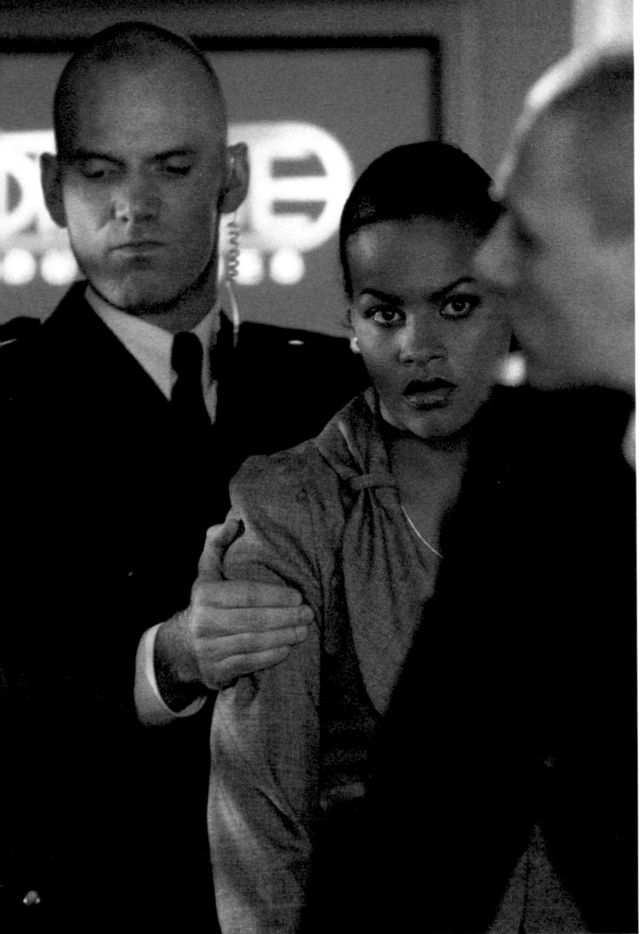

Penny is captured!

confident.

MISS FOSTER
We know you're in here. So why don't you make this nice and easy, and show yourself?

Donna in the cubicle, lifts her feet up, terrified.

MISS FOSTER (CONT'D)
I'm waiting.
(silence)
I warn you. I'm not a patient woman. Now, out you come.

Silence, Donna so scared, trapped.

MISS FOSTER (CONT'D)
Right, we'll do this the hard way. Get her!

The guards move forward - kick the door in on the first cubicle, one guard kicking, the other ready with his gun -

Empty.

Donna terrified.

They kick in the second cubicle - empty -

Donna clutching her knees, helpless -

They kick in the third cubicle -

And there's PENNY CARTER! Hiding!

MISS FOSTER (CONT'D)
There you are.

On Donna. Eh?!

As the guards haul Penny out, she's furious -

PENNY
I've been through the records, Foster! All your government clearances were based on fake evidence - there's something about those pills you're not telling us -

MISS FOSTER
Oh, I think I'll be conducting this interview, Penny.

And they're hauling Penny out of the door, gone.

Beat.

Donna opens her cubicle door a fraction, peers out.

CUT TO:

63. EXT. ADIPOSE INDUSTRIES ROOFTOP - NIGHT

THE DOCTOR opens the access door, steps out onto the roof. The lights of the city all around.

But he runs, fast, over to the edge -

Where there's a WINDOW CLEANER'S CRADLE. Lovely! Just what he needs. He starts to sonic the controls.

CUT TO:

64. INT. SALES CUBICLES - NIGHT

The room now dark. MISS FOSTER striding ahead, PENNY being dragged along by the TWO SECURITY GUARDS -

Penny (Verona Joseph) is restrained by Miss Foster's security guards (Ruari Mears and Claudio Laurini).

PENNY
- you've got no right to do this! Let me go!!

Behind them, through the door they first came through -

DONNA peeks through a tiny gap. Following.

CUT TO:

65. INT. ADIPOSE INDUSTRIES - NIGHT

WIDE SHOT, the WINDOW CLEANER'S CRADLE descending.

CUT TO CLOSER, THE DOCTOR in the cradle.

CUT TO:

66. INT. MISS FOSTER'S OFFICE - NIGHT

Office empty. At the windows, the WINDOW CLEANER'S CRADLE is just descending, THE DOCTOR sliding past -

But he ducks down out of sight as MISS FOSTER, the TWO SECURITY GUARDS and a struggling PENNY walk in -

MISS FOSTER
Sit there!

PENNY
I'm phoning my editor -

MISS FOSTER
I said *sit!*

CUT TO:

67. EXT. ADIPOSE INDUSTRIES - NIGHT

THE DOCTOR has stopped the cradle, now crouching down, to duck below the window level.

Then he presses his ear to the wall. Listening.

CONTINUES INTERCUT WITH SC.69, MISS FOSTER'S OFFICE.

CUT TO:

68. INT. AREA OUTSIDE MISS FOSTER'S OFFICE - NIGHT

Secretaries' area, in DARKNESS. DONNA creeps along. The only lights shine from MISS FOSTER'S OFFICE - it's got glass interior walls, but with blinds drawn, though there's still a clear glass panel on the door.

Donna crouches below the glass in the door. Listens.

CONTINUES INTERCUT WITH SC.69, MISS FOSTER'S OFFICE.

CUT TO:

69. INT. MISS FOSTER'S OFFICE - NIGHT

MISS FOSTER stands behind her desk, facing PENNY. The GUARDS have tied Penny's wrists to the chair with flex, now they stand to the sides.

INTERCUT with DONNA listening, crouched low, outside the office door; THE DOCTOR crouched low, outside the window.

PENNY
You can't tie me up! What sort of country d'you think this is?

MISS FOSTER
A beautifully fat country.

PENNY
(calmer, strong)
Come on then. Those pills. Miss Foster. What are they?

MISS FOSTER
You might as well have a scoop. Since you'll never see it printed.
(holds up a capsule)
This… is the spark of life.

PENNY
What's that supposed to mean?

MISS FOSTER
According to our literature, the capsule attracts all the fat cells, and then flushes them away. Well, it certainly attracts them, that part's true. But it binds the fat together, to form a body.

PENNY
What d'you mean, a body?

MISS FOSTER
I'm surprised you didn't ask about my name. I chose it well. Foster, as in foster mother. And these… are my children.

She opens the desk drawer, reaches in, plucks out…

FX: and puts an ADIPOSE on the desk. It waves.

ON THE DOCTOR & DONNA ONLY now, frustrated, unable to see.

PENNY OOV
…you're kidding me. What the hell is that?!

MISS FOSTER OOV
An Adipose. The creature is called, a Adipose. Sweet, isn't it?

'This… is the spark of life.'

This next speech OOV, covering the action below:

PENNY OOV
Is that… fat? It's made out of fat? Look. I'm sorry. I don't know what's going on here. I was only checking for safety, for legislation, for… Miss Foster, I promise you, I haven't filed a report with anyone, if you want me to go, and not say a word, then I'll go, I promise, I'll just go…

But from 'Sweet, isn't it?', Donna *has* to see, so she inches up to look through the glass panel…
At the same time, the Doctor *has* to see, so he inches up to look through the window…

(NB, Miss Foster, the desk, Penny & guards are at the front of the office, the Doctor & Donna a few feet further towards the back, so there's a clear space between the Doctor & Donna, who are directly opposite each other.)

The Doctor lifts his head up… looking left, to the desk.

Donna lifts her head up… looking right, to the desk.

Then the Doctor looks straight ahead, seeing -

Donna looks straight ahead, seeing -

The Doctor!!!!

Donna!!!??!

Big long moment, both just boggling, open-mouthed.

Then, all shot through the glass, in silence, big gestures:

Donna: OH!!!!

The Doctor: Donna???

Donna: Doctor!

The Doctor: but…what? Wha… WHAT??!?

Donna: oh! My! God!

'You!! I was looking for you!'

The Doctor: but… how???

Donna points at herself! It's me!

The Doctor: well I can see that!

Donna: oh this is brilliant!

The Doctor: but… what the hell are you doing there???

Donna's just so thrilled, she waves! Big smile!

The Doctor: but, but, but, why, what, where, when?

Donna points at him - you!! I was looking for you!

The Doctor: me? What for?

```
Donna does a little mime. I, came
here, trouble, read about it,
internet, I thought, trouble = you!
And this place is weird! Pills! So
I hid. Back there. Crept along.
Heard this lot. Looked. You! Cos
they…

And on 'they', she gestures and
looks towards Miss Foster.

Who is staring at her. As are the
guards. Penny, too.

Donna freezes. Oops.

Miss Foster then looks at the
Doctor. Calm:

                MISS FOSTER
    Are we interrupting you?

Donna stands, still framed in
the glass. Looks at Miss Foster,
speechless. Then at the Doctor.

The Doctor: run!!!

And Donna runs -

                MISS FOSTER (CONT'D)
    Get her!

The security guards head for the
door -

The Doctor holds the sonic, whirrs
it dead ahead -

Clunk! The door's locked, the
guards struggle with it -

Miss Foster turns to face the
Doctor -

                MISS FOSTER (CONT'D)
    And him!

The Doctor sonics the cradle-
controls, fast -

(FX?) Seen from inside the office,
through the window, the cradle
zooms up, fast, taking the Doctor
with it -
```

The Doctor gives Donna a chance to escape.

I'm very pleased with the Doctor and Donna's meeting. (Very pleased?! BLOODY DELIGHTED! If not ECSTATIC!) It's everything that I wanted it to be. It's so nice to write for such brilliant, skilful actors.

Also, today, funnily enough… I worked out what David's last words could be, one day, before his regeneration. I've stored that away.

FROM: BENJAMIN COOK TO: RUSSELL T DAVIES
MONDAY 3 SEPTEMBER 2007 13:40:54 GMT

RE: 4.1

>>I worked out what David's last words will be, one day, before his regeneration.<<

What? What?! WHAT??!!!

FROM: RUSSELL T DAVIES TO: BENJAMIN COOK
MONDAY 3 SEPTEMBER 2007 14:01:40 GMT

RE: 4.1

I'm not telling you. Ha ha ha. You've got to have something to wait for.

CHAPTER NINE

THE GREAT ESCAPE

In which Rose Tyler returns, the Controller of BBC One has second thoughts, and a little tusk makes a big difference

FROM: BENJAMIN COOK TO: RUSSELL T DAVIES
MONDAY 3 SEPTEMBER 2007 15:33:52 GMT

TODAY'S ANNOUNCEMENT

'No *Doctor Who* return until 2010,' declares BBC News.

'*Doctor Who* to return for fifth series in 2010,' says the official *Doctor Who* website.

How's the *Doctor Who* crew taken the news that there will be no Series Five in 2009?

FROM: RUSSELL T DAVIES TO: BENJAMIN COOK
MONDAY 3 SEPTEMBER 2007 15:54:06 GMT

RE: TODAY'S ANNOUNCEMENT

The weeks of work that bloody press release has taken! The RSC was going to announce that David is doing *Hamlet*, at a press conference on 11 September, so everything was timed for then… until the RSC brochure was sent out last week, mentioning David! Clearly, their PR is as good as ours. Numbskulls. So the news of no *Doctor Who* series in 2009 has all been a bit rush-released. Phil and Julie were going to talk to all the staff and heads of departments calmly and properly, but then had to run around like idiots on Friday instead, blabbing to one and all.

I'm a bit locked away here, so I'm not sure how it's gone down, though Julie and Phil say not too bad. Everyone has been aware of the rumours for ages, so I don't think anyone is very surprised. A lot of people said, 'I thought so.' Many of the staff are freelance, and this is how the freelance world works. Jess in the office was immensely pragmatic: she said she's been travelling about as a freelancer for ten years now, so she'll always get work.[1] The most worrying thing is for the crew, the regular crew on set every day, those that live in Cardiff. I haven't even time to ask those that I'm worried about – people like Lindsey Alford, who've moved lock, stock and barrel to Cardiff. I'm not sure where that leaves them. I can't leave this desk to find out. That's terrible. But there's the promise of work to come, the *Doctor Who* Specials, maybe *Torchwood*, maybe *Sarah Jane*, as well as bigger plans to move *Casualty* here when the new studio is built. Lindsey was in Bristol, on *Casualty*, before this, so she might stay, she might move

1 Production co-ordinator Jess Van Niekerk.

on. A freelancer's life. I'm the same. I can't think when anyone last asked me how I feel having to spend all this time in Cardiff, away from Manchester. It's just assumed, that's what you do. It's the distorting *Doctor Who* prism that makes today's announcement seem inflated; this sort of thing is normal in this industry.

Exciting, though. I like change.

Besides, it's not as lengthy a filming break as it might have been, because the BBC is just desperate for a Series Five as soon as possible. And Julie is hitting problems: it's terribly hard to raise the money for these Specials if BBC Worldwide isn't getting much in return. When there's no surrounding series to ameliorate the cost of a Special, the budget becomes frighteningly small. So, we'll still make the 2008 Christmas Special at the end of Series Four, and then, it's been decided, come back in January 2009 to make three more Specials – probably for Christmas 2009, New Year's Day 2010, and an Easter 2010 Special. Then Series Five will have a new production team. The show really only goes off air for 2009. And that's summed up weeks of really delicate discussions. Though the plans still keep changing!

FROM: BENJAMIN COOK TO: RUSSELL T DAVIES
MONDAY 3 SEPTEMBER 2007 23:30:14 GMT

RE: TODAY'S ANNOUNCEMENT

On days like this, when the press/internet/schedule is going crazy, is writing an escape? From real life? It is an escape, quite often, for people who write in their spare time, but it's your job, your career, and what you write affects the lives and careers of lots of other people. Frequently, for you, writing is the very thing that you try to escape from (all those diversion techniques, etc), but was it the opposite today?

FROM: RUSSELL T DAVIES TO: BENJAMIN COOK
TUESDAY 4 SEPTEMBER 2007 01:53:57 GMT

RE: TODAY'S ANNOUNCEMENT

Tricky, that one, about escapism. Hard for me to judge, because the time I spend writing is to the detriment of my family and friends, so am I escaping them? Am I choosing to be like this? 'Escape' implies a choice. Would I be like this anyway if I worked in Greggs? Would I spend all my time getting the lattice pastry on the chicken-and-ham pies correct? (The answer is yes.) To be honest, I have trouble with 'escapism' full stop. It's usually a derogatory term. Or condescending. At best, cute. Is the person who goes upstairs for a couple of hours a week to write a never-published work, or watch *Star Trek*, or play with a train set, actually escaping? It makes the pastime, whether it's a hobby or a job, seem tiny and silly, when it's a vital part of your life. It's best summed up by that encounter with the Time-Check Woman the other week. Writing is actually my way of engaging with the world, not escaping from it. I meet someone, I see something, and I'm breaking it all down into dialogue and story and rhythms. But that doesn't mean I'm escaping. It's not dreamland – clearly it's not, because I've built a multi-million-plus empire in South Wales out of it. Not that success is a measure of how real this is, although… well, it *is* a measure.

The very word 'fiction' implies another world, literally a different place, whereas no one claims that a dedicated sportsman is escaping his life, or a chef, or a nurse. But the poor writer – the sci-fi one especially – is seen as running away. Bollocks. This is real, for me, and it's tough, it's fun, it's practical, and it's very, very important.

I was in just the mood to answer that!

David . . . Hamlet role

Dr Who hold-up

BAD news for fans of Doctor Who – the show's fifth series has been shelved until 2010.

BBC bosses have had to postpone filming because star David Tennant will be playing Hamlet.

TV Biz revealed last month that he will go on stage with The Royal Shakespeare Company between next July and November.

Specials

That is when the actor – currently filming series four for next spring – would have been due to film a Dr Who 5.

However, David **WILL** make three specials over the coming months, to be aired in 2009.

He is set to quit the role after that, making way for a new Timelord in 2010.

An insider said: "Normally the Doctors do three series and then bow out."

Creator Russell T Davies is expected to stay for the 2009 specials, then hand over series five to another executive.

70. INT. STAIRWELL - NIGHT

DONNA bursts into the stairwell, runs up -

CUT TO:

71. EXT. ADIPOSE INDUSTRIES ROOFTOP - NIGHT

THE DOCTOR back at the top, clambering out of the cradle - runs across the roof -

CUT TO:

72. INT. MISS FOSTER'S OFFICE - NIGHT

TWO SECURITY GUARDS FIRE - PRAC GUNS -

PRAC FX: the locked door is shot into splinters!

Guards run through - MISS FOSTER following -

PENNY is left tied to the chair.

PENNY
What the hell is going on?!

FX: the ADIPOSE on the desk jumps up and down - such fun!

CUT TO:

73. INT. STAIRWELL - NIGHT

DONNA running up -

Donna is reunited with the Doctor.

THE DOCTOR running down -

And they meet on a landing!

She throws herself at him, hugs him!

DONNA
Oh my God, Doctor! I don't believe it! It's really you! You've even got the same suit, don't you change?

THE DOCTOR
Thanks Donna, not right now -

There's a *bang!* from a few floors below - he looks down -

His POV: the SECURITY GUARDS heading up -

And he grabs her hand, big smile!

THE DOCTOR (CONT'D)
Just like old times!

And they run up the stairs together -

CUT TO A FEW FLOORS BELOW -

More SECURITY GUARDS joining in, EIGHT of them storming up - MISS FOSTER following, talking into her WRISTWATCH COMMS -

MISS FOSTER
Cover is broken. Prepare maximum parthenogenesis. And summon… the Nursery.

CUT TO:

74. EXT. ADIPOSE INDUSTRIES ROOFTOP - NIGHT

THE DOCTOR & DONNA race out of the door - the Doctor sonics it shut - then run across the rooftop, to the CRADLE, where the Doctor frantically sonics the winch, taking loose wires out of his pocket and welding them to the controls -

And right from the word go, Donna's talking, top speed -

DONNA
- cos I thought, how do I find the Doctor? And then

I thought, just look for trouble, and he'll turn up! So I looked everywhere, spent all my money, searching - you name it, UFO sightings, crop circles, all those weird things in Cardiff, I investigated them all - like all that stuff with the bees disappearing, I thought, I bet he's connected, oh, I tried everything, but I found nothing, just nothing, but I kept on going, I checked everything - well, except for Christmas Day, all that stuff about a replica Titanic flying over Buckingham Palace, I mean, come on!, that's gotta be a hoax -

THE DOCTOR
What d'you mean, the bees are disappearing?

DONNA
I dunno, that's what it says on the internet, but on the same site, there were all these conspiracy theories about Adipose Industries, I thought, right, I'll take a look -

The access door starts banging, Guards on the other side.

THE DOCTOR
Right, in you get.

DONNA
In I get where?

THE DOCTOR
Into that.

DONNA
What am I getting into that for?

THE DOCTOR
To escape.

DONNA
We're escaping in that?

THE DOCTOR
Oh, I'd forgotten what it was like with you!

DONNA
Ditto!

CUT TO:

75. INT. INSIDE ACCESS DOOR, ROOFTOP - NIGHT

It's a hefty door, one GUARD slamming against it with his shoulder, other GUARDS piled up, waiting, as MISS FOSTER strides up the stairs -

MISS FOSTER
Get it open!

CUT TO:

76. INT. ADIPOSE INDUSTRIES ROOFTOP - NIGHT

THE DOCTOR & DONNA now standing in the CRADLE, the Doctor still making tiny changes to the controls with the sonic.

DONNA
But if we go down in this, they'll just call it back up again!

THE DOCTOR
No, I've locked the controls to a sonic matrix, I'm the only one who can control it -

And he holds up the sonic, whirrs it, with a big smile -

The cradle starts to descend -

BLAM! - THE ACCESS DOOR flies open - GUARDS charge out, though clearing centre to allow MISS FOSTER to stride out -

And she's calm, just holds up her PEN. Which glows with a blue light on the end, and whirrs.

The cradle jerks to a halt. It's lowered so that only the Doctor & Donna's heads are visible over the edge.

They look faintly ridiculous. Muttered:

DONNA
'I'm the only one who can control it.'

THE DOCTOR
Did I say I was perfect?

DONNA
Act like it.

Miss Foster strolling over to the edge, relaxed. (GUARDS with guns raised, standing a good distance back.) Calm, with the absurdity of the Doctor & Donna being just heads:

MISS FOSTER
Well, then.

THE DOCTOR
Evening.

DONNA
Hello.

THE DOCTOR
Lovely night.

MISS FOSTER
Wonderful. Evidently you're another offworlder, that thing would be…?

THE DOCTOR
Sonic screwdriver.

MISS FOSTER
Sonic pen.

THE DOCTOR
Nice. You can write notes with it! And if you were to sign your real name, that would be…?

MISS FOSTER
Matron Cofelia, of the Five-Straighten Classabindi Nursery Fleet, Intergalactic Class.

THE DOCTOR
A brood mother. Using Humans as surrogates.

MISS FOSTER
Subcontracted by the Adiposian First Family to breed new stock. Where else to look, but Earth? Living off the fat of the land.

DONNA
So those little things… they're made out of fat? But that woman last night, Stacy Harris, there was nothing left of her.

'Well, then.' Miss Foster makes an entrance.

MISS FOSTER
In a crisis, the Adipose can transmute bone and hair and internal organs. Though it does make them a little bit sick, the poor things.

DONNA
Poor Stacy, more like!

THE DOCTOR
Seeding a populated planet without permission is against galactic law, you must know that.

MISS FOSTER
Are you threatening me, down there?

FROM: RUSSELL T DAVIES TO: BENJAMIN COOK
TUESDAY 4 SEPTEMBER 2007 17:14:42 GMT

RE: TODAY'S ANNOUNCEMENT

Here's more script.[2] I've sent this to the office, too, so that they can start to prep – or just weep at – the window-cleaner's-cradle sequence…

2 As reproduced here, this latest instalment of script picks up the Adipose Industries rooftop scene two pages in.

MISS FOSTER
Are you threatening me, down there?

THE DOCTOR
I'm telling you to stop.

MISS FOSTER
Sorry, I can hardly resist saying this. Fat chance!

THE DOCTOR
I'm trying to help you, Matron. This is your one chance. Because if you don't call this off… then I'll have to stop you.

MISS FOSTER
If I were you, I'd concentrate on stopping gravity.

And she holds out her SONIC PEN, at one of the winches - (NB, the cradle is fixed to the roof with, basically, one winch on its right hand side, one winch on its left, each running the METAL CABLES which support the cradle).

THE DOCTOR
No no don't no - !

DONNA
No! No! No! -

PRAC EXPLOSION on the WINCH -

FX: THE DOCTOR & DONNA's heads PLUMMET out of shot - !

FX: THE DOCTOR & DONNA & CRADLE plummeting down, TOWER BLOCK FLOORS RACING past them - Donna screaming - !

FX: CU DOCTOR, with FLOORS RACING PAST behind him, holding out the sonic, whirring furiously -

FX: PRAC EXPLOSION on CU WINCH at one end of the CRADLE (with FLOORS RACING PAST B/G) -

WIDER on the CRADLE, halfway down the building, jerking to a sudden halt - the Doctor & Donna jolted, recovering -

CUT TO THE DOCTOR, sonicking the nearest window -

'We can get in through the window –'

THE DOCTOR
- hold on - we can get in through the window -

CUT TO THE ROOFTOP, Miss Foster looking over the edge, on her wristwatch comms -

MISS FOSTER
Deadlock the building!

CUT TO THE CRADLE, a *clunk!* of locks, the Doctor sonicking -

THE DOCTOR
Can't get it open!

DONNA
Well then, smash it!

And she's got a spanner from a workman's toolkit in the cradle, slams the window -

CUT TO INSIDE THE BUILDING, the Doctor & Donna hammering at the glass - but it's security glass, doesn't give -

CUT TO ROOFTOP, the Guards now at the edge, readying guns, pointing down - but -

MISS FOSTER
Don't be so stupid, we're in the middle of the City! I can make this look like a perfect accident…

She's calmly walking over to the left-hand-side winch. Holds the PEN against the metal cable -

PRAC FX: the CABLE burning, sparks flying out, like an oxyacetylene torch - the cable fraying -

CUT TO the CRADLE, both looking up, horrified -

DONNA
She's cutting the cable!!!!

CUT TO ROOFTOP, CU CABLE - PRAC FX, it SNAPS!!

FX, STUNT!, WIDE SHOT - the CRADLE tips, the LEFT HAND SIDE falling, the broken cable whipping downwards, the RIGHT HAND SIDE still connected, staying where it is, so the whole shebang falls to the left - THE DOCTOR & DONNA tumbling left, with Donna on the left (ie, camera left) -

CU the Doctor flailing out, to reach for -

FX: DONNA tumbling over the edge, screaming - !

THE DOCTOR slams into the left-hand wall of the cradle - the cradle now hanging vertically - and swinging a little - but it remains connected on the right-hand-side, so the left-hand-wall has become the floor -

The Doctor whipping his head over the side, to see -

THE DOCTOR
Donna - ?!

FX: DONNA hanging on, about 10 feet below, the GROUND far below her - she's clinging to the hanging left-hand-side cable. (There's, say, a spar of metal, formerly part of the winch, fixed to the cable, and Donna's actually holding on to that; she could never hold on to cable alone.)

DONNA
Doctor - !

THE DOCTOR
Hold on!

DONNA
I am!!

He grabs the cable, tries to heave it up -

FX: DONNA dangling - but not moving up -

It's impossible - but the Doctor looks up, realising what Miss Foster will do next -

CUT TO ROOFTOP, Miss Foster now walking casually over to the right-hand-side of the winch - PEN glowing, whirring -

FX: TOP SHOT of the Doctor (with Donna hanging far below him) as he leans out of the cradle, LOOKING UP, and pointing his sonic up, whirring -

CUT TO ROOFTOP -

Hold on, Donna! 'I am!!'

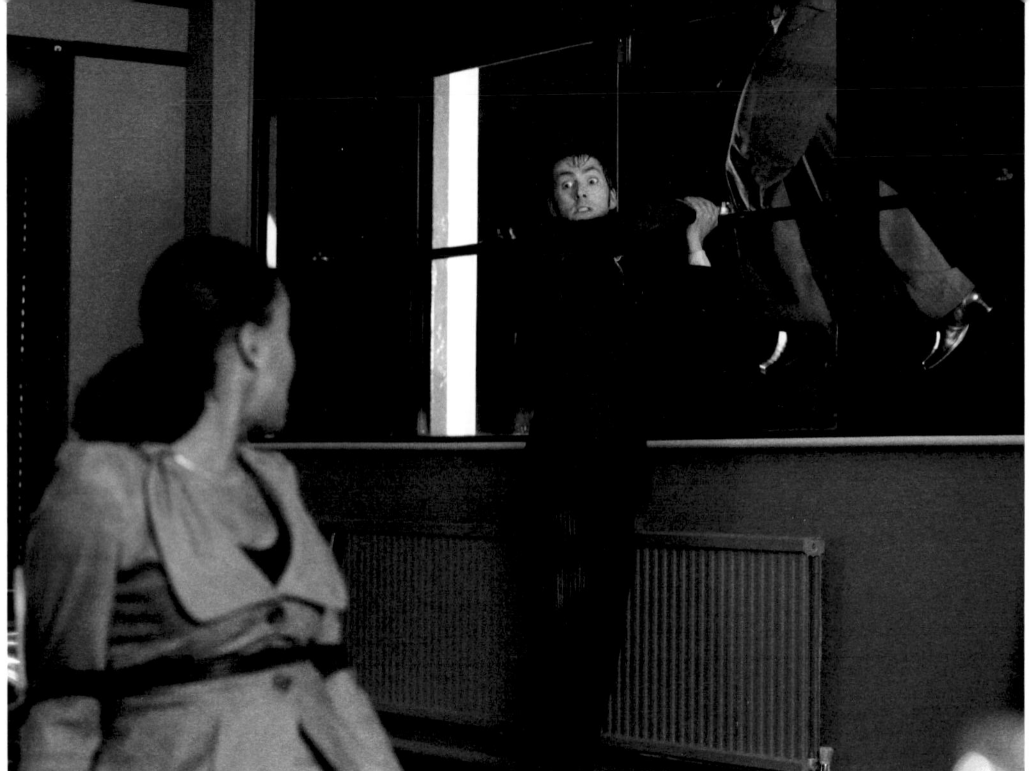

Penny's evening goes from strange to stranger.

FX: SMALL EXPLOSION on the PEN -

CU, Miss Foster drops it -

FX: SONIC PEN falling down, down, floors racing past b/g -

CUT TO the Doctor, leaning out, hand out -

CU his hand, he catches the pen!

And starts to sonic-pen the window nearest to him -

THE DOCTOR
That's better!

FX: Donna dangling -

DONNA
Get me up!! *Doctaaaa - !*

CUT TO:

76. INT. MISS FOSTER'S OFFICE - NIGHT[3]

PENNY, still tied to her chair. Looking out of the window.

DONNA's legs are hanging, kicking, outside the glass.

Strangely calm, given the circumstances:

PENNY
…what the hell is going on?

CUT TO:

77. EXT. ADIPOSE INDUSTRIES ROOFTOP/SIDE OF BUILDING - NIGHT

FX: DONNA dangling - and now raging -

DONNA
This is your fault! I should've stayed at home!!

CUT TO THE DOCTOR, window now open, about to crawl through -

THE DOCTOR
Won't be a minute!

FX: DONNA dangling -

DONNA
Don't leave me!

CUT TO ROOFTOP, MISS FOSTER looking down, with GUARDS.

MISS FOSTER
He's slippery, that one. And

3 The press launch scenes (numbered 13 and 14, set in the Cinema and Projection Booth respectively) have been combined so that the script is easier to follow, shifting all subsequent scene numbers, so the Doctor and Donna's face-off with Miss Foster on the rooftop – and the first part of the window-cleaner's cradle sequence – is now Scene 75, followed by this, Scene 76, of Penny in Miss Foster's office.

they can't be acting alone.
Our primary duty is to
protect the children.

And she strides towards the Access Door, Guards following -

CUT TO:

78. INT. STAIRWELL - NIGHT

THE DOCTOR running down, down, down -

CUT TO:

79. EXT. SIDE OF BUILDING - NIGHT

CU DONNA, struggling, holding on tight.

CU HER HANDS, clenched tight on the spar/cable.

FX: DONNA, the drop below…

CUT TO:

80. INT. STAIRWELL - NIGHT

THE DOCTOR running - busting through a door -

CUT TO:

81. INT. MISS FOSTER'S OFFICE - NIGHT

PENNY still tied to the chair as THE DOCTOR runs in - races to the window, DONNA's legs still kicking outside -

He sonic-pens the window, frantic -

PENNY
Is anyone gonna tell me
what's going on in this
place?

THE DOCTOR
What are you, a journalist?

PENNY
Yes.

THE DOCTOR
Just make it up.

And the window swings open - !

The Doctor reaching out to the LEGS -

THE DOCTOR (CONT'D)
I've got you - stop kicking!

CUT TO:

82. INT. STAIRWELL - NIGHT

SECURITY GUARDS running down, MISS FOSTER following, on WRISTWATCH-COMMS -

MISS FOSTER
Earth Report Cover is broken.
Tell the Adiposians, we're
going into premature labour.

CUT TO:

83. INT. MISS FOSTER'S OFFICE - NIGHT

DONNA just hopping down to the floor, breathless - being helped down by THE DOCTOR. PENNY still tied up.

DONNA
I was right. I was so right.
It's always like this with
you, isn't it?

THE DOCTOR
(kind)
You all right?

DONNA
(smiles)
Just about. Thanks.

THE DOCTOR
Right then. Off we go - !

And he runs out - Donna following -

PENNY
Oy!

The Doctor pops his head back round the door.

THE DOCTOR
Sorry.

He holds out the sonic pen, whirrs -

Penny's hands pull free, the flax loosened.

THE DOCTOR (CONT'D)
Now do yourself a favour,
get out!

And he's gone -

CUT TO:

84. INT. STAIRWELL - NIGHT

THE DOCTOR & DONNA run out - and down -

PAN UP, MISS FOSTER & SECURITY GUARDS two floors above, just heading down -

CUT TO:

85. INT. MISS FOSTER'S OFFICE - NIGHT

PENNY is doing her job, ransacking through files -

PENNY
Adipose… cellular basification…

She's about to run out of the door, with what she's found - stops dead. MISS FOSTER & GUARDS striding in.

MISS FOSTER
Tie her up!

PENNY
Oh you're kidding me -

CUT TO:

86. INT. ADIPOSE INDUSTRIES, DOWNSTAIRS CORRIDOR - NIGHT

THE DOCTOR & DONNA run along - the Doctor running to his STOREROOM from sc.55, yanks open the door, starts throwing out mops, buckets, etc. Donna stands back, bemused.

DONNA
Well, that's one solution. Hide in a cupboard. I like it.

THE DOCTOR
I've been hacking into things all day, cos the Matron's got a computer core running through the centre of the building, triple-deadlocked, but now I've got this -
(the sonic pen)
- I can get into it -

And he's heaving at the ENTIRE BACK WALL of the storeroom -

Which creaks and pulls away, like A HIDDEN DOOR -

Behind it, floor to ceiling: a COMPUTER WALL. Very distinct design, all golden curves and lights.

FROM: RUSSELL T DAVIES TO: BENJAMIN COOK
WEDNESDAY 5 SEPTEMBER 2007 01:24:20 GMT

FW: TEST AND DESIGN OF ADIPOSE

Look at the Adipose! The Mill sent me these to approve today. The one on the left, 'G', that's the one. Ha ha ha.

FROM: BENJAMIN COOK TO: RUSSELL T DAVIES
WEDNESDAY 5 SEPTEMBER 2007 01:28:28 GMT

RE: TEST AND DESIGN OF ADIPOSE

That is so cute! Am I the only one already thinking of the merchandising opportunities?

FROM: RUSSELL T DAVIES TO: BENJAMIN COOK
WEDNESDAY 5 SEPTEMBER 2007 01:39:29 GMT

RE: TEST AND DESIGN OF ADIPOSE

Yes, I'm thinking… well, that I've lost a bloody fortune by inventing these under a BBC contract! Talking of which…

It's all hitting the fan over Monday's press release. If I told you all the shenanigans, I'd have to type for 500 hours. Peter Fincham, having been talked through our plans for 2009 so many times, is reacting to the press release like it's brand new information. Seriously! Since

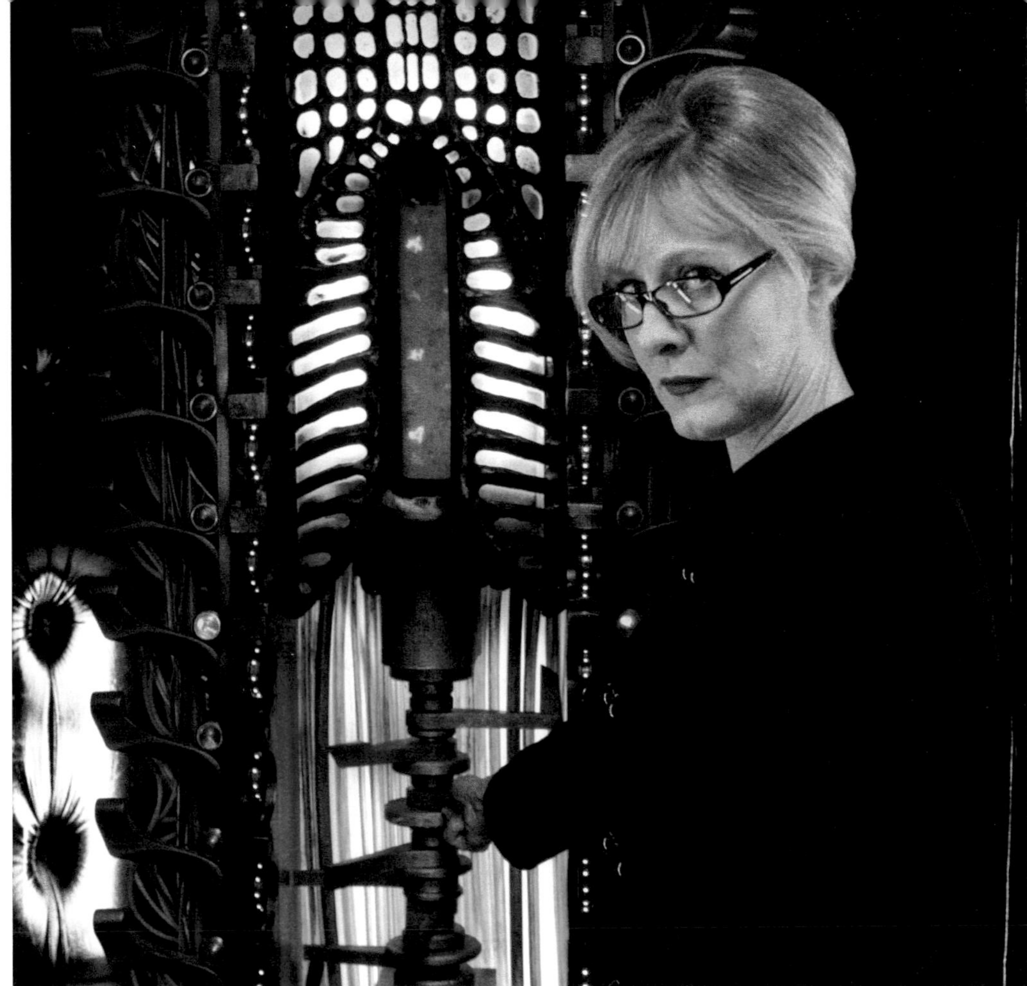

Miss Foster seduces the Inducer that's hidden inside Adipose Industries.

this stupid Queen business, he's in siege mentality.[4] He's been phoning up Julie: 'Why are we doing this?! *Why?!*' Maybe I'm getting paranoid, but I reckon if it escalates one more notch, just one, then his next step is to overrule Jane Tranter, magic a new production team out of nowhere, and have a complete new series in 2009. That's how much of an emergency it is. Interesting times.

FROM: BENJAMIN COOK TO: RUSSELL T DAVIES
WEDNESDAY 5 SEPTEMBER 2007 01:58:10 GMT

RE: TEST AND DESIGN OF ADIPOSE

Scary times! What other programme in Britain has had its 2010 commission headlined in the newspapers? Does the media hoo-hah of the last couple of days not affect your writing of 4.1 at all?

FROM: RUSSELL T DAVIES TO: BENJAMIN COOK
WEDNESDAY 5 SEPTEMBER 2007 02:13:04 GMT

RE: TEST AND DESIGN OF ADIPOSE

Oh, it drives me mad. I don't know a lot of what's going on; Julie keeps it from me, to protect my writing time, but tonight she was so tired and worn down and disheartened by it all that it came out in a great big blurb. Julie's outpouring only came about because I happened to mention that I was worried that David personally was taking a lot of flak for the 'gap year', like we'd done it in order for him to do *Hamlet*. In fact, we'd decided to pause anyway, ages ago – a decision taken *with* him, yes, but the *Hamlet* offer came up afterwards, when he knew that he had free time; we decided first. I suggested to Julie, off the cuff, that I could mention this in my column in *Doctor Who Magazine*, and Julie

4 In July 2007, at a press launch of the BBC's forthcoming autumn schedule, Fincham introduced a trailer for the documentary ***A Year with the Queen***, and told journalists that the Monarch had walked out of a photo shoot 'in a huff', after being asked to remove her tiara by photographer Annie Leibovitz. However, unknown to Fincham, the footage in the trailer had been assembled in the wrong order by production company RDF Media; the Queen had actually been walking *in* to the photo shoot. Fincham admitted the error, and initially rejected calls that he should resign.

blanched. And then the outpouring started, because she had to tell me how severe things were, in order to stop me saying anything to anyone. Not out of secrecy, but because the smallest word now becomes so inflammatory. Even to the BBC One Controller. Madness. *Doctor Who*! That little show. So bizarre.

But to answer your question… no, it doesn't affect my writing. Not one jot. Completely separate worlds. Doesn't intrude at all. Thankfully.

FROM: RUSSELL T DAVIES TO: BENJAMIN COOK
WEDNESDAY 5 SEPTEMBER 2007 23:57:56 GMT

MORE ADIPOSE

This is what I've done so far. I'm going to keep going and see if I can finish tonight. There's a Tone Meeting tomorrow…

```
86. INT. MISS FOSTER'S OFFICE -
NIGHT[5]

PENNY tied up again, as MISS FOSTER
stands back, the two SECURITY
GUARDS sliding back the wall behind
her chair - revealing an IDENTICAL
COMPUTER WALL to the storeroom's.

                PENNY
    What does that thing do?

              MISS FOSTER
    That's the Inducer. We'd
    planned to seed millions, but
    the 500 test subjects will
    have to do -
           (to the Guards)
    That Doctor and the woman.
    Find them. Get rid of them.

The Guards run out -

                                 CUT TO:

87. INT. ADIPOSE IND., DOWNSTAIRS
CORRIDOR/STOREROOM - NIGHT

THE DOCTOR on the floor, rewiring
the COMPUTER WALL, DONNA beside
him. He gives her a handful of
wires, and keeps using those wires
throughout, as they talk -

              THE DOCTOR
    Hold that -

                DONNA
    What are you doing?

              THE DOCTOR
    She's wired up this whole
    building. And we need a bit
    of privacy -

                                 CUT TO:

88. INT. ADIPOSE IND., DOWNSTAIRS
CORRIDOR #2 - NIGHT

The TWO SECURITY GUARDS charging
along, with guns -

They slam through a set of Fire
Doors -

FX: ARCS OF ELECTRICITY all
around the doorframe, zapping the
GUARDS - they fall to the ground,
unconscious -

                                 CUT TO:

89. INT. ADIPOSE IND., DOWNSTAIRS
CORRIDOR/STOREROOM - NIGHT

THE DOCTOR fiddling with two wires -

FX: tiny ARC OF ELECTRICITY, same
as sc.88.

              THE DOCTOR
    Just enough to stun them! But
    why's she wired it up, what's
    it all for…?
```

5 The brief scene in the Adipose Industries foyer, of Claire and the workers heading home, has been deleted, shifting all subsequent scene numbers, so the Doctor and Donna entering the storeroom is now Scene 85, followed by this, the new Scene 86, of Penny in Miss Foster's office.

The Doctor zaps Miss Foster's guards – only enough to stun them, mind.

Then he keeps working, intent. And in the pause, Donna is looking at him. Properly, now. Then, quiet & smiling (though he keeps working, she keeps handing him wires):

DONNA
You look older.

THE DOCTOR
Thanks.

Pause.

DONNA
Still on your own?

THE DOCTOR
Yeah. Well, no, I had this friend, Martha, she was called, Martha Jones, she was brilliant. And I destroyed half her life. But she's fine, she's good. She's gone.

DONNA
What about Rose?

THE DOCTOR
…lost.
(looks at her)
I thought you were gonna travel the world.

DONNA
Easier said than done. It's like, I had that one day with you, and I was gonna change, I was gonna do so much. Then I woke up the next morning, and it's the same old life. Like you were never there. And I tried, I did try, I went to Egypt, oh, I was gonna go barefoot and everything. But then it's all bus trips and guide books and don't-drink-the-water, two weeks later you're back home, it's nothing like being with you. I must've been mad, turning down that offer.

THE DOCTOR
What offer?

DONNA
To come with you.

THE DOCTOR
…you're coming with me…?

'She's started the program!'

DONNA
Ohh, yes please!

THE DOCTOR
…right.

COMPUTER WALL starts bleeping, ILLUMINATING!

DONNA
What's it doing now?

THE DOCTOR
She's started the program!

CUT TO:

<u>90. INT. MISS FOSTER'S OFFICE - NIGHT</u>

MISS FOSTER slams a final lever, crosses to the window. PENNY still tied to the chair.

MISS FOSTER
Mark the date, Miss Carter. Happy birthday. So many birthdays.

FX: ANGLE ABOVE MISS FOSTER, looking out, with the WHOLE OF LONDON glittering below…

CUT TO:

91. INT. WINE BAR - NIGHT

Smart, but not posh, like a Yates'. SYLVIA is out with the GIRLS - five women, her age, all dressed up for a night out, on the white wine. SUZETTE holding court -

SUZETTE
- I swear, that Adipose treatment, it's amazing, just look at me, look at my chin! Almost seven pounds in three days.

SYLVIA
It's like a miracle! And all of that from one little pill?

SUZETTE
I've been eating like normal, all you do is swallow the pill and…

She stops.

Holds her stomach. Feels something.

SYLVIA
You all right, love…?

SUZETTE
Yeah, I'm just… Funny sort of feeling, just…

THROW FOCUS, far behind her, at a separate table, a NICE MAN on date with a LADY. But he stands. Feels his stomach. Something wrong. The woman saying, 'What is it…?'

CUT BACK TO SUZETTE, just standing and turning to go -

SUZETTE (CONT'D)
Just… pop to the loo…

SYLVIA
Oh my God, Suzette!

SUZETTE
What…?

She turns, trying to see - because under her clothes, on her back, something is starting to move…

CUT TO:

92. INT. ROGER'S HOUSE - NIGHT

LIVING ROOM, ROGER just standing, feeling a bit odd. Puzzled. Lifts his shirt…

FX: the SKIN on his SIDE is moving, a squirming bump…

CUT TO:

93. INT. WINE BAR - NIGHT

SUZETTE trying to look at her back - SYLVIA going to her, the OTHER WOMEN staring, and other CUSTOMERS -

SUZETTE
What is it, what is it, get it out, *get it off me - !*

SYLVIA pulls down the back of Suzette's blouse -

FX: a LITTLE ADIPOSE waving!

Sylvia screams!! Then turns - cos there's another scream -

It's the LADY, cos the MAN is standing there, holding his shirt up, boggling, while -

FX: AN ADIPOSE stre-e-e-etches out and plops! onto the table in front of him!

WHIP PAN over to -

A YOUNG WOMAN at the bar, feeling her stomach, alarmed -

CUT TO:

94. INT. ROGER'S HOUSE - NIGHT

ROGER now lying on the floor,

'Get it off me!' Suzette (Sue Kelvin) gets a bit of a shock.

Sylvia Noble and her fellow bar patrons look on as the Adipose go on the march.

gobsmacked, as -

FX: his ADIPOSE stretches out of his side, separates, plop!

FX: the ADIPOSE trundles away across the carpet -

CUT TO:

95. INT. ROGER'S KITCHEN - NIGHT

FX: THE ADIPOSE hops through the cat-flap, gone!

CUT TO:

96. EXT. ROGER'S ESTATE - NIGHT

WIDE SHOT of the street, doors opening, PEOPLE standing there, some screaming, others just boggling, as -

FX: ADIPOSE run from one house, and another, FIVE of them scuttling into the night, all heading down the road together -

CUT TO:

97. INT. WINE BAR - NIGHT

FX: LOW ANGLE as SUZETTE'S ADIPOSE scuttles across the floor - PEOPLE standing back, terrified -

SUZETTE panicking in b/g, with the GIRLS consoling her, but SYLVIA is walking across to the door, stunned, open-mouthed, determined to follow the Adipose…

CUT TO:

98. EXT. WINE BAR - NIGHT

SYLVIA walks into the doorway, stunned…

It's a busy street, with pubs & restaurants and takeaways.

FX: HER POV, three ADIPOSE scuttling out of the pub opposite -

Whip pan -

FX: HER POV, TEN LITTLE ADIPOSE, in formation, scuttling down the middle of the road -

CUT TO A BLACK CAB, screeching to a halt -

CUT TO A CAR, slewing across the road, braking -

CUT TO THE DRIVER of another car,

stopped in the middle of the street, getting out of his car to just boggle -

PEOPLE on the pavement, pointing, some SCREAMING.

FX: THIRTY ADIPOSE marching down the middle of the road!

Sylvia yelps, looks down -

FX: CU another ADIPOSE, scuttling out of the Wine Bar, beetling between Sylvia's feet - !

CUT TO:

99. INT. MISS FOSTER'S OFFICE - NIGHT

PROFILE MISS FOSTER, at the window.

MISS FOSTER
Come to me, children. Come to me.

CUT TO:

100. EXT. STREET - NIGHT

FX: WIDE SHOT. THE MARCH OF THE ADIPOSE. Hundreds of little shapes marching in unison down the road. BYSTANDERS staring, pointing, screaming, keeping well back.

FX: GROUND LEVEL, ADIPOSE waddling along…

CUT TO:

March of the Adipose!

101. INT. ADIPOSE IND., DOWNSTAIRS CORRIDOR/STOREROOM - NIGHT

THE DOCTOR, frantic with the wires - DONNA helping -

THE DOCTOR
- so far, they're just losing weight, but the Matron's gone up to Emergency Parthenogenesis -

DONNA
And that's when they convert -

THE DOCTOR
- skeletons, organs, everything, five hundred people are gonna die!

CUT TO:

102. INT. WINE BAR - NIGHT

SYLVIA running back in -

Because SUZETTE is now on the floor, the GIRLS panicking - LOTS OF BUMPS are now writhing under her clothes -

The MAN is still standing, but horrified, as his clothes all start moving and flexing with bumps -

The YOUNG WOMAN at the bar is the same, scared, trying to press down the moving bumps in her clothes -

CUT TO:

103. INT. ROGER'S HOUSE - NIGHT

ROGER on the floor, rolling onto his side, trying to see -

LOTS OF BUMPS moving under the back of his shirt -

CUT TO:

104. INT. ADIPOSE IND., DOWNSTAIRS CORRIDOR/STOREROOM - NIGHT

THE DOCTOR still fighting - DONNA at his side -

THE DOCTOR
- gotta cancel the signal -

- and he takes out his GOLD CAPSULE

& PENDANT, wrapping a wire around it, connecting it to the computer-

THE DOCTOR (CONT'D)
This contains the basic signal, if I can switch it backwards, the fat goes back to being just fat -

CUT TO:

105. INT. MISS FOSTER'S OFFICE - NIGHT

MISS FOSTER at the COMPUTER WALL -

MISS FOSTER
Nice try. Double strength!

She slams a lever -

CUT TO:

106. INT. ADIPOSE IND., DOWNSTAIRS CORRIDOR/STOREROOM - NIGHT

ALARMS BLEEP - bad news, THE DOCTOR still with the GOLD CAPSULE and wiring -

THE DOCTOR
No, she's doubled it, I need -

On his feet - runs a few yards down the corridor, desperate -

THE DOCTOR (CONT'D)
- haven't got time - !!

- stops, runs back, grabs wiring - so fast, now -

THE DOCTOR (CONT'D)
- it's too far - can't override it - they're all gonna die - !

CUT TO:

107. INT. WINE BAR - NIGHT

SUZETTE, on the floor, panicking, as her clothes heave -

CUT TO:

108. INT. ROGER'S HOUSE - NIGHT

CU on ROGER, so scared, as his back writhes. About to separate…

CUT TO:

Donna's second Adipose pendant is just what the Doctor ordered.

109. INT. ADIPOSE IND., DOWNSTAIRS CORRIDOR/STOREROOM - NIGHT

CU DONNA, now, fixed, quiet, as THE DOCTOR works, frantic -

DONNA
What d'you need?

THE DOCTOR
- gotta double the base pulse - I can't - !!

DONNA
Doctor. What do you need?

THE DOCTOR
I need a second capsule, to boost the override, but I've only got the one, they're all gonna die -

And Donna holds up… HER GOLD CAPSULE & PENDANT.

The Doctor looks at her.

She looks at him.

The moment suspended. Just magic.

He smiles.

She smiles.

Then back to normal, as he grabs the SECOND CAPSULE off her, jams it

Matron Cofelia of the Five-Straighten Classabindi Nursery Fleet, Intergalactic Class. (You can call her 'Nanny'!)

into the wiring -

And the whole COMPUTER BANK goes dead!

CUT TO:

110. INT. WINE BAR - NIGHT

SUZETTE on the floor, SYLVIA & GIRLS crowding round her -

But Suzette's suddenly still.

SUZETTE
It's stopped. They've gone…

She's patting her clothes, incredulous. No bumps.

CUT TO MAN in b/g. Laughing, overjoyed! It's stopped!

CUT TO YOUNG WOMAN. Joy!

CUT TO:

111. INT. ROGER'S HOUSE - NIGHT

ROGER on the floor, suddenly calm. Lifts his head up. Pats his clothes. All flat. Nothing. It's stopped!

He starts to laugh, out of shock, but oh, the relief!

CUT TO:

112. INT. MISS FOSTER'S OFFICE - NIGHT

MISS FOSTER slamming levers on the COMPUTER WALL, but it's dead, no lights. PENNY still tied to the chair.

PENNY
What's happened?

MISS FOSTER
I think the Doctor happened. But we've still given birth to 700 Adipose. And the Nursery is coming.

FROM: BENJAMIN COOK TO: RUSSELL T DAVIES
THURSDAY 6 SEPTEMBER 2007 00:27:57 GMT

RE: MORE ADIPOSE

This episode will be responsible for *so* many kids wetting the bed. I hope they make Adipose soft toys. Or sponges! (Or squeezy stress balls. Yeah.)

FROM: RUSSELL T DAVIES TO: BENJAMIN COOK
THURSDAY 6 SEPTEMBER 2007 00:51:37 GMT

FW: ADIPOSE SHARP FANG

The Adipose stress ball? I'd have that! Here's the final design for the Adipose. I asked The Mill to give it one little fang, off centre, because… well, that's what makes a monster. A sharpened tusk! Like there's a *tiny* bit of nastiness to them. And it's funnier off-centre.

FROM: BENJAMIN COOK TO: RUSSELL T DAVIES
THURSDAY 6 SEPTEMBER 2007 02:59:35 GMT

IT'S 3AM. ARSE.

Finished 4.1 yet? Or have you fallen asleep at the keyboard? How's it going?

FROM: RUSSELL T DAVIES TO: BENJAMIN COOK
THURSDAY 6 SEPTEMBER 2007 03:15:07 GMT

RE: IT'S 3AM. ARSE.

It's going *very* well, thank you. The final pages are near. I suddenly sped up. How marvellous that you've been following this script in every detail (remember when it started with a jilted Penny, walking down the street, past the TARDIS?), and now it feels as though you're here for the final pages, keeping vigil.

FROM: BENJAMIN COOK TO: RUSSELL T DAVIES
THURSDAY 6 SEPTEMBER 2007 03:27:40 GMT

RE: IT'S 3AM. ARSE.

I'm keeping vigil with a glass of red wine. I'm reading Nicola Shindler's brilliant Huw Weldon Lecture from 2002. Apparently, Jimmy McGovern once said to Nicola that though he hates scenes that he's written being cut, he'd prefer for an audience to be confused for ten minutes than bored for even ten seconds. I like that.

FROM: RUSSELL T DAVIES TO: BENJAMIN COOK
THURSDAY 6 SEPTEMBER 2007 03:35:18 GMT

RE: IT'S 3AM. ARSE.

That lecture was fantastic. You'd love Nicola. She's like Julie, but ruder – and every bit as lovely. I often quote that Jimmy McGovern thing in Edits. In fact, tonight, I've been slicing through earlier scenes in 4.1 like a man possessed, cutting and trimming, because the page count is seriously freaking me out now.

I'm sending you what I've written so far. It's an odd ending to the alien story. Getting rid of the villain like this is… different. Normally, I don't give a hoot about swinging from comedy to darkness, but even I'm surprised by the way that this script is ricocheting to and fro. Of course, I'm terrified about the budget. I've spent about £500 million, so it'll have to calm down. Or I might ask them to axe BBC Three.

```
112. INT. ADIPOSE IND., DOWNSTAIRS
CORRIDOR/STOREROOM - NIGHT[6]

THE DOCTOR & DONNA, as the room
starts to rumble. Shudder.

                DONNA
    What the hell is that…?
```

6 The brief scene on Roger's estate – people screaming and boggling as Adipose run from one house – has been deleted, shifting all subsequent scene numbers, so the scene in Miss Foster's office after the Doctor has overridden the system ('I think the Doctor happened') is Scene 111, followed by this, the new Scene 112, of the Doctor and Donna in the storeroom.

THE DOCTOR
They're babies. They need a Nursery.

CUT TO:

113. INT. WINE BAR - NIGHT

SUZETTE sitting, exhausted, THE GIRLS all tending to her -

SUZETTE
...it just went, it just stopped...

The place starts to rumble. Shudder. Small CAMERA SHAKE.

SYLVIA
What the hell is it now - ?!

And she runs back to the door -

CUT TO:

114. EXT. WINE BAR - NIGHT

SYLVIA runs out. Stops dead. Looking up.

PEOPLE all around, looking up at the sky. The deep, low rumble shuddering away...

HIGH WIDE SHOT of the STREET - still in chaos, with cars having braked all over the place - EVERYONE staring up...

FX: A HUGE SPACESHIP gliding

overhead! Close Encounters-style, a black disc with BRIGHT LIGHTS UNDERNEATH.

On Sylvia, open-mouthed...

CUT TO:

115. EXT. HILLSIDE - NIGHT

GEOFF is sitting there with his TELESCOPE, and a CUPPA. Earphones on - only a CD Walkman, playing 'Spanish Eyes', Al Martino. Geoff's the happiest man in the world.

FX: BEHIND HIM, the SPACESHIP gliding over LONDON, way off in the distance.

His telescope's pointing the other way. He's got no idea.

CUT TO:

116. INT. MISS FOSTER'S OFFICE - NIGHT

PROFILE, MISS FOSTER at the window, looking up. Smiling.

The Nursery Ship arrives over Adipose Industries.

PENNY
What's that noise? What is it??

MISS FOSTER
My lift home.

And she strides out -

PENNY
You can't just leave me here!

But she does!

CUT TO:

117. EXT. ADIPOSE INDUSTRIES - NIGHT

FX: LOW ANGLE, looking up at the SPACESHIP, gliding to a halt like a vast halo above the Tower Block.

FX: in the street in front of the building, THE ADIPOSE ARMY. HUNDREDS of TINY SHAPES.

FX: LOW ANGLE, an ADIPOSE waving up at the SPACESHIP.

CUT TO:

118. INT. ADIPOSE IND., DOWNSTAIRS CORRIDOR/STOREROOM - NIGHT

The rumbling, shaking, stops. THE DOCTOR still packing wires back into the COMPUTER WALL, DONNA helping -

DONNA
When you say Nursery, you don't mean a crèche in Notting Hill?

THE DOCTOR
Nursery Ship - ohh, wait a minute -

One screen on the Wall has blinked into life. Strange alien script scrolling across - the Doctor fascinated.

DONNA
Hadn't we better go and stop them?

THE DOCTOR
Hold on, hold on… Instructions from the Adiposian First Family…

CUT TO:

119. EXT. ADIPOSE INDUSTRIES - NIGHT

MISS FOSTER strides out. Stands there. Triumphant.

MISS FOSTER
Children! It's time to go

The Adipose flag down their lift.

home. I'm taking you to meet your new mummy and daddy.

FX: HUNDREDS OF ADIPOSE in the STREET go 'yaaay!', happy.

Miss Foster looks up…

FX: *WHAM!* STRONG, WIDE, BLUISH BEAMS OF LIGHT shaft down from the SPACESHIP.

FX: VERY WIDE SHOT, the Tower Block with the SPACESHIP above, and BEAMS OF LIGHT from ship to ground.

MISS FOSTER (CONT'D)
Up you go, babies. Up you go!

FX: A BUNCH OF ADIPOSE in a BEAM OF LIGHT, and one by one, they begin to rise up, gently, into the air, wheee!

FX: WIDE SHOT, STREET, THE HUNDREDS OF ADIPOSE now in bluish BEAMS OF LIGHT, as they ALL begin to lift up, up…

FX: on MISS FOSTER, with little ADIPOSE lifting up gently, in the FOREGROUND, as she smiles:

MISS FOSTER (CONT'D)
That's it! Flying!

CUT TO:

120. INT. ADIPOSE IND., DOWNSTAIRS CORRIDOR/STOREROOM - NIGHT

THE DOCTOR still reading the screen -

THE DOCTOR
- she wired up the building, to convert it into a Levitation Post. Ohh, but it's worse than that - come on - !

And he's running, Donna following -

CUT TO:

121. EXT. ADIPOSE INDUSTRIES - NIGHT

Adipose all gone; MISS FOSTER steps forward, into the strong light from above. Deep breath, looking up…

MISS FOSTER
Now, get me out of here.

'That's it! Flying!' The Adipose – and their Nanny – are beamed up.

CUT TO:

122. EXT. ADIPOSE INDUSTRIES, ROOFTOP - NIGHT

THE DOCTOR & DONNA burst out -

And stop.

Awestruck; the light of the BEAMS reflecting off them, gently; all rather beautiful, as they look out…

FX: the sky full of ADIPOSE, the air glowing with BEAM-LIGHT, as hundreds of the little dot-sized creatures rise up…

The Doctor & Donna smiling.

DONNA
What you gonna do, then? Blow them up?

THE DOCTOR
They're just children. Can't help where they came from.

DONNA
Makes a change from last time. That Martha must've done you good.

THE DOCTOR
She did. Yeah, she did.
(beat, then cheeky)
She fancied me.

DONNA
Oh, Mad Martha, that one. Blind Martha. Charity Martha.

FX: CLOSER on one rising ADIPOSE; it gives a little wave.

Donna waves back. Then stops.

DONNA (CONT'D)
I'm waving at fat.

THE DOCTOR
Actually, as a diet plan, it sort of worked… There she is - !

FX: A DISTANCE AWAY - ie, away from the roof, over the street, MISS FOSTER is rising up, gently, in the same levitation beam. Around her, the LAST ADIPOSE rise up through shot, disappearing up, gone.

The Doctor runs forward, urgent - Donna following -

THE DOCTOR (CONT'D)
Matron Cofelia, listen to me - !

MID-SHOT, Miss Foster stops, suspended in the air (IE, NON-FX, shot against night sky). Calling across the night:

MISS FOSTER
I don't think so, Doctor. And if I never see you again, it'll be -

THE DOCTOR
- oh why does no one ever listen to me?! I'm trying to help! Just… get across to the roof, can you shift the levitation beam?

MISS FOSTER
What, so you can arrest me?

THE DOCTOR
Just *listen!!* I saw the Adiposian instructions! They

Sarah Lancashire braves green screen and a harness in preparation for Miss Foster's grisly high-rise demise.

know it's a crime, breeding on Earth, so what's the one thing they don't want to leave behind? Witnesses!

MISS FOSTER
Then you'd better run and hide.

THE DOCTOR
Not me! You!!

FX: WIDE SHOT, MISS FOSTER suspended in the beam… as the LIGHT SNAPS OFF. Darkness.

MID-SHOT Miss Foster looking left and right, held in the air for a second like a cartoon coyote. Then -

FX: WIDE SHOT as Miss Foster falls, plummets, screaming, out of the bottom of frame -

Donna turns to the Doctor, flinches, with the OOV *crunch!*

The Doctor puts his arm around her. So sorry.

Then both look up, hearing the whine of engines…

FX: ABOVE THEM, the SPACESHIP lifts up, up, up…

CUT TO:

123. FX SHOT - ABOVE THE EARTH

FX: A WINDOW crammed full of ADIPOSE. Mewling. They look sad. A little wave from one of them, bye bye.

FX: PULLING OUT, the WINDOW set in the SPACESHIP, and the Ship hurtles away, into space, away from Earth, gone…

CUT TO:

124. EXT. ADIPOSE INDUSTRIES - NIGHT

THE DOCTOR & DONNA stroll out. Exhausted. Calm. Way off in the distance, there are signs of the disruption - POLICE BARRIERS, FLASHING LIGHTS. An AMBULANCE and PARAMEDICS closer to the building (hiding the remains of Miss Foster).

The Doctor looks a the SONIC PEN, decides naah, chucks it away, gets out the SONIC SCREWDRIVER, points it up -

FX: a SMALL BLUE PULSE OF LIGHT flies up, into the sky…

DONNA
What's that?

THE DOCTOR
Sending a statement to the Shadow Proclamation. Reporting the Adiposian crime. Suppose the children will be taken into care. I hate being official, brrr.

PENNY appears. Staggering. She is still tied to her chair, having to hold it behind her. Wild-eyed and furious:

PENNY
You two! You're just… mad! D'you hear me?? Mad! I'm gonna report you! For madness!

She runs off towards the distant POLICE, like a lunatic.

DONNA
Some people just can't take it.

THE DOCTOR
Nope.

DONNA
And some people can! So, then. Tardis! Come on!

She grabs his hand, yanks him out of shot - !

CUT TO:

125. EXT. CITY STREET - NIGHT

The street from sc.50, DONNA running in, realising that her car is near the TARDIS, though a fair distance between them. THE DOCTOR is the definition of dubious.

DONNA
That's my car! That's like destiny! And I've been ready for this, I packed ages ago, just in case -

'Planet of the Hats, I'm ready!' Donna is prepared for life aboard the TARDIS.

And she's opening the boot, hauling out a suitcase, another, a carpet bag, a valise, a trolley-thing, two plastic bags -

She shoves them at the Doctor, piling them up in his arms -

DONNA (CONT'D)
- cos I thought, hot weather, cold weather, no weather, he goes anywhere, I've gotta be prepared -

THE DOCTOR
You've got a hatbox.

DONNA
Planet of the Hats, I'm ready!

She swings the boot shut, *slam* - !

JUMP CUT TO DONNA dumping her armfuls of stuff by the Tardis, THE DOCTOR standing back, still weighed down with luggage; so she's in the Tardis doorway, with him facing her, the opposite of the end of 3.X.

DONNA (CONT'D)
- I don't need injections, do I? Y'know, like when you go to Cambodia, is there any of that? Cos my friend Veena went to Bahrain, and… you're not saying very much.

THE DOCTOR
No! Just, um… travelling with me, you don't think you're, um…

DONNA
Don't think I'm what?

THE DOCTOR
A bit too, sort of…
(oh God)
Old?

DONNA
Oy! How old are you, spaceman?

THE DOCTOR
Nine hundred and three.

DONNA
Well then!
(beat)
How old?!

THE DOCTOR
No, but it's just... It's a funny old life, in the Tardis, it's not...

DONNA
(quiet, crestfallen)
You don't want me.

THE DOCTOR
I'm not saying that.

DONNA
But you asked me.
(silence)
Would you rather be on your own?

THE DOCTOR
...no. Actually, no.
(dumps luggage)
But the last time, with Martha, like I said, it got complicated. And it was all my fault. I mean...
(sighs)
I just want a mate.

DONNA
You just want TO MATE??!

THE DOCTOR
I just want A mate!

DONNA
I'm not mating with you!

THE DOCTOR
A mate, I want, a! Mate!

DONNA
Well, that's a relief! I'm not having any of that nonsense. You're a skinny streak of nothing.

THE DOCTOR
There we are, then. Okay!

DONNA
I can come?

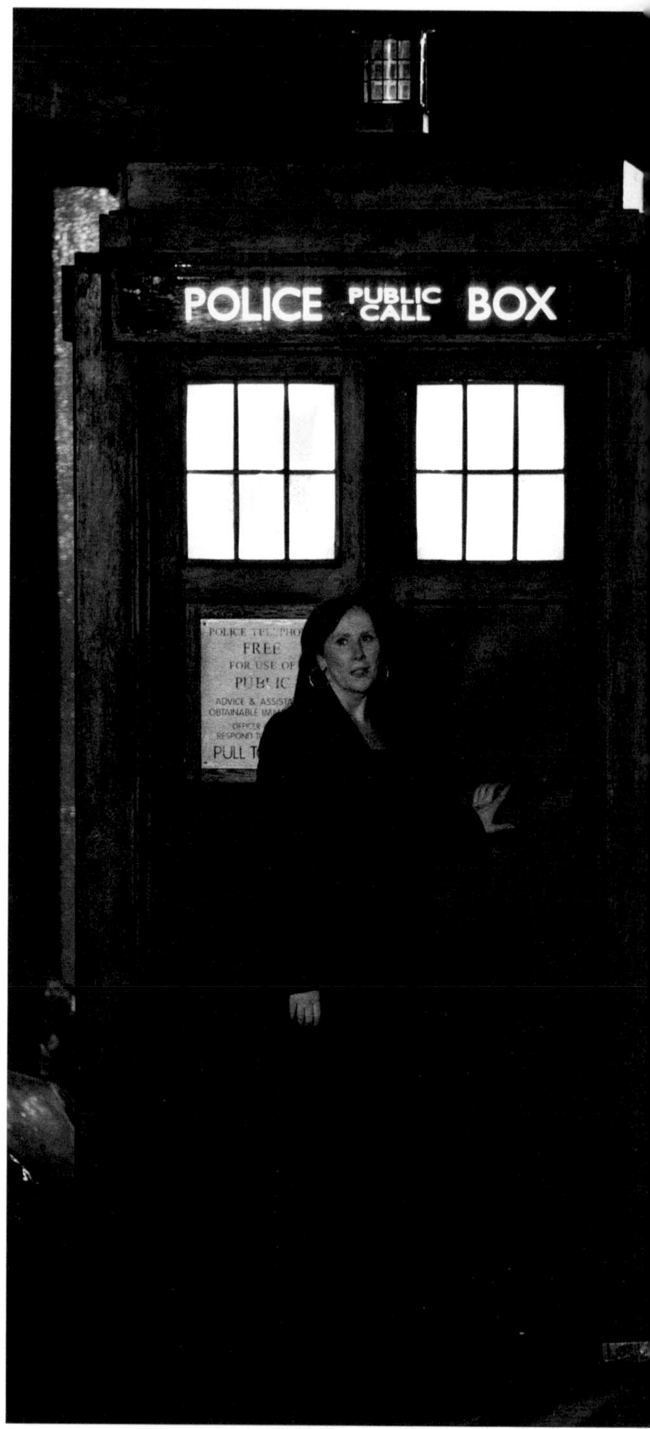

'I can come?' Donna Noble prepares to travel through time and space.

```
                THE DOCTOR
         Yeah. Course you can, yeah.

    She runs towards him, overjoyed -

                DONNA
         Ohhhh, that's just - !
              (no, diverts!)
         Car keys!

                THE DOCTOR
         What?

                DONNA
         I've got my mother's car
         keys! Back in a tick!

    And she's gone. The Doctor stands
    there for a second, looking at the
    luggage, wondering, what the hell…?
    But then crucially, he smiles.
    Starts picking up the bags.
```

Right. Must get back to work. The Special Guest Star is yet to appear…

FROM: RUSSELL T DAVIES TO: BENJAMIN COOK
THURSDAY 6 SEPTEMBER 2007 03:51:18 GMT

RE: IT'S 3AM. ARSE.

I have just typed the stage direction:

```
    It's ROSE TYLER.
```

FROM: BENJAMIN COOK TO: RUSSELL T DAVIES
THURSDAY 6 SEPTEMBER 2007 03:55:55 GMT

RE: IT'S 3AM. ARSE.

What?! She's made the cut?! I thought you didn't reckon on getting Billie back for more than one day's filming. This isn't her one day, is it?!

FROM: RUSSELL T DAVIES TO: BENJAMIN COOK
THURSDAY 6 SEPTEMBER 2007 04:00:24 GMT

IT'S 4AM. ARSE!

No, it's not her only day. But it's costing us. We've had to rearrange the schedule and pay people off. As ever, Julie sorted it all out. So stand by, here comes Rose…

```
    126. EXT. CITY STREET #2 - NIGHT

    DONNA hurrying along, ten-to-the-
    dozen, on her mobile -

    She's closer to the POLICE
    BARRIERS, a POLICE CAR with flashing
    lights, some PEOPLE at the barrier,
    looking on.

                DONNA
         - I know Mum, I saw it,
         little fat people, listen,
         I've gotta go, I'm gonna stay
         with Veena for a bit - yes,
         I know, spaceship! But I've
         still got the car keys -

    There's a litterbin, on a lamppost.

                DONNA (CONT'D)
         Look, there's a bin, on the
         corner of Brook Street and
         Alexander Road, I'll put them
         in there - yes, I said a bin,
         stop complaining, the car's
         just down the road, gotta go,
         really, gotta go, bye -

    And she puts the keys in the bin.

    Thinks. Then runs over to the
    barrier.

    OVER SHOULDER, WOMAN AT BARRIER,
    Donna going to her -

                DONNA (CONT'D)
         Listen, if this woman comes
         along, tall woman, blonde,
         called Sylvia, tell her -
         that bin there, okay? It'll
         make sense. That bin there!

    Donna runs off -
```

'Tell her – that bin there, okay?' Donna explains to a perfect stranger…

... but she's no stranger to us. It's Rose Tyler!

CUT TO REVERSE on the WOMAN at the barrier.

It's ROSE TYLER.

She's just quiet, solemn. Defeated. Turns and walks away.

FX: and Rose gently fades away...

CUT TO:

127. INT. TARDIS - NIGHT

DONNA pokes her head around the half-open door.

DONNA
Off we go then!

THE DOCTOR by the console, plus luggage. As Donna walks up the ramp to join him:

THE DOCTOR
Here it is! The Tardis! Bigger on the inside than it is on the -

DONNA
- oh I know all that bit, frankly you could turn the heating up.

THE DOCTOR
So! You've got the whole wide universe. Where d'you want to go?

DONNA
I know exactly the place.

THE DOCTOR
Which is...?

DONNA
Two and a half miles, that way.

One more scene to go! This is like a live transmission.

FROM: BENJAMIN COOK TO: RUSSELL T DAVIES
THURSDAY 6 SEPTEMBER 2007 04:03:02 GMT

RE: IT'S 4AM. ARSE!

A live transmission? Perhaps Graham Norton will bleed into our e-mails.[7] I can't go to bed now – it's the lethal cocktail of red wine, a speech by Nicola Shindler, and Rose Tyler. For God's sake, send, send, send!

7 In some regions, the first few minutes of the original BBC One broadcast of *Doctor Who* 1.1 were marred by the accidental mixing of several seconds of off-air sound from Graham Norton hosting *Strictly Dance Fever*.

Geoff spots Donna's blue box. Illustration by Russell T Davies.

FROM: RUSSELL T DAVIES TO: BENJAMIN COOK
THURSDAY 6 SEPTEMBER 2007 04:11:04 GMT

RE: IT'S 4AM. ARSE!

Graham Norton? Sound bleed? Oy, enough of that language!

Ahh, I just typed the last line. It's made me cry. How pathetic.

128. EXT. HILLSIDE - NIGHT

WIDE SHOT, GEOFF on his lonely mount.

He's pottering about with the TELESCOPE. Happy. A sip of tea. Gene Pitney on the earphones.

Then he looks through the eyepiece, focusing it…

Stops. Eh?! Looks up, without the telescope. But…?

Looks back through the eyepiece.

And then he's all excited!

FX: GEOFF'S POV. The night sky, with a LITTLE BLUE BOX spinning across the sky.

He calls off, as though she might come running -

GEOFF
But… Donna! Donna! It's the flying blue box!!

Looks back through the eyepiece.

Stunned. Whispers.

GEOFF (CONT'D)
Whaaaat…?

HIS POV: CLOSER on the TARDIS. DONNA standing in the doorway. Waving at him! Behind her, THE DOCTOR, and he gives a little wave, too.

GEOFF (CONT'D)
But that's… that's…

And he abandons the telescope. Waves up at the sky! With a great big *yahoo!*

FX: THE TARDIS spins away into space…

HIGH SHOT: on Geoff, on his little hillside, in the middle of the night, waving up at the sky and whooping with joy.

END OF EPISODE 4.1

DONE! All 58 pages. Ahh, I'm glad you were here. That was nice.

Three more scripts to go before I can take a holiday. No, four. Maybe five. Oh bollocks.

Greetings from
ROME
IANCARLO GASPONI

CHAPTER TEN

STILL FIGHTING IT

In which tight white pants are all the rage in Rome, the producer of *Doctor Who* makes a scene in a restaurant, and Steven Moffat says yes

FROM: BENJAMIN COOK TO: RUSSELL T DAVIES
THURSDAY 6 SEPTEMBER 2007 22:17:36 GMT

SO...

How did the Tone Meeting go? What does everyone think of the script? How shattered have you been today? I hope you're all right.

FROM: RUSSELL T DAVIES TO: BENJAMIN COOK
THURSDAY 6 SEPTEMBER 2007 23:18:24 GMT

RE: SO...

I'm fine. Knackered. Of course, at this time of night, I begin to wake up again. I've still got to read Helen Raynor's Sontaran two-parter tonight, which I'll have to start rewriting on Monday. We're going to cast Christopher Ryan (Mike from *The Young Ones*!) as the Chief Sontaran. And all the Sontaran extras will be the same height, because they're all really short and dumpy and angry. Sontarans *are* trolls. It makes sense.

The 4.1 script went down well, I think. Well, Julie said that she loved it, and so did Phil, though maybe they're just glad to see a script. But a Tone Meeting isn't really the time or place for opinions, just hard facts. (We'll have a proper script session soon, of course.) My God, that team is extraordinary. That script is impossible. The cradle sequence especially. Any other production team would chuck that out, but they just set about it, breaking it down, shot after shot, battling, wrestling, finding the right way to do it. It's a thousand times more difficult than it first seems, what with the Health and Safety implications. And all sorts of things you don't think of, like... with the cradle hanging vertically, plus a cable hanging down, which Donna is holding on to, the sheer height of that is about 30 feet, beyond anything our green-screen studio can manage. Or anyone's studio! Still, they battled on. Fighting. The best team in the world. I worry that there's going to come a nasty moment, when all the costs are added up. Big decisions to come, I fear.

As for me, I'll read the script back tomorrow night, in Manchester. But I think I love it. It feels good. I'm pleased that it's done. That feels miraculous. Most of all, though, I'm bothered by those two guards; the way that they get electrocuted in the doorway is so lame. I hate that scene. But I'm stuck with them. I tried everything in my head. I mean, Miss Foster needs two guards or she'd look weak. (In one of those late-night drafts that I sent you, I upped it to eight guards, which I then got rid of the next day, because two were hard enough to deal with!) I suppose they could stay with Miss Foster and be beamed up with her, but then they'd have to fall to their deaths with her, and that's just not as good. It's such a great image, Miss Foster floating up with her children, all on her own. Two extras would spoil it. Plus, if they're with Miss Foster, that means she never sent them to go and stop the Doctor, which is a bit stupid. She must *try* to stop him. But what else to do? Trap them in a lift? I've done a million lift scenes. And no soldier would be so daft as to use a lift in any emergency. Could the Doctor lock the stairwells, so they're stuck inside? Equally lame. Maybe Donna could find a way to knock them unconscious? Nah, that's rubbish. Quite apart from the fact that I can't think of a way for her to do that, I really don't like that sort of physical violence from the companion. Four years in, and I've rarely resorted to the Doctor or companion having to clobber someone unconscious. I'm sort of proud of that, though it does write me into corners. When trapped with a guard, I much prefer to write some sort of distraction – then run! Idiots punch. And punches can kill. Oh, listen to me.

That's why I was writing till gone 4am. I could work out everything else, but I've two irrelevant bloody security guards going round and round and round in my head. I woke up today, worrying about them. I've tried to cover it with fluffy dialogue, tried to make it look inbuilt in the plot; the Doctor can only electrocute them from a distance because Miss Foster has mysteriously 'wired up' the building. Why's she done that? Turns out, she's turned it into a 'Levitation Post'. Which is bollocks. There's a bloody big spaceship above, perfectly capable of beaming up everyone, like spaceships do. But all that dialogue is there to excuse the electrocuting-the-guards moment, a sure sign that something has gone wrong with the plot. Adipose, Stacy, capsules, cradles, levitation… and the one thing that's bugging me is the sodding security guards! It's the one bit that I don't *believe*.

Also, I'm still wondering about a couple of lines that I cut, to get 59 pages to 58: at one point, as the whole of London heads towards Emergency Parthenogenesis and everyone's clothes are writhing, Donna said, 'Do they have to be wearing their pendants?' The Doctor said no – having introduced the pendant as a trigger, it's unlikely that anyone would actually wear such a cheap and rubbish free gift. Well, maybe Suzette. 'They only have to touch the capsule once,' explained the Doctor, 'and it biotunes into them.' Nonsense, but sort of believable nonsense. And yet, in the middle of a crisis, with all those Adipose about to burst out of Roger and Suzette and Nice Man and 497 others… who gives a damn about those dull explanatory speeches? It's that old problem: how much do you explain to the audience, when the characters wouldn't waste time chatting about it? So, I'm still wondering about that. (Did you wonder about it?)

Miss Foster's guards prepare to be electrocuted, lamely.

Other than that – yes, I'm happy. I particularly love the litterbin. The fact that Donna would leave her mother's car keys in a bin, because she's rushing off to travel in time and space (and must worry that the Doctor will take off without her), is so mad that it's real! I absolutely believe the silliness of that scene. The daft things that people do.

FROM: BENJAMIN COOK TO: RUSSELL T DAVIES
FRIDAY 7 SEPTEMBER 2007 18.47.34 GMT

RE: SO...

I didn't wonder about the missing info-dump speech, but I did wonder whether you'd really get three people – Suzette, Nice Man and Young Woman – out of the 500 across London, all in the same wine bar at the same time. Bit of a coincidence.

FROM: RUSSELL T DAVIES TO: BENJAMIN COOK
MONDAY 10 SEPTEMBER 2007 16:56:14 GMT

RE: SO...

Sorry for being a bit quiet. I've spent three days going *clomp*. Those scripts don't half knacker you. My poor boyfriend, all he gets out of me on a weekend home is *clomp*. Still, I felt guilty, so I just went and bought him a car. Oh, but he so deserves it. If only for putting up with me and all this *Doctor Who* nonsense.

Phil is texting from Rome! How exciting. When do the rest of you get out there?

FROM: BENJAMIN COOK TO: RUSSELL T DAVIES
MONDAY 10 SEPTEMBER 2007 21:57:08 GMT

RE: SO...

I'm off to Rome on Tuesday. I hope the hotel has internet access.

FROM: RUSSELL T DAVIES TO: BENJAMIN COOK
TUESDAY 11 SEPTEMBER 2007 23:49:27 GMT

RE: SO...

It'd better have internet access. I want Roman Scandal!

I'm supposed to start rewriting the Sontaran episodes this week, but actually Helen deserves another crack at 4.4. Anyway, I'm still going *clomp*, so to hell with it.

Text message from: Ben
Sent: 13-Sep-2007 09:08
'And... action!' Filming in Rome has begun. It's looking fantastic. There's a mule on set, and chickens, and I'm standing on a replica Roman toilet to get a good view.

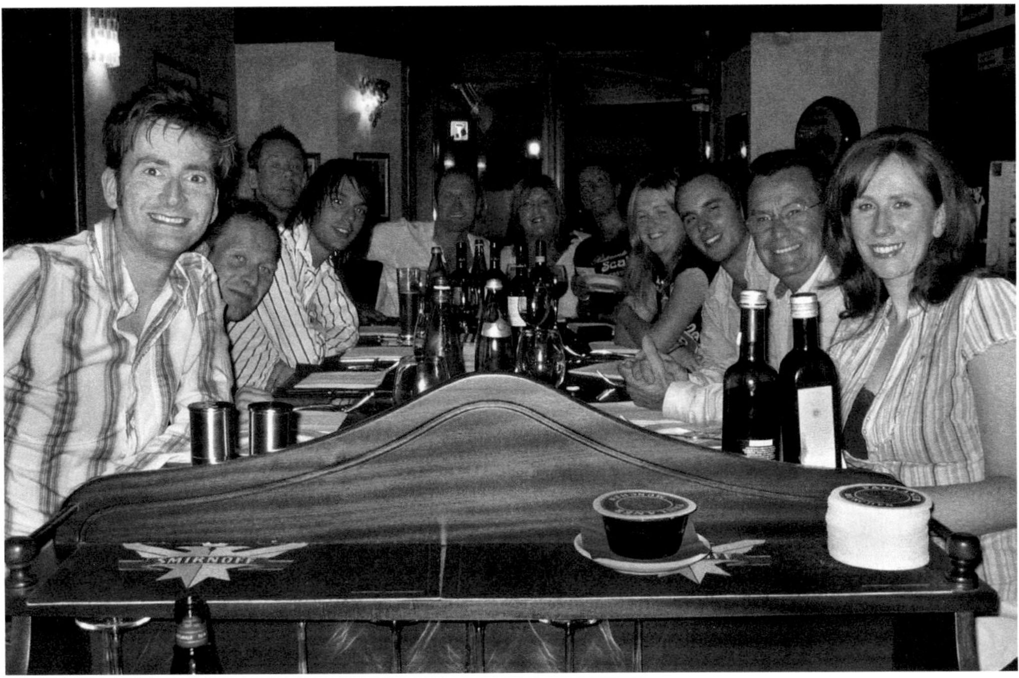

The cast and crew of *The Fires of Pompeii* enjoy the Italian nightlife. L–R: David Tennant, Colin Teague, Steve Smith, Benjamin Cook, Phil Collinson, Tracie Simpson, an Italian waitress (!), Sarah Davies, Andy Newbery, Ernie Vincze and Catherine Tate.

Text message from: Russell
Sent: 13-Sep-2007 09:46
A mule! Ha ha ha, how brilliant. Thanks for letting me know. Big kiss to Francois Pandolfo. In a strictly professional way.

Text message from: Russell
Sent: 13-Sep-2007 23:03
Hope all went well at Cinecittà today. It's very odd sitting here while everyone's abroad. I feel like the caretaker of a school.

Text message from: Ben
Sent: 13-Sep-2007 23:22
Filming went well. We're all on a night out in Rome. It's like St Trinian's on tour! Everyone has worked so hard today. How are things in the UK?

Text message from: Russell
Sent: 13-Sep-2007 23:43
It's all go here. We've just told Burn and Naoko that they won't be in the third series of *Torchwood*, because we're killing off Owen and Tosh. Madness in two countries simultaneously.

Text message from: Ben
Sent: 14-Sep-2007 00:24
There's a rat in our restaurant. Phil is standing on the table. The producer of *Doctor Who*! Oh, now he's asking for a discount. He says it's taken two years off his life.

Text message from: Russell
Sent: 14-Sep-2007 00:31
Tell him that makes him 41. That'll make him cross. Hey, if I were in a restaurant, scared of a rat, I'd cling to... ooh, Francois maybe?

Text message from: Ben
Sent: 14-Sep-2007 00:35
I'll suggest it to Phil.

Text message from: Russell
Sent: 14-Sep-2007 13:49
According to The Mill's list, we're 150 FX days over on 4.1. I have to suggest cuts. Damn.

Text message from: Ben
Sent: 15-Sep-2007 00:50
It's the night-shoot at Cinecittà! Is Francois' tunic supposed to be so short?

Text message from: Russell
Sent: 15-Sep-2007 00:55
We spent a long time MAKING Louise Page shorten it. Oh, the power!

Text message from: Ben
Sent: 15-Sep-2007 01:02
Colin Teague is worried about the shot of Francois climbing through the window of Lucius' quarters. Um – we'll see everything! Have you done this on purpose? Louise is not happy. She's insisting that Francois wears underwear.

Producer Phil Collinson leaps athletically onto a table because of (inset) a deadly, slavering Roman rat! Eeeek!

The night shoot for *The Fires of Pompeii* at Rome's legendary Cinecittà Studios.

Text message from: Russell
Sent: 15-Sep-2007 01:09
Exactly as I planned. Who d'you think wrote the climbing-through-the-window scene? Ha ha ha. I'm sure the Pyroviles invented tight white pants. I'll issue a pink page to that effect.

FROM: RUSSELL T DAVIES TO: BENJAMIN COOK
TUESDAY 18 SEPTEMBER 2007 23:50:05 GMT

ROMAN HOLIDAY

Are you back from Rome? The rushes are amazing. Oh, but here's tonight's script problem (this one has me stumped)… the one thing that we can't afford to shoot on 4.1 is the Doctor and Donna and Miss Foster having their conversation on the rooftop, with the Doctor and Donna already in the stationary cradle. As soon as the cradle falls, we're fine, bizarrely. We can afford the stunt, the Adipose, the End Of The Sodding World, but not that confrontation scene. (The reasons are too dull to go into. It involves the number of nights – just one, apparently – for which we can afford a crane and an actual cradle, as opposed to the cradle that we'll build in the studio for the stunt sequence against green screen.) Of all the things that I expected to be cut (which included the entire cradle sequence), I never expected that. The Doctor's whole confrontation with the enemy! Where the plot is explained! Bollocks.

Francois Pandolfo in the shortest toga known to man.

So… they escape to the roof, Miss Foster chasing, cut around the actual moment of descent to avoid the precise mechanism, so the Doctor and Donna are already heading down when Miss Foster nixes the equipment, and then we go into the stunt sequence as written, minimal changes. But then the Doctor and Donna run through the building, meet Miss Foster, and have that pivotal conversation… in a corridor? Or on a stairwell? That's a very flat, lame setting compared to a rooftop at night. It's just not good enough. And then what? The Doctor and Donna can't just run away. The Doctor would have to find some clever way to outfox Miss Foster and the guards, but then that raises the question: why didn't the Doctor do that in the first place, instead of trying to escape via the cradle? So, um…

FROM: BENJAMIN COOK TO: RUSSELL T DAVIES
WEDNESDAY 19 SEPTEMBER 2007 01:46:33 GMT

RE: ROMAN HOLIDAY

The rooftop dilemma! Don't you usually get around these things by having the Doctor talk to the villain over intercoms or TV screens?

FROM: RUSSELL T DAVIES TO: BENJAMIN COOK
WEDNESDAY 19 SEPTEMBER 2007 02:02:16 GMT

RE: ROMAN HOLIDAY

I just read the script again. I suppose the Doctor and Donna could escape from the cradle sequence into the building, and meet Miss Foster and the guards for the vital dialogue in the darkened sales-cubicles room. That's quite a good setting. Bit of space. Better than a corridor. In some ways, the heart of Miss Foster's empire.

And how to escape? It just struck me: the Doctor has a sonic screwdriver *and* a sonic pen. What happens when you hold two sonic devices together? I'll tell you what. You get wibbly-wobbly vibrations and guards clutch their ears for long enough to enable you to escape! That's what happens, because I say so. I hate using the sonic screwdriver as a solution, but that's what comes of making this an action-adventure series with a hero who doesn't carry a gun. Small price to pay. The episode has gone to great lengths to give the Doctor two sonic devices at the same time, so it'll look like I planned it all along.

FROM: RUSSELL T DAVIES TO: BENJAMIN COOK
THURSDAY 20 SEPTEMBER 2007 02:23:59 GMT

RE: ROMAN HOLIDAY

How's this? After the cradle sequence, Scene 84 is now the Doctor and Donna meeting Miss Foster in the sales cubicles (instead of earlier on the rooftop)...

```
84. INT. SALES CUBICLES - NIGHT

THE DOCTOR & DONNA burst through,
from one end -

Stop dead. As MISS FOSTER strides
through from the other end of the
room, both SECURITY GUARDS hoisting
up guns. A standoff; good distance
between the two parties.

            MISS FOSTER
Well, then. At last.

            THE DOCTOR
Evening.

               DONNA
Hello.

            THE DOCTOR
Nice to meet you. I'm the
Doctor.

               DONNA
And I'm Donna.

            MISS FOSTER
Partners in crime. And
evidently offworlders,
judging by your sonic
technology.

            THE DOCTOR
Oh! I've still got -
         (holds up)
Your sonic pen. Nice! I like
it. Sleek, it's kind of...
sleek.

               DONNA
Definitely sleek.

            THE DOCTOR
And if you were to sign your
real name, that would be...?

            MISS FOSTER
Matron Cofelia, of the
Five-Straighten Classabindi
Nursery Fleet, Intergalactic
Class.

            THE DOCTOR
A wet nurse. Using Humans as
surrogates.

            MISS FOSTER
I've been subcontracted by
the Adiposian First Family,
to sire a new generation,
after their breeding planet
was lost.

            THE DOCTOR
What d'you mean, lost, how
d'you lose a planet?

            MISS FOSTER
The politics are none of my
concern. I'm just employed,
by the parents, to take care
of the children.
```

'D'you know what happens if you hold two identical sonic devices against each other?'

DONNA
What, like an outer space Supernanny?

MISS FOSTER
If you like.

DONNA
So those little things, they're made out of fat, yeah? But that woman last night, Stacy Harris, there was nothing left of her.

MISS FOSTER
In a crisis, the Adipose can absorb bone and hair and internal organs. Though it does make them a little bit sick, the poor things.

DONNA
What about poor Stacy?!

THE DOCTOR
Seeding a Level Five planet is against galactic law.

MISS FOSTER
Are you threatening me?

THE DOCTOR
I'm trying to help you, Matron. This is your one chance. Because if you don't call this off… then I'll have to stop you.

MISS FOSTER
I hardly think you can stop bullets.

Both Guards raise guns, the click of safety catches.

THE DOCTOR
Oh, but hold on, one more thing! Before dying! D'you know what happens if you hold two identical sonic devices against each other?

MISS FOSTER
No.

THE DOCTOR
Nor me. Let's find out!

And with a huge grin, he holds SONIC PEN against SONIC SCREWDRIVER, whirrs!

CAMERA SHAKE, whole room VIBRATING! Miss Foster & Guards clutch their ears, in pain - Guards dropping guns -

Donna holding her ears, screeching, ow!

PRAC FX: GLASS WINDOW SHATTERS!

The Doctor holding on, juddering, actually loving this!

Miss Foster falls to her knees, in agony -

Donna gives the Doctor a shove -

DONNA
Come on!

Noise stops dead, as the Doctor & Donna leg it out -

Miss Foster recovering, furious. On WRISTWATCH-COMMS:

MISS FOSTER
Tell the Adiposians, the birthplan has been advanced. We're going into premature labour.

And she strides out, Guards following -

FROM: RUSSELL T DAVIES TO: BENJAMIN COOK
FRIDAY 21 SEPTEMBER 2007 23:41:24 GMT

LATEST 4.1

We saw the half-finished FX on 4.X today. The *Titanic* sailing over Buckingham Palace is so brilliant, we stood up and clapped! Amazing. We also realised, for the first time, that since the BBC's trouble with the Queen, it's probably a very good thing that we didn't trash the Palace after all. Phew.

Also, I've been tweaking 4.1 today, to lose some more FX days and in the light of notes from Julie and… well, YOU, actually! One of them is your note. When you wondered about the coincidence of so many of the 500 victims being in such close proximity, I realised that I'd made it 500 because initially I'd planned to kill them all, have them all do a Stacy rip-apart, before I decided that was just gruesome and undeserved. And expensive. (I'd thought 500 was a reasonable massacre!) Now they don't die, though, so I've upped it to 10,000 people, making the threat much bigger. So that little wonder of yours was brilliant. Thank you.

FROM: BENJAMIN COOK TO: RUSSELL T DAVIES
SATURDAY 22 SEPTEMBER 2007 00:57:00 GMT

RE: LATEST 4.1

Now, *that's* got to be worth ten per cent?

FROM: RUSSELL T DAVIES TO: BENJAMIN COOK
SATURDAY 22 SEPTEMBER 2007 01:03:52 GMT

RE: LATEST 4.1

Ha ha ha. No.

FROM: RUSSELL T DAVIES TO: BENJAMIN COOK
SATURDAY 22 SEPTEMBER 2007 13:26:21 GMT

RE: LATEST 4.1

I'm so behind with the 4.4 rewrites. I quite like what I'm thinking: lovely stuff with Donna returning home, having travelled in time and space; the Doctor's new attitude to UNIT (he doesn't like them – men with guns – he wouldn't); the Doctor knocking out a Sontaran with a tennis ball! It all feels good, but it's a lot of work.

Also, I forgot to tell you, I walked to Tesco yesterday, thinking about Gwen and Ianto defending the Torchwood Hub from advancing Daleks in 4.12! Daleks in the Hub! I was almost hyperventilating with excitement.

FROM: BENJAMIN COOK TO: RUSSELL T DAVIES
MONDAY 24 SEPTEMBER 2007 18:04:40 GMT

SARAH JANE

I've just seen Lis Sladen on the CBBC channel, being interviewed by a cactus.

FROM: RUSSELL T DAVIES TO: BENJAMIN COOK
MONDAY 24 SEPTEMBER 2007 18:26:40 GMT

RE: SARAH JANE

A Spanish cactus at that. Or was it Mexican? What happened to good-looking CBBC presenters?

Tonight, Jane Tranter and Julie Gardner are having dinner with Steven Moffat. The future starts here! Mind

The Doctor meets his old enemies the Sontarans once again in 4.4 *The Sontaran Stratagem*.

you, what if he says no? (He won't actually give an answer tonight. Months of negotiations, etc.) But Christ alive, what happens then? I can't even bear to think about it.

FROM: BENJAMIN COOK TO: RUSSELL T DAVIES
MONDAY 24 SEPTEMBER 2007 18:36:15 GMT

RE: SARAH JANE

Of course he won't say no. He won't, will he? He'll say yes. Who'd say no? It's the best job in the world.

FROM: RUSSELL T DAVIES TO: BENJAMIN COOK
MONDAY 24 SEPTEMBER 2007 19:03:04 GMT

RE: SARAH JANE

He might say no. I wonder. For starters, he's got kids and a wife. He works with Hartswood, which is practically his company. And now that he's writing stuff like *Tintin* for Spielberg, his agent might clobber him if he goes and does a TV show.[1] Plus, if someone else takes over from me, they'd be begging scripts off Steven anyway, so he'd still get to write *Doctor Who*. All the fun, none of the pain.

FROM: RUSSELL T DAVIES TO: BENJAMIN COOK
WEDNESDAY 26 SEPTEMBER 2007 00:54:36 GMT

RE: SARAH JANE

I just got a midnight e-mail from A. N. Other Writer. Having trouble with 'the basic linear causality' of an episode. *Basic linear causality?!* Do you see the crap that writers talk? Really, though, if you think of a script in terms like that, how the hell are you ever going to get anything written?

Text message from: Russell
Sent: 27-Sep-2007 09:05
Guess who we've got for Miss Foster? Sarah Lancashire!

Text message from: Ben
Sent: 27-Sep-2007 09:15
Brilliant casting! That's going to be one sexy mother foster!

1 Moffatt is scripting *Tintin* for directors Steven Spielberg and Peter Jackson. Filming is due to begin in September 2008.

FROM: RUSSELL T DAVIES TO: BENJAMIN COOK
THURSDAY 27 SEPTEMBER 2007 20:53:31 GMT

4.4 COMPLETED!

Another script done! Yes, I've finished 4.4. It's like a bloody production line. Well, it *is* a production line.

I admitted to Julie today that Tom MacRae's Episode 8 simply isn't right. Tom's script is good, and we could make it great, but I don't think it can ever be great enough. It's misconceived. This is entirely my fault: I don't like the concepts I gave him, and I don't like the overall tone of both 4.7 and 4.8 being comparatively light, fun episodes. Two in a row. I'm left with the prospect of having to write a replacement script myself. But I've no time. I'd have about three days! Even if I could do it in three days, I'd lose more time than that – for recovery. (Julie said today, 'This is the only job in writing where you actually talk about having Recovery Days!') We're going to wait a week, to get 4.5 dealt with, and then decide what to do about 4.8…

FROM: RUSSELL T DAVIES TO: BENJAMIN COOK
FRIDAY 28 SEPTEMBER 2007 16:11:31 GMT

THE MOFF

Steven just e-mailed me. He admitted, in an unguarded moment, that YES, HE'S GOING TO DO *DOCTOR WHO*! So that's exciting.

FROM: BENJAMIN COOK TO: RUSSELL T DAVIES
FRIDAY 28 SEPTEMBER 2007 16:21:45 GMT

RE: THE MOFF

That's great news. He'll be brilliant. As of tonight, I shall start e-mailing Steven Moffat instead. Goodbye, Russell.

FROM: RUSSELL T DAVIES TO: BENJAMIN COOK
FRIDAY 28 SEPTEMBER 2007 16:30:37 GMT

RE: THE MOFF

Have you read Steven's *Children in Need* script?[2] It's a hoot and very lovely. Next Sunday, 7 October, that's when they're shooting it at Upper Boat. Peter Davison

2 Moffatt wrote *Time Crash*, an eight-minute mini-episode of *Doctor Who*, for the BBC's *Children in Need* telethon. Broadcast in November 2007, it depicted an encounter between the Tenth Doctor and his former, fifth incarnation, played by Peter Davison.

Day! Poor Louise Page, trying to find a pair of striped trousers like the Fifth Doctor's! Did they *ever* make trousers like that?

FROM: RUSSELL T DAVIES TO: BENJAMIN COOK
FRIDAY 5 OCTOBER 2007 11:32:10 GMT

PETER FINCHAM'S ARSE

Terrible rumours flying around the BBC right now. It looks like Peter Fincham is resigning any minute – along with his Head of Press, Jane Fletcher, who's done more to support *Doctor Who* than I can ever tell you. Wonderful woman. All over this stupid bloody Queen business! It makes me sick. Further reports to follow…

Sorry for my silence over the last week. I'm snowed under like you will not believe. 4.5 is requiring a lot of work. A Tone Meeting on Monday! Filming any day now! Bloody hell. It's doing my head in. I'll tell you what's really crippling me: all my emergency solutions end up nicking stuff from what I've planned for 4.12/4.13. I'm robbing my own scripts to make these ones work. That's pissing me off profoundly.

Oh, and I've submitted the absolute final draft of 4.1, with post-read-through changes – a bit more explanation of the capsules and a couple of lines rephrased to sound more elegant. Also, your note on the scale of Miss Foster's scheme went further (see, you were right), so it's gone from 500 people, to 10,000, and now it's a million!

FROM: BENJAMIN COOK TO: RUSSELL T DAVIES
FRIDAY 5 OCTOBER 2007 21:32:17 GMT

RE: PETER FINCHAM'S ARSE

'BBC ONE BOSS QUITS OVER QUEEN ROW!' say the news reports.

So it's happened. This is madness.

FROM: RUSSELL T DAVIES TO: BENJAMIN COOK
SATURDAY 6 OCTOBER 2007 00:14:06 GMT

RE: PETER FINCHAM'S ARSE

I swear, I'd resign from this stupid organisation. Except I love *Doctor Who*, so what would be the point? The loss of Jane Fletcher is scandalous. Never has a woman worked so hard. She was completely wonderful. Oh, it makes my blood boil.

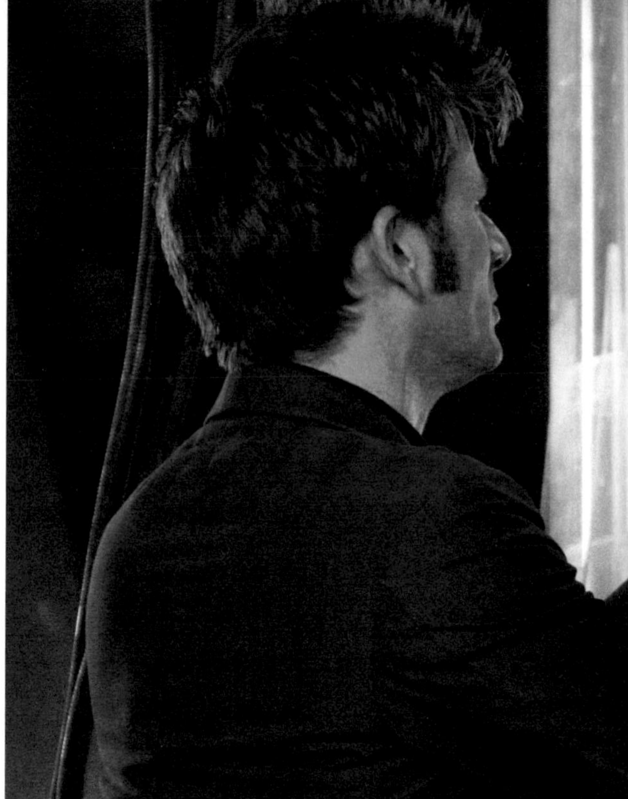

The Tenth Doctor (David Tennant) meets the Fifth Doctor (Peter Davison) in Steven Moffat's *Children in Need* mini-episode *Time Crash*.

Text message from: Russell
Sent: 7-Oct-2007 11:10
Davison Day! And I'm sat in the flat rewriting the bloody Sontarans. Bah! Have fun.

Text message from: Ben
Sent: 7-Oct-2007 11:22
You're not coming?! Your inner fanboy must be screaming a lament. Don't be daft. You've got to pop in. History in the making!

Text message from: Russell
Sent: 7-Oct-2007 11:45
If the universe implodes because two Doctors meet, at least I'll be a distance away. Oh, maybe I'll come along for a bit this afternoon.

FROM: RUSSELL T DAVIES TO: BENJAMIN COOK
MONDAY 8 OCTOBER 2007 04:33:42 GMT

FINISHED 4.5!

I've finished 4.5! That's 24 pages today! Plus a visit to Upper Boat! I'm exhausted. And it's the bleedin' Tone Meeting in a few hours. But I really did love today,

in studio. Sorry I had to leave before the end. I was quite sad for a bit afterwards, thinking how good Peter Davison looked. Proper lighting. Proper set. Brilliant dialogue. He should have been like that in the '80s. Never was.

If I keep up this rate of work, I could find the time to replace Tom MacRae's 4.8 with a completely new episode. It means writing two episodes, 4.8 and 4.11, in two weeks – yikes – but it can be done. Downside: it might kill me. Sooner or later, at this rate of work, a kidney is going to burst or something. Still. You can buy kidneys. I keep remembering that 4.8 is going to be our fiftieth episode. (Can you believe it? I still think the world has gone mad. For four years now. Four good years.) Tom's script is nice, it's clever, it's funny, but the truth is we can be more adventurous. Shame, to have an ordinary fiftieth episode, even if we're the only ones aware of the numbers.

FROM: BENJAMIN COOK TO: RUSSELL T DAVIES
MONDAY 8 OCTOBER 2007 12:59:42 GMT

RE: FINISHED 4.5!

>>Downside: it might kill me.<<

Upside: it might not.

How was the 4.4/4.5 Tone Meeting?

FROM: RUSSELL T DAVIES TO: BENJAMIN COOK
MONDAY 8 OCTOBER 2007 22:19:08 GMT

RE: FINISHED 4.5!

It might not? Yes, I like that. The thing is, it really could. Writing 24 pages yesterday took me 80 cigarettes. I will be able to say, honestly, that the Sontarans killed me.

The Tone Meeting was good, but I was so tired. I got a bit tetchy. Actually, I got a bit tetchy with good reason. One of the funny things about rewrites is, a lot of people aren't very good at deleting the old drafts from their heads. That's a particular problem when they're the producer or director! It's a really subtle, insidious thing that creeps in and makes scripts, or the production of scripts, indistinct. It drives me bananas when people start quoting from old drafts, in which the Sontarans had different motivations. It's more pernicious when it creeps into tiny, important details of character and backstory. Clarity and definition can go out of the window. That sort of creep and bleed is the reason – no, one of the reasons – why so much drama is neither here nor there. No definition. Drafts upon drafts. Muddling along.

Worth it in the end, though. For all its improvised, battling, freefall blundering, I think 4.5 is a rather marvellous episode. Best of all, it ends with a fantastic Doctor scene: that final confrontation with the Sontarans on their spaceship. I think that's bloody excellent. It's really hard to find new things for the Doctor, especially new climaxes, so I'm really chuffed with that. Hoo-bloody-ray.

FROM: BENJAMIN COOK TO: RUSSELL T DAVIES
TUESDAY 9 OCTOBER 2007 00:36:25 GMT

RE: FINISHED 4.5!

But haven't *we* both found it difficult to delete old drafts from our heads? Or you wouldn't have got tongue-tied when you bumped into [Miss X] in Oxford Street back in March, because you still had Penny-as-played-by-[Miss X] in your mind. And neither of us can read 4.1 without a certain pang when Penny pops up. That said, there's a difference, I know, between what we natter about in these e-mails and what's required from folk at Tone Meetings. When you're wearing your writer's hat (I imagine it's a beret, with pink tassels), old and new drafts are fluctuating in the quantum state of Maybe. However, in your executive producer's hat (a pith helmet, I reckon, with solar panels that power a miniature fan to keep you cool), you need to be more disciplined. Is that true? At this stage in production, is it easy enough to divorce your role as writer from your role as executive producer?

FROM: RUSSELL T DAVIES TO: BENJAMIN COOK
TUESDAY 9 OCTOBER 2007 22:00:36 GMT

RE: FINISHED 4.5!

I didn't mean that writers should delete old drafts from their minds; just producers and directors and anyone on the floor, hands-on making it. Maybe that sounds hypocritical, because I know it's easier said than done, but they have to concentrate on what they're making now, without confusing it.

I do find it easy to divorce my two roles. With my producer's hat on (it's lemon), if a scene becomes impossible or expensive or is simply dropped on the day because they ran out of time, then I can score a great big line through it. Even if I loved it. I won't moan or bleat or feel any substantial regret. It's something that writers in this country need to be trained in, like in the US. We still cling to that notion of the writer-eccentric (the slippers, the attic, the cardigan), which is a bloody nightmare on set. That sort of writer kicks up a fuss if a character is wearing a white shirt instead of a blue one. That sort of writer shouldn't be allowed near filming. Mind you, that writer-eccentric does allow you to get away with murder. Writers are allowed, professionally, to be stroppy and weird and angry and demanding and petulant and oversexed and drunk. As long as your writing is good, that behaviour is sort of revered. Even expected. We're allowed to misbehave, because it's seen as creative, like it's part of the job. Rubbish!

So many writers get credited as execs these days, because that's the goal, career-wise, for a writer. Half of them – most of them – don't know what exec'ing actually is, and couldn't do it, and don't want to. It cheapens the title. A while ago, a writer-friend of mine, a powerful writer – who shall remain nameless – was demanding an exec credit on a big ITV show of his, so he phoned me up, asking what jobs I did to earn that credit. I listed them all: casting actors, working with directors, production meetings with heads of department, rushes, Edits, Dubs, etc. He said, 'I don't do any of that.' I said, 'Sod off, then!' But he got his exec credit anyway, without taking on any of those duties. That's what pisses me off.

FROM: RUSSELL T DAVIES TO: BENJAMIN COOK
WEDNESDAY 10 OCTOBER 2007 12:51:53 GMT

MORE WORK, LESS MAYBE

I must update you on the Maybe, although it feels wrong calling it that now. 'Maybe' was nice and mystical back in February, when I was planning, not writing. Now I think the word is just 'Work'. It can't fluctuate so much any more. I have to make choices. Fix it. Write it.

One terrible thing is happening – and I can't stop it bleeding into my thoughts. Howard Attfield, who plays Donna's dad, has been ill. As you know, he's had cancer and chemo. The agent told us about it, but said that Howard was more than happy to do Series Four. And already I'm using that, in the story. That sounds terrible, but it's what happens; I start weaving it in. That, I think, has been part of the Donna and Geoff closeness that's crept into their scenes together in 4.1 and 4.4/4.5. (Look at me, absolving myself of blame by saying 'crept into', giving it a life of its own!) But now that we've started shooting 4.1 and Howard is on set… blimey, he's ill. He's not had chemotherapy; he's *having* it. Phil was talking to him about his scenes in 4.4/4.5, and Howard

Howard Attfield as Geoff Noble cheers Donna off on her adventures in the TARDIS. From the original version of 4.1 *Partners in Crime*.

said, lightly, 'That's if I'm still here.' He's dying. That lovely man is dying. And there it is feeding back into the scripts and onto screen. It can't not. That scene of Donna and Geoff on the hillside is utterly exquisite. Wonderfully shot. Beautifully acted by Catherine and Howard. Each draft and redraft over every little line of that scene was so worth it. It's one of best scenes that we've ever shot. But if you add this knowledge about Howard to what you're watching… well, it's heartbreaking. I watched the rushes and cried.

To be blunt: how do we plan ahead? What do we do? Talk about the Maybe being in a state of flux! I don't know what to do. Howard is supposed to be in 4.11 and 4.12/4.13, but… ouch. I'm writing his illness into the story (can I do that? Should I?), that Donna has to face the death of her father. That she always was. That she went looking for the Doctor on the day that Geoff was diagnosed. That she's running away – and will, one day, have to walk back and face it. And then Donna Noble grows up.

I can't talk about this too much more. I'm sorry, Ben. It feels obscene. It feels fascinating. It's sort of *too* fascinating. Does that make sense?

Elsewhere, this mysterious 4.8 that I haven't got time for has been building in my head. It had taken a fair old shape, when I happened to see *Jeepers Creepers 2* on ITV the other night… and it was exactly what I had in mind. Everyone trapped on a bus, with a monster outside. They stole my idea! Five years ago! Those time-travelling Hollywood bastards. My version is set on an alien planet. Donna is busy moonbathing, so the Doctor goes off on a tourist trip, in a tank-like bus thing. But we don't see the outside. No models, no CGI, apart from an establisher of the planet. This, literally, takes place on one set – inside the bus – which will have to seal off its windows, so let's say there's a big old powerful X-raying sun outside. So it's a box. It's a show set in a box. That'll help our budgets right now. The box sets off on its journey, with the Doctor and five or six other interesting people on board, but then it breaks down. There Is Something Outside. (Or is there?) They're trapped. Forty minutes of fear! Never leaving the box. God only knows how or what happens. I don't think we've the money for a monster, so it's sort of psychological terror.

At the heart of this, I've one idea that keeps nagging, because it feels so attractive and unnerving and plain terrifying. Whatever's outside the box, one woman inside becomes possessed by it – and she repeats everything that you say. She has no speech of her own; she just repeats everything. All the time. You know how it drives you mad when people repeat what you say? When kids do it? Imagine that *not stopping*. Forty minutes of it, inside a box, with the lights failing and the heat rising, and the paranoia building, and this woman (I like the name Sky), this woman with wild, staring eyes, *will not stop*. Worse than that – better than that – her repetition starts to synchronise! Her repeats get closer and closer to your words until they're overlapping. She's saying words at *exactly the same time as you!* Speeches would be laid out as:

```
        THE DOCTOR & WOMAN
What are you doing, what's
inside you, what is it…?
```

That's hard to shoot. That actress would have to learn the entire script. She wouldn't just say the Doctor's words, she'd say everyone's, no matter how fast it gets. Incredible moments where all the other characters are talking at once, and she sort of manages to say everyone's words at once, like talking in tongues. It's a real possession story. It's the tension of it that I love. The weirdness. Even the technical difficulty of shooting this becomes fascinating. All that production-tension creeping onto the screen. Also, it's key to the Doctor – or David's Doctor – because he uses words so well, and this is all about him losing his speech.

But how does it end? That, in truth, is why I'm a bit scared of commissioning myself here. Dragging those endings out of my head, that's what hurts, that's what makes me smoke and burn. Last week, when I was staring at 4.5 and had no idea how it ended, it was a great big raw screaming hole. It was a mindless panic. And it had to be fixed by Monday. It's horrible, looking into that. The blank space of an unknown ending. When I talk about being exhausted and recovering from a script, what I really mean is recovering, physically, from going through that fear. I'm not even going to qualify that with an 'Oh, how pretentious', though my fingers are dying to type a self-deprecating qualifier. No matter how difficult 4.11 and 4.12/4.13 are, I know how they end, so I've somewhere to head for. But I've no such luxury with 4.8. It's tempting me forward, but repelling me at the same time.

FROM: BENJAMIN COOK TO: RUSSELL T DAVIES
THURSDAY 11 OCTOBER 2007 15:10:56 GMT

RE: MORE WORK, LESS MAYBE

I hadn't realised that things were quite that serious for Howard. That's terrible. I only met him briefly on set for *The Runaway Bride*. He seemed to be having a good time. Very happy. Very twinkly. I really hope I see him again. It seems fitting that he should influence his character's path, and Donna's, to some extent.

Hey, I saw the report in the *Daily Star* the other day, that Billie and everyone is coming back for the series finale. How the hell do they find out this stuff?

FROM: RUSSELL T DAVIES TO: BENJAMIN COOK
THURSDAY 11 OCTOBER 2007 19:51:55 GMT

RE: MORE WORK, LESS MAYBE

Heaven knows! We're very worried about that. It's a top-level leak. Almost no one knows the full size of these plans. But what do we do? Suspect everyone? There's nothing we can do. Some sly little shit will have to be hot with their tiny victory. But talking to the *Daily Star*...! How dumb is that? At least *The Sun* has readers.

FROM: RUSSELL T DAVIES TO: BENJAMIN COOK
FRIDAY 12 OCTOBER 2007 20:54:46 GMT

RE: MORE WORK, LESS MAYBE

Poor Howard. It's looking bad. We're trying to bring his 4.4/4.5 scenes forward to film *next week*, plus any scenes from 4.11 that I can write in advance. It's that bad.

FROM: RUSSELL T DAVIES TO: BENJAMIN COOK
SATURDAY 13 OCTOBER 2007 03:33:46 GMT

RE: MORE WORK, LESS MAYBE

ATTACH: 4.8 (TOTAL PAGE COUNT: 9 3/8)

Oh well, I started 4.8. Like an idiot. I couldn't resist. I'm giving myself this weekend. If I can convince myself by Sunday night that there's a story in this Space Bus (I'm calling the Space Bus *Crusader Five*) – and a story that I can complete in time – then I'll keep going. Prep on 4.8 starts on Monday, so that's a handy deadline. If it doesn't work... well, I can keep it as a pet project; something will happen to it one day. Every idea gets used somewhere, eventually.

FROM: BENJAMIN COOK TO: RUSSELL T DAVIES
SATURDAY 13 OCTOBER 2007 12:31:17 GMT

RE: MORE WORK, LESS MAYBE

CRUSADER FIVE IS GO! I'm leaving for Newport in an hour, but I've just sat here and read what you've written of 4.8, so now I'm running late. Obviously, I'm Invisible Ben, so I can't tell you whether or not I enjoyed it. But I did enjoy it. More's the point, you sound as though *you're* enjoying this one. I'm on set tonight, through the night, for Miss Foster's confrontation with the Doctor and Donna, but send me more and I'll read it when I get back to the hotel at 6am.

FROM: RUSSELL T DAVIES TO: BENJAMIN COOK
SATURDAY 13 OCTOBER 2007 13:11:20 GMT

RE: MORE WORK, LESS MAYBE

I'm glad you enjoyed it. I'm still not sure. I've chosen the hardest thing to write, which is eight people all in one scene at the same time. That's why most drama consists of two-handers. Much easier. The sheer effort of keeping eight characters on the boil, while not forgetting anyone, but not delaying things by laboriously giving everyone their turn, is technically one of the hardest things to write.

Have fun on set. That episode is looking wonderful. I swear, the scene where the Doctor and Donna see each other through their respective windows is The Funniest Thing Ever. Certainly, the funniest thing that I've written for ages. You write and write and write, hoping to hit something *that* funny, and sometimes, rare times, you get there. Catherine plays a blinder. (She texted me afterwards to say, 'I'm petitioning them to bring back *Give Us a Clue*.') And then David raises his game and gets even funnier. Oh, I'm happy.

And Sarah Lancashire was born to play a villain.

Text message from: **Russell**
Sent: 13-Oct-2007 23:49
It's weird to think of everyone filming on a Saturday night. I don't think we've done this before. It robs me of my martyr status – I'm not alone! How goes it?

Text message from: **Ben**
Sent: 14-Oct-2007 00:30

How Russell originally imagined the passengers aboard the *Crusader 50* in 4.8 *Midnight*.

I was interviewing Sarah Lancashire when you texted. She said that your scripts are 'non-negotiable' and 'uncompromising', and that she 'believes every single beat of it'. The bribe worked, then?

Text message from: **Russell**
Sent: 14-Oct-2007 02:04
Ah, that's nice of her. I've known her for years. Always wanted to work with her – now she's an evil alien Supernanny! Who'd have thought?

Text message from: **Ben**
Sent: 14-Oct-2007 02:07
How goes Crusader Five? You have to work the number 50 into the script somewhere. Couldn't it be Crusader 50 instead?

Text message from: **Russell**
Sent: 14-Oct-2007 02:10
Oh, I forgot that! Right, the Space Bus is called Crusader 50 now. Good call.

FROM: RUSSELL T DAVIES TO: BENJAMIN COOK
SUNDAY 14 OCTOBER 2007 03:50:33 GMT

RE: MORE WORK, LESS MAYBE

ATTACH: 4.8 (TOTAL PAGE COUNT: 28 3/8)

This is hard work. Just laying it out on the page, just clearly explaining what's happening and timing it right. I think it works, it's scary, the concept is scary, but… I just don't know. My brain is bleeding. Good night.

FROM: BENJAMIN COOK TO: RUSSELL T DAVIES
SUNDAY 14 OCTOBER 2007 12:07:05 GMT

RE: MORE WORK, LESS MAYBE

Chatting to Phil on set last night, he mentioned Howard. He said that depending on how you write him into later episodes, it might be worth recasting – and reshooting the scene on the hillside – though Phil did stress that he really didn't want to. Is that an option, do you think?

I shared a car back to the hotel with Sarah. I hadn't realised that her dad was a writer, Geoffrey Lancashire, who wrote episodes of *Coronation Street* years before Sarah was in it. She's another one fascinated by what makes writers tick. Her theory is that you have to be slightly unhinged to be a writer. 'All the best writers are mad,' she said. Then again, it was 5am, so she could have been talking in tongues and I'd have duly nodded.

FROM: RUSSELL T DAVIES TO: BENJAMIN COOK
SUNDAY 14 OCTOBER 2007 12:22:16 GMT

RE: MORE WORK, LESS MAYBE

My brain is buzzing. This Space Bus script is driving me mad. Perhaps in a good way. I woke up with it whirring and whizzing through my head. I wish I had a Dictaphone, so I could babble out all the ideas. I'll keep going till tonight, then decide whether to abandon it or keep going. Or maybe I'll send it to Julie and Phil to decide. It's about to turn into a Balloon Debate – who to throw out of *Crusader 50*? I used to love Balloon Debates in school. Some kid would stand there droning, 'I am Florence Nightingale and I saved lots of lives,' some other kid would come back with 'I am Winston Churchill and I won the war,' and I'd just be sitting there thinking, *we throw someone out of a balloon?! Brilliant!* (Am I showing my age? Do they still have Balloon Debates? Do you know what I'm on about?)

Bless Sarah Lancashire, she's always been dying to write herself – so tempted by it, after years of watching her dad, who's well remembered and much loved in Manchester – and I used to nag her to start, but maybe she's wise. Maybe it's better, staying away. Who needs it? But she really is clever, isn't she? Much underestimated. You don't get to that status in the industry without a keen mind.

Poor Howard. That's the final option, to recast and reshoot. Oh, but that would be terrible. (A lot easier for us, though.) It doesn't bear thinking about.

CRUSADER 50

This is Russell's e-mail to Julie and Phil, accompanying the first two-thirds of his script for Episode 4.8…

FROM: RUSSELL T DAVIES
TO: JULIE GARDNER; PHIL COLLINSON
SUNDAY 14 OCTOBER 2007 19:54:43 GMT

2/3RDS OF 4.8

ATTACH: 4.8 (TOTAL PAGE COUNT: 40 6/8)

All right, you two. I'll keep going with this tonight, but here it is, so far – the first 40 pages of a new 4.8. It'll only take another day to finish, though that's a bit buggered because I have to go to London tomorrow. But I'm sending this now, because prep starts tomorrow, so I suppose we'd better make our minds up.

So. This, or Tom MacRae's! Don't make up your minds until you've read the attached. This is an odd script. And it's a tough read. Literally, it's hard to read sometimes. But I swear it *sounds* right, if you just let it flow. It's all atmosphere. It depends on the tension.

FROM: BENJAMIN COOK TO: RUSSELL T DAVIES
MONDAY 15 OCTOBER 2007 18:03:16 GMT

RE: MORE WORK, LESS MAYBE

What do Julie and Phil make of the Space Bus episode? Is it going to be yours or Tom MacRae's? And have you warned Tom yet?

FROM: RUSSELL T DAVIES TO: BENJAMIN COOK
TUESDAY 16 OCTOBER 2007 18:56:35 GMT

RE: MORE WORK, LESS MAYBE

ATTACH: 4.8 (TOTAL PAGE COUNT: 53 3/8)

They love it. Phew. However, in 4.1 news, Howard is so frail, he's broken his leg, so his wife, bless her, phoned up and admitted, 'I think we'd better stop.' He's definitely out. The terrible thing is, we couldn't claim insurance before for filming any replacement scenes, because we'd known that he was ill and took the risk. No insurance. But now that he's broken his leg, we have insurance money for a brand new hillside scene. That's weird. But we needed the money.

Yesterday, in the space of 12 hours, after deciding that Howard couldn't continue, I said that I wanted to rewrite it with Donna's grandad instead, so Howard and family won't have to see a new Geoff on screen – and Phil suggested Bernard Cribbins. Donna's grandad is the newspaperman from *Voyage of the Damned*! We phoned up Bernard's agent… and he's free! He loved his day with us, so he's on board. Well, not quite – money to sort out and all that – but technically the deal is done. Christ, this show can move fast sometimes. That was a blizzard of phone calls and e-mails. So, today, I've rewritten Geoff as Wilf. The newspaperman was Stan in 4.X, but I like Wilf better for a longer-running part. His name is never said on screen in 4.X, so all we have to do is change him to Wilf in the end credits.

Howard Attfield's scenes as Donna's dad, Geoff, in 4.1 were later reshot with Bernard Cribbins as Donna's grandfather, Wilf.

It's spooky, though, because that hillside scene is one of the few that I obsessed over in our e-mails – and here it is cropping up again. Of course, we're faced with the outrageous coincidence of the Doctor meeting the grandfather of the woman with whom he fought the Racnoss, the same woman who's about to track him down. Phil suggested reshooting the Christmas scene so that Bernard didn't appear twice. I said, 'No, let's make it the same man.' It's sort of funny. I've just rewritten 4.4/4.5 as well (it's been a hell of a day), in order to change the dad to the grandad. At the Nobles' house, Wilf recognises the Doctor, the Doctor recognises him, Donna realises that the Doctor and Wilf have met before, and Sylvia still has to recognise the Doctor from the wedding in *The Runaway Bride*, while handily adding that Wilf wasn't there because he had Spanish flu! That's the maddest scene ever. We could just ignore all these links, but we've a dedicated audience – not the fan-audience, but the other 7.9 million – so I think this casting needs to be acknowledged. And the fact that it's not any old actor, it's Bernard bloody Cribbins, sort of allows the madness.

Nonetheless, that fanboy part of me does have his teeth slightly on edge, so I'm going to take care of it in 4.11. When Rose is trying to get Donna to put history back on course, she's going to say something like, 'You met the Doctor, then your grandfather did, then you found the Doctor for a second time. That's not just coincidence. It's like the universe was trying to bind you to the Doctor. To stop this [the parallel world] from happening.' That's a fair bit of nonsense, and posits the universe, or at least destiny, as a sentient force, but it's kind of spooky. I like that. At the very least, it's saying, 'We know this is barmy.' The only time I try to rule out huge coincidence is when it actually *changes* the plot. But here it doesn't. It's just detail.

Yesterday continued to be weird. If my favourite thing in 4.1 is the hillside scene, my least favourite is those bloody guards being electrocuted in the doorway, isn't it? I never could think of a solution. Well, at 3.36am – I noted the time – my phone rings. They're on a night shoot – oh God, red alert – so I grab my phone and, sure enough, it's James Strong. Oh no, what's wrong?

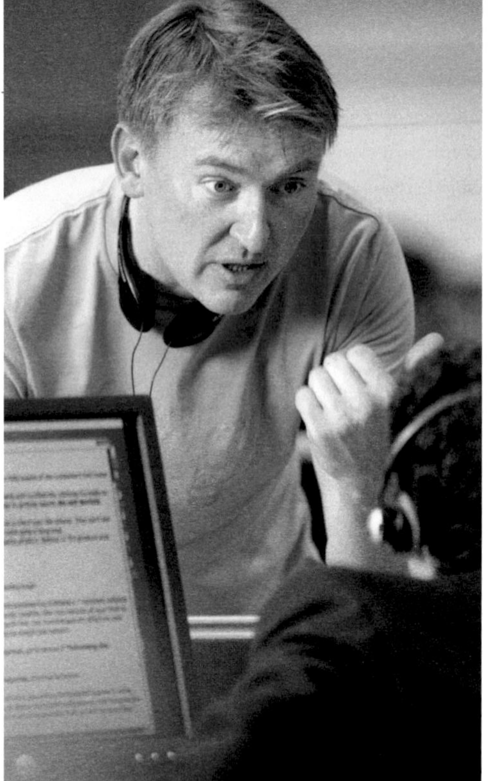

James Strong on location for 4.1 *Partners in Crime*.

```
                JAMES
Russell! David's asking,
about these guards, the ones
who get electrocuted. How
does the Doctor know where
they are, to electrocute
them?

                RUSSELL
Well, he doesn't. He's
discovered the wiring that
Miss Foster's used to
convert the building into a
Levitation Post, and he uses
that to electrocute all the
doorways.

                JAMES
Ah. Right.
              (pause)
They aren't coming through a
doorway.

                RUSSELL
Right. Why not?

                JAMES
The doorways here are
rubbish.

                RUSSELL
Oh-kaaay. So how do they
get electrocuted? In your
version?

                JAMES
They come through a sort of
archway.

                RUSSELL
So the archway electrocutes
them?

                JAMES
Yes.

                RUSSELL
But they don't actually touch
anything?

                JAMES
No.

                RUSSELL
And you've already shot this?

                JAMES
Yes.
              (pause)
The doorways really are
rubbish.

                RUSSELL
So the Doctor electrified
every single archway in the
building, with such strong
electricity that anyone
passing through one would get
electrocuted.

                JAMES
Yes! That works!

                RUSSELL
Good. Oh, and James? You tell
David that's your version.
Not mine.

                JAMES
Okay.

                RUSSELL
Night then.

                JAMES
Night.
```

And don't you love the way that I made myself sound good there? But it just proves something (poor James, it's not his fault at all): if something is a problem, it'll *always* be a problem unless you fix it. Like the best problems, it comes back to haunt you – on the page, on the shoot, in the Edit, on transmission. I failed to fix that. Clearly failed. It would always have gone wrong, somehow. It was wrong from the start. I bleated about it to you, but didn't actually do anything. Lesson learnt. Well, maybe.

FROM: RUSSELL T DAVIES TO: BENJAMIN COOK
WEDNESDAY 17 OCTOBER 2007 17:11:03 GMT

RE: MORE WORK, LESS MAYBE

No more Space Bus script yet. I sat with it last night and just couldn't get into it. If you're not into that script, if you're not devoted, and hooked, and scared, and passionate, it just reads like a bunch of boring people stuck in a box. Hopefully, this isn't true. I've just got to get in the mood and launch myself into it. I can finish it tonight, I reckon. Pompeii has adrenalised me.

But now I've got to phone Bernard Cribbins. It turns out that he thought he was travelling *in* the TARDIS! As a companion! So it looks as though that's about to go bollocks-up.

FROM: RUSSELL T DAVIES TO: BENJAMIN COOK
THURSDAY 18 OCTOBER 2007 04:17:59 GMT

RE: MORE WORK, LESS MAYBE

ATTACH: 4.8 (TOTAL PAGE COUNT: 53 3/8)

It's finished! See 4.8 as a belated birthday present, Ben. (God, I'm cheap.) Happy birthday! (It is the 17th, isn't it?) You old man.

Ian Bunting's design drawing for the *Crusader 50* in 4.8.

FROM: BENJAMIN COOK TO: RUSSELL T DAVIES
THURSDAY 18 OCTOBER 2007 13:43:38 GMT

RE: MORE WORK, LESS MAYBE

Thanks, Russell. That's one CREEPY episode! It scared the crap out of me. What's it going to do to the kids? Hey, I just thought – the monster knocking on the outside of the Space Bus *has no name*. Yes, that makes it creepier, but mightn't Gary Russell's head explode? How is he going to enter it into his Great Big Encyclopedia Of Everything In *Doctor Who* Ever? Won't somebody think of Gary Russell's mind?!

FROM: RUSSELL T DAVIES TO: BENJAMIN COOK
THURSDAY 18 OCTOBER 2007 21:02:29 GMT

RE: MORE WORK, LESS MAYBE

Your typing sounds somehow… older. Have you aged suddenly? Ha ha ha.

I'm coming down off that 4.8 rush. I keep saying things to people like 'I'm not tired', but I think that's bravado. Vanity, I suppose. I want to say 'I'm fine' and sound impressive, but this morning I found myself hobbling to the shops. Hobbling! And wheezing. My legs aching. My knee hurting. My ear's a bit deaf. I'm chronic. Bollocks I'm not tired. I watched old people walking past in the Bay, faster than me. Still, 4.8 seems to have gone down a treat. Ed Thomas is very excited about building the *Crusader 50* set. And I think I should call the episode *Midnight*. What do you think? Or maybe *Crossing Midnight*, but maybe that's pretentious. David has been sent the script tonight. I'm slightly dreading his response. All those lines! He's going to kill me.

It's the opposite of *Voyage of the Damned*, that script. In *Voyage*, a group of survivors are wonderful. In *Midnight*, they're awful. Humans at their worst. All paranoid and terrified. Much closer to the real world – or my view of the world. That's partly why it was so hard to write; the language is very stripped down, there are very few jokes or conversational riffs, all those things that I normally rely on. The characters haven't even got much backstory, which is odd, because Trapped People Dramas usually rely on that. But this one's about who they are now. Very bleak. ■

CHAPTER ELEVEN

STEVEN MOFFAT'S THIGHS

In which the Doctor gains a wife, Donna's fate is sealed, and *The Guardian* portrays Russell as giggling, primping and lipsticked

FROM: RUSSELL T DAVIES TO: BENJAMIN COOK
FRIDAY 19 OCTOBER 2007 01:16:49 GMT

RE: MORE WORK, LESS MAYBE

4.1 is cursed! Last night's filming had been rescheduled from its original date, because of the rain two nights ago, so we ended up shooting the Donna-goes-to-the-TARDIS-with-her-hatbox scene up against a nightclub, with *BAM BAM, BAM* music and crowds of drunk Welsh, literally, yelling. Very loud. On and on and on. The offstage noise is terrible. With David and Catherine soldiering on bravely. Take after take after take. Today, David sent Phil, Julie and me an e-mail, complaining – well, complaining is too strong a word for him. He was just genuinely sad, because it's a lovely scene and he thinks that their performances were constrained. Ideally, we'll have to reshoot.

This show is so well run that sometimes I forget that days like this are normal, if not inevitable. This is a walk in the park compared to most other shoots. On *Queer as Folk*, we had one day so bad that the police were called in. We were filming outside Stuart's flat, in a dead rough area, and the local pub turned its music up deliberately. When they discovered the show's name, they turned it up further still. It was blasting out. When we went in to ask them to turn it down, the crew was threatened with machetes!

Also last night, James called from the Nobles' kitchen, pointing out that Sylvia says that Donna is unemployed, though Donna is clearly in work clothes. Damn! Over the phone, I added a line: Sylvia saying, 'It's no good dressing up like you're job-hunting. You've got to *do* something.' I should have seen that one. It's terrible for Jacqueline King. No actor likes having a line added on the spot. (But I'm delighted that Jacqueline is back as Sylvia. You just smile when you see her on the rushes. She's so clearly a descendant of Jackie Tyler, and that's really good.) And then tonight it was Phil phoning from the set, asking if there should be extras in the street as Miss Foster addresses the masses of Adipose and levitates. I said, 'No! What would extras do? Stand there and boggle badly?' That's what Phil had thought, but he wanted to check.

FROM: RUSSELL T DAVIES TO: BENJAMIN COOK
SATURDAY 20 OCTOBER 2007 15:57:05 GMT

RE: MORE WORK, LESS MAYBE

I'm interviewed in *The Guardian* today. Yet another interview in which I'm portrayed as giggling, primping and lipsticked. In this one, I keep squeezing the journalist's arm and practically burst into tears at one point. What a load of bollocks. As if. I've read so many of those camped-up interviews now. I'm almost beginning to suspect it's true. That's sobering. I was asked to do *The South Bank Show* once, but I turned it down, because it was being directed by the man who did Paul Abbott's. That portrait of Paul was so accurate, it was terrifying. It captured all his mania and compulsion and repetition. I thought, if I saw myself through that director's eyes, I'd never be able to deny that it's true. Never see yourself.

FROM: RUSSELL T DAVIES TO: BENJAMIN COOK
TUESDAY 23 OCTOBER 2007 00:45:50 GMT

RE: MORE WORK, LESS MAYBE

In TV land, things are moving fast. Steven's agent came in today to talk to Jane and Julie about *Doctor Who*, and then Jane and Julie interviewed Julie's replacement. In a year or so, Julie will step down. She'll exec next year's Specials, but there will be a new exec for Series Five. Julie wants to either move to the US and work there or… well, all sorts of top-secret plans are being discussed. But the interview turned out to be quite emotional for her. It suddenly struck her that she's leaving. Her replacement – if he accepts – is going to be Piers Wenger. He only got into TV because he saw *Queer as Folk*, so naturally I like him. Very exciting. Very good news for the show. I hope he accepts. But no Julie! Imagine!

FROM: BENJAMIN COOK TO: RUSSELL T DAVIES
TUESDAY 23 OCTOBER 2007 13:48:55 GMT

RE: MORE WORK, LESS MAYBE

I've met Piers before. He's lovely, wonderful and clever, although quite different to Steven, I think, who's just as lovely, wonderful and clever, but in a different sort of way. Piers is softer and calmer. That contrast is exactly what the show would need, isn't it? What a team! (This is all horribly luvvie. I'm making myself retch. Shall I lie and say that they're both complete bastards and *Doctor Who* is doomed?) Who will complete the Holy Trinity? Who's going be the new Phil Collinson? What about Susie Liggat?

Steven Moffat and Sue Vertue on set for *Time Crash*.

FROM: RUSSELL T DAVIES TO: BENJAMIN COOK
TUESDAY 23 OCTOBER 2007 18:03:49 GMT

RE: MORE WORK, LESS MAYBE

As for the actual producer, no one is sure yet. I don't think Susie would want it. I think she likes to move on every so often. But I'm glad that you like Piers. On a personal level, he's a proper old-fashioned gentleman. I wouldn't feel that the show was getting an exec who'd say, 'Davies was rubbish! That era is gone! Sweep it away!' Mind you, maybe that's what the newcomer *should* say. I just want to be gently enshrined. In gold leaf. Is that too much to ask?

Oh, but 4.11 is due in on Monday! MONDAY!!! Think back to all those leisurely months when I was musing over that episode. Well, now it's here. I've less than a week. Although, a little bit of me is quite excited…

PARALLEL WORLDS

This e-mail exchange between Steven Moffat and Russell regards the similarities between their respective scripts for 4.10 and 4.11…

FROM: STEVEN MOFFAT TO: RUSSELL T DAVIES
THURSDAY 25 OCTOBER 2007 09:22:35 GMT

STUFF

Right, so I'm on Episode 10 now. It's coming just before Episode 11 (no flies on me!), which is the one where Donna is in a parallel existence, yeah? Living the life she would've led? Now, we've already had this conversation, but just to be extra careful…

One element of my Episode 10 is Donna finding herself in Girl's World, wondering what the hell happened, but starting to fit in, maybe falling in love (time moves differently there), with the Doctor trying to pull her back out – I'm trying to avoid spoilers here – as he runs about the Library, battling shadows and certain death.[1] How close are we, given the proximity? There are different ways I can play this, lots of different ways, so what do I have to avoid? For instance, the Girl's World is currently modern-day Britain, but that could change without huge upheaval. What do you think?

FROM: RUSSELL T DAVIES TO: STEVEN MOFFAT
THURSDAY 25 OCTOBER 2007 16:43:50 GMT

RE: STUFF

I suppose it is a bit of a worry, except mine's supposed to be delivered on Monday, so I get in first, ha ha. (Note the 'supposed'.) Episode 11 is a big What If story. Namely, what if Donna never met the Doctor? A nasty Time Beetle on her back causes this to happen. It's called *Turn Left*, because she turned left in the car one day to go for her job interview at HC Clements. If she'd turned right and gone for some other job, she'd never have met the Doctor. But time changes (thanks, Time Beetle!), she does turn right… and the Racnoss Webstar attacks, it's blown up, and the Doctor is pulled out of the wreckage, dead, because Donna wasn't there to tell him to stop. That's all seen from newsreaders' points of view – and by Donna, standing behind the crash barriers, just an ignorant bystander.

1 The 'modern-day boy' mentioned in the Series Four Breakdown as featuring in Moffat's Space Library episodes is now a little girl. She is custodian of an artificial world, referred to here as 'Girl's World', in which Donna finds herself trapped.

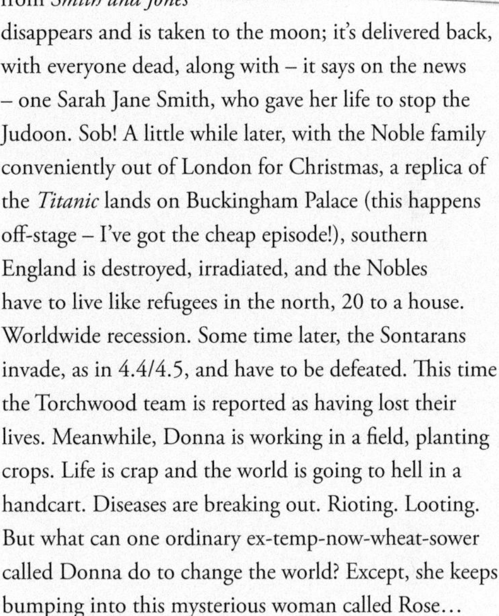

So then the world gets worse and worse, as alien events happen with no one to stop them. The hospital from *Smith and Jones* disappears and is taken to the moon; it's delivered back, with everyone dead, along with – it says on the news – one Sarah Jane Smith, who gave her life to stop the Judoon. Sob! A little while later, with the Noble family conveniently out of London for Christmas, a replica of the *Titanic* lands on Buckingham Palace (this happens off-stage – I've got the cheap episode!), southern England is destroyed, irradiated, and the Nobles have to live like refugees in the north, 20 to a house. Worldwide recession. Some time later, the Sontarans invade, as in 4.4/4.5, and have to be defeated. This time the Torchwood team is reported as having lost their lives. Meanwhile, Donna is working in a field, planting crops. Life is crap and the world is going to hell in a handcart. Diseases are breaking out. Rioting. Looting. But what can one ordinary ex-temp-now-wheat-sower called Donna do to change the world? Except, she keeps bumping into this mysterious woman called Rose…

Basically, Rose is working with UNIT, who have salvaged the TARDIS. They can use it to send Donna back in time to stop herself turning right instead of left. Except Donna fails, and everyone dies. No, I made up that last line! (Well, I'm making all of it up. We both are.) Still, 4.11 is pretty joyless – Christ, it's grim – so for God's sake, Steven, put some jokes in 4.10. But it doesn't sound too like Girl's World, does it? I suppose we both have Donna in an unreal world, but I can compensate for that by making it sound like a pattern. Does that help? Maybe I can combine both our plots by making it sound like dark forces are conspiring to separate her from the Doctor – first of all, Girl's World, now the Time Beetle, because Great Events are coming. Sort of saying, mystically, that the universe is trying to bind Donna to the Doctor, like they're meant to be together, because she has some Greater Purpose To Fulfil. I haven't quite worked out what that is yet, but I'll sort it out in 4.13. Er, somehow.

PARALLEL WORLDS (continued)

FROM: STEVEN MOFFAT TO: RUSSELL T DAVIES
THURSDAY 25 OCTOBER 2007 17:25:35 GMT

RE: STUFF

So these mighty powerful influence-anything-they-want-to forces are of a broadly mystical nature? One of my plans is to make it heartbreakingly hard for Donna to leave her other life. Maybe the Doctor could muse, in the final scenes, that the efforts made to keep Donna in Girl's World seemed over the top, almost like something else was at work…

FROM: RUSSELL T DAVIES TO: STEVEN MOFFAT
THURSDAY 25 OCTOBER 2007 18:10:25 GMT

RE: STUFF

I haven't worked out if it's heartbreaking for Donna to leave my parallel world. In theory, she should have a husband and kids so that changing reality means she has to lose them, as the ultimate sacrifice… hmm, but we're both heading in the same direction there, aren't we? Shall I leave that alone? Do you want that?

FROM: STEVEN MOFFAT TO: RUSSELL T DAVIES
THURSDAY 25 OCTOBER 2007 18:53:20 GMT

RE: STUFF

Exactly where I was going. Oops! Okay, you're going first anyway, and I'm on *Tintin* for the next week, so you could see if it works for you. Very broadly, in mine, Donna would have kids, but she'd realise that they're not real. Just as she's about to leave Girl's World, one of her children is clinging to her, because he's got a suspicion that he stops existing every time that his mummy isn't looking – oh, the heartbreak!

FROM: RUSSELL T DAVIES TO: STEVEN MOFFAT
THURSDAY 25 OCTOBER 2007 19:13:43 GMT

RE: STUFF

Ooh, no, that's brilliant. You have the kids. (You've got kids! You do better kids!) I've been struggling with my other-world husband and kids, because the world is going to hell, so their life isn't up to much, and I've got London destroyed, Donna picking hops (do you pick hops?), Rose and a gutted TARDIS… yeah, I've got enough to be going on with. Instead of making it How Can I Leave All This For A Different World In Which You Don't Exist?, I've got How Can One Ordinary Woman Change The Whole World?' Kids are yours!

Reproduced with kind permission

FROM: BENJAMIN COOK TO: RUSSELL T DAVIES
TUESDAY 23 OCTOBER 2007 22:28:53 GMT

RE: MORE WORK, LESS MAYBE

How much has 4.11 changed now that it's Donna not Penny?

FROM: RUSSELL T DAVIES TO: BENJAMIN COOK
WEDNESDAY 24 OCTOBER 2007 20:12:24 GMT

RE: MORE WORK, LESS MAYBE

Well, we haven't seen the pivotal 'turn' scene in 4.1 as I'd planned, because it doesn't fit Donna's new motive, but it's quite fun working out exactly when her life did turn left or right. I reckon – this has been Maybe-ing away for months now – that her vital moment was when she went for the job interview at HC Clements (HC Clements is back! Who'd have thought?), where

Above: Donna's parallel world in 4.11. Facing page: A more idyllic alternative existence, with husband Lee (Jason Pitt), in 4.10.

she was working as a temp when we first met her, in *The Runaway Bride*. But then the story locks down in pretty much the same way, so it's no worry. Well, it's a little continuity-fraught. More than I'd have liked. Now I've got to back reference as far as 3.X – in fact, to events before 3.X that we never saw – but I can handle that.

FROM: RUSSELL T DAVIES TO: BENJAMIN COOK
THURSDAY 25 OCTOBER 2007 20:18:38 GMT

RE: MORE WORK, LESS MAYBE

The rushes are in for the 4.1 wine bar scene. Brassy Suzette is a treat. It's exactly what I wanted – bizarre, panicky, funny and weird. Suzette's bubbling shirt is excellent. Nice stuff. But as for the ladies' toilets rushes – well, I'm a bit peeved. At the Tone Meeting, I stressed how vital it is that Penny and Donna should *not* be in neighbouring cubicles, or they'd both be aware of one another. And what have they gone and done? They're right next to one another! I might as well talk to thin air. That's a really subtle, important point, lost. I texted James. He texted back, saying, 'I completely forgot!' Yes. Yes, you did. I think we'll be able to cut around it slightly, but still that's a scene operating at 90 per cent instead of the full 100. That's a shame.

That's not quite a wrap on 4.1, because we have to reshoot Howard's stuff on the hillside. From what I hear, Bernard Cribbins is definitely in.

FROM: RUSSELL T DAVIES TO: BENJAMIN COOK
FRIDAY 26 OCTOBER 2007 20:44:09 GMT

STEVEN MOFFAT'S THIGHS

... are now mighty and impressive, because – mark the day – pending money and all that, the deal is done. As of today, Series Five is Steven's!

FROM: BENJAMIN COOK TO: RUSSELL T DAVIES
FRIDAY 26 OCTOBER 2007 21:04:32 GMT

RE: STEVEN MOFFAT'S THIGHS

Awesome news! I'm as delighted as you are... but are we *really* going to keep this subject line? I think I preferred 'Charlie Hunnam's Arse'.

FROM: RUSSELL T DAVIES TO: BENJAMIN COOK
SATURDAY 27 OCTOBER 2007 17:58:48 GMT

RE: STEVEN MOFFAT'S THIGHS

ATTACH: 4.11 (TOTAL PAGE COUNT: 11 3/8)

I started 4.11 today. Well, it made sense, what with prep starting on Monday! I'm going to overrun on this script now and miss the National Television Awards in the Albert Hall on Wednesday. I love that ceremony. I actually get to talk to *Hollyoaks* boys. This is a big event in my life. Damn.

Still, 4.11 is... interesting. A lot harder to rip through quickly, because it needs so much construction. The opening scenes in the Fortune Teller's den on the planet Shan Shen (where the Time Beetle jumps on Donna's back, and we flashback to Donna's life on Earth before she met the Doctor) are so complicated, with so much to be established, that they could have gone on for 20 pages. Even now, I don't get to the pre-titles cliffhanger until Page 7. I don't think it's ever been that late. After the titles, we're straight into the parallel world where Donna turned right instead of left, but I'm having a lot of trouble, because Steven has a sort of parallel-world Donna in 4.10, too. I'm having to write around his plans. But I can't wait to see what he's come up with.

In other news, we offered the part of Sky Silvestry in 4.8 to Lesley Sharp – and she's said yes! Brilliant! She needed some talking into it, because of the sheer amount of line-learning. I phoned her up and said we'd cast Jane Horrocks instead. She was hooting. I love Lesley.

FROM: BENJAMIN COOK TO: RUSSELL T DAVIES
SATURDAY 27 OCTOBER 2007 19:27:46 GMT

RE: STEVEN MOFFAT'S THIGHS

So you don't know what's coming in 4.10 until you read Steven's first draft? Doesn't he tell you? Do you really fight the spoilers?

FROM: RUSSELL T DAVIES TO: BENJAMIN COOK
SATURDAY 27 OCTOBER 2007 19:44:02 GMT

RE: STEVEN MOFFAT'S THIGHS

It's funny, isn't it? I ask him not to spoiler me. He's written 4.9 already, so I've read that. It's called *Silence in the Library*, and it has a character in it who I'm just sure is the Doctor's wife (!!!), but I don't like to ask. I want to find out in the second episode, like a viewer. It's the closest that I get to experiencing brand new *Doctor Who*. Not for long, though…

FROM: BENJAMIN COOK TO: RUSSELL T DAVIES
SATURDAY 27 OCTOBER 2007 19:56:11 GMT

RE: STEVEN MOFFAT'S THIGHS

I've been reading the Royal Television Society's Huw Wheldon Memorial Lecture that Nicola Shindler gave in 2002. (Random, I know, but what can I say? I'm a swot!) In it, she says:

> *There are a lot of ways to tell a story and, in my opinion, a lot of ways that shouldn't be used. I've got my pet hates, which drive the writers I work with mad. But they have to do a lot to persuade me to change my mind. I can't bear voiceovers and flashbacks. Interestingly, when you just lift them out of a script, it's amazing how well the story works without them, with no rewrites. I think they're often just a crutch for the writer and sometimes show lazy storytelling. I feel the same about voiceover. It's lazy. This is a visual medium, so don't have someone tell me what to think or what to watch; show me!*

Lesley Sharp as Sky Silvestry in 4.8 *Midnight*.

Bearing in mind, Russell, that you've just started writing an episode that hinges on flashbacks, I wonder whether you agree with Nicola. You also used flashbacks and flashforwards aplenty in *Casanova*, and even *The Runaway Bride* employed flashbacks to fill in Donna's backstory (and let's not get started on *Love & Monsters*), while there were voiceovers in *Bob & Rose* (I'm thinking of the scene where Bob is in a nightclub, surveying the talent), for example, so where do you stand on this? What are the dos and don'ts of flashbacks and voiceovers? Plus, from a technical point of view, how do you write them into a script?

FROM: RUSSELL T DAVIES TO: BENJAMIN COOK
SATURDAY 27 OCTOBER 2007 21:22:33 GMT

RE: STEVEN MOFFAT'S THIGHS

I'm with Nicola – I think you should beware. The techniques are too often being used to disguise the truth, the real story, the heart of the script. It's all pyrotechnics and glitter, fuelled by insecurity. That 'Where do you start a story?' question can become so overwhelming that the writer goes mad, firing out shots all over the place. 'I'll start here! And now! And backwards!' Oh, why not just get on with it and write the story? Nic's dissatisfaction comes, I think, from having read so many scripts where the techniques are masking the skill. If I'm reading something new, especially by someone new, I want to know that they can write, I want to know how their characters talk, how the pace skips along, how the story hooks me, how passionate the writer is, how much I feel the whole thing. I'm not interested in admiring the artifice and thinking, oh, that's clever.

Of course, those devices *can* work. I remember being very careful with the use of Old Casanova as narrator in *Casanova*. The presence of an old and very much alive man was in danger of robbing Young Casanova's experiences of any vitality or danger. I'll admit, I wrestled with that, but I was experienced enough to be aware of the dangers and subvert them. The sequence that I'm most proud of is Young Casanova's duel, where obviously he's going to survive (Old Casanova says afterwards, 'Well, you didn't think I was going to die, did you?'), but it worked because it forced me to look at the duel from a different angle – a more important angle – namely, *why* is it taking place? What is the Duke of Grimani (who Casanova is duelling) actually thinking? Which leads to devastating insights into Grimani's life. The duel is actually irrelevant.

Even with Peter O'Toole in the role, Old Casanova's appearances are limited, especially as the story goes on. There are huge chunks where he doesn't appear. Even then, the role of narrator is potentially flat and dull, so it was vital – oh, crucial – that Old Casanova had a plot of his own. He had his relationship with fellow servant Edith and, more vitally, his hope that his one true love, Henriette, was still alive. Without that, if he'd just been a dying old man, it would have been passive and uninteresting. Peter knew that. When he was first offered the part, he wasn't so interested, because he knew how dull a narrator is – and that Young Casanova could upstage the whole thing! It was only when Peter read it, when he saw that Old Casanova had a story, that he accepted.

Even with voiceovers, take care. The greatest TV example these days is *Desperate Housewives*, but you have to consider the bigger framework at play. Firstly, *Desperate Housewives* isn't one particular character's story: it's Life On Wisteria Lane. That overarching structure, that authorial stance, allows the voiceover. It's part of the whole show. It's part of the show's ethos. I could listen to that actress, Brenda Strong, for ever. That voice is seriously, beautifully cast. But more's the point, that character, Mary Alice, is dead. Added thrill! In a show about secrets, the omnipresent narrator allows us to see into people's hidden lives. It's at its best at the end of an episode, when Mary Alice's voiceover calmly leads us to an otherwise silent image – the New Handsome Neighbour has a gun in his kitchen! – so it's actually a clever, witty way of framing a cliffhanger.

David Tennant as the world's most famous lover in Russell T Davies' BBC Three drama *Casanova*. Inset: Peter O'Toole as the older Casanova.

Imagine how dull that Handsome New Neighbour scene would be if you just cut to his house, he's all on his own, he gets out a gun. Boring! The voiceover gives it a size and majesty; it leads you into the revelation and then quickly gets out, leaving you dangling. In a show that's seen as camp, pretty and funny, it's easy to miss how incredibly skilful that is.

That authorial/narrator's voice demands a certain wisdom, in summing up events, because often it says stuff along the lines of 'That's the thing about love…' That's hard to write. You can end up with the Hallmark Cards voiceover. 'That's the thing about love: it hurts and wounds, and yet, when it's pure, you'll never feel so safe.' Yuck! The voiceover is a honey trap for bad writing. It has to exist for more reasons than 'here's a sweet way to end the episode'. That's why Nic is warning against it.

As with all this stuff, you're never sure if you've got it right, even after transmission. The first draft of *Mine All Mine* started at the end – or almost at the end – of the story, with the Vivaldi family on stage in the middle of a public concert in Swansea, the Vote Vivaldi climax from Episode 5. You were thinking, who are they? Why's everyone cheering? They *what?!* They own the town?! 'Tell us how this all started,' the MC said to Max Vivaldi – and then, on Max, we flashbacked to the beginning of the story. Now, Nicola cut that, because she thought, never mind framing devices, don't distract me, just tell the story properly. In other words: get on with it! And I agreed with her. I lost that opening. But still, sometimes, in the dark hours, I wonder… if that had opened the episode, you'd have seen what's at stake for that ordinary family, right from the start. You'd have taken hold of an essentially ephemeral and even silly notion – 'I own Swansea!' – and made it concrete, powerful and alive. Without that, the starting point of the story was: man gets off train and gets into taxi. Hardly thrilling. The flashforward opening would have given you scale, crowds, cheering and fireworks. Hmm. Difficult to say. I'll always wonder.

From a technical point of view, writing them into a TV script, usually a flashback demands a scene break, because it's a different place or a different time. I'd write:

```
1. INT. BEN'S KITCHEN - DAY

BEN is back from Rome. He unpacks
his stuff, then leans against the
fridge, remembering…

                              CUT TO:

2. INT. ROME, RESTAURANT - NIGHT

A RAT runs across the restaurant!
PHIL screams!

                              CUT TO:

3. INT. BEN'S KITCHEN - DAY

BEN laughs at the memory.
```

That doesn't use the word flashback at all. Although, in fairness, we've been talking about flashbacks, so you're expecting one. If this were a brand new script, I might read that and think, eh? What just happened? What rat? It might be better to write:

```
2. FLASHBACK - INT. ROME,
RESTAURANT - NIGHT
```

Or even:

```
2. INT. ROME, RESTAURANT - NIGHT

FLASHBACK. Two nights ago. A RAT
runs across the restaurant! PHIL
screams!
```

The most important thing is that it's nice and clear, and doesn't piss off the reader. Don't say:

```
1. INT. BEN'S KITCHEN - DAY

BEN is back from Rome. He unpacks
his stuff, then leans against the
fridge and his mind goes back,
back, back, to two nights ago, when
he was so happy. On a CU of his
noble and yet careworn features…

MIX TO: white frames, which pulsate
and bleach, filling the frame, then
slowly bleed into fleeting defocused
images, as we gently flashback to
the sounds of Roma herself, the
pasta, the people, and the rat,
yes, the rat…
```

Blah, blah, blah, get on with it!

And voiceovers are simple:

```
1. INT. BEN'S KITCHEN - DAY

Ben is back from Rome. He unpacks
his stuff, then leans against the
```

```
fridge, remembering...

                    BEN V.O.
          I remember that wonderful
          night in the restaurant in
          Rome...
```

More often, I write 'V/O' instead of 'V.O.', just because I always have. Some people would write 'O.S.', which stands for 'Out of Sight'. However, in my multi-camera directing days, 'O.S.' meant 'Over Shoulder', so it makes me flinch. And don't write 'BEN OOV', because that's 'Out Of Vision', which literally means offstage but nonetheless present – i.e. there would be a second Ben calling through from the kitchen. (Maybe there is...? I know nothing about Chiswick.)

Donna finds herself trapped in a dream world – of sorts – in 4.10 *Forest of the Dead.*

FROM: BENJAMIN COOK TO: RUSSELL T DAVIES
SATURDAY 27 OCTOBER 2007 21:46:56 GMT

RE: STEVEN MOFFAT'S THIGHS

Like Nicola Shindler, in her Huw Wheldon Memorial Lecture, you must have pet hates that drive the writers you work with mad. The other month, you cited the list of three adjectives (and I was curious, fascinated, amused), but any others...?

FROM: RUSSELL T DAVIES TO: BENJAMIN COOK
SATURDAY 27 OCTOBER 2007 22:28:30 GMT

RE: STEVEN MOFFAT'S THIGHS

I'm hesitant to list any particular devices like Nicola does, because, as she'd admit herself, all her dislikes *can* work. (She produced *Casanova*, remember.) A writer should never cut him- or herself off from something that might be useful one day. I'd be mad to say, 'I'll never do flashbacks!' Then again...

Dream sequences. I hate dream sequences. I hate them in novels, too. If I come to a dream sequence, I turn the pages until it's over. Nothing ever happens in a dream. It's all symbolic. Pathetically symbolic. Why get symbolic when you can show me what's *really* happening? Also, have you ever read or seen a dream sequence that actually feels like a dream? Really? I think it's impossible. Dreams are so odd and dislocated. I've never seen one captured properly. Matt Jones fell foul of this on *The Impossible Planet.* The cliffhanger ended with Rose being possessed by the Devil – her eyes went black and she said, 'I am the Beast Incarnate!' or something. It was wonderful – but then the next episode opened on the Tylers' estate. Back home with Jackie and Mickey, but a strangely different Jackie and Mickey, doing mysterious things, speaking with the wrong voices, being generally spooky, because, well, it was a dream. Inside Rose's head. I simply couldn't bear it. I was convinced – I'm still convinced – that nothing of any dramatic merit can happen in a dream sequence. So out it went.

Mind you, isn't Steven planning a dream sequence for 4.10, with Donna trapped in a fake reality? But he'll write it so well, it'll prove me wrong. I think the point there is that the Doctor is trying to get Donna *out*, so that injects drama into the whole set-up.

Another pet hate – and you'll see this three times

a night on British TV – is scenes that end with one character storming off, and the other character just saying their name, plaintively or crossly. Angie storms out, and Tom just says, 'Angie!' Whenever that happens on TV, I sit there and say, 'Have you lost the use of your legs?' (I'm always talking at the TV. I love it.) Watch a week's output and count how many times a scene ends with the departing person's name being called out. It's not good enough! I could argue that people storm out of rooms very rarely. How often in your life have you actually stormed out? It happens 27 times a night on the TV. There has to be a better way. (The other night, on *Casualty*, a character storming out did at least have the good grace to say, 'Don't follow me!' That's some sort of solution, I suppose.) I don't think the writer even notices. They think it's acceptable. They've seen it happen 5,000 times, so they think it's natural. They're not really writing at all; they're just transcribing a weakened version of their overall television experience.

I can't even bear phone conversations that don't end in 'Bye'. *Everyone* says goodbye at the end of a phone call. Only a Wall Street banker or Joan Collins could conceivably just hang up. The laziness comes from having seen this on screen so many times that the writer thinks it's acceptable. Bad habits. This is my other favourite:

```
Angie goes to leave the room.

                ANGIE
    Well then, I'll see you
    later.

At the door, she stops, looks back.

            ANGIE (CONT'D)
    Oh, and Tom?

Pause. Tom looks at her.

            ANGIE (CONT'D)
    Thanks.

And she walks out.
```

NO ONE HAS EVER DONE THAT! Pure TV artifice. It drives me bonkers.

I can't bear dialogue that's forced into unnatural shapes because of production circumstances. For example, it's almost impossible to include 'Let's go to the cinema' dialogue anywhere in TV drama, in any form, because it's hard to know what's going to be on at the cinema when you transmit. I remember one, just once, many years ago on *EastEnders* – Ricky Butcher said that he wanted to go and see *The Adventures of Baron Munchausen*, which was actually showing in cinemas at the time! That sentence was so odd, but brilliant, by being so rare. I've never forgotten it. Otherwise, you should find ways to write around it, not have dialogue that goes: 'D'you fancy seeing that new film tonight?' 'Yeah, great, I'll come with you.' That's never been said in real life, ever. (What film? Which cinema?) It gets worse: 'I'll meet you at eight.' 'Okay, see you then.' (Meet you where? Your house? My house? Outside the cinema? Where at eight? *Where?!*) It really is the curse of the soap opera. They find it acceptable to say, 'Fancy trying that new restaurant in town?' 'Yeah, let's go tonight!' (What restaurant? Where in town? Is that it?!) *STOP IT!* Writing like that is pure laziness.

I, of course, make no mistakes ever.

Er...

FROM: RUSSELL T DAVIES TO: BENJAMIN COOK
SUNDAY 28 OCTOBER 2007 01:23:09 GMT

RE: STEVEN MOFFAT'S THIGHS

ATTACH: 4.11 (TOTAL PAGE COUNT: 14 5/8)

Is 4.11 wandering, do you think? It feels like it doesn't have a story other than wandering through previously established *Doctor Who* events from a new perspective.

FROM: BENJAMIN COOK TO: RUSSELL T DAVIES
SUNDAY 28 OCTOBER 2007 01:47:17 GMT

RE: STEVEN MOFFAT'S THIGHS

Well, surely that *is* a story in itself?

FROM: RUSSELL T DAVIES TO: BENJAMIN COOK
SUNDAY 28 OCTOBER 2007 02:56:16 GMT

RE: STEVEN MOFFAT'S THIGHS

But it feels a bit empty. New scripts often feel empty early on. But I can't help feeling that Donna should be falling in love and building up a life that then has to be sacrificed, instead of just... experiencing it all. But that avenue is closed off. I can't give her a husband and kids

In 4.11 *Turn Left*, the Noble family find themselves refugees from a London destroyed by the *Titanic* crashing into Buckingham Palace.

now, because Steven is doing that, so 4.11 becomes a sort of exaggerated clip show. Like it's sort of whimsical.

FROM: RUSSELL T DAVIES TO: BENJAMIN COOK
SUNDAY 28 OCTOBER 2007 23:45:35 GMT

RE: STEVEN MOFFAT'S THIGHS

I've had a terrible day. I'd half-forgotten that I had to give a talk at the Dylan Thomas Centre in Swansea this afternoon. I've been so busy that I hadn't paid it much attention. (All I've wanted to think about is Donna and Rose.) I opened the brochure last night, about 3am, just to check details – oh Christ, it's a full-blown posh lunch with Dylan Thomas's daughter and the Mayor and 200 guests all paying £25 to see me! And I hadn't prepared a thing! I had close to a panic attack this morning, running around, frantic, in a flop sweat. My head was exploding. My dad in the audience and everything! Needless to say, it went marvellously. I'm a bastard with a microphone. I'm genuinely, properly arrogant with a microphone. I can understand Hitler with a microphone.

I haven't had time to write more script, but I'm going to give it a go now, see how far I get. Hey, I don't know London geography. If Donna is in Chiswick and the Racnoss Webstar is heading for central London, what direction is that? At the moment, Donna says west, because they always say they're going 'up west' on *EastEnders*. But that's not correct from Chiswick, is it?

FROM: BENJAMIN COOK TO: RUSSELL T DAVIES
MONDAY 29 OCTOBER 2007 01:38:03 GMT

RE: STEVEN MOFFAT'S THIGHS

No, it's flying east. Chiswick is in West London. They say 'up west' on *EastEnders* because… well, that's in East London. And on that bombshell…

FROM: RUSSELL T DAVIES TO: BENJAMIN COOK
MONDAY 29 OCTOBER 2007 03:18:42 GMT

RE: STEVEN MOFFAT'S THIGHS

ATTACH: 4.11 (TOTAL PAGE COUNT: 20 2/8)

I've written a bit more, just so that they've 20 pages to be getting on with at the Production Meeting in the morning. Now I need sleep.

FROM: RUSSELL T DAVIES TO: BENJAMIN COOK
TUESDAY 30 OCTOBER 2007 02:05:44 GMT

RE: STEVEN MOFFAT'S THIGHS

ATTACH: 4.11 (TOTAL PAGE COUNT: 30 6/8)

Is 4.11 too adult? I've already taken out lines about the mass graves in the south of England. But I do like that creating-a-whole-different-world thing. It's hard to do, but an enjoyable sort of hard. One minute, Donna and her family are normal people. The next, they're impoverished and homeless, all in a few short scenes. I sort of believe it, that it could happen to any of us, all of us, in the blink of an eye. One day, I want to write a huge-scale adult series with that happening. It's good for Donna, too. I love writing her. There's an indestructible core to her, like she's always determinedly at a right-angle to events. I'd love to be like Donna.

FROM: RUSSELL T DAVIES TO: BENJAMIN COOK
TUESDAY 30 OCTOBER 2007 18:44:40 GMT

RE: STEVEN MOFFAT'S THIGHS

I'd been hoping that I'd finish 4.11 by tomorrow afternoon, so I could hotfoot it to the Albert Hall for the National Television Awards, but that's buggered. I'm getting nowhere today. I'm always planning dramatic arrivals that never actually happen. Maybe everyone does.

FROM: BENJAMIN COOK TO: RUSSELL T DAVIES
WEDNESDAY 31 OCTOBER 2007 20:28:46 GMT

RE: STEVEN MOFFAT'S THIGHS

I'm e-mailing you in the dark. If I switch the lights off, the trick-or-treaters won't know that I'm in. The National Television Awards start in half an hour. Are you there? (If you are, pointless question.)

FROM: RUSSELL T DAVIES TO: BENJAMIN COOK
WEDNESDAY 31 OCTOBER 2007 22:19:19 GMT

RE: STEVEN MOFFAT'S THIGHS

Happy Halloween! I'm stuck at home working, but I might as well have gone – I'm getting 50 texts a minute from the Albert Hall. Hey, *Doctor Who* won Most Popular Drama! And David is Most Popular Actor! He dedicated his award to his mum. I did that when I won Comedy Writer Of The Year, but then had 107 people coming up to me afterwards, saying, 'Your mother must be delighted.' I spent the evening saying, 'No, she's dead.' That put the dampeners on it.

FROM: RUSSELL T DAVIES TO: BENJAMIN COOK
WEDNESDAY 31 OCTOBER 2007 23:46:09 GMT

RE: STEVEN MOFFAT'S THIGHS

ATTACH: 4.11 (TOTAL PAGE COUNT: 55)

Sad news. Howard Attfield died this morning. We've just heard. Coincidentally, we're watching the first edit of 4.1

David Tennant and Freema Agyeman clean up at the 2007 NTAs.
Picture © David Fisher/Rex Features

tomorrow, which has the Geoff stuff edited into it, just so that we can get the feel of that sequence in the overall shape of the episode. That's going to be weird. Poor old Howard. It feels double-weird reading back the stuff in 4.11 where Sylvia and Donna mention Geoff.

Anyway, writing 4.11 is hard enough at the moment. Rose has to explain the whole situation to Donna. The problem is, the audience sort of knows what's going on, but you can't skip Donna's reactions, and there's so much to react to, so I have to keep it interesting, somehow new and slightly unexpected, while working out where to place what information and when. I'd hoped to finish tonight. Ah, sod it. That's enough for now. I've smoked too much.

FROM: RUSSELL T DAVIES TO: BENJAMIN COOK
THURSDAY 1 NOVEMBER 2007 11:55:03 GMT

RE: STEVEN MOFFAT'S THIGHS

I'm hotfooting it from the 4.1 Edit. First reaction: I am delighted. Mad, funny, weird, mental, it's oddly unpredictable, sort of unclassifiable. The genre keeps switching like crazy. There's a long way to go – I've three solid pages of notes, and Phil and Julie have tons more

– but I know we'll get it to where we want it. Actually, I think the loveliest moment is when the taxi driver pulls up and says, 'Stacy Campbell?' It's a small part for an actor, but he says it perfectly. And Donna looks so lost. The night and the street and the sudden calm are just perfect. It feels real, in that moment. A little, insignificant moment just crystallises into everything that I wanted.

FROM: BENJAMIN COOK TO: RUSSELL T DAVIES
THURSDAY 1 NOVEMBER 2007 14:23:44 GMT

RE: STEVEN MOFFAT'S THIGHS

Have you ever been disappointed at an Edit? Like, *really* disappointed? Crushingly disappointed? What do you do? Is it too late by then?

FROM: RUSSELL T DAVIES TO: BENJAMIN COOK
THURSDAY 1 NOVEMBER 2007 16:11:04 GMT

RE: STEVEN MOFFAT'S THIGHS

I live in a state of constant disappointment, but that's what makes you work harder, to act on that disappointment and eliminate it. The Edit tends to get skipped in all discussions of modern *Doctor Who*, like all we do is delete a few lines. But the Edit is tough, vigorous and merciless, because that's when you really shape all those words and pictures into the drama. It's like starting again. It's like production begins from scratch. No one ever takes the script into the Edit, because it's irrelevant by then. You're dealing with what you've got, not what you should have got. That's why we go through five, six, seven edits, with millions of notes from all of us, every time.

I'm making this sound very executive-driven, like Julie, Phil and I do all the work. Of course, the director and the editor do a hell of a lot before we even step in there. Having said that, *Doctor Who* has limited post-production time, so often we get to see the show at a stage when, really, the director and editor should spend another fortnight in there alone. But that's disingenuous, because we love going in there while it's still a bit raw. We know how to hammer something into shape. I'm always reading about interfering executives sitting in Edits, demanding that you shave a few frames off a shot, as a Great Evil Of Modern TV… but that's exactly what we do, and I think it's right. I suppose if your executive is a bonehead, you're in trouble. But then the US system is to lose the director from the Edit, so the producers take over completely.

A lot of what we do is eliminating the disappointment. Any moment that's only 90 per cent, we work at – try this, try that, cut it faster, lose that line, add music, play it off David, emphasise Catherine during that bit of dialogue – to make it a hundred per cent. Any moment that's only fifty per cent, we'll move heaven and earth to cut. You sharpen and concentrate it, until you like it. The more you watch something, the more you like it, the more you forgive it, the more inclined you are to accept its faults, and that's why you have to remember the impact of that very first viewing, always. The most awful viewing was the first Edit for *The Runaway Bride*, because the director, Euros Lyn, and his editor hadn't had time – in a tricky episode, with that motorway chase and everything – to put on any music. (We always watch with temporary guide tracks, like movie scores and things.) It was the flattest hour of *Doctor Who* ever, particularly when it's supposed to be a big, blousy Christmas episode. The music is so vital to this version of the show. God, that was dispiriting! I was gutted. It was like watching an episode where David has a bag over his head.

I'm just describing a writer's life, really – and a producer's, a director's, an editor's. Everything is a work in progress. Potential is never reached. Do you remember how worried I was, on *Voyage of the Damned*, that the passengers and crew of the *Titanic* would appear to be human? That it looks like they're from Earth instead of just visiting? We played about with giving them bindis and stuff, although we abandoned that idea. Well, just last night, it occurred to me that I should have simply had the people on the *Titanic* referring to 'the humans' a lot more. Like, a couple of dozen times, in the dialogue. It's so obvious! I can't believe it didn't occur to me earlier. Too late now, of course. Instead, we faffed about with sodding bindis. In 20 years' time, that'll still niggle me. It'll always be a work in progress.

FROM: RUSSELL T DAVIES TO: BENJAMIN COOK
FRIDAY 2 NOVEMBER 2007 03:12:03 GMT

RE: STEVEN MOFFAT'S THIGHS

ATTACH: 4.11 (TOTAL PAGE COUNT: 46 5/8)

Finito 4.11! I'm not sure it makes sense. Sod it, I'm posting it to the office now. They need prep. Ooh, I can

Above: The Doctor (David Tennant) and his 'daughter' Jenny (Georgia Moffett) in 4.6 *The Doctor's Daughter*. Facing page: Russell with original *Doctor Who* producer Verity Lambert. Photograph by Andy Short © *SFX Magazine* 2006

sleep tomorrow.

The best news is – I looked at my watch, thinking of telling you this, and it was 9.15pm tonight – I finally worked out how to write out Donna at the end of the series! This has been driving me mad. Quietly, desperately insane. There isn't time to tell you all the stuff going on in my head, but sometimes I leave out the most awful fears, because I don't even like admitting them to myself. It's been churning in my head – *how, how, how?* All day long, every day – *how?* She loves the Doctor, she loves travelling with him, she chose to be with him and went to extraordinary lengths to find him again, and she has precious little to go back to, so how could she leave? She gets injured? Dies? Sylvia dies? Donna gets lost in time, and I pick her up for one of the Specials (we find her years later, on an alien world, citizen of the universe, older and wiser, no longer needing the Doctor)? None of those ideas worked. They're all crap. They're all dull, actually. But then, tonight, I solved it. At 9.15pm. It's like it just went *wham!* Right now, I can't wait to write it. Huge stuff.

And I'm not going to tell you what it is! HA HA HA! It needs to sink into my head for a bit. But I don't think you should know. I think you should find out.

FROM: BENJAMIN COOK TO: RUSSELL T DAVIES
FRIDAY 2 NOVEMBER 2007 08:21:29 GMT

RE: STEVEN MOFFAT'S THIGHS

NOOOOOOOOOO!!!

Fine. I'll wait. Hmpf.

FROM: RUSSELL T DAVIES TO: BENJAMIN COOK
THURSDAY 8 NOVEMBER 2007 23:47:14 GMT

RE: STEVEN MOFFAT'S THIGHS

Episode 8 is shaping up nicely. We've cast Sam Kelly as Professor Hobbes, Lindsey Coulson as Val Cane, Daniel Ryan as Biff Cane (he was Rose's first boyfriend, Andy, in *Bob & Rose* – it's a Lesley/Daniel reunion!), and Rakie Ayola as the Hostess. That's an amazing cast. I'm so excited. Also, we've auditioned a very handsome Goth-type Jethro. Those eyes! His name is Colin Morgan. Oh, and did I tell you that we've cast Georgia Moffett as the Doctor's daughter in 4.6? Peter Davison's real-life daughter! She *really is* the Doctor's daughter! We didn't cast her for the publicity, honest. She's genuinely fantastic. She's going to have one hell of a career.

But I hit the roof the other day, because Episode 8

of *Sarah Jane* hasn't shaped up so nicely: it went out on the CBBC Channel with bloody atrocious credits. 'CASTING BY ANDY PRYGOR', that sort of thing! How amateur. I banged off an e-mail accusing Julie, Phil, Matthew Bouch and me of not looking after that show in post-production enough. We were all there for filming and the Edits, but then other work has overtaken us and we've neglected it. That was all a bit sour.

Also, I saw David and Catherine tonight, to explain the end of 4.13 to them. That went down a treat. Bloody lovely. They were enraptured. David kept on saying, 'That's *exactly* where it should end!' But I'm not going to tell you what that means.

FROM: RUSSELL T DAVIES TO: BENJAMIN COOK
WEDNESDAY 14 NOVEMBER 2007 00:14:58 GMT

SILENCE IN THE DISCO

I've been on the phone to Julie since 9.30pm. Sometimes the BBC is the maddest, stupidest place in the whole world. An example: it was proposed that the Christmas Special press launch – it's on 18 December – has a disco. Well, okay, fine. The place is booked until midnight. But the council says that the music has to stop by 11pm, so what happens between 11pm and midnight? Mrs Event Organiser says, 'I thought we could have a silent disco. It worked well when I was at MTV.' A silent disco – though you're 25 and probably know this – is when everyone puts on their iPods and dances in silence. At a *Doctor Who* press launch! To quote Julie, 'We're not launching bloody *Skins*!'

FROM: BENJAMIN COOK TO: RUSSELL T DAVIES
WEDNESDAY 14 NOVEMBER 2007 00:32:25 GMT

RE: SILENCE IN THE DISCO

Silent discos are fun. There was one at Glastonbury this year. Then again, there were Portaloos, pear cider, Lily Allen, and people swimming in their own excrement at Glastonbury, but none of that would go down very well at a *Doctor Who* press launch. You were right to scoff.

FROM: RUSSELL T DAVIES TO: BENJAMIN COOK
TUESDAY 20 NOVEMBER 2007 21:10:20 GMT

RE: SILENCE IN THE DISCO

This morning, we found out that lovely Sam Kelly, who was to be Professor Hobbes in 4.8, has been involved in a car crash and broken his leg. So he's out. We'll have to recast. Oh God…

I got a car back to Cardiff from Manchester last night, and it occurred to me, out of the blue, as we drove along… I should do a Davros origin story in 4.12/4.13! Like I did with the Master in *The Sound of Drums*. It sort of demands it, doesn't it? How did Davros become how he is? How did he get scarred? Well, he was Josef Mengele, wasn't he? The war, the wounded, the experiments. Blimey, that's good. (Interesting use of the word 'good', but you know what I mean.) Trouble is, in costing these episodes, I haven't allowed for that at all – digital mattes of Skaro, hospitals full of wounded – but it's worth pushing for, don't you think?

FROM: RUSSELL T DAVIES TO: BENJAMIN COOK
THURSDAY 22 NOVEMBER 2007 13:23:02 GMT

RE: SILENCE IN THE DISCO

I received an e-mail from Janet Fielding this morning. She used to run the Women in Film and Television organisation, and I'm due to go to the WFTV Awards on 7 December, to give a Lifetime Achievement award to Verity Lambert. David is going, too, if he can be released from the schedule. But the e-mail is devastating. Verity's cancer has returned. She's been taken into palliative care. Janet, bless her, is apologising, because now they want the award to be collected by a friend of Verity's. As if I'd mind! I don't like to intrude and ask how bad it really is, but…

Text message from: Russell
Sent: 22-Nov-2007 23:22
Verity Lambert died today. We've just heard. I'm ridiculously sad.

Text message from: Ben
Sent: 22-Nov-2007 23:32
I'm speechless. Tomorrow is *Doctor Who*'s 44th anniversary. None of us would be doing what we're doing if it weren't for her.

Text message from: Russell
Sent: 22-Nov-2007 23:36
I know. We're putting a dedication at the end of the Xmas Special.

Text message from: Ben
Sent: 22-Nov-2007 23:37
I was going to suggest it, but then realised that of course you'd be doing that. Quite right.

Text message from: Russell
Sent: 22-Nov-2007 23:57
Julie just said, 'Knowing our luck with graphics, it'll be spelt "Varsity Lamboot"!' I've been laughing so much, like you do when you're sad.

Text message from: Ben
Sent: 23-Nov-2007 00:02
I'm just glad that she lived to see *Doctor Who* become, once again, as brilliant and imaginative and important and loved as it was when she produced it.

Text message from: Russell
Sent: 23-Nov-2007 00:07
Yes! And she really did watch it. When I met her last year, she said, 'All those Daleks flying into Canary Wharf! I wish we could have done that.' Oh, but you did, Verity. You made it all.

FROM: RUSSELL T DAVIES TO: BENJAMIN COOK
SATURDAY 24 NOVEMBER 2007 13:01:49 GMT

RE: SILENCE IN THE DISCO

Yesterday's read-through of 4.8 was a bit disconcerting. (Everyone else was happy, but sod them.) It just sounded slight and unimportant and weak. Maybe whacking great CUs of fearful faces will sell it. Lesley synced so well with everyone – it was an astonishing performance – so it sounded interesting rather than scary. It even started to sound natural. I do worry that a thin conceit has become a whole episode. I know that I've taken a big risk. I'm a bit worried.

The read-through of 4.11, on the other hand, was magnificent. Rarely have I been so pleased in a read-through. Catherine blazed her way through it. She did something I've never seen anyone do before: she said a line, made it hugely funny, everyone roared with laughter, then she looked up, looked around, and she laughed too! It was a look of absolute pure delight. Great moment. Catherine's capacity to perform anything really frees me up, to go anywhere, to say anything. There's a great bit in that script, when Donna is being sacked, and there's a *whumph!* as the Royal Hope Hospital is returned to Earth, offstage, but she's so full of her own problems, she turns to the office and says, 'Well, isn't that wizard?!' There's something about that line that proves everything that I've been trying to say about dialogue, how free you can be, because I've never heard anyone say, 'Isn't that wizard?!' You'd never expect someone like Donna to say 'wizard'. It wouldn't seem to be in her vocabulary. I'm not even sure myself why Donna chooses it. But it works. Somehow, for reasons that I can't even articulate, 'wizard' is exactly right for that moment. Moments like that, I like my writing.

Text message from: Russell
Sent: 25-Nov-2007 18:19
Guess who we've cast as the Professor in 4.8? David Troughton!

Text message from: Ben
Sent: 25-Nov-2007 22:10
Here's a marvellous thing: David Troughton appeared in the 50th *Doctor Who* serial, *The War Games*, back in 1969... and now you've cast him in the 50th episode of the revived series. FANBOY OVERLOAD!

Text message from: Russell
Sent: 25-Nov-2007 22:19
It was meant to be! FANBOY GLEE! Hey, Billie is in town tonight. She starts filming 4.11 tomorrow. Rose Tyler is back!

FROM: RUSSELL T DAVIES TO: BENJAMIN COOK
THURSDAY 29 NOVEMBER 2007 23:45:19 GMT

RE: SILENCE IN THE DISCO

Everything is firing on all cylinders at the moment. We've two episodes filming at once, so it's only to be expected. Catherine and Bernard are brilliant together in 4.11, as are Catherine and Billie. Although, watching the 4.8 rushes is an odd experience, because it's all being shot in sequence. I'm seeing the story unfold, literally, day by day. The cast is starting to go stir-crazy on that

The cast of 4.8 *Midnight*. L–R: Val Cane (Lindsey Coulson), the Hostess (Rakie Ayola), Professor Hobbes (David Troughton), the Doctor (David Tennant), Jethro Cane (Colin Morgan), Dee Dee Blasco (Ayesha Antoine), Biff Cane (Daniel Ryan) and Sky Silvestry (Lesley Sharp). Inset: Donna stays behind to moonbathe! Illustration by Russell T Davies.

Crusader 50 set. They did the monster-knocking-on-the-outside-of-the-bus scene today. Both David and Lesley texted to say, 'We're scared to death!' More importantly, Colin Morgan is beautiful. You meet him in real life and think, yeah, nice, sweet. But he's one of those lucky bastards that the camera absolutely loves. All cheekbones and black hair and *mmm!* He's a seriously excellent actor, too. Every line, he makes a really interesting choice.

I would describe to you the fear and bile that's rising up with the approach of writing the series finale, but I can't bear to. Oh, that cold clutch of fear. Steven wrote to me today, saying, 'Don't you feel like sticking your head out of the window and yelling, "I DON'T KNOW WHAT I'M DOING!!!"' Yes, absolutely. Solidarity. Fear is always the same. Different worries with different scripts, but the same baseline fear.

FROM: BENJAMIN COOK TO: RUSSELL T DAVIES
FRIDAY 30 NOVEMBER 2007 00:02:56 GMT

RE: SILENCE IN THE DISCO

It can't all be fear and bile, can it? Aren't there bits of 4.12/4.13 that you're really looking forward to writing?

FROM: RUSSELL T DAVIES TO: BENJAMIN COOK
FRIDAY 30 NOVEMBER 2007 00:24:48 GMT

RE: SILENCE IN THE DISCO

It's not all fear and bile, no. Like, I've worked out the end to 4.13 – well, not the very end, that's Donna, but the climax to the plot and all the Dalek stuff. I went into a frenzy, playing Murray's Series Three soundtrack CD full-blast. I actually stood up and walked around the room. For ages, just striding. And hitting things. I was sort of banging work surfaces and stuff. Sometimes that happens. After about 20 minutes of frenzy, I was actually crying. In a good way. With relief. With happiness, actually. Because it works. I really think it works and will be magnificent. Right now, I believe in it with all my heart. So that's good. That's not fear and bile.

Of course, it's only one of a thousand problems solved – I don't know how I get everyone to the right positions yet, that's the tricky thing, the geography – but the sheer joy of that resolution is fantastic. It's so *Doctor Who*. It's so Doctor. It's so Donna. Sod off, Davros, you've no chance!

FROM: RUSSELL T DAVIES TO: BENJAMIN COOK
SATURDAY 1 DECEMBER 2007 14:35:44 GMT

RE: SILENCE IN THE DISCO

In the early hours of this morning, Steven Moffat delivered 4.10! At last! It's brilliant, of course. Such an imagination, it's staggering. I'm not sure I understand it yet, but then I read it at about 3am. We're trying to get Kate Winslet for River Song, who's sort of the Doctor's wife, and Michael Gambon or Ian McKellen for Dr Moon. Fat chance!

I've just returned from Shan Shen, the fabled Chino planet. I have voyaged to the stars! In an alley behind Cardiff's Royal Infirmary. It's an amazing set. Smoke, lanterns, chickens, peppers, alien fruit… and it's only for two short scenes! It's starting to piss down now, but that's probably made it more *Blade Runner*-y. It's unsettling, though, going on set, because I feel such a stranger. Almost a fraud. All I do is type the words 'Shan Shen', that's easy, and then all those people have to slave away on a Saturday, in the rain, to create the bloody thing. I actually feel guilty. Julie and I laugh about what the crew must think of us when we turn up on set, because inevitably you're met with 'Nice of you to join us', like we've left our catamites and Leisure Palaces to walk amongst the workers. People talk as though you've never been on a set before, almost saying, 'This is the camera. This is the director. You'll have to be quiet because we're going for a take,' forgetting that we've spent 20 years on different sets in every sort of circumstance. You see yourself becoming that oft-joked-about, never-on-set producer. Like all that experience was for nothing. Hey ho.

Text message from: **Russell**
Sent: 03-Dec-2007 22:14
We've just played the Christmas episode to Kylie, in London. She clapped and laughed and cried and even sang a bit. What a weird night!

Text message from: **Ben**
Sent: 03-Dec-2007 22:19
Send her my love. Actually, she's probably forgotten who I am.

Text message from: **Russell**
Sent: 03-Dec-2007 22:21
Oh, she's disappeared off into the night now. She's probably forgotten me already. She is not of this mortal Earth.

Above: Russell T Davies, Debbie Chazen and Kylie Minogue – who is not of this Earth – in the bar of Cardiff's St David's Hotel in July 2007. Below: A Cyberman.

Text message from: **Ben**
Sent: 03-Dec-2007 22:22
Yes. She's stardust.

FROM: RUSSELL T DAVIES TO: BENJAMIN COOK
THURSDAY 6 DECEMBER 2007 14:05:57 GMT

CRUSADER 52?

Time for an update. Phil wasn't part of the discussions about Donna's parallel worlds in both 4.10 and 4.11. Coming to it clean – this is why it's good to have someone coming to it clean – he's thrown his hands up in horror and said that we can't run both episodes consecutively. Yikes! He's right, of course. He wondered whether we should ask Steven to write out Donna's parallel life completely, but it's way too integral. And I've known about it all along, so it's my fault. As a result, we're shifting the transmission order. Steven's two-parter becomes Episodes 8 and 9, *Midnight* becomes Episode 10, and then Episode 11 remains the same, so there's a one-episode buffer in between Donna's two parallel worlds.

Tragically, that means that *Midnight* is no longer our fiftieth episode. My fanboy heart is broken. It might as well be the *Crusader 52* now. What a shame. (And we've lost your marvellous David Troughton/fiftieth episode fact!) Hand on heart, though, I think the new order is good. All the experimental stuff gets shifted further back in the series. I worry that running *Midnight* and *Turn Left* consecutively means two lower-budget episodes in a row – but actually that was the same as *Love & Monsters* and *Fear Her*, and the ratings went up, week on week, so I'm worrying for nothing. That doesn't stop me worrying, though, but there we go.

Elsewhere, in Maybe land, it's a pit of despair! I even hesitated over that exclamation mark, because that's making it sound like fun. I know I had that moment of joy the other day, but it hasn't lasted. There's a greater fear, of course, and that's Christmas 2008. That's doing my head in, above and beyond 4.12/4.13. I haven't a clue – and it has to be written in February! I keep thinking of ways to escape. I could tell them that there just won't be a Christmas 2008 episode. 'Tough!' What would happen? The world wouldn't end. But Julie would die. I couldn't bear to let her down that much.

I'm not sure about Cybermen in the snow, in Victorian times. Would it be a retread of *The Unquiet Dead*? I spent a day wondering if the court of Henry VIII would be better, but that's not Christmassy enough. You'd have a banquet, but no turkey. It'd be flagstones, knights, swords and funny trousers, none of which feels Christmas Day enough. Plus, translating Victorian into Tudor is hardly a solution; it's just a disguise. How about something completely new? After the *Torchwood* press launch in London on Monday, I spent the night in a large, faceless Paddington hotel. I couldn't sleep, so I went for some ice at 2am. All the big, wide corridors were empty. Not a noise. The machine on Floor 2 wasn't working, so I went up to Floor 3. Still empty. The lift shafts were sort of humming, almost roaring. It was eerie. And I imagined, what if I was a dad and I'd left my family in the room, and when I got back… they were gone? Just gone. That's the start of a *Doctor Who* story! The whole hotel is empty, at Christmas, like it's been taken out of time or something, and creatures are beginning to stir, and the only other person in existence is this man called the Doctor. That sort of thing. Nice. But random. In need of an awful lot of thought – and I have to write this in February, so there's not enough time to develop it. I'm stuck with random, mad thoughts, desperately trying to plug a gap, but none of them quite working. It feels lousy. Sometimes I think, if I just died, all of this would go away. That begins to feel like a good option. It wouldn't be letting anyone down. I'd be blameless and free and martyred. Ridiculous, I know.

FROM: BENJAMIN COOK TO: RUSSELL T DAVIES
THURSDAY 6 DECEMBER 2007 15:18:15 GMT

RE: CRUSADER 52?

It's lucky that you're an atheist, then. Bugger all on the other side, and you know it. You'd *hate* that.

Besides, if you died, I'd never find out what's in store for Donna Noble. Reason enough to keep going, Russell.

Text message from: **Russell**
Sent: 07-Dec-2007 15:22
Are you on set today? I hope the *Crusader 52* is fun.

Text message from: **Ben**
Sent: 07-Dec-2007 15:26
I am on set, and it'll always be the *Crusader 50* to me. I helped name this bus! What am I supposed to do with my David Troughton/50th episode fact now, eh? The horror.

Text message from: **Ben**
Sent: 07-Dec-2007 16:16
Hold the presses! I've just realised, *Midnight* IS still the 50th episode of new *Doctor Who*… to be shot! Filming on *Turn Left* started one day earlier, didn't it? So this is still (sort of) the 50th something after all. My fanboy mind is delighted.

Text message from: **Russell**
Sent: 07-Dec-2007 16:18
Ha ha ha, oh, your fanboyness! I love it. Yes, *Turn Left* started a day earlier, so it definitely came first. That's cheered me up. I'll sleep easier in my bed tonight.

CHAPTER TWELVE

HOLDING THE LINE

In which working on *Doctor Who* is likened to al-Qaeda, Russell loses his trousers in Soho, and Catherine Tate sparks a major diplomatic incident

FROM: RUSSELL T DAVIES TO: BENJAMIN COOK
FRIDAY 7 DECEMBER 2007 21:09:20 GMT

RE: CRUSADER 52?

Huge movements on Series Five. Piers Wenger has said yes to Julie's job – to the whole job, Head of Drama at BBC Wales, everything. However, with the usual *Doctor Who* madness, *The Guardian* has got hold of it, so a press release has had to go out, announcing Julie's departure… in 18 months' time! This is the only job where that gets reported so far in advance! Even Tony Blair kept us guessing for longer.

It's our production manager Tracie Simpson's farewell party on Monday. First Tracie, then it'll be Phil, and now Julie is off. It's the end, slowly. Piers and Steven had a train journey back from Cardiff together on Tuesday, so you could say that work on Series Five has already begun. That's weird. Actually, it doesn't feel weird – I'm not sure I feel anything at all about it. But as a fanboy – how exciting! That's a brilliant team.

FROM: RUSSELL T DAVIES TO: BENJAMIN COOK
MONDAY 10 DECEMBER 2007 03:21:07 GMT

RE: CRUSADER 52?

I spent today considering one tangible thing: whether to destroy New York in 4.12. That would be fun, wouldn't it? The idea came from the fact that all the Doctor's companions are found in England. I've a chance to expand on that, create a bigger world. Maybe Martha is in New York? She'd have to be saved, maybe by trying some experimental UNIT teleport that zaps her out of the building before Dalek lasers hit. The only survivor! It suits Martha, that lone warrior feel, and brings her back to England with an easy zap. But destroying New York has its problems: it leaves heavy repercussions for the rest of *Doctor Who* history, because there's no reset button. I worry about that. Series Five is bound to have episodes set on modern-day Earth – and that might be hard to establish, because it'd be a very wounded world. It even deflates the end of 4.13, with the Doctor flying

Cribbins v. the Daleks – the rematch! Illustration by Russell T Davies.

planet Earth back home, all happy and hooray… except for that smouldering crater with millions dead! These e-mails do influence things, definitely, because now I'm thinking, no, destroying New York is a bad choice. Typing it out in this e-mail made me realise that, but it's good to spend a day considering the option. This is the only job in the world where you can do that. Unless you work for al-Qaeda, I suppose. I might not destroy New York at all, but the thought is a good indication that I need to work harder to establish a worldwide feel.

I'm definitely doing Bernard Cribbins and the paint gun, though. Did I tell you this? He phoned me up a while back – I love getting phone calls off Bernard – and said, 'Is it true we're meeting the Daleks in the last episodes?' 'Yes, Bernard.' 'I've fought them before, you know!'[1] 'I know, Bernard, it was 41 years ago.' 'I've always had this great idea,' he said. 'You know those paint gun things? You could take out a Dalek with a paint gun, cos it's only got one eye. Bit of paint on the eye, it'd be blinded!' I was hooting. I said, 'I'll see what I can do.' It could be brilliant – if only because Bernard Cribbins requested it. I'd better not tell the rest of the cast that I'm taking requests!

FROM: BENJAMIN COOK TO: RUSSELL T DAVIES
MONDAY 10 DECEMBER 2007 03:28:47 GMT

RE: CRUSADER 52?

Look, 03:21 that last e-mail was sent! Do you never sleep? Once again, we're both still up at ridiculous o'clock. Why don't we just work in offices, Russell? Wouldn't that be easier? Don't you think? Go on, tell me why you don't work nine-to-five in an office. Why isn't that the life for you?

FROM: RUSSELL T DAVIES TO: BENJAMIN COOK
MONDAY 10 DECEMBER 2007 04:05:01 GMT

RE: CRUSADER 52?

It's funny you should ask, because I *did* work in offices, in TV, for years and years, but I never fitted those hours. When I was storylining the soap *Revelations*, I was locked in an office with a brilliant man called Paul Marquess, who went on to create *Footballers' Wives*. We had such a laugh. One of the best times of my working life. I refused to start work at 9am. I physically couldn't. We'd be in the office at 9am every day, but we'd just hoot and gossip. We fancied a man down the corridor, called Tony Gregory, and invented excuses to walk past his door 15 times a day. We'd sit with Pritt Stick and Tipp-Ex and the photocopier, and invent *Revelations* paperback covers. We had a trainee called Jim who we'd torment all day, because he was the token straight in a sea of gays. But then, around about 4pm, we'd start work – and we'd be there till gone midnight, because then we'd work hard and properly. I loved storylining. Those ideas were watertight and insane. Looking back, I probably drove Paul mad. Every so often, he'd say, plaintively, 'Can we do some work now?' But I'd be busy cutting out cast photos and giving them moving mouths like Captain Pugwash, so I could act out the shows in puppet form! I was making a nine-to-five office job fit me. But that was the mid '90s,

1 Bernard Cribbins played police constable Tom Campbell in the 1966 movie *Daleks – Invasion Earth 2150 AD*, based on the 1964 *Doctor Who* television serial *The Dalek Invasion of Earth*.

when I was already set on leaving to become a writer. I knew what I wanted. I was only storylining *Revelations* so that I'd get to write the best episodes. But before that…

I read those interviews with people who say 'I knew that I wanted to become a writer when I was six years old' with such envy. I didn't know. For a long time. Partly because being a writer didn't even seem like an option. It was like wishing to be a pop star or a mountaineer or a pianist. In my head, I was writing all the time, in the sense of making up stories, but I thought that was just *thinking*. Like, that's how people think. I thought everyone did it. Daydreaming. Doodling. Literally doodling – I'd draw all the time. All that energy went into cartooning. Just as a hobby, but a compulsive hobby. Everything I drew, I'd expand into stories. When I was 15, 16, I'd imagine being a Marvel artist. (A careers teacher said, 'You're colour blind. You'll never work in the graphics industry if you're colour blind', and crushed that dream dead.) Even at Oxford University, I poured all that energy into drawing. I had a cartoon strip in the student newspaper. I'd illustrate the Student Handbook. Far more important to me than lectures. After Oxford, I went to Cardiff to do a postgraduate course in Theatre Studies, because I couldn't think what else to do with my life, but even then I was drawing all the time. I covered my bedroom wall with my own artwork. I became a poster designer for Cardiff's Sherman Theatre. Drew some of my best stuff ever. One of my first TV jobs was illustrating a *Jackanory*-type show for BBC Wales.

When I landed my first producing job, on *Why Don't You…?*, a magazine show with a gang of kids showing you things to do in the school holidays, my real passion was the Fact Pack, a free photocopy that we'd send out to viewers, packed with games, recipes, puzzles and stuff. I started to expand the illustrations into cartoon adventures. I was meant to be illustrating recipes, which was boring, so I thought it'd be fun if I brought a Potato to life. Then he needed someone to talk to, so I added an Egg and a Plastic Cup. They started to grow personalities, way beyond the gags. Potato was bullish and verbose, Egg was simple and sweet, Plastic Cup was sarky, sly and undoubtedly gay. Their simple lives started to develop into stories. I drew one where the Stationery Cupboard went to war with the Kitchen, which is still one of the best things I've ever done. Eventually, whole pages of the Fact Packs were given over to them, and their adventures became more and more epic. I was obsessive about it. At one point, I started sort of seeing a very nice hairdresser called Mark, but I had a Fact Pack to complete and gave it more time than I did him. Eventually, he said, 'This is never going to work. That drawing's more important to you than I am.' He was right. Obsession sounds like a bad thing, but it was more like love. I loved those cartoons. I still do.

During all this, I had the day job on *Why Don't You…?* proper. That was the office job. Organising schedules, material, rehearsals and stuff. Edits. Dubs. Lunch in the canteen. The nine-to-five job. But I glided through that. The real stuff, the creativity, for me, was drawing Potato fighting Paperclips, at night, at home, in the cartoons – and then the same thing started to happen to my *Why Don't You…?* scripts. I started to dramatise them. I couldn't help it. Scenes would link together. Gags would become running jokes. The kid presenters grew screen personalities – one daft, one cheeky, one mad – so that they could interact better. They started to have adventures. One week, they went off to explore Loch Ness, to find the Loch Ness Monster. That episode was the first time that I realised what I'd done. I remember, clearly, going home and thinking, take out the recipes and I've just written a drama! I only realised it after I'd written it. Not everyone liked it, of course. The Head of Children's Television, Anna Home, did comment, 'It's not supposed to be a drama. You're failing the magazine content.' That was true. I guess that was an official slap-down. But I ignored it. Like you do. You're cheeky when you're young.

Why Don't You Just Switch Off Your Television Set And Go Out And Do Something Less Boring Instead? Like read Russell's lovely Fact Pack!

In my final year on *Why Don't You...?*, for my very last episode, I really went for it: recipes and puzzles and makes were chucked out of the window, and the *Why Don't You...?* gang found themselves trapped in their cellar with an insane supercomputer, which they defeated with an electric, lemon-powered skateboard. We *tripled* the ratings! Turning it into a drama sent that show from 0.9 million to 2.9. We were carried around Television Centre in a ticker-tape parade (not really, but almost). After I left, the show went back to its magazine format… and ratings fell to 0.9 million again. Hah! Seriously, that was me realising how powerful drama can be, how it can draw you in and build an audience. But I only did it because I like stories. Storytelling just bleeds out. Of course, much of it was disguised as drawing. I can still see cartooning in my work (cue internet insults), in the speed and the fast cuts, the visual gags, the pacing of the dialogue, but now my hobby is my life. That's why I never think of it as work, really, no matter how much hard graft I actually do. Even if no one ever saw this stuff, I'd be doing it anyway.

Nowadays, by the way, I run screaming from the notion of nine-to-five office life. Four years on *Doctor Who*, and I've never had an office. Never even had a desk. It'd be handy sometimes, to have somewhere to escape to or sit and think on my own when trapped in BBC Wales, but it wouldn't work. I'd end up drawing on the walls.

FROM: BENJAMIN COOK TO: RUSSELL T DAVIES
MONDAY 10 DECEMBER 2007 10:07:36 GMT

RE: CRUSADER 52?

>>I never think of it as work, really, no matter how much hard graft I actually do. Even if no one ever saw this stuff, I'd be doing it anyway.<<

I believe that. I'm going to quote it back at you next time it all gets too much. I'm going to make you write it out and stick it above your computer!

FROM: RUSSELL T DAVIES TO: BENJAMIN COOK
MONDAY 10 DECEMBER 2007 23:39:02 GMT

RE: CRUSADER 52?

I've just got back from Tracie Simpson's surprise farewell party. It was a genuine surprise, I think. She looked shell-shocked, instead of acting all fake-surprised. I think we really got her! Wonderful party. You can just tell that it's going to escalate all night. They're going to be off their heads. I've come home, genuinely sad. Deeply sad, actually. It's starting to sink in: this is the beginning of the end. Phil gave a beautiful speech. He described our very first block of filming, back in 2004, when, after one week, we were three weeks behind. Oh, those dark, dark days. With all our massive experience, we still had no idea how to make a show like *Doctor Who*. No one did. Tonight, Phil said, 'We had the BBC's new flagship in tatters, just one week in.' They were filming on the Tyler's estate, and Phil just couldn't take it any more. He burst into tears. He phoned Julie. Julie calmed him down, and then she said those fateful words: 'I'm sending you someone.' That someone was Tracie. From the next day onwards, the whole show ran better. We got it made thanks to Tracie. And in the history of *Doctor Who*, she's going to look like a footnoted crewmember. Amazing woman. Every single person in that room tonight loves her.

Departing Production Manager Tracie Simpson, with David Tennant.

Anyway, gobsmacking 4.11 rushes today. No kidding, one of the finest pieces of acting I have ever seen – when Catherine realises that she's going to die. She's crying with horror. Absolutely perfect. I texted her to say thanks. She's a very private person, I'm never a hundred per cent sure what she thinks about things, but she texted back: 'I'm so lucky to be doing all this. It's wonderful to be part of it.' That made me happy. Very happy. For many hours. But then I had a terrible conversation with Julie…

I'd e-mailed her asking about delivery dates. She e-mailed back saying that 4.12/4.13 is due by 7 January, and 2008 Christmas Special (officially designated 4.14) is due by – gulp – 18 February. Ten minutes later, she phones up:

```
                JULIE
I know why you're asking.
This is impossible, isn't it?

               RUSSELL
Well, I'll try.

                JULIE
No, but this is really
impossible, isn't it?

               RUSSELL
Well... it's bad.

                JULIE
Do you think you can do it?
```

'A better world takes its place…' Donna's hope is misplaced in 4.11 *Turn Left*.

```
               RUSSELL
Episodes 12 and 13, fine, I'll
have that done. Maybe not all
by the 7th, but certainly 12,
and enough of 13 to be going
on with, and a good synopsis
of the ending for you to work
from.

                JULIE
But then you'll have to work
on that, rewriting it and
getting the FX to budget.
That's another two weeks at
least. That leaves you three
weeks for Christmas 2008. Can
you do it?

               RUSSELL
Um...

                JULIE
I have a plan of attack.
First option is the worst
case scenario: we just don't
do a Special for Christmas
2008.

               RUSSELL
Oh.

Long, long pause. Telephone wires
humming. Then JULIE says, quietly:

                JULIE
That 'oh' is the happiest
I've heard you sound in four
or five years.

               RUSSELL
I just said 'oh'!

                JULIE
No, that was a very big 'oh'.

               RUSSELL
I meant 'oh', that's all,
just 'oh'.

                JULIE
That 'oh' was like, oh the
relief. It was joyous.

               RUSSELL
But what would the channel
say?

                JULIE
They'd be devastated.

               RUSSELL
Then we can't do it.
```

```
                JULIE
We have to, if you can't
write it.

                RUSSELL
But in times like this, when
we're scared of the schedule
and feel like running away
or stopping, you always say,
hold the line. We hold the
line. You always say that.

                JULIE
Right. Then that's what
we'll do.

                RUSSELL
We hold the line?

                JULIE
We hold the line.
```

So we're blundering on. Into the darkness. That conversation has scared me. Julie is going to try to find money to give us an extra week so that we can stand down for seven days before filming 4.14. That would give me an extra week to write, so the deadline would be 25 February. Julie never, ever gives up. She fights. Also, she leads you into conversations like the one above. You find yourself speaking your darkest fears. They become tangible so that you can deal with them. You're not alone.

I think I would back down and give up if BBC One didn't have a new Controller, Jay Hunt, whose appointment was announced last week. We need her on our side, we need her to be waving the flag for *Doctor Who*, more than ever, so that we're not slipping back to become an also-ran. It's absolutely the wrong time for *Doctor Who* to fall out of the schedules. So. We hold the line. I keep going.

Which means I'm going to start 4.12, right…

… now.

FROM: BENJAMIN COOK TO: RUSSELL T DAVIES
TUESDAY 11 DECEMBER 2007 00:04:56 GMT

RE: CRUSADER 52?

You've started! (But have you *really* started?)

One question (but answer it later – don't let me distract you from 4.12): filming Series One, back in 2004, how, after one week, is it possible to be three weeks behind schedule?

Catherine Tate, Julie Gardner and David Tennant gather in composer Murray Gold's London flat for the transmission of 4.1 *Partners in Crime*.

FROM: RUSSELL T DAVIES TO: BENJAMIN COOK
TUESDAY 11 DECEMBER 2007 02:20:47 GMT

4.12

Julie is so sad tonight. She's crying. It really has hit home. The slow end. Funnily enough, it's sort of helping me – makes me determined to write. All those brilliant people on the crew, I've got to write something excellent for them, something that's worth all their time and effort. Yeah, how noble. That'll evaporate by tomorrow.

>>filming Series One, back in 2004, how, after one week, is it possible to be three weeks behind schedule?<<

It's the amount that you plan to complete each day. For his speech at Tracie's party, Phil had dug out our very first callsheets, and we couldn't believe them. Like, we'd planned four pages on the Tyler's estate in the morning – that was just the morning! – then a move across London and another four pages, with monsters and FX and closing off Whitehall. That number of pages – or more – is quite normal for most dramas, but we discovered that *Doctor Who* is more like four to five pages a day. That's why, after that first week, we had a backlog of three weeks' material still to shoot. (I can't believe that it was actually three – I think that's become a good legend – but the point still stands.) It was terrifying. And guess what Julie said? 'Hold the line!' I was offering to rewrite, to cut, to scale down, to seriously change the vision of what the show should be, to make it achievable, but no – 'Hold the line!' And we did, and we learnt, and we got more realistic, and faster, and better.

Anyway, 4.12 has begun. As an opening seven pages, it could hardly be more exciting…

```
1. EXT. SUBURBAN STREET - DAY

An ordinary day. Perfectly normal
street. Nice and quiet.

A MILK FLOAT buzzes its way along,
stops. The MILKMAN gets out, takes
bottles to a house, as, a distance
away…

FX: the grind of engines, and the
TARDIS appears.

THE DOCTOR comes racing out! Stops
dead. DONNA steps out, both looking
round, both wired.

                THE DOCTOR
    It's fine, it's fine,
    everything's fine. Nothing's
    wrong. All fine!
            (yells across)
    'Scuse me! What day is it?

                MILKMAN
    Saturday.

                THE DOCTOR
    Saturday. Good. I like
    Saturdays.

                DONNA
    …so I just met Rose Tyler?

                THE DOCTOR
    Yep.

                DONNA
    But she's locked away in a
    parallel world, yeah?

                THE DOCTOR
    Exactly. If she could cross
    from her parallel world, to
    your parallel world, then
    that means the walls of the
    universe are breaking down.
    If Rose is trying to come
    back… then everything's
    ending.

                DONNA
    And what does Bad Wolf mean?[2]

                THE DOCTOR
    Well, basically, it's an
    inverted retroactive self-
    inculcated autosuggestive
    paradoxical mnemonic.

                DONNA
    In English, Spaceman!

                THE DOCTOR
    Bad Wolf means trouble!

And frustrated, he runs back into
the Tardis, Donna follows -

Door slams shut.

The milkman is strolling back to
his float. But he hears a noise.
A rattling. Ting-ting-ting. Glass.
He looks…

The empty bottles in their crates
are shivering, just a little. Ting-
ting-ting…

He walks closer, puzzled…

They rattle, harder. Shaking.

The milkman looks round. Tiny,
fractional CAMERA SHAKE.

He sees a couple of slates slide
off a roof…

HIGH SHOT on the Milkman, as he
looks up. At the sky.

In horror.

                                CUT TO:

2. INT. TARDIS - DAY

THE DOCTOR at the console, frantic.
```

2 At the end of 4.11, Rose tells Donna to warn the Doctor: 'She said… two words,' remembers Donna. The Doctor: 'What two words? What were they? What did she say?' Donna: 'Bad wolf.'

DONNA calmer.

THE DOCTOR
Readings normal. No disturbance in the vortex. Spatial exorhythms all constant…

DONNA
Thing is though, Doctor. No matter what's happening, and I'm sure it's bad, I get that, but… Rose is coming back. Isn't that good?

And for the first time, he allows himself the biggest smile.

THE DOCTOR
Yeah.

WHUMPH! CAMERA SHAKE, just one, big jolt. Then nothing.

DONNA
What the hell was that…?!

THE DOCTOR
Wasn't us - came from outside -

- and he's running down the ramp, opens the door -

FX: the door opens onto black, empty space. Just dusty swirls of gas and a few lonely rocks tumbling past.

THE DOCTOR (CONT'D)
…what?! But… *what???*

Donna joining him.

DONNA
We're in space. How did that happen, what did you do?

The Doctor runs back to the console - slamming switches - impossible! - running from lever to lever -

THE DOCTOR
But… we haven't moved, we're fixed - can't be! The Tardis is exactly where it was, we haven't budged an inch - but - !

He runs all the way back to Donna. Stunned.

THE DOCTOR (CONT'D)
The Tardis is in the same place. We've stayed still. But the Earth has gone. The entire planet! It's gone!

FX: the Doctor & Donna in the Tardis doorway, the whole box visible, hanging in space and dust and rocks.

CUT TO BLACK.

Bring up CAPTION:

Far across the universe…

MIX TO:

3. INT. UNIT HQ, NEW YORK CITY - NIGHT

Darkness. PRAC SPARKS fizzing. Image resolving, into a CU of MARTHA JONES, lying on the ground, as she lifts her head. Stunned, dazed, shakes it off. Over this, CAPTION:

NEW YORK.

She lifts herself up. It's an office block, smart, swanky, all desks & smoked glass, though now in disarray, everything having been jolted about, though now still. Other WORKERS & UNIT SOLDIERS picking themselves up from the floor.

MARTHA
What was that? Some sort of earthquake, or…? Jalandra, you all right? Wikowsky? Anyone hurt?

Mutters of 'No,' 'I'm okay,' etc. Everyone slowly standing.

MARTHA (CONT'D)
We've lost power. Someone get the lights back on. DaCosta! See to it! Right now! Suzanne, you okay?

SUZANNE is by the window. Looks at Martha. Terrified.

SUZANNE
Martha. Look at the sky.

MARTHA
Why, what is it?

SUZANNE
Just look at the sky.

CUT TO:

4. INT. THE TORCHWOOD HUB - NIGHT

CAPTAIN JACK HARKNESS, picking himself up off the floor. Shakes it off, stunned for a second, and over that, CAPTION:

CARDIFF.

CAPTAIN JACK
Woah! What happened, was it the Rift? Gwen, you okay? Ianto?

Looking round; place in disarray, wires and rubble everywhere, GWEN COOPER, IANTO JONES getting to their feet.

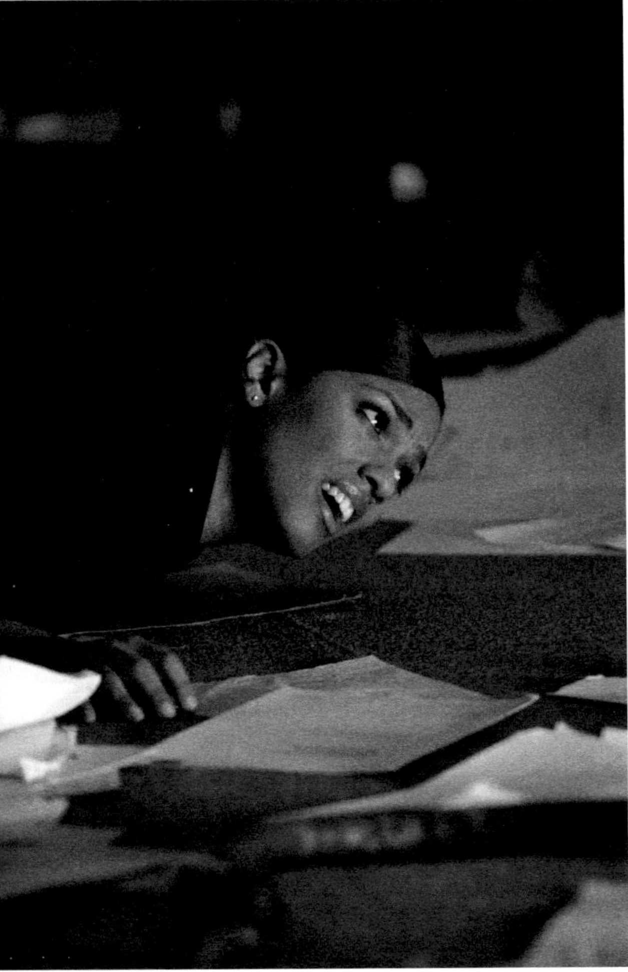

'Some sort of earthquake?' UNIT medic Martha Jones (Freema Agyeman) feels the Earth move in New York City.

GWEN
Whole place just went mental!

IANTO
No broken bones. Slight loss of dignity. No change there then.

GWEN
The whole city must've felt that - the whole of South Wales!

CAPTAIN JACK
I'm gonna take a look outside -

He runs out, the circular door *chunk-chunk-chunking* open...

Ianto has reached his computer. Grim.

IANTO
Little bit bigger than South Wales.

CUT TO:

5. EXT. NOBLES' HOUSE - NIGHT

Over the front door, CAPTION:

LONDON, CHISWICK.

Then it opens, WILF comes out, SYLVIA behind him, Wilf ready for action with a cricket bat.

WILF
That wasn't an earthquake, that was aliens! I'll bet my pension! What d'you want this time, where are you?! C'mon! You green swine!

SYLVIA
Dad...

WILF
You stay inside, Sylvia. They always want the women!

SYLVIA
No, Dad, just look. Oh my God. Look at the sky.

HIGH SHOT, both looking up, in horror...

CUT TO:

6. INT. SARAH JANE SMITH'S ATTIC - NIGHT

CU SARAH JANE SMITH, on the floor, dazed. Bring up CAPTION:

LONDON, EALING.

She stands. The attic in disarray. Her son, LUKE, also standing, recovering. She runs to him, big hug.

SARAH JANE
Luke, are you all right…?

LUKE
Felt like some sort of cross-dimensional spatial transference.

SARAH JANE
But it's night! It wasn't night, it was eight o'clock in the morning… Mr Smith! I need you!

PRAC FX: STEAM! Walls open, fold back, and MR SMITH, the supercomputer, glides out, *ta-daaaa!*

SARAH JANE (CONT'D)
Ohh, I wish you'd stop giving that fanfare - tell me, what happened?

MR SMITH V/O
I think you should look outside, Sarah Jane.

SARAH JANE
Just tell me!

MR SMITH V/O
You will find the visual evidence more conclusive than my current theoretical datastreams.

Cross, huffing, Sarah Jane storms out, Luke following -

CUT TO:

7. EXT. SARAH JANE SMITH'S HOUSE - NIGHT

SARAH JANE & LUKE run out. Stop dead.

HIGH SHOT, BOTH looking up. In horror.

SARAH JANE
…that's impossible…

CUT TO:

8. EXT. ROALD DAHL PLASS - NIGHT

HIGH SHOT. CAPTAIN JACK looking up. Horror.

CAPTAIN JACK
…that's just impossible…

CUT TO:

9. INT. UNIT HQ, NEW YORK CITY - NIGHT

CU MARTHA, in the window. Looking up. In horror.

MARTHA
…it can't be…

CUT TO:

10. EXT. SUBURBAN STREET - NIGHT

The MILKMAN now picking himself up off the floor. Broken milk bottles & crates all around. But as he shakes his head, dazed, he looks round, feeling…

PRAC WIND blasts across him. He shields himself, stares…

FX: HARD CRACK OF WHITE LIGHT, and -

ROSE TYLER appears! Armed with a great big sci-fi gun!

She looks up at the sky.

ROSE
Right. Now we're in trouble.

FX: CAMERA BEHIND ROSE, PANNING UP to see the WHOLE NIGHT SKY. Space, all blue-and-gold clouds and swirls of gas. With DOZENS OF PLANETS suspended there, filling the entire vista, all shapes and sizes, all colours, some ringed, some rocky, some gently moving. A new galaxy.

HIGH SHOT on Rose, looking up; she clicks her gun, *ka-chik!*

ROSE (CONT'D)
And it's only just beginning.

CUT TO TITLES

In Ealing, London, Sarah Jane Smith (Elisabeth Sladen) and her son Luke (Thomas Knight) watch the skies.

I'm stopping now, not because I'm tired but because I'm terrified. It's taken seven pages to get this far into the plot, which means that this episode might be 5,000 pages long! I'm going to have to get it moving.

FROM: BENJAMIN COOK TO: RUSSELL T DAVIES
TUESDAY 11 DECEMBER 2007 15:53:26 GMT

RE: 4.12

The Hub! Sarah Jane's attic! Chiswick! Only another 4,993 pages to go, Russell. Hurry up!

FROM: RUSSELL T DAVIES TO: BENJAMIN COOK
TUESDAY 11 DECEMBER 2007 17:55:06 GMT

RE: 4.12

I haven't even opened 4.12 today. I'm flinching slightly. It's like I wrote that in a blur. I can feel the million problems ahead. No, the zillion.

But I was asked on holiday today. By a 71-year-old woman in Cardiff Bay! I bumped into Gary Russell while I was having my daily coffee in the Bay – at Coffee Mania, and the fact that the man serving there was voted seventh in Wales' Most Eligible Bachelors has *nothing* to do with it – and we had a chat. Me and Gary, not me and Mr Eligible. Then Gary plodded on his way, to the dentist, and that's when the 71-year-old approached me. She said, 'I'm going to Malta in January, and I think the perfect travelling companion would be an older gay man.' Older?! Let alone the gay bit! I was just sitting there having a coffee. I wasn't exactly wearing a dress.

FROM: BENJAMIN COOK TO: RUSSELL T DAVIES
TUESDAY 11 DECEMBER 2007 18:22:33 GMT

RE: 4.12

Gary Russell got you a holiday to Malta? In January? Maybe he should go with her. Now, there's a drama. I'd have said yes like a shot. You've missed out, Russell.

Now that you're into 4.12/4.13, with its not inconsiderable cast list, I'm interested in how your approaches to writing, say, Rose, Martha and Donna differ? Is it *what* different characters say or *how* they say it that defines them, makes them 'come alive', makes them distinguishable?

FROM: RUSSELL T DAVIES TO: BENJAMIN COOK
TUESDAY 11 DECEMBER 2007 18:51:14 GMT

RE: 4.12

That's tricky. I don't type 'DONNA' and then think, now, how would she say this…? The fact that I've typed 'DONNA' means that she already has something to say. You can worry too much about speech patterns, about imposing different styles on the words, one for Rose, one for Donna, one for Martha, one for Sarah Jane. They're all women, on the side of good, in a sci-fi world, so their speeches aren't going to be radically different. It's not so much what they say, as why they say it and when.

But I suppose there's a basic characteristic that I bear in mind. An essence. Rose is open, honest, heartfelt, to the point of being selfish, wonderfully selfish. Martha is clever, calm, but rarely says what she's really thinking. Donna is blunt, precise, unfiltered, but with a big heart beneath all the banter. But we come back to what I was saying ages ago about turning characters. If Rose can be selfish, then her finest moments will come when she's selfless. If Martha keeps quiet, then her moments of revelation – like her goodbye to the Doctor in *Last of the Time Lords*, or stuck with Milo and Cheen in *Gridlock* – make her fly. Donna is magnificently self-centred – not selfish, but she pivots everything around herself, as we all do – so when she opens up and hears the Ood song, or begs for Caecilius' family to be saved, then she's wonderful.

FROM: RUSSELL T DAVIES TO: BENJAMIN COOK
WEDNESDAY 12 DECEMBER 2007 03:14:05 GMT

RE: 4.12

The line is holding! So far. Here's some more…

```
11. INT. TARDIS - DAY

THE DOCTOR frantic, running
round the console, DONNA just as
desperate, following -

                DONNA
   - but what d'you mean, gone?
   It's not been destroyed, has
   it?

              THE DOCTOR
   No, it was more like a shift,
```

'That's fearsome technology.' The Doctor tries to find the missing Earth.

```
   like a teleport beams you
   from one place to another,
   yeah? But on a massive scale.
   It's been taken! Someone has
   stolen planet Earth!

                DONNA
   What about my mum? And
   Grandad?

              THE DOCTOR
   Give me a chance! If I follow
   the path, we can find them...

                DONNA
   Doctor, I'm not stupid! Move
   a planet, and all the air
   gets ripped away! They're
   dead, aren't they?

              THE DOCTOR
   Maybe not. You can move whole
   planets and keep them intact,
   I've seen it before -
```

DONNA
What about the sun?! They've lost the sun! Even if they're breathing, they're gonna freeze!

THE DOCTOR
I don't know, Donna, I just don't know, I'm sorry, I don't know…

Quieter, Donna on the edge of tears.

DONNA
That's my family. My whole world.

THE DOCTOR
More than that! Move one planet, all the others shift. The whole solar system is gonna fall apart.

DONNA
I don't care about Jupiter!

THE DOCTOR
Yeah, but right now, there's a gravity echo, keeping the orbits intact. We've got about seven hours till the whole thing collapses. Seven hours to find the Earth!

DONNA
Then where is it? Come on! It's not exactly small!

THE DOCTOR
There's no readings. Nothing. Not a trace. Not even a whisper. Whoever moved the planet… ohh, that's fearsome technology.

DONNA
So what do we do?

THE DOCTOR
We've got to get help.

DONNA
Where from?

THE DOCTOR
Donna. I'm taking you to the Shadow Proclamation. Hold tight!

Slams lever, the Tardis lurches -

CUT TO:

12. FX SHOT - PLANETARY ARRAY

FX: WIDE SHOT, dozens of PLANETS grouped in a vast sphere.

FX: CLOSER, one huge GREEN PLANET slowly shifting its orbit, to reveal THE EARTH behind it.

FX: CLOSER, SLOW ZOOM IN. Over this, BRING IN RADIO VOICES, mixing them over each other, rising and falling…

CHINESE VOICE V/O
<Citizens are being ordered to stay indoors, food and water will be rationed by the Central Government…>

FRENCH VOICE V/O
<This is the end of days, the Apocalypse has come, and the Human Race shall fall, we are but motes of dust in the eyes of God…>

RUSSIAN VOICE V/O
<Is there anyone out there? This broadcast is on behalf of Planet Earth. If you can hear this, please respond. Repeat, is there…>

MIX TO:

13. INT. NEWSREADER STUDIO - NIGHT

TRINITY WELLS REPORTS! Trinity to CAMERA, with graphics straplines: *Worldwide emergency. Planets appear in skies…*

AMNN
AMNN
WORLDWIDE EMERGENCY
PLANETS APPEAR IN SKIES
INITIALLY ASSUMED TO BE VISUAL ANOMALIES, ASTRONOMERS HAVE NOW DISCOVERED THAT

Trinity Wells (Lachele Carl) Reports!

TRINITY WELLS
The United Nation has issued an edict, asking the citizens of the world not to panic. So far, there's no explanation for the 17 planets which have appeared in the sky…

MIX TO:

14. INT. TV DEBATE STUDIO - NIGHT

Newsnight-type show, an ELDERLY PROFESSOR arguing:

PROFESSOR
- quite clearly, the planets didn't come to us, we came to them! Just look at the stars! We're in a completely different region of space, an unknown region -

MIX TO:

15. INT. THE NEW PAUL O'GRADY SHOW - NIGHT

PAUL O'GRADY at his desk, in fine form. Audience hooting.

PAUL O'GRADY
I look up, there's all these moons and things! Have you seen 'em? I thought, what was I drinking last night? Furniture polish?

MIX TO:

16. INT. THE TORCHWOOD HUB - NIGHT

IANTO at his computer, watching Paul O'Grady, laughing.

CAPTAIN JACK is at a second workstation, calls across:

CAPTAIN JACK
Ianto. Time and a place.

IANTO
He is funny, though. Sorry.

And he crosses to Jack -

CAPTAIN JACK
Gwen! Come and see!

GWEN just heading across the upper gantry, from the hothouse -

GWEN
Coming -
(on her mobile)
Rhys, I've got no idea, just stay indoors.[3] Oh, and phone my mother, tell her, I dunno, tell her to take her pills and go to sleep.
(stops, quiet, upset)
I'll come home. Soon as I can. I promise. Love you. Big idiot.

Hangs up, all professional again, runs to join -

Jack & Ianto, information scrolling across screen -

CAPTAIN JACK
Someone's established an artificial atmospheric shell. Keeping the air, and holding in the heat.

IANTO
Whoever's done this… wants the Human Race alive. Given the circumstances, that's a plus.

Ianto taps button, calls up GRAPHICS MAP OF PLANETARY ARRAY.

IANTO (CONT'D)
D'you recognise any of those planets?

CAPTAIN JACK
Not so far.
(stabs buttons)
Running a news check…

IANTO
There's only one headline at the moment.

CAPTAIN JACK
Searching for sightings of a blue box. Anywhere! That Doctor of mine, he travels in a blue box. And right now, we need him.

GWEN
What's that?

CAPTAIN JACK
What's what?

3 Rhys Williams (played by Kai Owen) is Gwen's boyfriend, later husband, in *Torchwood*.

The stars of *Doctor Who* spin-off *The Sarah Jane Adventures*. L–R: Maria Jackson (Yasmin Paige), Luke Smith (Thomas Knight), Sarah Jane Smith (Elisabeth Sladen) and Clyde Langer (Daniel Anthony).

GRAPHICS MAP: one of the PLANETS shifting, revealing, behind it, right at the CENTRE OF THE ARRAY… a SMALL RED BLIP.

All three faces clustered together, close, scared:

GWEN
That's not a planet…

CUT TO:

17. INT. SARAH JANE SMITH'S ATTIC - NIGHT

SARAH JANE in front of MR SMITH, the same GRAPHICS MAP showing the ominous RED BLIP. LUKE b/g on mobile.

MR SMITH V/O
The reading seems to be artificial in construction.

SARAH JANE
What, like a space station?

MR SMITH V/O
Sitting at the heart of the web.

SARAH JANE
Less of the metaphors, Mr Smith. Can we see it, can we get closer?

MR SMITH V/O
Reconfiguring scanners…

Luke coming off the phone, joining Sarah Jane.

LUKE
They're fine, Maria and her dad, they're still in Cornwall.[4] I told them to stay indoors.

SARAH JANE
And Clyde?[5]

LUKE
He's with his mum -

MR SMITH V/O
Sarah Jane. It seems the object is baffling all scans. Nonetheless, I have detected movement. Observe.

4 Maria Jackson (played by Yasmin Paige) and her father, Alan (Joseph Millson), are Sarah Jane's neighbours in *The Sarah Jane Adventures* Series One and, initially, Two.

5 Clyde Langer (played by Daniel Anthony) is a friend of Sarah Jane's and Luke's in *The Sarah Jane Adventures*.

ON SCREEN: GRAPHICS, as DOTS fly out of the RED BLIP. Lots and lots of them, in formation.

On Sarah Jane & Luke; he's delighted, she's scared.

LUKE
Spaceships!

SARAH JANE
And they're heading for Earth.

CUT TO:

18. INT. UNIT HQ, NEW YORK CITY - NIGHT

The place has been repaired a bit, lights back on, STAFF & SOLDIERS hurrying about. Though it's an office, one section has UNIT-HQ-TYPE CONTROLS, as in 4.4, manned desks (inc. SUZANNE) laid out with SCANNER SCREENS, COMPUTERS, etc.

UNIT General Sanchez (née Slade), played by Michael Brandon.

GENERAL SLADE
Tracking two hundred objects. Earthbound trajectory! Geneva is calling a Code Red, everyone to positions! Immediately! Dr Jones, if you're not too busy.

MARTHA is a good distance away, on her mobile.

MARTHA
Trying to phone the Doctor, sir.

GENERAL SLADE
Good move, soldier! Any luck?

MARTHA
I'm not a soldier, I'm a medic. But there's no signal, I can't get through. This number can call right across the universe, it never breaks down. They must be blocking it. Whoever 'they' are.

GENERAL SLADE
We're about to find out. They're coming into orbit.

GRAPHICS: two hundred DOTS all around the Earth.

I'm stopping now. I need to think ahead. There are three or four interesting options for what happens next, and I need to find the right one. It's an odd script, isn't it? The concept is so huge that the dialogue is quite perfunctory and plot-based. I'm fighting to get any character in there. The Doctor and Donna have to talk about plot, plot, plot – it would sound mad if they didn't (although 'I don't care about Jupiter!' makes me laugh) – and the others are talking in that sort of brusque signature dialogue. Like Martha's 'I'm not a soldier, I'm a medic'. Signature dialogue is saying 'This is who I am'. It's very obvious, but the size of the cast demands those simple distinctions. Also, I'm strangely aware of people watching this for the first time, even though it's an unashamed continuity-fest, so all the characters are stating their presence, as if for newcomers. And Ianto is quietly stealing the show. This is deliberate, so that Gareth David-Lloyd will love me. I'm only half-joking. Somewhere in the subconscious, I think you cast handsome men so that you can impress them. Yeah, and it really works. Well, maybe one day. Oh, just once.

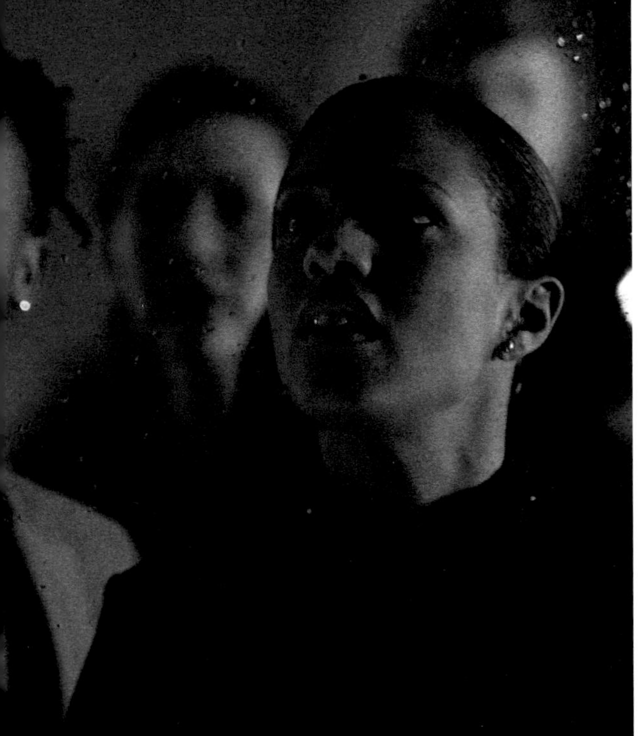

UNIT operatives Suzanne (Andrea Harris) and Martha (Freema Agyeman).

I'm still fighting to keep the cost down. I wrote the last few scenes with loads of FX – Dalek space station, Dalek saucers, hurtling towards Earth – but I need the money later on. It was spectacular, but expensive, so I deleted all the FX and made the whole thing work with cheap radar graphics. I think it's better, actually. Captain Jack, Sarah Jane and Martha can't see what's happening, not until the ships really arrive, which makes them more helpless. Good rewrite. Even if we could afford the FX, I think I'd keep it like that now.

FROM: BENJAMIN COOK TO: RUSSELL T DAVIES
WEDNESDAY 12 DECEMBER 2007 03:36:30 GMT

RE: 4.12

The Shadow Proclamation! Ooh, this is good! (Invisible Ben is on holiday in Cornwall. With Maria and her dad.) Hey, the professor on the *Newsnight*-type show in Scene 14 should so be Richard Dawkins. I bet he'd do it.

You say that you're considering three or four interesting options now. What are they?

FROM: RUSSELL T DAVIES TO: BENJAMIN COOK
WEDNESDAY 12 DECEMBER 2007 14:27:34 GMT

RE: 4.12

Richard Dawkins! Brilliant! I'm going to try that. Leave Invisible Ben in Cornwall. Visible Ben is full of good ideas. Mind you, if I was invisible and in Cornwall with Maria's dad, I know what I'd be doing…

The options… hmm, I haven't woken up with much clarity. I had a bad night's sleep, and woke up in a sort of panic attack at about 5am, with vivid, weird images of Daleks and Martha and stuff. That, for the record, has never happened before. Maybe 'options' is the wrong word. It's more that I'm struggling with two contradictory directions. I want two things to happen: I want all the companions to link up, via their computers and phones, to combine their technology to send a signal that'll tell the Doctor where they are; at the same time, I want all these companions to hit the streets in the middle of the Dalek invasion, like freedom fighters in the night. I want both of these things to happen. I know all the scenes of both sequences, and now I'm trying to mesh them, to get the best of both worlds. Also, I'm trying to find the right moments for the Doctor and Donna's story to advance. The correct order. With a hundred choices. I always believe there's a correct order, a sequence that makes everything sing. I've just got to find it.

FROM: RUSSELL T DAVIES TO: BENJAMIN COOK
WEDNESDAY 12 DECEMBER 2007 15:49:36 GMT

RE: 4.12

Rather than do some real work, I've changed ELDERLY PROFESSOR to RICHARD DAWKINS. Nice one.

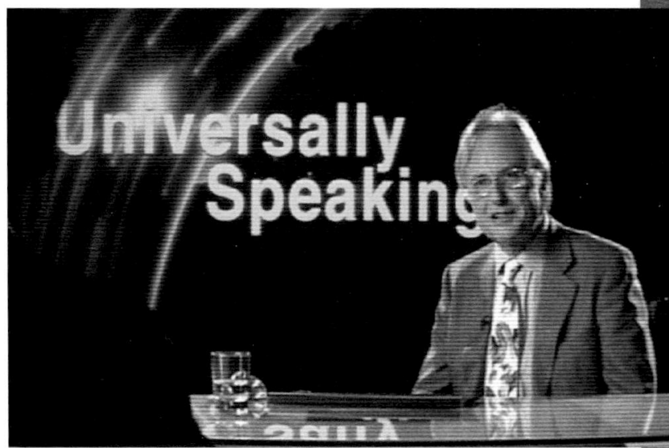

Professor Richard Dawkins makes a cameo in 4.12. Thanks to Ben!

MOFFAT'S NUMBER FIVE

December 2007, and work on Series Five is well under way...

FROM: STEVEN MOFFAT TO: RUSSELL T DAVIES
MONDAY 10 DECEMBER 2007 15:20:22 GMT

THE FUTURE

Russell! When you've some time, can we have a chat? I've a few practical points that I'd like to talk over with you. And since I'm starting to think about this for real (blimey!), I'm realising that I probably shouldn't hide myself away from spoilers like the whimpering fanboy that I am. Is it okay if I read your finale scripts when they're done, just in case there are any crossovers with all the nonsense currently in my head? If I wait to see the episodes, I'll be deep in new stuff, courses will be set, and it wouldn't be the first time that we've both blundered into the same idea.

One other thing, which I've been meaning to say. You're always so kind and positive, you'd never let it show, but I realise it can't be easy to hand over a show like this one – so please understand, I appreciate that and I'm hugely grateful for the chance that I'm getting. I'll try not to be some irritating little Scottish bastard measuring up your house for curtains. And boy do I need some more macho metaphors.

FROM: RUSSELL T DAVIES TO: STEVEN MOFFAT
MONDAY 10 DECEMBER 2007 20:35:22 GMT

RE: THE FUTURE

D'you know what? It *is* easy to hand over this show, now that I know it's to you. No kidding. No niceties. If it were going to some *Holby* committee, or some idiot, or some stranger, I'd be terrified, in a good old-fashioned fanboy way. But it's you. It's simply you. I think that's glorious. And I've genuinely had enough, while still loving it with all my heart. That feels good, getting out while still loving it. (Imagine going off *Doctor Who*!!!) So I'm really, really happy. You're not just measuring for curtains, you nonce. You're knocking down that wall, building an extension – hell, abandoning the whole thing, declaring it unsafe, and building a brand new house in its place. Like there's any stopping you!

When are we having this famous chat, then? I'm in London for the launch on 18 December. What if I came early? Are you free? Or how about the day after? Stories are beginning to prey on my mind, too. I'll park the Doctor wherever you need him. You decide! If you decide on more of an overlap, then the Specials can contain Series Five elements that'd be absolutely yours. I know, I'm so noble! But it's all for the good of the show. That's all that matters. If I'm taking time to think of the three Specials, and you've started formulating a whole series – oh, go on, you've started already, haven't you? – then we'll just swap roles, so you go first, you tell me what you're planning (not in too much detail, thank you – think of my fanboy heart), and I'll make sure that the Specials lead seamlessly into Series Five. That should work.

New showrunner Steven Moffat on the TARDIS set – pondering the future? Inset: Moffat and outgoing producer Phil Collinson.

FROM: STEVEN MOFFAT TO: RUSSELL T DAVIES
TUESDAY 11 DECEMBER 2007 11:47:26 GMT

RE: THE FUTURE

I'm so glad that you still love it. I've asked you every year, but I was too nervous to this time. That's honestly a relief to hear.

FROM: STEVEN MOFFAT TO: RUSSELL T DAVIES
WEDNESDAY 12 DECEMBER 2007 09:37:50 GMT

RE: THE FUTURE

Actually, never mind all that, I'm wittering like a girl. I've worked out my opening episode! It's good, honest!

FROM: RUSSELL T DAVIES TO: STEVEN MOFFAT
WEDNESDAY 12 DECEMBER 2007 10:30:45 GMT

RE: THE FUTURE

I *knew* it! Exciting, isn't it?! Oh, I bet you're having fun.

>>I'm so glad you still love it<<

No kidding. Every second. Bloody love it.

FROM: RUSSELL T DAVIES TO: BENJAMIN COOK
THURSDAY 13 DECEMBER 2007 02:21:32 GMT

RE: 4.12

Here's some more. Scary page numbers. I thought I'd be on Page 12 by now, but these events have taken me up to Page 20 already. I've thought about this for so long that I've become used to it, so it seemed smaller, more compact, in my head. I'm thinking ahead now and cutting huge chunks of future story as I go. New York has now becoming a pain in the arse, because it traps Martha there and her escape – 'Project Indigo' – is many pages long. It might have to be sacrificed.

```
19. EXT. SHOPPING STREET - NIGHT

Big, wide street, like St Mary's.
PEOPLE running past, screams,
yells, panic on the streets -
clearing past ROSE, who's striding
along, determined.

A DRUNK MAN is standing in the
middle of the road, happy.

                  DRUNK MAN
      End of the world, darlin'!
      End of the stinkin' world!

                    ROSE
      Have one on me, mate.

Hears a smash of glass, an alarm
sounds. She heads off -

                                CUT TO:

20. INT. ABANDONED COMPUTER SHOP
- NIGHT

Alarm blaring. ROSE's feet crunch
over broken glass, the shop door
broken. Following her in and PAN UP
to reveal…

Big shop, abandoned, strangely
bright and white. Empty, except for
two LOOTERS, shoving laptops into
a sack. They look at Rose, don't
care, keep scavenging. Feisty:

                    ROSE
      All right, you two. You can
      put that stuff down, or run
      for your lives. No. You can
      put that stuff down, AND run
```

for your lives. Bit new to this. Like the gun?

And big smile, she hoists it up, *ka-chik!*

The looters run!

JUMP CUT TO Rose, settling down in the empty shop (alarm off, now), tapping away at one of the display computers.

On screen:

CUT TO:

21. INT. NEWS 24 STUDIO - NIGHT

NEWSREADER TO CAMERA:

NEWSREADER
- unconfirmed reports say that a fleet of ships is descending towards Earth… We don't know who they are, or where they're from…

CUT TO:

22. INT. NOBLES' LIVING ROOM - NIGHT

Newsreader cont. ADR, SYLVIA kneeling in front of the TV, awestruck, calling WILF in. He's on the mobile.

SYLVIA
Dad! Come and see! It's on the telly! Who are you phoning?

WILF
I'm trying to get Donna, there's no reply. Where is she?

SYLVIA
They're saying spaceships!

CUT TO:

23. INT. THE TORCHWOOD HUB - NIGHT

CAPTAIN JACK, GWEN, IANTO, gathered around one screen. GRAPHICS: 200 BLIPS now around the Earth.

GWEN
Can we get visuals?

CAPTAIN JACK
Too far away. They're still at 3000 miles. Who are they?!

His mobile rings, he answers, caller-ID'ing, big smile -

CAPTAIN JACK (CONT'D)
Martha Jones! Voice of a nightingale! Tell me you put something in my drink!

CUT TO:

24. INT. UNIT HQ, NEW YORK CITY - NIGHT

INTERCUT WITH THE TORCHWOOD HUB.

MARTHA on mobile. Controlled panic in b/g. Throughout Martha & Jack, SUZANNE, at her RADAR, is counting down -

SUZANNE
Two thousand eight hundred miles… Two thousand five hundred miles… Two thousand miles and lowering…

While in the hub, IANTO counts down…

IANTO
27 hundred miles… 21 hundred miles… 19 hundred miles…

But they're CUTAWAYS. Also CUTAWAY to the GRAPHICS BLIPS, as and when. But mainly INTERCUTTING Martha & Jack:

Ianto Jones (Gareth David-Lloyd), Captain Jack Harkness (John Barrowman) and Gwen Cooper (Eve Myles) keep vigil in the Torchwood Hub.

'Well, I met this soldier in a bar...' Captain Jack on fine form. Illustration by Russell T Davies.

MARTHA
No such luck, have you heard from the Doctor?

CAPTAIN JACK
You're the one with a superphone.

MARTHA
I can't get through.
(quiet, scared)
What the hell is happening, Jack?

CAPTAIN JACK
Wish I knew. Where are you?

MARTHA
New York.

CAPTAIN JACK
Oh! Nice for some.

MARTHA
Just on a field trip. Medical Director on Project Indigo.

CAPTAIN JACK
Hey, d'you get that thing working?

MARTHA
(smiles)
Indigo's top secret, no one's supposed to know about it.

CAPTAIN JACK
Well, I met this soldier in a bar, long story.

IANTO
When was that?

CAPTAIN JACK
Keep counting, you!

GWEN
Fifteen hundred miles, and accelerating. They're almost here.

CUT TO:

25. INT. SARAH JANE SMITH'S ATTIC - NIGHT

SARAH JANE & LUKE at MR SMITH, displaying the SAME GRAPHICS.

MR SMITH V/O
Sarah Jane, I'm receiving the first visuals from Jodrell Bank.

SARAH JANE
Well, put them through!

FX: ON SCREEN. Fuzzy image. As 1.13, HUGE BRONZE SAUCERS, studded with rivets, descending through the PLANETARY SKY.

CUT TO:

26. INT. THE TORCHWOOD HUB - NIGHT

CAPTAIN JACK, seeing the IMAGE, winded, as though punched. So scared. He actually steps back, shaken, very quiet.

CAPTAIN JACK
...no. Ohh no...

GWEN
Jack, what is it? Who are they? D'you know them? Jack?

CUT TO:

27. INT. UNIT HQ, NEW YORK CITY - NIGHT

MARTHA on her mobile. All UNIT STAFF staring at a central screen, displaying the IMAGE. Martha in cold dread:

MARTHA
Jack… That design. Bronze. With rivets. Is that what I think it is…? Jack? Jack??

CUT TO:

28. INT. THE TORCHWOOD HUB - NIGHT

CAPTAIN JACK is no longer on the phone. He's hugging a scared GWEN & IANTO; kisses Ianto on the top of his head, then Gwen. Like a farewell.

CAPTAIN JACK
There's nothing I can do. I'm sorry. We're dead.

CUT TO:

29. INT. SARAH JANE SMITH'S ATTIC - NIGHT

SARAH JANE terrified, which scares LUKE.

LUKE
Mum? D'you recognise them?

SARAH JANE
I've seen… something like them. Long time ago, but…

And she hugs him, crying.

SARAH JANE (CONT'D)
You're so young. Oh God. You're so young.

CUT TO:

30. INT. ABANDONED COMPUTER SHOP - NIGHT

ROSE, alone, staring at the computer screen. So upset. Her worst fears. She's crying, just a little.

Then she pulls herself together. Picks up her gun. Strides out. Work to do.

Now, SC.31-34 INTERCUT WITH SC.35-40:

CUT TO:

31. INT. NOBLES' HOUSE - NIGHT

WILF & SYLVIA watching the events of sc.35-40 on TV.

CUT TO:

32. INT. UNIT HQ, NEW YORK CITY - NIGHT

MARTHA & UNIT watching sc.35-40 on the big screen. (Don't see the screen here; ADR Trinity Wells will describe an American equivalent of events, a saucer approaching the White House, landing - but OOV!).

CUT TO:

33. INT. SARAH JANE SMITH'S ATTIC - NIGHT

SARAH JANE & LUKE, watching sc.35-40 on MR SMITH.

CUT TO:

34. INT. THE TORCHWOOD HUB - NIGHT

GWEN & IANTO watching the events of sc.35-40 on a computer, CAPTAIN JACK in b/g, on his mobile, desperate:

CAPTAIN JACK
This is Captain Jack Harkness, I'm calling from Torchwood - I don't care, just tell the Prime Minster to get out of there!!

So sc.31-34 are layered in with:

CUT TO:

35. INT. NEWSREADER STUDIO - NIGHT

NEWSREADER TO CAMERA:

NEWSREADER
- reports are confused, but… It's being said, one of the saucers is descending towards Westminster…

CUT TO:

'The Human Harvest will commence!' Big Ben is destroyed by a Dalek saucer. Illustration by Russell T Davies.

36. FX SHOT

(NB, sc.36-40 now entirely experienced as grainy TV FOOTAGE.) HANDHELD CAMERA capturing SAUCER, as it descends on WESTMINSTER.

CUT TO:

37. EXT. CITY STREET - NIGHT

GRABBED HANDHELD SHOTS of PEOPLE, running, looking back, and up, in terror, fleeing from the saucer.

CUT TO:

38. EXT. CIVIC BUILDINGS - NIGHT

HANDHELD CAMERA, from a DISTANCE, capturing PRIME MINISTER AUBREY FAIRCHILD, TWO AIDES and a BRITISH ARMY COLONEL walking up to a scaffolding platform, like someone has quickly arranged a public meeting.

(NB, no need for real Whitehall, just civic-type buildings in darkness b/g, all shot close, grabbed, shaky).

NEWSREADER OOV

…we're getting pictures live from Westminster, we're seeing Prime Minister Aubrey Fairchild… It seems he's coming forward. To greet the visitors.

FX: WHIP PAN from Aubrey to a HANDHELD SHOT of a SAUCER, lowering down…

CUT TO HANDHELD Aubrey & staff, buffeted by wind, but remaining resolute, holding their ground…

CUT TO:

39. EXT. CITY STREET - NIGHT

GRABBED HANDHELD SHOTS - PEOPLE still running, but some have stopped. Looking up in awe. Terror. One man joyous.

CUT TO:

40. EXT. CIVIC BUILDINGS - NIGHT

HANDHELD CAMERA jerkily ZOOMS INTO CU AUBREY FAIRCHILD, as he goes to a microphone-stand. A brave man.

AUBREY FAIRCHILD
Visitors to Earth. We welcome you. We ask you for help, in this strange wilderness. But most of all, I seek to reassure you… The Human Race comes in peace.

FX: HANDHELD WHIP-PAN over to the SAUCER, as a huge BRONZE DOOR begins to lower…

CUT TO AUBREY & STAFF, HANDHELD, their fear, their hope…

(Still INTERCUT WITH SC.31-34, Wilf & Sylvia staring, Sarah Jane holding Luke, terrified, saying quietly 'No, no, don't, no…', Captain Jack now back at the screen with Gwen & Ianto, muttering, 'Get out of there, just get out…')

FX: HANDHELD, the DOOR completing its descent, to become a RAMP. Beyond, the interior of the ship: PITCH BLACK.

And then…

Just a voice.

DALEK
Exterminate!

FX: HANDHELD, ENERGY BOLT shoots out of the pitch-black -

FX: HANDHELD, AUBREY struck, skeleton, he screams & dies!

FX: HANDHELD: a SWARM OF DALEKS flies out!

CUT TO:

41. INT. CRUCIBLE COMMAND DECK - NIGHT

THE CRUCIBLE is the Dalek ship at the heart of the web. Huge, dark space, with 1.13-type designs. Start close, shot tight, DALEK 1 gliding into position -

DALEK 1
Dalek fleet in battle formation!

- tracking across DALEK 2, then 3,

The Daleks mass aboard the Crucible and prepare to become the masters of Earth.

then 4, gliding in -

DALEK 2
All systems locked and primed!

DALEK 3
Crucible at 90% efficiency!

DALEK 4
The Human Harvest will commence!

CUT TO:

42. INT. UNIT HQ, NEW YORK CITY - NIGHT

STAFF *running* to and fro now - chaos - alarms sounding - GENERAL SANCHEZ yelling out -

GENERAL SANCHEZ
Battle stations! Geneva declaring Ultimate Code Red! Ladies and gentlemen, we are at war!

WHUMPH! Whole room shakes, PRAC RUBBLE from the roof -

Martha running to the window - looking out - horrified -

CUT TO:

43. FX SHOT - NEW YORK

FX: DALEK SAUCERS gliding over NEW YORK at night! LASER BEAMS shoot down, EXPLOSIONS in the city!

CUT TO:

44. INT. CRUCIBLE COMMAND DECK - NIGHT

DALEK 1, spinning round on the spot -

DALEK 1
Supreme Dalek approaching!

CUT TO DALEK 4, spinning round on the spot -

DALEK 2
Supreme Dalek on the Bridge!

CUT TO the back of the chamber - a PLATFORM four feet or so off the ground, with a mighty metal ARCHWAY at the back, DOORS within

The Supreme Dalek – the first red Dalek ever in TV *Doctor Who*. The films got there first in 1966, mind you...

the archway now sliding open, LIGHT & PRAC STEAM FX of HYDRAULICS blasting out, as -

THE SUPREME DALEK glides out. A red Dalek; deep metallic red. It stays on its raised platform, its throne.

SUPREME DALEK
Stage One of the New Masterplan initiated! Soon, the Crucible will be complete! We have waited long for this glorious time. Now the Daleks are the masters of Earth!

CUT TO ALL PRAC DALEKS, swivelling to face the Supreme:

ALL DALEKS
Daleks are the masters of Earth!

FX: WIDE SHOT. With MULTIPLICATION OF PRAC DALEKS on FLOOR LEVEL, above and around that - tiers of balconies, all dark metal, with CG DALEKS gliding to and fro, some FLYING. The Daleks at their most powerful! All chanting:

ALL DALEKS (CONT'D)
Daleks are the masters of Earth!!!

FROM: RUSSELL T DAVIES TO: BENJAMIN COOK
THURSDAY 13 DECEMBER 2007 23:32:18 GMT

RE: 4.12

The Doctor is about to arrive at the Shadow Proclamation, but warning bells are ringing. He's meant to stride in with Donna, into some great hall, and, in a The Mill/Neill Gorton extravaganza, walk past every creature we've ever had. Krillitanes swooping. Judoon stomping. Slitheen farting. Maybe even an Isolus fluttering past. I've even thought of a way to include Margaret Slitheen, fleetingly.[6] But now I'm dreading it. It's going to eat up money. Money that is clearly better spent on the Dalek invasion of Earth. So I'm stalling. I hate writing something that might never be made. I haven't the time to waste! Trouble is, Will Cohen is *dying* to animate this sequence. He's been looking forward to it for months. So I'm writing to you instead of getting on with it. But I think typing that was therapy.

FROM: RUSSELL T DAVIES TO: BENJAMIN COOK
FRIDAY 14 DECEMBER 2007 02:05:49 GMT

RE: 4.12

I'm giving up for tonight. Just not connecting. I set myself the target of reducing 20 pages to 18. I failed, but lost a page and a half, so that's not too bad. It all helps. I lost the Bad Wolf stuff at the beginning, because… well, that was 4.11. Move on! Its explanation was only a gag anyway.

I have to go to Manchester this weekend, because it's my boyfriend's birthday, and then Swansea, because it's my dad's birthday too – same day! – so work on this is royally buggered. I hate interrupting a script. It's hard to get the momentum back.

FROM: RUSSELL T DAVIES TO: BENJAMIN COOK
FRIDAY 14 DECEMBER 2007 19:35:54 GMT

RE: 4.12

The Judoon are back! Bo! Klo! Fo! To! Mo!

```
45. INT. TARDIS - DAY

In flight, THE DOCTOR running round
the console -

              THE DOCTOR
   I'm trying to announce our
   arrival. No good just turning
   up! But that's weird… All
   frequencies jammed. They're
   on some sort of Red Alert…

He looks up.

DONNA is just standing against the
rail. She's been crying, doesn't
like to show it. He goes to her,
kind.

          THE DOCTOR (CONT'D)
   I'll find them, Donna. I'll
   travel this whole wide
   universe to find them, I swear.
   It's not just your home. That
   daft little planet is the
   closest thing I've got.

              DONNA
   Yeah. Sure.

ALARMS! The Doctor runs back to the
console -

              THE DOCTOR
   We're here! The Shadow
   Proclamation!

                              CUT TO:

46. FX SHOT

THE SHADOW PROCLAMATION. DMP only;
a huge installation, metal sc-fi
towers ranged across a series of
linked asteroids, hanging in space,
like a Roger Dean painting.
```

The Shadow Proclamation in all its glory.

6 Blon Fel-Fotch Pasameer-Day Slitheen (played by Annette Badland) appeared in *Doctor Who* 1.4/1.5 and 1.11, having appropriated the identity and skin of human MI5 official Margaret Blaine. Following an encounter with the Doctor, Blon was regressed to an egg and returned to the hatchery on Raxacoricofallapatorius.

'Every creature we've ever had. Krillitanes swooping, Judoon stomping, Slitheen farting. Maybe even an Isolus flying past...' The Shadow Proclamation, as Russell imagined it. Illustration by Russell T Davies.

Over that, the sound of the Tardis engines…

CUT TO:

47. INT. SHADOW PROCLAMATION LOBBY - NIGHT

CLOSE ON THE DOCTOR & DONNA - who's recovering, brave face on - both stepping out -

THE DOCTOR
- right, the first thing we've got to do is -

Stops dead, as a PLATOON OF JUDOON march past, big, heavy boots stomping, left to right - the Doctor & Donna nipping through a gap in the formation, pushing forward -

THE DOCTOR (CONT'D)
- whoops, 'scuse me, sorry -

FX: THREE KRILLITANES swoop down, the Doctor & Donna brushing them off, still pushing forward -

DONNA
Oy! Get off!

THE DOCTOR
Keep your wings in, you lot!

- then stopped by TWO VESPIFORMS, buzzing right to left -

THE DOCTOR (CONT'D)
- oh, mind those stings, thank you -

The Doctor & Donna then stopping to look properly. Gulp.

FX: WIDE SHOT. Big, white, open smart-sci-fi-building. Filled with CROWD MULTIPLICATION JUDOON, CROWD MULTIPLICATION SLITHEEN, a few HATH, two HELMETED SYCORAX, and CROWD MULTIPLICATION SPACE-EXTRAS - some in big opera cloaks, SISTERS OF THE WICKER PLACE MAT from 1.2, plus a lot of MONKS & NUNS. Also, SHADOW POLICE - like Judoon, but Human, in big stompy black uniforms. Flying through the air, KRILLITANES, VESPIFORMS, GELTH. And in one corner, a huge 15ft ADIPOSE, mewling. All busy, chaotic, emergency!

Peter McKinstry's draft design of the Shadow Proclamation.

CUT BACK TO the Doctor & Donna.

DONNA
Is it always this busy? What is the Shadow Proclamation anyway?

THE DOCTOR
Police. Outer space police.

DONNA
Name like that, I was expecting all druids and cloaks and incense.

THE DOCTOR
You should meet the Brotherhood of Darkened Time. That's the accountants.

TWO SLITHEEN & BABY SLITHEEN walk

past, fast -

DONNA
Cor, what a stink!

THE DOCTOR
That's the Slitheen -

The Slitheen turn round, furious -

SLITHEEN
We are not Slitheen! Slitheen are criminals! We are Jingatheen!

THE DOCTOR
Sorry. Easy mistake. Tell me, what's everyone doing here?

SLITHEEN
The whole universe is on red alert! Planets have disappeared! Dozens of them! We have lost Clom!

THE DOCTOR
Clom's gone?!

SLITHEEN
Clom's gone!

DONNA
What's Clom?

SLITHEEN
Our twin planet! Without it, Raxacoricofallapatorius will fall out of the sky!
(turns to go)
We must phone home -
(to Baby Slitheen)
- this way, Margaret.

Baby Slitheen talks with the VOICE OF MARGARET BLAINE:

BABY SLITHEEN
Take me home, Daddy, I don't like the nasty policemen!

THE DOCTOR
...Margaret...?

DONNA
Come on, you!

And she shoves him forward, out of frame -

CUT TO A RECEPTION DESK, manned by Judoon, one unmasked with RHINO HEAD. (All monks & nuns & opera-types crowding b/g, no FX.)

A GRASKE is standing on the desk, furious.

'Sco! Bo! Tro! No! Flo! Jo! Ko! Fo! To!' Donna and the Doctor face the bureaucratic might of the Judoon. Inset: A Slitheen... sorry, a Jingatheen!

GRASKE
Planet gone! Not good! Very bad!

THE DOCTOR & DONNA walking up, the Doctor just scooping the Graske off the desk and putting him down out of frame -

THE DOCTOR
'Scuse me, big fella -
(to the Judoon)
I'd like to report a missing planet. Another one. It's called Earth -

JUDOON
Sco! Bo! Tro! No! Flo! Jo! Ko! Fo! To!

THE DOCTOR
Lo! Kro! To! Sho! Maho?

JUDOON
Sco! Sco! Blo! Do! Mo!

DONNA
Hold on, I thought the Tardis translated alien languages?

THE DOCTOR
Judoon are too thick.

DONNA
(to the Judoon)
Listen, you big Rhino. Earth. Missing. Six billion people!

Judoon holds out its translator, at her face.

'What are you doing, zoo boy?'

DONNA (CONT'D)
Oy, what's it doing, what's that for, what are you doing, zoo boy?

The Judoon clips the translator into its chest-port. We hear Donna's words back, fast, *'Oywhatsitdoingwhatsthatf...'*

JUDOON
Language assimilated. Designation: Earth English.

DONNA
Right, good, that's better, thanks - we need to report a missing planet, Galactic Location five delta omega -

JUDOON
Take number. Stand in line.

DONNA
But this is important!

JUDOON
Take a number. Stand in line.

The Doctor takes a number from a supermarket-style dispenser -

THE DOCTOR
Number one-six-two-five-eight-nine-

Looks up. DISPLAY: number 003.

THE DOCTOR (CONT'D)
You're only on number three!
(psychic paper)
I have been sent by the Judoon High Council, top priority, Ambassador Number One -

JUDOON
Stand in line.

THE DOCTOR
(to Donna)
I said so, thick!!
(to Judoon, angry)
My name is the Doctor, I need to see the Chief Constable, right now, I can help you -

The Judoon raises its gun -

JUDOON
Stand in line!

The Doctor steps back - other MONKS

& NUNS pile in, taking their place. The Doctor & Donna just figures in the crowd.

He puts his arm round her.

CUT TO:

<u>48. INT. SHADOW PROCLAMATION LOBBY - NIGHT</u>

A LINE OF JUDOON stomping past…

Clearing to reveal DONNA, sitting alone. Haunted. MONKS, NUNS, SYCORAX, etc, all around her. She glances across.

At a distance, THE DOCTOR, at the RECEPTION DESK, surrounded by CROWD. He's filling in paperwork, arguing with Judoon.

Donna looks front. Lost in thought.

And as she stares into space…

Real sound fades away…

As she hears…

A heartbeat.

SLOW ZOOM IN on Donna staring to the distance, lost…

As it calls to her…

Then…

The moment breaks, as a FIGURE steps in foreground. Donna snaps out of it, looks up:

An ELDERLY NUN. Grave. Staring at her.

DONNA
Sorry, I was just…

ELDERLY NUN
There was something on your back.

DONNA
How d'you know that?

ELDERLY NUN
You have been marked, child.

DONNA
(chilled)
What does that mean?

ELDERLY NUN
You are something new.
Something terrible and new.
(touches her cheek)
Oh, but destiny is cruel. I'm so sorry for your loss.

DONNA
…my whole planet's gone.

ELDERLY NUN
I mean the loss that is yet to come. God save you.

And the Nun turns and goes.

Donna shaken, disturbed.

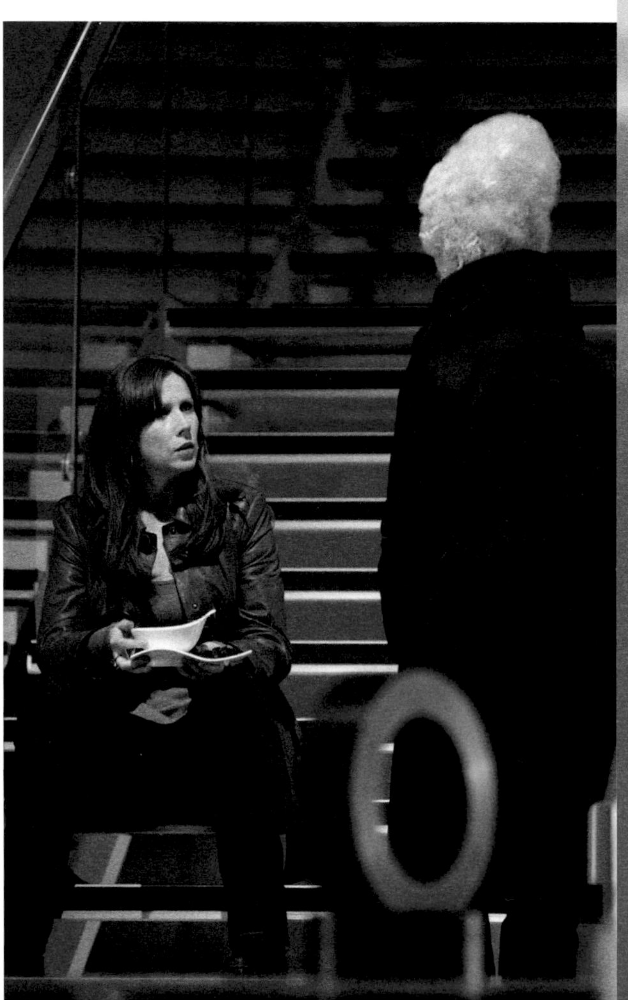

'I'm so sorry for your loss.' Donna finds some sympathy at the Shadow Proclamation. But it's not for her missing planet…

```
CUT TO THE DOCTOR, at the desk.
Head down, scribbling through
piles of Judoon paperwork,
angry.

A SHADOW SOLDIER (ie, Human)
steps into extreme foreground.

               SHADOW SOLDIER
      Can I help you with that,
      sir?

                THE DOCTOR
      Triplicate! You've
      got 24 planets
      missing, and you
      need forms in
      triplicate! I'm the
      one and only person
      who could help, but
      no one's listening
      to me!

             SHADOW SOLDIER
      I can listen. I
      did last time. And
      you saved my life,
      Doctor.

The Doctor looks up -

And the Shadow Soldier
is MIDSHIPMAN FRAME!
```

I leave you with 4.12 cliffhanging on the best possible words! It may not be possible, but we'll see. I enjoyed typing it.

And I wrote the expensive stuff. It's actually the touch of a keystroke to delete it all. The same effect can be achieved with Judoon and a couple of Slitheen. Nice to try, though. I expressed my fears to Will, and he said, 'Oh, go on, do it!' So I did.

FROM: RUSSELL T DAVIES TO: BENJAMIN COOK
SATURDAY 15 DECEMBER 2007 14:09:44 GMT

ARSE, ARSE, ARSE!

I was hoping for a quiet weekend. No such luck. Catherine has just said on Jonathan Ross's radio show that this is David's last series! Poor Catherine. My heart sank. You could almost hear her swallowing the words as she said them. In fairness, it's so hard on *Doctor Who* to remember what's true and what isn't, what's possible and what's just speculation. But now it has all gone mad! Press on the phone! BBC News 24 is going to run it as a banner! It's like they threaten us. The biggest fight now, in your post-Hutton BBC, is to stop our Press Office from making a statement. Most people weren't listening to Jonathan Ross's show, for Christ sake! Just let it lie as rumour and gossip. 'No,' they say, 'we must have a "line".' So what's The Line?

FROM: BENJAMIN COOK
TO: RUSSELL T DAVIES
SATURDAY 15 DECEMBER 2007
14:22:15 GMT

RE: ARSE, ARSE, ARSE!

Why does the BBC have to confirm or deny anything? Shouldn't the BBC just shut up? Wouldn't that be less damaging?

FROM: RUSSELL T DAVIES
TO: BENJAMIN COOK
SATURDAY 15 DECEMBER 2007
14:37:48 GMT

RE: ARSE, ARSE, ARSE!

Exactly! But it's a hard argument to maintain. Once this juggernaut starts rolling, it's difficult to stop – and it threatens to undermine Series Four. We all – Julie, Jane, David and me – have to work out an official response. That's David's call, really, though it's our job to help and protect him. And, of course, we've lost Jane Fletcher, who used to handle this magnificently. She's sorely missed.

We've just spoken to David. He's asked us to confirm, 'No decision has been made.' Poor bastard. He's the one who has to face the press on Tuesday night.

Everyone wants a piece of *Doctor Who* these days. Press interviews, launches, and signing hundreds upon hundreds of autographs – all in a day's work for the tireless David Tennant, pictured here in his trailer.

FROM: BENJAMIN COOK TO: RUSSELL T DAVIES
SATURDAY 15 DECEMBER 2007 17:39:31 GMT

RE: ARSE, ARSE, ARSE!

BBC News is reporting that David is leaving *Doctor Who*. Russell, how has your day gone since Catherine's gaffe? What goes through your mind when something like this happens? Honestly?

FROM: RUSSELL T DAVIES TO: BENJAMIN COOK
SATURDAY 15 DECEMBER 2007 21:12:29 GMT

RE: ARSE, ARSE, ARSE!

I get frustrated, really, because there's a barrage of confusing information about the show. If you're listening to all the news reports over the past few months – not as a hardcore fan, but as a more casual viewer – you'd have this bizarre whirlwind impression of the Doctor with three companions, and then the show is going off air because David regenerates, except he doesn't, and then Rose goes with him, and then James Nesbitt takes over or has he started already…? We sound *confused*. Publicity and public image depends on a strict, simple picture. A man and his police box. But now we sound like a mess. I really, really worry that we sound like old news, or bad news, or boring news. I worry profoundly about that. On Tuesday, at the press launch, all the journalists will want to know about this, putting David under terrible pressure and obscuring the point of the evening.

Meanwhile, this afternoon, the second wave started. I've given so many interviews over the years, a lot of journalists have my mobile number. I always give an interview on the condition that they don't use the number again. But of course they do. I'm thick. They phone up from BBC Stoke, BBC Cornwall, BBC Humberside, Galaxy FM, every bloody Radio Backyard. Though the BBC itself is by far the worst. When they talk about BBC cutbacks, they can start with those hopeless stringers sitting in Nowhere Land, imagining that they can break a big story by digging through their contact list. I suppose it's their job, and maybe sometimes it works, but imagine if I gave an exclusive to BBC Strathclyde!

The third wave is not just asking for a quote, but asking me to go on this chat show, that chat show, *Newsbeat*, you name it. The BBC has something called

The Grid, a depository of phone numbers, which any BBC journalist can consult. I've asked a thousand times for my number to be taken off The Grid. It never is. People even deny its existence! So more and more calls come in, from complete strangers. I sort of hit my stride by late afternoon, telling them to sod off. If they persisted, I took their name and told them that I'm making a formal complaint within the BBC. That usually works. Eventually, I just stopped answering my phone. By tonight, it calmed down. But now it's out there, uncontrollable, on BBC News, everywhere, reported as fact. It can't be unsaid, ever. It's *Doctor Who*, for Christ's sake! You'd think we'd assassinated the Prime Minister. What the hell is it like on *real* news?

FROM: BENJAMIN COOK TO: RUSSELL T DAVIES
SUNDAY 16 DECEMBER 2007 00:48:39 GMT

RE: ARSE, ARSE, ARSE!

Amid all of this, what's Catherine saying on the matter? She must realise the storm that she's created. Poor Catherine.

FROM: RUSSELL T DAVIES TO: BENJAMIN COOK
SUNDAY 16 DECEMBER 2007 01:30:43 GMT

RE: ARSE, ARSE, ARSE!

That's the one thing I haven't asked. I don't like to. Like you, I wonder what she's said to David. Probably nothing. It was just a mistake, must have been, and they both adore each other, big time, so it'll just blow over, I presume. That's the last thing we need, actor wars. But they're both too intelligent for that.

Hey, I had the bloody *Mail* today describing me as having 'a large, soft, expressive face'. How bloody sexy do I feel? Soft!!!

FROM: BENJAMIN COOK TO: RUSSELL T DAVIES
MONDAY 17 DECEMBER 2007 15:42:36 GMT

RE: ARSE, ARSE, ARSE!

Is that the *Mail*'s article claiming that more than one companion in Series Four will 'confuse things', that it isn't 'very feminist that *Doctor Who* has gone from one assistant to a virtual harem', and describing Captain Jack's 'flamboyant sexuality' as a 'disruptive axis'? Is the jury still out on whether interviews with the *Daily Mail* are a good idea, Russell? Didn't your boyfriend tell you that he'd rather you didn't grant them interviews? I think I agree with him on this one...

FROM: RUSSELL T DAVIES TO: BENJAMIN COOK
MONDAY 17 DECEMBER 2007 16:08:47 GMT

RE: ARSE, ARSE, ARSE!

Far worse was the article's description of Martha as 'always going to be second best to Rose', followed immediately by a quote from me, making it sound as if *I'd* said second best! I'm still waiting to find out if Freema has seen that. I had a feeling that journalist was going to be dodgy, but I went ahead with it anyway. Why? Well, in the end, it's two pages in the *Daily Mail*. A great big photo of David and Kylie, a reminder that it's transmitted on Christmas Day (they printed the wrong time, of course – twice), and that's what matters. Harsh, but true. It's publicity. Moreover, that's two pages on me and my success, as a gay man, in a paper that vilifies homosexuality. Visibility is a good way of changing things, and that'll do me. As long as you don't get paid by them. I'd never accept that.

But it hasn't been a great weekend. On top of everything, Andy Pryor has discovered that Russell Tovey is in a play, *The Sea*, at the Theatre Royal Haymarket, from January to April, so that's our recording block buggered. (I really should have checked first.) Midshipman Frame was going to be vital. I had a lot of that planned out. And now... hmph. He would have been a junior soldier in the Shadow Proclamation. (After the *Titanic*, I imagined that he'd sort of followed the Doctor's example and set out to do good.) He could have helped the Doctor cut through the red tape at the Proclamation, but – and this is the best bit – when the Doctor goes on the run from the authorities, I wanted Frame to go with him. He'd become a companion! The Doctor, Donna and Alonso, on board the TARDIS, searching for the Earth. What a great team! But not for long. When they arrive on the Dalek ship in 4.13, then *zap!* Frame is killed! I wanted that to hurt. I wanted to show how cold the Daleks are, how vicious Davros is, how much danger they're all in, so Alonso would have had to go. Except now he won't be in it at all. That's stalled a plot. What do I do instead?

Russell T Davies and Julie Gardner pose for the press at the launch of *Voyage of the Damned*, in December 2007. Picture © Jonathan Hordle/Rex Features

Text message from: **Ben**
Sent: 17-Dec-2007 22:16
How are you feeling about tomorrow's press launch, Russell? Also, will there be nibbles?

Text message from: **Russell**
Sent: 17-Dec-2007 23:28
I'm dreading it. But there will be nibbles.

FROM: BENJAMIN COOK TO: RUSSELL T DAVIES
WEDNESDAY 19 DECEMBER 2007 11:20:01 GMT

RE: ARSE, ARSE, ARSE!

As press launches go, that wasn't too bad... was it? Well, the Science Museum was a fun choice of venue, at least.

FROM: RUSSELL T DAVIES TO: BENJAMIN COOK
WEDNESDAY 19 DECEMBER 2007 23:01:36 GMT

RE: ARSE, ARSE, ARSE!

I'm home now. I've been here for hours. I've been meaning to answer your e-mail about last night's launch, but I couldn't face it. I hated it. *Hated* it. I still feel sour.

It started badly. Me and Julie were running late. We had to rush for the train to London. We're always rushing. London is even more of a rush, because of the traffic, so Julie had to get changed in my hotel. She's running around in her bra and knickers – actually, it was a camisole. I had to ask, 'What's that called?' Like we're an old married couple. 'Why d'you have to moisturise your legs?' 'I shaved them yesterday.' 'Who's gonna know?' 'Oh, thank you!' (I'll leave you to guess who's who there.) Then we rushed to meet David and Jane for a drink. We had to work out The Line. Catherine claimed that David is leaving, so what's The Line on that? A one-line response, to be elaborated on at will, but one essential response from all of us, coordinated. I used to laugh at this, but it's needed if you're facing journalists. And what if the new BBC One Controller demands a 2009 series? What if someone asks about David's mother? Have we confirmed how long Catherine is staying for? What are we saying about Billie? What's The Line, The Line, The Bloody Line?! Except people are late, and gossiping, and pleased to see each other, so half The Lines don't even get discussed. Too late, we're behind schedule, go, go, go, into the cars, hurry up –

Actually, I'm making this sound funny. It wasn't funny. It was awful. At the first venue, where we met for a drink beforehand, I pretended that I didn't have any cigarettes, just so that I could walk out of the bar and away down the street for 15 minutes on my own. Head buzzing with Lines. Freezing cold. Christmas decorations. Best time I had all night.

When we arrived at the Science Museum – well, that's when it hits you, the sheer size of it. That launch was

David Tennant faces the press *en masse* at the *Voyage of the Damned* launch. Elisabeth Sladen and Camille Coduri keep smiling in the background.
© Richard Young/Rex Features

massive. A proper BBC event. We'd been chosen. It's good that we're chosen, it's important for the show, but I didn't enjoy it. It feels wrong somehow. It feels like it doesn't fit our show. We make the programme big, blousy and ballsy, but I think it's still sort of intimate, a daft little show, no matter how many spaceships are on display. It's certainly not corporate. That press launch was corporate. And there was no time to see anyone. Quick hello to my agent, I'm trying to see if Camille Coduri has turned up, I'm trying to see if you're there, but no time for that, there are people whose job it is to herd you in front of the journalists…

Next second, it's that parade of cameras, GMTV, BBC Breakfast, BBC News, *Newsround*, and you find yourself spouting The Lines, like a puppet. Worse, you slip into showbiz speak. I find myself saying things like 'There are lots of great surprises coming up.' Who talks like that?! Real people don't talk like that! In the middle of the line-up, I say hello to Russell Tovey. He's in front of GMTV. I'm with *Newsround*. We both look embarrassed. You can't say hello properly with lights and cameras in your face. Then you get shoved in front of the radio journalists, which is worse, because they're all in one gaggle, so ten different shows want ten different quotes, all at once. You have to be funny and sarky for *Newsbeat*, factual for Radio 2, factual-but-edgy for Radio 5, bland for Galaxy, all at the same time. That's probably where I go wrong. I should be myself. But everyone has a lot of different selves. I think that's why an evening like this is so dispiriting: I'm left wondering, who am I? And the funny thing is, while I hate it, I'm very aware that if, say, David is following me down the line, then no one actually wants to talk to me anyway. I'm left feeling like nothing again, but in a different way. The vanity!

Then it's the screening. We're hustled to our seats. 'That's Russell Tovey's boyfriend,' someone points out

– and a whole fantasy night dies in my mind. We sit at the front, but The Lines are still buzzing in my mind, and everyone is doing a post-mortem on what just happened with the journalists. 'What did they ask? What did they say? Were they friendly? Did they ask about Catherine?' A hundred times over, in whispers – while Bernard Cribbins is saying hello, so that switchback personality is still flickering to and fro. 'Hello, Bernard!' (The journalists were fine) 'How are you?' (What did David say?) 'Nice to see you.' (Who's giving the first speech?) 'Wait till you see it!' (Where's my radio mic?)

Lights down, it begins… and I feel totally disconnected from it. I don't laugh. I don't cry. It's the size again – *Doctor Who* on a giant screen with 500 people watching. Not that a *Doctor Who* movie couldn't work, but *Voyage of the Damned* isn't a movie, it's for TV, so it looks wrong, sounds wrong. I sat there thinking about the differences between film and TV. I can see it in action. TV cuts faster, spends much more time in CU, so it looks awful on a big screen, too choppy, too close, too amateur. It's a clumsy and jittery piece of work, blown up. The lovely sound mix, on a sound system this big, is distorted, everything divided into clean, separate tracks – music from over there, booms from over there, all unrelated – instead of the proper mix you get on a telly. It's like a grotesque version of itself. It's a cheap tart. I just stare, feeling nothing. I love *Voyage of the Damned*, and this is making me hate it. Julie keeps saying, 'There's too much bass. Should we alter the bass?' until I snap, 'Leave it, just shut up.' And then I feel bad all night for snapping at her. She never complains. She's used to me doing that. I always snap at the one who'll take it. Is *that* who I am?

After the screening, we get speeches praising me. I would rather die, I swear. I just wish they'd stop it. I don't recognise that person at all. That's not modesty – I think I'm brilliant! – but I'm not the person in those speeches. It just gets so awkward. Do you clap when everyone claps you? I do, but then I feel stupid. I'm imagining someone saying, 'Look at that tosser clapping himself!' It's very hard to stop a clap once you've started. Then it's the Q&A. I hate the Q&A. I hate any Q&A. I'm 44 and balding and putting on weight, in a cheap suit because nothing else was clean and my alarm didn't go off; the last thing I want to do is sit in front of 500 people. I feel so self-conscious. But no one's asking Russell Tovey, Gray O'Brien or Clive Rowe any questions, and I feel responsible for them. Also, I'm trying to stop myself being 'funny', because I can put on 'funny' in front of a crowd, as a mechanism, but that default usually means swearing or being filthy, and there are kids in the audience, so I'm all constrained. At the same time, I'm scanning the audience for that journalist with a killer question – like the man from *The Times* at the *Rise of the Cybermen* press screening, who implied that the *Doctor Who* crew had been paid off by Motorola because a mobile phone logo was visible! He actually, literally, accused that brilliant crew of being corrupt, of accepting back-handers. And it escalated. The day after that, *The Times* phoned Motorola and other mobile companies asking if they had illegal deals with the *Doctor Who* crew, while we had to send the episode back to The Mill for all accidentally seen logos to be digitally removed, at quite some cost. That's how serious some dumb-arse little question can get. So I'm waiting, waiting, waiting, all the time, for some snake question like that.

Then it's the party afterwards. But I can't relax. It's all work. In three hours, I have half an apple juice and half a Coke. I have to speak to everyone. That's my job. Signing autographs for kids, which is nice, but then the MPs, the bloody MPs, then a man from the Youth Hostelling organisation ('Have you ever Youth Hostelled?'), then BBC bosses (so I have to be nice and ask for more programme money), then more MPs – they never, ever say which party they represent. For all I know, I could be thanking a Tory. Oh, but there's Annette Badland, except I haven't time to say hello. Actors and friends fly past. The people that you want to see get snatched away. I pop out for a cigarette, but there's Mark Thompson, the BBC Director-General, so suddenly I sound like this professional robot. And then he makes it clear that he knows that Steven is taking over, so suddenly I feel like yesterday's robot. And then more MPs, and they're getting red-wine mouths. Everyone is trying to grab a bit of you. 'I run this website. Will you join and endorse it?' 'Can we do dinner?' 'Can we, can we, can we?'

The one time I do get five minutes to myself, one of the sci-fi-magazine men is drunk and won't leave me alone, while I'm fending off his sly, smiling insults ('That was a fun episode, wasn't it? Just fun!'), and then I find myself with two gay boys who work as researchers in Parliament, and they're gorgeous, but it turns out that they're with the Shadow Secretary of Something. I'm thinking, would I sleep with a Tory? But then they're telling me that they were 13 when *Queer as Folk* was on, and I realise that I'm as old as George Bernard Shaw to them. They keep talking about how they watched *Queer as Folk* in secret on portable TVs in their bedrooms, so essentially we're talking about wanking, which is weird. Then it turns out that one of them knows the exact date of my mother's death, which is completely out of leftfield and the last thing that I want to think about. I've spent six years trying not to think too much about that, so I move on. But then someone else appears and he's all 'Why don't I ever see you? Why won't you have a cigarette with me? You have a cigarette with everyone else. Why not me?' I'm thinking, oh shut *up!* And then more bloody MPs, and there's the nice man from *The Guardian*, all smiles and hellos, the same man who wrote a *Guardian* blog last week describing *Doctor Who* as the Most Overrated TV Show Of The Year, but I'm smiling back, because they can write what they like. And it goes on and on and on. When I say I hate it, I'm really so unhappy – and smiling like an idiot. A hundred versions of me, and every single one sounds like a fool.

Then it ends. Back to the hotel. So wound up. I don't get to sleep for hours. I just sit there, watching skiing and late-night poker on TV. Starving. I have a Coke and a Bounty from the mini bar. I worry about the price. On my wage, I worry about the price of a Bounty! And I sit there replaying everything I said to everyone, and all the people I missed, and all the stupid jokes I made, and I hate it. I hate myself. I just don't like myself very much. Well, who ever does? But when that self has been such a public self, all night, I feel prostituted, exaggerated, indistinct and stupid.

Still, the next morning is funny. I wake up, still sour. The 4.11 Edit is in Soho at 10am, so I wear my jeans and stuff, carry my suit on a hanger, go into Soho, have a coffee, buy the papers, have another coffee. After half an hour, I realise that my hanger is feeling rather light. I look. The trousers have slid off. I've lost my trousers. In Soho. I have to retrace my route through the cafes and newsagents, asking, 'Have you seen my trousers?' I never find them. Some tramp is looking smart for Christmas! But when I get to the Edit, I tell Phil, Julie, Graeme and Susie this story – and they laugh so hard, for so long, that I realise: *this* is why I love this job. These people. And whoever I am, if these people are my mates, then I can't be doing too bad.

This shot, from the cover shoot for *The Writer's Tale*, shows just how tall Russell really is... at least compared to designer Clayton Hickman.

FROM: BENJAMIN COOK TO: RUSSELL T DAVIES
THURSDAY 20 DECEMBER 2007 11:11:38 GMT

RE: ARSE, ARSE, ARSE!

I'm still laughing at your missing trousers! But I'm surprised that you're so worried about how you came across at the launch. I can understand you not enjoying it, and thank you for such honesty, Russell, but you're fantastic at dealing with the press, at putting on that public face. At least, you looked as though you knew what you were doing – how far to push it, and when, and with whom. You were asked who, living or dead, you'd like to see play the Doctor, and you answered 'Hitler' – *and actually got away with it!* Confident. Funny. Impassioned. It's sort of a shame that you don't think so.

FROM: RUSSELL T DAVIES TO: BENJAMIN COOK
THURSDAY 20 DECEMBER 2007 12:13:44 GMT

RE: ARSE, ARSE, ARSE!

Thank you. That cheered me up. I suppose what I'm saying is summed up in your phrase 'putting on that public face', because that's not a natural thing to do. I do know I'm good at it, but then that becomes a pressure in itself. People are expecting me to be good. You can sort of see why famous people go mad. I get one zillionth of that fame lark. Imagine being really famous, and famous for your face, your looks, your voice, famous for just being you. That's why the likes of Britney Spears and Amy Winehouse go berserk. I think it's one long cry of 'Who am I?'

FROM: BENJAMIN COOK TO: RUSSELL T DAVIES
THURSDAY 20 DECEMBER 15:35:34 GMT

RE: ARSE, ARSE, ARSE!

I meant to ask, did you finally meet up with Steven Moffat yesterday, in London, for that coffee? (Nice coffee, was it? Milk? Sugar?)

FROM: RUSSELL T DAVIES TO: BENJAMIN COOK
THURSDAY 20 DECEMBER 16:44:19 GMT

RE: ARSE, ARSE, ARSE!

It was a latte. Freezing, because I wanted to sit outside and smoke. Poor Steven. A kid called Karim recognised us and asked for a photo, and Steven said, 'You'll never know how historic this moment is!' But it was lovely. No great emotions. Well, I had a good time and we had a good chat, but I don't usually get emotional about stuff like that. Except in a good way. I *like* change. I love it when people move and leave and swap around. It felt good, healthy and natural.

I went for our coffee, full of things to tell Steven. I was bristling with them. But as soon as we sat down, I thought very clearly: I don't need to tell him any of this stuff. He knows scripts, he knows writers, he knows what's what. And he knows what he wants to do. He'll invent his own way of doing things. Experience – it's useless! Mostly we talked about the rewriting process, though it's a hard thing to discuss. As I talked, I thought I sounded power-mad. Genuinely. So I clammed up about it after a while. I didn't like the sound of myself. If anything, I felt a good old fanboy thrill down my spine, because Steven talked about the future in terms of … well, to the extent that I said, 'Don't tell me any more!' I want to find out as a viewer. I was even surprised, because I was half-expecting there to be a No Old Monsters rule under The Moff. But no. So that felt good.

I love this show, completely, and yet I will leave it without blinking. I've always been like that. I suppose I care about myself more than I care about any TV show. What I mean is… a funny thing happened that day. As Steven and I left Soho, we bumped into an ex of mine, Gareth. Lovely man, so we had a nice chat. As I wandered off with Steven, I explained that Gareth was my ex, and then I found myself saying, 'Actually, he's my *only* ex. I've only ever had two boyfriends, and he was one of them.' I'd never consciously thought that before, never mind said it out loud. I'm 44, and I've only had two proper relationships. Is that weird? I mean, I knew that to be the case, obviously, and yet I'd never really looked at the facts before so simply and easily. Two boyfriends! Just two! Steven must have thought I was really odd – not for only having two boyfriends, but for the way that I said it, because I was spelling it out, in words, carefully and slowly, for my own benefit. So really, for me, that – and losing my trousers – was what the last couple of days was all about. Not *Doctor Who*. ■

CHAPTER THIRTEEN

THE CHRISTMAS INVASION

In which Davros exposes himself, a former Prime Minister bites the dust, and millions watch *Voyage of the Damned*

FROM: RUSSELL T DAVIES TO: BENJAMIN COOK
FRIDAY 21 DECEMBER 2007 02:02:51 GMT

THE ABOMINATION IS INSANE

Look, more script! Not enough, though. But also too much, because I'm on Page 32 when I should be on Page 23 or something. I'm not going to fit it all in. Still, I went back and revised the end of Scene 47 and wrote a brand new Scene 48, cutting the stuff with Donna and the Elderly Nun ('There was something on your back'), which I'm keeping for a bit later…

JUDOON
Stand in line.

THE DOCTOR
(to Donna)
I said so, thick!!
(to Judoon, angry)
You! Designate my language!

JUDOON
You speak Earth English.

THE DOCTOR
Go on then. Double check!

Judoon holds up its translator, the Doctor speaks into it -

THE DOCTOR (CONT'D)
Mary had a little lamb, its fleece was white as snow, and everywhere that Mary went, her lamb was sure to go.

The Judoon clips the translator into its chest port - the Doctor's words play back, '*Maryhadalittlelambitsfleecewas…*' but overlaid with a thousand jabbering babbles -

The Judoon begins to shake! Shudder!

With a roar, it throws off the translator -

PRAC FX: it hits the floor and explodes!

All Judoon raise weapons at the Doctor & Donna! *Click* of metal! EXTRAS fall silent, the whole room staring. Donna follows the Doctor's lead, both putting their hands up.

JUDOON
Designation: impossible! You speak six million languages simultaneously!

THE DOCTOR
And all six million languages would like a word with the Chief Constable. Right now.

CUT TO:

48. INT. CHIEF CONSTABLE'S OFFICE - NIGHT

Large, cool, clinical sci-fi room, like Lazarus' office or Mrs Wormwood's.[1] Big desk, behind which: the CHIEF CONSTABLE. Tough, efficient woman, 40s, black uniform.

THE DOCTOR & DONNA facing her, with TWO HELMETED JUDOON GUARD, plus the UNHELMETED JUDOON CAPTAIN.

CHIEF CONSTABLE
Time Lords are the stuff of legend. They belong in the myths and whispers of the Higher Species. You can't actually be *real*.

THE DOCTOR
More to the point, 24 missing planets! Can you give me a list? What's gone missing where?

The Chief Constable presses a button. On a BIG SCREEN (Ood-Hospitality-size), small representations of, and information about, 24 planets, each in a separate box.

CHIEF CONSTABLE
The locations range far and wide, across all galactic vectors. But all disappeared at the exact same moment. Leaving no trace.

THE DOCTOR
Clom. Callufrax Minor. Jahoo. Shallacatop. Woman Wept. Flane...

CHIEF CONSTABLE
As far as we can tell, they've got nothing in common. Different sizes,

1 *Doctor Who* 3.6 and *The Sarah Jane Adventures* 1.X respectively.

'Time Lords are the stuff of legend.' The Tenth Doctor, as drawn by Russell T Davies.

different ages. Some populated, some not. But all unconnected.

DONNA
What about Pyrovillia?

CHIEF CONSTABLE
I'm sorry?

DONNA
Donna, Donna Noble, Human, every bit as important as Time Lords, thank you. But way back, in Pompeii, d'you remember? That Lucius bloke said that Pyrovillia had gone missing.

CHIEF CONSTABLE
Pyrovillia is a cold case, it vanished two thousand years ago, it's got nothing to do with this -

DONNA
And the Adipose Breeding Planet, d'you remember?

THE DOCTOR
...lost, she said it was lost... Chief Constable, d'you mind...?

He starts fiddling with the controls on her desk.

THE DOCTOR (CONT'D)
If we make this a 3-D representation...

FX: in front of the desk, floating mid-air, GRAPHICS of the 24 PLANETS, grouped in an array. Static.

THE DOCTOR (CONT'D)
Now, if we add Pyrovillia... And the Adipose World, then...

Looks up -

FX: Two more PLANETS appear in the floating GRAPHIC. But the Doctor seems to be disappointed...

THE DOCTOR (CONT'D)
...where else, where else...? If planets have been taken out of time, and not just space, then... Oh! The Lost Moon of Poosh!

Stabs a button -

FX: a small MOON appears amongst the 24, and then...

As they stare...

FX (AND REPEAT): PLANETS rearrange themselves, quick spin, settle into a new pattern. A *moving* pattern. Slow orbits.

CHIEF CONSTABLE
What did you do?

THE DOCTOR
Nothing. They rearranged themselves. Into the optimum pattern. Ohh, but look at that! 27 planets in perfect balance! Self-perpetuating motion! Come on! That is beautiful!

DONNA
Doctor, don't get all Spaceman, what does it mean?

THE DOCTOR
All those worlds fit together like pieces of an engine.

CHIEF CONSTABLE
Generating massive kinetic energy.

THE DOCTOR
It's like a powerhouse! The tension of those planets would provide enough energy to... what? What is it, what are they building, what??

DONNA
And who's they?

THE DOCTOR
(dark)
Someone tried to move the Earth before. Long time ago. I wonder...
(goes to Donna)
But the thing is Donna, to get that balance, you need the planets completely intact! It depends on every little thing, the heat, the atmosphere, even the matrix of life on the surface! It means the Earth is still intact! They're still alive!!

DONNA
Ohh, thank you - !

'All those worlds fit together like pieces of an engine.'

Big hug!

CUT TO:

49. INT. CRUCIBLE COMMAND DECK - NIGHT

SUPREME DALEK addressing his MINIONS:

SUPREME DALEK
Engaging Earth forces! Battle Plan Five! No military prisoners! Attack! Destroy! EXTERMINATE!!

CUT TO:

50. FX SHOTS

FX: DALEK SAUCER, set against the PLANETARY SKY, disgorging HUNDREDS OF DALEKS!

FX: DALEKS swoop foreground, and behind them, THE VALIANT! Shooting LASER BEAMS! (Below, the shores of Britain.)

FX: LASER BEAMS slice through a ROW OF DALEKS, they EXPLODE!

FX: FLEET OF DALEKS, the SAUCER above them, rain down FIRE -

FX: the VALIANT EXPLODES!

CUT TO:

51. INT. TORCHWOOD HUB - NIGHT

CAPTAIN JACK, GWEN, IANTO, running separately from one terminal to another, trying to follow the battle, with a babble of despairing MILITARY RADIO VOICES over COMMS, ADR -

CAPTAIN JACK
The Valiant is down!

GWEN
Airforce retreating over North Africa! Daleks landing in Egypt -

IANTO
We've lost Geneva! Geneva is down!

Captain Jack running to his mobile, desperate -

CAPTAIN JACK
Martha, get out of there -

CONTINUES INTERCUT WITH UNIT HQ, NEW YORK.

CUT TO:

52. INT. UNIT HQ, NEW YORK CITY - NIGHT

INTERCUT WITH TORCHWOOD HUB.

MARTHA on mobile headset, on the floor - the room in greater disarray, papers, desks, chairs scattered, PEOPLE running - as Martha bandages the head of a dazed, injured SOLDIER -

MARTHA
I can't, Jack, I've got a job to do -

WHUMPH! Whole room shakes, PRAC RUBBLE falls -

CAPTAIN JACK
They're targeting military bases, and you're next on the list -

MARTHA
I'm needed. And I'm staying.

Looks up - GENERAL SANCHEZ & a SOLDIER stand above her.

GENERAL SANCHEZ
Doctor Jones. You'll come with me.

MARTHA
I haven't finished -

GENERAL SANCHEZ
Leave him. And that's an order. Project Indigo is being activated. Quick march!

CUT TO:

53. INT. UNIT HQ, NEW YORK CITY, LONG CORRIDOR - NIGHT

Long, long, featureless corridor. MARTHA being marched along by GENERAL SANCHEZ & SOLDIER, like a prisoner -

MARTHA
- but we can't use Project

'Washington, can you hear me? This is New York!' UNIT prepares to battle the invading Daleks.

Indigo, it hasn't been tested, we don't even know if it works -

CUT TO:

54. INT. UNIT HQ, NEW YORK CITY - NIGHT

SOLDIERS running to and fro, SUZANNE on desk-microphone -

SUZANNE
Washington, can you hear me? Repeat, Washington, can you hear me, this is New York City -

PRAC EXPLOSION - BIG ONE! - the office DOORS blow open -

Suzanne & others thrown to the floor -

Then, as she gets back to her feet, she sees…

FOUR DALEKS glide through the smoke, into the office.

SOLDIERS OPEN FIRE, PRAC FX BULLETS -

FX: SPARKS ricochet off the Daleks, as they line up -

DALEKS
Exterminate!

FX: SUZANNE is hit, screams, reduced to a SKELETON, dies -

CUT TO:

55. INT. UNIT HQ, NEW YORK CITY, LONG CORRIDOR - NIGHT

At the end of the long corridor, a big bank-vault-like steel door. The SOLDIER now swinging it open.

Inside: GLOWING WHITE WALL, and a HARNESS on a display-stand, all metal clips and buckles. To Martha:

GENERAL SANCHEZ
Put it on, fast as you can -

Still INTERCUT WITH SC.51, TORCHWOOD HUB, Jack yelling -

CAPTAIN JACK
Martha, I'm telling you, don't use Project Indigo, it's not safe -

GENERAL SANCHEZ
You'll take your orders from UNIT, Doctor Jones, not Torchwood -

Martha starts to haul it on, buckle up, the soldier helping, buckles clicking into place, and during this -

MARTHA
But why me?

GENERAL SANCHEZ
Because you're our only hope. Of finding the Doctor.
(quieter, sad)
Now face me, Martha. Look at me. And follow these instructions. If there's no Doctor. If no help is coming… Then with the power invested in me by the Unified Intelligence Taskforce, I authorise you to take this.

From his pocket: an electronic KEY, a square of metal, on a chain. Martha knows what it means, horrified.

GENERAL SANCHEZ (CONT'D)
The Stattenheim Key.

MARTHA
…I can't take that, sir.

GENERAL SANCHEZ
You know what to do. For the sake of the Human Race.

PRAC EXPLOSION at the far end of the corridor -

The soldier runs forward, gun ready -

GENERAL SANCHEZ (CONT'D)
Doctor Jones. Good luck.

He salutes her. Then turns, pulls out his revolver -

FOUR DALEKS appear through SMOKE at the far end -

Soldier & General Sanchez open fire, standing in front of Martha, shielding her to the last -

CUT TO sc.51 continued, CAPTAIN JACK in the HUB -

CAPTAIN JACK
Martha, don't do it! Don't - !!

MARTHA
(quiet)
Bye Jack.

FX: SANCHEZ & SOLDIER hit by DALEK FIRE, SKELETONS -

And Martha reaches up, pulls two cords on the harness, like parachute rip-cords, closes her eyes, and PULLS -

FX: MARTHA vanishes in a TELEPORT GLOW!

CUT TO:

56. INT. TORCHWOOD HUB - NIGHT

CAPTAIN JACK furious, slams the desk. Then silence. GWEN & IANTO looking at him, fearing the worst.

GWEN
What happened? Did they get her?

CAPTAIN JACK
…I don't know.

IANTO
What's Project Indigo?

CAPTAIN JACK
Experimental teleport. Salvaged from the Sontaran ship. But they're like kids with a toy, they don't know how it works, they haven't got coordinates, or stabilisation. She could be anywhere.

GWEN
But… alive?

CAPTAIN JACK
Or scattered into atoms.
(pause)
She's gone. Martha's down.

CUT TO:

'The Abomination is insane.' Dalek Caan, damaged by his Emergency Temporal Shift into the timelocked Time War.

57. INT. CRUCIBLE COMMAND DECK - NIGHT

DALEK 1 glides up to the SUPREME DALEK'S platform.

DALEK 1
Earth forces defeated!

SUPREME DALEK
Commence the landings. Bring the Humans here! Prepare the Crucible!

Then, over COMMS, a cold, clever, quiet voice:

VOICE OOV
Supreme Dalek. Is there news?

SUPREME DALEK
Earth has been subjugated!

VOICE OOV
I mean, is there news of him?

CUT TO:

58. INT. CRUCIBLE LOWER DECK - NIGHT

(Command deck redressed.) More sinister, quiet, empty. A dark, echoing space, with three free-standing Dalek-type computer banks arranged in a wide semicircle.

Still, only the voice. A FIGURE hidden in shadow.

SUPREME DALEK OOV
Negative! No reports of Time Lord or Tardis. We are beyond the Doctor's reach!

CU on a DALEK base, gliding forward…

VOICE
If I had not elevated you above crude emotions, I could almost mistake that tone for one of victory. Beware your pride.

Travelling up the base, to find CU HAND. A metal hand, chrome, with elegant, multi-jointed fingers, hovering above a buttons & switches built into a panel…

SUPREME DALEK OOV
The Doctor cannot stop us!

VOICE
And yet, Dalek Caan is uneasy.

The HAND flicks a switch.

With the figure deep foreground, out of focus - a SPOTLIGHT SLAMS ON, far across the room, throwing into harsh relief, on a platform of its own…

A weird shape, like a Dalek has been opened, gutted and melted, its harsh lines now curved and warped.

SUPREME DALEK OOV
The Abomination is insane.

VOICE
Show respect. Without Dalek

Caan, none of this would be possible.

DALEK CAAN
...he is moving, in the dark, and the wild and the lonely places...

Its voice is childlike, sing-song, mad. CUT CLOSER. In the middle of the warped shell sits the DALEK MUTANT, tentacles stirring; but this creature is burnt and blackened. Though its eye still stares.

VOICE
Do you speak of the Doctor? Tell me! Can you see him?

DALEK CAAN
...he is coming. Quietly slowly quickly, the bad, bad man. Oh creator of us all. He is coming...

Hey, guess what else? We've cast Alex Kingston as River Song in Steven's two-parter! ALEX KINGSTON! I bloody love her. Alex Kingston is the Doctor's wife! And Dr Moon is Colin Salmon. Classy cast.

FROM: RUSSELL T DAVIES TO: BENJAMIN COOK
SATURDAY 22 DECEMBER 2007 03:04:00 GMT

RE: THE ABOMINATION IS INSANE

I got rid of that whole Dalek descent on Westminster (Scenes 31–40). It's the Daleks – why are they so diplomatic? When I read that back to myself on Thursday night, having been away from the script for three days, I found my eyes skipping over those scenes, and I woke up this morning and thought, get rid of them. I needed to lose some pages anyway. You have to go down those blind alleys sometimes. Scenes 25–32 now go like this...

25. INT. SARAH JANE SMITH'S ATTIC - NIGHT

SARAH JANE & LUKE at MR SMITH, displaying the SAME GRAPHICS.

MR SMITH V/O
Sarah Jane, I'm receiving a communication from the

Silence in the Library's Professor River Song (Alex Kingston) indulges in some sonic-screwdriver rivalry with the Doctor (David Tennant).

Earthbound ships. They have a message for the Human Race.

SARAH JANE
Put it through, let me hear.

Sarah & Luke listen, the sound of radio-whine, tuning in...

And then...

That old, terrible voice:

DALEKS OOV
Exterminate! Exterminate! *Exterminate!* EXTERMINATE!

SARAH JANE
No...

On Sarah Jane. Staggered. The terror.

CUT TO:

26. INT. TORCHWOOD HUB - NIGHT

CAPTAIN JACK, hearing the 'Exterminate!' - which remains constant over these scenes - winded, as though punched.

CAPTAIN JACK
...no. Ohh no...

GWEN
Jack, what is it? Who are they? D'you know them? Jack?

CUT TO:

27. INT. UNIT HQ, NEW YORK CITY - NIGHT

All UNIT STAFF frozen, listening. 'Exterminate!'

CU MARTHA. Terrified.

CUT TO:

28. INT. TORCHWOOD HUB - NIGHT

'Exterminate' continues. CAPTAIN JACK is hugging GWEN & IANTO; kisses Ianto on the top of his head, then Gwen.

CAPTAIN JACK
There's nothing I can do. I'm sorry. We're dead.

CUT TO:

29. INT. SARAH JANE SMITH'S ATTIC - NIGHT

SARAH JANE hugs LUKE. He's scared. Because she's crying.

SARAH JANE
You're so young. Oh God. You're so young.

CUT TO:

30. INT. ABANDONED COMPUTER SHOP - NIGHT

ROSE, alone, staring at the computer screen. Hearing 'Exterminate!' Her worst fears. She's crying, a little.

She pulls herself together, picks up her gun, strides out -

CUT TO:

31. EXT. SHOPPING STREET - NIGHT

ROSE steps out of the computer store. Looks up.

FX: MASSIVE DALEK SAUCER roars overhead! Shoots LASER!

PRAC FX: HUUUGE FIREBALL EXPLOSION in the street!

CUT TO:

32. FX SHOT

FX: FLEETS OF DALEK SAUCERS sweeping over the EARTH!

This is followed by Scene 33 (what used to be 41) on the Crucible Command Deck, shifting all subsequent scene numbers, so Scene 50 (originally 58) is now the first one in the Crucible Vaults, ending with Dalek Caan's 'He is coming…', followed by Scene 51 in the Chief Constable's Office…

51. INT. CHIEF CONSTABLE'S OFFICE - NIGHT

Lights low, quiet, all strangely calm. THREE JUDOON, one UNHELMETED, standing back, on guard. THE DOCTOR hunched over the terminal, with the CHIEF CONSTABLE, frustrated.

THE DOCTOR
…there's nothing. No echo. No decay. 27 planets have got to leave some sort of trace…

CHIEF CONSTABLE
Perhaps if we scan for Zygma Energy.

THE DOCTOR
Tried it. I'll try again…

But all this seen from a distance. By DONNA. She's exhausted, sits alone towards the back of the room.

She sighs, just sits there.

The Dalek invasion of Earth commences.

And then…

SLOW ZOOM into Donna. She's just staring to the middle distance, lost in thought. But as the zoom creeps closer…

Natural sound lowers, muffled, then fading to nothing…

Bring in a new sound…

Softly, but getting stronger…

A heartbeat.

Donna just staring.

Closer on her…

Louder…

Closer…

And…

She snaps out of it as someone steps into foreground - It's an ALBINO SERVANT. A gaunt, white woman, 20s, humble, swathed in black robes. She offers Donna a china bowl.

ALBINO SERVANT
You need sustenance. Take the water. It purifies.

DONNA
Thanks.

Donna takes the bowl, then. But the Albino stays, staring.

DONNA (CONT'D)
…sorry, what are you looking at?

ALBINO SERVANT
There was something on your back.

DONNA
How d'you know that?

ALBINO SERVANT
You are something new. Something terrible and new.
(sad smile)
I'm so sorry for your loss.

DONNA
…my whole planet's gone.

ALBINO SERVANT
I mean the loss that is yet to come. God save you.

The Albino walks away, Donna watching, unnerved, then -

The Doctor, sharp, calling across -

THE DOCTOR
Donna! Come on! There must be something, think!

DONNA
What sort of something?

THE DOCTOR
Some trace of the Earth, just think - was there anything happening back in your day? Any sort of warning? Like, electrical storms? Freak weather? Patterns in the sky?

DONNA
Well how should I know? Um… not really, no, I don't think so.

THE DOCTOR
(turns away, brusque)
Oh never mind -

DONNA
…although… There was the bees disappearing.

THE DOCTOR
The bees disappearing… The bees disappearing. *The bees disappearing!*

And he's leaping round the terminal, stabbing buttons -

CHIEF CONSTABLE
How is that significant?

DONNA
Well, we've got these insects, on Earth, called bees, little flying things, and they were starting to disappear. They stopped colonising.

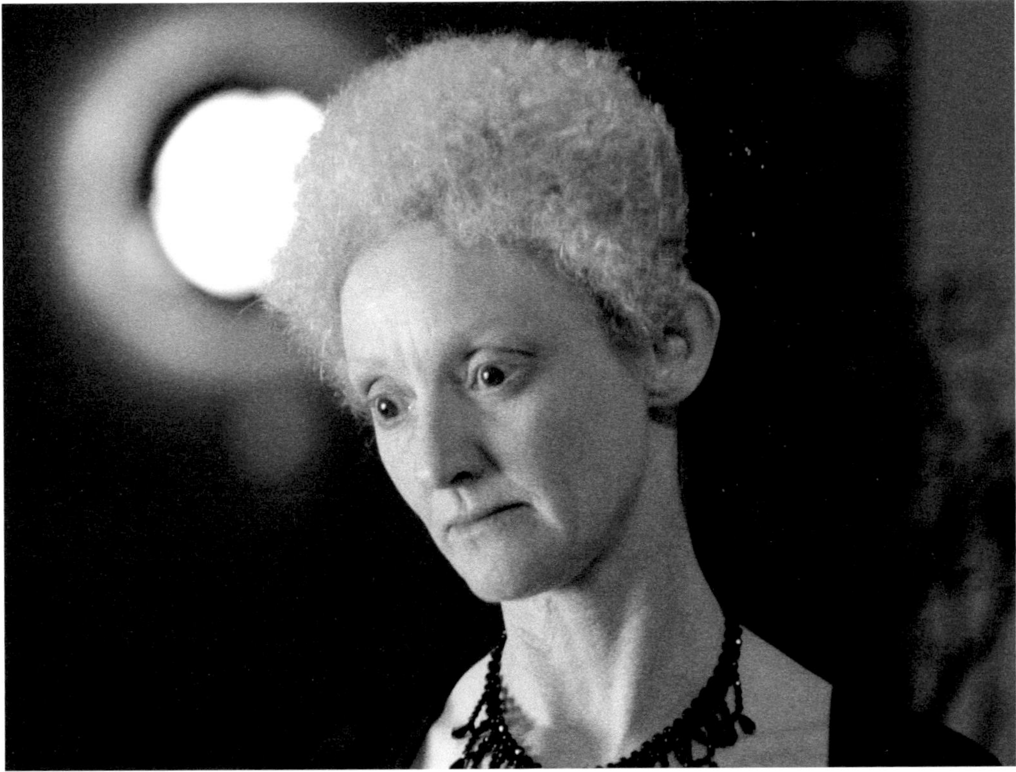

'Perhaps if we scan for Zygma Energy?' The 'Chief Constable' of the Shadow Proclamation.

Some people said it was pollution, or mobile phone signals -

THE DOCTOR
Or! They were going back home!

DONNA
Back home where?

THE DOCTOR
The planet Melissa Majoria!

DONNA
Are you saying bees are aliens?!

THE DOCTOR
Don't be so daft. Not all of them. But if the Migrant Bees felt something coming, and escaped… Tandocca!

CHIEF CONSTABLE
The Tandocca Scale…

THE DOCTOR
(to Donna, busy)
The Tandocca Scale is a series of wavelengths used as a carrier signal by Migrant Bees. Infinitely small! No wonder we didn't see it, it's like looking for a speck of cinnamon in the Sahara, but look -

Donna runs to join him, seeing on the terminal -

GRAPHICS: a MAP OF SPACE, with tiny, thin, dust-like trails scattered across…

DONNA
And that's the Tandocca thing?

THE DOCTOR
If the teleport was using the Tandocca Scale… we can follow the path…

DONNA
And find the Earth?!

THE DOCTOR
Oh yes!

And he's running out of the room - !

CUT TO:

52. INT. TARDIS - NIGHT

THE DOCTOR running round the console, happy, with DONNA -

THE DOCTOR
Tandocca, Tandocca, Tandocca… We're a bit late, the signal's scattered. But it's a start!

He runs down the ramp -

CUT TO:

53. INT. SHADOW PROCLAMATION LOBBY - NIGHT

THE DOCTOR pops his head out of the door. THE CHIEF CONSTABLE stands a distance back, formal, with a FULL GUARD OF ALL JUDOON. (In b/g, the SPACE EXTRAS, monks & nuns etc, chaos still continuing, but way back from the Tardis.)

THE DOCTOR
I've got a blip! Just a blip! But it's definitely a blip!

CHIEF CONSTABLE
Then according to Shadow Proclamation Protocols, I will have to commandeer your equipment and transport.

THE DOCTOR
…oh, really, what for?

CHIEF CONSTABLE
We have to assume that the planets were stolen with hostile intent. The Seven Hundred Societies have declared war, Doctor. Right across the universe. And you will lead us into battle!

THE DOCTOR
Right, yes, course I will. I'll just go and… get you the key…

And he slams the door -

CUT TO:

54. INT. TARDIS - NIGHT

THE DOCTOR runs back to the console - slams levers - !

THE DOCTOR
Off we go then!

CUT TO:

55. INT. SHADOW PROCLAMATION LOBBY - NIGHT

The wheeze and grind of ancient engines starts up…

CHIEF CONSTABLE furious. JUDOON raise weapons, *ka-chik!*

CHIEF CONSTABLE
Doctor! I order you to stop! D'you hear me? Stop right now!

FX: WIND sweeps across, and the TARDIS melts away…

CUT TO:

56. INT. TARDIS - NIGHT

In flight. THE DOCTOR busy with the controls, all energised. DONNA smiling.

DONNA
So the Shadow Proclamation's got guns, and soldiers, and spaceships, but no, we're gonna face someone big enough to steal 27 planets, all on our own. Two of us!

THE DOCTOR
Just you and me!

Big smile from both - then holding on as the Tardis lurches -

CUT TO:

57. FX SHOT

FX: THE TARDIS spinning away into the distance, a brave little box, through a HUGE VISTA OF OUTER SPACE.

I'm not very fond of the Shadow Proclamation. The Chief Constable is the most thankless part ever. She has to say terrible sci-fi lines like 'Perhaps if we scan for Zygma Energy' and 'The Tandocca Scale…' Some poor actor! Giving her detail, flesh and interest would just rack up the page count, so she's terribly stripped down. I keep wondering if I should cut the Shadow Proclamation completely, but without it… well, the Doctor would sit in the TARDIS, scanning things, until, yes, he finds the Earth. It would be strangely domestic. No struggle, no journey, no obstacles. He has to have a journey. Should the Shadow Proclamation be replaced with something more mystic, like a trip to a barren world to consult some psychic hermit? But that's equally bollocks. I hate that sort of spooky crap.

Also, I can feel the start of a cold. I *cannot* have a cold. I just can't. I won't.

FROM: RUSSELL T DAVIES TO: BENJAMIN COOK
SUNDAY 23 DECEMBER 2007 02:40:20 GMT

RE: THE ABOMINATION IS INSANE

I went back and fixed the Chief Constable. Her main problem was being a Chief Constable, so I decided – and it's funny how that e-mail to you yesterday clarified my worries – that since she has to say lame sci-fi lines, she can only work if she's a sci-fi creature. I've renamed her the Shadow Architect, made her albino and weird (hair scraped into a black snood, red eyes, solemn, swathed in black robes), and given her a slight mysticism – not hermit-in-a-cave mysticism, just an albino freakiness – so that she's sort of interesting now. Not fascinating, just interesting.

Right, here's more…

```
58. EXT. SUBURBAN STREET #2 - NIGHT

CU on a DALEK spinning round on the
spot.

              DALEK 1
   All Humans will leave their
   homes! The males, the
   females, the descendants; you
   will come with us! Resistance
   is useless!

FX: MULTIPLICATION WIDE SHOT.
PEOPLE leaving every home - couples
hugging, scared, some with hands
up, KIDS looking scared, but all
walking to the centre of the road,
to form a line. MULTIPLICATION PRAC
```

'All Humans will leave their homes! The males, the females, the descendants!' Daleks – Invasion Earth 2008 AD.

'Good splodge of paint, they're blinded!' Wilf (Bernard Cribbins) and Sylvia (Jacqueline King) hide in the shadows.

DALEKS on guard. From one house: SCARED MAN, WIFE and 14 Y/O SON, walking out.

SCARED MAN
Where are you taking us?

DALEK 1
Daleks do not answer Human questions! Form a line!

CUT TO WILF. He's a good distance away, hidden in the shadows of an alley. Grim. Holding a PAINT GUN.

SYLVIA, terrified, creeps up behind him, whispers:

SYLVIA
Dad. Please come home. They're leaving our street alone.

WILF
I've got a weapon!

SYLVIA
It's a paint gun!

WILF
Exactly! Those Dalek things, they've only got one eye! Good splodge of paint, they're blinded!

But then they look back to the street, hearing -

SCARED MAN
We're not going! D'you hear me? Laura, get back in the house! Simon! Get inside!

Wife & son run back to the house, the man throws a brick -

- which just bounces off the Dalek, *clang!*

SCARED MAN (CONT'D)
Get back in the sky, get back where you came from, and leave us alone!

And he follows his wife, runs into the house - the front door slams shut -

THREE DALEKS calmly glide in front of the house. (All the PEOPLE standing, staring, frozen, terrified.)

DALEK 1
Maximum extermination!

FX: ALL THREE DALEKS FIRE, three constant beams -

(PRAC FX? CG?): ALL THE WINDOWS OF THE HOUSE BLAST OUT!

CUT TO Wilf & Sylvia, horrified.

WILF
...monsters.

SYLVIA
Please, Dad. Come home.

And Wilf goes with her. They run away, into the shadows...

In the street, the Daleks turn to the lined-up people.

DALEK 1
Now march! You will be taken to the Crucible!

And the people, scared, defeated, begin to march...

CUT TO:

<u>59. EXT. SUBURBAN STREET #3 - NIGHT</u>

WILF & SYLVIA run out of the alley, into a new street -

Where one solitary DALEK faces them, middle of the road.

DALEK 2
Halt! You will come with me!

WILF
Will I heck!

And he lifts his PAINT GUN, fires -

SPLAT! Yellow paint on the Dalek's eyestalk!

The Dalek twitches, shudders, but -

DALEK 2
Engaging bodywork repair!

FX: CU EYESTALK, yellow paint smokes, evaporates, gone.

SYLVIA
I warned you...

DALEK 2
Hostility will not be tolerated! Exterminate! Exterminate! Exterm -

PRAC FX: *WHOOMPH!!!* THE DALEK BLOWS UP!

Wilf & Sylvia flinching back, dazed, staring...

THROW FOCUS: behind the shattered Dalek: ROSE TYLER. With her great big, now-smoking, sci-fi gun.

ROSE
You're Donna Noble's family, right? I'm Rose Tyler. And I need you!

CUT TO:

Rose Tyler – Dalek Killer!

60. INT. NOBLES' HOUSE, LIVING ROOM - NIGHT

WILF passing ROSE his phone, but both despairing...

WILF
I tried calling her. But I can't get through!

ROSE
My phone's the same, like they're out of range or something.

WILF
She's still with the Doctor, I know that much! Last time she phoned, it was a planet called Midnight. Made of diamonds!

SYLVIA watching them like they're mad.

SYLVIA
What the hell are you two on about?

WILF
Donna. She's out there, in space, with that Doctor. She travels with him. Fighting aliens!

SYLVIA
Oh don't be ridiculous!

WILF
The sky is full of planets! We're being invaded by pepper pots! And you're calling me ridiculous!

But Rose sits, defeated.

ROSE
You were my last hope. I thought if you knew where Donna was... But if we can't find the Doctor...
(pause)
The Daleks have won.

CUT TO:

61. INT. TORCHWOOD HUB - NIGHT

GWEN at a terminal, IANTO at a second. But CAPTAIN JACK is just sitting on the floor, a distance away. Defeated. Over this, RADIO VOICES of Daleks at work. Quiet:

GWEN
They're taking people off the streets. What for? Jack? What do they need them for?

Both looking at Jack. No reply.

GWEN (CONT'D)
Well, that's a great strategy. Nice one, Jack, yeah. Let's just all give up!

CAPTAIN JACK
(bitter, quiet)
Still don't get it, do you? It's the Daleks. There is nothing we can do. Nothing.

And that scares Gwen & Ianto more than anything.

WIDE SHOT Hub, all useless. Just victorious Dalek voices.

CUT TO:

62. INT. SARAH JANE SMITH'S ATTIC - NIGHT

Dalek RADIO VOICES carry over, via Mr Smith. But SARAH JANE & LUKE are sitting well back. Quiet, helpless.

'What do they need them for?' Gwen refuses to give up.

'You can stop them, can't you, Mum?'

LUKE
You can stop them, can't you, mum? You'll think of something. You always do.

SARAH JANE
Not this time.
(looks up)
Where is he?

WIDE SHOT. The two of them, alone.

CUT TO:

63. INT. TARDIS - NIGHT

THE DOCTOR at the console, with DONNA, but -

THE DOCTOR
…it's stopped.

DONNA
What d'you mean? Is that good or bad? Where are we?

The Doctor reads the scanner. In awe…

THE DOCTOR
The Medusa Cascade.

CUT TO:

64. FX SHOT

FX: the TARDIS, small, just spinning slowly on the spot. Around it, the blue-and-gold gas-clouds seen backing the Planetary Array. But with no planets. Just empty space.

CUT TO:

65. INT. TARDIS - NIGHT

THE DOCTOR still at the scanner. Quiet, worried.

THE DOCTOR
I came here when I was just a kid. 90 years old. It was the centre of a Rift in time and space…

DONNA
But where are the planets?

THE DOCTOR
Nowhere. The Tandocca trail stops dead. End of the line.

DONNA
So what do we do?

No reply. The Doctor's frozen, standing still, lost.

DONNA (CONT'D)
Doctor? What do we do?
(no reply)
Don't do this to me. Tell me. What are we gonna do?

THE DOCTOR
…I don't know.

DONNA
Don't say that. Don't you dare. You never give up. Doctor! Think of something! Please.

The Doctor just steps back. Against the rail. Powerless.

Which scares Donna to death. She puts her hands to her face, dismayed, close to tears.

WIDE SHOT of the Tardis, neither of them moving. Helpless.

Bring in score, over this. Haunting, lyrical music…

MIX TO:

66. INT. TORCHWOOD HUB - NIGHT

Music over: CAPTAIN JACK still hunched on the floor, against the wall. IANTO sitting separately, desolate. GWEN sitting apart, upset, hearing, under the music; Dalek radio voices; the sound of the world ending.

All dead and hopeless.

MIX TO:

67. INT. SARAH JANE SMITH'S ATTIC - NIGHT

Music over: SARAH JANE just holding LUKE. Dalek radio voices in b/g, victorious.

Sarah Jane Smith, with no hope.

CUT TO:

68. INT. NOBLES' HOUSE, LIVING ROOM - NIGHT

WILF on the settee, hugging poor SYLVIA, who's crying. ROSE sitting alone. Haunted, defeated. Distant Dalek voices from the street barking commands.

And then…

A sound.

Like a radio tuning in, white noise shashing. And under the noise, fluctuating…

A WOMAN'S VOICE.

(SC.66, 67, 68 continuing, intercutting them constantly.)

IN THE HUB. GWEN looks up. Hearing…

WOMAN'S VOICE
…can anyone hear me? The Subwave Network is open. You should be able to hear my voice. Is there anyone there…?

CUT TO SARAH JANE'S ATTIC. Luke hearing this.

LUKE
Who's that…?

SARAH JANE
Someone calling for help. Nothing we can do.

LUKE
But look at Mr Smith.

MR SMITH's CRYSTAL DISPLAY has been replaced by a screen of white noise. A face, lost in static.

CUT TO NOBLES' LIVING ROOM. ROSE looking up…

The Nobles have got an old COMPUTER on a dresser. The screen is shashing with white noise, an obscured face…

WOMAN'S VOICE
…if you can hear me, then please respond. This message is of utmost importance. And we haven't got much time…

ROSE
I know that voice…

CUT TO THE HUB, GWEN moving to the computer.

GWEN
Someone's trying to get in touch.

CAPTAIN JACK
Whole world's crying out.

GWEN
But I've heard that voice before.

IANTO
Sounds like… Can't be.

CAPTAIN JACK
Just leave it.

WOMAN'S VOICE
Captain Jack Harkness. Shame on you. You will stand to attention, sir, and answer me!

CAPTAIN JACK
Whaaat…?!

And he runs to Gwen's terminal, Ianto going with him - Jack stabs a button, and the screen clears, to reveal -

Penelope Wilton returns as... oh, you know who she is!

HARRIET JONES!

CAPTAIN JACK (CONT'D)
I don't believe it.

HARRIET
(shows passport)
Harriet Jones. Former Prime Minister.

CAPTAIN JACK
I know who you are!

CUT TO THE NOBLES' HOUSE, Rose yelling at the screen, which now shows Harriet.

ROSE
Harriet! I'm here! Ohhhhh, she can't hear me -
(to Wilf)
Have you got a webcam?

WILF
(of Sylvia)
She wouldn't let me, she says

they're naughty.

ROSE
I can't speak to her!

CUT TO SARAH JANE'S ATTIC, HARRIET on Mr Smith's screen. Sarah Jane running to Mr Smith, energised, with Luke.

HARRIET
And you, Sarah Jane Smith, 13 Bannerman Road, are you there?

SARAH JANE
I'm here! That's me! Sorry ma'am.

HARRIET
Good, now let's see if we can all talk to each other.

She leans forward, presses a button.

On Mr Smith's screen, Gwen's terminal, and the Nobles' computer, the image divides into four; displaying COMPUTER POVs of HARRIET, JACK, SARAH JANE, the fourth square still just white noise. (Rose, Wilf & Sylvia, staring at the same display, listening to every word, unable to speak.)

CUT TO:

69. INT. HARRIET'S COTTAGE - NIGHT

(Still intercutting sc.66, 67, 68, all the way to sc.72)

HARRIET sitting at her COMPUTER. Lovely old house in the country, classy. On screen, Harriet can see herself, Torchwood, Sarah Jane, and the fourth panel of shash.

HARRIET
The fourth contact seems to be having trouble getting through.

ROSE
That's me! Harriet! That's me!

HARRIET
I'll just boost the signal…

And the FOURTH PANEL shashes, resolves into…

MARTHA!

MARTHA
…hello…?

Reaction in the Hub!! Joy!

CAPTAIN JACK
Martha Jones!!

IANTO
She made it!

GWEN
Oh my God, you're alive!

Rose pissed off.

ROSE
Who's she? I want to get through!

CAPTAIN JACK
Martha, where are you?!

CUT TO:

70. INT. JONES' HOUSE - NIGHT

CLOSE ON MARTHA, b/g hidden, at

'Let's see if we can all talk to each other.'

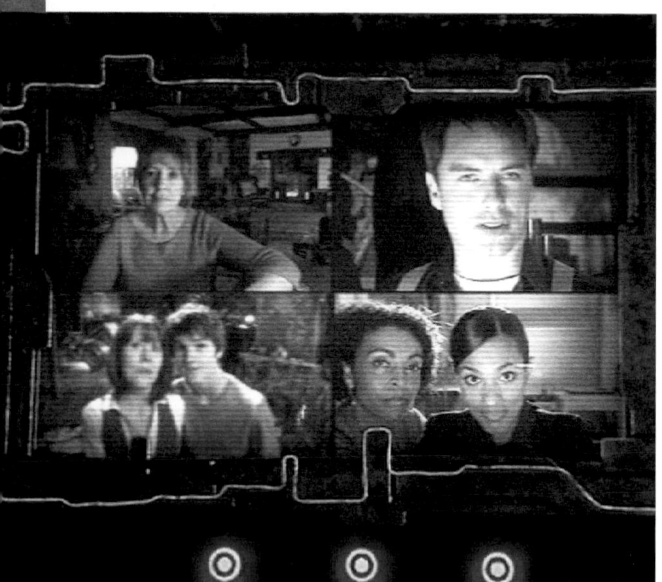

Project Indigo takes Martha Jones to the one place she wants to be – back home with her mother, Francine (Adjoa Andoh).

laptop & webcam, smiling.

MARTHA
I guess Project Indigo was more clever than we thought. One second I was in Manhattan…

WHITEOUT, FLASHBACK SC.47, MARTHA vanishing, WHITEOUT TO -

CUT TO:

71. INT. JONES' HOUSE - EARLIER THAT NIGHT

MARTHA in the harness, on the floor, dazed. Looking up…

MARTHA V/O
Next second… Maybe Indigo tapped into my mind. Cos I ended up in the one place I wanted to be.

Only now REVEAL this as the JONES' HOUSE, as Martha sees -

MARTHA
…mum!

FRANCINE JONES! Standing, staring, astonished!

Francine runs to Martha. Hugs her.

WHITEOUT -

CUT TO:

72. INT. JONES' HOUSE - NIGHT

(INTERCUTTING WITH SC.66, 67, 68 and now 69.)

MARTHA at the laptop, now REVEALING FRANCINE sitting next to her - not visible on the webcam image.

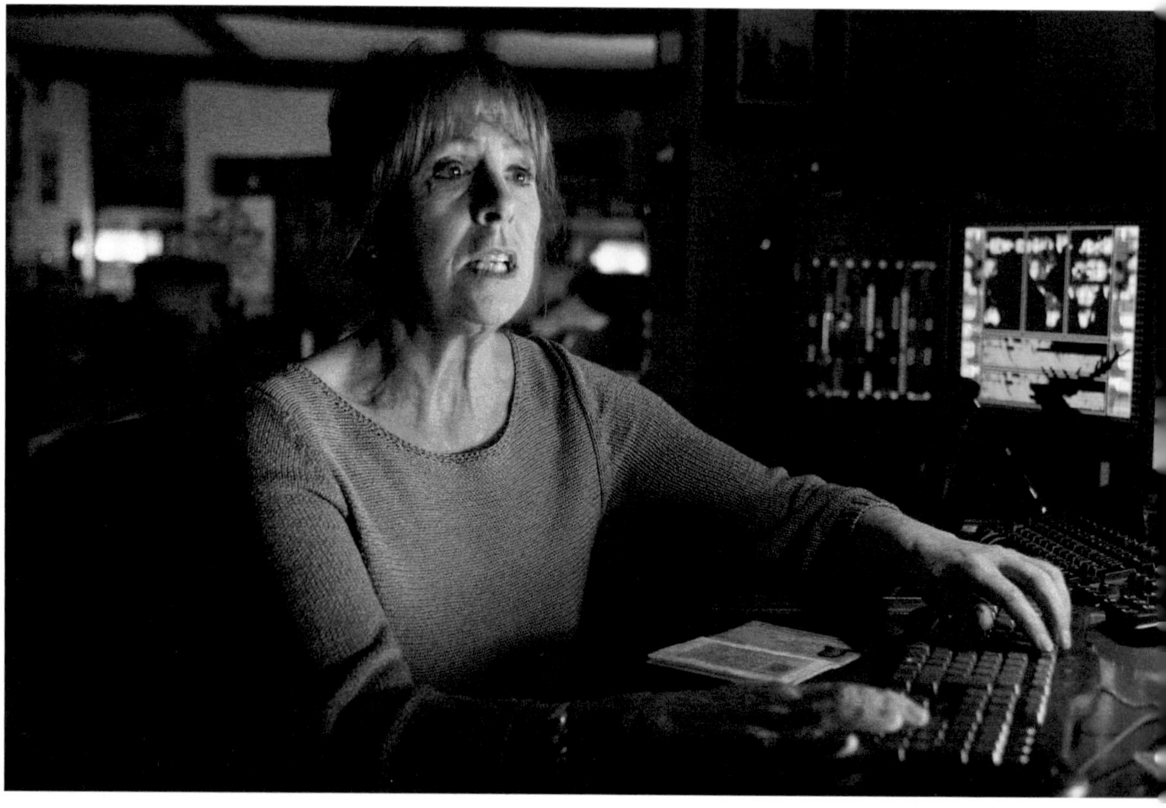

Harriet Jones activates the Subwave Network – thanks to Mr Copper.

FRANCINE
You came home. At the end of the world, you came back to me.

MARTHA
(to the computer)
But then all of a sudden, it's like the laptop turned itself on.

HARRIET
It did. That was me.
(passport)
Harriet Jones, former Prime Minister.

MARTHA
Yes, I know who you are.

HARRIET
I thought it was about time we all met. Given the current crisis. Torchwood, this is Sarah Jane Smith.

CAPTAIN JACK
I've been following your work. Nice job with the Gorgon.

SARAH JANE
Yeah, well I've been staying away from you lot. Too many guns!

CAPTAIN JACK
All the same, might I say… Looking good, ma'am.

SARAH JANE
(bashful)
Really? Oh. Thank you.

HARRIET
Not now, Captain. And Martha Jones, former companion of the Doctor -

ROSE
Oy! So was I!!

MARTHA
But how did you find me, in my mother's house?

FRANCINE
Oh, don't tell me, the Prime Minister was tapping my phone. Again!

HARRIET
This, ladies and gentlemen, this… is the Subwave Network. A sentient piece of software. Programmed to seek out anyone and everyone, who can help to contact the Doctor.

MARTHA
What if the Daleks can hear us? They're outside, they're everywhere -

HARRIET
No, that's the beauty of the Subwave, it's invisible.

SARAH JANE
What, and you invented it?

HARRIET
I developed it. It was created by the Mr Copper Foundation.

CAPTAIN JACK
Excuse me, ma'am, but, if you're looking for the Doctor… didn't he depose you?

HARRIET
He did. And I've spent a long time wondering about that. Whether I was wrong. And he was right.
(pause)
But I stand by my actions, to this day. Because I knew this would happen. I knew, one day, the Earth would be in danger, and the Doctor would fail to appear. I told him so myself. And he didn't listen. So I've dedicated my retirement to prepare for this moment.

WILF
Marvellous woman, I voted for her.

SYLVIA
You did not!

MARTHA
But we've tried - the Doctor's got my phone, on the Tardis, but I can't get through.

ROSE
Nor me! I was here first!

HARRIET
That's why we need the Subwave. To bring us all together. That phone is a link with the Tardis, and if we boost the signal… If we combine forces, and transmit with the power of the Torchwood Rift, and a Zylok computer, perhaps we can find him.

CAPTAIN JACK
…that could work!

SARAH JANE
Mr Smith, does that make sense?

MR SMITH V/O
It is 50% possible.

GWEN
50% is better than nothing!

LUKE steps forward into Sarah Jane's shot. Excited:

LUKE
But Mr Smith can do better than that! He can link up with every telephone exchange on Earth! What if we get the whole world to call Doctor Jones's number, all at the same time? Every phone, every modem, every router! Billions of phones, calling out, all at once!

CAPTAIN JACK
Brilliant! Who's the kid?

SARAH JANE
That's my son!

CAPTAIN JACK
Captain Jack Harkness, nice to meet you.

SARAH JANE
And he's 14.

We won't keep that line, but ha ha ha.

```
                HARRIET
      Then I suggest we start work.
      People are dying out there -

                IANTO
      But, um... excuse me, sorry,
      Ianto Jones, hello. But if
      we start transmitting, this
      Subwave Network is going to
      become visible. I mean, to
      the Daleks.

                HARRIET
      Indeed. And they will trace
      it back to me. But my life
      doesn't matter. Not if it
      saves the Earth.

Silence. Then Captain Jack salutes
her.

             CAPTAIN JACK
      Ma'am.

                HARRIET
      Thank you, Captain. And I'll
      say this for the Doctor, he
      chooses his companions well.
      God bless you all. Now then.
      Let's begin.
```

FROM: BENJAMIN COOK TO: RUSSELL T DAVIES
SUNDAY 23 DECEMBER 2007 07:30:09 GMT

RE: THE ABOMINATION IS INSANE

'Have you got a webcam?'

'She wouldn't let me. She says they're naughty.'

Ha ha ha ha ha! And three cheers for Bernard's paint gun. But surely, before repairing itself, the Dalek should say, 'MY VISION IS IMPAIRED! I CANNOT SEE!'…? Isn't that kind of obligatory?

Has Penelope Wilton signed up already? Or do negotiations start now?

FROM: RUSSELL T DAVIES TO: BENJAMIN COOK
SUNDAY 23 DECEMBER 2007 10:32:01 GMT

RE: THE ABOMINATION IS INSANE

I'm glad you like the webcam joke. I love putting gags in the middle of The End Of The World, although that gag works because Wilf isn't being funny; he really means it. At the launch on Tuesday, as he was leaving, Bernard said, 'Are we doing that paint gun thing?' I said yes, and he was astonished. He was like, 'Really?!' What a lovely man. So no matter how many pages I'm over, I'm not cutting that. I know what you mean about 'My vision is impaired' – it's a proper Dalek catchphrase, isn't it? – but, while he's saying that, Wilf and Sylvia would run away. It's already slightly dodgy that they just stand there.

God knows about Penelope Wilton. Julie and Phil have been nagging me to pay off Harriet's ending in *The Christmas Invasion* since… well, since *The Christmas Invasion*. (What a great episode title that was!) She's very hard to book, because she's so in demand. We only got her on *Bob & Rose* by the skin of our teeth. Imagine if we hadn't! That's why she's limited in this script to one location, one day's work. Easier to book. Julie has been expecting it, but I doubt she's laid any groundwork, because she can't until a script is in. We can't do anything until after Christmas now, but oh, fingers crossed. If not, I'm afraid it'll have to be Mr Copper from *Voyage of the Damned*. That would work. But I hope it's Harriet.

FROM: RUSSELL T DAVIES TO: BENJAMIN COOK
SUNDAY 23 DECEMBER 2007 11:40:13 GMT

RE: THE ABOMINATION IS INSANE

Ah! Got it! The Dalek says 'My vision is *not* impaired!' Good joke. Fanboy joke.

FROM: RUSSELL T DAVIES TO: BENJAMIN COOK
MONDAY 24 DECEMBER 2007 03:24:43 GMT

RE: THE ABOMINATION IS INSANE

I didn't finish. Damn and crap and bollocks! I don't think I've got time tomorrow. I haven't bought a single card or present yet, and I have to go to Swansea tomorrow night. Christmas with my blind dad. I sit and describe to him what's happening on TV. 'The Host have hooked arms with the Doctor, and they're flying him up, up, up through the ship…' I have a laugh doing that. I make things up. 'They're on fire!' There's no budget when you're blind.

I keep making cuts to 4.12 as I go along. Donna's 'I don't care about Jupiter!' has gone. I thought that was a good line once; now I think it's stupid. But Harriet Jones has certainly brought the whole episode to life. I'll be gutted if we can't book Penelope. She just gives it so much heart.

Silence. Then Captain Jack salutes her.

CAPTAIN JACK
Ma'am.

HARRIET
Thank you, Captain. But people are dying out there, on the streets. That's enough talk. Let's do it!

CUT TO:

71. INT. CRUCIBLE COMMAND DECK - NIGHT[2]

ALARM BLARES! FOUR DALEKS spin round to the SUPREME DALEK -

DALEK 1
Emergency! Unknown network transmitting!

DALEK 2
Identified as Subwave Network!

SUPREME DALEK
Trace it! Find it! Destroy!

CUT TO:

72. INT. TORCHWOOD HUB - NIGHT

Action, fast - CAPTAIN JACK & GWEN running from one terminal to the other, stabbing buttons like crazy -

IANTO hauling a big co-axial cable across the floor, to join it up to the terminals -

CAPTAIN JACK
Rift Power activated!

GWEN
All terminals coordinated!

IANTO
National grid online - giving you everything we've got!

CUT TO:

73. INT. SARAH JANE SMITH'S ATTIC - NIGHT

SARAH JANE & LUKE slamming levers together -

SARAH JANE
Connecting you to Mr Smith!

LUKE
All telephone networks combined!

CUT TO:

74. INT. JONES' HOUSE - NIGHT

MARTHA with FRANCINE, connecting her mobile to the laptop -

MARTHA
Sending you the number - now!

CUT TO:

75. INT. HARRIET'S COTTAGE - NIGHT

HARRIET stabbing buttons -

'Emergency! Unknown network transmitting!'

2 Scenes 61 (in the Torchwood Hub) and 62 (in Sarah Jane's attic) have been deleted, shifting all subsequent scene numbers, so Captain Jack saluting Harriet is now Scene 70, followed by this, Scene 71, on the Crucible Command Deck.

HARRIET
Opening Subwave Network to maximum -

Only now revealing that her COMPUTER is surrounded by extra SERVERS & HARD DRIVES & WIRES, all now illuminating, LIGHTS flashing, huge hum of power!

CUT TO:

76. INT. SARAH JANES' ATTIC - NIGHT

SARAH JANE & LUKE, as NEW LIGHTS around MR SMITH blaze -

SARAH JANE
Receiving you! Go on, Mr Smith, make that call!

MR SMITH V/O
Calling the Doctor!

CUT TO:

77. INT. NOBLES' HOUSE, LIVING ROOM - NIGHT

ROSE watching, clutching her mobile.

ROSE
So am I!
(to Wilf & Sylvia)
Get your phones! Any phone! Dial that number!

CUT TO:

78. INT. TORCHWOOD HUB - NIGHT

CAPTAIN JACK, GWEN, IANTO, all busy, slamming switches -

CAPTAIN JACK
Aaaand sending - !

FX: ARCS OF ELECTRICITY SHOOT UP THE WATER-TOWER -

CUT TO:

79. EXT. ROALD DAHL PLASS - NIGHT

FX: ARCS OF ELECTRICITY shoot up the WATER TOWER, and at the top, they become concentric circles of blue, old-fashioned transmitter graphics, pulsing out, *bip-bip-bip…*

CUT TO:

80. FX SHOT

FX: HIGH SHOT - DALEK SAUCER zooms past foreground - clearing to reveal THE SOUTH WALES COAST, with CONCENTRIC CIRCLES pulsing out of CARDIFF! *Bip-bip-bip…*

FX: WIDE SHOT OF EARTH, in the PLANETARY ARRAY, CONCENTRIC CIRCLES spreading out, *bip-bip-bip*, into the universe…

CUT TO:

81. INT. TARDIS - NIGHT

WIDE SHOT. THE DOCTOR & DONNA standing apart. Defeated.

Then…

Bip-bip-bip…

Both look up. Look round. What…?

And realise - !

THE DOCTOR
The phone!!!

DONNA
Martha's phone!!!

Both diving for it - both listening, heads together -

THE DOCTOR
Martha?! Is that you??

But the phone is just going *bip-bip-bip-*

THE DOCTOR (CONT'D)
It's a signal! She's calling us!

DONNA
Can we follow it?

THE DOCTOR
Just watch me!

And he's at the controls like a wild thing -

CUT TO:

82. INT. CRUCIBLE COMMAND DECK - NIGHT

ALARMS still sound, DALEKS at computer banks.

DALEK 1
Signal cannot be stopped!

SUPREME DALEK
Find the point of origin!
Find and exterminate!

Again, the cold, calm voice:

VOICE OOV
I warned you, Supreme One…

CUT TO:

83. INT. CRUCIBLE VAULTS - NIGHT

WIDE SHOT, the FIGURE gliding forward, still a silhouette, a Dalek base with what appears to be a man, sitting inside..

VOICE
Just as Dalek Caan foretold.
The Children of Time are
moving against us. It is
their destiny.

DALEK CAAN is giggling, insane.

DALEK CAAN
One of them will die. Ohh,
one of the pretty Children
will die.

CUT TO:

84. INT. CRUCIBLE COMMAND DECK - NIGHT

SUPREME DALEK furious -

SUPREME DALEK
All of them will die!
Exterminate!

CUT TO:

85. INT. TORCHWOOD HUB - NIGHT

PRAC EXPLOSIONS from the terminals & from IANTO'S CABLING -

CAPTAIN JACK
Keep it going!! Come on
Doctor! Answer the call!

CUT TO:

86. INT. JONES' HOUSE - NIGHT

HOUSE LIGHTS flickering. MARTHA

'Find the point of origin! Find and exterminate!'

clutching her phone, almost praying. FRANCINE holding her mobile too.

MARTHA
Come on, come on, come on…

CUT TO:

87. INT. NOBLES' HOUSE, LIVING ROOM - NIGHT

HOUSE LIGHTS flickering. ROSE clutching her mobile, WILF his, SYLVIA hers. Willing them to work. Then Rose holds hers up like an offering…

HIGH SHOT, ROSE & MOBILE. And she's desperate.

ROSE
Find me, Doctor. *Find me.*

CUT TO:

88. INT. TARDIS - NIGHT

THE DOCTOR
Got it!!! Locking on!

WHOOMPH!, whole Tardis shakes, and plunges into RED LIGHTING STATE! And it keeps SHAKING, SHUDDERING.

Holding on tight, but they both laugh! Exhilarated!

CUT TO:

89. INT. TORCHWOOD HUB - NIGHT

More PRAC EXPLOSIONS from the terminals, but gleeful -

CAPTAIN JACK
I think we've got a fix!

GWEN
Is it him?!

CAPTAIN JACK
Who else could it be?

CUT TO:

90. INT. SARAH JANE SMITH'S ATTIC - NIGHT

PRAC EXPLOSIONS from MR SMITH, SARAH JANE & LUKE keep going -

SARAH JANE
Mr Smith now at 200%! Come on, Doctor!!

CUT TO:

91. INT. TORCHWOOD HUB - NIGHT

CAPTAIN JACK & GWEN frantic in b/g, IANTO at his terminal -

IANTO
Harriet! A saucer's locked on to your location, they've found you!

CUT TO:

92. INT. HARRIET'S COTTAGE - NIGHT

HARRIET
I'm aware of that. Just keep transmitting.

Behind her, PRAC FX: SIDE-ON to the French windows, as they blast open, WHITE LIGHT AND SMOKE raging through, the sound of a saucer landing… Harriet composed, calm, keeps working, doesn't even look round.

CUT TO:

93. INT. TARDIS - NIGHT

RED LIGHT, WHOLE PLACE SHAKING. PRAC FX: SHEETS OF FLAME erupting from under the central grid. PRAC EXPLOSIONS from the console! THE

'The phone call's pulling us through!'

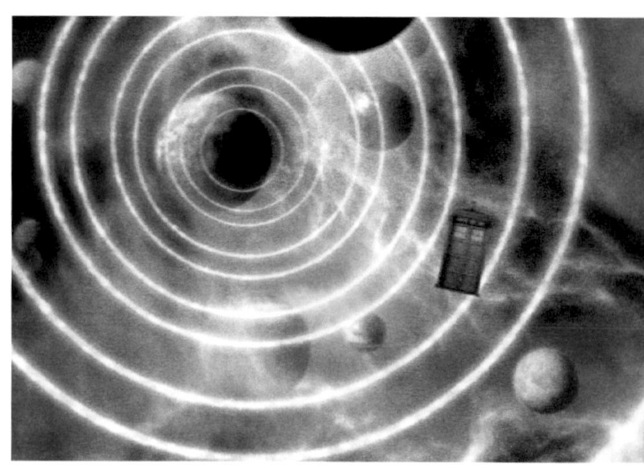

'We know who you are.' The Daleks track down Harriet.

DOCTOR & DONNA clinging on -

THE DOCTOR
We're travelling through time!

DONNA
What, they're in the future?

THE DOCTOR
One second in the future! But the phone call's pulling us through!

CUT TO:

94. INT. HARRIET'S COTTAGE - NIGHT

HARRIET calm, pressing a final button.

HARRIET
Captain. I'm transferring the Subwave Network through to you. You're in charge now. Good luck.

CAPTAIN JACK OOV
Harriet, get out of there!

HARRIET
And tell the Doctor from me. He chose his companions well. It's been an honour.

And she stands, turns. With dignity.

THREE DALEKS gliding through her French windows, face her.

She holds up her passport.

HARRIET (CONT'D)
Harriet Jones. Former Prime Minister.

DALEK 1
We know who you are.

HARRIET
Oh, you know nothing. Of any

Human. And that will be your downfall.

CU DALEK...

DALEK 1
Exterminate!

CUT TO:

95. INT. TARDIS - NIGHT

WILD LURCHING now, PRAC FLAME, EXPLOSIONS -

THE DOCTOR
Here we go - !

CUT TO:

96. FX SHOT

FX: TARDIS, with the empty Medusa Cascade as b/g, being battered by concentric circles of HARD, BLAZING WHITE LIGHT -

CUT TO:

Harriet Jones's last stand.

97. INT. TARDIS - NIGHT

THE DOCTOR
Three! Two! *One!*

DONNA
Come *onnnnnnn!*

CUT TO:

98. FX SHOT

FX: TARDIS buffeted by WHITE CIRCLES, which then rip free -

FX: and suddenly, all is calm, the TARDIS spinning free, into the now-visible PLANETARY ARRAY, the 27 planets, the Earth - like the whole system just ripped into sight -

CUT TO:

99. INT. TARDIS - NIGHT

Calm again. THE DOCTOR & DONNA at the scanner, overjoyed.

THE DOCTOR
27 planets! And there's the Earth!

DONNA
Why couldn't we see them?!

THE DOCTOR
The entire Medusa Cascade has been put a second out of synch with the rest of the universe. Perfect hiding place, a tiny little pocket of time. But we found them!

The scanner fizzes, whines, tuning in. The Doctor puzzled.

THE DOCTOR (CONT'D)
What's that...? Hold on. Some sort of Subwave Network...

And on screen, the four part-image; TORCHWOOD, SARAH JANE, MARTHA. With Harriet's square now just static.

But CAPTAIN JACK, GWEN, IANTO, SARAH JANE, LUKE & MARTHA can see the Doctor - they're all going mental!

But while ROSE can see him - he can't see her!

Merry Christmas!

I won't be back online until Friday now. Days off! Maybe a break will do me good. Although, I'll just be thinking about the script. It's Christmas Eve, and I'm dying to get back to work already. I'd better work out what that bloody Osterhagen Key does. (It was called the Stattenheim Key in earlier drafts, but I prefer Osterhagen. I went on a website of German surnames to find that.)

Text message from: **Russell**
Sent: 25-Dec-2007 12:28
Merry Xmas, Benjamino! Shame there's nothing good on TV tonight...

Text message from: **Ben**
Sent: 25-Dec-2007 15:34
Oh, I don't know, I'm counting down the minutes till *To The Manor Born*! Ha! Merry Xmas to you and yours. I'm stuffed already. I'll have put on a stone by the time *Voyage of the Damned* is on.

Text message from: **Ben**
Sent: 25-Dec-2007 20:10
Watching *Doctor Who* with the family is so stressful. But it went down well.

Text message from: **Russell**
Sent: 25-Dec-2007 20:13
Various members of my family are now bleeding and wounded because they TALKED!!! For the love of Clom! The punishments will continue all night. Still, I might be biased, but I loved that Special. It worked well with the kids here too – just as it should.

Text message from: **Ben**
Sent: 26-Dec-2007 09:56
So what do you make of the viewing figures? An overnight estimate of 12.2 MILLION! OH MY GOD! Many congrats.

Text message from: **Russell**
Sent: 26-Dec-2007 10:08
F*****G HELL!!! I'm phoning Phil, Julie's phoning me, we're all going mental!

Text message from: **Russell**
Sent: 26-Dec-2007 11:31
Twelve point two!!! I just thought I'd spell it out in words to see how good it looks. I'm still laughing. I can't get over those figures. I am reeling. Everyone is so happy.

Text message from: **Ben**
Sent: 26-Dec-2007 11:38
And to think, just a week ago, you were walking around Soho with no trousers. That's some comeback, Russell.

Text message from: **Russell**
Sent: 26-Dec-2007 11:45
I hope my lucky trousers played some part in our ratings victory.

Text message from: **Ben**
Sent: 26-Dec-2007 11:51
The final, consolidated figure will be closer to 13 million, surely? That's incredible. It must make all the stressing worthwhile?

Text message from: **Russell**
Sent: 26-Dec-2007 12:42
Oh yes, it does. Mind you, it's swiftly followed by the terrifying thought: NEXT YEAR! But sod that for now. You've got to take time to enjoy it.

FROM: RUSSELL T DAVIES TO: BENJAMIN COOK
THURSDAY 27 DECEMBER 2007 23:44:10 GMT

12.2 MILLION!!!

I'm back in Cardiff. I wasn't supposed to be back until tomorrow, but there's too much work to do, so I made my farewells. All is quiet and still in Cardiff Bay. Lovely.

I can't face opening 4.12. It feels like something that I

wrote aeons ago. I've cancelled going to Billie's wedding next week. That's the last thing I need right now. Shame, but it had to be done. The script is more important. And that much-threatened cold is now descending over me fast. I'm snivelling away and starting to cough. Nooooo to the cough! The cough took me out for five weeks last year.

FROM: RUSSELL T DAVIES TO: BENJAMIN COOK
SATURDAY 29 DECEMBER 2007 03:13:47 GMT

RE: 12.2 MILLION!!!

I've reduced the 50 pages down to 48 today, which feels good. It's just trims and stuff. That milkman at the beginning is bugging me. I'd lose half a page if I cut him and his bottles and just had the *whumph* from inside the TARDIS… but I love that milkman. It's so ordinary and calm. He remains for now. Also, I've added an important piece of dialogue for Donna, in her Albino Servant conversation, where she says that she can type at 100 wpm:

```
            ALBINO SERVANT
    You are something new.

                DONNA
    Not me, love. I'm just a
    temp. Shorthand, filing, 100
    words per minute, fat lot of
    good that is now. I'm no use
    to anyone.
```

Is 100 wpm fast? She should sound a bit above average, but I don't know average typing speeds.

FROM: BENJAMIN COOK TO: RUSSELL T DAVIES
SATURDAY 29 DECEMBER 2007 10:16:13 GMT

RE: 12.2 MILLION!!!

Yes, 100 wpm is a bit above average. She has plenty of secretarial experience, so you could even go up to 110 wpm, I think. You'd better check that, though, or I'll have ruined *Doctor Who* ('An otherwise faultless production…') and you'll get complaints.

FROM: RUSSELL T DAVIES TO: BENJAMIN COOK
SUNDAY 30 DECEMBER 2007 02:28:05 GMT

RE: 12.2 MILLION!!!

Here's more… but it's absolute bollocks. I wanted to finish tonight, but I haven't. I failed. This cold is getting worse. My eyes are streaming and I can't see the sodding keyboard. Plus, this is now way, way, *way* too long. Seriously, I need another ten pages. I'm writing stuff that I know I'm going to cut. There are a couple of pages of lovely dialogue where finally the Doctor and Donna link up, over the scanner, with Jack, Martha and Sarah Jane, and Donna meets them all… but it's all going to be cut, I can tell. That's pissed me off. Dialogue that I've been dying to write, and now I've written it with a faint heart, because it's cuttable. What a waste of time and energy.

```
             THE DOCTOR (CONT'D)
    What's that…? Hold on. Some
    sort of Subwave Network…

And on screen, the four part-image;
TORCHWOOD, SARAH JANE, MARTHA. With
Harriet's square now just fizzing
static.

All yelling, SC.99, 100, 101, 102
intercut, fast -

                              CUT TO:

99. INT. TORCHWOOD HUB - NIGHT[3]

CAPTAIN JACK overjoyed, yelling at
the screen - all screens now show
only a Tardis-scanner-POV, the
Doctor & Donna -

                CAPTAIN JACK
    Where the hell have you
    been?! Doctor, it's the
    Daleks, they've taken control
    of the Earth -

                    GWEN
    Oh, he's a bit nice. I
    thought he'd be older. You
    say Doctor, you think older.

                    IANTO
    He's not that young.

                              CUT TO:

100. INT. SARAH JANE SMITH'S ATTIC
- NIGHT

SARAH JANE yelling at the image of
the Doctor -
```

3 Scene 21 (in the News 24 Studio) has been deleted, shifting all subsequent scene numbers, so the Doctor picking up the Subwave Network on the TARDIS scanner is now Scene 98, followed by this, Scene 99, in the Torchwood Hub.

SARAH JANE
It's the Daleks, they've got a ship, it's called the Crucible -
(can't help herself)
And look! Doctor, I've got a son! This is Luke!

CUT TO:

101. INT. JONES' HOUSE - NIGHT

MARTHA overjoyed, yelling at the image of the Doctor -

MARTHA
It's the Daleks, can you hear me? Doctor? The Daleks!! They're still alive, not just Dalek Caan -

CUT TO:

102. INT. NOBLES' HOUSE - NIGHT

WILF & SYLVIA overjoyed, staring at the image -

SYLVIA
That's Donna!

WILF
I told you! That's my girl!

But ROSE is heartbroken. The Doctor can't see her. Quiet:

ROSE
Doctor. It's me. I came back.

CUT TO:

'Doctor. It's me. I came back.'

103. INT. TARDIS - NIGHT

ALL INTERCUT - and SC.99, 100, 101, 102 keep running - with THE DOCTOR, with DONNA, smiling at the four-part scanner image -

DONNA
That's Martha! But who's the rest of them?!

THE DOCTOR
That must be Torchwood. And Sarah Jane! Ohhh, aren't they brilliant?

DONNA
And who's he?

THE DOCTOR
Captain Jack. Don't. Just don't.
(at the screen)
All right, all right, stop talking, all of you, one at a time -

They keep babbling. The Doctor gets out a whistle. Blows!

Silence.

THE DOCTOR (CONT'D)
That's better! Now! Nice to see you all, but we can have a chat later, how's it going down there? Captain, situation report!

CAPTAIN JACK
Well, basically… it's the Daleks!

THE DOCTOR
I thought so. No one else could be this clever.

CAPTAIN JACK
Harriet Jones brought us all together, but… They found her. She gave her life.

THE DOCTOR
…I wasn't there. She said so.

MARTHA
But the Daleks died, we saw it happen, there was only one left -

ROSE
Oh, been there, love.

SARAH JANE
But they're not killing everyone, they're taking people on board their spaceship, we don't know why -

THE DOCTOR
Just tell me… Has there been any sign of Rose?

CAPTAIN JACK
Rose Tyler? But that's impossible.

ROSE
I'm here! *I'm here!!*

THE DOCTOR
Nope, that's how bad things are, there's far more at stake than just the Earth. So! Millions of Daleks. Humans being captured. 27 planets forming a gigantic super-engine. What do we do?

And all the lights in the Tardis go dark! Scanner blank. Huge booming voice echoes out:

SUPREME DALEK OOV
You will surrender to Dalek control!

In the Hub, Sarah Jane's Attic, Jones', Nobles' House, all the screens go dead.

MARTHA
Doctor? Doctor!

CAPTAIN JACK
We've lost him!

ROSE
No, not now, no - !

SARAH JANE
Mr Smith, where is he?

MR SMITH V/O
I regret, the Doctor's vehicle is caught in a Dalek tractor beam.

CUT TO:

104. FX SHOT

FX: a HUGE DALEK SAUCER above the tiny TARDIS, with a MASSIVE BLUE BEAM OF LIGHT enveloping the police box.

CUT TO:

105. INT. CRUCIBLE COMMAND DECK - NIGHT

FX: SAME WIDE SHOT as sc.34, extra levels and FX DALEKS, the SUPREME DALEK at the centre, victorious.

SUPREME DALEK
This is victory! This is destiny! We have the Doctor!

CUT TO PRAC DALEKS, swivelling round from controls -

DALEK 1
Tardis locked and powerless!

DALEK 2
It will be brought to the Crucible!

CUT TO:

106. INT. TARDIS - NIGHT

Darkness, THE DOCTOR & DONNA holding on to the console -

THE DOCTOR
They're taking us to the centre of the web.
(sonics scanner)
Let's have a look… Ohh, now that's what I call a space station!

CUT TO:

'That's what I call a space station!' The TARDIS and the Crucible.

Old Blue Eye is back! Davros (Julian Bleach) returns.

107. FX SHOT

FX: TARDIS, in its BLUE BEAM, sweeps past foreground, revealing, at the centre of the PLANETARY ARRAY, THE CRUCIBLE. A mighty Dalek space station; a central riveted, bronze GLOBE, with SPIKES radiating out, like arms.

FX SHOT X 2: CLOSER on the CRUCIBLE, sweeping round it.

CUT TO:

108. INT. CRUCIBLE COMMAND DECK - NIGHT

The FOUR DALEKS at the CONTROLS:

DALEK 1
Tardis approaching!

CUT TO SUPREME DALEK, hearing again, the calculating voice:

VOICE OOV
Supreme One. Bring him to me.

SUPREME DALEK
Negative! Every word spoken by The Doctor is a contamination!

CUT TO:

109. INT. CRUCIBLE VAULTS - NIGHT

The SHADOWED FIGURE gliding forward on its Dalek base…

Into the LIGHT. REVEALING: DAVROS.

Half-man, half-Dalek, his face withered, an artificial blue eye blazing in his forehead. His torso swathed in a tunic like a black leather straitjacket. The metal hand always suspended above the Dalek-base's switches.

DAVROS
Ohh, but I'm ready for him. I have been ready for so many years. Through endless wars and boiling skies. It is right and fitting that the Doctor should bear witness to the resurrection, and the triumph, of Davros. Lord and Creator of the Dalek Race!

CUT TO:

110. INT. TARDIS - NIGHT

Darkness. THE DOCTOR peering at the scanner.

THE DOCTOR
…that station's about 200 miles across. Right at the centre of the kinetic energy field. It must be soaking up power! But what for…? Look at that shape, like arms, reaching out, ready for something, ready for what…?

But DURING THIS: SLOW ZOOM in on DONNA. Ostensibly looking at the scanner, but actually looking ahead…

Lost in thought again.

And the Doctor's voice fades out; the noise creeps in…

The heartbeat…

Pounding.

Donna staring…

Louder…

And…

Suddenly snapped out of it -

THE DOCTOR (CONT'D)
Donna!

DONNA
What?

THE DOCTOR
I said, are you ready?

DONNA
Yes! What for?

THE DOCTOR
Tractor beam! Don't give me tractor beam! I rode this Tardis through a Time War! We flew through the Gates of Elysium right over the head of the Dalek Emperor's Nightmare Child. So! I've seen enough! Shall we go?!

DONNA
Allons-y!

The Doctor slams controls -

LIGHTS come back on! The room lurches -

CUT TO:

111. FX SHOT

FX: the TARDIS rips free of the BLUE BEAM!

FX: THE EARTH, with a tiny Tardis spinning down, down, down, towards it…

CUT TO:

112. INT. CRUCIBLE COMMAND DECK - NIGHT

ALARMS SOUND!

DALEK 1
Tardis has broken free!

DALEK 2
The Doctor has escaped!

SUPREME DALEK
Find him! Find him! Find him!

CUT TO:

113. INT. CRUCIBLE VAULTS - NIGHT

DAVROS furious, turning to face DALEK CAAN.

DAVROS
He will go to planet Earth! To find his precious Human allies!

DALEK CAAN
And death is coming. Ohh, such a death, sir. Everlasting death for the most faithful companion…

Tonight, this feels like a space-opera runaround. I don't like it much. It's too big, it's daft, the Doctor arrives too late and does nothing all episode. It's lame shit. It feels like we're going to spend millions of licence-fee-payers' money on silly rubbish. That's not the right mood to write in. And now tomorrow is buggered, because my boyfriend is coming to Cardiff for the New Year, but I must keep writing. I promised him that I wouldn't work over the next few days. Even though he has the patience of a saint, he's going to kill me. It's all going to get tense, and that's no mood to write in either.

FROM: RUSSELL T DAVIES TO: BENJAMIN COOK
SUNDAY 30 DECEMBER 2007 20:06:21 GMT

RE: 12.2 MILLION!!!

Sorry about last night's outpouring. I lost control of it. I woke up this morning, telling myself the thing that I have to tell myself a million times: I'm in control of it, it's not in control of me. I've reworked everything from Scene 103 onwards. I'm in a better mood now. I should finish tonight, but this cold is streeeeeaming now, so I'll send now in case I don't…

103. INT. TARDIS - NIGHT

INTERCUT with SC.99, 100, 101, 102 - THE DOCTOR & DONNA, smiling at the four-part scanner image -

DONNA
That's Martha! But who's the rest of them?!

THE DOCTOR
That must be Torchwood. And Sarah Jane! Who's that boy? She's got a what?! Oh, aren't they brilliant?

DONNA
And who's he?

THE DOCTOR
Captain Jack. Don't. Just don't.

DONNA
It's like an outer space Facebook.

THE DOCTOR
…everyone except Rose.

CUT TO:

104. INT. CRUCIBLE VAULTS - NIGHT

CU DALEK CAAN. Writhing, giggling.

DALEK CAAN
He is here. The Dark Lord is come. Ohh the trap is closing…

CUT TO THE SHADOWED FIGURE, gliding on its Dalek base.

VOICE
Supreme One. This Subwave Network. I would address it; give me access.

CUT TO:

105. INT. CRUCIBLE COMMAND DECK - NIGHT

SUPREME DALEK on its throne, listening:

'We meet again.' Davros addresses his oldest enemy once more.

VOICE OOV
It is him. You know it's him. His very presence causes ripples in space and time; you can feel him. Let him see me!

SUPREME DALEK
Access granted!

CUT TO:

106. INT. TARDIS - NIGHT

The SCANNER fizzes, goes to static…

DONNA
We've lost them!

THE DOCTOR
No, there's another signal coming through. There's someone else out there. Can you hear me…?
(dares to hope)
Rose…?

The VOICE floats out, calm and wise and contemptuous… And the Doctor is *horrified.*

VOICE OOV
Doctor. Your voice is different. And yet, its arrogance is unchanged.

THE DOCTOR
No. But you're dead.

CUT TO SC.100 CONTINUED, SARAH JANE'S ATTIC:

SARAH JANE
Not him. Ohh, not him…

VOICE OOV
After all the bloodshed and devastation, the endless wars and the boiling skies… We meet again.

CUT TO:

107. INT. CRUCIBLE VAULTS - NIGHT

INTERCUT with sc.99, 100, 101, 102, 106, all watching the image of DAVROS, now in CU on all the screens.

The SHADOWED FIGURE gliding forward on its Dalek base…

Into the LIGHT. REVEALING…

DAVROS.

Half-man, half-Dalek, his face withered, an artificial blue eye blazing in his forehead. His torso swathed in a tunic like a black leather straitjacket. The metal hand always suspended above the Dalek-base's switches.

DAVROS
Welcome to my new Empire, Doctor. It is only fitting that you should bear witness to the resurrection, and the triumph, of Davros. Lord and Creator of the Dalek Race!

Silence.

Hold. The Doctor just staring. Lost.

Donna more alarmed by his silence than by anything. Quiet:

DONNA
Doctor…?
(pause; kind)
It's all right. We're in the Tardis. We're safe.

Which brings the Doctor back. Still staring:

THE DOCTOR
…but you were destroyed. In the very first year of the Time War. At the Gates of Elysium. I saw your command ship crash and burn.
(beat)
I tried to save you.

DAVROS
But it took one stronger than you. Dalek Caan himself.

CUT TO DALEK CAAN, shivering, gleeful.

DALEK CAAN
I flew into the wild and fire, I danced and died a thousand times.

DAVROS
Emergency Temporal Shift took him back into the Time War itself.

THE DOCTOR
But that's impossible! The entire war is timelocked!

DAVROS
And yet he succeeded. Oh, it cost him his mind. But imagine! A single, simple Dalek succeeded where Emperors and Time Lords failed. A testament, don't you think, to my remarkable creations?

THE DOCTOR
Then, Dalek Caan… I salute you.

DAVROS
At last, you come to worship.

THE DOCTOR
And you made a new race of Daleks…?

DAVROS
I gave myself to them. Quite literally.

And he opens his tunic, just a little…

'I gave myself to them. Quite literally.'

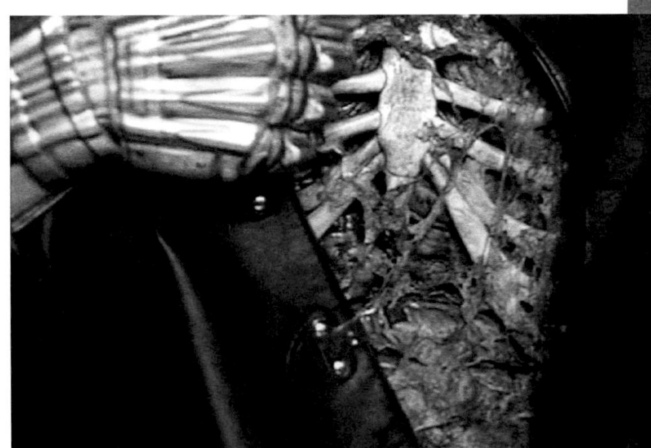

Inside: OPEN RIBS, organs underneath, the skin peeled away.

DAVROS (CONT'D)
Each one grown from a cell of my own body. New Daleks. True Daleks. I have my children, Doctor; what do you have, now?

THE DOCTOR
Davros. After all this time. Everything we saw. Everything we lost. I have only one thing to say to you.
(pause)
Bye!

And he slams the controls - !

CUT TO:

108. FX SHOT

FX: the TARDIS spins, wild, tumbling down, down, down towards THE EARTH.

CUT TO:

109. INT. CRUCIBLE COMMAND DECK - NIGHT

SUPREME DALEK
Emergency! Locate the Tardis! Find the Doctor!!

CUT TO:

110. INT. CRUCIBLE VAULTS - NIGHT

DAVROS
He will go to planet Earth! To find his precious Human allies!

DALEK CAAN
And death is coming. Ohh, such a death, sir. Everlasting death for the most faithful companion…

CUT TO:

111. INT. TORCHWOOD HUB - NIGHT

Screens now dead -

IANTO
The link's been cut -

GWEN

A squad of Daleks invades the Torchwood Hub! Illustration by Russell T Davies.

But where's he going, where's the Doctor?!

CAPTAIN JACK
(grabs mobile)
Martha. Now listen to me. Do exactly as I say…

CUT TO:

112. INT. CRUCIBLE COMMAND DECK - NIGHT

DALEKS 1 & 2 swivelling round to the SUPREME DALEK:

DALEK 1
Subwave Network rerouted. New

BRAKKA-BRAKKA-BRAKKA!
YAAAAA!
EXTERMINATE IANTO!
EXTERMINATE GWEN!
EXTERMINATE TORCHWOOD!
DALEKS IN TORCHWOOD!

location: Torchwood!

SUPREME DALEK
Exterminate them, at once!
Exterminate Torchwood!

CUT TO:

113. INT. TORCHWOOD HUB - NIGHT

IANTO calling GWEN over to his terminal, CAPTAIN JACK on the mobile in b/g -

IANTO
Dalek saucer heading for the Bay. They've found us.

CUT TO JACK, rattling off, fast -

CAPTAIN JACK
- you lift the central panel, there's a string of numbers, the numbers keep changing, but the fourth number keeps oscillating between two different digits, tell me what they are -

CUT TO:

114. INT. JONES' HOUSE - NIGHT

MARTHA, with FRANCINE watching, has opened the central panel of the INDIGO PROJECT, revealing a small

```
readout, displaying eight different
numbers which constantly change -

                 MARTHA
     It's a four, and a nine, we
     could never work out what
     that was -

                              CUT TO:

115. INT. TORCHWOOD HUB - NIGHT

CAPTAIN JACK on the mobile -

               CAPTAIN JACK
     That's the teleport base
     code. And that's all I need,
     to get this thing working
     again!

His WRIST-STRAP! He taps in -

            CAPTAIN JACK (CONT'D)
     Oscillating four and nine -
                 (mobile)
     Thank you, Martha Jones!

Jumps up, to GWEN & IANTO -

            CAPTAIN JACK (CONT'D)
     - I've gotta go, I've gotta
     find the Doctor, I can lock
     this thing onto the Tardis,
     I'll come back, I promise
     you, I'm coming back -

                 GWEN
     Don't worry about us! Just
     go!

                 IANTO
     We'll be fine!

               CAPTAIN JACK
     You'd better be.

He presses the wrist-strap button -

FX: CAPTAIN JACK disappears in a
teleport glow -

Gwen & Ianto left alone, quiet.

                 GWEN
     'We'll be fine.'

                 IANTO
     What else could I say?

WHUMPH! From above, CAMERA SHAKE,
RUBBLE from the roof.

HIGH SHOT, Gwen & Ianto looking up;
a distant 'Exterminate!'

                 GWEN
     They're here...
```

FROM: RUSSELL T DAVIES TO: BENJAMIN COOK
MONDAY 31 DECEMBER 2007 04:35:22 GMT

RE: 12.2 MILLION!!!

FINISHED! I finished at about 1am, but it was 63 pages long, so I've been sitting here since then, whittling it down to 58. But it's still too long; it should be around 54. It's hard to tell with action scripts. When the FX budget is over – way over! – that'll help me prune back even more…

```
114. INT. SARAH JANE SMITH'S ATTIC
- NIGHT[4]

SARAH JANE rushing, grabbing coat,
bag, keys -

                MR SMITH V/O
     Tardis heading for Vector 7,
     grid reference 665.

                    LUKE
     But there are Daleks out
     there!

                 SARAH JANE
     I know, I'm sorry, but I've
     got to find the Doctor - don't
     move, don't leave the house,
     don't do anything -

                MR SMITH V/O
     I will protect the boy, Sarah
     Jane.

                 SARAH JANE
     I love you. Remember that.

And close to tears, she runs out -

                              CUT TO:

115. EXT. SARAH JANE SMITH'S HOUSE
- NIGHT

Fast, wild - SARAH JANE runs to her
car -
```

4 Scene 83 (on the Crucible Command Deck) has been deleted, and Scenes 11 and 113 (both in the Torchwood Hub) have been combined, shifting all subsequent scene numbers, so Captain Jack teleporting from the Hub is now Scene 113, followed by this, Scene 114, in Sarah Jane's attic.

'I've got to find the Doctor!' Sarah Jane races into action.

JUMP CUT TO the CAR racing off, fast -

CUT TO:

116. INT. NOBLES' LIVING ROOM - NIGHT

SYLVIA & WILF in b/g, ROSE so determined, on her mobile -

ROSE
Control? I need another shift. Lock me on to the Tardis - now!
(turns to others)
I'm gonna find them. Wish me luck!

WILF & SYLVIA
Good luck - !

FX: HARD CRACK OF WHITE LIGHT, ROSE vanishes - !

CUT TO:

117. EXT. BIG WIDE STREET - NIGHT

CLOSE ON THE DOCTOR & DONNA, stepping out of the Tardis -

CUT WIDER. Big, wet, empty street, maybe a CROSSROADS, as wide and as echoing as possible. Deserted suburbia. They look round. Doorways open. Abandoned cars. Eerie.

DONNA
Like a ghost town.

THE DOCTOR
Sarah Jane said they were taking the people. But what for? Think, Donna, when you met Rose in that parallel world, what did she say?

DONNA
Just… the darkness is coming.

THE DOCTOR
Anything else?

DONNA
Why don't you ask her yourself?

The Doctor looks at her, eh?

Donna is just smiling. The Doctor looks the other way…

Far off in the distance, as far away as possible, on a cold and empty ordinary street…

A woman. Walking towards them.

ROSE.

And the Doctor smiles.

CUT TO Rose. And she smiles. The best smile.

She starts to run.

The Doctor starts to run.

Rose running.

The Doctor running.

Across the distance.

Donna stays where she is; so happy for him.

Running closer…

And closer…

And…

With the Doctor & Rose running on a north-south axis, then to the west, gliding out of darkness, into sight -

A DALEK!

DALEK 1
Exterminate!

Rose sees it -

The Doctor sees it -

FX: THE DALEK FIRES -

FX: the beam glances across the side of the Doctor's torso, just nicking him, but with an awful skeleton-ghost half-appearing across one side of his body -

- and he falls -

FX: fourth axis, to the east, TELEPORT GLOW, CAPTAIN JACK appears - in that same second, he's firing the DEFABRICATOR GUN -

PRAC FX: DALEK EXPLODES!

CUT TO THE DOCTOR on the ground. Rose reaching him. He's alive, but shivering, in a cold sweat, in agony -

ROSE
You're alive, I've got you, it missed, look, you're alive, I'm here, Doctor, it's me -

THE DOCTOR
…hello!

'Long time... no see...' Picture © Rex Features

ROSE
Hi.

THE DOCTOR
Long time… no see…

ROSE
Yeah, been a bit busy, y'know.
(drops pretence)
Don't die, oh my God, don't die.

Jack reaching them - Donna also running up -

CAPTAIN JACK
Get him into the Tardis, quick!

CUT TO:

118. INT. TORCHWOOD HUB - NIGHT

GWEN runs up to IANTO, hands him a MACHINE GUN, with one for herself -

IANTO
But they don't work against Daleks!

GWEN
I am going out fighting. Like Owen. Like Tosh. What about you?

IANTO
Yes ma'am!

CUT TO:

119. INT. TARDIS - NIGHT

Slam! THE DOCTOR falls down on to the floor, shuddering -

ROSE & DONNA with him, CAPTAIN JACK standing back, grim -

DONNA
What do we do?! There's gotta be some sort of medicine, or -

CAPTAIN JACK
Just step back. Rose! Do as I say, and get back! He's dying. And you know what happens next.

ROSE
(crying)
But he can't. Not now. I came all this way.

'But he can't. Not now. I came all this way.'

'... It's starting...'

DONNA
What d'you mean, what happens next?!

But the Doctor holds up one hand, staring at it...

FX: that old, golden glow playing across his hand...

THE DOCTOR
...it's starting...

CUT TO:

120. EXT. STREET NEAR SARAH JANE'S - NIGHT

SARAH JANE's car screeches round a corner - brakes!

She's driven right into a semicircle of THREE DALEKS. All now swivelling around on the spot to face her.

DALEK 1
All Human transport is forbidden!

SARAH JANE
I surrender! I'm sorry!

DALEK 1
Daleks do not accept apologies! You will be exterminated!

ALL DALEKS
Exterminate! *Exterminate!*

And Sarah Jane coves her head with her arms -

CUT TO:

121. INT. TORCHWOOD HUB - NIGHT

GWEN & IANTO face the circular door. Raise guns, *ka-chik!*

PRAC FX: small explosions around the door, it rolls back -

REVEALING A DALEK!

CU GWEN & IANTO yell, bloodlust, pure rage, and open fire!

CUT TO:

'Daleks do not accept apologies! You will be exterminated!'

```
122. INT. TARDIS - NIGHT

DONNA standing back, CAPTAIN JACK
just pulling ROSE back, away from
THE DOCTOR, so the three of them
stand together -

            CAPTAIN JACK
   Here we go! Good luck,
   Doctor!

And the Doctor is just hauling
himself to his feet…

               DONNA
   Someone tell me what's going
   on!

               ROSE
   When he's dying. His body. It
   repairs itself. It changes.
              (upset)
   But you can't!

            THE DOCTOR
   Sorry. Too late.
              (smiles)
   I'm regenerating.

FX: THE DOCTOR throws his head
back, splays out his arms -
VOLCANIC GOLDEN ENERGY blasts out
of his arms, his neck -

Donna, Rose, Captain Jack flinch
back, shield their eyes -

FX: HIGH SHOT on the Doctor's head,
tilted back, as the Tenth Doctor's
features disappear into the GOLDEN
INFERNO -

                    END OF EPISODE 12!
```

What a cliffhanger! And now I'm going to go and have a cold. Properly.

FROM: BENJAMIN COOK TO: RUSSELL T DAVIES
MONDAY 31 DECEMBER 2007 13:07:59 GMT

RE: 12.2 MILLION!!!

For once, just for once, could 4.12 *not* finish with a 'Next Time' trailer? Put a 'TO BE CONTINUED' graphic or something – anything! – but it'd spoil that amazing cliffhanger if we see the Doctor up and about in the trailer. Is the plan to convince people that this is David's swansong as the Doctor?

The explosive cliffhanger to 4.12 *The Stolen Earth*.

This is all very exciting. How are you feeling about it? What have Julie and Phil said? They'll have read it by now, won't they?

FROM: RUSSELL T DAVIES TO: BENJAMIN COOK
MONDAY 31 DECEMBER 2007 13:57:38 GMT

RE: 12.2 MILLION!!!

You're right, actually. A black, silent 'TO BE

CONTINUED' card would be amazing. There are bound to be TV trailers that week, but you could just show lots of Daleks and a repeat of 'I'm regenerating…' We never send out preview discs of the last episode, so we might just get away with it. What a laugh! I feel happy now. Very. I think the script has lived up to the concept's promise.

Julie got back from New York this morning, sat down in the Virgin lounge to read it, but then Phil arrived to pick her up. She texted me: 'He's on time! He's never on time! I'm only on Page 30!' She's left in high suspense, but now she's got Billie's wedding all day and won't be able to read it till tonight. But I never send scripts to Phil at the same time as Julie. Maybe I should, but the whole thing is a headache to him – it's a terrifying budget sheet – so I leave him in peace. For now.

Of course, stopping has meant that this cold is sweeping over me. My hands are swollen. That's not good. What does that mean? Hey, what are you doing tonight? Dancing in fountains? I'm so sick and bleeargghhh, I'm just going to sit in front of the TV with my old fella and herald in the New Year from my armchair.

FROM: BENJAMIN COOK TO: RUSSELL T DAVIES
MONDAY 31 DECEMBER 2007 14:09:05 GMT

RE: 12.2 MILLION!!!

I'm out in Covent Garden tonight, and then on to Trafalgar Square – or maybe the Victoria Embankment to watch the fireworks.

Well, a rest should do you good. It'll give you a chance to shake off the cold. At least it won't take you five-and-half hours to get home tonight! Pity me.

Happy New Year, Russell.

FROM: RUSSELL T DAVIES TO: BENJAMIN COOK
MONDAY 31 DECEMBER 2007 14:16:27 GMT

RE: 12.2 MILLION!!!

Happy New Year to you, Benjamino! Seriously, my favourite thing about this year? This correspondence. I have loved it. It's been something new. New is good. I'm so glad that you thought of doing this. Thank you.

Get home safe. Subwave Network closing down. Good night.

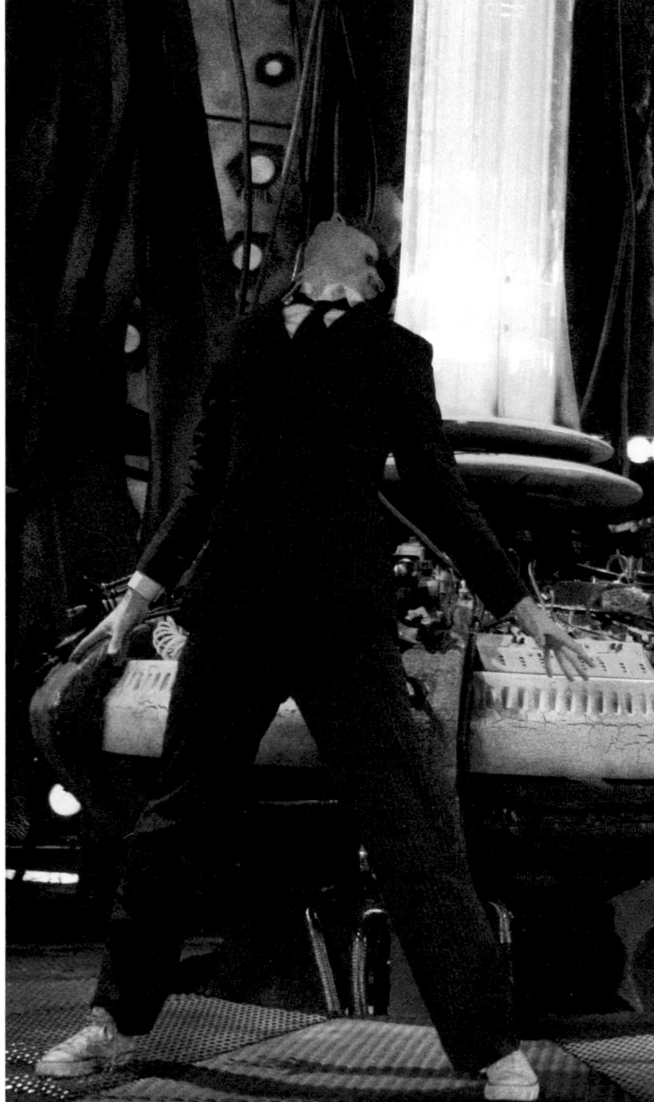

David Tennant records his 'regeneration' on the TARDIS set.

CHAPTER FOURTEEN

DAY OLD BLUES

In which Russell hits rock bottom, the Daleks learn German, and Young Davros has a scream on Skaro

FROM: RUSSELL T DAVIES TO: BENJAMIN COOK
SATURDAY 5 JANUARY 2008 18:25:27 GMT

HAPPY NEW YEAR?

I'm starting to feel human again. I've spent half of the last week in bed. It's only a cold, but being a smoker makes it vicious. Yes, it's all my own fault. And I'm dying for a cigarette now!

The prep date for 4.12/4.13 is Monday, but they'll only have 4.12. There's plenty of work in that to be getting on with. Actually, I still haven't officially submitted 4.12; only you and Julie have read it so far. I keep meaning to go over it again, to reduce the page count, but then I sit here and cough, and want a cigarette, and fail to do anything. I'll give it the weekend. And I'll start 4.13. Any day now. Late already. Oh God.

New Year? They sold us a pup. It's the Old Year, with a bit of nail varnish.

FROM: RUSSELL T DAVIES TO: BENJAMIN COOK
SATURDAY 5 JANUARY 2008 19:29:50 GMT

RE: HAPPY NEW YEAR?

I've just realised, you sent me that first e-mail on 18 February... and that's now my exact deadline for 4.14. It's a year! Blimey. A year of sitting in this bloody chair. I'm depressed now.

FROM: BENJAMIN COOK TO: RUSSELL T DAVIES
SATURDAY 5 JANUARY 2008 20:38:30 GMT

RE: HAPPY NEW YEAR?

That's just the cold talking. Trust me, you've loved every minute of it! Ha ha.

>>I never think of it as work, really, no matter how much hard graft I actually do. Even if no one ever saw this stuff, I'd be doing it anyway.<<

Is now a good time to quote the above back at you?

FROM: RUSSELL T DAVIES TO: BENJAMIN COOK
SATURDAY 5 JANUARY 2008 20:45:23 GMT

RE: HAPPY NEW YEAR?

Ha ha ha.

No.

FROM: RUSSELL T DAVIES TO: BENJAMIN COOK
WEDNESDAY 9 JANUARY 2008 22:51:15 GMT

RE: HAPPY NEW YEAR?

Work is like… oh, fear and panic. It's like trying to peg down a tent in a gale. (That's not going to win at the Analogy Awards, is it?) You've a huge piece of canvas flapping in all directions. It's a nightmare, you're going to lose the lot, you peg one thing down, but that's no help, then you get another peg in, but that's still not enough, but gradually, slowly… like, I still haven't a clue what Martha and Sarah Jane are doing, but suddenly, today, I realised where they should end up, about 30 minutes into 4.13. And why they're there. And what connects them. It was like slamming two strong pegs into place, at the same time. All the panic, the flap and the fury seemed a little less. It was some sort of progress. In other words, it's all thinking, no writing.

I bumped into Freema in the Bay today. Big hug, hello, then I walked back to my flat, thinking about Martha in 4.13. I closed the door, and then I actually, really, said out loud to myself, all alone, 'You cannot let her down.' I really did that. Sometimes I say scary motivational things to myself out loud. Like it helps! It doesn't.

The good news is, Harriet Jones is back! Penelope Wilton says yes! Apparently, she said yes straight away, no doubt, no hesitation, bang, done. *Brilliant!* I wasn't expecting it to be that easy. So that's a thrill. She'll face the Daleks!

FROM: BENJAMIN COOK TO: RUSSELL T DAVIES
WEDNESDAY 9 JANUARY 2008 23:04:17 GMT

RE: HAPPY NEW YEAR?

>>'You cannot let her down.'<<

But why do you never talk about letting *yourself* down? Doesn't that worry you as much?

'You cannot let her down.' Russell motivates himself to give Freema Agyeman a proper send-off in 4.13 *Journey's End.*

FROM: RUSSELL T DAVIES TO: BENJAMIN COOK
THURSDAY 10 JANUARY 2008 16:46:53 GMT

RE: HAPPY NEW YEAR?

I've been thinking about your question a lot. It struck a chord. It's partly because letting down Freema or Catherine or David or the production team *does* mean letting myself down. If we end up with a rubbish series finale, I'll be gutted. My God, I'll be suicidal. 'They' and 'me' exist simultaneously in that equation. They work for me, with me, because of me.

At the same time, the question went deep, because… well, this is kind of hard to say, but I never have, in my work, let myself down. Not ever. Not really. Not profoundly. Is that an outrageous thing to say? But that's why I'm successful. I'm good at what I do. I work exceptionally hard. That doesn't mean everything that I've done has been brilliant or that every script that

I've written has been good, but actually every piece of work has been done with good intent, to the best of my abilities, within the limits of my own talent and stamina. Every Single Thing. Even some bloody awful Granada sitcoms that I was coerced into, where I ended up using a pen-name. Rotten scripts, rotten to the core… but I couldn't have made them better, at the time. I gave them everything. For all their awfulness, I still have a strange pride in them. I put everything into work. Everything. It's not always enough, and hindsight shows me a thousand different ways that I should have done things, but that's natural; I don't beat myself up over that. Or maybe I'm blind to the proper disasters. Maybe you have to be, to keep working. The problem is, there's no consolation in the above. I've only really thought about this when you posed the question.

But it's more than that… this is where it becomes a difficult question, in that it starts to define me, because I let myself down in a million other areas. I let myself down in my relationship with my father, in not phoning my sisters from one year to the next, in not giving my boyfriend enough time. When I do give him time, I mess that up too. I let myself down personally by smoking badly, eating badly, living badly. Do you see? *That's* where I let myself down. The real stuff. All the time. Is that because I work so hard? Or do I work so hard to absolve myself from blame? This is where work and life are simply indivisible. Ah, but that's what writing is. Looking at yourself all day, every day. Whether I'm thinking about monsters, gay men, religion, comedy… it's all me, in the end. With no answers and no clarity. Just more questions.

Text message from: Russell
Sent: 11-Jan-2008 13:57
Final viewing figures for Voyage of the Damned: 13.3 million!!!

Text message from: Ben
Sent: 11-Jan-2008 14:04
That's immense! Well done all. Hey, I'm texting you from a tunnel in Barry Island, on location for *The Doctor's Daughter*. I'm huddled in a corner, drinking soup. David texted me yesterday: 'It's not cold, actually – we're underground. It does smell like a wino's breath, though.'

Text message from: Russell
Sent: 11-Jan-2008 18:28
I'm sat here doing no work. I'm scared now. Proper scared.

FROM: RUSSELL T DAVIES TO: BENJAMIN COOK
SATURDAY 12 JANUARY 2008 03:14:22 GMT

RE: HAPPY NEW YEAR?

It's only two pages. Don't get excited. An easy two pages. I always knew how to get out of those cliffhangers. I only did this tonight so that I don't wake up tomorrow in blind misery without even a file that says '4.13'…

```
1. INT. TARDIS - NIGHT

REPEAT last TWO FX shots from
4.12 - the Doctor exploding with
light, CU on his head surrounded by
energy, then -

On DONNA, ROSE, JACK, flinching from
the light, but staring -

FX: full length on THE DOCTOR, his
head still a volcano, as he swings
round, aims both arms together -
both still channelling the golden
energy - pointing across the room,
downwards - so the energy shoots
out like a gun, hitting -

FX: the HAND-IN-JAR, bubbling like
crazy - the whole jar shuddering as
it's blasted by GOLDEN LIGHT -
```

The Doctor pours his regeneration energy into his handy spare hand.

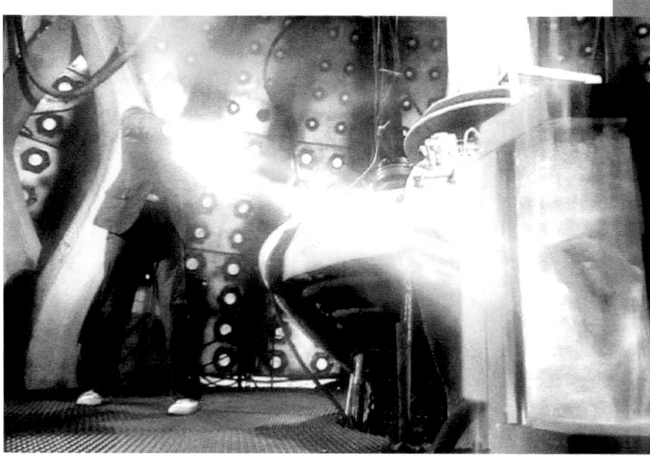

CUT TO closer on Donna, Rose, Jack, watching…

FX: full length on the Doctor - and now he's bowing his head, in alignment with his arms, three beams of energy shooting across and into the jar -

FX: MID-SHOT on the Doctor, energy pouring out of his neck, until, suddenly, *schwup!*, it STOPS! Gone!

And there's the Doctor. Blinking. Same as ever.

THE DOCTOR
Now then. Where were we?

CUT TO:

2. EXT. STREET NEAR SARAH JANE'S - NIGHT

REPEAT, THREE DALEKS surrounding SARAH JANE'S CAR - CUT TO -

FX: behind her car, a HARD CRACK OF WHITE LIGHT (exactly like Rose's in 4.12/10) and standing there -

MICKEY! Carrying a big SCI-FI GUN (again, like Rose's) - FX: and he's firing, *BLAM! BLAM! BLAM!*, three shots, in an arc -

Mickey Smith (Noel Clarke) to the rescue.

'Us Smiths gotta stick together!'

FX? PRAC? one, two, three, the DALEKS explode!

And silence. Sarah getting out of the car, staggered.

SARAH JANE
…Mickey Smith.

MICKEY
Us Smiths gotta stick together!

CUT TO:

3. INT. TORCHWOOD HUB - NIGHT

GWEN & IANTO firing like mad, ready to die…

Until they stop. Lower guns. Puzzled. Eh…?

FX: the REVERSE. The DALEK in the doorway… Just frozen. And, like dots, suspended in the air, BULLETS.

Gwen walks forward…

FX: CU on her as she steps closer to the BULLETS, just hanging in the air. She lifts a hand, touches the air…

FX: small RIPPLE in the air, an invisible wall hanging between the inside of the Hub, and the Dalek &

bullets.

GWEN
What the hell…?

CUT TO:

4. INT. TARDIS - NIGHT

FX: THE DOCTOR kneeling by the HAND-IN-JAR, which is still boiling with the GOLDEN ENERGY. He blows on it, like cooling a cuppa, and the energy fades.

THE DOCTOR
There now, d'you see, used the regeneration energy to heal myself, then before it could go any further, I siphoned off the rest of it into a handy bio-matching receptacle, namely, my hand, that hand there, my handy spare hand, I thank you, what d'you think?

ROSE
…you're still you?

THE DOCTOR
I'm still me. Rose Tyler. We were in the middle of saying hello.

And she runs to him!

Hugs him. He hugs her. The biggest hug. Laughing.

'What the hell…?' Something strange is happening in the Hub.

CUT TO DONNA & CAPTAIN JACK, watching, all smiles.

DONNA
You can hug me, if you want.
(he laughs)
No, really, you can hug me.

FROM: RUSSELL T DAVIES TO: BENJAMIN COOK
SUNDAY 13 JANUARY 2008 01:43:22 GMT

RE: HAPPY NEW YEAR?

Steven Moffat e-mailed me earlier and said, almost in passing…

> *Another thing: I've started. I've written the first few pages of my first episode. Couldn't stop myself. It was like incontinence. Well, hopefully not* completely *like incontinence. But anyway.*

He's started! Oh my God, I'm old news.

FROM: RUSSELL T DAVIES TO: BENJAMIN COOK
SUNDAY 13 JANUARY 2008 19:52:22 GMT

RE: HAPPY NEW YEAR?

Yesterday was bad. Rock bottom, really. I went a bit mad. I ended up walking around the Bay at 3.30 this morning. But I think it forced some good thoughts out. I want to work tonight, but I feel so tired. Oh, moan, moan, moan. We'll get there.

FROM: BENJAMIN COOK TO: RUSSELL T DAVIES
SUNDAY 13 JANUARY 2008 20:15:19 GMT

RE: HAPPY NEW YEAR?

What good thoughts? It can't all have been doom and gloom…

FROM: RUSSELL T DAVIES TO: BENJAMIN COOK
SUNDAY 13 JANUARY 2008 21:18:31 GMT

RE: HAPPY NEW YEAR?

Mainly, it's the pattern of this episode. The chessboard. Who ends up where. I don't know how to get them there. The Doctor needs to be taken prisoner by Davros so that Davros can taunt him and, more handily, explain the plot. (This is where the Supreme Dalek is messing me up, because he's an additional element in an already busy cast. Life would be much better if the Dalek

Crucible had just one badass in charge. But I simply can't bear it when Davros is in charge of the Daleks. They wouldn't let him; it reduces them to soldiers.) So, the Doctor with Davros, yes... but which companion in that room with them? I'd always imagined that it'd be Donna. I've a brilliant Donna-showing-compassion-for-Davros scene in mind. Plus, this is Donna's series; putting the Doctor with Rose weights the whole drama too heavily in her favour. And in some ways – which become important later on – Donna should have been in this room for a while. Simultaneously, the plot is demanding that Donna is in the TARDIS, touching the hand-in-a-jar, so she becomes the biological catalyst for Doctor #2 to be grown out of the original Doctor's hand. That's why Doctor #2 is half-human, because he's part-Donna, which gives him one heart. This means that when he goes to live in the parallel universe, with Rose, at the end, he's going to age at a normal rate, so they'll be a proper couple. None of that 'You'll wither and die while I stay the same' lark. It's the final solution to their biggest problem as a couple. Donna has to be in the TARDIS as Doctor #2 appears. So she spends most of the episode with him, right?

But hold on – look at your other options – because if Rose is going to spend the rest of her life with Doctor #2, shouldn't *she* be with him in the TARDIS as he springs into existence – and they spend the rest of the episode together, riffing off each other, both liking each other. And Doctor #2 is half-human, remember, so he can be more overtly sexualised than the original. Do you see how neat that is? If I don't take that option, she'll have to meet Doctor #2 in the last ten minutes. Pretty quick to fall in love. So, right, take that option – but that requires Donna to bond with the hand-in-a-jar, then think no more of it, waltz out of the TARDIS, with the original Doctor, to become Davros' prisoner, leaving the Doctor #2 birth to happen as if she'd had nothing to do with it. That's wrong. That's very wrong.

Also, it's a major piece of work simply to get the original Doctor out of the TARDIS with one companion, plus Jack, and to leave the other companion inside. Why would one stay behind? Why would Rose stay behind? Why would Donna stay behind? The other option: Rose *and* Donna stay in the TARDIS. Donna creates Doctor #2, while Rose is instantly attracted to him, and all three spend the episode together.

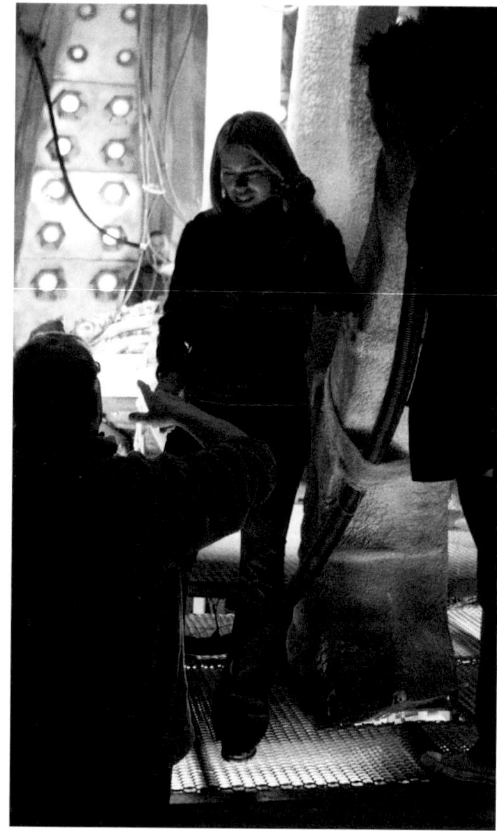

Graeme Harper offers direction to Billie Piper, while Noel Clarke and David Tennant listen in.

Feels wrong, doesn't it? These scenes demand that the companion is alone, not two women together. The loneliness of it. And then the triumph! Remember way back, when I had to rewrite 4.5 very quickly, I told you that I'd stolen some of 4.12/4.13's plot to make 4.4/4.5 work? Well, here it is, coming back to haunt me. I stole the Donna-alone-in-the-TARDIS thread, where she finds herself alone on the Sontaran ship, and now I've got Donna alone in the TARDIS again in 4.13. It feels so similar. I've robbed myself. So maybe Rose should be in the TARDIS alone...?

FROM: RUSSELL T DAVIES TO: BENJAMIN COOK
SUNDAY 13 JANUARY 2008 21:34:36 GMT

RE: HAPPY NEW YEAR?

Oh, you asked me what good thoughts I'd had. I answered with the problems I've got! You only hear what you want to hear. Or maybe good thoughts and problems are the same thing.

FROM: RUSSELL T DAVIES TO: BENJAMIN COOK
MONDAY 14 JANUARY 2008 15:21:50 GMT

RE: HAPPY NEW YEAR?

I did no work last night. I went to bed. Set the alarm on my mobile, as usual. Placed my mobile far away from the bed, as usual. But then got a sheet of A4 and wrote on it in big, black Magic Marker: 'WORK, YOU STUPID ****!' That did the trick. I've been working since 11am…

```
5. INT. TORCHWOOD HUB - NIGHT

FX: GWEN & IANTO now staring at
the mid-air bullets and the frozen
DALEK.

                    GWEN
    It's like… everything got
    suspended in time. The whole
    Hub.

                    IANTO
    Wait a minute, the Time
    Lock - !

He runs to a terminal, Gwen
following. On the run:

                    GWEN
    What's a Time Lock? Well,
    I can see what a Time Lock
    is, that's a Time Lock, but
    where's it from?

                    IANTO
    It's a defence programme.
    Tosh was working on it, I
    thought she never finished
    it, but…
              (at terminal)
    She did! The Hub's sealed off
    in a time bubble, nothing can
    get in!

                    GWEN
    And we can't get out?

                    IANTO
    There is that.

                    GWEN
    But Jack's out there!

                    IANTO
    Nothing we can do. Not
    without unlocking that Dalek.

                    GWEN
    We can't just sit here!

                    IANTO
    No choice. We're trapped.
    It's all up to Jack, now.

HIGH SHOT, Gwen & Ianto looking up…

                    GWEN
    Jack, and that Doctor of his…

                                        CUT TO:

6. INT. TARDIS - NIGHT

CAPTAIN JACK hugging ROSE! In b/g,
THE DOCTOR busy, flicking switches,
DONNA opposite Rose & Jack.

                    CAPTAIN JACK
    - and you, Rose Tyler! You've
    got some explaining to do!
    The things you did to me!

                    ROSE
    What d'you mean, what did
    I do - ? Oh! Donna, I saw
    your mum, and your Grandad,
    they're okay -

                    DONNA
    Oh thank God - wait a minute,
    you didn't tell my mother
    where I am?

                    ROSE
    I had to, sorry!

                    DONNA
    Ohhh, she's gonna kill me -

                    THE DOCTOR
                   (still busy)
    Oy, oy, anyway, domestics!
    Leave it! We can catch up
    later! Right now, we need a
    plan! We've got 27 planets
    sitting in the Medusa
    Cascade, we need to find out
    what the Daleks are doing,
    and why, and how's your
    mother by the way?

                    ROSE
    She's fine! Same as ever.

                    THE DOCTOR
    And the baby?
```

'Oy! Domestics!'

ROSE
Yeah, she had a boy!

DONNA
Oy! Domestics!

CAPTAIN JACK
(at the scanner)
Doctor! We've got Daleks outside! They've found us!

CUT TO:

7. EXT. BIG WIDE STREET - NIGHT

FOUR DALEKS now grouped around the TARDIS in a circle.

DALEK 1
Report! Tardis has been located!

CUT TO:

8. INT. CRUCIBLE COMMAND DECK - NIGHT

On the SUPREME DALEK.

SUPREME DALEK
Bring it to me! Bring the Doctor here! Initiate temporal prison!

CUT TO the FOUR DALEKS at their posts on ground level:

DALEK 2
Temporal prison initiated!

CUT TO:

9. EXT. BIG WIDE STREET - NIGHT

FX: with the FOUR DALEKS grouped a distance back, a horizontal circle of BURNING WHITE LIGHT around its midriff surrounds the TARDIS. Like it's been hoop-la'd.

DALEK 1
Temporal prison in place!

CUT TO:

10. INT. TARDIS - NIGHT

LIGHTS GO DOWN! Sound of power dying. Not complete darkness, but shadowy and spooky. THE DOCTOR frantic -

THE DOCTOR
They've got us! Power's gone! Some kind of chronon loop -

DONNA
But we're safe, aren't we? Nothing can get inside the Tardis.

THE DOCTOR
Daleks can.

ROSE
You told me, nothing can get through those doors.

THE DOCTOR
Daleks can.

CAPTAIN JACK lifts up the still-attached EXTRAPOLATOR!

CAPTAIN JACK
But you've got an Extrapolator shield! Nothing can override that -

THE DOCTOR
Daleks! Can! All right?! Last time we all fought the Daleks, they were scavengers and hybrids. This is a fully

fledged Dalek Empire, they can
do anythi- woah!

- as the Tardis lurches, all
stumble -

CUT TO:

11. EXT. BIG WIDE STREET - NIGHT

On DALEK 1, gliding backwards a
little -

DALEK 1
Transferring Tardis to the
Crucible.

FX: WIDER, DALEKS watching as the
HOOP-OF-LIGHT-TARDIS lifts off the
ground a few feet…

CUT TO a *good* distance away. SARAH
JANE & MICKEY in an alley, in
shadows, just running up, staying
hidden, seeing -

FX: the HOOP-OF-LIGHT-TARDIS
accelerates, whooshes up into the
sky, becomes a dot of light, gone.
In whispers:

MICKEY
They've got him!

SARAH JANE
Mickey, that teleport thing,
can you use it? If they've
taken the Doctor to the Dalek
spaceship, then that's where
we need to be -

'Transferring TARDIS to the Crucible.'

Mickey takes his 2.13 yellow-
pendant from his pocket -

MICKEY
It's not just a teleport,
it's a Dimension Jump, man.
This thing rips a hole in
time and space -

SARAH JANE
But can we use it?!

MICKEY
Not yet, it burns up energy,
needs half an hour in between
jumps -

SARAH JANE
Then put down your gun.

MICKEY
Do what?!

SARAH JANE
If you're carrying a gun,
they'll shoot you dead. We
need to be taken prisoner.

And without waiting for him, deep
breath, she steps out into the
middle of the street, with her
hands up -

SARAH JANE (CONT'D)
Daleks! I surrender!

The Daleks turn to face her.

DALEK 1
All Humans in this Sector
will be taken to the
Crucible!

Mickey, in shadows, muttering:

MICKEY
She's bloody mad!

Gives his gun a kiss. Puts it down.
Steps out, hands up.

MICKEY (CONT'D)
And me! I surrender!
(mutters at Sarah)
Whether I like it or not.

CUT TO:

12. INT. JONES' HOUSE - NIGHT

FRANCINE on the mobile. MARTHA's
got the INDIGO PROJECT, tapping

numbers into the readout; she's taking the numbers off a UNIT website, on the laptop, SECURITY LEVEL RED.

FRANCINE
Still no reply.

MARTHA
(still tapping away)
We've lost contact with the Subwave, and the Tardis. So it's up to me!

FRANCINE
What are those numbers?

Martha starts hoisting on the Indigo Project, buckling up.

MARTHA
Grid references. Now Jack's explained the base code, I know how this teleport works. I think. But you stay indoors, there's no Daleks on this street, you should be all right, just keep quiet.

FRANCINE
But where are you going...?

MARTHA
I'm a member of UNIT. And they gave me the Osterhagen Key. I've got to do my job.
(upset)
I'm sorry.

FRANCINE
What for...?

Martha goes to her. Close to tears. Kisses her.

MARTHA
Love you.

Martha steps back. Readies the rip-cords. Francine scared:

FRANCINE
Martha. What's an Osterhagen Key? Tell me. What does it do??

MARTHA
...it's not my fault.

And crying, now, she pulls the cords -

FX: MARTHA VANISHES in the teleport glow!

On Francine. Shaken, upset.

CUT TO:

13. EXT. GERMAN FOREST - NIGHT

CU MARTHA on the ground. Dazed, blinking, recovering.

GRAPHIC: *GERMANY, 50 miles outside Bremmen.*

Martha stands, looks round. It's dark, dense forest; not woodlands, proper forest. Middle of nowhere. Spooky.

Martha hears something, turns -

FX: way off in the distance, DALEKS, in the air, gliding slowly through the trees. Though not heading towards her.

GERMAN DALEKS
Exterminaten! Exterminaten!

If you go down to the woods today, you're sure of a big surprise!

Martha heads off in the opposite direction. Scurrying away into the darkness. On a mission.

CUT TO:

14. FX SHOT

FX: THE HOOP-OF-LIGHT TARDIS sailing away from EARTH, through the PLANETARY ARRAY.

CUT TO:

```
15. INT. TARDIS - NIGHT

Still low-light. THE DOCTOR, DONNA,
ROSE, CAPTAIN JACK, all grouped
around the console. Grim:

                DONNA
    Where are they taking us?

              CAPTAIN JACK
    On the scanners, there was a
    massive Dalek ship. Sitting
    at the centre of the planets.
    They're calling it the
    Crucible.

                DONNA
    You said all these planets
    were like an engine. But what
    for?

              THE DOCTOR
    Rose? You've been in a
    parallel world. And that
    world's running ahead of this
    universe. You've seen the
    future. What was it...?

                ROSE
    The darkness.

                DONNA
    The stars were going out.

                ROSE
    One by one. We looked up at
    the sky. And they were dying.
    Entire constellations. And
    at the same time, the walls
    between dimensions started
    to weaken. We'd been building
    this machine, a Dimension
    Cannon, so I could... Well...

              THE DOCTOR
               (smiling)
    What?

                ROSE
    So I could come back.
              (he grins)
    Shut up. But all of a sudden,
    it started working. Like,
    everything was starting to
    collapse. Not just our world,
    not just yours. But the whole
    of reality.

A low-level beep from the scanner,
the Doctor runs to it:

              THE DOCTOR
    Here we go. The Crucible!
    And not, I think, the one in
    Sheffield.

                                CUT TO:

16. FX SHOT

FX: the HOOP-OF-LIGHT TARDIS swoops
past CAMERA, revealing, in all its
glory: THE CRUCIBLE.

FX: CLOSER, CAMERA gliding around
the ship; a huge GLOBE, many
miles in diameter, all studded and
riveted bronze, with six bristling
metal ARMS radiating out of its
centre.

FX: a tiny hooped TARDIS being
drawn inside the ship.
```

FROM: BENJAMIN COOK TO: RUSSELL T DAVIES
MONDAY 14 JANUARY 2008 18:05:36 GMT

RE: HAPPY NEW YEAR?

GERMAN DALEKS!!! They've always been German, really, haven't they?

FROM: RUSSELL T DAVIES TO: BENJAMIN COOK
MONDAY 14 JANUARY 2008 18:53:18 GMT

RE: HAPPY NEW YEAR?

I've gone one better now: I Babel Fish-ed some dialogue for them, so now they're saying:[1]

```
                DALEKS
    Halt! Oder Sie werden
    geabschaffen! Sie sind ein
    Gefangener des Daleks!
```

Even then, I had a proper little conversation with myself about how Daleks would communicate in foreign countries – and how we, as the audience, would hear it. This tapped into another ponder, namely how much of the TARDIS translation facility Martha would have kept with her once she stops being a proper companion. Not much, I decided, or there would be all these polylingual ex-companions all over the place. That ability has to fade. Martha would hear German, so we should hear German. Daleks don't talk in standard English anyway, and would

1 Babel Fish is a web-based application that translates text from one of several languages into another.

adapt to each country or planet. And yes, German, how apt for a bunch of Nazis.

FROM: RUSSELL T DAVIES TO: BENJAMIN COOK
TUESDAY 15 JANUARY 2008 03:11:59 GMT

RE: HAPPY NEW YEAR?

I'm terrified that there's no room for Jackie. I think we've asked Camille Coduri to keep the whole filming block of four weeks free, but now she's only going to be needed for one day at the end, when we return to Bad Wolf Bay. That's been worrying me all night. I e-mailed Julie about an hour ago, to ask where we stand with Camille and her agent. Not that Camille would complain, of course, but we're talking a living wage here. It's not fair. I did wonder, in my Julie e-mail, if Jackie could team up with Mickey and Sarah Jane (poor Julie hasn't even read 4.13 and won't know what I'm on about), but I regarded that as a desperate, last-minute option. Funny thing is, as the thought settles in, I realise that it could be rather good. It spoils the clean dynamic of the two Smiths together, but Jackie always comes up with good dialogue, and the thought of her and Sarah Jane is a bit tempting.

But would Jackie's early arrival bump up the length of the script? Also, I *really* worry that since Jackie has given birth and has little Tony at home (Tony Tyler!), she'd never enter a bloody battle zone. She'd stay at home. So I don't know what's best for the story, and I don't know what's good manners professionally. Still, today's new stuff is rather marvellous...

```
17. INT. TARDIS - NIGHT

The room bumps, a landing. All
scared:

            THE DOCTOR
    We've arrived.

            CAPTAIN JACK
    What do we do?

            THE DOCTOR
    Not much choice. If we don't
    go out, they'll get in.

            ROSE
    But they'll kill us. Last
    time we walked onto a Dalek
    ship, they were shooting like
    maniacs.

            THE DOCTOR
    But this time it's Davros.
    Our only chance is, he wants
    us alive.

Now, slow track in to Donna,
dialogue fading in b/g; again,
she's staring into space. Lost in
thought.

Hearing...

The heartbeat...

Closer and closer on Donna...

(This dialogue fading away b/g:)

            CAPTAIN JACK
    What about that Dimension
    Jump? Could you use it to
    get out?

            ROSE
    Needs twenty minutes to
    recharge. And anyway. I'm not
    leaving.

            THE DOCTOR
    What about your teleport?

            CAPTAIN JACK
    It's dead. They must have a
    cancellation signal.

            THE DOCTOR
    Right then. All of us.
    Together, yeah? Donna?
                (beat)
    Donna?

She snaps out of it.

            DONNA
    Yeah.

He thinks she's just scared:

            THE DOCTOR
    I'm sorry. There's nothing
    else we can do.

            DONNA
    Yeah, I was just... I know.

Psyching themselves up:

            THE DOCTOR
    Right then.

            ROSE
    Daleks.
```

CAPTAIN JACK
Ohh God.

THE DOCTOR
It's been good, though, hasn't it, yeah? All of us, all of it. Everything we did. You were brilliant. And you were brilliant. And you were brilliant.

DONNA
You're not bad either.

THE DOCTOR
Oh, I'm brilliant too. Or I was.
(pause)
Right. Blimey.

And he turns, they walk down the ramp…

The Doctor opens the door…

SCENE CONTINUES INTERCUT WITH -

CUT TO:

18. INT. CRUCIBLE COMMAND DECK - CONTINUOUS

INTERCUT WITH SC.17, INT. TARDIS.

THE DOCTOR steps out, deep breath…

THE DOCTOR
Ohhhkay…

Then ROSE, then CAPTAIN JACK…

INT. TARDIS, on DONNA, following them; she's just a few feet down the ramp, but…

She stops.

Staring.

Hearing, again…

The heartbeat.

The Doctor, Rose and Captain Jack step clear of the Tardis - staring at the Daleks, not seeing that Donna's stopped.

FX: WIDE SHOT, as 4.12/35, MULTIPLICATION DALEKS floor level, TIERS above, FLYING DALEKS, SUPREME DALEK on its platform:

SUPREME DALEK
Behold, Doctor! Behold the might of the true Dalek Race!

'Behold the might of the true Dalek Race!' Rose, the Doctor and Jack face the Supreme Dalek.

CUT TO DONNA. Still inside.

In her head…

The heartbeat…

She turns. As though entranced. Looking back into the Tardis… at what…?

Outside, the Doctor calls to her:

THE DOCTOR
Donna, come on, you're no safer in there…

She turns back towards the Doctor's voice, still lost…

Schwup! the Tardis door slams shut!

THE DOCTOR (CONT'D)
Donna? Donna!!

Donna snaps out of it! Runs to the door, yanking it -

DONNA
Doctor? What have you done? Oy! I'm not staying behind!!

THE DOCTOR
It wasn't me, I didn't do anything!
(to Supreme Dalek)
What did you do?!

SUPREME DALEK
This is not of Dalek origin.

THE DOCTOR
No, just stop it, she's my friend, now open the door and let her out -

Inside, banging on the door:

DONNA
Doctor! What's going on?!

Outside, to the Supreme Dalek:

THE DOCTOR
Please, stop playing games, just let her out -

SUPREME DALEK
This is Time Lord treachery.

THE DOCTOR
It wasn't me!

ROSE
The door just closed on its own!

SUPREME DALEK
Nevertheless. The Tardis is a weapon. And it will be destroyed!

FX: HIGH ANGLE on the TARDIS - with Rose & Captain Jack already a few feet back, the Doctor, at the Tardis door, jumps back just in time - as a simple panel of the black floor slides open, a trapdoor, and the Tardis drops through, like a stone, gone - !

INT. TARDIS CAMERA SHAKE, Donna thrown against the rail -

INT. CRUCIBLE, the Doctor yelling at the Supreme Dalek -

THE DOCTOR
What are you doing? Bring it back!!

INT. TARDIS, Donna clinging to the rail for dear life -

DONNA
Doctaaaaaa - !

CUT TO:

19. FX SHOT

FX: the TARDIS shooting down a plain metal shaft -

CUT TO:

20. INT. CRUCIBLE COMMAND DECK - NIGHT

THE DOCTOR runs to the SUPREME DALEK's platform, raging -

THE DOCTOR
What have you done, where's it going?!

SUPREME DALEK
The Crucible has a core of Neutronic Energy. The Tardis will be deposited into the core.

THE DOCTOR
But you can't, you've taken the defences down, it'll be

Donna is trapped inside the TARDIS as it plunges into the burning heart of the Crucible.

torn apart!

CUT TO:

21. FX SHOT

FX: the TARDIS rattles down the shaft -

FX: WIDE SHOT the CORE. DMP of a METAL ROOF above, with the lower half of frame filled with BOILING WHITE ENERGY. The small TARDIS falls out of a panel in the roof, down -

FX: REVERSE, the TARDIS falling into FULL-FRAME WHITE BOILING ENERGY. Disappearing into it!

CUT TO:

22. INT. TARDIS - NIGHT

DONNA pulling her way back to the console, as -

PRAC FX: a row of ROUNDELS SHATTER, as though the portholes are made of GLASS - outside, just WHITE LIGHT & SMOKE -

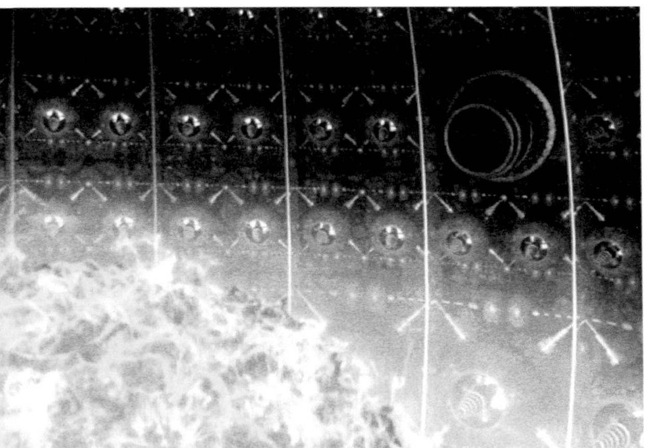

Donna ducks down, yelping -

PRAC FX: more ROUNDELS shatter!

CUT TO:

23. INT. CRUCIBLE COMMAND DECK - NIGHT

ROSE & CAPTAIN JACK running to THE DOCTOR -

ROSE
But Donna's still in there!

CAPTAIN JACK
Let her out!!!

SUPREME DALEK
Earthwoman and Tardis will perish together. Observe!

FX: OPPOSITE the Supreme Dalek, a big VIEWSCREEN zips into existence, mid-air, showing the FX shot from sc.24. Then cut to that shot full frame -

CUT TO:

As roundels shatter all around her, Donna feels the heat.

24. FX SHOT

FX: THE TARDIS in a bed of BOILING WHITE ENERGY.

FX: CLOSER, the WINDOWS in the doors SHATTER -

CUT TO:

25. INT. TARDIS - NIGHT

PRAC FX: THE DOOR-WINDOWS blasting out, white light outside -

Donna is on her knees, by the console, coughing - smoke in the air, heat blasting through - she's helpless -

FX: WIDE SHOT, widest shot possible, showing BEAMS OF WHITE LIGHT blasting through almost every ROUNDEL, now -

CUT TO:

26. INT. CRUCIBLE COMMAND DECK - NIGHT

ROSE & JACK watching the viewscreen, THE DOCTOR desperate -

THE DOCTOR
Please, I am begging you, I'll do anything, put me in her place, you can do anything to me, I don't care, just get her out of there!

Pause. Then the SUPREME's eyestalk swivels. Looks down.

SUPREME DALEK
Continue.

THE DOCTOR
…what?

SUPREME DALEK
Begging. It befits you.

CUT TO THE FOUR DALEKS, 2 and 4 swivelling round -

DALEK 2
Tardis integrity decreasing!

DALEK 4
Destruction imminent!

CUT TO:

27. INT. TARDIS - NIGHT

On DONNA. Trapped. Light and smoke all around her, but…

Suddenly, she's calm.

Hearing…

The heartbeat.

And she looks…

Knowing where it's from.

She's near the HAND-IN-JAR. It's bubbling away, and -

FX: GOLDEN ENERGY swirling around it.

Donna hypnotised. Reaching out…

FX: the JAR, the ENERGY…

She reaches closer…

Holding out one hand…

FX: CU DONNA'S HAND as she reaches for the GLOWING JAR… and as she touches it -

FX: DONNA AND JAR, as GOLDEN ENERGY whooshes around them both, enveloping her body, Donna transfixed, shuddering, a GOLD LIGHTSTORM twisting between them both -

FX: CU Donna, swathed in ENERGY -

FX: CU on the jar as it SHATTERS, the ENERGY dissipating -

Donna thrown back - !

CUT TO:

28. INT. CRUCIBLE COMMAND DECK - NIGHT

THE DOCTOR, ROSE & CAPTAIN JACK staring up at the (OOV) viewscreen - but the Doctor winces, ow! -

ROSE
What is it?

CAPTAIN JACK
You've been connected to that Tardis for hundreds of years. You're feeling it die.

The Doctor gives Donna a hand, without even being in the room!

THE DOCTOR
But why did the door close…?

CUT TO:

29. INT. TARDIS - NIGHT

Light & smoke all around. Donna on the floor, her old self, snapping out of it. But she looks. What the hell…?

THE DOCTOR'S HAND is now lying on the grille.

Donna sits up. Stares…

FX: GOLDEN LIGHT plays around the hand…

Donna staring - not hypnotised now, just gobsmacked -

FX: WIDER on the hand, as the GOLDEN LIGHT spreads out from it, taking the rough shape of a GLOWING PRONE BODY. No features, just humanoid-shaped energy.

Donna open-mouthed!

FX: MID-SHOT as the GLOWING BODY sits up!

And as Donna stares…

FX: the ENERGY *schwupps* away, fast, gone, and there is -

THE DOCTOR! An identical Doctor! Naked! (Mid-shot only.)

DONNA
..it's you.

THE DOCTOR #2
Oh yes!

DONNA
You're naked.

THE DOCTOR #2
Oh yes!

CUT TO:

30. INT. CRUCIBLE COMMAND DECK - NIGHT

Staring up at the screen. ROSE takes THE DOCTOR's hand.

SUPREME DALEK
Total Tardis destruction in ten rels, nine, eight, seven, six…

CUT TO:

31. INT. TARDIS - NIGHT

MID-SHOT on THE DOCTOR as he pops his head up, over the console, and, with a grin, stabs one particular button -

CUT TO:

32. FX SHOT

FX: THE TARDIS, in the BOILING WHITE LIGHT… fades away.

CUT TO:

33. INT. CRUCIBLE COMMAND DECK - NIGHT

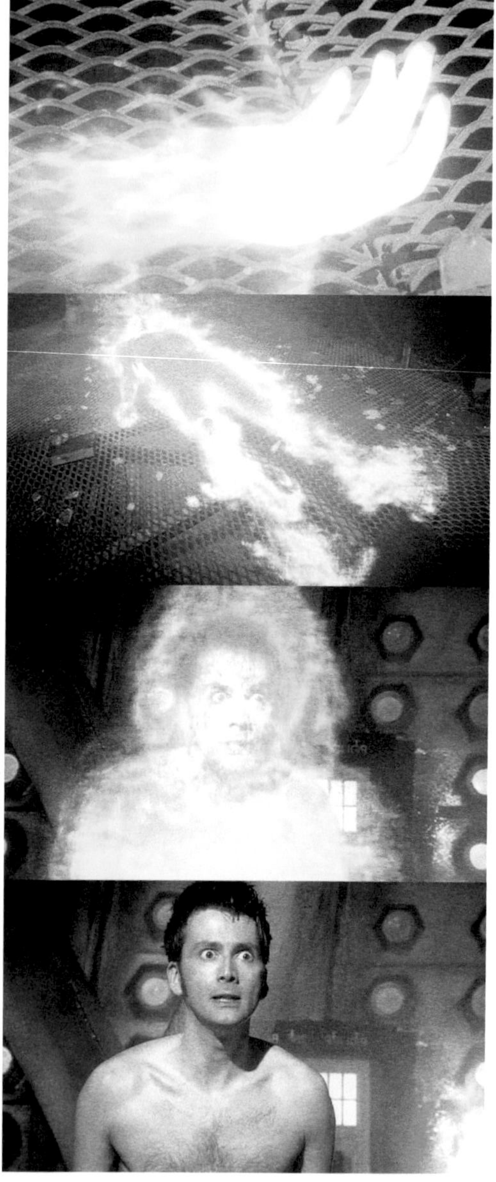

'Oh yes!' A new Doctor is born.

THE DOCTOR, ROSE & CAPTAIN JACK staring up as -

SUPREME DALEK
The Tardis has been destroyed. Now tell me, Doctor. What do you feel? Anger? Sorrow? Despair?

THE DOCTOR
...yeah.

SUPREME DALEK
Then if emotions are so important, surely we have enhanced you?

CAPTAIN JACK suddenly spinning round - revolver in hand!

CAPTAIN JACK
Yeah, well feel this - !

He fires at the Supreme Dalek -

FX: BULLETS *tzing!* off, SPARKS, the SUPREME DALEK fires -

SUPREME DALEK
Exterminate!

FX: BEAM hits him, CAPTAIN JACK skeleton'd, falls, dead.

'Exterminate!' Captain Jack is blasted by the Daleks.

Rose horrified, runs to him, kneels by his body -

ROSE
Jack! Oh my God! Ohhh no...

The Doctor goes to her.

THE DOCTOR
Rose, come here, leave him...

ROSE
They killed him.

THE DOCTOR
I know. I'm sorry.
(touches Jack's head; knowing)
Good man, Captain.

'But you promised him to me.' Davros is anxious to get his hands... er, hand on the Doctor.

(to Rose)
Come on. Nothing we can do.

The Doctor & Rose stand, holding each other.

THE DOCTOR (CONT'D)
So! You still haven't killed me, and there's got to be a reason for that. Where is he?

DAVROS OOV
I have been watching. With quite some fascination, Doctor.

FX: VIEWSCREEN. DAVROS, in his CRUCIBLE VAULT.

DAVROS
It is time we met. As veterans of war. So many wars.

SUPREME DALEK
You have been warned, Davros. The Doctor is a contamination.

DAVROS
But you promised him to me. The Doctor, and the Children of Time.

```
                THE DOCTOR
                (vicious)
      Promised? Ohhh, yes yes yes,
      I get it - Davros, you're
      not in charge! That thing's
      the boss, yeah? Daleks rule
      supreme, so what does that
      make you? Servant? Slave?
      Court jester? Pet?

                  DAVROS
                  (cold)
      Send him to me.

FX: VIEWSCREEN vwips! out of sight,
off.

              SUPREME DALEK
      Escort them to the Vault.

As TWO DALEKS glide over to the
Doctor & Rose -

           SUPREME DALEK (CONT'D)
      What of the Human cargo?

                 DALEK 1
      Test subjects now boarding.

               THE DOCTOR
      What sort of tests? What are
      you doing with this Crucible-
      thing?

              SUPREME DALEK
      You are the playthings of
      Davros, now. Take him!

As the Daleks manoeuvre around the
Doctor & Rose, the Doctor glances
across -

CAPTAIN JACK is on the floor.
Face down. But alive! Keeping
very still, his eye catching the
Doctor's.

The Doctor catches the look. Then
turns and goes, with Rose and the
Dalek escort.
```

FROM: BENJAMIN COOK TO: RUSSELL T DAVIES
TUESDAY 15 JANUARY 2008 13:16:44 GMT

RE: HAPPY NEW YEAR?

>>I e-mailed Julie about an hour ago, to ask where we stand with Camille and her agent.<<

And what has Julie said? What will decide: the story or the desire to give Camille a fair crack of the whip?

>>I *really* worry that since Jackie's given birth and has little Tony at home (Tony Tyler!), she'd never enter a bloody battle zone.<<

You could say the same of Sarah Jane, though. She has Luke waiting for her back home. If the world is about to end, I suppose you do whatever necessary to save that world and the people in it that you care about most.

FROM: RUSSELL T DAVIES TO: BENJAMIN COOK
TUESDAY 15 JANUARY 2008 13:40:41 GMT

RE: HAPPY NEW YEAR?

Julie has more or less told me to do what I want. Although, unusually for Julie, who always says 'write what you want', she did add, 'A bit more for Jackie would be great, though,' so I think that's a hint. I'm tempted to see what a Sarah/Mickey/Jackie combo would be like, so I might try it out this afternoon. I do love Jackie. But in the end: story wins. In the past, we've booked actors and then paid them off in order to get rid of them. A producer – a bad producer – will always say, 'But we've contracted them, we're paying them!' And I always reply, 'Yes, but we're paying them anyway, so it doesn't matter if they're in it or not.' Plus, you do spend less on them if you don't use them, on overnights and per diems. So there.

I don't think I need to worry about a reason for Mickey needing Jackie. That *would* start to get convoluted. I'm already having to shoehorn in lines about Dimension Jumps needing another half-hour to recharge and awful caveats like that, to stop the cast teleporting all over the place. Instead, I think it's very Jackie to just turn up. Like a nag. 'I'm not staying behind! Where's my daughter?!' There, motivation in one line, accurate character work and a bit of a laugh.

FROM: RUSSELL T DAVIES TO: BENJAMIN COOK
TUESDAY 15 JANUARY 2008 14:53:03 GMT

RE: HAPPY NEW YEAR?

I was on Page 19 and set myself a target: if I could add Jackie and make trims here and there so that the end result is *still* 19 pages, then she could stay. And I have. So she is. Hooray! She first appears in a new Scene 5:

```
5. EXT. BIG WIDE STREET - NIGHT

SARAH JANE about to run off,
```

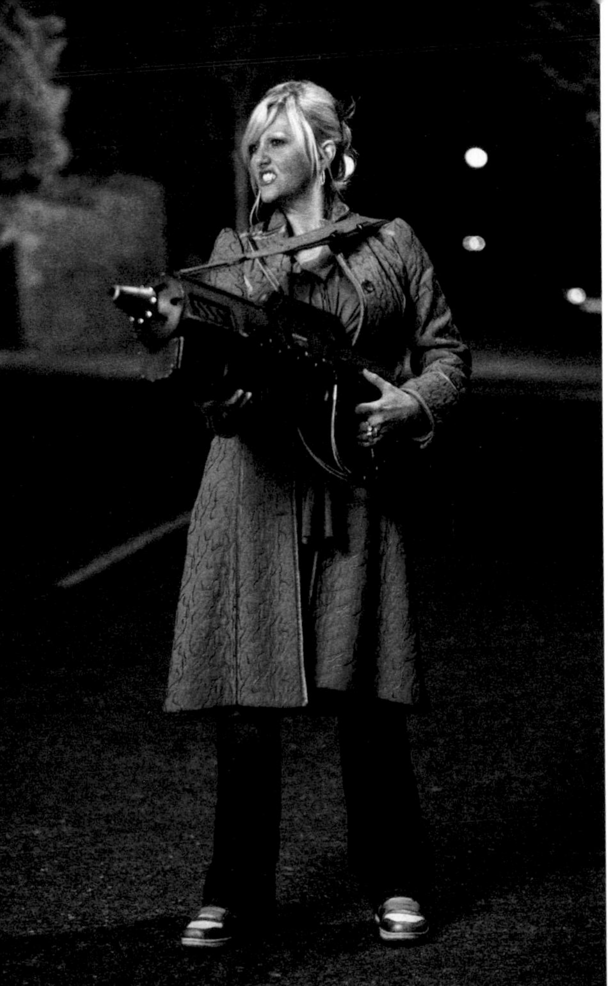

Jackie Tyler (Camille Coduri) makes it to the party after all.

grabbing her bag from the car -

SARAH JANE
The Tardis landed on Dexeter Road, come on, we can't take the car -

But MICKEY turns, as he's hit by PRAC WIND -

MICKEY
Ohhh no, I told her, I said, you can't come! She never listens - !

FX: HARD CRACK OF WHITE LIGHT, and standing there - JACKIE TYLER! With a big sci-fi gun.

MICKEY (CONT'D)
That gun is bigger than you!

JACKIE
I am not staying behind! Not while my daughter's in danger, now where is she?
(big smile at Sarah)
Jackie Tyler. Rose's mum.

Sarah looks at her like the world has gone mad.

Then she just turns and runs - Mickey & Jackie following -

And then, of course, she's in (what's now) Scene 12, where Sarah Jane and Mickey (and now Jackie) surrender themselves to the Daleks.

FROM: RUSSELL T DAVIES TO: BENJAMIN COOK
WEDNESDAY 16 JANUARY 2008 02:21:45 GMT

RE: HAPPY NEW YEAR?

35. EXT. SQUARE - NIGHT[2]

Ordinary square, not town-centre, just a suburban open space. A row of PEOPLE being marched along, all scared, defeated, hands-on-heads. DALEKS guarding them. In the line: SARAH JANE, MICKEY & JACKIE.

DALEK 1
Prisoners will stand together!

CUT TO WIDER, the line joining a group of AS MANY EXTRAS AS POSSIBLE. All hands-on-heads. Muttering, as they join:

MICKEY
Great idea, this was. Next time you need saving...

SARAH JANE
How did you find me, anyway?

JACKIE
Oh, he's always going on about you, Sarah Jane this and Sarah Jane that. I think he's got a bit of a thing about you.

SARAH JANE
(pleased)
Really? Is that true?

2 The addition of Scene 5 (introducing Jackie) has shifted all subsequent scene numbers, so the extermination of Captain Jack on the Crucible Command Deck is now Scene 34, followed by this, Scene 35, in a suburban square.

JACKIE
As a mother figure.

SARAH JANE
Oh, right, thanks.

DALEKS now gliding back:

DALEK 1
Test subjects ready for transport!

MICKEY
Test subjects?! What does that mean – ?!

FX: WIDE SHOT, the ENTIRE GROUP in a TELEPORT GLOW -

CUT TO:

36. INT. DALEK CORRIDOR - NIGHT

CU ON A DALEK, barking instructions:

DALEK 1
Prisoners will march in this direction. Immediately!

WIDER: a CORRIDOR on the Crucible; dark metal, industrial. Full of the GROUP OF PEOPLE, still hands-on heads, including SARAH JANE, MICKEY & JACKIE. DALEKS on guard.

They start to march towards Dalek 1. Sotto:

MICKEY
Testing what, though?

Mickey, Sarah Jane and Jackie are marched aboard the Dalek ship.

SARAH JANE
We're on board the Crucible, that's the important thing. One step closer to the Doctor…

CUT TO:

37. EXT. GERMAN FOREST - NIGHT

MARTHA making her way across rough ground, bracken. It's cold, dark, creepy. But she keeps going.

CUT TO:

38. EXT. COTTAGE, GERMAN FOREST - NIGHT

MARTHA steps out on to a rough track. Heading towards…

A COTTAGE. Standing on its own, in the forest. Sinister; dark and abandoned. But somehow, sort of… waiting.

As she walks closer…

A voice calls out, in German.

OLD WOMAN
<There's no one here. Whatever you want, just go away. Leave me alone.>

She's old, hostile, standing by the cottage door.

MARTHA
<My name is Martha Jones.>

OLD WOMAN
<I don't care who you are.>

MARTHA
<UNIT operative five six six seven one. Rank, medical officer.>

OLD WOMAN
<They said you might come.>
(in English, now)
The accent, what is that? London?

MARTHA
Yeah.

OLD WOMAN
I went to London. Long time ago. You travel, a long way.

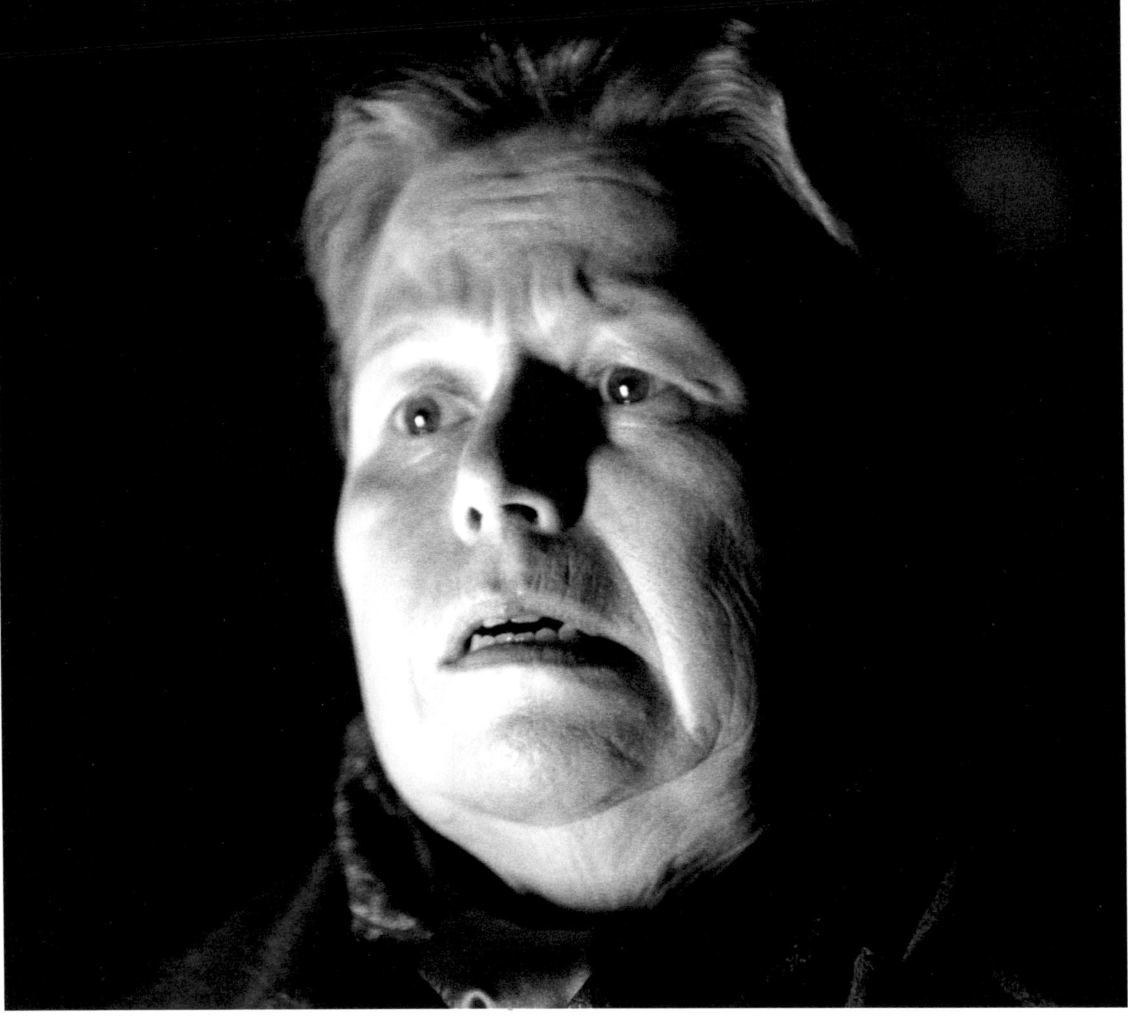

'I went to London. Long time ago.' Martha meets the real guardian of the Osterhagen Station – an Old Woman (Valda Aviks).

```
MARTHA
Thought this place was
supposed to be guarded.

OLD WOMAN
They were soldiers, jah.
Boys. I brought them food,
every day. When die Alptraume
came from the sky… They ran.

MARTHA
They're meant to stay on
duty.

OLD WOMAN
They had families, lovers,
children. They went home to
die. But not you, I think…?

MARTHA
I've got a job to do.

And she walks past the old woman,
heads inside.
```

I can feel already that the Martha stuff is in the wrong place. It should come later. But I'll let it stand for now. Lindsey Alford has someone lined up to translate the German dialogue properly tomorrow.

FROM: RUSSELL T DAVIES TO: BENJAMIN COOK
THURSDAY 17 JANUARY 2008 02:41:51 GMT

RE: HAPPY NEW YEAR?

I've added two scenes – a new 37 and 38 – with Donna and Doctor #2:

```
37. FX SHOT

FX: THE CRUCIBLE. And the TARDIS
fades into sight, gliding along,
spinning slowly (the windows
repaired now, intact).

CUT TO:
```

38. INT. TARDIS - NIGHT

Back to its spooky LOW-LIGHTING STATE. THE DOCTOR #2 is by the door, smoothing the now-intact windows (portholes fixed too); he's now in the BLUE SUIT, though jacketless.

THE DOCTOR #2
All repaired. Lovely. Sssh!

And he runs back to the console. DONNA is there; just boggling at him. As he shucks on his jacket:

THE DOCTOR #2 (CONT'D)
Silent running. Like they do in submarines, so no one can hear us. Can't even drop a spanner. Don't drop a spanner!
(of the suit)
I like blue. What d'you think?

DONNA
You. Are. Bonkers.

THE DOCTOR #2
Why, what's wrong with blue?

DONNA
Is that what Time Lords do? Lop a bit off, grow another one? You're like… worms!

THE DOCTOR #2
No, I'm unique. There's never been another like me, not ever. Cos all that regeneration energy went into the hand. Look at my hand! Love that hand! But then you touched it, wham! Instantaneous biological metacrisis, I grew, out of you. Still. Could be worse.

DONNA
Oy! Watch it, spaceman!

THE DOCTOR #2
Oy! Watch it, Earthgirl!… Oh. I sound like you. I sound all sort of… rough.

DONNA
Oy!

THE DOCTOR #2
Oy!

Donna gets acquainted with the newly grown Doctor.

DONNA
Oy!!

THE DOCTOR #2
Spanners! Sssh!
(realising)
But I must've picked up a bit of your voice, that's all. Is it? Did I? No! Oh you are kidding me, no way!
(feels chest)
One heart. I've got one heart! This body's got only one heart!

DONNA
What, like you're Human?

THE DOCTOR #2
Ohhh that's disgusting.

DONNA
Oy!

THE DOCTOR #2
Oy!

DONNA
Stop it!

THE DOCTOR #2
But I am… No, wait, I'm… part Time Lord, part Human. Well isn't that wizard?!
(smiles)
You did that, Donna! You!

DONNA
It's like… I kept hearing that noise, that heartbeat…

THE DOCTOR #2
That was me. My single heart. Cos I'm a complicated event in time and space, it must have rippled back. Calling to you.

DONNA
Why me?

THE DOCTOR #2
Cos you're special.

DONNA
Don't be daft, no I'm not.

THE DOCTOR #2
But you are, you're… Oh. You really don't believe that, do you?
(of his own head)
I can see, Donna. What you're thinking. All that attitude. All that lip. Cos all this time… you think you're not worth it.

DONNA
(quiet)
Stop it.

THE DOCTOR #2
Shouting at the world. Cos no one's listening. Why should they?

DONNA
(hurt)
Doctor. Stop it.

THE DOCTOR #2
(goes to her, kind)
But look at what you did. No, it's more than that, it's like… we were always heading for this.

CU Doctor & Donna over the next speech; PAINT THIS with silent flashbacks; Donna the Bride, arriving in the Tardis; Donna in 4.1, seeing him again; Wilf; then sc.50 from 4.1, Donna leaving her car as the Tardis appears behind it.

THE DOCTOR #2 (CONT'D)
You came to the Tardis. Then you found me again. Your Grandad! And your car, Donna, your car, you parked your car right where the Tardis was going to land, that's not coincidence, oh we've been blind. Something's been drawing us together. For such a long time.

DONNA
You're talking like… destiny. There's no such thing, is there?

THE DOCTOR #2
Then what is it? Who is it…?

DONNA
(sad smile)
Still doesn't mean I'm special. I was just moved into the right place.

THE DOCTOR #2
Stop saying that. You're wonderful. I wish you could believe that.

DONNA
Yep. Still. I've done what I need to do, now.

THE DOCTOR #2
(stares to distance)
No, it's like there's more… Like the pattern's not complete, the strands are still drawing together… But heading for what?

This is followed by Martha making her way through the forest, and then arriving at the cottage. Of course, the additional two scenes with Donna and Doctor #2 shift all subsequent scene numbers, so Martha's first encounter with the old German woman is now Scene 40, followed by this, 41, inside the cottage…

41. INT. COTTAGE - NIGHT

Inside, it's dark, bare. MARTHA knows what to do, goes straight to an internal wall. Pulls a wooden table and chair away from it. Then takes down a picture, off the wall. Behind it: a PALM PRINT READER. Martha places her palm over the screen. It glows, beeps -

During this, the OLD WOMAN stays in the doorway. Talks to Martha; Martha keeps her back to her, focused on the job.

OLD WOMAN
London, in those days. To see it! So much glamour. That was the word, glamour. And I was so young.
(pause)
I heard the soldiers talking. Many times. They would speak of the Osterhagen Key.
(pause)
I think London must be changed now, yes? But still. The glamour.

- and on the beep, a DOOR slides open in the wall. Opening into a metal box; a LIFT.

And Martha hears a click. A safety catch.

Looks back round.

The Old Woman is pointing a revolver at her. Scared.

OLD WOMAN (CONT'D)
You will stop. You will not go.

But Martha remains utterly calm. Fixed.

MARTHA
I've got no choice.

OLD WOMAN
I know the Key. What it does. <You are the nightmare! It's not them, it's you! I should kill you, right here, right now!>

MARTHA
Then do it.

And Martha just steps into the lift.

The Old Woman lowers her gun, defeated, shaking.

OLD WOMAN
<You're going straight to Hell!>

As the door closes on her, quieter:

MARTHA
I know.

CUT TO:

Martha descends into the depths of Osterhagen Station One.

Davros has the Doctor just where he wants him.

42. INT. LIFT SHAFT - NIGHT

The lift descending…

CUT TO:

43. INT. LIFT/OSTERHAGEN STATION ONE - NIGHT

MARTHA in the lift. It pings, stops. Door opens…

She steps out into OSTERHAGEN STATION ONE. A small room, lined with plain COMPUTER BANKS. One chair, one desk. On the desk, a panel, designed to fit the Key.

Martha looks at one wall. FOUR SMALL TV SCREENS, labelled CHINA, ALASKA, ARGENTINA, LIBERIA. All showing static. Martha clicks a button, opening comms.

MARTHA
This is Osterhagen Station One. Is there anyone there? Repeat, this is Osterhagen Station One. My name is Martha Jones. Can anyone hear me…?

CUT TO:

44. INT. CRUCIBLE VAULTS - NIGHT

CU DAVROS.

DAVROS
Activate the Holding Cells.

CU THE DOCTOR - BRIGHT WHITE SPOTLIGHT slams down on him.

CU ROSE - BRIGHT WHITE SPOTLIGHT slams down on her.

WIDE SHOT. DAVROS in his chair, the Doctor under a vertical shaft of light, Rose in another, both a good distance apart, deliberately separated.

DAVROS (CONT'D)
Excellent. Even when powerless, a Time Lord is best contained.

THE DOCTOR
Good to know you're scared of me.

Said reaching out, and, just as he thought -

FX: A RIPPLE of forcefield, in the shape of the LIGHT-SHAFT.

Davros glides over to him.

DAVROS
It is time we talked, Doctor. After so very long. After the -

THE DOCTOR
- no no no, we're not doing the nostalgia tour, you can keep the photo albums, Davros, I want to know what's happening, right here, right now, cos the Supreme Dalek said Vault, yeah? We're in the Vault? As in, dungeon? Cellar? Prison? You're not in charge of the Daleks, are you? They've got you down here like, what, a servant? Slave? Court jester? Pet?

DAVROS
(rattled)
We have… an arrangement.

THE DOCTOR
Yeah, you do all the work, they get all the glory! And then what? Cos they hate you, Davros, the Daleks hate you, for being flesh, soon as they're finished with you, they'll kill you all over again!

Davros glides towards Rose.

DAVROS
So very full of fire, is he not? And to think. You crossed entire universes, to find him again.

ROSE
How d'you know that…?

'She is mine. To do as I please.' Rose is a prisoner of Davros.

THE DOCTOR
Leave her alone.

DAVROS
She is mine. To do as I please.

ROSE
Then why am I still alive? What's all this for?

DAVROS
You must be here. It was foretold. Even the Supreme Dalek would not dare to contradict the prophecies of Dalek Caan.

Across the ROOM, *slam!*, DALEK CAAN illuminates on its plinth.

DALEK CAAN
…so cold and dark and hot, and the Doctor burns at the centre…

ROSE
What is that thing?

```
            THE DOCTOR
A Dalek. But it flew through
the Time Vortex. Unprotected.

            DAVROS
Caan did more than that,
he saw Time. Its infinite
complexity and majesty,
burning in his mind. And he
saw you. Both of you.

            THE DOCTOR
Saw what? Dalek Caan? What
did you see?

            DALEK CAAN
The Doctor will be here. At
the end of everything. The
Doctor and his Children of
Time.
        (giggles)
And one of them will die.

            THE DOCTOR
Was it you, Caan? Did you
kill Donna? Why did the
Tardis door close?, tell me!

            DAVROS
          (gleeful)
Ohh that's it! The anger!
The fire! The rage of a Time
Lord who butchered millions,
there he is!

The Doctor boiling; but he makes
himself shut up.

            DAVROS (CONT'D)
Why so shy? Show your
companion. Show her your true
self. Dalek Caan has promised
me that, too.

            DALEK CAAN
At the time of the ending.
The Doctor's soul will be
revealed.

            THE DOCTOR
...what does that mean?

            DAVROS
We'll discover it together.
Our final journey. Because
the ending approaches; the
testing begins!

            THE DOCTOR
Testing of what?

            DAVROS
The Reality Bomb.
```

The Doctor meeting Davros! (You'll noticed that I've moved some of his dialogue from the earlier scene on the Crucible Command Deck – the one where Captain Jack is exterminated – to this most recent one.) Davros is hard to write. It's so easy to find yourself starting every line with 'So, Doctor…' and all that crap.

FROM: BENJAMIN COOK TO: RUSSELL T DAVIES
THURSDAY 17 JANUARY 2008 20:52:24 GMT

RE: HAPPY NEW YEAR?

I've just watched the first episode of Series Two of *Skins*. *Radio Times* biked it over to me. I'm interviewing Bryan Elsley for them next week. Oh, Russell… it's much better than Series One. I'm ridiculously happy about that. I can't wait for you to see this second series when it airs on E4 next month. Also, it seems that the blond gay one, Maxxie (played by Mitch Hewer), is the lead for the first half of the series, so you've *got* to watch. You're Number One Gay!

FROM: RUSSELL T DAVIES TO: BENJAMIN COOK
THURSDAY 17 JANUARY 2008 21:04:03 GMT

RE: HAPPY NEW YEAR?

Good for *Skins*! I mean that. I will watch, because I feel quite attached to that show, if only because we talked about Series One so much. (And did I mention Tony in his pants?) Isn't Tony all crippled and sick in Series Two? That's one way to reinvent a character. You can tell that Beautiful Maxxie is the new lead by the way that he dances half-naked through the trailer. And into my arms. Oh, they know their trailers, those *Skins* boys.

I fell asleep this afternoon. Bad move. I only woke up 20 minutes ago. Still a bit dazed. I spent today rearranging things (I've got Jackie and Mickey arriving at the same time now, in the same FX shot – of course, duh, how stupid was I?) and seeding information in the right place. I realised that Rose spent time in 4.11 telling Donna that she was super-important for reasons *beyond* 4.11's plot, but now she forgets to mention it to her, so I fixed things like that. Also, I realised that the Doctor is happily pointing to his hand-in-a-jar at the beginning, with Rose just standing there. Rose should be like, 'What?! Your hand *what?!*'

FROM: RUSSELL T DAVIES TO: BENJAMIN COOK
THURSDAY 17 JANUARY 2008 23:50:31 GMT

RE: HAPPY NEW YEAR?

I am writing. Jackie Tyler is about to die. I love Jackie about to die!

FROM: BENJAMIN COOK TO: RUSSELL T DAVIES
FRIDAY 18 JANUARY 2008 00:10:09 GMT

RE: HAPPY NEW YEAR?

You can't kill Jackie Tyler! She has a son now!

Kill him instead.

FROM: RUSSELL T DAVIES TO: BENJAMIN COOK
FRIDAY 18 JANUARY 2008 02:59:55 GMT

RE: HAPPY NEW YEAR?

I've started to write rubbish now. Always a sign. A sign saying: 'STOP'. I really wanted to write more, which means that I won't finish tomorrow after all, and then I have to go to Hull this weekend. I cut two scenes – Scenes 5 (where Jackie arrives, because she and Mickey now arrive together in Scene 2) and 35 (prisoners being marched along in the town square) – but added a new scene straight after Martha's descent in the lift shaft:

```
40. INT. DALEK CORRIDOR - NIGHT

CAPTAIN JACK, lying dead on a
PALLET, TWO DALEKS either side.

                DALEK 2
   Commence disposal.
   Incinerate!

A PANEL in the wall slides open.
Then the PALLET slides in, Jack's
body disappearing through, gone.
Panel closes.

                DALEK 3
   Disposal completed.

Both Daleks glide away.

Pause, slow TRACK IN to the closed
panel, and...

Jack slides it open! Poking his
head through. RED LIGHT behind him.
He's gasping; it's hot in there!
```

This has shifted subsequent scene numbers, so Davros meeting the Doctor (originally 44) is now Scene 43, followed by this, Scene 44, in the Crucible Test Area…

```
44. INT. CRUCIBLE TEST AREA - NIGHT

SARAH JANE, MICKEY, JACKIE & PEOPLE
being escorted by DALEKS through
a door, joining OTHER PRISONERS.
Looking up:

                MICKEY
   This place is massive...!

FX: WIDE SHOT. The 'corridor' is
a vast space - like, if not the
same as, the UNIT WAREHOUSE from
4.11, sc.45 onwards. Dark, cold
metal, industrial, with added DMP
BUTTRESSES leading up to the roof.
CROWD & DALEK MULTIPLICATION; many
people arranged in groups, leading
away into the distance, Daleks
guarding them.
```

DALEK 1
Prisoners will stand in designated area! Move!

As they walk forward, one WOMAN collapses to her knees, exhausted. The Dalek glides over.

DALEK 1 (CONT'D)
On your feet. On your feet!

Fast, Sarah Jane looking round - she's next to a door - no Daleks looking - gets out the SONIC LIPSTICK, whirrs, the door opens soundlessly - she hisses, 'Mickey!' -

He spins round - hisses 'Jackie!' - runs - !

Jackie is a few feet ahead, looks back - turns -

But the Dalek turns away from the now-standing woman, its sucker-arm cutting across Jackie.

DALEK 1 (CONT'D)
You will move forward!

Jackie stopped, looking across -

The door closing on a horrified Sarah Jane & Mickey -

CU TO OTHER SIDE OF THE CLOSED DOOR, a small, dark space.

MICKEY
We can't just leave her - !

'We can't just leave her!' Jackie is in terrible danger...

... while Sarah Jane and Mickey watch in horror.

SARAH JANE
No Mickey, wait - !

The door has a GLASS PANEL. And on the TEST AREA side, a DALEK glides in front of the door, stations itself there. Facing into the Test Area, not seeing, behind it: Sarah & Mickey looking through the glass panel, in horror, at:

Jackie - with a glance back, not wanting to give them away - having to join the rest of the GROUP.

DALEK 1
Prisoners will stand still. Testing will commence in thirty rels.

Jackie is standing next to the woman who fell.

WOMAN
What do they mean? What are they testing, what are they gonna do?

DALEK 1
Test cycle initiating.

The sound of power building, a deep, throbbing hum...

JACKIE
Reckon it's that thing there...

Jackie & woman looking up.

FX: ROOF. They're standing under a WIDE METAL CIRCLE, with a PALE WHITE CENTRE. Which starts to PULSE.

CUT TO:

45. INT. CRUCIBLE COMMAND DECK - NIGHT

SUPREME DALEK with DALEKS gliding to and fro f/g, busy.

SUPREME DALEK
Testing calibration of Reality Bomb! Firing in 20 rels, 19, 18…

CUT TO:

46. INT. CRUCIBLE VAULTS - NIGHT

SUPREME DALEK'S countdown continues OOV, 17, 16, 15…

DAVROS gliding forward, THE DOCTOR & ROSE still trapped.

DAVROS
You will bear witness, Doctor. Behold the apotheosis of my genius.

FX: VIEWSCREEN blinks on, MID-AIR, showing FX SHOT 1 from sc.44, the WIDE SHOT of CRUCIBLE TEST AREA.

CUT TO:

47. INT. CRUCIBLE TEST AREA - NIGHT

SUPREME DALEK'S countdown continues OOV, 8, 7, 6, 5…

SARAH JANE & MICKEY trapped behind their door, THE BACK OF THE DALEK visible through the glass panel, JACKIE & CROWD beyond that. Hushed, but fierce -

MICKEY
We've got to get her out!

SARAH JANE
We can't!

MICKEY
But that's Jackie!!

CUT TO:

48. INT. CRUCIBLE COMMAND DECK - NIGHT

SUPREME DALEK
…2, 1, zero! Activate planetary alignment field!

CUT TO:

49. INT. CRUCIBLE VAULTS - NIGHT

WHOLE ROOM SHUDDERS. THE DOCTOR staggering in the spotlight -

THE DOCTOR
What's a Reality Bomb? Davros! What are you doing??

And Davros *giggles*.

CUT TO:

Davros has a bit of a giggle. Possibly.

50. INT. TARDIS - NIGHT

Room SHUDDERS. THE DOCTOR #2 & DONNA stagger, recover - running to the scanner -

THE DOCTOR #2
What was that...?
(reads display)
It's the planets. The 27 planets! Look at them!

CUT TO:

51. FX SHOT

FX: THE PLANETARY ARRAY. Close on a number of planets. They begin to SHINE with HALOES OF ENERGY. Rising and falling, like a programmed sequence, flaring with light around their circumference, falling, then rising again...

FX: WIDER SHOT of the ARRAY, the PLANETS FLARING...

CUT TO:

52. EXT. NOBLES' HOUSE - NIGHT

WILF standing outside, looking up. The sound of power, throbbing all around. SYLVIA in the door, scared.

SYLVIA
- Dad, get off the street, there's still Daleks out there -

WILF
But look at it Sylvia. What are they doing up there...?

FX: LOW ANGLE WILF, the PLANETARY ARRAY SKY above him, the PLANETS halo-ing in sequence...

CUT TO:

53. INT. CRUCIBLE TEST AREA - NIGHT

JACKIE, the WOMAN & all the PEOPLE looking up in horror...

FX: ABOVE, the CENTRE OF THE CIRCLE pulsing, brighter...

Jackie looks across, helpless.

SARAH JANE & MICKEY, trapped behind their door, the DALEK still stationed in front. Staring, mute, terrified.

CUT TO:

54. INT. CRUCIBLE VAULTS - NIGHT

THE DOCTOR, ROSE, DAVROS stare up at the OOV viewscreen...

THE DOCTOR
But that's Neutronic Energy... Flattened by the alignment of the planets into a single string... No! Davros, you can't! *No!*

CUT TO:

55. INT. TARDIS - NIGHT

THE DOCTOR #2 & DONNA at the scanner -

THE DOCTOR #2
Single-string neutrinos compressed into... No way!

CUT TO:

56. FX SHOT

FX: WIDE SHOT, PLANETARY ARRAY, noise reaching a crescendo as ALL THE PLANETS SHINE WITH HALOES together!

CUT TO:

57. EXT. NOBLES' HOUSE - NIGHT

CU WILF & SYLVIA shield their eyes, as a terrible WHITE LIGHT shines down on them...

CUT TO:

58. INT. CRUCIBLE TEST AREA - NIGHT

JACKIE, WOMAN & PEOPLE looking up...

FX: CENTRE OF THE CIRCLE now GLOWING! FIERCE!

CUT TO SARAH JANE & MICKEY, desperate -

A *ping*. Mickey realises! Gets out his YELLOW-PENDANT!

MICKEY
Thirty minutes - !!

His face at the glass. Holding the pendant! At Jackie. Mouthing the words, frantic, 'It's recharged, use it!'

Jackie gets out her YELLOW-PENDANT. Upset, to the woman:

JACKIE
I'm sorry.

She presses the centre.

FX: HARD CRACK OF WHITE LIGHT, she VANISHES -

CUT TO JACKIE - slam, straight into a hug with Mickey! She's now in their closed-off section. But during all this, the noise is building, building, building…

Sarah Jane is still staring through the glass. Horrified.

FX: THE CENTRE OF THE CIRCLE now BLINDING -

FX: THE PEOPLE. As they begin to… divide. Their bodies, clothes, everything, slowly, even gently, floating into discrete particles. No pain, just dissolution.

FX: CLOSE on the WOMAN, as she divides into particles…

The Reality Bomb is tested.

FX: WIDE SHOT TEST AREA, all the CROWD MULTIPLICATION PEOPLE becoming like floating dust… and the DALEKS remain intact.

CU Sarah Jane, Mickey, Jackie, staring at the window…

FX: the PARTICLES drift into floating DUST, into NOTHING.

A Dalek glides forward into the empty space.

DALEK 1
Test completed.

FX: WIDE SHOT with DMP BUTTRESSES, and MULTIPLICATION DALEKS. But empty, so empty; not a remnant of the people.

CUT TO:

59. FX SHOT

FX: WIDE SHOT, PLANETARY ARRAY. The SHINING HALOES fade away. NOISE powers down, gone.

CUT TO:

60. EXT. CRUCIBLE VAULTS - NIGHT

(Viewscreen gone now.) DAVROS quiet, triumphant:

DAVROS
The unravelling of life itself. A success, wouldn't you say?

THE DOCTOR
And that was just a test…?

ROSE
What is it, what happened?

DAVROS
Electrical energy, Miss Tyler. Every atom in existence is bound by an electrical field. The Reality Bomb cancels out it out. And that test was focused on living subjects only. The full transmission will dissolve every form of matter.

ROSE
…the stars are going out.

THE DOCTOR
The 27 planets. They become one, vast transmitter. Blasting that wavelength...

Davros gradually building in pitch, to classic Hitler-rant:

DAVROS
Across the entire universe. Never stopping, never faltering, never fading. People and planets and stars will become dust, and the dust will become atoms, and the atoms will become nothing. And the wavelength will continue! Through the Rift at the heart of the Medusa Cascade! Into every dimension! Every parallel! Every single corner of creation! This is my ultimate victory, Doctor! The destruction of *reality itself!!*

You wouldn't believe the stuff that I'm cutting as I go along. Stuff that I'd planned in my head, but then, no, too expensive or too long or just rubbish, so I never write a word of it. Even though it was alive and possible until… ooh, yesterday. Like, Doctor #2 and Donna were going to go back to the Shadow Proclamation and enlist a fleet of Judoon ships! And attack the Medusa Cascade! Blimey! Madness, I know. It would have been good, though. Roughly ten FX shots of Judoon ships flying and attacking Dalek saucers, etc.

FROM: RUSSELL T DAVIES TO: BENJAMIN COOK
SATURDAY 19 JANUARY 2008 03:24:20 GMT

RE: HAPPY NEW YEAR?

59. INT. CRUCIBLE COMMAND DECK - NIGHT[3]

THE SUPREME DALEK, as invigorated as Davros:

SUPREME DALEK
Test: successful! Prepare for maximum detonation!

'All hail the Dalek Race!'

FOUR DALEKS
We obey!

SUPREME DALEK
The Daleks will not simply rule the universe! We will be the universe! All hail the Daleks!

FX: WIDE SHOT, all the DALEKS chanting:

ALL DALEKS
All hail the Dalek Race!

CUT TO:

60. INT. CRUCIBLE VAULTS - NIGHT

THE DOCTOR & ROSE still in SPOTLIGHTS; looking up, hearing the sound of MASSIVE HYDRAULICS. DAVROS calmer, now:

DAVROS
It begins! Finally, we will

3 Scenes 49 and 52 have been cut, shifting all subsequent scene numbers, so Davros' Hitler-rant ('The destruction of *reality itself!!*') is now Scene 58, followed by this, Scene 59, on the Crucible Command Deck.

'I saw the surface of the planet only once...' Young Davros observes the ruined world of Skaro. Illustration by Russell T Davies.

achieve all that I have ever wanted. Peace. Everlasting peace.

THE DOCTOR
They'll kill you, Davros. Once it's done. Cos the Daleks despise you, for being flesh. Ohh, you will be exterminated.

DAVROS
As I said, Doctor. Peace.

Silence, as Davros glides away from them. Hold.

Only the noise of huge hydraulics from above. The Doctor looking up, trapped, helpless.

But Rose is looking at Davros. She's quiet, sad:

ROSE
What happened to you? I mean your face. Your eyes. What happened?

DAVROS
Are you showing me pity, Miss Tyler?

ROSE
Someone must have. Once upon a time.

DAVROS
(quiet)
Not for so many years. But I was like you, back then. Walking tall, so young and so proud. On a world called Skaro. A world at war.

ROSE
With who...?

DAVROS
With each other. My race, the Kaleds, in perpetual battle against the Thals. My very first memory; hiding underground, with the screams of battle above. I saw the surface of the planet, only once...

On CU Davros...

MIX TO:

61. EXT. SKARO - DAY

FX: CU DAVROS, the MAN. Gaunt, strong, in a dirty-white medic's coat. FX for the BOILING RED SKY behind him...

FX: REVERSE. DAVROS a small

figure on a VAST PLAIN. DMP of a RUINED WORLD. A shattered domed city; weird, warped cliffs in the distance. NUCLEAR CLOUDS in the sky.

CUT TO:

62. INT. CRUCIBLE VAULTS - NIGHT

DAVROS
And I swore, then. To end it. I pledged my life, to help my people, to ensure their survival.

CUT TO:

63. INT. HOSPITAL WARD - DAY

These images are now cranked up, wild & jittery, only glimpsed. It's like a WORLD WAR I WARD. But WINDOWLESS, underground. INJURED SOLDIERS, bandaged, WOMEN in simple nurses' uniforms, running, panicking.

JUMP CUTS of DAVROS the MAN, going from bed to bed. Studying one SOLDIER, opening his eyelid, shining a torch; preparing a syringe; injecting the soldier. The soldier thrashing in agony; Davros & Nurse holding him down.

DAVROS OOV
I studied the soldiers. Their frailty. Their pain. I sought to find a way, to free them from the agonies of the flesh. And then…

PRAC FX: EXPLOSION, Davros silhouetted against FIRE -

Glimpsed, jagged images - nurses - screaming - running -

CU Davros, his head now BALD, red, peeling; holding both hands over his face, so he can't be seen. He's screaming.

CUT TO:

64. INT. CRUCIBLE VAULTS - NIGHT

DAVROS
…I became victim myself. Perhaps it was necessary. To inspire me.

THE DOCTOR
…except you weren't helping those soldiers. You were

'The one thing Davros isn't expecting, is another me!' Doctor #2 puts the finishing touches to his device.

experimenting on them. You even experimented on your own family. Twisting the evolution of the Kaled Race, until they became the Daleks.

DALEK CAAN
(giggling)
We were born! Out of blood!

DAVROS
(still at Rose)
Can you imagine? I had one idea! An idea that has never stopped. Rolling out across the centuries. I have slept, and woken, and died, and every time I open my eyes, there they are. My Daleks. Outlasting eternity. And all from one man!

THE DOCTOR
Oh, but every time you open your eyes, Davros… There's me.

CUT TO:

65. INT. TARDIS - NIGHT

DOCTOR #2 at work, feverish, building things out of the console itself, a handheld DEVICE of wires & bits & pieces.

THE DOCTOR #2
- and the one thing Davros isn't expecting, is another me!

DONNA
So what's that thing…?

THE DOCTOR #2
Davros gave himself away, back on the Subwave. He said one thing, that gives us hope. Cos it's all down to you and me now, Donna, we're the only ones left…

CUT TO:

66. INT. CRUCIBLE TEST AREA, ANTECHAMBER - NIGHT

MICKEY ducking down as a DALEK

glides past, seen through the glass panel. To SARAH JANE, behind him:

MICKEY
There's Daleks everywhere! We're never gonna find the Doctor, there's nothing we can do -!

WHAM! A BIG PANEL OF METAL in the wall is booted out -

And there's CAPTAIN JACK! Clambering out!

CAPTAIN JACK
Just my luck, I climb through two miles of ventilation shafts, chasing life signs on this thing -
(the wrist strap)
And who do I find? Mickey Smith. Boy, is this a bad day.

MICKEY
You can talk, Captain Cheesecake.

Then a big grin, and they give each other a hug.

CAPTAIN JACK
Good to see ya. That's beefcake.

MICKEY
Yeah, and that's enough hugging.

CAPTAIN JACK
We meet at last, Sarah Jane.

Turning to her, with a big smile and a salute. But he stops dead. Sarah Jane is quiet.

SARAH JANE
There is something we can do.
(close to tears)
You've got to understand. I've got a son. Down there on Earth. He's only 14 years old.
(pause)
I brought this.

From her bag, she holds up…

A TINY DIAMOND. On a chain.

FX: a small SHINE of STARLIGHT around it, then gone.

SARAH JANE (CONT'D)
It was given to me by a Verron Soothsayer. He said… This is for the End of Days.

CAPTAIN JACK
Is that…?

He takes it. Holds it up. In awe:

CAPTAIN JACK (CONT'D)
A Warp Star.

MICKEY
Gonna tell me what a Warp Star is?

CAPTAIN JACK
A warpfold conjugation trapped in a carbonised shell. It's an explosion, Mickey. An explosion waiting to happen.

CUT TO:

67. INT. OSTERHAGEN STATION ONE - NIGHT

FULL FRAME CHINESE WOMAN on TV SCREEN; she's young, scared.

CHINESE WOMAN
…this is Osterhagen Station Five. Are you receiving, Station One?

CUT TO MARTHA, watching the screens.

Chinese Woman (Elizabeth Tan) in Osterhagen Station Five.

MARTHA
I've got you. That makes three of us. And three is all we need.

Her REVERSE: THE TV SCREENS. Chinese Woman on the CHINA screen, a YOUNG MAN on LIBERIA - he's tense, grim - the other two screens showing static. (Woman & Man shot against identical Osterhagen Station walls)

CHINESE WOMAN
My name is Anna Zhou, what's yours?

MARTHA
Martha Jones. What about you, Station Three? You never said.

LIBERIAN MAN
I don't want my name on this. Given what we're about to do.

CHINESE WOMAN
So what happens now? Do we do it?

MARTHA
No. Not yet.

CHINESE WOMAN
UNIT instructions say, once three Osterhagen Stations are online -

MARTHA
Yeah, well I've got a higher authority, way above UNIT. And the Doctor would give them a choice.

CUT TO:

68. INT. TARDIS - NIGHT

THE DOCTOR #2 building his DEVICE, DONNA with him.

THE DOCTOR #2
…it's a z-neutronic biological inversion catalyser.

DONNA
Earthgirl, remember?

THE DOCTOR #2
Davros said, he built those Daleks out of himself. His genetic code runs through the entire race. If I can use this, to lock the Crucible's transmission onto Davros himself…

DONNA
It blows up the Daleks!

THE DOCTOR #2
Biggest backfire in history!

Bleep from the scanner, Donna runs to it -

DONNA
Better hurry up, then. I reckon they're starting!

CUT TO:

69. INT. CRUCIBLE COMMAND DECK - NIGHT

SUPREME DALEK exultant:

SUPREME DALEK
Open Crucible transmission field! Prepare for full activation!

CUT TO:

70. FX SHOT

FX: WIDE SHOT, THE CRUCIBLE, as mighty METAL PANELS around the globe begin to grind and slide back…

FX: CLOSER, revealing massive METAL CIRCLES, like those in the Test Area, but huge. The Crucible ready to transmit.

CUT TO:

'Prepare for full activation!'

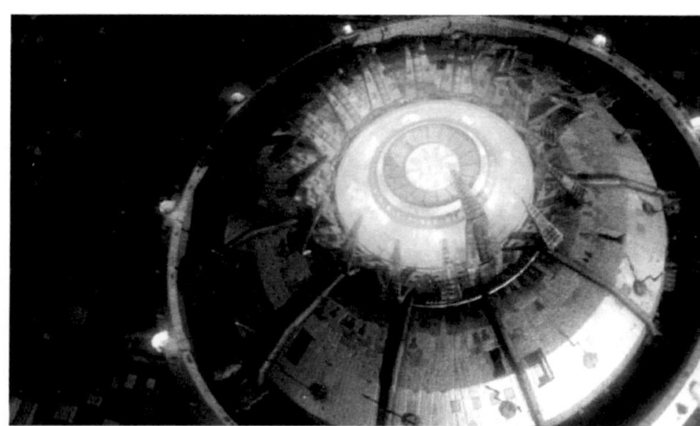

The Doctor is helpless.

71. INT. CRUCIBLE COMMAND DECK - NIGHT

DALEK 4 swivels round to face the SUPREME DALEK:

DALEK 4
Incoming transmission! Origin: Planet Earth.

SUPREME DALEK
Display!

FX: VIEWSCREEN *vwips* into existence, mid-air, and on screen:

CUT TO:

72. INT. OSTERHAGEN STATION ONE - NIGHT

MARTHA, looking up at a WALL-MOUNTED CAMERA. Scared, brave.

MARTHA
This is Martha Jones. Representing the Unified Intelligence Taskforce, on behalf of the Human Race. Can you hear me?

CUT TO:

73. INT. CRUCIBLE VAULTS - NIGHT

THE DOCTOR, then ROSE, turning round to see:

THE DOCTOR
Whaaat…?

FX: VIEWSCREEN MID-AIR, SC.72 CONTINUED, MARTHA to CAMERA.

MARTHA
I repeat. Calling the Dalek Crucible, can you hear me?

THE DOCTOR
Put me through.

DAVROS
It begins. As Dalek Caan foretold.

DALEK CAAN
The Children of Time will gather. And one of them will die.

THE DOCTOR
Stop saying that! Put me through!
(to viewscreen)
Martha! Where are you?!

MARTHA
(upset)
Doctor. I'm sorry. I had to…

DAVROS glides forward; loving this.

DAVROS
Ohh, but the Doctor is powerless. My prisoner! State your intent.

'Doctor, I'm sorry. I had to…'

MARTHA
I've got the Osterhagen Key. Leave this planet and its people alone. Or I'll use it.

THE DOCTOR
Osterhagen what?, what's an Osterhagen Key?!

MARTHA
There's a chain of 25 nuclear warheads, placed at strategic points beneath the Earth's crust. If I use this key… they detonate. And the Earth gets ripped apart.

THE DOCTOR
What?! Who invented that?! Well, someone called Osterhagen, I suppose - Martha, are you insane?

MARTHA
The Osterhagen Key is to be used… if the suffering of the Human Race is so great. So without hope. That this becomes the final option.

THE DOCTOR
That's never an option!

MARTHA
Don't argue with me, Doctor! Cos if the Daleks need these 27 planets for something, what if it becomes 26? What happens then? Daleks? Would you risk it?

ROSE
(smiling)
Oh she's good.

THE DOCTOR
That's not good!

MARTHA
Who's that?

ROSE
My name's Rose. Rose Tyler.

MARTHA
(genuine, sad smile)
Oh my God. He found you.

CUT TO:

74. INT. CRUCIBLE COMMAND DECK - NIGHT

DALEK 3 swivels round:

DALEK 3
Second transmission, internal!

SUPREME DALEK
Display!

FX: VIEWSCREEN *vwips* into a SECOND SCREEN next to the first (Martha stays in-vision, listening to all this), displaying:

CUT TO:

'Oh my God. He found you.' Martha realises that Rose has returned.

75. INT. CRUCIBLE TEST AREA, ANTECHAMBER - NIGHT

CAPTAIN JACK, with SARAH JANE, MICKEY & JACKIE, looking up at a WALL-MOUNTED CAMERA. Captain Jack holding the DIAMOND, which is wired up to cables he's pulled out of the wall.

CAPTAIN JACK
Captain Jack Harkness, calling all the Dalek boys and girls, are you receiving me? Don't send in your goons, or I'll set this thing off!

CUT TO:

76. INT. CRUCIBLE VAULTS - NIGHT

INTERCUTTING with SC.72, Osterhagen Station, SC.74, Command Deck (the Supreme Dalek quietly monitoring all this) and SC.75, Test Area Antechamber.

ROSE
But… he's still alive!

THE DOCTOR
Mickey…?! Jackie??
(to viewscreen)
Captain, what are you doing?

CAPTAIN JACK
I've got a Warp Star. Wired into the mainframe. I break this shell, the entire Crucible goes up.

THE DOCTOR
But…! It's - you can't - ! Where did you get a Warp Star?!

SARAH JANE
From me. Had no choice. We saw what happened to the prisoners. And if that was just a test…

CAPTAIN JACK
I'll do it! Don't imagine I wouldn't. I'm ready.

MARTHA
It's the Crucible. Or the Earth.

ROSE
(grinning)
Fantastic, now that's what I

Jackie, Mickey, Jack and Sarah Jane with the Warp Star.

call a ransom! Doctor…?

The smile falls from her face, seeing him.

He is *devastated.* Knowing what Davros is going to say:

DAVROS
And the prophecy unfolds.

DALEK CAAN
The Doctor's soul is revealed.

DAVROS
The man who abhors violence. Never carrying a gun. But this is the truth, Doctor! You take ordinary people and fashion them into weapons. Behold your Children of Time, transformed into murderers. I made the Daleks, Doctor. You made this.

THE DOCTOR
(weak)
…they're trying to help.

DAVROS
But already, I have seen them sacrificed. The Earth woman, who fell, opening the Subwave Network -

THE DOCTOR
Who was that…?

ROSE
Harriet Jones. She gave her

life, to get you here.

THE DOCTOR
Harriet…

And CU Doctor, pained, and PAINT with fleeting, silent images; Harriet from 1.4, 1.5, 2.X. At her finest.

DAVROS
And how many more? Just think!
(powerful)
How many have died?! In your name??

CLOSER on the Doctor, like this is hitting him - rapid, silent images of Jabe, 1.2; Pete Tyler, 1.8; Controller, 1.12; Lynda, 1.13; Sir Robert, 2.2; Mrs Moore, 2.6; the Abzorbaloff faces of Mr Skinner, Bridget, Ursula, 2.10; the Face of Boe, 3.3; Dalek Sec, 3.5; Chantho, 3.11; Astrid, 4.X; Luke, 4.5; Jenny, 4.6; River Song, 4.9; Hostess, 4.10.

Silence.

The Doctor just staring into space. Raw.

Davros so quiet, so clever:

DAVROS (CONT'D)
This is my final victory, Doctor. I have shown you… yourself.

Hold. And then -

CUT TO:

77. INT. CRUCIBLE COMMAND DECK - NIGHT

THE SUPREME DALEK utterly calm, even casual.

SUPREME DALEK
Engage defence pattern five.

DALEK 1
Transmat engaged!

CUT TO:

78. INT. OSTERHAGEN STATION ONE - NIGHT

FX: MARTHA disappears in a TELEPORT GLOW - yelling -

MARTHA
Nooo - !

She was holding the OSTERHAGEN KEY; it falls on to the desk, clunk, unused.

CUT TO:

79. INT. CRUCIBLE TEST AREA, ANTECHAMBER - NIGHT

FX: JACK, SARAH JANE, MICKEY, JACKIE disappear, TELEPORT -

The DIAMOND & WIRING fall to the floor, clunk, unused.

CUT TO:

80. INT. CRUCIBLE VAULTS - NIGHT

FX: TELEPORT GLOW, MARTHA appears, over by THE DOCTOR's spotlight, falling to the floor - WHIP PAN ACROSS, TELEPORT GLOW, SARAH JANE, CAPTAIN JACK, MICKEY, JACKIE appear, over by ROSE's spotlight, half-stumbling together.

'Mum, I told you not to.' Rose is horrified to see that Jackie is aboard the Crucible.

'Guard them!' The Children of Time become the prisoners of Davros.

DAVROS
Guard them!

The THREE SILENT DALEKS glide away from their three free-standing WORKSTATIONS, cover the new arrivals.

ROSE horrified, to see Jackie.

ROSE
Mum. I told you not to.

JACKIE
I couldn't leave you.

MICKEY
We'll get you out of here.

ROSE
Don't be so stupid, how?!

Martha goes to the Doctor, reaching out…

MARTHA
I'm sorry…

THE DOCTOR
Don't. Forcefield.
(quiet, pained)
Never do that again. Never.

Davros holding court.

DAVROS
And the final prophecy is in place. The Doctor and his Children of Time, as witnesses!

DALEK CAAN
They will see the end of all things.

DAVROS
Supreme Dalek! The time has come! Detonate the Reality Bomb!

CUT TO:

81. INT. CRUCIBLE COMMAND DECK - NIGHT

SUPREME DALEK
Activate planetary alignment!

CUT TO:

82. FX SHOT

REPEAT FX SHOTS, SC.50, SHOTS 1 and 2, the PLANETS beginning to HALO, then the WIDE SHOT of the PLANETARY ARRAY, haloing.

FX: THE CRUCIBLE. The OPEN CIRCLES on the surface of the Crucible from sc.70 begin to PULSE, shining, brighter…

FX: CLOSER on one CIRCLE, pulsing, brighter…

CUT TO:

83. INT. CRUCIBLE COMMAND DECK - NIGHT

SUPREME DALEK
Reality Bomb detonation in 150 rels, 149, 148…

CUT TO:

84. INT. CRUCIBLE VAULTS - NIGHT

SUPREME DALEK COUNTDOWN continues, OOV, 147, 146, 145…

THE DOCTOR trapped in his spotlight, raging -

THE DOCTOR
You can't, Davros, just listen to me, just *stop* - *!!!*

And Davros is giggling. Insane!

CUT TO:

85. INT. FX SHOT - NIGHT

FX: CAMERA sweeping around the CRUCIBLE, its open CIRCLES, flaring with power…

CUT TO:

86. INT. CRUCIBLE VAULTS - NIGHT

SUPREME DALEK COUNTDOWN continues, OOV, 126, 125, 124…

MARTHA, DALEK guard nearby, to THE DOCTOR in his spotlight -

MARTHA
But what does it do?

THE DOCTOR
It destroys everything! Every single thing.

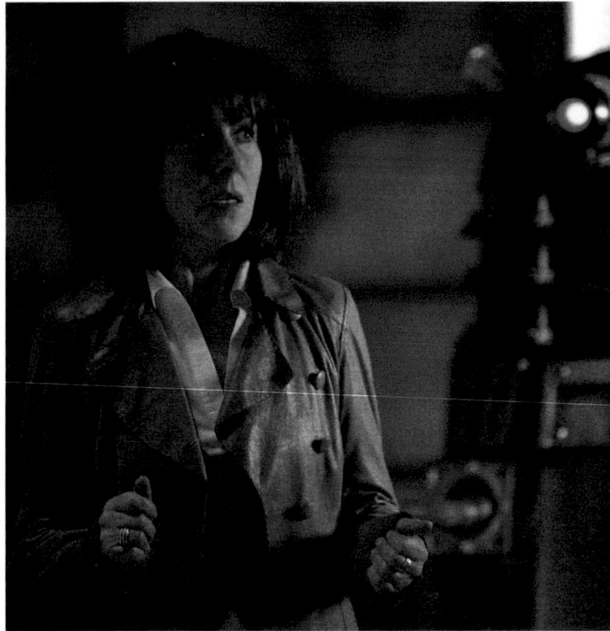

Sarah Jane hears a familiar wheezing, groaning sound…

MICKEY suddenly roars with rage - running past his DALEK guard, the Dalek swivelling too late - towards Davros -

Davros lifts his metal hand.

FX: an ARC OF ELECTRICITY zaps across, cutting Mickey down -

Mickey on the floor - alive, breathing hard, hurt.

DAVROS
Nothing can stop the detonation, Doctor! Nothing and no one!

CUT TO:

87. INT. TARDIS - NIGHT

THE DOCTOR #2, DEVICE in hand, slams down the controls -

THE DOCTOR #2
Maximum power!!!

THE LIGHTS COME BACK ON! SHINING! Time Rotor rising…

THE DOCTOR #2 (CONT'D)

Ready for this, Earthgirl?!

DONNA

Oh yes!

And he slams the final lever - they lurch - !

CUT TO:

88. INT. CRUCIBLE VAULTS - NIGHT

SUPREME DALEK COUNTDOWN continues, OOV, 99, 98, 97…

On THE DOCTOR, in his spotlight.

But then he turns, slowly, incredulous, hearing…

The familiar grind of ancient engines.

CUT TO ROSE, looking round, hearing it. It can't be…? PRAC WIND begins to sweep across the room.

The noise rising, stronger than ever, magnificent!

MARTHA blasted by WIND, shielding her face, but staring…

DALEKS swivel to look.

All eyes on one spot, directly opposite Davros…

CAPTAIN JACK standing tall in the wind, staring…

SARAH JANE blasted by the wind, but starting to smile.

JACKIE blasted by the wind, staring…

The noise is a SYMPHONY now, engines rising and falling…

MICKEY, on the floor, sits up, recovering - but grinning!

SUPREME DALEK COUNTDOWN, OOV, 60, 59, 58…

The Doctor blasted by wind, boggling.

THE DOCTOR

But that's…

DAVROS shocked.

DAVROS

…impossible!

And like a miracle…

At the centre of the Vault, directly opposite Davros, a good 20 feet or so away, like a temple of light and wind…

FX: THE TARDIS appears!

'… Impossible!'

And the door opens!

DOCTOR #2 stands there, backlit by PURE WHITE LIGHT inside the Tardis, as in Pompeii. He's holding the DEVICE!

On the Doctor:

THE DOCTOR

What??!

On Rose:

ROSE

What??

On Captain Jack:

CAPTAIN JACK

Brilliant

And then Doctor #2 is running -

SLOW MOTION RUN. HERO SHOT. Running straight towards Davros, towards CAMERA. Across the empty space.

Davros reveals another trick up his sleeve...

Holding out the DEVICE...

Davros slowly backing away, staring, open-mouthed.

SLOW MOTION RUN, Doctor #2, closer...

But too late -

The Doctor, trapped in his spotlight, calls out -

THE DOCTOR
Don't - !

And Davros calmly lifts his METAL HAND -

FX: ARC OF ELECTRICITY from Davros to Doctor #2 - !

And Doctor #2 hits the ground like a stone - !

The DEVICE skitters across the floor.

Hope, joy, excitement, all stopped dead.

DAVROS
Activate Holding Cell.

And a SPOTLIGHT slams down on Doctor #2, just as he's recovering, hauling himself to his feet.

Suddenly -

DONNA is running out of the Tardis, desperate -

DONNA
- I've got it -

She scoops up the DEVICE -

Runs to one of the FREE-STANDING WORKSTATIONS -

But as soon as she's there -

DONNA (CONT'D)
I don't know what to do! I don't know what to <u>do</u>!

THE DOCTOR
Donna - !

FX: DAVROS shoots out an ARC OF ELECTRICITY -

FX: ELECTRIC ARC hits Donna, and it's vicious, hard - (stunt?) - she goes flying, hits the floor, hard.

Again, the Device slides across the floor -

FX: DALEK fires -

Martha, Sarah Jane, Jackie and Rose 'stand witness' to Davros' master plan.

```
PRAC FX: DEVICE explodes, shatters!

                DAVROS
   I was wrong about your
   warriors, Doctor. They are
   pathetic!

NB, FX: DOCTOR DUPLICATION as and
when on WIDE SHOTS; Doctor #2 now
standing, to the Doctor -

             THE DOCTOR #2
   Human biological metacrisis.

              THE DOCTOR
   Never mind that!

                DAVROS
   Stand witness, Time Lord!
   Stand witness, Humans! The
   end of the universe is come!
```

Unfinished. But that's what I call a cliffhanger!

Text message from: **Russell**
Sent: 19-Jan-2008 19:32
Jane Tranter has just agreed to make 4.13 a 60-minute Special!

Text message from: **Ben**
Sent: 19-Feb-2008 20:15
No need to worry so much about page count. Good news.

FROM: RUSSELL T DAVIES TO: BENJAMIN COOK
MONDAY 21 JANUARY 2008 01:47:02 GMT

RE: HAPPY NEW YEAR?

Just so you know exactly what happened on Saturday… I got *really* worried about page count. I can cut down anything, but this was getting absurd. The clincher for me was cutting two very simple, seemingly unimportant lines at the top of Scene 43 in the most recent draft. After Davros has activated the Holding Cell, he said, 'Excellent. Even when powerless, a Time Lord is best contained.' And then the Doctor said, 'Good to know you're still scared of me.' Cuttable, yes… except they're *not*, because those are two introduction lines to a big scene, they're a pause, a settling, a statement of intent. Signature dialogue. A signature that's saying, 'These two are going to talk now.' I thought, if I'm having to cut *that*, I'm in serious trouble. Let alone other stuff, like the fact that I was now writing in such shorthand that Davros didn't have time to recognise Sarah Jane, that I didn't have time in the TARDIS for the Doctor to tell Captain Jack and Rose to put down their guns…

So I forwarded the script to Julie, saying what trouble we were in, to the extent of wondering: does something massive need to be cut? Like Sarah Jane? Or Torchwood? Something intrinsic, not just line-trims. Julie read it, loved it, phoned Jane and got instant authorisation for a 60-minute Special! It's not that simple, of course – Julie now needs to find funding, and contract Graeme and all departments and the actors for another week – but if anyone can do it, she can. What support, though. Amazing.

FROM: RUSSELL T DAVIES TO: BENJAMIN COOK
MONDAY 21 JANUARY 2008 02:46:36 GMT

RE: HAPPY NEW YEAR?

I'm only tootling through that script tonight, slipping back lines that I wish I hadn't cut, such as this exchange between the Doctor and Rose in the Crucible Vaults, just after Davros has said that he wants 'Everlasting peace'…

An extended running time for 4.13 means that Rose can finally ask the Doctor to finish that sentence from Bad Wolf Bay.

Julian Bleach discusses a scene with director Graeme Harper, while (insets) Phil Collinson and David Tennant get terribly excited at seeing Davros for the first time!

```
Silence, as Davros glides away from
them. Hold.

Only the noise of huge hydraulics
from above. The Doctor looking up,
trapped, helpless.

Then, quiet, intimate, across the
distance:

                    ROSE
      You never did finish that
      sentence.

                 THE DOCTOR
      What sentence...?

                    ROSE
                  (smiles)
      Like you don't know. Last
      time I saw you. On Bad Wolf
      Bay. You said, 'Rose Tyler...'

                 THE DOCTOR
      ...isn't it cold?

                    ROSE
      Come on. Properly.

                 THE DOCTOR
      Does it need saying?

                    ROSE
      Yeah.

Pause; sad smile between them.

Then, just as quiet:

                   DAVROS
      Such intimacy. So different
      from the Doctor I once knew.
```

That's the sort of thing I mean, the sort of stuff that I was having to leave out by compressing into shorthand. It's at the heart of the whole thing. It'll pay off beautifully at the end. Of course, this script has to be ready for the Tone Meeting on Wednesday (it's going to be an endless meeting – we haven't even got the right amount of practical Daleks, let alone all the ones that I'm blowing up!), and I've just upped the page count, which gives me even more pages to write. Ah, something always bites me on the arse. That's a lot of work.

LEPHONE
E OF
SSISTANCE
CARS
ALL CALLS

CHAPTER FIFTEEN

TIME FOR HEROES

In which *Skins* is the best thing on TV, Russell gets chicken pox, and Rose Tyler is a terrible racist… possibly

FROM: RUSSELL T DAVIES TO: BENJAMIN COOK
TUESDAY 22 JANUARY 2008 02:37:55 GMT

RE: HAPPY NEW YEAR?

I've almost finished… but I'm still a way off. I'm wondering whether to stay up and finish it. Technically, I *have* to, because this is supposed to be distributed to everyone tomorrow morning, but I don't know, I've had a weird day. I feel a bit strange, a bit dizzy and sick, just not myself. I've been typing away, without music, in silence. Normally, I love writing series finales. I get a real buzz. I'm not getting a buzz this time. It's laughable to think that I ever imagined fitting all this into 45 minutes. That's not helping. I feel stupid.

I'll send this now, if only because that'll help me stop for half an hour, have a break, see how I feel. I'm not sure I should continue, feeling like this, with big and lovely scenes to come. I feel like I might spoil them.

```
              DAVROS
    Stand witness, Time Lord!
    Stand witness, Humans! Your
    strategies have failed! Your
    weapons are useless! The end
    of the universe is come!

SUPREME DALEK OOV COUNTDOWN -

Ten!

On Doctor #2, looking up at the
viewscreen, helpless -

Nine!

On Sarah Jane, Captain Jack &
Jackie, looking up, helpless -

Eight!

On Donna, dazed, hauling herself up
on the workstation -

Seven!

On Mickey, looking up, helpless -

Six!

On Martha, looking up, helpless -

Five!
```

On Rose, looking up, helpless -

Four!

On the Doctor, looking up, helpless -

Three, two, one -

As Donna breathes in, clearing her head - instantly better! - flexes her hands, like a typist about to type, and stabs, very precisely, ONE BUTTON.

FX: *vwip!* VIEWSCREEN BLINKS OFF.

The sound of massive power, fading down and dying.

Everyone: eh??

Everyone looks at each other, puzzled…

And then at Donna. She's at the controls of the workstation. In her element:

DONNA
Aaaand, closing all Z-Neutrino relay loops with an internalised synchronous back-feed reversal loop - that button there!

She stabs it -

CUT TO:

93. EXT. FX SHOT[1]

FX: CRUCIBLE, METAL GATES now closing over the CIRCLES.

CUT TO:

94. INT. CRUCIBLE COMMAND DECK - NIGHT

The FOUR DALEKS agitated -

DALEK 1
System in shutdown!

DALEK 2
Detonation negative!

1 Four short scenes have been added – Scenes 60 (Dalek saucers leave Earth in formation), 61 (Wilf and Sylvia watch them leave, and Wilf says, 'Going where, though? And Donna's still out there. Ohh, it's not over yet, sweetheart…'), 62 (Dalek saucers in formation around the Crucible) and 76 (the Supreme Dalek says, 'Send transmission to the Vault. Continue to monitor'), shifting all subsequent scene numbers, so the Supreme Dalek's countdown is now Scene 92, followed by this, Scene 93, an exterior shot of the Crucible.

SUPREME DALEK
Explain! Explain! EXPLAIN!!

CUT TO:

95. INT. CRUCIBLE VAULTS - NIGHT

ALL staring at DONNA! (All fast now, whole scene:)

THE DOCTOR
Donna?! But… you can't even change a plug!

DONNA
D'you wanna bet, Time Boy?

DAVROS
You will suffer for this - !

He lifts his hand -

FX: ELECTRICITY ARCING around his own hand, but not travelling. Davros screams in pain.

DONNA
Oh, bio-electric dampening field with a retrogressive arc inversion? Done that! Next?!

DAVROS
Daleks! Exterminate her!

The three DALEKS swivel, to face her, guns ready -

Donna stabs a sequence of buttons -

Click - click - click! Guns not working! Their eyestalks stare down

Davros gets a shock, thanks to Donna.

Donna and Doctor #2 ponder their options.

at their guns, puzzled.

DONNA
What, macrotransmission of a K-filter wavelength blocking Dalek weaponry in a self-replicating energy blindfold matrix? Come on! Give me something difficult!

THE DOCTOR
But! How did you work that out…? You, you, you're…

THE DOCTOR #2
…Time Lord! Part Time Lord!

DONNA
Part Human! Oh yes! That was a two-way biological metacrisis - half Doctor, half Donna!
(another button)
Holding Cells deactivated!

The SPOTLIGHTS above the Doctor, Doctor #2 & Rose slam off -! As Jackie runs to Rose, big hug - everyone still boggling at Donna, at what's happening -

DONNA (CONT'D)
Well don't just stand there, you skinny boys in suits! Get to work!

The Doctor runs to one WORKSTATION, Doctor #2 to the third -

DAVROS
Stop them!

A Dalek glides up to the Doctor, sucker outstretched -

DONNA
Oh I like this one, watch this -

She stabs buttons -

The Daleks start to shudder. Croak. Squawk. Jerk. Arms, eyestalks juddering, out of control.

DONNA (CONT'D)
Aaaand spin -

Stabs a button -

The Daleks begin to revolve on the spot -

DONNA (CONT'D)
Aaaand, the other way -

Stabs a button -

They revolve in the opposite direction! (And they now stay like this, jerking, changing directions,

'What is happening?? Explain!' The Supreme Dalek begins to feel the effects of Donna's interference.

throughout.)

THE DOCTOR
What's that??

THE DOCTOR #2
What did you do?!

DONNA
Used the biofeedback shielding to exacerbate the Dalekenium interface, thus inculcating a trip-stitch circuit breaker in the psychokinetic threshold manipulator!

THE DOCTOR
Of course!

THE DOCTOR #2
But that's brilliant!

THE DOCTOR
That's… revolutionary! Why did we never think of that?!

DONNA
Cos you were just Time Lords, you dumbos, lacking that little bit of Human, that gut instinct that comes with Planet Earth - I can think of ideas you two wouldn't dream of in a million years! Oh, the universe has been waiting for me! Now let's send that trip-stitch all over the ship!
(hands poised)
Did I ever tell you? Best temp in Chiswick, 100 words per minute!
(to the Doctors)
Go!

And then she's slamming levers, spinning switches -

The Doctor & Doctor #2 doing the same, gleeful -

CUT TO:

96. INT. CRUCIBLE COMMAND DECK - NIGHT

The FOUR DALEKS start to jerk, convulse, and spin - !

DALEK 1
- system - malfunctionnnn - !

DALEK 2
- out of control - !

DALEK 3
- motor casing interference- !

DALEK 4
Help me! Help me! Help *meeeeee* -

The SUPREME DALEK is juddering, on its plinth, though maintaining more control than the others:

SUPREME DALEK
What is happening?? Explain!

FX: WIDE SHOT, CROWD MULTIPLICATION DALEKS on FLOOR LEVEL, CGI DALEKS up above - all jerking, spinning, shaking -

SUPREME DALEK (CONT'D)
This cannot be! This cannot be!

CUT TO:

97. INT. CRUCIBLE VAULTS - NIGHT

CAPTAIN JACK running for the Tardis, goes inside -

DONNA pressing buttons like mad - everything still *fast* -

DONNA
Come on, boys, we've got 27 planets to send home! Activate Magnetron!

She is slamming switches like mad -

The Doctor is slamming switches like mad -

Doctor #2 is slamming switches like mad -

INTERCUTTING between them, as they slam away, feverish, but glancing at each other, loving this, each other -

Davros gliding forward -

DAVROS
You will stop! Stop this at once -

Captain Jack running out of the Tardis, carrying his DEFABRICATOR - and throwing the SCI-FI GUN to MICKEY, who's now fully recovered, on his feet - catches the gun, smiling -

Mickey swings the gun round on Davros:

MICKEY
How d'you like some of this - ?

THE DOCTOR
Mickey, *don't!*

And Mickey stops himself from firing, just in time. Deep breath. Keeps the gun aimed, guarding DAVROS.

MICKEY
Just stay where you are, mister.

The tables turned, Mickey holds Davros at gunpoint.

And Jack runs to one juddering DALEK -

CAPTAIN JACK
Outta the way!

Gleeful, he shoves the Dalek - it glides, out of control, still twitching, to the edge of the room -

MARTHA does the same to her Dalek, heaves - it glides away -

SARAH JANE does the same to the THIRD DALEK, so they're all out of harm's way, though they keep shuddering -

CUT TO Donna, at her workstation:

DONNA
Right then? Ready?

THE DOCTOR
Ready!

THE DOCTOR #2
Ready!

All three slam a final switch -

DONNA
Aaaand reverse!

CUT TO:

98. FX SHOT

FX: ONE, TWO, THREE PLANETS vanish from the ARRAY -

CUT TO:

99. INT. CRUCIBLE VAULTS - NIGHT

THE DOCTOR, DOCTOR #2 & DONNA working away, fast -

THE DOCTOR
Off you go, Clom!

THE DOCTOR #2
Back home, Adipose 3!

DONNA
Shallacatop, Pyrovillia and the Lost Moon of Poosh, sorted!

CUT TO:

100. FX SHOT

FX: FOUR, FIVE, SIX, SEVEN, EIGHT

Martha, Jack, Rose and Jackie celebrate their victory over Davros and the Daleks.

PLANETS gone - !

CUT TO:

101. INT. CRUCIBLE VAULTS - NIGHT

THE DOCTOR, DOCTOR #2 & DONNA, still working away, fast -

ROSE
Is anyone gonna tell us? What the hell is going on?!

CU Donna, PAINT WITH FLASHBACKS to SC.27, 29, Donna, the energy, the hand-in-jar, as she explains -

DONNA
He poured all his regeneration energy into his spare hand, I touched the hand, he grew out of that - but that fed back into me! But it just stayed dormant

in my head till the synapses got that extra little spark, kicking them into life, thank you, Davros!

PAINT with Donna getting hit by electricity, SC.92 - then a NEW IMAGE, part of sc.92 but not seen before -

CU on Donna, having been thrown against the WORKSTATION, just recovering, lifting her head, as…

FX: a GOLDEN GLOW burns in her eyes.

DONNA (CONT'D)
Part Human, part Time Lord, and I got the best bit of the Doctor, I got his mind!

SARAH JANE
So there's three of you?

ROSE
Three Doctors?!

CAPTAIN JACK
Oh, I can't tell you what I'm thinking right now.

MARTHA
D'you mean, she's like Jenny…?[2]

THE DOCTOR
No, that was just biology, Donna's a brand new creation. So unique that the Time Lines were converging on you. A Human Being with a Time Lord brain!

DAVROS
But you promised me, Dalek Caan! Why did you not foresee this?

But Caan is insane, bubbling with laughter!

The Doctor looking at Caan (keeps working), realising:

THE DOCTOR
Ohh, I think he did… Something's been manipulating the Time Lines, all the way from the start. Getting Donna Noble to the right place at the right time.

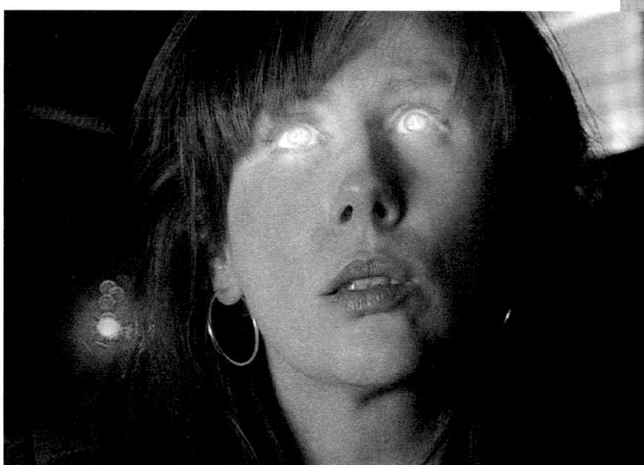

A brand new creation – a Human with a Time Lord brain.

2 The Doctor's daughter, Jenny, created by a Progenation Machine in *Doctor Who* 4.6, was part Time Lord.

'I saw the truth of us, Creator, and I decreed: no more.' Dalek Caan finds his conscience.

DALEK CAAN
This would always have happened; I only helped, Doctor.

DAVROS
You betrayed the Daleks!

DALEK CAAN
I saw the Daleks. What we have done, throughout Time and Space. I saw the truth of us, Creator, and I decreed: no more.

CUT TO:

102. INT. CRUCIBLE COMMAND DECK - NIGHT

THE FOUR DALEKS jerking, spinning -

But the SUPREME DALEK is stronger than the rest:

SUPREME DALEK
The machinations of Davros… are to blame… I will descend… to the Vault!

PRAC? FX? On its platform, the SUPREME DALEK begins to lower through the floor…

CUT TO:

103. INT. CRUCIBLE VAULTS - NIGHT

CAPTAIN JACK looking round -

CAPTAIN JACK
Heads up!

PRAC? FX? THE SUPREME DALEK descending, surrounded by SMOKE and LIGHT, majestic.

SUPREME DALEK
Davros! You have betrayed us!

DAVROS
It was Dalek Caan!

SUPREME DALEK
The Vault will be purged! You will all be exterminated!

'Feel this!' Captain Jack destroys the Supreme Dalek.

FX: on ground level now, it fires -

FX: BEAM, PRAC FX EXPLOSION, THE DOCTOR'S WORKSTATION explodes - he jumps clear, in time -

CAPTAIN JACK
Like I was saying. Feel this!

FX: Captain Jack FIRES the DEFABRICATOR GUN -

FX: BEAM, PRAC(?) EXPLOSION - the SUPREME DALEK EXPLODES!

The Doctor at the shattered workstation -

THE DOCTOR
We've lost the Magnetron! And there's only one planet left. Guess which one? But we can use the Tardis -

And he runs for the Tardis, heads inside -

CUT TO:

104. INT. TARDIS - NIGHT

THE DOCTOR running to the console -

Stabbing controls, fast -

CUT TO:

105. INT. CRUCIBLE VAULTS - NIGHT

DOCTOR #2 & DONNA still working away -

THE DOCTOR #2
Holding Earth stability, maintaining atmospheric shell -

But quiet, voice carrying across the room:

DALEK CAAN
The prophecy must complete.

DAVROS
Don't listen to him!

DALEK CAAN
I have seen the end of everything; it must surely happen, Doctor.

The Doctor #2 & Donna look at each other. Grim; knowing what that means.

Captain Jack, Donna and the Doctor work to send all the planets back where they came from.

THE DOCTOR #2
...yeah.

DONNA
(of the Tardis)
He'd try and stop us.

THE DOCTOR #2
He's not here. And with or without a Reality Bomb, this Dalek Empire's big enough to slaughter the cosmos.

DONNA
(deep breath)
Right then.
(twists controls)
Maximise the Dalekenium feeds.

THE DOCTOR #2
And, blast them back - !

Both slam down -

PRAC? FX? THE THREE DALEKS, in different corners, EXPLODE!

CUT TO:

106. INT. TARDIS - NIGHT

CAMERA SHAKE, sound of EXPLOSIONS -

THE DOCTOR horrified - runs out -

CUT TO:

107. INT. CRUCIBLE VAULTS - NIGHT

THE DOCTOR runs out of the Tardis - CAMERA SHAKE, SOUND OF EXPLOSIONS ABOVE, ALL flinching - furious, at Doctor #2 -

THE DOCTOR
What have you done?

THE DOCTOR #2
Fulfilling the prophecy.

They flinch, huge *BANG!* from above - PRAC RUBBLE FALLS -

CUT TO:

108. INT. CRUCIBLE COMMAND DECK - NIGHT

PRAC? FX? THE FOUR DALEKS still spinning, out of control, voices squawking, as they EXPLODE -

FX: CROWD MULTIPLICATION DALEKS, floor level, all EXPLODING -

FX: WIDE SHOT, all CGI DALEKS EXPLODING!

CUT TO:

Explosions rip through the Dalek Crucible.

109. EXT. FX SHOT - NIGHT

FX: the FLEET, SAUCERS beginning to EXPLODE!

FX: THE CRUCIBLE, EXPLOSIONS ripping across the surface -

CUT TO:

110. INT. TORCHWOOD HUB - NIGHT

PRAC? FX? - THE DALEK in the doorway EXPLODES!

GWEN & IANTO duck!

IANTO
Woah!

GWEN
There goes the Time Lock!

CUT TO:

111. INT. CRUCIBLE VAULTS - NIGHT

CAMERA SHAKE, NOISE OF EXPLOSIONS -

PRAC FIRE bursting out of the WORKSTATIONS, THE DOCTOR #2 & DONNA stepping back from them -

PRAC RUBBLE falling from the ROOF -

THE DOCTOR furious, at DOCTOR #2 & DONNA -

THE DOCTOR
I want a word with you. Both of you! Now get inside!

FX: DOCTOR MULTIPLICATION as DOCTOR #2 runs into the Tardis, then Donna, the Doctor staying by the door -

THE DOCTOR (CONT'D)
All of you inside! Marthaaaa! Sarah Jane! Rose, Jackie, Jack, Mickey, all of you - run!!

- they run - each running past the Doctor, into the Tardis -

THE DOCTOR (CONT'D)
In! In! In! In! In! In - !

CUT TO:

112. INT. TARDIS - NIGHT

- as THE DOCTOR #2 stands by the

As the Crucible begins to burn, the Doctor looks for Davros amidst the devastation.

door, counting them in -

MARTHA, then SARAH JANE, then ROSE & JACKIE, then CAPTAIN JACK, then MICKEY, as they whiz past him, up the ramp -

THE DOCTOR #2
- Martha - Sarah Jane - Rose - Jackie - Jack - Micketty McMickey!

CUT TO:

113. INT. CRUCIBLE VAULTS - NIGHT

THE DOCTOR flinches back -

GIRDER & RUBBLE fall from the ROOF, centre - forming a low barrier of tangled metal, separating him from Davros, who's a good distance away, rippling with HEAT HAZE.

CAMERA SHAKE - THE DOCTOR, calling across -

DAVROS now behind RUBBLE, PRAC FLAMES rising around him -

THE DOCTOR
Davros! Come with me!

DAVROS
Never!

THE DOCTOR
I can save you!

But Davros is cold, simply pointing at him.

DAVROS
Never forget, Doctor. You did this. I name you, for ever, as the Destroyer of Worlds.

PRAC (plus FX?) FLAMES rise up around Davros.

He screams. More anger than rage.

And he is gone from sight.

CU on the Doctor, trying to see,

but there's SMOKE & DUST & HEAT HAZE in the air. And then, he's strangely calm.

Looking across.

At DALEK CAAN. Its voice soft, somehow carrying across:

DALEK CAAN
One will still die.

PRAC FLAMES rise up in front of Caan, obscuring him.

The Doctor still staring. Unnerved. Already, realising…

Then he runs back into the Tardis -

CUT TO:

114. INT. TARDIS - NIGHT

ALL inside, THE DOCTOR running to the console -

THE DOCTOR
And, off we go - !

The Time Rotor starts rising and falling…

CUT TO:

115. FX SHOT

FX: CLOSE ON EXPLOSIONS breaking out all over the CRUCIBLE -

FX: WIDE SHOT, THE WHOLE CRUCIBLE BLASTING APART!

FX: then calm, in contrast, THE TARDIS fades in, spinning gently above THE EARTH, with its MEDUSA CASCADE B/G.

CUT TO:

116. INT. TARDIS - NIGHT

(NB, FX: DUPLICATION DOCTOR for selected shots.)

SARAH JANE
But what about the Earth? It's stuck in the wrong part of space!

THE DOCTOR
All in hand.

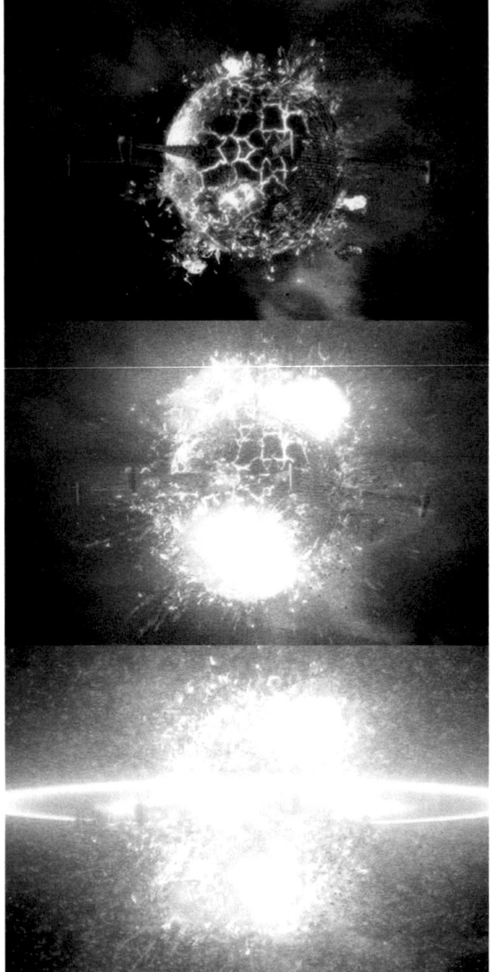

The Crucible succumbs.

(at the scanner)
Torchwood Hub! This is the Doctor! Are you receiving me?

CUT TO:

117. INT. TORCHWOOD HUB - NIGHT

GWEN & IANTO at a terminal, excited, seeing THE DOCTOR (on his TARDIS SCANNER POV) -

GWEN
Loud and clear! Is Jack there?

CUT TO:

118. INT. TARDIS - NIGHT

INTERCUT WITH SC.117 CONTINUED, TORCHWOOD HUB.

THE DOCTOR
Can't get rid of him!
(looks closer)
Tell me, Gwen Cooper, were you born in Llandaff?

GWEN
My grandparents were.

THE DOCTOR
Thought so, Rift genetic multiplicity, funny old world - now, Torchwood, I want you to open up that Rift Manipulator! And send all that power to me!

IANTO
Doing it now, sir!

Ianto taps in a program -

THE RIFT MANIPULATOR in the WATER TOWER rises and falls…

GWEN
What's that for?

THE DOCTOR
It's a towrope. Now then, Sarah Jane, what was your son's name?

SARAH JANE
Luke! He's called Luke! And the computer's called Mr Smith!

THE DOCTOR
(at the scanner)
Calling Luke and Mr Smith! This is the Doctor!

CUT TO:

119. INT. SARAH JANE'S ATTIC - NIGHT

INTERCUT WITH SC.118 CONTINUED, TARDIS.

LUKE seeing THE DOCTOR (SCANNER POV) on MR SMITH's screen -

LUKE
Is mum there? We saw the Crucible explode, is she all right?

THE DOCTOR
Oh, she's fine and dandy,

The Doctor and Sarah Jane call Luke and Mr Smith.

Luke, K-9 and Mr Smith, in Sarah Jane's attic.

now Mr Smith, I want you to harness the Rift Power and loop it around the Tardis, got that?

MR SMITH
I regret, I will need remote Tardis basecode numerals.

THE DOCTOR
Blimey, that's gonna take a while -

SARAH JANE goes to the scanner -

SARAH JANE
No, let me! K-9! Out you come!

REPEAT FX from SJA 1.10, K-9 materialising in the Attic.

K-9
Affirmative, Mistress!

THE DOCTOR
Oh, good dog! K-9, give Mr Smith the basecode!

K-9
Master! Tardis basecode now being transferred. As instructed!

K-9 trundles forward, attaches its nose-antenna to Mr Smith.

Now, the Doctor walks around the console, giving people a position, placing their hands on certain controls -

THE DOCTOR
Now then, you lot - Sarah, hold that down - Mickey, you hold that, keep it to the left -
(to all)
Cos d'you know why this Tardis is always rattling about the place?
(to Rose)
Rose, that, there.
(to all)
It's designed to have six pilots. And I have to do it single handed!
(to Martha)
Martha, keep that level.
(to all)
But not any more!
(to Jack)
Jack, there you go, steady that -
(to all)
Now we can fly this thing -
(to Jackie)
No, Jackie, don't touch anything, just stand back -
(to all)
- like it's meant to be flown! We've got the Torchwood Rift, looped around the Tardis by Mr Smith, and we're gonna fly Planet Earth back home! Right

The TARDIS tows planet Earth across the universe.

L–R: Sarah Jane (Elisabeth Sladen), Mickey (Noel Clarke), Doctor #2 (stunt double Collum Sanson-Regan), Rose (Billie Piper), the Doctor (David Tennant) and Donna (Catherine Tate). Inset: Luke and K-9 ride the planet home. Illustration by Russell T Davies.

then! Off we go!

He pulls a big lever - all holding on excited -

CUT TO:

120. FX SHOT

FX: THE TARDIS shoots forward, foreground, out of frame, then behind it, THE EARTH MOVES! As it sweeps foreground -

FX: REVERSE, and the STARS round the EARTH warp into NEEDLES OF LIGHT, a classic SPACE TUNNEL! Earth flying down it!

CUT TO:

121. INT. SARAH JANE'S ATTIC - NIGHT

CAMERA SHAKE, things flying around in b/g. But LUKE is holding on to MR SMITH, laughing. K-9's ears whirring away.

CUT TO:

122. INT. TORCHWOOD HUB - NIGHT

CAMERA SHAKE, GWEN & IANTO hanging on to the shuddering terminals for dear life. Things falling all over the place. But they're loving it, whooping! Cheering!

CUT TO:

123. INT. NOBLES' HOUSE - NIGHT

CAMERA SHAKE! WILF & SYLVIA staggering about - shelves falling, lamps flying, ornaments flying, both trying to catch things, whoops - !

CUT TO:

Earth's greatest heroes – and a pair of Doctors – save the world one more time.

124. INT. JONES' HOUSE - NIGHT

CAMERA SHAKE, but FRANCINE sits on the floor, safe. FURNITURE & STUFF flying and tumbling foreground, she's just staring - what the hell is happening now?!

CUT TO:

125. FX SHOT

FX: SPACE TUNNEL, NEEDLES OF LIGHT. The TARDIS whooshes through from foreground, disappearing into the distance, followed by THE EARTH!

CUT TO:

126. INT. TARDIS - NIGHT

ROOM GENTLY SWAYING. THE DOCTOR, ROSE, SARAH JANE, MARTHA, CAPTAIN JACK, MICKEY at the controls. The Doctor calling out instructions to each of them - left a bit, right a bit, keep it steady, not so fast, that button there...

THE DOCTOR #2 & DONNA standing back at the rail, both helping with instructions - Mickey, hold it down, Sarah, the one on the left, etc. But really, just loving it.

And JACKIE, opposite rail, holding on, just smiling away.

INTERCUT this whole sequence, on each of them, these heroes, flying the Tardis, and taking their planet back home.

CUT TO:

127. FX SHOT

FX: THE NEEDLES fade down to ordinary STARS, the SPACE TUNNEL dispersing, THE EARTH slowing...

FX: THE TARDIS, set against an ordinary starscape now, whooshes

Success! Rose and the Doctor share a hug as the Earth is restored.

through frame -

FX: and there's the EARTH! Static! Back in its rightful place! SUNRISE just curving over the horizon.

CUT TO:

128. INT. TARDIS - NIGHT

And they all CLAP! Big, lasting applause! Wild! So happy!

Then - for example - MICKEY high-fiving CAPTAIN JACK. ROSE gives MARTHA a hug. DONNA pushes SARAH JANE out of the way to hug JACK. JACKIE hugs THE DOCTOR.

Any combination, all combinations. Just the joy of it.

CUT TO:

129. INT. NOBLES' HOUSE - DAY

LIGHT streaming through the windows!

WILF and SYLVIA, the biggest hug! Dancing! Laughing!

CUT TO:

130. EXT. JONES' HOUSE - DAY

FRANCINE opens her front door. Crying with happiness.

Above, the BLUE SKY. The most ordinary day.

PANNING UP until the sky fills the frame...

FROM: BENJAMIN COOK TO: RUSSELL T DAVIES
TUESDAY 22 JANUARY 2008 02:51:08 GMT

RE: HAPPY NEW YEAR?

>>It's laughable to think that I ever imagined fitting all this into 45 minutes. That's not helping. I feel stupid.<<

Yeah, but with the best will in the world, Russell, plenty of writers don't have enough story in their heads to fill 30 or 45 minutes of drama, let alone an hour. So think yourself lucky. Or gifted. But not stupid.

FROM: RUSSELL T DAVIES TO: BENJAMIN COOK
TUESDAY 22 JANUARY 2008 02:58:51 GMT

RE: HAPPY NEW YEAR?

You're too wise. That's actually worked on me. Right, I'll continue. Might as well forge on. More soon.

FROM: RUSSELL T DAVIES TO: BENJAMIN COOK
TUESDAY 22 JANUARY 2008 05:06:50 GMT

RE: HAPPY NEW YEAR?

In 40 minutes, Tesco opens for more cigarettes.

FROM: RUSSELL T DAVIES TO: BENJAMIN COOK
TUESDAY 22 JANUARY 2008 06:23:04 GMT

RE: HAPPY NEW YEAR?

Bloody hell. I must be five pages from the end. Just five. This is a long haul. But the return to Bad Wolf Bay is quite nice. Next, I have to write out Donna, but I can't bear it. I LOVE HER! Right, off to Tesco now, then I'll finish.

FROM: BENJAMIN COOK TO: RUSSELL T DAVIES
TUESDAY 22 JANUARY 2008 06:27:02 GMT

RE: HAPPY NEW YEAR?

STAY! WHERE! YOU! ARE!

Oh, all right, go to Tesco. But don't get run over by a bus on your way back. That would be *very* annoying.

FROM: RUSSELL T DAVIES TO: BENJAMIN COOK
TUESDAY 22 JANUARY 2008 06:27:58 GMT

RE: HAPPY NEW YEAR?

I just thought that. If I fell into the Bay, no one would know what happens to Donna!

I won't fall into the Bay.

FROM: RUSSELL T DAVIES TO: BENJAMIN COOK
TUESDAY 22 JANUARY 2008 06:46:00 GMT

RE: HAPPY NEW YEAR?

I didn't fall into the Bay. Mmm, croissant. Still warm. I love a little shop.

FROM: BENJAMIN COOK TO: RUSSELL T DAVIES
TUESDAY 22 JANUARY 2008 06:49:16 GMT

RE: HAPPY NEW YEAR?

Did you get hit by a bus, though?

FROM: RUSSELL T DAVIES TO: BENJAMIN COOK
TUESDAY 22 JANUARY 2008 06:54:39 GMT

RE: HAPPY NEW YEAR?

Yes, I'm typing from the ambulance. They say I'll never dance again. In fairness, I've had my day.

FROM: RUSSELL T DAVIES TO: BENJAMIN COOK
TUESDAY 22 JANUARY 2008 07:37:28 GMT

RE: HAPPY NEW YEAR?

This to too sad for words! I can't type because I'm crying!

FROM: BENJAMIN COOK TO: RUSSELL T DAVIES
TUESDAY 22 JANUARY 2008 07:41:49 GMT

RE: HAPPY NEW YEAR?

It's 7.40am. You've been writing through the night. You're allowed to cry. (What are you going to be like at the Final Mix? We'll bring tissues.)

FROM: RUSSELL T DAVIES TO: BENJAMIN COOK
TUESDAY 22 JANUARY 2008 07:49:29 GMT

RE: HAPPY NEW YEAR?

I can imagine Julie at the Final Mix. She'll die! I haven't even written Wilf's last speech yet. That's going to kill me.

Dawn over the Bay is very beautiful. How's Chiswick?!

FROM: BENJAMIN COOK TO: RUSSELL T DAVIES
TUESDAY 22 JANUARY 2008 07:56:43 GMT

RE: HAPPY NEW YEAR?

Chiswick is fearing for the welfare of Donna Noble.

FROM: RUSSELL T DAVIES TO: BENJAMIN COOK
TUESDAY 22 JANUARY 2008 09:54:58 GMT

RE: HAPPY NEW YEAR?

It all ends in Chiswick. That's so funny.

Oh, enough! Have it.

Phew.

Blub.

```
131. EXT. PARK - DAY

A beautiful, wide, rolling PARK.
THE TARDIS sitting there.

Door opens, THE DOCTOR & SARAH JANE
step out -

            SARAH JANE
  Y'know, you act like such a
  lonely man. But look at you.
  You've got the biggest family
  on Earth!
            (big hug)
  Gotta go. He's only 14. Long
  story. And thank you!

                            CUT TO:

132. INT. TARDIS - DAY

B/G, MARTHA & CAPTAIN JACK just
heading down the ramp, DONNA on her
mobile, talking to Gramps, DOCTOR
#2 talking to ROSE (and getting on
a treat), but…

On MICKEY, private moment with
JACKIE. He hugs her. Quiet:

            MICKEY
  Gonna miss you. More than
  anyone.

            JACKIE
  What d'you mean? The Doctor's
```

taking us back home, isn't he?

MICKEY
That's the point.

CUT TO:

133. EXT. TARDIS - DAY

CAPTAIN JACK & MARTHA already walking away.

THE DOCTOR
And go straight back to UNIT, get rid of that Osterhagen thing!

MARTHA
Will do!

CAPTAIN JACK
D'you know, I'm not so sure about UNIT these days. Maybe there's something else you could be doing…

And Captain Jack takes Martha's hand, as they walk off…

MICKEY steps out of the Tardis.

THE DOCTOR
Where are you going?

MICKEY
I'm not stupid. I can work out what's happening next.

And hey, I had a good time in that parallel world. But my Gran passed away. Nice and peaceful. She spent her last years living in a mansion! But there's nothing left for me there, now. Certainly not Rose.

THE DOCTOR
What will you do…?

MICKEY
Anything! Brand new life! Just you watch me! See ya, boss.

Holds up his fist. They knock knuckles. Big smile.

Then Mickey's running, after Captain Jack & Martha -

MICKEY (CONT'D)
Hey, you two - !

CAPTAIN JACK
Oh I thought I'd got rid of you…

And the Doctor watches them go. Smiling.

Then turns, goes back into the Tardis.

CUT TO:

134. INT. TARDIS - DAY

THE DOCTOR going to the console, past DONNA, ROSE, JACKIE, DOCTOR #2 (no FX, just a double) -

THE DOCTOR
Just time for one last trip. Darlig Ulv Stranden. Better known as…

CUT TO:

135. EXT. BAD WOLF BAY - DAY

FX: THE TARDIS MATERIALISES. Wide open beach.

Caption: *Bad Wolf Bay, Norway.*

JACKIE walking out, THE DOCTOR #2 & ROSE follow, then THE DOCTOR & DONNA; the Doctor & Donna stay by the Tardis. FX: DOCTOR DUPLICATION

'See ya, boss.' Mickey Smith heads off to a brand new life.

Jackie and Rose return to Bad Wolf Bay, in Norway, in the company of the new, blue, half-Human Doctor.

as and when, though not often.

JACKIE
Well, fat lot of good, this is! Back of beyond. Bloody Norway! I'll have to phone your father.

THE DOCTOR #2
Oh, I never said, congratulations - you had a baby boy! What did you call him?

JACKIE
Doctor.

THE DOCTOR #2
Really?!

JACKIE
No, you plum. He's called Tony.

THE DOCTOR #2
Tony Tyler? Okay. Nice.

But Rose is looking back at the Tardis (dialogue has taken them a good 20 feet away, good distance). At the Doctor.

ROSE
…but I don't understand. What are we doing?

THE DOCTOR
We're leaving you. With your family. In the parallel universe.

DONNA
The walls of the world are closing. We'll have to go soon. It's a dimensional retroclosure - see, I really get that stuff now!

ROSE
But… I came all that way. To find you.

THE DOCTOR
And you've got me. Well. Him.

ROSE
(cautious, to #2)
But… are you the same?

THE DOCTOR #2
Same man. Same memories. Same… thoughts. But a little bit better.

ROSE
In what way?

THE DOCTOR #2
Well. Better for you. I've only got one heart.

ROSE
Which means…?

THE DOCTOR #2
I'm part Human. Specifically, the ageing part. I'll grow old. And never regenerate. I've only got one life, Rose Tyler. And I'm spending it here.

ROSE
One heart…?

And she puts her hand on his chest. So intimate, now.

THE DOCTOR
He's a bit too Human, for my liking. Too fast in destroying those Daleks. He needs someone to look after him, Rose. Someone like you.

DONNA
They're not listening.

THE DOCTOR
No, they're not, are they?

Because Rose & Doctor #2 are just staring at each other.

ROSE
I stood here. On the worst day of my life. You still haven't finished that sentence.

THE DOCTOR #2
What sentence?

ROSE
'Rose Tyler…

THE DOCTOR #2
…isn't it cold?'

ROSE
Oh, you really are the same!

THE DOCTOR #2
Mmm, not quite.

And he kisses her!

Big proper kiss!

But on the Doctor. The original. Denied this.

Doctor #2 & Rose separate. So happy.

JACKIE
Actually… that was weird!

THE DOCTOR
Tell you what, here you go -

Throws them a chunk of CORAL - Doctor #2 catches it.

Whatever he whispered to her, it certainly did the trick!

THE DOCTOR (CONT'D)
This universe is in need of defending. Chunk of Tardis. Grow your own.

THE DOCTOR #2
But that takes thousands of years.

THE DOCTOR
No, because…

DONNA
…if you shatterfry the plasmic shell and modify the dimensional stabiliser to a foldback harmonic of 36.3, you accelerate growth by the power of 59!

THE DOCTOR/THE DOCTOR #2
We never thought of that!

DONNA
I'm just brilliant!

THE DOCTOR
The Doctor. In the Tardis. With Rose Tyler. Just as it should be.

ROSE
(to the Doctor)
But I didn't think… What about you? You gonna be all right?

THE DOCTOR
Oh, I've got madam.

DONNA
Human with a Time Lord brain, perfect combination! We can travel the universe for ever. Best friends! And equals, just what old skinnyboy needs, an equal!

FX: the TARDIS lamp flares, the box groans.

THE DOCTOR
We've got to go. This reality's about to be sealed off. For ever.

ROSE
Bye then. Good luck!

THE DOCTOR
And you, Rose.
(to Donna)
Come on, in we get.

Donna goes inside.

JACKIE
And thank you, Doctor.

THE DOCTOR
Look after Tony!

Mentioning Tony makes Rose turn to Jackie, to give her a great big hug, just so happy.

Leaving just the Doctor & Doctor #2 staring at each other.

And a terrible look passes between them.

Doctor #2 mutters something. 'Sorry.'

The Doctor just nods, grave. Then turns, goes into the Tardis.

Rose turns back, smiling, takes Doctor #2's hand, to watch:

FX: WIDE SHOT, Doctor #2, Rose & Jackie standing there, on Bad Wolf Bay, as the TARDIS… fades away.

And then the three of them walk away, to their new life.

CUT TO:

136. INT. TARDIS - NIGHT

In flight. DONNA at the console, operating it, like it's normal. THE DOCTOR opposite. Watching. So quiet.

DONNA
I thought, we could try the planet Felspoon! Just cos… what a good name! Felspoon! Apparently, it's got mountains that sway, in the breeze, mountains that move, can you imagine?

THE DOCTOR
…and how d'you know that?

DONNA
Cos it's in your head! And if it's in your head, it's in mine!

'And how does that feel?' The Doctor grimly observes Donna.

She's moving round the console, he follows, carefully.

THE DOCTOR
And how does that feel?

DONNA
Brilliant! Fantastic! Molto bene! Great big universe, packed into my brain! D'you know, you could fix that chameleon circuit if you just tried hotbinding the fragment-links and superseding the binary, binary
(can't stop)
Binary, binary, binary, binary, binary, binary - I'm fine!

She's scared now. Because she knows.

DONNA (CONT'D)
Naaah, never mind Felspoon, d'you know who I'd like to meet? Charlie Chaplin! I bet he's great, Charlie Chaplin, shall we do that? Go and see Charlie Chaplin? Shall we? Charlie Chaplin? Charlie Chester? Charlie Brown, no, he's not real, he's fiction, friction, fixing, mixing, Rickston, Brixton -
(pain)
Ow - !
(stops. Quiet)
Oh my God.

THE DOCTOR
There's never been a Human-Time Lord metacrisis before now. And you know why.

DONNA
Because there can't be.

He goes closer to her. She's almost scared of him.

DONNA (CONT'D)
I want to stay.

THE DOCTOR
Look at me, Donna. Look at me.

She does. Both close. And Donna is crying.

DONNA
I was gonna be with you. For ever.

THE DOCTOR
I know.

DONNA
Rest of my life. Travelling. In the Tardis. The DoctorDonna.[3] Oh, but I can't go back. Don't make me go back. Doctor. Please.

THE DOCTOR
Donna. Oh, Donna Noble. I'm sorry.
(pause)
Goodbye.

And he holds his hands to her temples. Still crying:

3 In 4.2, the Ood describe the Doctor and Donna as 'DoctorDonna'.

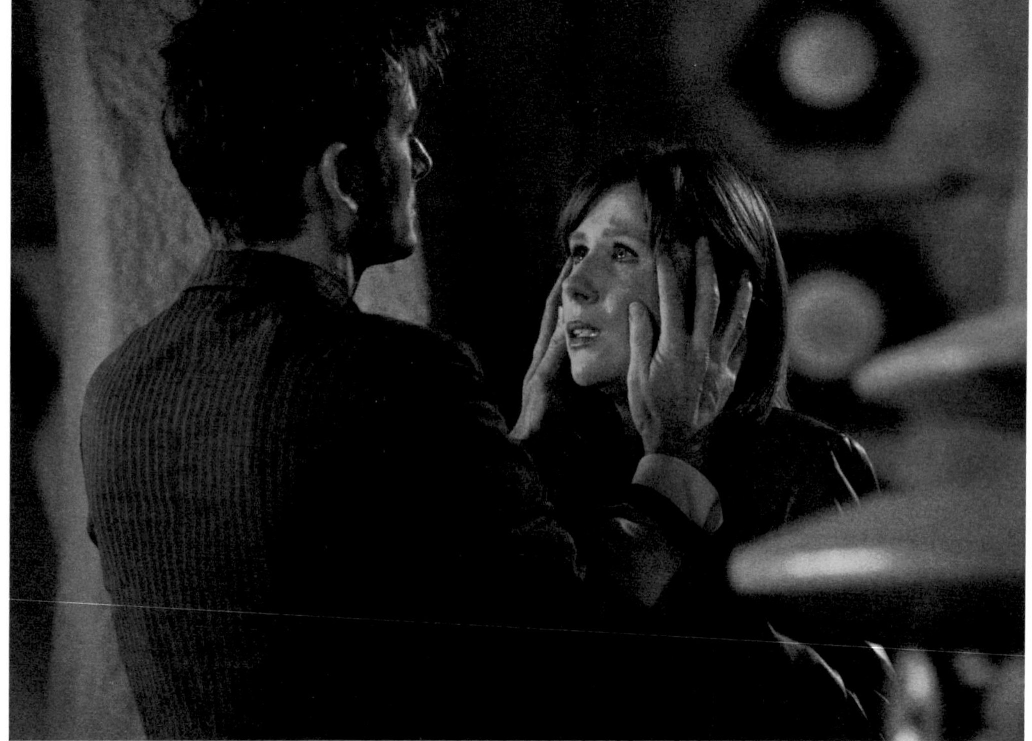

'Don't make me go back!' The Doctor must erase Donna's memories to save her life.

DONNA
No, please, no, no, no…

But she falls unconscious; he catches her, lowers her down.

CUT TO:

137. INT. NOBLES' HOUSE - NIGHT

The doorbell is ringing, ringing, ringing, ringing. WILF bounding down the hall, happy -

WILF
That must be her!

He opens the front door -

In the street, the TARDIS. But Wilf sees only THE DOCTOR, stooping down, DONNA unconscious at his feet. Desperate:

THE DOCTOR
Help me.

CUT TO:

138. INT. DONNA'S BEDROOM - NIGHT

CU DONNA, on her bed, unconscious, still clothed.

THE DOCTOR stands above her. Calmer. WILF in the doorway.

The Doctor turns and goes. Closes the door, darkness.

CUT TO:

139. INT. NOBLES' HOUSE, FRONT ROOM - NIGHT

Low light. THE DOCTOR sits with WILF & SYLVIA. Wilf so sad; Sylvia less forgiving, as he explains:

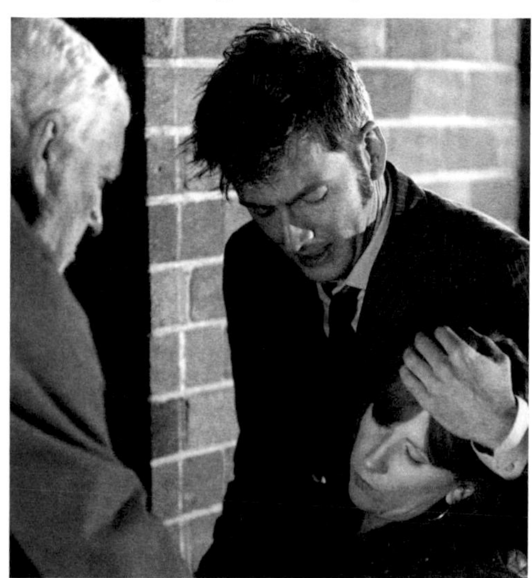

'That version of Donna… is dead.'

THE DOCTOR
She took my mind, into her own head. But that's a Time Lord consciousness. All that knowledge. It was killing her.

WILF
But she'll get better now…?

THE DOCTOR
I had to wipe her mind, completely. Every trace of me, or the Tardis, anything we did together, anywhere we went… had to go.

WILF
All those wonderful things she did -

THE DOCTOR
I know. But that version of Donna… is dead. Cos if she remembers, just for a second, she'll burn up. You can never tell her. You can't mention me, or any of it. For the rest of her life.

SYLVIA
But the whole world's talking about it, we travelled across space.

THE DOCTOR
And it'll just be a story. One of those Donna Noble stories. Where she missed it all, again.

WILF
But she was better, with you.

SYLVIA
Don't say that.

WILF
But she was.

THE DOCTOR
I just want you to know… That there are worlds out there, safe in the sky, because of her. That there are people, living in the light, and singing songs of Donna Noble, a thousand million light years away. They will never forget her. While she can never remember.
(pause; upset)
And for one moment. One shining moment. She was the most important woman in the whole wide universe.

SYLVIA
She still is. She's my daughter.

THE DOCTOR
Then maybe you should tell her that, once in a while.

And suddenly - DONNA walks in. As normal as can be.

DONNA
I was asleep! On my bed! In my clothes! Like a flippin' kid, what d'you let me do that for?
(to the Doctor)
Sorry, don't mind me. Donna!

THE DOCTOR
I'm… John Smith.

SYLVIA
Mr Smith was just leaving.

DONNA
My phone's gone mad! 32 texts! Veena's gone barmy, she's saying 'planets in the sky!', what have I missed now? Nice to meet you!

And she's gone.

Donna is her old self once again, tragically.

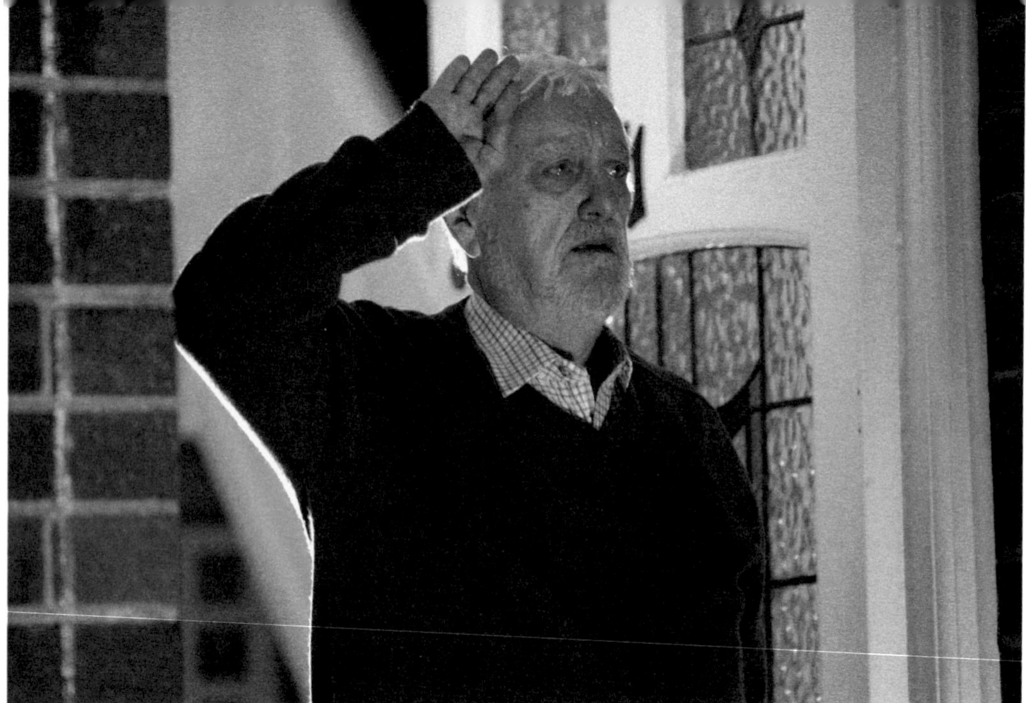

'I'll look up. On her behalf!' Not a dry eye in the house as Wilfred Mott bids the Doctor goodbye.

Silence. Wilf dismayed. Then, cold:

SYLVIA
As I said. I think you should go.

CUT TO:

140. INT. NOBLES' HOUSE, KITCHEN - NIGHT

DONNA on her mobile, making a cuppa.

DONNA
Don't be so stupid! How thick d'you think I am?! Planets! I'll tell you what that was, dumbo, it's those two-for-one lagers you get down the offy cos you fancy that little man with the goatee!
(hooting)
That's the one! I've seen you!

And THE DOCTOR can't help it; pops his head round.

THE DOCTOR
Um. Donna. I was just going.

DONNA
Yeah, see ya -
(turns her back, on the mobile)
Tell you what though, you're wasting your time with that one, cos Susie Mair, she went on that dating site, and she saw him - no, listen, this is important! Susie Mair wouldn't lie! Unless it's about calories!

During that, on the Doctor. Taking a last look at her.

Then he goes.

CUT TO:

141. EXT. NOBLES' HOUSE - NIGHT

WILF & THE DOCTOR in the doorway. It's now RAINING.

THE DOCTOR
You'll have quite a bit of this. Atmospheric disturbance. Still, it'll pass. Everything does. Bye then, Wilfred.

The Doctor walks into the rain; Wilf stays in the doorway.

WILF
But, Doctor… What about you, now? Who have you got? I mean, all those friends of yours…

THE DOCTOR
They've all got someone else. Still. That's fine. I'm fine.

WILF
I'll watch out for you, sir.

THE DOCTOR
You can't ever tell her.

WILF
No, but… Every night, Doctor. When it goes dark. And the stars come out. I'll look up. On her behalf. I'll look up at the sky, and think of you.

So simple, so heartfelt, that the Doctor could cry.

THE DOCTOR
…thank you.

And before he loses it, he walks away.

WIDE SHOT, the Doctor walking to the Tardis. In the rain. Wilf just a silhouette in the doorway.

The Doctor goes inside.

FX: THE TARDIS LAMP flares, the grind of ancient engines…

CUT TO:

<u>142. INT. NOBLES' HOUSE, KITCHEN - NIGHT</u>

DONNA on her mobile. But in the distance, the grind and roar of the old Tardis engines echoes across…

And just for a second, Donna looks up.

Stares into space. As though remembering….

But then. Back to normal. For ever.

DONNA
No, so what did she say then? Did she? Well she's lying! She is!

CUT TO:

<u>143. EXT. NOBLES' HOUSE - NIGHT</u>

The Tardis noise now fading away. And all alone in the doorway, in the rain…

WILF salutes.

WIDE SHOT. The Tardis has gone. Only the rain. And Wilfred Mott gently closes the door.

CUT TO:

<u>144. INT. TARDIS - NIGHT</u>

WIDE SHOT. In flight.

THE DOCTOR, all alone. He's a bit bedraggled, from the rain. Looks up at the Time Rotor.

Lost in thought.

Deep breath. Move on. He starts wandering round. Flicking switches. Recovering himself.

Nice and slow, taking his time. All the time in the world.

Then, eventually, there's a small bleep from the scanner. He wanders over. Only half interested. Studies it.

Then more curious…

THE DOCTOR
What…?
(looks closer)
What?
(closer)
Whaaaat????!

The Doctor. Alone again.

```
And he's bending over, fascinated,
unable to see -

TWO CYBERMEN rearing up behind
him!!!

                    END OF EPISODE 13
```

FROM: RUSSELL T DAVIES TO: BENJAMIN COOK
TUESDAY 22 JANUARY 2008 10:03:01 GMT

RE: HAPPY NEW YEAR?

And now, ten minutes after pressing send, I'm remembering all the lines and moments that I meant to put in. Always the way. I only remembered the Ood's 'DoctorDonna' five minutes ago, and bunged it in.

FROM: BENJAMIN COOK TO: RUSSELL T DAVIES
TUESDAY 22 JANUARY 2008 10:23:19 GMT

RE: HAPPY NEW YEAR?

Poor, poor Donna. That's worse than death, isn't it? I think *I* might cry! At least Wilf remembers.

Donna was much better than Penny Carter would have been.

FROM: RUSSELL T DAVIES TO: BENJAMIN COOK
TUESDAY 22 JANUARY 2008 10:30:07 GMT

RE: HAPPY NEW YEAR?

I know, imagine forgetting the Doctor! Catherine is *begging* to make an appearance in *The Sarah Jane Adventures*, because it's her daughter's favourite show, but I'm sitting here going, 'But *how?!*'

FROM: RUSSELL T DAVIES TO: BENJAMIN COOK
TUESDAY 22 JANUARY 2008 23:03:08 GMT

RE: HAPPY NEW YEAR?

I slept all afternoon. Fresh as the proverbial. People seem happy with the script, though Phil was seen to be weeping. Not at the sad ending; at the budget!

FROM: BENJAMIN COOK TO: RUSSELL T DAVIES
TUESDAY 22 JANUARY 2008 23:29:31 GMT

RE: HAPPY NEW YEAR?

You cried when writing Donna's goodbye, even though you knew what was coming, and now Phil is in tears... aren't you worried that it might be *too* sad for some viewers, especially the younger ones?

Also, if this isn't an odd question, why have you written that final scene with the Cybermen? What exactly do you think it adds to the plot? Isn't it a bit... superfluous?

FROM: RUSSELL T DAVIES TO: BENJAMIN COOK
WEDNESDAY 23 JANUARY 2008 00:04:57 GMT

RE: HAPPY NEW YEAR?

The final scene? Well, same reason as ever, really. Like the runaway bride appearing in the TARDIS at the end of *Doomsday*, like the *Titanic* crashing into the TARDIS at the end of *Last of the Time Lords*, to end on an upbeat note. To say that the story isn't over, don't stop watching *Doctor Who*, ever. The Doctor's life never stops, no matter how sad things get. Dry your tears, move on. New adventures to come. Otherwise, you might remember *Doctor Who* as a sad and bleak thing, which is maybe not so good if you're eight years old.

But am I worried that some viewers might find Donna's departure *too* sad? Not remotely. Not for a single second. I believe, hugely, massively, that TV isn't there to make you smile. Drama certainly isn't. That ending is devastating. I hope it's never forgotten. I hope people cry for years. In 70 years' time, kids watching it now will be in old folks' homes, saying, 'Oh, why couldn't Donna Noble have remembered just one thing?!' There's this

On the Dalek Crucible set at Upper Boat Studios, the cast and crew of 4.12/4.13 celebrate the end of principal photography.

great misconception that the Slitheen are for kids and episodes like *Human Nature* and *The Family of Blood* are for adults. In fact, adults can enjoy daft green monsters, and kids can appreciate emotional, grown-up drama. Pixar understands that perfectly. JK Rowling does. If kids are upset, then they're feeling something, and kids feel things vividly. The death of a goldfish is like the end of the world. It's keen, real and powerful for them. But that doesn't make it something to be avoided. If they can reach that state through fiction, well, they're actually experiencing something wonderful. And important.

Of course, very young kids might not get it, because forgetting has no analogy with their lives. They understand grief and loss, that's easy, because they've all lost that goldfish, grandparent, mother, favourite pen, or been lost in a crowd, so they get it when they see the Doctor lose Rose to a parallel world, or Nemo's dad lose his son in *Finding Nemo*, or Harry Potter see his dead mum and dad in the Mirror of Erised. It has an echo within them, whereas simply *forgetting* someone doesn't. What happens to Donna is actually, beneath its simplicity, a fairly sophisticated sci-fi idea, so I think a lot of younger kids might be puzzled. Or bored. That's why Wilf, with his lonely salute, is so important, because you can register his loss. For adults, too, he really sells the moment. But I can't think of a way in which a kid could think, even unconsciously, that's happened to me.

Then again, you can never predict how kids will react. They're bloody clever. All that instinct. The writer Pete Bowker tells the best *Doctor Who*-viewing story ever. His son, Eric, watched *Doomsday*, and didn't particularly react to Rose's departure, but then the bride, Donna, appeared in the TARDIS at the cliffhanger, and Eric turned to his dad and said, 'It's all right now, cos the good fairy has appeared to make the man better.' And that's not just cute: Pete said that to see such engagement with a story, so emotionally and pictorially, for the first time ever, was actually a family triumph.

FROM: BENJAMIN COOK TO: RUSSELL T DAVIES
WEDNESDAY 23 JANUARY 21:39:11 GMT

RE: HAPPY NEW YEAR?

How was today's Tone Meeting? Did you make it through? (Or are you still there? Have they locked the doors?)

FROM: RUSSELL T DAVIES TO: BENJAMIN COOK
THURSDAY 24 JANUARY 2008 00:22:08 GMT

SKINS WINS!

I just got a text from the Broadcast Awards – *Skins* Series One has beaten *Doctor Who* Series Three! You've been e-mailing the wrong person, Benjamino. You should be doing – no, wait for it –The Life Of Bryan. Ha ha ha.

The Tone Meeting wasn't as endless as I thought. I'm not about to say that 4.13 is easy, no way, but actually there's a lot of sleight of hand. The end of the universe actually takes place in six or seven separate rooms, three of which are standing sets, with a lot of spectacle purely CGI. I think it's achievable. (Remember me saying this. Next week the bills come in and I will bleed!) And that team is so excellent now. Piers was there to observe, and at times I thought, to him, we must be talking in shorthand. 'Scene 43, Shot 2, is a mid-shot green screen, no reverse, like in *Doomsday*, yeah?' There was a great moment when I was despairing of finding a location for the Crucible Test Area. I said, 'Let's face it, we're not going to find a big enough space that fits Dalek design. I might have to cut this sequence.' And Ed Thomas said, 'Oy! I thought you were made of better stuff. Four years on this job and you've never wimped out before.' I loved him for saying that.

It was Phil's last Tone Meeting. We had a strange round of applause. Strange, because it was sad.

Text message from: **Russell**
Sent: 24-Jan-2008 19:44
On set today, Alex Kingston walked up to me and shouted through her spacesuit helmet, 'Can you write me a part as a lipstick lesbian?!' I love moments like that.

Text message from: **Ben**
Sent: 24-Jan-2008 20:18
It's great going on set at the moment, isn't it? Everyone is just gutted by what's in store for Donna in 4.13!

Text message from: **Russell**
Sent: 25-Jan-2008 11:16
Bernard Cribbins just phoned me up: 'I have read Episode 13. I have been crying for two days.'

FROM: BENJAMIN COOK TO: RUSSELL T DAVIES
SATURDAY 26 JANUARY 2008 00:22:08 GMT

RE: SKINS WINS!

Where do you stand with the Christmas Special right now? How's life in the Christmas Maybe?

FROM: RUSSELL T DAVIES TO: BENJAMIN COOK
SUNDAY 27 JANUARY 2008 09:00:23 GMT

RE: SKINS WINS!

Lordy God. Panic. I've been having a lot of thoughts – nothing coherent, not yet – for ages, but the rush of scripts has been so great that I haven't had time to tell you. Cybermen, Victoriana, a swordfight on the roof with Cybershades (Cyberman heads in flowing black robes, like wraiths, sort of creepy half-Cybermen), workhouse kids as slaves… That's all the normal plot stuff. The real heart of it is the beginning: the Doctor arrives, hears a damsel in distress, the Doctor steps forward to save her… when this *other* man swings in, dashing, brilliant, amazing, clever, witty, saves the day. The Doctor says, 'Who are you?' The man says, 'I'm the Doctor!' Good scene. The Doctor becomes *his* companion. I like that. Sweet. There will be a beautiful

David Morrissey in 4.14 *The Next Doctor.*

woman too, of course, but really it's the Doctor paired with a new Doctor. That's a lovely story and it's got great potential. It would be wonderful if I had a month or two to let it stew. But it's due in three weeks! I can hardly bear to look at it. The furnace!

Quite apart from the time in which I have to write it, it's like relaxing-after-the-thirteenth-episode-is-delivered is hardwired into me. I can feel bits of my brain and body closing down. It's Herculean to keep going. And I'm not Hercules. I'm really, properly, feeling old. I used to have the stamina to steamroller through this sort of schedule, but it's lacking now. The last time I had my eyes tested, the optician asked my age and said, 'You'll need bifocals soon. Your lenses won't be able to cope with reading for much longer.' Lo and behold, a few months later, it's like someone's thrown a switch. Suddenly, overnight, my glasses are on and off, on and off. Proper, undeniable ageing. You sort of think it'll never happen, but your body has other ideas.

Nah, it's worse than that. It's not just Grumpy Old Men stuff. Far worse is the snaky little thought: if you had some coke, you'd have twice the energy and stay awake for longer. I haven't thought that seriously for years. This is the first time, in ten years or so, of thinking, I *need* it. I know it's bollocks, I know, I know. I think I needed to type it out to see how stupid it looks.

FROM: RUSSELL T DAVIES TO: BENJAMIN COOK
THURSDAY 31 JANUARY 2008 01:11:06 GMT

RE: SKINS WINS!

Well, 4.13 is 170 FX days over! I've found about 88 to cut, and Phil has found 120, but they're a bit severe, so I'm fighting them off. Never mind, we'll get there, I'm sure of that. It's just that the actual getting there is such a slog.

I know what's *really* preying on my mind, though, and stopping me moving onto the Christmas Special. Julie said, 'That scene on Bad Wolf Bay isn't working, is it?' And she's absolutely right. I love a good note, because it's like someone has articulated the voice at the back of your head. That scene doesn't work. I have always known that, from the moment I typed it out, but I don't know how to fix it. Rose has to be stupid to fall in love with Doctor #2. No matter what I do, that's not her Doctor. I can Elastoplast over it by saying that Doctor #2 needs Rose, but that's slight. You don't *feel* that. Why doesn't Rose hop into the TARDIS and go with the real Doctor? The walls of the universe are open enough for her to pop to and fro. She's always wanted to get him back, so why does she stay on Bad Wolf Bay? The hardest thing of all in that scene – and Billie might yet have problems with it – is getting Rose to walk away from the TARDIS in the first place, disguised by that funny Jackie dialogue. That, indeed, is the problem with the whole scene, that Rose has to act out of character to stay on Bad Wolf Bay. She's utterly, marvellously selfish, and would push past anyone to get to her Doctor.

I have to work out whose scene it is, too. In many ways, it's the Doctor's, the real Doctor's. David thinks it's a tragic scene, because it's all about the original, but that's exactly what has reduced Rose's intelligence; she's doing what the plot demands, not what *she'd* demand. That's always wrong. But follow Rose's impulse and we're off into... well, plots that we can't shoot, pages of arguing, the Doctor denying her a life with him for no good reason other than my need to tie up the loose ends. Oh, it's driving me mad. In *Doomsday*, Bad Wolf Bay was the best scene ever, and now I've made it the location of the most unconvincing scene ever – and I don't know how to fix it. All sorts of false notes are chiming. I think I hate the kiss. That's when Rose's intelligence is zero. It makes me feel nothing, when I should be feeling everything.

When I get this stuck, I start lying to myself. I tell myself that the Bad Wolf Bay scene mustn't be that sad, because the really sad scene is Donna's departure. You can't have tragedy after tragedy. Well, there's a certain amount of sense in that, but it's still a lie. I'm telling myself that to soothe myself for not getting the scene right in the first place. I'm supposed to be thinking about 4.14, but this Bad Wolf Bay scene has become a logjam in my head. It's all I can think about. Julie first made her comment about five days ago, and I've been thinking about it ever since. One thing I do know: this isn't a couple-of-lines rewrite. It's more fundamental. Julie keeps e-mailing with suggestions, like Rose saying to the original, 'But he's not you', which only makes me say, 'So why stay with him?!' This isn't a dialogue problem. There's no sentence that will paper over the cracks. It's a plot rewrite. I've got the story wrong. And that's massive, potentially. In an episode that's already over-length (it's been timed at 67 minutes, damn it – this is getting ridiculous) and over-budget, how do I think of a new story?!

FROM: BENJAMIN COOK TO: RUSSELL T DAVIES
THURSDAY 31 JANUARY 2008 01:41:18 GMT

RE: SKINS WINS!

Yes, I suppose the original Bad Wolf Bay scene, in *Doomsday*, worked because the Doctor and Rose *had* to be separated. This scene isn't working because they choose to be. The imperative has gone. Ouch!

FROM: RUSSELL T DAVIES TO: BENJAMIN COOK
THURSDAY 31 JANUARY 2008 01:51:04 GMT

RE: SKINS WINS!

Well, exactly. And that raises another problem: if I work out a version in which they *have* to be separated, aren't I repeating the first bloody version? Argh! Do you see?

FROM: RUSSELL T DAVIES TO: BENJAMIN COOK
MONDAY 4 FEBRUARY 2008 10:45:39 GMT

RE: SKINS WINS!

I've made further FX cuts. Not just for FX, but also for page count. Firstly, the Shadow Proclamation Lobby has gone. Completely. Slitheen, space extras, monks and nuns. Poor Louise Page – I hope she hasn't spent money on this already. (As we have with Margaret Slitheen's voice. Annette Badland has already recorded her line!) Hey ho, something substantial had to go. The TARDIS now lands directly in the Shadow Architect's office. We'll still need the Judoon – they'll be there with some 'Bo! Klo! Fo!' dialogue – but we only have four of them now.

All the stuff on Skaro with the Young Davros has been cut, too. The FX, plus the ward and the nurses and the soldiers, everything. It's heartbreaking, but what can you do? Will Cohen is devastated.

However, I have asked for two extra FX shots – that's all we need – around Rose. Brand new ones. Similar to the Voidstuff shots with the 3D glasses in *Doomsday*. This should fix the problems with her plot. The Voidstuff surrounds anyone who crosses from one universe to another, so I can say that it's now contaminated or something, as though – because of the Daleks' dimension-rupturing – it's become lethal if you're in the wrong universe. Rose has to stay in the parallel world – or she'll die. She has no choice.

Text message from: Russell
Sent: 04-Feb-2008 22:04
I feel... blurgh! I get dizzy every time I turn my head. My eyes are all puffed up. Oh well, it'll pass. I have to get on with work tomorrow. It can't wait any longer.

FROM: RUSSELL T DAVIES TO: BENJAMIN COOK
TUESDAY 5 FEBRUARY 2008 14:15:12 GMT

RE: SKINS WINS!

Chicken pox! I've got bloody chicken pox!!! I woke up today like a *Doctor Who* monster. More lumps and bumps than… well, my normal lumps and bumps. I feel like crap. I'm going back to bed now. Must not scratch.

FROM: BENJAMIN COOK TO: RUSSELL T DAVIES
WEDNESDAY 6 FEBRUARY 2008 01:08:38 GMT

RE: SKINS WINS!

Chicken pox?! Didn't you get it out of the way when you were a kid? It's supposed to be less of a bastard when you're young. (Sorry, not helping.) My mum used to make me go round to play at the houses of kids with chicken pox, hoping that I'd catch it!

Text message from: Ben
Sent: 06-Feb-2008 19:45
Feeling any better? Today was fun. I was on set for *Silence in the Library*. Swansea in the sunshine! Gorgeous set. AMAZING lunch.

Text message from: Russell
Sent: 06-Feb-2008 19:51
Amazing lunch? In Swansea?! I'm worse today, because I was allergic to the pills, so my mouth blew up till I was having trouble breathing. I had to go to casualty. On a Wednesday morning. Not glamorous. Now my lips are so big, I look like a cartoon duck.

Text message from: Ben
Sent: 06-Feb-2008 20:18
Casualty?! Russell, I hope you aren't working tonight. That shouldn't be your priority. For once, let other people sort out the shit.

Russell promised Noel Clarke that Mickey would be brought back in *Torchwood* Series Three.

Text message from: Russell
Sent: 06-Feb-2008 20:22
I know, you're right, I'll stop soon. But no one else can rewrite this bastard script. I'll work till Friday, then I can stop and have a whole weekend off in lovely Manchester.

Text message from: Russell
Sent: 07-Feb-2008 12:16
I'm hobbling today. It's on the soles of my feet. There ain't no dignity.

FROM: RUSSELL T DAVIES TO: BENJAMIN COOK
SATURDAY 9 FEBRUARY 2008 18:18:09 GMT

RE: SKINS WINS!

Manchester, hooray! My boyfriend, my clothes, my CDs, my… everything. Even my full-sized Dalek in the hall. (I've got to get rid of that. It's too much like work now.) With a bit of luck, I can stay here for ten days or so, but I'm itchy, scratchy and tired, and I still have to rewrite 4.13. And I just realised, my plan to make the Bad Wolf Bay scene work – the one involving Voidstuff – won't work, because I'd forgotten that Mickey has to be free to stay in our universe. Bollocks. Julie's upset. She's saying, 'Leave Mickey in the parallel universe,' and I'm saying, 'Too late! We promised Noel that we'd bring him back in *Torchwood* Series Three.'

FROM: BENJAMIN COOK TO: RUSSELL T DAVIES
SATURDAY 9 FEBRUARY 2008 19:01:46 GMT

RE: SKINS WINS!

Why not have Rose admit that she's a terrible racist and she wants to stay in the parallel world to rid herself of Mickey? Yes, that'll do. Rose Tyler: Terrible Racist. That's not just an idea, it's a spin-off.

FROM: RUSSELL T DAVIES TO: BENJAMIN COOK
SATURDAY 9 FEBRUARY 2008 19:24:12 GMT

RE: SKINS WINS!

That's brilliant! Or maybe Freddie Ljungberg, Russell Tovey and Charlie Hunnam could run past in speedos, and Rose thinks, hmm, okay, I'll stay here, thank you very much. That would work.

FROM: RUSSELL T DAVIES TO: BENJAMIN COOK
MONDAY 11 FEBRUARY 2008 23:55:16 GMT

RE: SKINS WINS!

I watched the new *Skins* tonight, finally. But, but, but…

that first episode is EXCELLENT! What a change. What a show! Moments of absolute beauty – like Tony with Maxxie's mum, when she has to help him piss, and then they started laughing, that was perfect. The tiny little fact that Maxxie's mum used to clean for Tony's mum. I loved it.

FROM: BENJAMIN COOK TO: RUSSELL T DAVIES
TUESDAY 12 FEBRUARY 2008 01:57:01 GMT

RE: SKINS WINS!

I'm glad you're watching. It's much better, isn't it? It's extraordinary and fascinating that they had to destroy Tony in order to let the show breathe. I hear rumours that Series Three will have an almost entirely new cast, to keep the show about 17- and 18-year-olds. I think that's an incredible idea. Brave, aren't they?

How are you feeling today?

FROM: RUSSELL T DAVIES TO: BENJAMIN COOK
TUESDAY 12 FEBRUARY 2008 13:15:36 GMT

RE: SKINS WINS!

Sick as a dog. The moment I stopped work, everything leapt on me. Today, it's bronchitis! And I still haven't rewritten 4.13.

FROM: RUSSELL T DAVIES TO: BENJAMIN COOK
MONDAY 18 FEBRUARY 2008 02:14:07 GMT

RE: SKINS WINS!

I've whittled down 4.13 from 78 pages to 71. That's a miracle. I can't believe I'm delivering the final draft on the day that they start filming! That's horrific.

The Bad Wolf Bay scene still isn't working, but do you know what? No one's giving me good notes on it, when they should, so sod it. It's slightly better now, and I've cut the kiss between Rose and Doctor #2, but it still sucks. After the Doctor and Jackie dialogue ('No, you plum. He's called Tony'), the scene plays out like this:

```
But Rose is looking back at the
Tardis (dialogue has taken them a
good 20 feet away, good distance).
At the Doctor.

                ROSE
...but hold on. I spent all
that time, trying to get away
from this place. So I could
find you. I'm not going back
now.

             THE DOCTOR
But you've got to. Cos we
saved the universe at a cost,
and the cost, is him.
          (ie, Doctor #2)
He's too dangerous to be left
on his own.

           THE DOCTOR #2
You made me.

             THE DOCTOR
Exactly. You were born in
battle. Full of blood and
anger and revenge.
            (to Rose)
Remind you of someone? That's
me, when we first met. And you
made me better. Now you can
do the same for him.

                ROSE
...but he's not you.

             THE DOCTOR
He needs you. That's very me.

                DONNA
It's better than that,
though. Don't you see what
he's giving you?
          (to Doctor #2)
Tell her, go on.

           THE DOCTOR #2
I look like him. Think like
him. Same memories, same
thoughts, same everything,
except... I've only got one
heart.

                ROSE
Which means...?

           THE DOCTOR #2
I'm part Human. Specifically,
the ageing part. I'll grow
old. And never regenerate.
I've only got one life, Rose
Tyler. I... could spend it with
you. If you want.

                ROSE
You'll grow old... at the same
time as me?

           THE DOCTOR #2
Together.
```

'He needs you. That's very me.'

ROSE
That's…

Scared, tempted, she puts her hand to his chest. Feels his heartbeat. So intimate, now.

Moment broken by the Doctor -

THE DOCTOR
Oh, and don't forget this -

Throws them a chunk of coral - Doctor #2 catches it.

THE DOCTOR (CONT'D)
This universe is in need of defending. Chunk of Tardis. Grow your own.

THE DOCTOR #2
But that takes thousands of years.

THE DOCTOR
No, because…

DONNA
…if you shatterfry the plasmic shell and modify the dimensional stabiliser to a foldback harmonic of 36.3, you accelerate growth by the power of 59!

THE DOCTOR/THE DOCTOR #2
We never thought of that!

DONNA
I'm just brilliant!

THE DOCTOR
The Doctor. In the Tardis. With Rose Tyler. Just as it should be.

ROSE
But… what about you?

THE DOCTOR
Oh, I'm fine, I've got madam.

DONNA
Human with a Time Lord brain, perfect combination! We can travel the universe for ever. Best friends! And equals, just what old skinnyboy needs, an equal!

The Tardis groans.

THE DOCTOR
We've got to go. The walls of the universe are repairing themselves -

ROSE
But I'll see you again, yeah?

THE DOCTOR
We can't. Now the Reality Bomb's been destroyed, the dimensions are closing again. This parallel is about to be sealed off. For ever.

Rose steps forward, a little -

ROSE
But it's still not right. I came back for you.

THE DOCTOR
And you've got me! As him! Go on. Test him!

Doctor #2 walking forward to join Rose.

ROSE
Okay. If you've got the same memories… When I last stood here. On the worst day of my life. What was the last thing you said to me?

THE DOCTOR #2
I said, 'Rose Tyler.'

ROSE
And how was that sentence gonna end?

He leans in close. Gentle.

And he whispers.

It's the most powerful moment; he steps back again, he and Rose just staring at each other. Awestruck. Dazzled.

And that's all the Doctor needs to see.

Heartbroken.

Donna knows it too, glancing at him.

Then the Doctor turns, goes into the Tardis, Donna following -

Rose only looks round as she hears the door slam - !

She runs a step forward -

ROSE (CONT'D)
No - !

FX: the Tardis fades away...

Rose stands there. Upset. But behind her, Doctor #2 walks forward again. He reaches out.

He holds her hand.

WIDE SHOT, Jackie standing back, Rose & Doctor #2 hand in hand, looking at the now-empty beach.

Rose leans against him.

And hold.

I know exactly what's wrong with it: it's too complicated. Emotionally, I mean. It has no echo, no resonance, it's empty sci-fi. When the Doctor and Rose were separated into parallel universes in *Doomsday*, that felt like every love you've ever lost – even if it's only the ones that you've lost in your head, like teenage virgins pining over love songs in their bedroom. But when you've been separated into different universes, but now have a double of the man that you loved, who's not quite the same, but who's better because he's mortal, but worse because he's not the original… well, you're going beyond human experience. There's no parallel with real life. No equation. Therefore, no feeling.

I got carried away with the double Doctor idea.

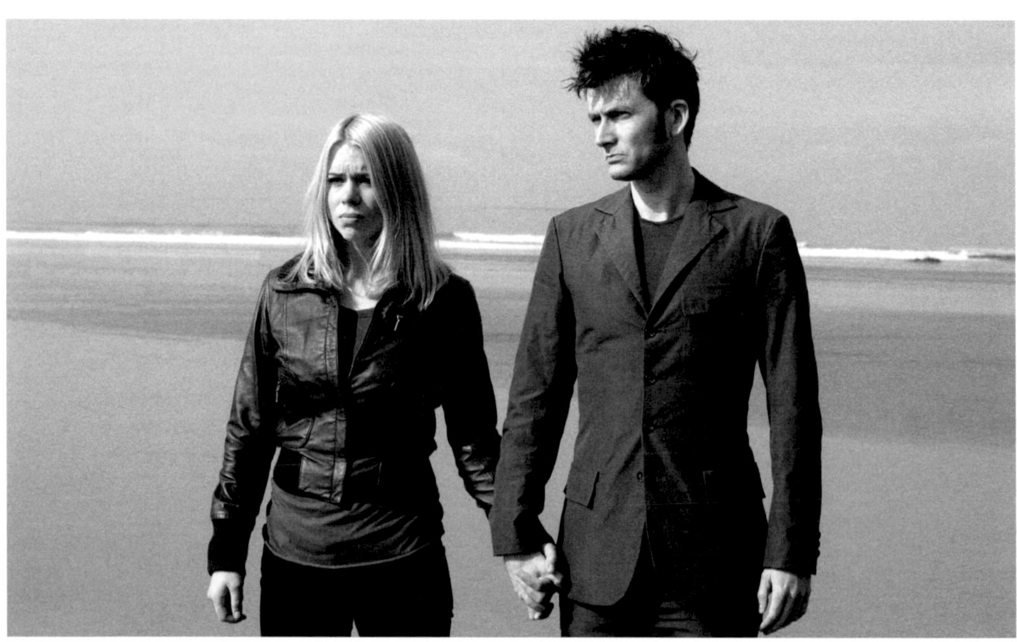

Rose Tyler and Doctor #2 will grow old together, in a parallel universe. Sob!

Originally, that was just going to happen right at the end, but then I remember saying in one of my e-mails to you, 'If you've got two Doctors in 4.13, why not use them both?' Which I have done. Which means that I've written myself into a corner. Doctor #2 isn't a quick, throwaway idea that I can jettison now; he's integral to the whole of 4.13. I think that proves that sometimes you can have too long to think about ideas. They don't always grow; sometimes they fester.

FROM: BENJAMIN COOK TO: RUSSELL T DAVIES
MONDAY 18 FEBRUARY 2008 02:22:06 GMT

RE: SKINS WINS!

I agree with some of what you said about the Bad Wolf Bay scene (you're right, it's still not *quite* working), except for the bit about Rose's departure, as written, having no resonance. We've all loved someone and it hasn't worked out, for whatever reason, so we've found someone else. We've moved on. Even the teenage virgins find someone real, someone who exists beyond the posters on their bedroom walls. And yet we know – we always know – that the next love is *not* the same, they're *not* as good, we're settling for second best. We're all just making do. Like Judith in *The Second Coming*, we're all hoping that someone better will come along, someone as incredible as our First Love or as perfect as the girl or boy in the posters on our bedroom wall. Or is that just me? Oh God…

FROM: RUSSELL T DAVIES TO: BENJAMIN COOK
TUESDAY 19 FEBRUARY 2008 14:18:55 GMT

RE: SKINS WINS!

I take your point about accepting second best, making do with Doctor #2, and how we can all recognise that, because we've all done it (we lie to kids, we tell them that those bedroom posters are fantasies – bollocks, they're the *best!* Everything else is a pale imitation), but the problem is, none of us does it THAT QUICKLY. Not in three pages. Accepting second best is a quiet, passive condition – universal, yes, but you have to slide that into a drama. It's what Rose has done with Andy in *Bob & Rose*, it's what Vince does when he goes out with Cameron in *Queer as Folk*… they're making do with compromises and imagining themselves happy, wishing themselves happy, even if it isn't true. But no one does that in a crisis. It's gradual.

I'll think on. I'm sure that I'm going to rewrite that scene again before it's shot.

FROM: BENJAMIN COOK TO: RUSSELL T DAVIES
TUESDAY 19 FEBRUARY 2008 22:05:31 GMT

RE: SKINS WINS!

I wonder whether Rose's decision works *because* it's quick. If she had time to think about it, of course she wouldn't stay on Bad Wolf Bay. As I read it, Rose accepts second best, Doctor #2, because her Doctor, the original Doctor, manipulates her into doing so. That's why it happens so suddenly. The whole 'He's too dangerous to be left on his own' speech – 'He needs you. That's very me.' Ouch! The original Doctor knows how to hit a nerve, doesn't he? He's pushing Rose away, making a magnificent sacrifice, because he loves her. (And we've all done that with someone we love, haven't we?) That's why you describe him in the script as 'Heartbroken'. You're hung up on the idea that Rose must be dumb to choose to stay on Bad Wolf Bay, but she doesn't choose, does she? Not really. He does.

FROM: RUSSELL T DAVIES TO: BENJAMIN COOK
FRIDAY 22 FEBRUARY 2008 18:08:59 GMT

PANIC!!!

Sorry I haven't written for a few days. On Monday, I've just two weeks to write the Christmas script… and I haven't a clue. There have been no Maybe thoughts while I've been ill, and now I'm worried because I'm still feeling ill. I've got this cough that I can't shake off, I'm losing sleep because I'm coughing so much, and naturally I think it's cancer because, well, that's what smokers think. I'm cocking things up like buggery here. I'm going back to Cardiff on Monday. I need to be there, to lock myself away, to panic some more and bang my head against the wall.

FROM: BENJAMIN COOK TO: RUSSELL T DAVIES
FRIDAY 22 FEBRUARY 2008 19:16:03 GMT

RE: PANIC!!!

>>I never think of it as work, really, no matter how much hard graft I actually do. Even if no one ever saw

this stuff, I'd be doing it anyway.<<

Ahem.

FROM: RUSSELL T DAVIES TO: BENJAMIN COOK
FRIDAY 22 FEBRUARY 2008 19:18:16 GMT

RE: PANIC!!!

SOD OFF!

You're right, though.

Text message from: Ben
Sent: 25-Feb-2008 23:12
Please don't tell me you missed tonight's Skins...?! How shocking was Sid's dad's death? That long, lonely day in Sid's house, that was just wonderful. Bryan Elsley, all is forgiven!

Text message from: Russell
Sent: 26-Feb-2008 00:32
That episode was brilliant. BRILLIANT! Isn't it weird? Skins has got so much better by bringing the parents right into the centre and by sidelining the shagging and clubbing somewhat. In some ways, it's the opposite of what it was. Bloody marvellous, though.

FROM: RUSSELL T DAVIES TO: BENJAMIN COOK
SATURDAY 1 MARCH 2008 16:28:17 GMT

RE: PANIC!!!

I've rewritten Bad Wolf Bay again. Finally, I've got it right! It starts as before with the exchange between the Doctor and Jackie, and then:

```
But Rose now looks back at the
Tardis (dialogue has taken them a
good 20 feet away, good distance).
At the Doctor.

                ROSE
     ...but hold on. This is the
     parallel universe, right?

             THE DOCTOR
     You're back home.

                DONNA
     And the walls of the world
     are closing again, now
     the Reality Bomb never
     happened. It's a dimensional
     retroclosure - see, I really
     get that stuff now!

                ROSE
     No, but I spent all that
     time, trying to find you. I'm
     not going back now.

             THE DOCTOR
     But you've got to. Cos we
     saved the universe at a cost,
     and the cost, is him.
             (ie, Doctor #2)
     He destroyed the Daleks. He
     committed genocide. He's too
     dangerous to be left on his
     own.
```

Then the scene continues as before, with the Doctor explaining that Doctor #2 is 'Full of blood and anger and revenge', Doctor #2 telling Rose that he's part-human, and the original Doctor chucking them a lump of TARDIS, and then:

```
The Tardis groans.

             THE DOCTOR
     We've got to go. This reality
     is sealing itself off. For
     ever.

Rose steps forward, a little -

                ROSE
     But it's still not right. Cos
     the Doctor's still... you.

             THE DOCTOR
     And I'm him!

Rose looks at them both. And takes
control. The two Doctors; the most
important decision of her life...

                ROSE
     All right. Both of you.
     Answer me this. When I last
     stood here, on this beach,
     on the worst day of my life,
     what was the last thing you
     said to me?
             (to the Doctor)
     Go on. What was it?

             THE DOCTOR
     I said, 'Rose Tyler.'

                ROSE
     And how was that sentence
```

The kiss is back in there – and so is Rose Tyler!

```
    gonna end?

                  THE DOCTOR
    ...does it need saying?

She turns to Doctor #2.

                  ROSE
    And you. Doctor. What was the
    end of the sentence?

And he smiles. He leans in close.
Gentle.

And he whispers.

It's the most powerful moment; he
steps back again, he and Rose just
staring at each other. Awestruck.
Dazzled.

Then suddenly, on impulse, she
leans forward, pulls the Doctor
down by the lapel -

And kisses him!

And that's all the original Doctor
needs to see.

Heartbroken.

Donna knows it too, glancing at him.

Then the Doctor turns, goes into
the Tardis, Donna following -

Rose & Doctor #2 separate only as
they hears the door slam -
```

Basically, I've given more of the decision to Rose, put her in control, and used that control to push away the original Doctor. And the kiss is back in! Then the scene finishes as before: Rose saying, 'No – !', as the TARDIS fades away, Doctor #2 taking her hand, and a wide shot of the now-empty beach. Julie is happy, David is happy, phew, good. Series Four, final rewrite, done.

FROM: BENJAMIN COOK TO: RUSSELL T DAVIES
SATURDAY 1 MARCH 2008 16:47:51 GMT

RE: PANIC!!!

Ahh, that's the one! That Bad Wolf Bay scene is better now, isn't it? Never mind Julie and David… are *you* happy with it, Russell?

FROM: RUSSELL T DAVIES TO: BENJAMIN COOK
SATURDAY 1 MARCH 2008 17:13:56 GMT

RE: PANIC!!!

I am delighted. That is such a weight off my mind. Knowing that it wasn't working was driving me mad. It hung over me, during Chicken Pox Fortnight. Literally, all the time. I tell you what helped: I watched the footage of the 4.12/4.13 read-through. They filmed it for *Doctor Who Confidential*, then edited it together fast so that I could see it – and they had to read the first draft of 4.13, because that's all that I'd written. It was so slow! (I'd been worried that cutting all that history-of-Davros stuff had gutted the script and left it a bit vacuous, but then I realised that it's the best cut I could have made, because the read-through drags terribly around about those scenes.) I could see what worked and what didn't, and I realised how good the kiss was, but equally that the kiss had no consequence. That's why it wasn't earning its place. But it's obvious, in the end, isn't it? The scene is about Rose choosing between two Doctors. So, on the last draft, finally, I've written clearly, obviously, Rose making that choice. Rose is in control.

The rushes have helped, too. When Rose is in the TARDIS with Doctor #2, Billie is looking at him with sheer *lust*. As only Billie can do! That, too, puts the power into Rose's hands. The mechanics start to work…

FROM: RUSSELL T DAVIES TO: BENJAMIN COOK
MONDAY 3 MARCH 2008 23:50:38 GMT

RE: PANIC!!!

Hey, did you see *Skins* tonight? Blimey! It's not afraid to take risks, is it? It's a different show each week. A lot like *Doctor Who*, actually. But every episode has such a strong, wonderful, unique voice. I don't know whether that comes from Bryan Elsley or from his team of young writers. But *Skins* makes me feel so out of touch with domestic drama. I kind of dread going back to writing that stuff, like it's something I've forgotten. No, not forgotten, something that I've moved too far away from. And a world which is working perfectly well without me. Damn them!

Sometimes I think of giving up writing, and that thought seems utterly wonderful. Like bliss. Like a release. Freedom. Imagine having no deadlines ever again. Sometimes I think very strongly that I really could stop for ever. That shouldn't feel so brilliant, should it? I don't know. Maybe it's the pox talking. No, it's just the middle-aged businessman talking, that's all. But I do get so tired of Scene 1, Scene 2, Scene 3, on and on and on. Maybe I should try to write a book...?

FROM: BENJAMIN COOK TO: RUSSELL T DAVIES
TUESDAY 4 MARCH 2008 00:07:55 GMT

RE: PANIC!!!

You couldn't stop writing, Russell. You wouldn't last six months.

How does a writer know when they've found their voice, do you think? *Can* you know? Or is it for others to tell you? Must your voice be unique? Aren't writers – like musicians – imitators by trade? Does finding your voice begin with imitating other, more accomplished writers, do you think?

FROM: RUSSELL T DAVIES TO: BENJAMIN COOK
TUESDAY 4 MARCH 2008 02:18:21 GMT

CYBERMAN ARSE

Ha ha, you're right, I couldn't stop writing for ever. Not even for six months. What would I do? I'm a slave to this job. Oh dear...

Look, I finally started 4.14. Christ, I hate starting. It just says: such a long way to go. Funny to think, the last Christmas script, that was the very first script that I ever sent you, and now we're onto next Christmas already. This one hasn't exactly got Kylie and the *Titanic*, but it's got a different sort of hook...

```
1. INT. TARDIS - NIGHT

REPEAT the end of 4.13; THE DOCTOR
alone. He walks around the console.
A bleep from the scanner, he
studies it…

            THE DOCTOR
   What?
            (looks closer)
   What??
            (even closer)
   Whaaaat???

And he's bending forward, staring,
not noticing… the TWO CYBERMEN
rearing up behind him!!

NEW MATERIAL. The Doctor spins
round - !

          THE DOCTOR (CONT'D)
   What?!
```

Cybermen in the Victorian snow in 4.14 *The Next Doctor*.

FX: THE TWO CYBERMEN… fade away…

The Doctor looks round, hearing a *whoosh*…

FX: THE TWO CYBERMEN reappear, fading up at the top of the ramp. Both flailing, slowly, as if falling…

The Doctor takes a step towards them, boggling!

FX: and the two CYBERMEN fade again. A second later, one fades back into existence, right by the wooden door; it's as though they're phasing through the Tardis.

FX: CU that Cyberman fades, gone.

The Doctor runs to the console, throwing levers -

THE DOCTOR (CONT'D)
Falling through the Vortex! But heading for where…?

The Tardis lurches, CAMERA SHAKE! The Doctor running around the console, feverish, levers, buttons, switches, then -

Bump! Landed! The Doctor runs to the door, heading out -

CUT TO:

2. EXT. VICTORIAN STREET - DAY

THE DOCTOR steps out of the Tardis.

Snow! In a STREET MARKET. It's a working-class area of London, all busy and bustling…

Vendors, cocky lads, working girls, crones, braziers, beggars in doorways, hot chestnuts, smoke, steam, the works.

The Doctor walking through. Gradually relaxing into a smile. Soaking it in. He's loving it, the sheer colour and bustle and noise; this is what he travels for.

Throughout all this, a CAROL can be heard; a new Murray Gold Christmas Carol. Jolly & sinister, like the best hymns. The Doctor passes the CAROLLERS, stops for a listen.

Then he wanders on, calls out to an URCHIN:

THE DOCTOR
You there, boy, what day is this?

URCHIN
Christmas Eve, sir!

THE DOCTOR
In what year?

URCHIN
You thick or something?

THE DOCTOR
Oy! Answer the question!

URCHIN
Year of our Lord 1851, sir.

THE DOCTOR
Good, right, fine, and I don't suppose you've seen any men, sort of tall, sort of metal, men made of metal, with ears, like handles, big handle things, metal, no…?

The best title for this episode would be *The Two Doctors*… but maybe not. *The New Doctor*, perhaps? Or *The Next Doctor*? I quite like *The Next Doctor*. I'm glad to have started, though worried by what's to come. I had a fair bit of Cybermen-in-Victoriana worked out, but this two Doctors story, the *real* story, is so strong that it's sort of knocking out everything else. That's good. It shows that it's a strong concept. But it's kind of left me clutching broken bits of story. Then again, a lot of that Cybermen stuff was dark – graveyards and things – whereas this new stuff is fun and lively, it's even going to get knockabout, and that's good for Christmas Day.

You ask how a writer finds their voice. Now, *that's* a question! Everyone has a voice, in life and in print, but finding it in print takes time. There's no technique for finding it, I don't think, and it's never a hundred per cent individual. Yes, imitate like hell. Everyone does. But I'm not sure that it happens on purpose; it's a natural process. We all do it in speech, maybe even with thought. I can hear conversational riffs in my speech patterns that are torn from my friends, dozens of people, and writing is the same. Gaining a voice, whatever that is, comes with experience and practice – and the writing, again, is indivisible from the person. Your voice tends to be something that other people talk about, about you. It's not something that you think about much yourself, and certainly not whilst writing. I never – *never* – sit here thinking, what's my voice? You might as well ponder, who am I? It is, in fact, exactly the same thing. You can wonder your whole life and you'll never get an answer to that.

After all these years of wondering, I've never realised those last four sentences quite so clearly! This Great Correspondence does me good.

So the voice exists simply because you exist. You find your voice by writing, by experience. It doesn't matter what exactly you're writing, just that you *are* writing. Then one day someone will say, 'You've really found your voice with that piece', and you'll think, eh? Really? Everyone said it to me on *Queer as Folk*. It was kind of obvious, an easy remark, since that series was so close to home – so close that it still staggers me to watch it from afar, now. I did, in some ways, find my voice, but I wasn't aware of it. All this analysis exists outside the script. I just got on with it and wrote the next piece.

You can see voices in scripts, can't you? The difference between Steven's and mine? And it's always such a reflection of the person. I mean, look at Steven: he's all tough and Scottish, full of lethal gags (both in life and in script), and quite a lustful man, I think, a writer clearly driven by sex. More significantly, under that gruff exterior, a wonderful and romantic man, who hates to give that away – except in his writing. Again, again, again, scripts don't just live in Script World; they exist alongside everything else that you love and hate in your whole, wide, mad, lovely life. You copy from – or rather, are influenced by – everything.

I'm sure a lot of this e-mail correspondence amounts to Handy Tips, and that's fine, but everyone should find their own way to write. You must. Thing is, copying isn't just copying; it's selecting. It's not a dumb process. You can be aware of the fact that, yes, you've taken that phrasing or spacing off me, or Moffat, or Bryan Elsley or whoever, but what you're not so consciously aware of is the stuff that you're choosing *not* to use. If, say, you happen to like my one-line-pause technique, you'll know that you lifted it off me. At the same time, you'll have discarded techniques from my scripts that you don't like. That's not merely copying, but selecting, editing and adapting. It's a good, intelligent process of choosing, not imitating. So grab it all. From anyone. Read scripts, lots of them. Not just *Doctor Who* scripts. Go into the TV department of your nearest bookshop, grab any and every script book and bury yourself in them.

If you're thinking of writing your first script (oh, go on!)... well, I know what it's like. It's so easy to put off. Maybe you just don't write until you're ready, but I worry that's too easy an excuse, because then you could spend your whole life being not-quite-ready. You've got to start. The kids writing *Skins* are in their teens and early twenties! There is no time to waste! The whole world is full of unwritten scripts. There's a marvellous bit in *Peer Gynt* where he's surrounded by Songs, and they sing, 'We are songs, / you should have sung us. / A thousand times / You have curbed and suppressed us. / In the depths of your heart / we have lain and waited... / We were never called forth – / now we poison your voice.' That must feel terrible – and obviously feels true of everyone, even if you've written as many books as Stephen King or Agatha Christie. Don't be stifled and strangled.

It's so important to start writing, because then the process never, ever ends. Finding your voice isn't the last stage, just another stage along the way. You reach the top of that mountain, only to see a whole bloody, endless range of mountains waiting beyond. You've a million more things to reach for, a million more variations on your voice to articulate. Because your writing always lacks something. Mine does, Moffat's does, even Paul Abbott's does, everyone's does, and that's why we spend the rest of our lives, still typing away in the dark, trying to get better. Until we die.

There's a note to end on!

NINETEEN DAYS LATER...

David Tennant and two Cybermen film the (original) final scene of 4.13, with First Assistant Director Simon Morris in the background.

FROM: BENJAMIN COOK TO: RUSSELL T DAVIES
SUNDAY 23 MARCH 2008 02:04:12 GMT

HELLO AGAIN!

I've been thinking. I know, I know, I really should stop doing that. It only leads to trouble. But there's something I've been meaning to say. Something that's been bothering me. It's about 4.13. Bear with me…

It's a nine-out-of-ten script. One thing is standing between that nine and a ten… and it's the final scene. Back in January, I remember asking you why exactly that scene was there at all. 'To end on an upbeat note,' you said. To remind us that there are 'new adventures to come'. But I can't help thinking… doesn't that defeat the object of that ending? It's *supposed* to be sad. It's meant to be tragic. The Doctor and Rose are parted again (for ever this time?), and Donna – oh, poor Donna – is right back where she started, with no recollection of how amazing a person she can be. That's tear-jerking. Maybe a little bit bleak. But also it's brilliant, deeply affecting and, above all, an incredibly brave ending. It's noble! And then the bloody Cybermen pop up in the TARDIS and… well, that spoils it a bit. It's too easy. It's not even shocking. It's a bit rubbish, really. It's a watered-down version of the endings to Series Two and Three, even down to the 'What? What?? Whaaaat???' gag. Ending on Wilf, standing there in the rain, saluting the Doctor, or on the Doctor alone in the TARDIS… isn't that a hundred times better? What does that scene with the Cybermen add to the plot? Nothing at all. So what if you leave us in floods of tears? That's good television. That's *great* television.

Besides, you don't really need a scene at the end that throws forward to the Christmas Special: for the first time in four years, you'll have filmed the Special by the time that Episode 13 airs, so you can include a trailer after the end credits. Moreover, what's the one thing in *The Next Doctor* script that doesn't really work either? The opening scene! (Well, isn't it? You know it is.) The Doctor pushes some buttons on the TARDIS console and – oh, look – the Cybermen disappear. If you cut the final scene of 4.13, you can cut the opening scene of 4.14, the cliffhanger resolution, and improve both episodes immeasurably. C'mon, you know it makes sense.

Invisible Ben is dead. Long live Visible Ben. Etc. Ha ha. Tell me to sod off if you want.

FROM: RUSSELL T DAVIES TO: BENJAMIN COOK
SUNDAY 23 MARCH 2008 02:35:31 GMT

RE: HELLO AGAIN!

Damn it, Benjamino, I'll do anything for a ten-out-of-ten script. But… but… yes, it's a sad ending, yes, it's tragic, but that's not the keynote of *Doctor Who*, is it? Well, maybe it's becoming so. But this is a show about danger and monsters and a mad man in a blue box. The Doctor versus the monsters, that's what you get from the Cybermen ending. The tragedy of poor Donna – it's like a death – I don't think that's the right note to end on. The finality of it. You could almost turn your telly off and say, 'Right, that's the end', and it's my job to make sure that people never, ever do that. The story goes on, the Doctor survives. The final scene does add to the plot, because it's a *new* plot. Yes, I've done that 'What? What?? Whaaaat???' twice before, but that's the point. It's a running gag. I'd like to think that it's almost expected now. Imagine it without that ending. People would be saying, 'What, no "Whaaaat???"…?'

Hmm. I'm saying all that, but… well, you have tapped into something there, maybe, because there was a problem with that scene. They had to phone me from set. The problem being: how wet is David? He's just stepped out of the rain, then he's got to run straight from that TARDIS scene and directly into the Christmas Special, chasing Cybermen. But he can't spend the whole of 4.14 soaking wet. Over the phone, we reached a compromise: David is a bit tussled, he's dried off his jacket, so it's a few minutes later when he meets the Cybermen. That's what they shot. But it's one of those on-the-spot decisions that's put my teeth on edge. (My fault.) You should feel that the Doctor has just left Wilf, that he's still thinking of Donna. By putting in an offstage break, it's kind of interrupted the sadness. Plus, they didn't shoot the-Doctor-walking-around-the-console-sadly for long enough. You can imagine the music swelling, the tragedy of it all… but not for only ten seconds! We need longer, so we've already set that aside for a reshoot. Gaps are opening up in that scene.

But I do like it. Honestly. You should see it. When the Cybermen stand into shot, it's like… wow! Cybermen! Great ending!

FROM: RUSSELL T DAVIES TO: BENJAMIN COOK
TUESDAY 25 MARCH 2008 22:30:02 GMT

RE: HELLO AGAIN!

Do you know what? It takes time. For notes to sink in, sometimes. And I've kept thinking about what you said, about the Cybermen. It's kept niggling. Partly because you've spent most of these e-mails being Invisible Ben, so for you to pipe up, you must feel it strongly…

Oh God. What I'm saying is: you're right. I *think* you're right. Hand on heart, when you get a good note, it chimes with something that you're already thinking. Right at the back of my mind, I think I'd always thought, right from the moment I typed that last scene, that the runaway bride was brilliant, the *Titanic* was brilliant, and the Cybermen… aren't. They're kind of a poor cousin to those first two cliffhanger surprises. Catherine Tate and the world's most famous ship were just gobsmacking. Cybermen, not so much. I knew that. It just took me a long time to hear it.

And I'd completely forgotten that we'll have shot the material to run a proper Christmas Special trail. Good point! Everything I'm saying about 'new adventures to come', we can achieve that after the credits.

Also, we're way over on the 4.14 FX list, and Scene 1 has a good 15 days of FX, as the Cybermen vanish and tumble through the Time Vortex, heading for Victorian England. If I cut those 15 days, we'd be back on track. Plus, plus, plus… yeah, the thought of the Doctor landing in Scene 1 of 4.14, just arriving, fresh and happy and unbound by continuity to 4.13, is rather lovely. New episode, new start, Christmas Day, off we go. And another thing – I've been thinking about this a lot! – confronting the bride and the *Titanic* was fun, but starting 4.14 with Cybermen phasing in and out of reality is such a sci-fi opening. In a bad way. It's kind of off-putting. Besides, if we're reshooting the end of 4.13 anyway, the Doctor can now be wet and bedraggled and sad, so that problem is solved too.

Oh, all right, you win! Well, hold on, I'll talk to Julie tomorrow. She does love her 'What? What?? Whaaaat???'

Text message from: Russell
Sent: 26-Mar-2008 14:06
Benjamino! I just talked Julie through changing the end of 4.13 – no cliffhanger, no Cybermen, run a trail instead – and she likes it! I told her it was my own idea, so hah! I hope that script gets a 10/10 from you now...

Text message from: Ben
Sent: 26-Mar-2008 17:25
Much better! Yes, it's a 10/10 episode now.

Text message from: Russell
Sent: 26-Mar-2008 18:25
You and this correspondence have changed the script! The whole ending to the series! Now the world is going to spin off its axis. Beware the power, Ben. Power corrupts! No, but seriously. Thank you. See you later.

■

APPENDIX 1

A LETTER TO BRYAN ELSLEY

FROM: RUSSELL T DAVIES TO: BRYAN ELSLEY
SUNDAY 20 APRIL 2008 12:35:56 GMT

HELLO

Dear Bryan,

I hope you don't mind me writing out of the blue. I cadged your e-mail address off a mutual friend of ours, Charles Martin.

But anyway, hello. I'm a writer too. I'm the *Doctor Who* man. I've always wanted to meet you. I think you're brilliant, but now I've been driven to cadging e-mail addresses, because I had to write and say that *Skins* is just PHENOMENAL. I bloody love it. I enjoyed the first series, but the second series just flew. It became something so rare, and beautiful, and wise, and funny, and brave, and mental and new. Ending with a final episode that was just about perfect. Nothing's ever perfect! But that was!

And I've got to say, the penultimate episode, when you took that dazzling, huge, brilliant leap to New York, was one of the most amazing things that I've ever seen. I've never seen a story take such a jump. I can't imagine how you even thought of that. But it was lucid, and true, and heartbreaking, and I will never forget it.

I'm going to sound like a stalker soon, so I'll stop in a minute, but also I think everything you've done with that young writers' team is wonderful and shames the rest of us. I read an interview with you, years ago, in the *Sunday Times*, I think, where you spoke about new forms of narrative, how our TV-watching generation is becoming outdated and the next generation will have new ways of storytelling. I just nodded, sadly. But then you went out and did something about it! You're an inspiration.

So thank you for *Skins*. Good luck with the next series. And good luck with the BAFTAs tonight. If you don't win, it's a scandal!

All the best,
Russell

FROM: BRYAN ELSLEY TO: RUSSELL T DAVIES
MONDAY 28 APRIL 2008 16:45:18 GMT

RE: HELLO

Dear Russell,

I'm sorry that it's taken so long to reply to your lovely e-mail. I've just acquired a baby and it's 20 years since I had my last one, so I've had to be sent away for re-education.

Anyway, I'm finally back in my office and just want to say thank you for being so encouraging. It means a lot to me, because you're the writer who, a few years ago, reassured me that it was still possible to do something meaningful, funny and entertaining in TV drama, and that these things can coexist, just at the point when I was about to give up trying. It's hard to relate just what *Queer as Folk* meant to me, but I'm sure lots of people say that to you. I just hope that isn't boring or frustrating, given all the other fantastic work that you've done. It happens to be true, that's all.

Next year on *Skins*, on Series Three, we're kind of pushing it out. All the writers except me are under 23, and four of them under the age of 20. All the characters are gone, to be completely replaced with a set born from the imaginations of the young creative team. The possibilities of going on our arses are too numerous to think about. We'll be hanging on for dear life again. If you ever fancied coming by our writers' meeting on a Wednesday afternoon and spending half an hour telling a bunch of kids how you go about things, we would be so happy. In the meantime and failing that, it would be nice to finally meet up at some point.

We didn't get the BAFTA, of course. Quite a long evening when your award comes and goes in the first 45 seconds...

Best regards,
Bryan

APPENDIX 2

FROM RUSSELL TO STEVEN

WORKS REFERENCED

DOCTOR WHO
AND ITS SPIN-OFFS (in chronological order)

***Doctor Who* (1963–present)** – an alien known as 'the Doctor', a Time Lord, with the ability to regenerate into a new body and personality, at least 12 times, in order to cheat death, travels through time and space in a ship called the TARDIS, which is disguised as a London police box. The show ran on the BBC from 1963 to 1989, with seven successive actors playing the Doctor. A TV movie starring Paul McGann was made in 1996. The show was revived in 2005, produced by BBC Wales (most of the show is filmed in and around Cardiff), with Russell T Davies as showrunner:

- **Series One (2005)** – starring Christopher Eccleston, Billie Piper and John Barrowman
- ***The Christmas Invasion* (2005)** – Christmas Special, starring David Tennant and Piper
- **Series Two (2006)** – starring Tennant and Piper
- ***The Runaway Bride* (2006)** – Christmas Special, starring Tennant and Catherine Tate
- **Series Three (2007)** – starring Tennant, Freema Agyeman and Barrowman
- ***Voyage of the Damned* (2007)** – Christmas Special, starring Tennant and Kylie Minogue
- **Series Four (2008)** – starring Tennant, Tate, Piper, Agyeman, Barrowman and Elisabeth Sladen
- ***The Next Doctor* (2008)** – starring Tennant and David Morrissey

***Doctor Who Confidential* (2005–present)** – BBC Three's behind-the-scenes companion show

***Torchwood* (2006–present)** – adult-themed *Doctor Who* spin-off show, created by Russell, concerning the Cardiff branch of a covert agency, the Torchwood Institute, led by Captain Jack Harkness (Barrowman), that investigates extraterrestrial incidents on Earth. Series One débuted on BBC Three in October 2006, and Series Two on BBC Two in January 2008

***The Sarah Jane Adventures* (2007–present)** – BBC One's *Doctor Who* spin-off show for children, created by Russell, focusing on investigative journalist Sarah Jane Smith (Elisabeth Sladen)

OTHER SHOWS
WORKED ON BY RUSSELL T DAVIES

***Bob & Rose* (2001)** – Russell's six-part ITV romantic drama focusing on a gay man falling in love with a woman

***Casanova* (2005)** – Russell's three-part BBC drama telling the life of eighteenth-century Italian adventurer Giacomo Casanova (David Tennant)

***Coronation Street* (1960–present)** – ITV soap, created by Tony Warren, set in a fictional street in Lancashire. Russell was a storyliner in the mid 1990s, also writing the direct-to-video special *Viva Las Vegas*

***Dark Season* (1991)** – Russell's six-part BBC teen drama telling of the adventures of three adolescents and their battle to save their school from the actions of the sinister Mr Eldritch

***Families* (1990–1993)** – ITV daytime soap, created by Kay Mellor, following two families: the Thompsons, based in Cheshire, England, and the Stevens, living in Sydney, Australia. Russell wrote various episodes

***Mine All Mine* (2004)** – Russell's five-part ITV drama about Max Vivaldi, who believes that the city of Swansea belongs to him – and is proved right!

***Queer as Folk* (1999)** – Russell's Channel 4 drama series chronicling the lives of three men in Manchester's gay village around Canal Street

***Queer as Folk 2* (2000)** – two-part TV special concluding the *Queer as Folk* story

***Revelations* (1994)** – short-lived Granada/Carlton soap opera, devised by Russell

***The Grand* (1997–1998)** – hotel-set ITV period drama, written by Russell

***The Second Coming* (2003)** – Russell's two-part ITV drama concerning the realisation of Steve Baxter (Christopher Eccleston) that he's the Son of God

***Why Don't You...?* (1973–1995)** – BBC children's magazine show, which Russell produced and directed between 1988 and 1992

OTHER TV SHOWS DISCUSSED

***Blue Peter* (1958–present)** – BBC magazine programme for children

***Buffy the Vampire Slayer* (1997–2003)** – US drama

series, created by Joss Whedon, about a young woman, Buffy Summers, chosen by fate to battle against vampires, demons, and the forces of darkness

***Casualty* (1986–present)** – BBC medical drama, created by Jeremy Brock and Paul Unwin, based around the fictional Holby City Hospital

***Coupling* (2000–2004)** – BBC sitcom, created and written by Steven Moffat, about a group of thirtysomething friends

***Desperate Housewives* (2004–present)** – US drama series, created by Marc Cherry, following the lives of a group of women, seen through the eyes of their dead neighbour, and the secrets that lie beneath the surface of suburbia

***Early Doors* (2003–2004)** – BBC sitcom, created and written by Craig Cash and Phil Mealey, set in a small pub, The Grapes, in Manchester

***EastEnders* (1985–present)** – BBC soap, created by Julia Smith and Tony Holland, set in the fictional Albert Square in the East End of London

***Fawlty Towers* (1975–1979)** – BBC sitcom, created and written by John Cleese and Connie Booth, set in a fictional Torquay hotel

***Give Us a Clue* (1979–1997)** – ITV's gameshow version of charades, which ran until 1992; BBC One attempted a revived version in 1997

***High School Musical* (2006)** – US TV movie musical, written by Peter Barsocchini and made by the Disney Channel, concerning students and rival cliques at a fictional high school in New Mexico

***I, Claudius* (1976)** – BBC adaptation of Robert Graves' *I, Claudius* and *Claudius the God* novels, scripted by Jack Pulman

***Jekyll* (2007)** – six-part BBC drama series, written by Steven Moffatt, starring James Nesbitt as a modern-day descendant of Dr Jekyll, who has begun transforming into a version of Mr Hyde

***Life on Mars* (2006–2007)** – BBC drama series, created by Matthew Graham, Tony Jordan, and Ashley Pharoah, about a policemen, Sam Tyler (John Simm), who's hit by a car in 2006, and wakes up in 1973

***Longford* (2006)** – one-off Channel 4 drama, written by Peter Morgan, about Moors Murderers Ian Brady and Myra Hindley

***Most Haunted* (2002–present)** – Living TV show based on investigating purported paranormal activity

***Neighbours* (1985–present)** – Australian soap opera, created by Reg Watson, set in Ramsay Street, a cul-de-sac in the fictional suburb of Erinsborough

***The New Paul O'Grady Show* (2006–present)** – Channel Four chat show presented by comedian Paul O'Grady; originally ran on ITV (under the title *The Paul O'Grady Show*), from 2004 to 2005

***Only Fools and Horses* (1981–2003)** – BBC sitcom, created and written by John Sullivan, focusing on brothers Derek and Rodney Trotter's attempts to get rich

***The People's Quiz* (2007)** – BBC Saturday-night quiz show (full title: *The National Lottery People's Quiz*), hosted by Jamie Theakston

***Primeval* (2007–present)** – ITV sci-fi drama, created by Adrian Hodges and Tim Haines, about a team of scientists that investigates anomalies in time and deals with creatures that travel through

***The Royle Family* (1998–2006)** – BBC sitcom, created by Caroline Aherne and Craig Cash, about the working-class Royle family, who rarely do anything other than watch television, chat, eat, smoke, and drink

***Skins* (2007–present)** – E4/Channel 4 drama, created by Brian Elsley and Jamie Brittain, about a group of sixth-formers growing up in Bristol

***Star Wars* (set to début in 2010)** – US science-fiction series, yet to be given an official title, focusing on characters from the galaxy of the *Star Wars* movies

***The South Bank Show* (1978–present)** – ITV arts magazine show

***Teletubbies* (1997–2001)** – BBC series for pre-school children; created and written by Anne Wood CBE and Andrew Davenport

***The X Factor* (2004–present)** – ITV talent show contested by aspiring pop singers

MOVIES DISCUSSED

***Dangerous Liaisons* (1988)** – based on a play, by Christopher Hampton, about eighteenth-century French aristocracy; in turn based on eighteenth-century novel *Les Liaisons dangereuses* by Pierre Choderlos de Laclos

***Finding Nemo* (2003)** – computer-animated movie, produced by Pixar and Disney and written by Andrew Stanton, Bob Peterson and David Reynolds, telling the story of a clownfish, Marlin, in search of his son, Nemo

***Grease* (1978)** – film musical about students at the fictional Rydell High School in 1959. Written by Bronte Woodard, and based on Jim Jacobs and Warren Casey's 1972 musical of the same name

***The Great Mouse Detective* (1986)** – animated Disney movie based on the children's book series *Basil of Baker Street* by Eve Titus. It draws heavily on the tradition of Sherlock Holmes, with a heroic mouse who consciously emulates the detective

***Jeepers Creepers 2* (2003)** – horror movie, directed and written by Victor Salva. The movie is a sequel to the earlier *Jeepers Creepers*

***Monsters, Inc.* (2001)** – computer-animated movie, produced by Pixar, set in Monstropolis, a city inhabited by monsters and powered by the screams of children

***The Poseidon Adventure* (1972)** – concerns the capsizing of a fictional ocean liner, and the struggles of a handful of survivors to reach the bottom of the hull before the ship sinks. It is scripted by Wendell Mayes and Stirling Silliphant, and based on a novel by Paul Gallico. The movie has been remade twice: as a television special in 2005, with the same name, and a theatrical release, *Poseidon*, in 2006

***The Simpsons Movie* (2007)** – animated movie based on TV sitcom/cartoon series *The Simpsons*, created by Matt Groening, following the lives of the residents of the fictional US town of Springfield

***Sliding Doors* (1998)** – concerning the life of a woman who's fired from her job; the plot then splits into two parallel universes, which run in tandem. It is written and directed by Peter Howitt

OTHER WORKS DISCUSSED

***Asterix and the Laurel Wreath* (1972)** – the eighteenth volume of the *Asterix* comic book series (original French title: *Les Lauriers de Cesar*), by René Goscinny (stories) and Albert Uderzo (illustrations), following the exploits of a village of ancient Gauls as they resist Roman occupation

***A Christmas Carol* (1843)** – novella by Charles Dickens, telling the Victorian morality tale of miserly Ebenezer Scrooge, who undergoes profound redemption over the course of one night as four ghosts visit him

***Chain Reaction* (1991–present)** – host-less chat show, first broadcast on BBC Radio 5 in 1991, then revived on BBC Radio 4 in 2005. Each week, a famous name interviews another famous name; and the interviewee goes on to be the following week's interviewer

***The Cherry Orchard* (1904)** – Anton Chekhov's last play, concerning a once-wealthy family as they return to their estate in Russia shortly before it is auctioned off

***Death in the Clouds* (1935)** – mystery novel by Agatha Christie, featuring Belgian detective Hercule Poirot

'Eleonora' (1842) – short story by Edgar Allan Poe, considered by many biographers to be autobiographical

Goldilocks and the Three Bears – fairy tale that first became widely known in 1837 when Robert Southey composed it as a prose story, *The Story of the Three Bears*, collected in his book *The Doctor*, although it was probably based on an even older story in the oral tradition

***Hamlet* (1599–1601)** – a play written by William Shakespeare, telling how Prince Hamlet of Denmark exacts revenge on his uncle for the murder of his father. The exact year of writing remains in dispute

***Harry Potter and the Deathly Hallows* (2007)** – the seventh and final book in JK Rowling's *Harry Potter* series of fantasy novels about the adventures of the eponymous adolescent wizard

***How I Write: The Secret Lives of Authors* (2007)** – an anthology of writings by various provocative authors, includes letters, essays, photographs and memorabilia; edited by Dan Crowe and Philip Oltermann

***Peer Gynt* (1867)** – a play, written in verse, by Henrik Ibsen

***Prisoner of Trebekistan* (2005)** – a book by Bob Harris, about Alex Trebek, presenter of US quiz show *Jeopardy*

***Six Characters in Search of an Author* (1921)** – play written by Luigi Pirandello. During rehearsals for a play, six characters turn up and insist on being given life

***Starship Titanic* (1998)** – a computer game designed by Douglas Adams and made by The Digital Village, of which Adams was a founding member. The game takes place on a spaceship called the *Titanic*, which has crash-landed on Earth

***Ten Little Niggers* (1939)** – detective novel by Agatha Christie (later editions re-titled *And Then There Were None*), about ten people, trapped on an island, killed according to an old nursery rhyme

INDEX

INDEX